Numbers from Nowhere

Numbers
from
Nowhere

The American Indian

Contact Population Debate

David Henige

University of Oklahoma Press : Norman

Also by David Henige

(Editor) *Colonial Governors from the Fifteenth Century to the Present*
  (Madison, 1970)
The Chronology of Oral Tradition: Quest for a Chimera (Oxford, 1974)
(Editor) *Works in African History: An Index to Reviews, 1974–1978*
  (Waltham, 1978)
In Search of Columbus: The Sources for the First Voyage (Tucson, 1991)
The Princely States of India: A Chronological Checklist of Their Rulers
  (San Bernardino, forthcoming)

E
59
P75
H45
1998

Library of Congress Cataloging-in-Publication Data

Henige, David P.
    Numbers from nowhere : the American Indian contact population
    debate / David Henige.
        p.   cm.
    Includes bibliographical references and index.
    ISBN 0–8061–3044–X (cloth : alk. paper)
    1. Indians—Population. 2. History—Methodology.   I. Title.
E59.P75H45   1998   97–50252
304.6'08997—dc21   CIP

Text design by Alicia Hembekides.
Text is set in Sabon with equations in Gill Sans.

The paper in this book meets the guidelines for permanence and durability
of the Committee on Production Guidelines for Book Longevity of the
Council on Library Resources, Inc. ⊗

1 2 3 4 5 6 7 8 9 10

For those who would agree that life tastes better with a little salt.

Calculations in cases where there is no Principle to calculate from, no given number or Rule to begin at, should never obtain too much upon us; the judging by or from such Calculations leads Men, of otherwise great Penetration, oftentimes into fatal Mistakes, such as at least touch the Reputation of the Understandings and Judgment; as sometimes such as expose them to contempt; such were the Guesses of that great Pretender to politick Arithmetick, Sir William Petty, whose Calculations of the Numbers of the Houses, and Families, and Inhabitants in London, and other populous Cities, were not erroneous only, but we may say have since been prov'd absurd, and even ridiculous.

—Daniel Defoe,
Plan of the English Commerce (London, 1730)

Contents

Acknowledgments

The lengthy germination of the present work has entailed recurring and burgeoning debts. The first of these must be to William Denevan, who first interested me in the matter. As noted in chapter 1, this was entirely inadvertent and ultimately perhaps not even welcome. Just the same, Bill Denevan was unfailingly gracious during our discussions, and I came to appreciate the clarity of his arguments. I have always considered *Native Populations of the Americas,* the work he edited on the subject, to be the very model of the way in which editorial responsibilities can be fulfilled with objectivity and thoroughness. I hope that although he is retired, he is not yet done with the issue.

I owe an even greater—and in some ways an even older—debt to the staff of the Interlibrary Loan Department at the University of Wisconsin—Madison. For thirty years I have badgered them mercilessly, but they have withstood the barrage and acquired for me hundreds and hundreds of books and articles, an endeavor in which, I daresay, there is no real end in sight. So, Joy Brandenburg, Tom Maloney, Madeline Quigley, and Judy Tuohy, many thanks indeed!

My colleague Vicki Hill was ever willing to help me deal with materials in German, and for certain discussions herein this was by no means unimportant. I am grateful to another colleague, Suzanne Hodgman, for her efforts, again over about thirty years, to acquire materials from and about Latin America. These have been so successful that I would guess that my opportunities for immediate gratification have been in the 90-percent range, which helped enormously, indeed crucially, in achieving and maintaining momentum. Other colleagues in the libraries here have refrained from objecting strenuously to my sometimes insistent efforts to look at new materials as they arrive, for doing this has enabled me to add a serious leaven of productive serendipity to what otherwise might pass for nothing but system.

Bruce Fetter, Jan Vansina, and Paul Hair each read an earlier, and less well-organized, draft, and each contributed insights about how to proceed—as well as how not to. This ability to tap surrogate objectivity has, I believe, much value, though I suspect that all three might rightly think I should have followed their suggestions somewhat more closely in certain respects.

Robert McCaa might be surprised to find himself thanked here, because he disliked my approach on several counts. Nonetheless, by expressing his reasons for this, he helped me to recognize in time that I had not done enough to justify my purpose and strategy. Because of his comments, I should at least come closer to the mark, and I hope that what I have added will lessen his disappointment.

John Daniels also read the manuscript, but what I appreciate most is the extraordinarily lucid and dispassionate way in which he set about discussing the complicated history of this debate. I envy this ability but recognize that it is not my way, and in any case it would not be entirely appropriate in the present circumstances. Just the same, I refer every reader to his conspective article in the *William and Mary Quarterly* cited in the bibliography. It is *the* place to become oriented to the debate.

There can be no moment more humbling for an author than turning to the copy-edited version of his or her work to discover that text, arguments, and organization once thought flawless are in fact riddled with minor flaws, and even some not so minor. In the sensible author chagrin quickly gives way to gratitude and relief. Exposing weaknesses is particularly beneficial to the author who happens to be acting as critic, and I am very grateful to Jane Kepp for ensuring that this work is less flawed than it was before it fell into her hands. Readers will benefit from the added clarity and consistency, while reviewers, I hope, will have fewer targets to aim at.

At best solitary, scholarly research and writing is at worst a selfish pursuit, and I seem to be at it constantly. Jan Behn has put up with this for a long time and has gone so far as to assist at various stages when her quite superior keyboarding and troubleshooting skills were required.

I dedicated my last work to Pierre Bayle, who did so much to make skepticism respectable under the most trying of conditions but who always kept an open mind about possibilities, though not about probabilities. Although the dedication is different this time around, there remain better reasons than ever to express continuing appreciation for Bayle's groundbreaking work.

Finally, it would not be at all inappropriate to thank many of those whom I have termed High Counters. Clearly, I disagree with their premises, and so, necessarily, with their conclusions, but I can only admire the assiduity and earnestness with which they press them. Their success in the scholarly and public spheres is hardly an accident, and their prolificness has been so great that I could not even consider the possibility of confronting the bulk of it.

Numbers from Nowhere

Do Numbers Lie?

*Combined with Geoffrey's keen sense of narrative technique and dra-
matic structure, his revisionist strategies imparted a certain plausibility to his history. So many vivid stories, such circumstantiality and
completeness, such a novel viewpoint. Could this all be wrong?*

—Michael J. Curley, *Geoffrey of Monmouth*

*The method I take to do this is not yet very usual; for instead of using
only comparative and superlative Words, and intellectual Arguments,
I have taken the course . . . to express myself in Terms of Number,
Weight or Measure.*

—William Petty, *Economic Writings*

In his *Republic,* Plato noticed the centrality of numbers and their use:
"'Come,' said I, 'if we are unable to discover anything outside of
these, let us take something that applies to all alike.' 'What?' . . . 'This
trifling matter,' I said, 'of distinguishing one and two and three. I
mean, in sum, number and calculation. Is it not true of them that
every art and science must necessarily partake of them?'"[1] In this
book I want to discuss some effects of taking this centrality so seriously that a set of numbers—both the numbers in the sources and the
arithmetical procedures to which they have been subjected—have become icons, indeed almost idols.

"Probably no single issue has greater implications for the
ethnohistory of the Indian peoples of North and South America than
the depopulation resulting from the virgin soil epidemics that accompanied European contact."[2] These words begin a review essay of two
books on the subject of native depopulation and reflect a widely held
opinion about the defining need to understand the phenomenon by
seeking to measure it. Measurement is to be done by, first among other

things, somehow calculating the population of the various regions of the Americas in 1492 or shortly after. As the passage suggests, even those not particularly interested in the numbers themselves believe that seeking to establish them is useful, if not downright epochal.[3]

Discussing recent trends indicating that the precontact Americas were by no means the paradise some would have them, Clark Larsen argues that

> estimation of population size at contact is not a trivial issue. Rather, knowledge of the size of native population at the time of contact engenders a better understanding of the magnitude and variability of population decline throughout the Americas after 1492; it allows us to examine adaptations and history of native groups that inhabited the New World at the time of contact; it sheds light on the rate and timing of the spread of Old World pathogens; and, overall, population size changes provide a rough measure of health status alterations.[4]

This point of view is easy to accept in the abstract. Since there are no direct data available on the question, however, the issue immediately and abidingly becomes one of methodology and, even more, of epistemology.[5] For this and other reasons, the enterprise of estimating the contact population by calculating smaller numbers and projecting them onto a larger canvas has been a part of American history from the beginning, but it has gathered a great deal of momentum in the last half century, becoming more comprehensive and more complex, and with these, more confident. Along the way it has come to serve as a classic specimen of a movement, that is, a venture in which class solidarity, a large leaven of intuitive belief, and a militant sense of mission are dominant characteristics. In the present study I examine this movement in specific, if limited, ways: how its members unearth and treat evidence; how they deal with criticism; whether they generate self-criticism as a standard operating procedure; how their work mirrors the larger currents of the times; and whether it is advisable, indeed possible, to treat depopulation as a qualititative phenomenon infinitely capable of being quantified. In particular I seek to provide a larger historical context in which to treat both numbers and the means of reaching them.

Several of the ideas in this work have been with me for a long time. One day in 1976 a friend told me that he was taking a seminar on determining the contact population of the Americas. I knew nothing about the matter, but somehow the notion intrigued me. As I recall, my first question to myself, no doubt based on my ignorance, was, how is this possible? Hoping to find the answer, I secured permission to sit in on the course as an observer. I learned that the purpose was to guide each student to some subset of the New World population and direct him or her to determine a range of population possibilities at contact or zenith, using the available sources and quantitative techniques. Although I had no assignment, I began to look into the readings and was soon struck by the attempt of Sherburne Cook and Woodrow Borah to estimate the population of Hispaniola in December 1492, when Columbus's little expedition first reached the island.[6] I found myself reflexively skeptical of their argument that in the first decade after that event Hispaniola's population dropped by more than 6 million people. Even the novel spin they gave their sources did not, it seemed to me, invest those sources with the tensile strength they required.

I began to look at the reviews of their essay, which had been published about five years earlier. My own epiphanic moment arrived when I read in one of these that Cook and Borah had "uncovered" 8 million people in precontact Hispaniola.[7] Looking back, it seems as though it was at that very moment that I felt obliged to dissent. I was later to realize that I had fortuitously stumbled on work by Cook and Borah that was generally less well regarded than their principal work on central Mexico. But looking at their Mexico work did nothing to convince me that the difference was more than one of degree—that parallel ways of looking at the past and at our own role as historians were at work in both instances.

My interest in the subject of population estimates persisted in the midst of other concerns, and since my first encounter with the debate I have returned to the issue several times, usually in response to specific stimuli.[8] I was hardly alone in my criticism throughout the two decades since 1976, and I half expected—and fully hoped—that a colloquy would develop in this matter. It hardly seemed possible that it would not—after all, rather astonishing claims of magnitude and precision were being made on the basis of the most exiguous evidence.

Such a debate has never developed. Of course, by the very nature of their business, the critics of high estimates were engaging in colloquy, though usually with the dead. But the triangular and quadrangular aspects of true discussion simply never materialized, as the High Counters—that is, most of those who have attempted during the past forty years to put numbers to the inhabitants of the Americas when the Europeans began arriving—continued to argue their case without taking account of counterarguments and with little change in tactics and conclusions. Evidence continued to be subjected to over-refined statistical applications, and charts and diagrams proliferated. Otherwise, the High Counters continued to admire and to be encouraged by one another, and they maintained a striking faith in the accuracy and applicability of a narrow range of sources which they seldom subjected even to trial doubts.

Eventually their lack of response intrigued me as much as their methodology did. It struck me that refusing to come to terms with criticism proves a most effective way of prolonging one's position. As well, the High Counters have had the considerable advantage of tapping into a receptive vein of public and scholarly opinion, one that was thoroughly aired during the recent Columbian quincentenary. So they have not found it necessary to justify their case to the public at large; merely stating it repeatedly has been surprisingly sufficient.[9]

At the heart of the High Counters' enterprise is an ensemble of assumptions, each of which must be true if their conclusions are to be accepted. These assumptions include—but are not limited to—the following: that early European observers could count or estimate large numbers closely; that they wanted to do just this, reckoning precision a virtue; that they actually did so; and that these counts were transmitted into and through the written sources accurately.[10] In this book I deal with all but the second of these, and I see the first and third as different in the abstract but in practice much the same. In order to grant the benefit of any possible doubts, chapter 6 treats not large numbers but small ones, and not the protean Other but the presumably less problematical Self.

Many of the attitudes at issue are encapsulated in a statement by Linda Newson which, though made more than ten years ago, still represents the state of play well:

> There is still considerable controversy over the size of the population of Latin America and the Caribbean on the eve of the Spanish conquest. Estimates vary from 7.5 million to between 80 and 100 million and the variations reflect not only the type of evidence used but also the methodology and basic philosophy of researchers. There is a wealth of documentary evidence available for making such estimates. It includes accounts of the early conquistadors, soldiers and explorers, later administrative reports, including counts made for the assessment of tribute and labour services, church and missionary records, as well as some native accounts and recorded traditions.[11]

Perhaps the principal attribute of this point of view is its certainty in the efficacy of the sources and methods available for modern students of the problem. In this book I take issue with virtually every point Newson raises, not least with the apparently innocuous phrase "considerable controversy."

———

A brief word about terminology is in order. Some of those with whose work I disagree have taken umbrage at my use of the term "High Counters" to describe them. They think it demeans and oversimplifies their work. They might well be right; nonetheless, I prefer to continue using the term since it is undeniable that all of them have calculated, if not actually counted, and even more obvious that they have consistently and insistently arrived at numbers that are higher, sometimes by orders of magnitude, than those that appeared in earlier works on the same subject. One of the emphases in the present work is the reasons for, as well as the methods that have resulted in, this concomitant increase of both postulated population levels and certainty.

My intention originally was to write an integrated and comprehensive account of the ebb and flow of the debate, focusing on the writings and arguments of the High Counters. This quickly proved too ambitious; in its place is a series of essays that are disparate and self-contained yet not, I think, so much so that their aggregate does not offer a reasonable assessment. The aim is to be comprehensive without necessarily being systematic. Although the intent is to produce a whole greater than the sum of its individual parts, many of these parts should be able to stand alone in terms of presenting a coherent argument.

While some might regard Julius Caesar, the Black Hole of Calcutta, and the contact population of the Guaraní as odd dance partners indeed, I conceive of this work as taking a broad "numbers in history" approach to the contact population issue. The High Counters have generally concentrated on making their case at the expense of grasping the wider implications of the issues they raise. But this kind of arithmetic, lacking as it does so many of its parts, is necessarily an outcome of epistemology, and this epistemology in turn requires the broadest possible canvas in order to justify itself. The examples adduced here have at least one important commonality: they all bear on the question of the use—and most certainly of the abuse—of numbers, as well as on the study of this phenomenon from the earliest times to the present.

Colloquy should be the essence of scholarly communication. Often enough, such colloquy takes the form of debate—that is, at least one of the parties, by disagreeing with the methods or conclusions of the others, argues that it is premature to pretend to have arrived at a resolution, or offers a different one. Of all the disciplines, history ought to show the greatest propensity for colloquy, for the past has not been particularly benevolent in preserving itself for the edification of the present. The accessible evidence is meager, and in order to be true to that exiguousness, historians must be willing to adopt epistemological positions that encourage expansion rather than contraction.

Some scholarly debate is carried out within a small group of cognoscenti, while some is closely attuned to the particular mores of its time and place and reaches out to a larger audience. Some debate exists only long enough to stimulate the search for further evidence, while some is endless, ebbing and flowing according to cycles of fashion or the infusion of new evidence or new methods to quarry older evidence more imaginatively. The principal reason for the longevity of most debates is simply that the evidence necessary to resolve matters does not exist or has not been found. Sometimes, of course, the terms of the debate require amounts of evidence that are unattainable, and so the debate flourishes in an atmosphere of pretense and hope, perhaps making minor advances across the terrain of evidence that are offset by commensurate losses. The aim is to convince without being able to demonstrate. In the circumstances, disputants are forced to take liberties with evidence and presentation, for to maintain rigorous standards would be to abandon the contest as unwinnable.

―――――――

Few ongoing scholarly debates in the field of history so typify this nature of things as that over the size of the contact population of the Americas. In one form or another it has persisted for more than five centuries. During this time the terms of discussion and investigation have changed in appearance but remained remarkably alike in substance and even in form. During the past fifty years or so the debate has taken on new life, has expanded by leaps and bounds, has incorporated new arguments and new forms of discourse, has brought in conscripts from a remarkably broad range of disciplines, and has reached new heights and depths of outrage and outrageousness. One crucial thing that has not changed much, however, is the amount of direct evidence available to answer the question. Columbus and Las Casas and Oviedo had no data available to support either their regional or their hemispheric opinions; despite the intervening centuries, Kroeber, Borah, Dobyns, and others who have more recently addressed the matter of the contact population have had exactly as much direct evidence available to them.

To some, this will seem a harsh, even unsupportable, point of view. The first purpose of the present work is to show how justified—however unwelcome—this line of reasoning is. That done, it discusses the results of this finding on the course and content of the debate, which has intensified precisely as if new evidence had come to hand, or at least demonstrably better ways of exploiting existing evidence. In the process, other points will necessarily be raised, although I am by no means sanguine that there are invariably answers.

Of these additional points, perhaps the most interesting, though also the most inscrutable, is, why do so many historians, anthropologists, and demographers believe that it is acceptable scholarly practice to marshal arguments in support of sometimes very narrow population ranges for areas and periods for which not a scintilla of applicable evidence exists? The result is a body of historical methodology predicated on a series of conventions almost peculiar to the field—for example, using secondary sources, including translations, in place of primary sources in the original languages; imputing to archaeological evidence a great deal more explanatory power than it can possibly possess; using sources credulously, tendentiously, and anachronistically; ignoring sources and arguments that do not fit the prefabricated argument; and applying sophisticated but largely inapplicable quantitative techniques to an immensely disparate body of data that lack the required validity.

I have tried studiously, but I suspect unsuccessfully, to avoid extended discussions of motivation—what has prompted this surge in forlorn attempts to answer a thoroughly unanswerable question. Just the same, something must be said, and I wish that it could be less conjectural. Since these attempts have been solely in aid of raising the predicated figures, I can only assume that a Zeitgeist has been at work and has combined with a cadre and coterie spirit to enable and encourage this activity, in much the same way that very different circumstances combined to produce much lower counts a few academic generations earlier. At its broadest level it is a matter of going along with the times rather than with the evidence. Beyond this surmise, I hesitate to go.

———

This study is about counting and calculating—counting in the past and calculating in the present. More generally, it is about measuring, and most specifically of all it is about mismeasuring and misinterpreting. Behind all this, the work is necessarily also a study of belief systems, credulousness, and anachronism. Since the numbers offered by both early and modern counters can never be proved inaccurate, the most that can be accomplished is to demonstrate that the observational, psychological, or methodological underpinnings are faulty. This requires a context broader than the subject itself—and certainly broader than any that the High Counters have sought to provide. Indeed, I will argue that the reluctance of the High Counters to look beyond their particular area of interest is by itself a ruinously fatal methodology.

Referring to those who would doubt the claims of the early chroniclers as to the numbers of Indians they encountered, Woodrow Borah expressed bemusement: "What emerges out of this distrust is the extraordinarily interesting idea that there existed in people of earlier generations a general impulse to exaggerate numbers."[12] Ignoring Borah's implied belief that the present generation is exempt from this failing, and the further implication that he found the past's numerical skills quite up to his own, the present study draws widely on the wealth of evidence which indicates beyond cavil that despite such efforts at rehabilitation, the most interesting thing about Borah's astonishing claim is precisely that it is supported by so little evidence and contradicted by so much.

Another context I examine is the circumstances in which the results of the High Counters have been allowed to flourish and to spread ever more widely.[13] It is the same context that produced a quincentenary so different from its predecessor a century before. Particularly, it is a context that produced works with titles such as *The Conquest of Paradise* and *American Holocaust,* both of which embrace the results of the High Counters with untrammeled enthusiasm.[14] These studies, and others like them, argue that because the Americas (and Oceania) were the only places outside the Old World disease pool, they were also the only places where population increased steadily until the end of the fifteenth century or so, unaffected by recurring epidemics or, it seems, natural disasters. Concomitantly, when European diseases did strike, they were unusually devastating. The last of these suggestions is undoubtedly true, but unless the others are as well, there is no pressing need to infer particularly high numbers in these societies.

———————

The extraordinary lengths to which those wishing to postulate contact population levels will go are crystallized by a comment made more than fifty years ago by Francisco Loayza. In editing the chronicle of

Cristóbal de Molina, Loayza supplied an editorial comment to Molina's account of Spanish cruelties in the former Inca empire. Based on a couple of comments by later observers, Loayza declared that "it is easy to extract the total population of the Inca empire" in 1532. He went on:

> And here [is] the forceful eloquence of the numbers. *1,500,000* inhabitants, according to the Viceroy Francisco de Toledo, were alive forty years after the conquest, the result of a depopulation of some 30% of a particular people. To ascertain the exact population of this people, multiply by *30* the first quantity, and you would obtain the desired result; this is the total population of the Inca empire before the conquest, that is, forty-five million, *45,000,000*, neither a person more nor a person less—because the numbers are the numbers.

Loayza went on to argue that only with a population of this magnitude could the Incas have undertaken the large-scale public works programs attributed to them. These and "the agricultural system" provide "convincing proof for accepting absolutely such a population density."[15]

It is hard to imagine now that Loayza was serious—certainly both his logic and his arithmetic were in a class of their own. Just the same, his comment provides a short course in the most extreme methods and results of the High Counters. Although none of them has expressed so pathological a respect for numerical methodology, most have treated the numbers they accept or generate with the same high regard.[16]

Following Loayza's method, if not formally then in its barest bones, the methodology of the High Counters can be contained in a simple algebraic formula. Solving for X, the population size at or just before the time of contact, it would be something like this: $X = e (a + b + c + d)$. The variable a is a number mentioned in some postcontact estimate recorded in a source and which the High Counters take to be a relatively small subset of the total population—tax-paying male adults, for example. The variable b is the number attributed to another subpopulation (e.g., adult males of taxable age exempt from taxation for various reasons); c and d are yet other subpopulations (perhaps women of all ages and children under a certain age); and e is a depopulation ratio concocted to take the population level back to precontact times. It is an equation in which no more than one part is recorded, and even that one part is not necessarily known.

Typically in these exercises, variables *b*, *c*, and *d* combined are held to outnumber variable *a* by about four or five to one, while the total population at the count (that is, variables *a* through *d*) is reckoned to be no more than one-third to one-twenty-fifth of the contact population. Thus, the contact population, or *X*, is calculated to be as great as *a* × 5 × 25, or 125 times as great as the number of people actually counted on the occasion in question. In this process *a* becomes merely the starting point in an arithmetical whirling dervish in which *b*, *c*, *d*, and especially *e* have a habit of growing inversely to the size of *a*. Whatever the other methodological assumptions of High Counters might be, they depend intimately on making this formula seem to work. In this process *a* is given special tolerance since it is likely to be the only element of the equation for which an actual number is available. As such this number is generally held to be above reproach, no matter how high, how round, or how implausibly secured it might be. And *a* is never permitted to represent all the people at a given time and place but only some proportion, usually a small one (10–25 percent), of the whole population.

———

In the chapters to come, readers may find what they regard as inordinate attention to the High Counters' handling of sources. Just the same, it is always justifiable to judge a historiographical enterprise by the way it uses its sources. At first I had assumed that Cook and Borah's handling of the Hispaniola evidence was an aberration required by the magnitude of their task, but I was to find that this was not so—that the High Counters have consistently had trouble coming to full and fair terms with the evidence. In studying their writings for some twenty years, I have learned that they generally treat their sources in a way that falls remarkably short of the standards historians expect of each other. In almost every instance I have looked at, certain patterns have shown themselves: clearly tendentious selectivity in identifying, consulting, and interpreting sources; devising unacceptable translations; relying on such translations in lieu of the originals; quoting out of context; failing to test the reliability of sources; and, with that failure, an inevitable, if anachronistic, credulity.

The second reason for this concern is embodied in Albert Crosby's comment that forms the point of departure for chapter 9. In it Crosby remarks favorably on the way in which High Counters handle sources, while disparaging their predecessors and their critics for failing to do the same. The work of Crosby, who is not quite a quantifier himself but one who would probably count himself a fellow traveler, has been aimed at the intelligent nonspecialist and has been rightly and widely influential. His invidious contrast between those who rely on "tradition" and those who rely on "much research and analysis of original sources" is both uncannily evocative of the rhetoric of the High Counters and likely to have the effect of persuading interested parties that it is correct. In contrast, I am interested in showing that in their work the High Counters are all too often less rigorous and more tendentious than those they criticize.

None of what follows is to suggest that those who counted low were more likely to have estimated the actual population of the Americas in 1492 more accurately than those who now count high. They were, however, less pretentious in their work and their discourse and therefore more in harmony with the modest probabilities for success. Clearly, the High Counters have learned to talk a better battle, as we see (to cite just one recent example) in Linda Newson's remark that "the historical demography of the contact period has now become one of the most productive research fields in New World history, drawing scholars from an ever-widening range of disciplines."[17] Substitute "prolific" for "productive" and Newson's statement is on target, but as it stands it treats the concept of productivity in a confined and inchoate way.

My line of reasoning here is not to suggest that historians should remain either docilely quiescent or invincibly suspicious in the face of refractory source material. Rather, the argument is that we should feel obliged at least to tether, rather than tie, ourselves to the sources' testimony as a point of departure, and to accept or reject any evidence only after applying rigorous criticism, whether linguistic, textual, contextual, or transmissional.

One good reason to begin by doubting is that there are at least three particularly alarming things about numbers in sources. They can be easily changed, whether accidentally or purposefully; the changes, however minor paleographically, can be momentous; and changes in numbers are more likely than changes in letters to evade even the closest scrutiny. Adding a zero at the end of an Arabic number multiplies it by ten; adding an integer before an existing number can multiply it by much more than ten (e.g., 10,000 can easily become 910,000).[18] It is hard to think of comparable examples involving letters. Worse yet, changing a number does not advertise itself to readers, especially readers far removed in time and mental outlook. Few changes in number render a context unintelligible enough to arouse suspicion immediately. The most a change does is to render it unlikely—or, occasionally, when physical laws or known measurements are involved, impossible—and even then further knowledge is required to recognize the impossibility. So changing a number is seldom self-evident.[19]

————

Having outlined the predispositions that inform my argument, I should say something about the ways in which I develop it. As noted, I had originally intended a case-by-case study of the High Counters' stormy encounters with the sources. This would have been a perfectly feasible approach, but it would also have been repetitive, ultimately uninteresting, and above all gloomy and soporific. No less worrisome, the approach suffers the severe handicap of decontextualizing the discussion at the expense of the insights to be gained from a wider view of the question of numbers. In the end it seemed preferable to approach the issue in a variety of complementary ways.[20]

The present work came to be divided roughly into two parts. The first and larger one addresses the concepts, procedures, and results of the High Counters as they have gone about estimating the aboriginal population of the Americas. It includes several case studies—of both populations and High Counters. The second part is more complicated and diffuse, and some might view it as slightly irrelevant. It deals with similar issues over a much broader spectrum of time and space—the sort of "numbers in history" exercise mentioned earlier. It is occasioned by my belief that the High Counters operate very much *in vacuo*, devising standards of probability and treating sources in the New World situation as if they represent something of a novel case. The treatment here is far from wholly satisfying, since the corpus of work on which to draw is truly immense; one result is the strange-bedfellows outcome mentioned before. But it should give a flavor of how neatly the High Counter debate fits into a much longer-standing tradition.

In this widely conspective approach, it will seem at times as though I have padded note citations unmercifully. Perhaps so, but this seems unavoidable and even beneficial considering that my purpose is to show that cavalier use of numbers in sources and credulous use of sources in the larger historiographical world have been widespread, and that although credulity may have waned, it has by no means died out. In aid of this I use the notes to carry references to these cases instead of offering either a laborious case-by-case-by-case analysis or, worse, another argument supported largely by discourse and rhetoric.[21]

The temptation to be broadly comparative is reinforced by the frequency with which High Counters and others constantly express hope that somehow the defects in the data will be overcome. In speaking of the contact population question, for instance, Calvin Martin conceded that "[t]his is of course an extremely difficult question to answer" but managed at the same time to see an end to the tunnel, since he went on that "it may be true that we are some years away from wholly reliable estimates of the aboriginal population for the hemisphere and its constituent parts."[22] Far away from the Americas, Nicholas Postgate expressed a similar wistful hopefulness about Abu Salabikh in the mid-third millennium B.C.: "[E]ven if an absolute figure for the city's population remains frustratingly elusive," hope must not be extinguished.[23]

Finally, a word about what this work does not aim or claim to be. One reader in particular felt that I should approach the matter on the level of, for example, critiquing Cook and Borah's use of the *suma de visitas de pueblos,* discussed in chapter 4. It seems to me, however, that at the moment there is greater need for a way-of-thinking approach than for a way-of-doing approach. Earlier criticisms, both my own and those discussed herein, have not succeeded in stemming the tide of thinking that presumes the possibility of reaching defensible and definitive numbers for the contact population of the Americas. In part because of this, and in part because I believe that epistemology must precede and guide methodology in most things, I intend this work largely to establish a case for the need of such critiques in the hope that it might stimulate more of them and that they in turn will be more effective.

Just the same, I have not eschewed completely the chance to pursue some microcriticism on both textual and arithmetical levels, wherever it seems helpful in making a particular argument clearer. Indulging in too much of this, however, would result only in forcing readers to oscillate too often between analytical planes, and I thought it more important to devote attention instead to the manifold comparative evidence regarding both source criticism and arithmetical exercises. Readers are urged to consult relevant works as cited for more particulars while bearing in mind that much yet remains to be done.[24]

Let me conclude these preliminary comments by citing an observation, more in the nature of a challenge, made about a century and a half ago by E. G. Squier. It was not issued in a completely dispassionate spirit, but for all that it is a sentiment that bears being brought front and center.

> Whoever announces a discovery to the world, in any branch of research, must expect to have it subjected to every test sanctioned by the rules of evidence. Nor should it be a matter of complaint, if this scrutiny should be conducted with apparent severity towards themselves, particularly when, as in this instance, we have no collateral evidence to which appeal may be had in support of [the] presumed discovery.[25]

The Historiographical
Career of One Number

*The only proper way to criticize [existing figures] is to displace them
by more accurate figures.*

— Moheau,
Recherches et considérations sur la population de la France

*I dislike churches, and had I my way, I would write on every church,
chapel and cathedral only one line:—Important if true.*

—A. W. Kinglake, quoted by Richard B. Ince in
*Calverley and Some Cambridge Wits
of the Nineteenth Century*

After having ravaged parts of Spain for more than two decades, the
Vandals, finding themselves beset in turn by the more powerful Visigoths, looked afield—and saw North Africa, one of the most pros-
perous regions of the Roman empire. In A.D. 429 the Vandals crossed
from Spain en masse. Some sixty years later, Victor of Vita described
the crossing of the Strait of Gibraltar as a fixed and formal occasion:

> A large number made the crossing, and in his cunning duke Geiseric, in-
> tending to make the reputation of his people a source of dread, ordered
> then and there that the entire crowd was to be counted, even those who
> had come from the womb into the light that very day. Including old
> men, young men and children, slaves and masters, there was found to be
> a total of 80,000. News of this has spread quickly, until today those ig-
> norant of the matter think that this is the number of their armed men.[1]

Victor's narrative is the only extant account of this occasion
that includes a number, although Procopius, writing sixty years later,

said something that seems at first similar. Speaking of Geiseric's organization of his North African conquests, Procopius wrote: "The Vandals and the Alani he arranged in companies, appointing over them no less than eighty captains, . . . making it appear that his host of fighting men in active service amounted to eighty thousand."[2]

Victor's story—and in particular his figure of 80,000—has found remarkable favor in modern circles interested in the matter of barbarian numbers. Even those who doubt the figures in the sources for other barbarian groups find themselves more charitably inclined toward this particular number. This recognition typically takes the form of using the number without comment, thus treating it as unexceptionable.[3]

Stronger, more explicit, claims have also been advanced. Hans Delbrück, who was otherwise severely critical of the numbers of barbarians in the sources, was disposed to accept this figure so long as it was held to represent the entire population.[4] J. B. Bury, citing the circumstances of the count, felt that the figure had "particular claims on our attention."[5] Marc Bloch thought the total low and asked whether we ought to be "hypnotized by a raw number," but decided that yes, we should, in this instance.[6] A.H.M. Jones thought that estimates of Germanic hordes were "for the most part grossly exaggerated," with "the one exception" of the Vandal census.[7] Perry Anderson claimed that "[t]he only reliable figure for the size of the first invasions is that of the Vandal community, which was counted by its chiefs . . . and numbered 80,000."[8] Josiah Russell remarked that "[i]t is generally believed that the 80,000 assigned to the Vandals . . . is a real number based upon an exact count."[9]

Like others, Pierre Riché was grateful for the datum, commenting that whereas figures ranging from 70,000 to 500,000 had been advanced for the number of Visigoths who invaded Spain, "we know at least that the Vandals were 80,000 when they crossed the Strait of Gibraltar."[10] Dietrich Claude thought that Victor's testimony was "a secure datum" that allowed plausible speculation about the sizes of other barbarian groups, while for R.A.G. Carson the number was "an accepted estimate."[11] José Orlandis found the number "plausible."[12] Arthur Ferrill was categorical, regarding Victor's figure as a "major benchmark, the one certain figure," even while he was uncertain whether or not it was inclusive.[13] Michel Rouche confused his readers by first asserting that "a host [of Vandals] 80,000 strong" crossed into Africa and later speaking of "some 84,000 [*sic*]" Vandals on the occasion.[14] Finally, E. A. Thompson declared that Victor's information was "the only figure that is certain" and extrapolated from it to calculate at "rather less than 200,000" the number of barbarians who entered the Roman empire in 406.[15]

Outstripping these is the remarkable accolade that E. F. Gautier conferred on this uncorroborated datum. After referring to the question of barbarian "effectives" and commenting that "in no other matter has the popular imagination and, following it, the imagination of the chroniclers, taken such liberties with verisimilitude and reality," Gautier went on to say that with Victor's 80,000, "we are in the presence of a particular case." Gautier concluded with a remarkable statement: "[T]he official result of this census, known to everyone, constrained by the nautical knowledge of the Andalusian population, [and] transmitted from mouth to mouth in the form of a wholly dry number fixed once and for all, does not leave any play to the imagination."[16]

―――――――

Although Victor's text seems definite enough, there remains some dispute as to whom Geiseric had counted. Jakob Haury and Ludwig Schmidt argued over whether Geiseric had counted females as well as males.[17] By arguing the negative, Haury in effect more than doubled the figure in Victor's account. In turn, Otto Seeck, taking his cue from Procopius, went still further: Victor was defining not the Vandal population as a whole, or even the males, but only fighting men.[18]

The contrary view—that Geiseric's census was a universal one—is often justified by the argument that the count was to determine how many ships would be needed to transport the Vandals across the Strait of Gibraltar. Herwig Wolfram goes the farthest in this regard by chastising the Goths for having "neglected to take such a precautionary measure, . . . which is why they never . . . left any figures about the size of their people."[19] However, Wolfram is by no means alone in his assumptions about why Geiseric counted.[20] Justine Randers-Pehrson gives credence to the figure because "[t]here had to be an accurate determination of the number of vessels needed for the crossing to Africa," with the result that "this time the count must have been more trustworthy than usual."[21] This modern rationalization is all rather peculiar. In the first place, it blithely rejects Victor's testimony in the search to find reasons to accept his number.[22] Worse yet, it overlooks the most likely interpretation of Victor's own wording in this regard—that Geiseric counted his people *after* they had debarked.[23]

As we see, such suggestions are in no way countenanced by Victor's text beyond casual juxtaposition.[24] At some point the Vandal leaders must have given thought to just this problem, as did William of Normandy in 1066 and General Dwight Eisenhower in 1944. Even so, such views, which are never explicitly defended, can only be regarded as ex post facto attempts to find a rational explanation for this problematic narrative and in the process to lend legitimation to the number it provides.

Although grounds for belief in Victor's number are seldom expressed, we might suspect two reasons for it. The first is simply, as Henri Irenée Marrou put it, that "without [Victor's account] the history of [North] Africa at the end of the fifth century would be an almost blank page."[25] A second reason is that Victor's circumstantial and categorical account is central to larger arguments about barbarian numbers generally, as well as numbers of their fighting men.

———————

Arguing that "[a] more intriguing matter is the number itself," Walter Goffart has recently shown that the figure of 80,000—or rather figures in multiples of eight and forty—were clichés in the literature ranging from the Bible to writings of the later Roman empire.[26] A few others have also expressed doubts.[27] It seems possible, though, to discredit Victor's account solely on its own testimony.[28]

As the passage reads, it is clear that Victor believed—or wrote as if he believed—that both the crossing and the count occurred on the same day, with the second apparently following the first. This is clearly an impossibility, but one that he appears not to recognize. Then, too, his argument that Geiseric ordered the count in order to impress his enemies renders Geiseric less "cunning" than stupid. Numbers wielded for the immediate benefit of others—whether statistics collected on crowd sizes or numbers of homeless estimated—need have no relation to reality, since it is only the impression that matters. If Geiseric intended this as a piece of propaganda, it would have been equally effective, and much less troublesome, merely to put his preferred figure abroad.

Nor does it seem useless to ask where Victor got his information so much later. Was it from public report (i.e., propaganda) handed down to the next generation?[29] No ratio of ships to people could have mattered so much that Geiseric would have undertaken the consequential labor of counting 80,000 persons. The Vandals apparently were under no grave duress to leave Spain immediately but were making a deliberate choice to relocate operations. Minimizing the number of round trips across the Strait of Gibraltar should not have been a particular consideration; hence there was no need to correlate numbers of people with numbers of ships.[30] And, since a round trip would have taken no more than a few hours, would Geiseric not have used a shuttle system that guarded against a disastrous shipwreck?

Victor's figure has been put to nondemographic purposes as well. J. Le Gall's principal argument for a landborne rather than a seaborne passage from Tangier to Hippo, which the Vandals besieged the next year, was that the Vandals could not have commandeered enough ships to make the voyage "all at the same time."[31] Le Gall's conclusions—that the journey was made overland because it must have been—has generally been accepted, as have, by extension, his reasons for adopting them.[32]

Wolfram best explains the argument that derives the most benefit from believing Victor. Commenting on the difficulties and controversies in archaeologically pinning the Visigoths down in France, he observes that "[o]f course no one openly declares his biases but smuggles them in through the 'most reasonable' of human inventions, statistics." Speaking of the disparity in modern estimates of numbers of Visigoths at the time (from 100,000 to more than 200,000), he goes on:

> The origin of all the problems is Gaiseric's count of his Vandals in 429 in his efforts to procure enough ships. . . . Gaiseric . . . counted his people, supposedly right up to eighty thousand. Historians then complete the calculation. If the Vandals had a certain size but still ran away from the [Visi]Goths, the victors must then have been even more numerous: the results of such calculations are the statistics mentioned above.[33]

In short, historians have tapped Victor's account of Geiseric's census to serve as the basis for a series of assumption-laden extrapolations designed to impute figures to all the invading "hordes" of the fourth and fifth centuries. Nonetheless, when all is said and done, Goffart's observation remains compellingly true: "How many Vandals and other barbarians Geiseric led into Africa continues to be anybody's guess."[34]

———

One number in one source—this is the legacy of Victor of Vita's 80,000 Vandals. The context of the number and its reception illustrate remarkably well many of the elements that we will look at later in this work. First there is the text itself. It is not hard to find it unpersuasive. Victor offers the number, but not the source of his information. Then he provides an explanation—Geiseric's "cunning"—that belies itself because it requires us to believe that Geiseric undertook his count only to formulate a number that would have served his alleged purpose just as easily if he had plucked it from thin air. Finally, Victor seems to say that all the counting, as well as the debarkation, occurred during a single day ("then and there" [*ilico*]). To treat this passage as history requires a powerful will to believe.

The lesson in this story, however, is that there exists just this will. The wanness of Victor's story has proved no impediment to a century of firm and vigorously pronounced belief in aid of securing a number that historians could convince themselves was irrefutable enough to build on—and on.[35] Historians have believed in the number seriously enough to dispute its meaning: did Victor intend it to represent all the Vandals or just males? Or did he even consider the issue in these terms? In the process they impute to Victor an explanation—the need to calculate transport requirements—that is certainly more plausible than his own, but hardly plausible enough. In particular, Victor's number has been used to create new numbers and in the process to rehabilitate old ones—a practice that underlies the enterprise of those who would put numbers to American Indians at the time of first contact.

Treating in such depth a single figure from the historical record, then, serves as a useful entrée to the discussions that follow, few of which can be so comprehensive. Victor's 80,000 is more than just synecdoche, though; it is also a symbol of the divers ways of belief that pervade the treatment of such numbers when they appear. Most often Victor's number has been accepted without demur as a by-product of other sets of concerns. Nearly as often it has been defended and justified and then used for specific demographic and logistical arguments. Only occasionally has it been contextualized and rejected.

Higher Numbers, Higher Ground

Any present attempt to ascertain by means of the literature on the subject, the Indian numbers in pre-Columbian or even early historic times, within the present area of the United States, must be through a maze of contradiction and confusion. Although the examination should be confined to authorities who did not twaddle about imaginary millions and at least pretended to furnish statistics, even those are only valuable for comparison, and when corroborated by the tests of probability and possibility applied of late years by science to all historiographers.

—Garrick Mallery,
"The Former and Present Number of Our Indians"

Whatever mental reservations one may have as to the probability of the incident, by no sound application of the laws of historical testimony can it be disproved, save by the appearance of contrary evidence yet undiscovered.

—Jarvis M. Morse,
"John Smith and His Critics"

In the 1930s the population of the western hemisphere at the time of the arrival of the Europeans was estimated at 8 million. Some fifty years later it was asserted that on the morning of 12 October 1492, no fewer than 51.6 million American Indians were living in central Mexico alone, and up to 70 million were living elsewhere.[1] This represents a change in orders of magnitude, nothing less than a paradigm shift. But unlike most such shifts, this change was not grounded in an increase in the amount of direct evidence available. In fact, during this fifty-year period there was no change in the evidence at all—

in 1935 there was no direct evidence available, and today there is none either.

On the contrary, this fifteen-fold increase in the postulated contact population was based on instrument rather than evidence. Newly introduced European diseases, which had enjoyed some popularity as an engine of population decline in the eighteenth century and before, once again became the chief means used to explain a much greater decline—a classic deus ex machina. Views on the number and variety of these diseases, the timing of their impact, the extent of their spread, and the mortality they inflicted have all undergone changes. While there is no a priori reason to argue that lower hemispheric or regional estimates are more likely to be true than higher ones, the latter depart from sound historical method by requiring more assumptions, by demanding more explanations for greater losses, by making the silence of the sources even more mystifying, and by treating the testimony of these sources as unexceptionable to an alarmingly greater degree.

————

The enterprise of the High Counters is only the latest in a long line of attempts to put population numbers to all or large parts of the globe. Some of these efforts were perfunctory, even formulaic. Giovanni Battista Riccioli assigned people to various parts of the world in practically geometrical fashion and almost as an afterthought.[2] Apparently it was what cosmographers did.[3] In 1721 Montesquieu published his *Lettres persanes,* an example of the epistolographic technique advocating a particular line of reasoning by putting the arguments into the mouths of fictitious characters.[4] Montesquieu was firmly of the opinion that the world he lived in was in a state of steady, probably irreversible, decay, not least in terms of its population. This he saw not as growing but as declining at such a rate that "the earth will be a desert in a thousand years."[5] He offered no figures but asserted nonetheless that modern Greece had only "a hundredth" of its ancient population; that France was "nothing" compared to the picture Caesar had painted of it nearly two thousand years before; that the city of Rome had once been as populous as any of the European states in his time; and that in the Americas "we cannot find . . . the fiftieth part of the men who once formed great empires there."[6] Montesquieu concluded that "[a]fter a calculation as exact as possible in such circumstances, I have found that there is on earth scarcely a tenth of the people living in ancient times."[7] He left it to his readers either to agree with him on faith or disagree on the grounds of lack of argument.[8]

In his arguments Montesquieu was by no means alone, or even

particularly extreme. At about the same time he was writing, Benito Jerónimo Feijóo y Montenegro was waging his own war on behalf of high populations in the remote past. Buoyed by the astronomical numbers in biblical and classical sources, and betrayed by the procreative marvels detailed in what turned out to be the account of an imaginary voyage, Feijóo hesitated only momentarily on the way to positing enormous population possibilities.[9] And before either Montesquieu or Feijóo, there was Denis Pétau (1583–1652), who in his turn calculated that in less than three hundred years after the flood, Noah's progeny numbered about 700 billion.[10] Although such calculations are likely to produce only bemused mirth nowadays, their progenitors saw them as perfectly reasonable and plausible hypotheses arising from their particular intellectual worlds. From all appearances, they trusted in the veracity of the sources they had before them, as well as in the extrapolative measures they heroically applied to them.[11]

One who agreed wholeheartedly with all three of these early high counters was Robert Wallace, whose ambitious *A Dissertation on the Numbers of Mankind, in Antient and Modern Times* attempted to quantify Montesquieu's apocalyptic but vague concern and joined him in urging that the population of the present was markedly lower than that of ancient times. Wallace was not particularly interested in the size of his own world's population and was content to suggest that its inhabitants were "many more than 4675 [million], and many fewer than 34720 millions." But perhaps it "does not really contain more than 1000 millions"—coincidentally, the same figure Riccioli advanced.[12]

Displaying a much greater interest in earlier times, Wallace devised a rate of population increase such that, by his reckoning, there could have been above 400 billion people available to be swept away by Noah's flood. He decided, however, that this would have "overstocked the earth long before the deluge," requiring a lower rate of population increase than he had tentatively posited.[13] The flood, of course, required that the process begin again, this time with only a few couples to start the ball rolling. Since by his calculation the length of time between the flood and the time of Alexander the Great was half again that of the Adam-to-Noah period, presumably the population was able to increase to several times antediluvian levels.

To support this contingency, Wallace assiduously fished through the Bible and other classical sources for signs of immense populations and was able to net a large number of large numbers. Some were promising indeed: for instance, that the small Greek city-states of Sicily had populations as large as 800,000.[14] Or that the tiny island of

Aegina in Greece, only twenty miles in circuit, possessed not fewer than 470,000 slaves, never mind the free population.[15] Wallace sought further support for his thesis in estimates of army sizes and, to a lesser degree, of cities and larger areas. These he found aplenty, and his attitude toward them is not wholly unfamiliar. Effectively, he gratefully accepted them just as he found them. There was no hint that he doubted the reliability of any of his sources. On the few occasions when testimonies diverged, Wallace merely averaged the differences and proceeded apace. To arrive at total population figures, he adopted various conversion factors which he tried to gear to particular circumstances. Nonetheless, whenever these proved too low for his argument, he treated the numbers recorded in his sources as referring only to adult males, often despite clear evidence to the contrary—another familiar tactic.[16]

Wallace's estimate of the population of ancient "Belgium" provides a handy microcosm of his method. Taking the warrior figures for eleven tribes that Caesar mentioned in his *De Bello Gallico* at face value, he found that they totaled 298,000.[17] But, he supposed, these were not "all the fighting men in Belgium," but maybe only five-eighths of them, which increased the actual number of soldiers to 496,666. Multiplying by four gave him 1,986,664 inhabitants. But "there were many who were either in the condition of slaves, or only employed in agriculture, and in such mechanic arts as were thought unworthy of brave men. . . . And if we make this lower order of persons to have been thrice as numerous as the rest . . . we must reckon the inhabitants of Belgium about 8,000,000."[18] By dint of such heroic and repeated efforts, Wallace had no trouble at all in concluding his exercise by claiming that the earth was several times more densely populated in ancient times than in his own.[19]

Wallace's attempt to demonstrate that in ancient times there were immense populations prompted David Hume to respond in kind.[20] Hume met Wallace on his own ground, using many of the figures Wallace had adduced, but he drew distinctly different conclusions.[21] After pointing out that even in the eighteenth century no one knew the exact populations of European cities and states, he asked a question that has yet to be answered for the Americas (and which, in his own way, Wallace had asked, if only to ignore it): "How can we pretend to calculate those [numbers] of ancient cities and states, where historians have left us such imperfect traces?"[22] Hume then sought to counter Wallace point by point, sometimes, but not often, by impugning the same sources. In fact, for a renowned skeptic, Hume found it surprisingly difficult to disbelieve the ancient sources. He asserted that Diodorus Siculus, Dionysius of Halicarnassus, and Appian were "all historians, orators, and philosophers, whose testimony is unquestioned."[23] He found himself unable to disagree seriously with the numbers stated by Caesar in his *Gallic War,* and he believed an implausible figure of Diodorus Siculus's simply because he "very seriously insisted on" it.[24]

Thus Hume found it possible to mix doubt and belief in almost equal measures but confined the former to his contemporaries, leaving the ancients almost unscathed. His concluding statement, though, has considerable relevance for recent attempts to measure past populations: "The humour of blaming the present, and admiring the past, is strongly rooted in human nature, and has an influence even on persons endued [*sic*] with the profoundest judgment and most extensive learning."[25]

Although it failed to withstand the test of time, Wallace's work is important for the present discussion because he carried it out so elaborately and in aid of a particular philosophy, and because his methodology so closely mirrors that of later attempts to estimate other populations. Of course, this could hardly have been otherwise. Written records for overall population figures are notoriously lacking, whereas estimates of the sizes of armies are legion. The question for Wallace, and for his successors, was simply to decide what proportion of what population the armies in question represented. As we will see, the policy that Wallace inaugurated (or perhaps perpetuated)—a policy of minimizing this proportion—has proven to be popular, regardless of the ambient circumstances and regardless as well of the quality of the evidence.

———————

The genesis of today's High Counter movement can be traced back to the 1930s, with the work of Carl Sauer, even though he was not much of a counter himself.[26] Sauer's work, emphasizing Indian political and economic achievements before the arrival of the Europeans, broke new ground and provided an impetus for others to go even farther. They did so by, among other things, assigning higher and higher population levels to various Indian groupings throughout the hemisphere, on the assumption that there was a high correlation between population density and societal complexity. Because Sauer and his disciples were largely at the University of California, this line of demographic reasoning soon came to be christened the Berkeley School, a label by which it is still known, long after the dissemination of its views far and wide.[27]

Disagreement and debate about the contact population of the Americas is nothing new. As Woodrow Borah pointed out, "[t]he positions have remained strangely fixated [*sic*] since the eighteenth century, and even earlier."[28] At the end of the eighteenth century, for instance, Francisco Saverio Clavigero heatedly debated arguments expressed somewhat earlier by Cornelius de Pauw.[29] Looking at the basis of Clavigero's argument, which was that the Aztec empire probably had as many as 30 million inhabitants, is akin to a visit out of time, because it anticipated so remarkably the modus operandi of today's High Counters. He relied uncritically on the early chroniclers—indeed, he robustly defended them against the insinuations of de Pauw. He regarded population as the defining index of economic and military power. He resented the vexatious intrusion of someone who was no more than "a Prussian philosopher."[30] He found ways to multiply numbers in the sources by other numbers of his own devising. He found remarkable "uniformity" in the welter of different estimates these sources offered. He found it incredible even to imagine that "many Spanish and Indian writers should all agree to exaggerate the population of those countries, and not one amongst them show some respect for posterity." He asserted that the missionaries led "an exemplary life" and that of their veracity "there can be no doubt." He conjured up "counts" that according to his own sources were eyeball estimates at best. Clavigero concluded indignantly that "if all this which we have said is not sufficent to convince M. de Paw [*sic*], in charity I advise him to take himself off to a hospital."[31] In all, it was an apt prelude to many of the terms and the tenor of the debate that was to recrudesce nearly two centuries later.[32]

4

Damning the Torpedos

I had, also, during many years followed a golden rule, namely, that, whenever a published fact, a new observation or thought came across me, which was opposed to my general results, to make a memorandum of it without fail and at once; for I had found by experience that such facts and thoughts were far more apt to escape from memory than favourable ones. Owing to this habit, very few objections were raised against my views which I had not at least noticed and attempted to answer.

—Charles Darwin,
The Life and Letters of Charles Darwin

But the peculiar evil of silencing the expression of an opinion is, that it is robbing the human race; posterity as well as the existing generation; those who dissent from the opinion, still more than those who hold it. If the opinion is right, they are deprived of the opportunity of exchanging error for truth; if wrong, they lose, what is almost as great a benefit, the clearer perception and livelier impression of truth, produced by its collision with error.

—John Stuart Mill,
On Liberty

There is no better way to become acquainted with the High Counter philosophy and methodology than to look at the movement's industrial gold standard. This is the work that Sherburne Cook, Lesley Simpson, and Woodrow Borah carried out, severally and individually, from the 1940s to the 1960s on the population of central Mexico in the sixteenth century. One of the earliest efforts to formulate contact population estimates, it remains the most extensive of all such projects and has probably had the most influence both inside and outside the movement. Both the methods and their results were quickly incorporated into an overall argument from which further regional studies sprang like tributaries of a major river.

Those who would count high in other areas of the Americas have been lavish in their appreciation of the work of Cook, Simpson, and Borah. According to N. D. Cook, "the majority of researchers . . . recognize that the Borah and Cook [and Simpson] work is the most accurate and hence the most reliable of what we now have."[1] Linda Newson agrees, regarding their work as "an exhaustive analysis of documentary sources."[2] Horacio Larraín Barros declared that "both authors handle with equal facility the historical and ecogeographical information, and their work is placed clearly within the perspective of an extremely rich human and ecological geography."[3] Darcy Ribeiro spoke of "new sources and more precise criteria" that produced estimates "better founded than [those of] their predecessors."[4]

It is no surprise that central Mexico came to serve this role. By all accounts it was the most densely populated area the Spaniards ever encountered, as well as the one for which early postcontact documentation is most ample. It was only natural that population estimates of various parts of the area occurred early and with fair regularity. Servando Teresa de Mier propounded one of the earliest, and still the highest, of these estimates. One of the ideological giants of the Mexican independence movement, Mier held that the population of the "kingdom of Mexico" had once been "a hundred million." Perhaps sensing the implausibility of his claim, Mier hastened to add that this "calculation is not exaggerated" and that the figure heralded a remorseless population decline.[5] In this way the matter of population decline in New Spain became one of the planks in Mier's nationalist platform.[6]

———

One of the salient characteristics of the High Counters is the obduracy with which they ignore criticisms of their work. In the debate over the contact population there has been so little colloquy that the very word "debate" risks being a misnomer. Here I look at several examples in which other scholars have criticized the methods that Cook, Simpson, and Borah adopted for central Mexico. Sometimes this criticism can be regarded as friendly, inasmuch as the critics are sympathetic to the notion of very high but calculable population levels at contact; sometimes it cannot.

Cook began the discussion in a cautious and vague manner in a paper published in 1948. There he asserted only that central Mexico's population at contact was probably "far higher" than the 2.5 million he postulated for the area when Teotihuacán was at its height nearly a thousand years earlier.[7] This proved to be merely an opening gambit, and the matter quickly escalated. Before proceeding, however, it would be useful to say a few words about the *suma de visitas de pueblos* of approximately 1548, a collection of data that survives as a compiled document. Cook and Borah's interpretation of these data in their 1960 book *The Population of Central Mexico in 1548* accounted for a dramatic change in their methods and results.[8]

The *suma* was the first known attempt systematically to count, or account for, the Indian population of New Spain, but the document as we have it covers only about half the towns known to exist there at the time. The numbers in the *suma* are considerably lower than those for the next comparatively broad count, which took place in 1563, and this had led some to assume population growth in the interval.[9] However, since Cook and Borah had become committed to the notion that the Indian population of New Spain declined inexorably and continuously throughout the sixteenth century, they had no choice but to believe that although the *suma* undoubtedly counted people, it must not have counted all of them, even for the towns it encompassed.[10] As they put it in one of their classic *ex hypothesi* formulations: "It is clear . . . that at the time of the *suma* inquiries there were substantial groups in the Indian population who for one reason or another were exempt from payment of tribute to the Spanish overlords, and that such groups were excluded from any count of the tributary population."[11] In this way they gave themselves the task of determining what proportion of the population was excluded from the count and to add this number to the aggregated figures in the *suma*. The result would be the total Indian population of central Mexico in 1548, and it would be a much higher figure than that which was recorded for 1563.

These self-imposed ground rules governed Cook and Borah's every interpretation of the *suma* data. The numbers in the *suma* itself amounted to 1,366,499, but Cook and Borah argued, for instance, that this was only 43 percent of the adult population on the plateau and 65 percent of the adult population in the coastal areas.[12] By the time they finished with these data, they had turned them into their own estimate of 7,392,000, an increase of about 440 percent.[13]

Despite all, this finding presented Cook and Borah with several dilemmas created by Cook and Simpson's earlier work. In the event, they showed that they were open to criticizing this earlier work—the results if not the method. In the first place, Cook and Simpson had previously estimated that there had been 6,427,466 Indians in about

1540.[14] Since the *suma* count came on the heels of a severe epidemic, it seemed impossible that there were more Indians alive eight years later. One of the estimates must be wrong. They decided it was the earlier, lower, one.

A second dilemma related to Cook and Borah's use of early chroniclers' estimates of armies, houses, and cities. These estimates, of course, remained the same, even while Cook and Borah were increasing their "meaning" by a factor of 2.5. This uncongenial state of affairs required that they dispense with their earlier arguments about the relationship of these numbers to total population. These warrior counts became hors d'oeuvres to whet the appetite for the calculations that followed, which Cook and Borah now deemed to have no systematic relationship to the numbers in the chronicles.[15]

Finally, in 1948 Cook and Simpson had rejected using the information in the *suma* because they believed it was "a compilation of extant materials," that "the data included in it extend over the period 1531–1544," and that "there are wide differences in its treatment of the various provinces—differences in time, in methods of gathering, and in criteria of evaluation." Moreover, "very important sections of the country" were omitted, which was true enough. More importantly, "the estimates given in the *suma* are demonstrably too low."[16] In 1960 Cook and Borah briefly alluded to this earlier position but offered no explanation for why they had come to feel that the counts were sufficiently simultaneous to be blended together in a kind of numerical gumbo.[17] Once inadmissible as a source, the *suma* now became the basis for all kinds of arithmetical manipulation and projection. Given Borah and Cook's deterministic model, which described an invariable course and outcome once the assumptions had been slotted into place, this use of the *suma* was entirely predictable.

Borah and Cook breathed life into a fear that George Kubler had expressed more than a decade earlier. Reviewing Cook and Simpson's *Population of Central Mexico in the Sixteenth Century,* Kubler had worried about several of their procedures and assumptions and offered a critique as cogent as any since. He considered that "the attempt to value these early estimates positively is useful and provocative, providing it elicits protest." He continued, presciently: "There is always danger that for another generation we shall read that it has been 'proven' that the 1519 population of central Mexico was 11,000,000."[18]

Little could Kubler have realized how right—and how wrong—he would be. Considerably less than a generation later, Cook, now joined by Borah, decided not to wait but to reject the premises behind the figure of 11 million themselves. They chose a characteristic way to do this. Instead of acknowledging Kubler's strictures, they more than doubled their earlier figure, by means of the same set of premises and procedures that had led to it in the first place.

In turn, this new and higher estimate necessarily implied a much greater rate of depopulation than they had previously suspected, and because Cook and Borah operated on the principle that depopulation curves were not seriously affected by ambient circumstances, they inevitably found it necessary to seek a population for 1519 that was much in excess of their earlier estimate.[19] To do this they combined new calculations and extrapolations based on the 1548 *suma* with an interpretation of certain postconquest tribute records, particularly the *Codex Mendoza* and the *Matrícula de tributos*. Since the pictographic tribute records mentioned no numbers of people at all and contained a good deal of ambiguity as to amount, distribution, and periodicity of tribute, Cook and Borah were forced time and time again into artificial respiration in order to keep various equations alive. By the time the dust had settled, their new estimate was no less than 25.2 million, based on a range of 20 million to 28 million.[20]

The nature of the data in the *suma* congenially allows anyone to choose from a smorgasbord of information precisely those parts that suit a particular appetite. The effects of this are perhaps clearest in Borah and Cook's introduction to their discusssion of the conversion factors they eventually adopted. There they laid out several definitions (*casados, tributarios, vecinos, indios*) and concluded that "all the[se] terms were approximately synonymous and interchangeable at the time of the *suma*."[21] Even before finishing the paragraph in which this slightly hedged statement occurred, Borah and Cook removed the qualification: now the term *casado* was "equivalent to and interchangeable with *vecino*, or head of household, *indio*, and 'tributary.'" It thus provides," they concluded, "a stable factor in terms of which other relations may be calculated."[22]

Proceeding in this fashion permitted Borah and Cook to recruit what to others had seemed disparate data, call them the same, and commence counting. In agreeing that all oranges were also apples, however, there was the danger that Borah and Cook had simply ignored the complexities of the usages in the sources, and presumably of the conditions on the ground, in order to achieve the required breakthrough.

This was particularly the case since the equating process involved so few data—only one source was cited. It is hardly an uninteresting citation, however. Referring to a series of five brief reports submitted by Augustinian friars years after the *suma*, Borah and Cook asserted that these "expressly declare[d] tributaries and *casados* to be synonymous" and then cited an example: "Tiene este dicho pueblo [Xantetelco] quatrocientos yndios poco más o menos, juntos por su horden, pues estos quatrocientos yndios son casados que se llaman tributarios."[23] They were exactly right in their specific citation, but the conclusion they drew from it might not be. After all, of the nearly sixty population figures given in these reports, this is the *only* one explicitly to make this equation, suggesting that the writers had made this point simply because it was so unusual and that they had not made the sweeping equation Borah and Cook attributed to them. The use of "este dicho pueblo" supports such a view.

Borah and Cook continued with a passage from another letter in the set: "[S]uman los tributarios deste pueblo [Totolapan] y sus subjetos 2952 más 839 viudos y viudas." The point in quoting this is unclear since it adds nothing to their argument. Nonetheless, there is something of interest in these figures—the pueblo-by-pueblo subtotals underpinning it aggregate to only 2,715 tributaries and 779 widowers and widows.[24] Either only 92.8 percent of the adult men were tributaries or the Augustinians were unable to add (or to count?). Neither alternative is a good sign.[25] Nor is the fact that Borah and Cook failed to notice the discrepancy, or at least to comment on it.[26]

Borah and Cook concluded, oddly, that "[s]ince the reports are of 1569–1570 [in fact, they are all dated 1571], this usage is a survival of older custom."[27] Here is perfectly circular reasoning, for they impute to their unwitting source their own opinion that the equation *tributario = casado = vecino = indio* existed early enough to be incorporated into the 1548 *suma*. Actually, what these reports have to say about this relationship is little more than that in one particular town, Xantetelco, at one particular time, the Augustinians thought that all the adult male Indians happened to be married, and that in another town, Totolapan, figures could lie.

Small but repeated operational decisions such as these made it possible for Borah and Cook—and would make it possible for anyone else—to arrive at any number whatever for the total population, depending only on their particular menu selections. This circumstance encouraged objections to any particular strategy.

It is not hard to understand why anyone with a modest allotment of skepticism would find such remorseless massaging of the available data repugnant. Not surprisingly, even while most students of the *suma* agreed that its compilers were not concerned with tabulating every Indian in central Mexico, many were taken aback by an argument that it had in fact recorded only one in four or five. They did not swallow Pierre Chaunu's facile dictum, "The sources have spoken."[28] Unlike Chaunu, many students of the subject clearly recognized—it was no secret—that the sources had been spoken for. The question was whether the ventriloquists had done their job well.

Others, less committed to a single overarching demographic schema, questioned Borah and Cook's use of the *suma* and the cascade of results that eventuated. The first of these was Angel Rosenblat, who published an extended critique of Borah and Cook's study in 1967.[29] Rosenblat began by stating the obvious—that Borah and Cook had been forced to supplement the data in the *suma* by extrapolating from population estimates dating from a couple of decades later. He charged that for Tlaxcala they relied on what were eyeball estimates and then used them in such a way that "the 50,000 tributaries" in them "were converted into 630,000 inhabitants." Finally, he discerned some examples of double-counting in which Borah and Cook had confounded towns and provinces and used their data more than once.[30]

These sins constituted what Rosenblat termed "the first manipulation." He went on to question the proportion of the whole that these tributaries represented. Borah and Cook had argued that the *suma* ignored the chiefly and noble class, the young and the women, the old and sick, and the slaves. This assumption, Rosenblat suggested, "appears based, almost entirely, on pure supposition and on poorly interpreted readings" of the sources. To support his reasoning, he discussed about forty examples cited by Borah and Cook, which, he argued, all indicated that the proportion of these excluded categories was much less than 50 percent of the whole and was very often zero. If true, then Cook and Borah's addition of about 1.5 million excluded-category people—their "second manipulation"—was "in large part gratuitous."[31]

Rosenblat then turned to his "third manipulation," which was merely the reflection of the second: the addition of *mayeques*, or chiefly retainers, who, according to Borah and Cook, constituted about 35 percent of the whole population. Rosenblat noted how tiny the sample was from which Borah and Cook had drawn their inferences—figures from seven localities spread over twenty-seven years and amounting to only about thirty thousand people.[32] Rosenblat wondered why there was not more evidence for this allegedly numerous group or, for that matter, why the Spaniards, who everlastingly complained about the shortage of manpower, would have tolerated such a large class of exempt people.[33] He concluded by citing a number of eyewitness accounts which suggested that the Spaniards were not acting nearly as uncharacteristically as Cook and Borah supposed. In fact, Ropsenblat charged, Cook and Borah had greatly magnified the number of excluded *mayeques*.[34]

Rosenblat concluded that a base population of about 1,366,500 for central Mexico in 1548 was acceptable; that Borah and Cook's addition of 1,572,883 "inhabitants" based on their new extrapolation was "exaggerated"; that their calculation of 1,469,609 exempt (i.e., noncounted) Indians was "unsustainable"; that perhaps as many as 300,000 belonged to this group; that likewise, Borah and Cook's estimate of 1,830,000 *mayeques* should be reduced to 300,000; and that at most there were 10,000 slaves rather than 50,000. For Rosenblat, then, the population of "all of New Spain" in 1548 was about 3,176,000, or just about 41 percent of Borah and Cook's estimate of 7,817,000 for the same area.[35]

These criticisms led Rosenblat to speculate on the possibility of arriving at a reasonable estimate of the population in 1519. He observed that "this complex system of calculations, in which each supposition is based on another series of suppositions, is very vulnerable."[36] The larger suppositions were that the population of central Mexico in 1548 was 7.8 million, that it had declined at a steady and precipitous rate since 1519, and that the postconquest tribute records could, if discriminatingly used, enable scholars to transform the codices' pictures into numbers simply by applying more suppositions to the problem.[37]

Rosenblat picked out a few of Borah and Cook's more egregious assumptions about the value and periodicity of certain tribute payments and the relationship of these to numbers of people, and he showed how fatuous some of these assumptions had to be, since they were entirely unsupported by evidence not of Borah and Cook's own devising.[38] In this case Rosenblat did not offer an estimate of his own.

In sum, Rosenblat gathered an extended bill of indictment against Borah and Cook's use of the *suma de visitas* to devise a population estimate for 1548, let alone for 1519. Perhaps the most salient aspect of this criticism was the way in which Rosenblat pressed home the impression that this use was consciously designed in part and in sum to educe the largest possible population.

What effect did Rosenblat's sweeping criticisms have on Borah and Cook? Did his strictures goad them into a point-by-point response? Hardly. The only discernible responses were a review and a single sentence in each of two of the pair's more obscure articles.[39] In the first sentence, buried in a footnote, Borah and Cook—quite unfairly since Rosenblat had offered no guesses in this case—stigmatized him as "very much an upholder of very low [*sic*] estimates of pre-Conquest population" and referred readers to Rosenblat's *Población de América en 1492* "for the temper and kind of discussion."[40] In the second, Borah noted that "[t]he readings, interpretations, and adjustments [in the *suma de visitas* of 1548] have been objected to at length by Angel Rosenblat, *La población de América en 1492.*"[41] Period. Even this token gesture disappeared in a slightly revised version of that essay which appeared several years later.[42]

It would seem that essays entitled "Materials for the Demographic History of Mexico, 1500–1960," "An Essay on Method," and "Family and Household in Mexican Enumerations since the Spanish Conquest," all by Cook and Borah and all published four years after Rosenblat's critique, would have provided them ample opportunity to respond to his critique with more than a contemptuous shrug.[43] But, no—Rosenblat's 1967 work makes their bibliography but is otherwise mentioned only for Rosenblat's views on Hispaniola, and then only to be dismissed.

Nor in any of Borah's later, largely retrospective, works does he mention Rosenblat's criticisms, which, it would be no exaggeration to say, strike at the heart of his and Cook's entire enterprise. As a result, a wonderful opportunity for early and fruitful dialogue was jettisoned. To determine whether this is typical of their reaction to other criticism, let us look at the interactive pattern between Cook and Borah and their critics.

———————

William Sanders was the next critic to take aim at Cook and Borah.[44] For whatever reasons, Sanders's efforts have remained more visible over time than those of any other critic, and his estimates are the ones cited in counterpoise to Cook and Borah's. Like that of Rosenblat, Sanders's criticism was intended to be comprehensive and to stake out an alternative position on a range of issues. Like Rosenblat, as well as later critics, Sanders focused on Cook and Borah's use of the *suma* of 1548 and on the way in which they interpreted the codices that appear to contain preconquest tributary data.

Sanders began by suggesting that Cook and Borah were willing to put rather more faith in the accuracy of the *suma* numbers than they warranted. He pointed out ways and means and reasons why such data were fudged in the early postconquest period and suggested that the case of Cortés's own estates, which Cook and Borah regarded as typical, was in fact "exceptional, perhaps unique," even if conveniently accessible and congenial to their argument.[45]

Sanders next turned to what had become the crux of the *suma* affair—the conversion factors that Cook and Borah used. As we have seen, the the two were disposed to descry a very large excluded population, large enough certainly to ensure an extrapolated total population many times larger than the one that appeared on paper. Sanders concluded, as have all Cook and Borah's critics in this respect, that their multipliers were based on too small and too atypical a sample. Again like other critics, Sanders found it hard to imagine a population of excluded categories that was more than double the population of those who actually were included in the *suma* arithmetic, and he regarded Cook and Borah's "statistical manipulations to arrive at a figure for the tax-exempt population in 1548" to be their "weakest argument."[46] He thought that the sample they used to calculate the percentage of excluded categories was too small—11 of 1,200 localities, 9 of them outside central Mexico.

Like Rosenblat, Sanders could only disagree that there were still other large categories not included in the *suma* count. Nor did Sanders think that the *mayeques* could really have amounted to 35 percent of the whole population, again agreeing with Rosenblat. Sanders pointed out that Cook and Borah agreed that the *mayeques* accounted for only about 10 percent of the population in 1563, forcing them to argue that this group had declined faster than any other segment of the population, for reasons they never divulged. Sanders took exception as well to Cook and Borah's habit of averaging small samples and very wide ranges, as if this could be a valid procedure *in vacuo*. Although not as forceful as Rosenblat in his rejection of Cook and Borah's premises— allowing, for instance, a higher proportion for various exempted groups—Sanders unquestionably regarded their handling of the *suma* data as deficient in almost every respect.

Sanders had similar, if less stringent, objections to some of the results of Cook and Borah's estimates for later periods as well, but I will discuss only his criticism of their contact estimates. These were as might be expected. Sanders felt that Cook and Borah (and earlier Simpson) were unnecessarily ingenuous in relying on warrior and house counts and on claims of baptismal prodigies. In particular, he took them to task for relying so heavily on Cortés and López de Gómara, and he cited Bernal Díaz del Castillo in contradiction, though Sanders seems not to have noticed how the High Counters had shanghaied him.[47] Turning his attention to Cook and Borah's second—and "independent"—way of determining the contact population, tribute data, Sanders pointed out some of the intractable problems in using these sources for that purpose, but he was less specific than others were to be later.[48]

In the end, Sanders mitigated some of his criticism by offering at least partial estimates of his own, succumbing to the temptation that his own arguments should have squelched. Rightly treating carrying capacity as a ceiling concept, and drawing on a combination of archaeological and ethnographic evidence, Sanders offered some regional estimates but never pulled them together into a single figure. William Denevan did this for him in his conclusion to the volume in which Sanders's essay appeared, and ever since, this figure—11.4 million, "derived proportionally from Sanders"—has been linked with Sanders's name.[49]

Because Sanders's critique had first appeared in a mimeographed segment of a large and complicated site report, it might be that Cook and Borah felt no need to respond to it, depending on its relative inaccessibility to all but the most dedicated investigator. Its reappearance in Denevan's *The Native Population of the Americas,* however, would seem to have increased the stakes. Nonetheless, in their studies in *Essays in Population History,* Cook and Borah eschewed the opportunity to deal with Sanders, just as they had declined to recognize Rosenblat's criticisms.[50]

In 1978, B. H. Slicher van Bath published a paper in which he subjected parts of Cook and Borah's modus operandi to close scrutiny and leveled several fundamental criticisms.[51] He was especially concerned with the conversion factor Cook and Borah had used to determine total population from "casados." Cook and Borah had defined a *casado* as "a married man, unequivocally," whereas Slicher van Bath suggested that "in many cases" it was more likely that *casados* referred to *both* men and women.[52] Whenever this happened, of course, it would be necessary to reduce the conversion factor by as much as one-half.

Slicher van Bath pointed out that in determining that the average family size in postconquest central Mexico was 4.5 persons, Cook and Borah merely compounded an unrepresentative sample with a simplistic averaging factor between 4.0 and 5.0, both obviously on the high side for a population declining as rapidly as Cook and Borah claimed. Moreover, as time passed after the conquest, it became inappropriate to treat *casado* and *tributario* as interchangeable terms and thus as having interchangeable values.

Slicher van Bath next looked at Cook and Borah's ratio of *casados* per house. This, he thought, was also too high. He reminded readers that "[a]fter 1520 population drops dramatically; nevertheless [according to Cook and Borah] the number of families per house increases. One can only conclude that the number of houses declined even more rapidly than the population."[53]

In explaining their ratio of about two *casados* and their families per house, Cook and Borah argued that the extended family had come to replace the nuclear family as a result of the conquest, the evidence for this being precisely the high *casados*-to-house ratio—and nothing else. Preoccupied with this notion, Cook and Borah explained away the rare low ratio in the southern Toluca valley as the result of "a system [that] must have been a personal preference of the inspector"; they added that "it foreshadows a type of formulation very commonly employed by the enumerators of the late eighteenth century," without suggesting what the implications of either part of this extraordinary observation might be.[54] Explanations of this kind about the creation of a crucial source that is otherwise taken to be reliable seem nothing less than Pandora's boxes, opening themselves to, practically entreating, dangerous criticism, unless one agrees that only a handful of census takers thought along these lines, and then only in unwitting anticipation of assisting demographers several centuries later.

At any rate, using their sample, Cook and Borah decided that for central Mexico a ratio of 1 *casado* per 2.96 persons was legitimate. Based on one sixteenth-century count and, remarkably, the 1940 census of Mexico, they argued that for the sixteenth century the figure 2.96 did not include children under four years of age, so it became necessary to allow for this group, and the ratio then became 1 to 3.29.[55] Rounded off, it became 1 to 3.3, while that of *tributarios* (all *casados* were *tributarios* but not all *tributarios* were *casados*) was 1 per 2.8 persons. Slicher van Bath then pointed out that other figures from the same period, but outside Cook and Borah's sample, gave appreciably higher ratios, as high as 1 to 4.4. In closing, Slicher van Bath expressed unamplified doubts about the percentages of nobles excluded from the counts of *tributarios*, the populousness of the coastal regions of

New Spain, and the notion that population declined inexorably rather than spasmodically.[56]

Slicher van Bath was not a High Counter basher. In fact, he concluded that Cook and Borah had overestimated the 1520 population by only about 15 percent even while they underestimated the population between 1570 and 1605, so that the depopulation curve was less steep in his interpretation than in theirs.[57]

While Slicher van Bath's conclusions are not dramatically different from Cook and Borah's, his criticisms of their assumptions, particularly of their willingness to see small samples as representative and their propensity to choose the higher alternative, are fundamental. Even though Slicher van Bath's article appeared in a fairly obscure journal, one might expect its arguments to have been met in fair combat by Borah (Cook by that time was dead) or by others who subscribed to his premises and conclusions either for central Mexico or elsewhere.

—————

Two years later Rudolph Zambardino advanced further critical scrutiny of Cook and Borah's central Mexico work.[58] A statistician, Zambardino was disappointed that although Cook and Borah had employed various statistical concepts in their work, they had ignored others. In particular, they had ignored those procedures designed particularly to allow for error in the use of evidence, or for weak evidence.

Zambardino began by noting that a figure of more than 25 million for central Mexico would make it "the most densely inhabited sizable area in the world" of its time.[59] While this possibility could not be ruled out completely, it seemed unlikely enough to require some awareness and defense. Zambardino went on to reiterate the well-known statistical concept that multiplying variables decreases probability, while increasing the number of variables, especially when these are of low to average probability, has a devastating effect on the overall probability of any statistically based argument. As for Cook and Borah's numerous variables, Zambardino felt that they had "a much greater margin of error . . . due to their nature or to the paucity of the data from which they can be derived."[60] Because of this, sound statistical method required that conclusions be expressed in ranges that accommodated "error bounds," ranges that might vary so widely as to be unusable. Zambardino put the problem this way:

> The justification for using the multipliers method is simply that there are no alternatives. However, the results obtained tend to become so in-

accurate as to be meaningless if the number of multipliers increases and/or their approximation is poor. In such cases all the values in the range are possible and fully consistent with the data used. Although there may be compensation of errors, it would be misleading to try quantifying this possibility in terms of the mean or of other values: with only a few numbers involved, using statistical theory largely amounts to whistling in the dark.[61]

Simply put, the case for any number in the range is no better or worse than for any other number, and 5,692,397 would be statistically no less valid than, say, 25,200,000.

Zambardino joined Cook and Borah in regarding their 1568 population estimate as their most accurate, but even so he felt that, statistically speaking, their figure of 2,650,000 should be expressed as a range, 2.2 million to 3.0 million. For the 1580 estimate, for which the data were less certain, the range would come close to getting out of control, 1.3 million to 2.5 million. For 1590, the range would be somewhat smaller, and so on for later estimates based more and more closely on counts from more and more areas.

Turning to Borah and Cook's estimate of population in 1548, Zambardino naturally zeroed in on their assertion that in the *suma de visitas* underpinning this extrapolation, *tributario* referred to only some adult men, requiring fairly large multipliers to reach total population.[62] He had no trouble establishing the debilitating effects of *petitio principii* in Cook and Borah's arguments, as well as some outright inconsistencies and errors, all of which destroy their premise that if *tributarios* are not treated as they would prefer, an "unaccountable" population increase between 1548 and 1568 would result.

Zambardino then challenged Cook and Borah's rather winsome argument that the enumerators would—indeed, *must*—have been instructed to count tributaries only, so that all numbers actually recorded needed to be multiplied by a substantial conversion factor. As for Cook and Borah's assumption that a large leaven of the population—nobles and slaves—were not included at all, Zambardino, like Rosenblat, noted that this assumption was based on only a very small sample of records, much too small to "lend support to the thesis that this was the recommended and/or normal practice."[63] For Zambardino it meant a population range in 1548 of 2.6 million to 4.5 million, which contrasts with Borah and Cook's point estimate of 7,817,000.

The farther back the extrapolation extends and the more exiguous the extant evidence becomes, the more indefinite the ranges of probability inevitably grow, as Zambardino made clear when he fixed his discussion on Borah and Cook's projections for 1532 and 1519. Compounding the problem is the fact that for these estimates Cook and Borah calculated goods and services rather than people. Zambardino concentrated on the arithmetical aspects of the case. For instance, he noted how, for convenience, Cook and Borah treated all situations as alike by devising an average quota per family that ignored differences in time, place, social status, and other considerations. He concluded, rather mildly, that "[d]ue to the lack of tributary uniformity, the application of a single average quota to all of the towns involved is prone to error."[64] Zambardino concluded that the best estimate possible for the 1532 population of central Mexico was a range from 2.7 million to 35 million! He naturally concluded that this was "meaningless" and that it would be better to extrapolate from the much narrower ranges of later years.

Turning to the contact population, Zambardino concluded that "the attempt to derive a population figure from this [tribute] information is even more prone to intrinsic error than the 1532 estimate."[65] He noted that Cook and Borah had used this method for four of eleven regions, merely added 10 percent to their 1532 estimates for three other regions, and for the remaining regions used a combination of assumptions deriving from their estimates for 1532 and 1568, a procedural *omnium gatherum* unlikely to induce confidence. The best Zambardino could do with this was to suggest a range of 2.2 million to 28 million, but he conceded that in doing so he had "usually assumed margins of error much lower than warranted."[66] Presumably, any less optimistic assumptions would have created ranges near infinity.

Zambardino then discussed an important aspect of Cook and Borah's working method—their claim that they had tested their 1519 figures independently and found the results so close that they should be held to corroborate one another. If so, of course, there would be, despite the presumptiveness of so much of Cook and Borah's method, some hope that their results could be rehabilitated. But as Zambardino pointed out, the two methods—tribute-based calculations (which provided a figure of 25.2 million) and extrapolation from later estimates (which provided a figure of 27,650,000)—are not independent at all, since their backward projection is based on Cook and Borah's own estimates and not on actual data. Thus they tend sharply toward self-fertilization. Zambardino might have added that exercises that claim to be "independent" are actually thinly disguised forms of *peti-*

tio principii and are necessarily ubiquitous in the High Counter literature, since there exist no data for contact populations anywhere that do not require extensive reconfiguring and extrapolating. The case of central Mexico is merely the paradigm of the problem and its attempted solution.[67]

Perhaps surprisingly, Zambardino concluded with his own estimates, expressed, of course, as ranges. He suggested that the contact population of central Mexico was somewhere between 5 million and 10 million in 1519, between 2.7 million and 4.5 million in 1548, between 2.2 million and 3.0 million in 1568, between 1.3 million and 2.5 million in 1585, and between 1.1 million and 1.7 million in 1595. Taking the midpoint in each case, he postulated a decline from 7.5 million to 1.4 million, or a depopulation ratio of a little more than five to one, significantly less than Borah and Cook had suggested. In doing so, Zambardino emphasized that his figures were "based *exclusively* on the evidence used and published by Borah and Cook."[68] By this Zambardino underscored that Cook and Borah had merely made a series of choices in aid of reaching a very high population estimate, and that he in turn had done the same, while defining his limits differently. Implicit in his procedure was the inference that anyone could use the data generated by Cook and Borah, define his or her own goals, and arrive at a figure that would both have surface plausibility and match the goals.[69]

Zambardino's article appeared in a mainline historical journal and must have quickly come to the attention of those High Counters interested in central Mexico.[70] But what they might have thought about his trenchant and sophisticated criticism we cannot know, since they offered no response at the time and have offered very little since.[71]

―――――――――

In 1978 I published my own criticism of Cook and Borah's work on postcontact Hispaniola, admittedly an especially inviting target. There I argued that they had ignored dissenting evidence, had operated with tendentious translations, had postulated that an epidemic unknown to the historical record had struck down millions of Hispaniola Indians within just a few years, had relied too uncritically on certain writings, particularly those of Las Casas, and had committed various other sins against commonly accepted historical method. I hoped (and presumably I speak for Slicher van Bath, Zambardino, and others) that by striking at the heart of their argument I would bring forth a more reasoned defense of their approach and results, although I did not imagine that they would be able to find new sources that would fill so many crucial gaps—evidence, for instance, of a previously unknown and universal census taken immediately on Columbus's return to Hispaniola on his second voyage.

Nothing. Still, I thought that perhaps there would be a response that tried in its turn to discover and capitalize on the weak points in my own argument, whether of logic, translation, or interpretation. Still nothing. Years later I found Borah congratulating Francisco Guerra for "a fine piece of sleuthing" for conjuring up an epidemic to account for Indian depopulation on Hispaniola. But from that day to the present there has been no attempt to refute my criticisms.[72]

It is true that in looking at Hispaniola, Cook and Borah were also looking away from the kinds of evidence for later periods that existed for Mexico, which seriously reduced their chances for plausible extrapolation. It is equally true that their brief study of depopulation on Hispaniola seemed to be more avocation—and evocation—than vocation. Even so, it had a purpose, which was to buttress their Mexican work by attempting to show that even a relatively small island with a civilization for which there is no evidence of urbanization was teeming with millions of Indians. Clearly, they realized that if their arguments for Hispaniola could be accepted, it would strengthen their hand for central Mexico immeasurably.

At the same time, pursuing a course there successfully would have opened up much of the Americas for similar treatment. We have no more quantitative information about the Amazon rain forest or California or the St. Lawrence valley than we have for Hispaniola, but a successful excursion into the last would provide a much-needed thin end of the wedge for the rest. All in all it seemed then—and now— that Borah had much to gain by attempting to disarm any criticism of his and Cook's work on Hispaniola.

———

In addition to direct criticisms of Cook and Borah's quantitative methods, there have been discussions of some of their sources that should have given them pause. Frances Berdan discussed several of the cruxes that inhibit successful interpretation of the data in various Aztec tribute documents on which Borah and Cook relied so heavily in their *Aboriginal Population*. The first, and probably the most important, is simply whether or not these sources directly relay information from the preconquest period. Berdan pointed out that the *Matrícula de tributos* "does retain the indigenous style and, by assumption, the indigenous content."[73] Assumptions that our sources are as pristine as we would like them to be are commonplace, often necessary, and always tempting, but we do not usually know whether they are also true.

The *Matrícula de tributos* carries annotations in Nahuatl and Spanish which themselves must be *post*conquest, whatever the status of the data in the pictographs. Besides being later additions, these annotations are often ambiguously phrased, as if they represent some doubt in the annotators' minds as to their meaning. Berdan pointed out that the potential for duplication is serious here, owing to the necessity for "oral transmission rather than visual copying." As a result, Berdan preferred to use the information in the pictographs proper, whereas Cook and Borah preferred the annotations whenever these were available, despite the fact that they can be only early *interpretations* of the raw data in the pictographs. It would be as if a historian using nineteenth-century colonial dispatches were to use the minutes added to them in the metropolis while ignoring the texts themselves.

Be that as it may, problems with the codices are particularly rife in the area of foodstuffs, and Berdan raised the question of the value of some of the items listed as "tribute." When they are shown bunched together, for instance, do they represent a bin of mixed items, or was each item intended to represent a separate bin? If the latter—as Cook and Borah argue in assuming the higher option—then the value of the tribute increases proportionately, and, by their methodology, so does the number of people paying it.[74]

Berdan pointed as well to problems involved in reconciling overlapping but not identical tribute periods, as well as discrepancies among various tribute documents in terms of how frequently the pictured tribute was paid. Obviously, the more often it was paid, the more food and other products were required, and, *ex hypothesi,* the more people were needed to produce them. Again, in the case of mantas (cloaks or blankets), Cook and Borah chose to proceed on assumptions that produced much higher tribute figures.[75] Berdan emphasized the effects of this when she pointed out that a series of maximal assumptions could produce figures twenty times as great as those produced by the same series of minimal assumptions.[76]

Although her arguments were not couched as explicit comments on Cook and Borah's work, which she mentioned only in passing, Berdan's interpretation is both severally and severely at odds with theirs. Her conclusions applied to their methodology would derive a much lower population for central Mexico. Along the way—also, apparently, not intentionally—Berdan demonstrated how implacably

Cook and Borah opted for the interpretive alternative that produced the highest possible number.

In using the tribute records to infer numbers of people, Cook and Borah displayed the same propensity to treat the data as stand-ins for much larger figures that they had with the *suma de visitas*. A pronounced example of this was their argument that in cases where there is a modern need to decide between semiannual and eighty-day intervals for the delivery of certain tribute, the latter were intended. In large part their justification consisted simply of suggesting that partway through the transcription one of the annotators of the *Codex Mendoza* indicated this but did not retrace his work: "It is as though the reading of the amounts multiplied by only two [i.e., semiannually] accorded ill with the annual totals of tribute the interpreter knew [*sic*] to be paid."[77]

If the codices postdated the conquest by even a few years, they were subject to the beginnings of changes in cultural norms and, even more, to new economic and political imperatives, for the Spaniards were quick to impose themselves in both respects. If they were produced under the circumstances of this transitional stage, both their form and their content would have been affected, and it would be especially difficult to stipulate just what forms such differences might have taken. Just the awareness of a more effective way to convey information—by words rather than pictures—must have had a striking effect.

In a way, though, Borah and Cook's decisions about quantity and periodicity of tribute, as well as consumption levels, are less significant than their belief that the amount of tribute was intimately related to numbers of people and that the *Codex Mendoza* and *Matrícula de tributos* were both accurate (and accurately transcribed) and representative of the Aztec empire as a whole.[78] In recent years a great deal of research has been conducted on the tribute system of the Triple Alliance, and much of it complements Berdan's work by suggesting that the data in these codices do not deserve the implicit faith that Borah and Cook enthusiastically bestowed on them as surrogates in sufficiency.[79] For instance, in looking at a particular area directly subject to Tenochtitlan (other areas paid tribute to Texcoco or Tlacopan), Frederic Hicks concludes that tribute-paying groups were a motley crew. The typical group "would probably not have been a whole town, but a small *calpolli*, or 'minor ward' whose residents shared such a tribute obligation to pay directly to Tenochtitlán." Other such groups would owe tribute locally. As a result, "[o]nly those that tributed to Tenochtitlán, and who did so through the *calpixqui* [tax collectors] hierarchy, were part of the tribute provinces depicted in the *Mendoza* and the *Matrícula*."[80] In short, the data in these sources represented tribute received at Tenochtitlan, but not elsewhere.[81] If so, then they have even less value as a demographic gauge than Borah and Cook's critics have suspected.[82] Or else even 25 million was much too low an estimate.

In studying a tribute codex from Heuxotzinco dating from 1531, Noguez illustrates both the complexities and the "exaggerations" that characterize it. Whether through mistranscription or hyperbole, its figures imply 32,000 loads of maize (or more than 80 a day) and nearly 10 million mantas per year![83] To be sure, one could assume that such distortions and irregularities were not a feature of precolonial tribute recordkeeping—that the *Codex Mendoza* and *Matrícula de tributos* were as right as the Huexotzinco codex was wrong. This would imply both that the Aztec enforcement system was more efficient (by using pictographs instead of words) and the will to comply greater. Regrettably, there is no evidence for either of these counterintuitive presumptions.

The circumstances in which the surviving tribute figures were compiled suggest that applying arithmetic to them is wholly valueless. The critics have said very little about Borah and Cook's inclination to treat tribute as a fixed and symmetrical set of procedures, little influenced by time, space, or ambient conditions.[84] In adopting this procedure they are not without company—the temptation to take the part for the whole has inevitably been widespread. For instance, until 1939, when W. E. Lunt destroyed the notion, it was commonplace to infer English population in the early Middle Ages by assuming that taxes were uniformly applied and collected.[85]

Even more to the point are the ambiguities posed by the simple question, why should we expect the tribute levels listed in the postcontact codices to be correct, that is, accurate? It would have been miraculously ingenuous of the Indians to eschew the chance to secure new and lower tribute rates from their new rulers, who, after all, had not been around when the Aztecs collected tribute and could not have been sure just what this was. One can imagine a negotiating process in which the first step would be the Indians' advancing the lowest figures they thought might pass muster. Some of these would have been accepted and others rejected, prompting further negotiation, so that in the end the figures in the surviving codices were sometimes lower, sometimes higher, and sometimes, but not very often, exactly the same as the actual preconquest figures, which themselves might or might not have been collected. If more tribute figures ended up being lower than higher, as seems hardly improbable, then, by Cook and Borah's line of argument, again the population was even greater than 25 million. Since we can doubt this, we must also doubt that the method they used was reliable.[86]

Indeed, this brings to the front the whole vexed question of the authenticity and reliability of such postconquest documents, whether or not they relate to tribute. In writing of some fraudulent (late-seventeenth-century masquerading as from the 1520s) documents from Oaxaca, Kevin Terraciano and Lisa Sousa are alarmed that "[t]he issue of fraud and forgery raises the unsavory prospect that indigenous groups or individuals may have knowingly lied to obtain their goals." They go on to note how resistant modern scholars have been to this notion.[87]

Their chagrin is understandable, their frisson of surprise rather less so. They go on to quote from a study of another area in the region, whose author, Stephanie Wood, aptly summed things up: these documents are "the product of reasonable people trying to meet an impossible demand—to produce a written and/or pictorial record that they either never had or had lost."[88] If modern scholars are to be equally reasonable, we must in our turn accept the fact that any particular document emanating from the early postconquest period and professing to relate to Aztec times is more likely than not to be fraudulent in some respects.[89]

About fifty years later the Indians were offered another chance to comment on preconquest tribute, in a series of *visitas* carried out between 1579 and 1582. Generally, they responded to the relevant question utterly predictably: they had paid no tribute or they did "not know" whether they had. When they had more to say, it was usually couched in unspecific terms. As might be expected, few respondents were inclined to be their own worst enemies in this regard.[90] To presume that they were less inclined to self-interest in the 1520s would be the triumph of hope over common sense.[91]

———

The cumulative effect of the criticisms of Rosenblat, Sanders, Slicher van Bath, Zambardino, and Berdan was to challenge virtually every one of Cook and Borah's presumptions, methods, and results in their studies of the contact population of central Mexico. Individually and severally, they criticized the following aspects of Cook and Borah's central Mexico work: their subjectivity in determining the "value" of crucial categories such as *casados* and *tributarios;* their decisions about how much of the Indian population to exclude from (i.e., add to) the surviving counts, and how to compensate for this in adjusting population totals; the submerging of this crucial subjectivity in a numerical flood; their use and interpretation of the pictorial data in the codices; their tendentious translations; their equally tendentious statistical procedures; their drawing universal conclusions from inadequate samples; their lack of internal consistency in argument and arrayal of data; their defining and applying categories anachronistically; and their spuriously claiming the fortuitous convergence of ostensibly independent lines of approach for the contact population. From their work emerge implicit criticisms as well—for instance, that Borah and Cook's handling of crucial terms was so aberrant that even a strictly appropriate statistical method could not have rescued the enterprise, although it might have masked its deficiencies better.

For most scholars such accusations would be a call to arms, but in this case arms have remained stacked. In the fifteen years or so since the appearance of the last of these challenges, Borah has ignored them entirely and has been joined in his silence by most of the other High Counters. Borah's determined silence resisted the temptation to discuss, or even to mention, any of his critics in an article published in 1984 and entitled "Some Problems of Sources." It would seem that the problems he had in mind were those of others. Only William Denevan referred to the work of Slicher van Bath and Zambardino, and then in a bibliographical essay that was not a place for extended commentary, or one likely to achieve high visibility.[92]

In attempting to arrive at the most plausible model of population levels for the basin of Mexico through computer simulation involving a number of variables variously tested, Thomas Whitmore sees Zambardino's work largely as "provid[ing] an initial set of guidelines to determine a reasonable figure for the confidence limits of the uncertainty bounds." This remark suggests that he regards the greatest value of Zambardino's work as offering promise for more specific or narrower ranges, rather than as warning of the futility of such exercises.[93] In contrast to rare references to Zambardino and Slicher van Bath, Whitmore cites Cook and Borah's work scores of times, even though his own choice for a reasonable population for the basin of Mexico in 1519—about 1.5 million—is not much more than one-half that postulated by Cook and Borah.[94] As a result of the mindset Whitmore exemplifies, Cook and Borah's figure of approximately 25 million for central Mexico continues to enjoy all the fruits of incumbency, resting, it would seem, on the laurels it had garnered before the mid-1970s. It (or numbers very much like it) continues to be the single most cited figure both within and, even more, outside the field.[95]

Ross Hassig, writing on Aztec military matters, notes in passing that "Cook and Borah estimate the immediate pre-Conquest population at better than 25 million with a decline of 95 percent by the end of the sixteenth century." To drive the point home further, he follows with a table headed "Population estimates for central Mexico, 1519–1608," composed entirely of Cook and Borah's figures, as if these were completely unchallenged.[96] In a later work Hassig repeats himself almost verbatim.[97] Cecilia Rabell has recently recapitulated the criticism of Borah and Cook and added her own: that they have been insufficiently demographic by ignoring population dynamics in favor of population levels. Even so, she relegates the critics to a footnote, without detailing any of their arguments.[98]

If only a fraction of the criticisms that have been leveled against Cook and Borah's procedures is justified, then their estimate of some 25 million people for central Mexico is totally meaningless, a monument to persistence and salesmanship but hardly a testament to statistical method, rigorous source criticism, or internal logic. It seems extraordinary that, given the state of play in the matter, so few realize that one of two things should happen: either the critics are met and defeated on their own terms, point by point, or the work of Cook and Borah is abandoned and the task begun anew. It seems to me that Zambardino in particular has showed how fruitless any such new beginning is likely to be, particularly if the method remains intact while the methodology is retooled according to individual taste. This state of affairs, in which a particular orthodoxy is allowed to retain its status in the face of disabling criticism, brings us to the matter of the sociology of knowledge.

Woodrow Borah is on record with a low opinion of the value of what he calls "controversy." As he put it: "My impression of controversy is that 98 percent of it is heat, and 2 percent may be useful."[99] This might help explain his continuing silence, but it falls well short of justifying it. It is akin to an incumbent officeholder's admitting that he has suddenly gone off elections. Knowledge advances through debate, dispute, and dissent as much as by any other means. Of course, discovering new evidence is crucial, but differences of opinion are often the very stimulus for such a search. And evaluating that evidence is not likely to be nearly as straightforward as Borah appears to believe. No one looking at the broad sweep of historical and scientific interpretation over the centuries would imagine for a moment that forty-nine out of every fifty disputes have been unuseful. If this were so, we might still see ourselves as inhabiting a geocentric universe, ridicule continental drift, trace our ancestry to Noah, or believe that the first people were long-lived giants.[100]

The ways in which some of the High Counters characterize their own work might have a palling effect. Sheer bluster has been a discursive strategy prominently employed. For instance, Borah writes this about one of his and Cook's studies: "The study is based upon careful textual criticism of early reports and comments, using the methods developed by Lorenzo Valla, the editors of the *Acta Sanctorum,* and the school of Saint Maur—in short, methods accepted universally by historians."[101] The study in question?—their claim that the population of Hispaniola in 1492 was somewhere between 2.5 million and 14,560,000, most probably about 8 million.[102] Despite these grandiloquent claims, which must give pause to anyone who would compare the textual work of the High Counters and that of the Bollandists, this particular attempt at high counting has found the fewest adherents of their entire corpus.[103]

Borah and Cook—in this case—adopted a straightforward narrative strategy that eschewed introspection, either of themselves or of their sources. They defended their choices, but not by showing them to be best choices by pitting them against other possible arguments.[104] Data are snatched from here and from there and duly quantified, so that the act of quantifying stands surrogate for other acts such as comparing procedures and assessing sources in context.

The weaknesses of this approach are illustrated in Cook and Borah's failure ever to explain their most momentous decision—to use the *suma de visitas* after Cook and Simpson had rejected it little more than a decade earlier. This might suggest, for instance, that it was Simpson who found it wanting earlier but that Borah took a more tolerant view of it. Or it might mean that in the interim they (whoever "they" happened to be in this partnership at any particular time) concluded that the *suma* needed to be employed rather than wasted, and then proceeded to try to overcome its defects.

On several occasions Cook or Borah or both of them refer to estimates lower than theirs as "very low," as if they represent a kind of indefensible extreme position.[105] Earlier, Pierre Chaunu, arguing that Las Casas never "invented" a number but that these were invariably "administrative in origin," was even more emphatic, if not abu-sive—introducing along the way what has become a recurring term to describe those with whom one disagrees: "It is as such that [high numbers] must be treated, weighing them one by one to a delicate balance with a prudent historical criticism, not reject them globally. The hypercritic, once again, is only the most dangerous form of the absence of critical spirit, an excuse for indolence, an illusion of intelligence for dullards."[106] Surely this nicely phrased preemptive strike could, if taken seriously, inhibit at least some potential dissidents, which presumably was not the least of its purposes.

Of course, Chaunu confounded "globally" with "reflexively" and "skeptics" with "dullards," and both he and Borah, as well as others, confuse doubt with disbelief.[107] They also oversimplify the concept of doubt by confounding Pyrrhonist doubt, which is designed to stimulate devil's advocacy in order to approach surer knowledge in a dialectical fashion, with academic doubt, the paradoxical certainty that nothing can be certain.

———

In accepting Borah and Cook's figures, Ross Hassig does an unusual thing: he notes the objections of Slicher van Bath and Zambardino and the alternative estimates of Sanders, even if as succinctly as possible. He defends his own choice of the highest figures rather perfunctorily, arguing that "they are the most thoroughly analysed and I regard them as the reasonable high estimates."[108] There is a lot to wonder about in this sentence. First, Borah and Cook's estimates are not "analysed" at all; as for the sources, they are, if anything overanalyzed, but Hassig owes his readers a good deal more justification than simple assertion. The last part of this sentence clearly implies that Hassig has gone to the trouble of comparing Borah and Cook's figures with other "high estimates" and has found the latter unreasonable. The only higher estimates are Henry Dobyns's, which, while they might well be deemed unreasonable, ought at least to be mentioned as the basis of comparison and choice.

Still, others have not gone even this far. In a general article aimed at the quincentenary audience, Georges Baudot discussed the matter of the contact population of central Mexico. Citing the works of Borah and Cook—and for relief, Dobyns—Baudot could only conclude that the size of this population was 25.2 million, and that it dropped in various places to various figures, all as cited by . . . Borah and Cook.[109] In the chapter in the *Cambridge History of Latin America* devoted to sixteenth-century Mexico, Nathan Wachtel cited only Borah and Cook's figures and failed to indicate either that there were serious criticisms of these numbers or that alternative figures had been advanced in their place.[110] The Cambridge histories view themselves as uncomplicated, virtually archival, and thoroughly authoritative records of the past, and the opinions expressed in them are likely to attract a particular measure of belief.[111]

Studying social change in the Mezquita valley, Elinor Melville devoted considerable attention to the definition of *tributario*. She found that the totals generated by her definition "agree fairly well" with Borah and Cook's own estimates. This is reasonable, perhaps even encouraging, but if she had taken any overt cognizance of the literature of disagreement on the matter, this concordance might have been less. Conversely, if she had brought it into her discussion, it could have converted her assertion into an argument.[112] In her study, meant for nonspecialists, Frances Berdan, even though she did not apparently accept Cook and Borah's figures, nonetheless cited only them.[113] Also interested in determining what constituted the category *tributario* in the various counts of the sixteenth century, and even though disagreeing seriously with Cook and Borah's estimate of population, Prem, Dyckerhoff, and Feldweg still used their work on the subject as the point of departure for their own, without ever referring to Rosenblat or Slicher van Bath.[114]

Rudolf van Zantwijk offers the most extraordinary—and depressing—perspective of all. Speaking of Aztec agriculture, he writes:

> Nearly all the land that could be cultivated with the available technology was put under cultivation. This makes more plausible the enormous population density in the central provinces of the Aztec empire shown by Cook and Borah in several of their studies. These large population figures were received at first with great skepticism by other scholars. The heated debate over this issue following publication of the studies has quieted, and the differences in projected population numbers have dwindled to a margin of a few million, as we can see from the calculations of Slicher van Bath.[115]

Perhaps collegial courtesy impelled Van Zantwijk to cite his Dutch colleague as the only dissenter, but his statement suggests a woeful lack of awareness of the unanswered arguments of Rosenblat, Zambardino, Sanders, and others, every one of whom has offered estimates much lower than those of Slicher van Bath. This is not to mention those who feel that the matter is not susceptible to estimating at all. All that distinguishes van Zantwijk's formulation from those of others mentioned here is that he says what others only imply—that the issue, if not settled in the sense of being demonstrable, has reached an equilibrium in which a figure in the mid-20 millions holds forth.[116]

I close this discussion by treating in more detail the rhetorical strategies that Cook, Simpson, and Borah deployed to deflect criticism and persuade skeptics. Several instances have already been cited—the idea here is to draw these several strands together to give a clearer picture. The rhetorical strategies of the High Counters follow the standard route: establish that knowing the population is crucial to understanding more interesting problems; declaim the possibility of achieving such knowledge; and eventually iterate and reiterate that this possibility has been realized.

Actually, the argument that knowing the level of the contact population of central Mexico is essential for most other concerns appears more frequently in the writings of more recent students of the subject. For Hassig, "[t]he size of the native population [of Mexico] at Conquest is crucial to an understanding of many of the subsequent events in New Spain."[117] Prem, Dyckerhoff, and Feldweg all but repeat the comment verbatim: "The density and the absolute number of the indigenous populations are . . . crucial elements in considering the configuration and workings of Prehispanic societies." They continue:

> It is vital for evaluating problems like the economic situation, the stress on food production, the necessity of additional food procurement (e.g., by means of tribute or even, as recently advocated, by cannibalism) and the requirements of reducing the population through special military campaigns. All these doubtlessly essential questions require for their solution a sound demographic basis.[118]

Believing this, of course, can lead only to increasingly operose efforts to acquire such "knowledge." Along the way, it risks persuading us to believe as well that we have devised a population estimate that can resist all attempts to compromise or destroy it—something that, as we have seen, seems impossible, despite both repeated attempts to reach a reasonable degree of probability and repeated reluctance to admit the state of legitimate discord.

Knowing the specific effects of population levels and resource-crisis risks become a game of round-and-round-the-mulberry-bush. If the population is presumed to be high, then the carrying capacity is assumed to be at least high enough to have continued to support that population in one way or another. Conversely, if carrying capacity is deemed to be low, then lower population must follow to the degree that societies continued to survive and, if we are to believe the Spanish chroniclers, even to thrive. In short, there must be some piggybacking correlation between the two, no matter which is treated as the pig and which the back.[119]

Added to this are the many protean variables that ineluctably accompany the carrying-capacity arguments, including consumption requirements, the amount of arable land as defined by the technology available, the crops sown on it, the efficiency of this production, and its nutritional value in part and in whole. Manipulating any of these ripples throughout the process. We see this in the various attempts to suggest "average" nutritional requirements for central Mexican Indians.[120] Each of these is necessarily based on modern data deemed to be sufficiently comparable and on assumptions about workload levels, lifestyle, degree of comparability between pre- and postconquest situations, and the like.[121] And each is appreciably different from all the others, which in turn affects the other variables and, ineluctably, calculations of general population.[122]

The unacceptably but unavoidably broad latitude residing in the carrying capacity argument is amply demonstrated in Miguel Alvarez Ossorio y Redín's attempt to calculate the population of Roman Spain. Adopting the usual procedures, Ossorio estimated that this was as much as 78 million people. No wonder he was puzzled by the fact that the present population of Spain and Portugal was (or so he thought) only about one-sixth of its former level.[123] For us this result is simply outlandish—after all, the current population of the Iberian peninsula is scarcely 50 million—but it must have seemed plausible to Ossorio, and presumably to his audience. Our deeming it impossible three centuries later is really no indication that the present generation has finally harnessed the extrapolative excesses of the carrying capacity argument, for these are truly inherent and suffer from being virtually invulnerable to effective counterproof.

The High Counters' belief that population continuously declined forces them into an extrapolative bed of Procrustes in which any independence of action is subordinated to mathematics. Thus, any Indian newly found at a later date requires a ripple-effect backward projection using a multiplier consistent with the period involved—the later the discovery, the greater the multiplier. Evidence showing that 100,000 theretofore unknown Indians were living in a certain locality at the end of the sixteenth century would require adding as many as

2 million Indians to the contact population, in a kind of demographic peristalsis.

Would an additional population of 2 million for central Mexico matter if all evidence showed that the resources were or were not adequate to dealing with it? Would a population of 30 millon matter in the same circumstances? Only when the issues of carrying capacity and population levels are treated entirely separately—if that is possible at all—can there be progress toward reaching demonstrably plausible probability levels. As it stands, the two notions have become all but alter egos, each used for and determined by the needs of the other.

The High Counters continually lay stress on *agreement*. If looked at just right, the argument goes, the early sources can be seen to agree with one another; in turn, as Borah and Cook were to reiterate, their own estimates merely reconstituted and quantified this agreement, which had been ruptured by the advocates of lower figures. Thus, Borah closed his review of Rosenblat's *La población de América* with a ringing endorsement of the sources that Rosenblat had dared to doubt: the critics "must provide a framework of explanation which will encompass the testimony of the tribute counts and the overwhelming agreement of recorded testimony by sixteenth-century Spaniards and Indians."[124]

Earlier, Cook and Simpson had begun their first study of central Mexico by referring to "sources so varied and independent that their essential agreement cannot be fortuitous."[125] And, as we will notice later, Cook and Simpson (and later Borah) all but libeled Díaz del Castillo by referring to his chronicle as "supplement[ing] the statements of Cortés to an extraordinary degree" in regard to population levels.[126] Another example of this strategy is the claim that "[t]hese data were analyzed and yielded a population total for central Mexico of 7,800,000."[127] Obviously only the method yielded the figure; the data were vigorously massaged.

Perhaps the most egregious—and certainly the most ironic— example of the impossible demands that the High Counters put on the concept of agreement occurs in their discussion of their own work. In their last publication on the matter, in which they estimated the contact population of central Mexico at more than 25 million, Cook and Borah looked back on their earlier work. To our surprise, if not theirs, they found it remarkably consistent, and presumably therefore more credible: "We have arrived at population figures for the Spanish period that *agree essentially* with those of the [1948] Cook-Simpson study, although specific estimates differ."[128] The figures are given in Table 1.

Table 1. Estimates of Native Population in Central Mexico Drawn from Cook and Simpson, *The Population of Central Mexico in the Sixteenth Century* (1948), and Cook and Borah, *The Aboriginal Population of Central Mexico on the Eve of the Spanish Conquest* (1963)

1948		1963	
Year	Population	Year	Population
1519	11,000,000	1519	25,200,000
1540	6,400,000	1532	16,800,000
1548	6,300,000		
1565	4,400,000	1568	2,650,000
1580	1,900,000		
1595	2,500,000	1595	1,375,000
1607	2,000,000	1605	1,075,000

These two arithmetical interpretations of population decline in central Mexico agree only that it existed and was reasonably precipitous. But every observer from Díaz del Castillo to Angel Rosenblat already knew this much, even if he or she did not always care to couch it arithmetically or apocalyptically. Beyond that, it would be hard to find two more different notions; thus, for instance, Borah and Cook disagree with Cook and Simpson more than Cook and Simpson disagree with Sanders!

Despite the irony of this last example, in general the notions of independence and agreement are inextricably tied—in the sense that without the former, the latter is meaningless. Cook, Simpson, and Borah were fully aware of this, as they demonstrated in their frequent assertions that a source or a procedure was independent of other sources and procedures.[129] The inescapable problem in assessing claims of independence is that with the same hands at the controls, independence would require nothing less than Cook, Simpson, and Borah's being forced to accept the clear testimony of unambiguous evidence not susceptible to more than one interpretation. Needless to say, the set of conditions governing the exercise falls very far short of attaining this.[130]

———————

It is hardly to be expected that Cook and his colleagues would look kindly on their critics. Generally, as we have seen, they have preferred not to look at all.[131] While we can deprecate their reticence as un-obliging, it might have some advantages over their practice when they do come to grips with dissent. A popular way to defuse criticism is to treat doubt as unwholesome, counterproductive, sterile, even expedient. Borah expressed this feeling in 1966 when he wrote that "[c]redence requires less faith than inflexible disbelief."[132] Cook and Borah also cited Alonso de Zorita's observation that "fraud and error" characterized tax assessments. This notion is naturally anathema because it stigmatizes virtually all the High Counters' careful arithmetic as "garbage in, garbage out." Therefore, "[o]n [undefined] examination, it is clear that this passage sketches a partisan view of the history of tribute assessment in central Mexico."[133] Of course it does, but Cook and Borah's opprobrium rests oddly when it rests on Zorita, whose integrity and prolonged and close experience with just the matter of tribute assessment was unrivaled. Even odder, perhaps, neither Cortés nor Tapia nor Motolinía is ever described in such derogatory terms.

No less odd is Borah's comment on Rosenblat, whose arguments, he charged, were "based essentially upon an intricate series of rejections, selections, and alternative readings of documents." He went on to lament that "[u]nfortunately, as the technique is used in [Rosenblat's] essay, scholars can disagree endlessly about which source is reliable, which ought to be discarded, which interpretation of the text is correct, and so on."[134] The comment is reminiscent of two mirrors set opposite one another so that they reflect the same image innumerable times.

Cook, Simpson, and Borah do not fail entirely to address their arithmetical philosophy; they address it most often in their analysis of the *suma de visitas*. What they say proves to be less heartening than perplexing. Many comments are Manichaean, couched in good versus bad dichotomies in which the former emerge triumphant. Thus they admit that their "results can hardly be held to be more than an indication of probable order of magnitude in the individual cases," but they continue, in almost Panglossian fashion and surely against the rules of probability, that this doesn't really matter since "over a reasonably large number of instances selected without conscious bias they yield a result that is reasonably valid."[135]

This desperately *faute de mieux* tenor is also evident in another comment in the same work: "In spite of the faults of this method of calculation, however, the means can be used in calculating probable populations in 1568, for at least the general order of magnitude of the result will be valid. Furthermore, no other mode of approach will yield more dependable information."[136]

This sensation of shoulder-shrugging arithmetic is reinforced throughout Cook and Borah's work. In speaking of the disparate data in the *suma de visitas,* they reveal a truly extraordinary modus operandi: "If two or more values are available, we average them. This procedure may distort the value for a given town, but in the treatment of hundreds of cases, such errors cancel one another."[137] Underlying these sentiments is a single philosophy—that any number of numerical wrongs can somehow still make an arithmetical right, if only "the proper procedures" are employed.

Each of Cook, Simpson, and Borah's four major studies of central Mexico is graph-ridden. Sometimes this is to good effect, but too often one suspects bamboozlement. Take the series of four graphs entitled "Visita number," in which various aspects of the coverage of the *suma de visitas* of 1548 are encompassed.[138] There might be value in these for hard-core statisticians who are also interested in the subject at hand, but those wondering about either the reliability of the source or Borah and Cook's wholesale extrapolations from it are unlikely to be impressed and certainly will not be edified. A point to bear in mind in considering these tables, charts, and maps is simply that graphics are a particularly effective and efficient form of rhetoric. Graphical representation of quantitative operations is commonplace and often clarifying, but graphic display sacrifices nuance. A more serious aspect of the graphic argument is its hegemonic nature; it seeks to browbeat its audience into a submission based on a fear of doubt and hence a grudging, but no less effective, acceptance.[139]

Cook and Borah's figures for central Mexico have enjoyed a relatively free ride for over thirty years.[140] We see Michael Crawford, for example, finding Cook and Borah's highest estimate conceivable and even considering that Dobyns's still higher estimate is "not preposterous."[141] All things considered, perhaps the most salient characteristic of this recent drive to establish the contact population of central Mexico is its astonishing coarseness. Throughout, arithmetical exercises transcend—indeed, overcome—issues of population dynamics. The estimate of 25 million is *nothing else but* an arithmetical projection based on other arithmetical projections, and it fails to take into account any form of population dynamic except mortality. At least the even higher estimate of Fray Servando de Mier had the appeal of a *cri de coeur*. In the circumstances, one might have expected that the figure 25 million, as well as the premises and procedures that underlay it, would have perished during incubation. But as we have seen, it persists almost miraculously, successfully resisting every attempt to deprive it of authority even while it is unable to sustain any plausibility.

No more than this is needed to account for Cook and Borah's Olympian detachment, which has smothered any responsive and productive colloquy and left only a series of isolated incidents characterized by Cook and Borah's failure to bring continuity even to their own work by explaining changes of direction, estimation, and source evaluation. This leads to disjuncture and a thread of Ariadne that is broken at the first turn in the road. Long ago Francis Bacon identified this resistance of incumbent ideas to change:

> The human understanding, once it has adopted opinions, either because they are already accepted or believed, or because it likes them, draws everything else to support and agree with them. And although it may meet a greater number and weight of contrary instances, it will, with great and harmful prejudice, ignore or condemn or exclude them by introducing some distinction, in order that the authority of those earlier assumptions may remain intact and unharmed.[142]

Cook and Borah expose the reasons for their lack of caution when they remark rather plaintively that "[t]he data in our sources [are] the only figures we had on which to base our estimate." Not disheartened, they add immediately that the figures, fortunately in the circumstances, "are in all probability reliable within fairly small margins of error."[143] The sentiment smacks wonderfully of the tenet of "providential preservation" that literalist biblical scholars have propounded to allow themselves to proceed unimpeded. Whatever else the work of Cook, Simpson, and Borah might be, it is testimony to the advantages of silence in the face of criticism; to the tenaciousness of interpretations that fit existing ideologies well; and to the persistence of untutored acceptance of numbers.

Complementing Darwin's view on the value—indeed the needfulness—of criticism, Richard Levin argues that "we cannot hope to prove any proposition unless we look for negative evidence that might contradict it." He goes on that "many of us ignore [this] point, because of the tendency of our minds . . . to look only for positive evidence that confirms a proposition we want to prove."[144] Levin's case study happens to come from Shakespeare studies, but he is likely to agree that he could have found another in central Mexico.

Excursus

The sources for postcontact population are seldom antiphonal. Rather, they are the missionaries quoting numbers of baptized, from whom nothing is heard, or the royal tribute collectors providing ambiguous and contradictory data without rebuttal—cases of taxation without representation. Differences of opinion certainly surfaced in these sources, but they tend to be explained in ways that do not necessarily call into question the process of counting.

The case of the count carried out in the Tarascan kingdom in 1523–24, however, raises issues that strike dangerously close to the heart of the Cook-Borah enterprise. Only fragments covering five jurisdictions seem to have survived, but these are of especial interest because they purport to include "house" counts made by both the Indians and the Spaniards. In only 5 of 153 such counts do the two figures agree. In the remaining cases, the counts carried out by the Spaniards are higher, usually much higher, than those reported by the Indians, so that the final tallies are 1,237 houses, if the Indians are to be believed, and 3,213 houses, if the Spaniards were accurate.[145] That is, the Spaniards reckoned that there were more than five houses for every two the Indians could find.

Benedict Warren argues that the differences spring from the fact that "both were given by interested parties" and that the Spaniards "could very easily have counted unoccupied houses and would have tended to exaggerate the number of potential tributaries."[146] Although this makes sense, it is hard to credit the latter reason alone for the inordinate discrepancies. For instance, there are cases in which the Indian count showed only one house in a locality and the Spanish count showed five, and there are numerous others in which the difference is even greater. Could the Spaniards have been so unaware of the occupancy status of so many dwellings? And why were they unoccupied in the first place? Since he is not interested in establishing the contact population of Michoacán, Warren does not pursue these questions.

Sergio Navarrete Pellicer, on the other hand, does attempt to suggest population levels for sixteenth-century Michoacán. Like Warren, he regards it as "feasible" that the Indians would attempt to minimize their numbers in order to avoid forced labor. Like Warren, too, he points out that the Tarascans were evidently successful in hiding from the Spaniards the very existence of many small settlements.[147]

In contrast to Warren, however, Navarrete Pellicer believes that "the Spanish count does not appear to be exaggerated," because, he thinks, the purpose of the Spanish reconnaissance was to "register with the greatest possible objectivity" the potential of the area to bear the encomienda system. In fact, he goes beyond this by characterizing the Spanish numbers as "low or conservative" because of the Tarascan success in "a patent concealing of population."[148] Consequently, Navarrete Pellicer concludes that "[t]he numbers of inhabitants in the relevant areas in this [the Spanish] count must be considered incomplete but representative."[149] He then proceeds to use these figures for his own calculations, using a multiplier of 11.2 persons per "house," and duly arives at a total figure for the five jurisdictions of 36,007.[150] In the process he simply ignores the figures proffered by the Indians.

This argument is unconvincing, even peculiar, for, although Navarrete Pellicer actually speaks of "the concealment of houses," it is difficult to imagine that much concealment could have been carried out in areas visited by, or known to, the Spaniards. Remember that the different Spanish and Indian counts presumably referred to the same congeries of houses, and that it is probably more difficult to hide the existence of houses than it is of villages and individuals. In effect, in choosing "houses" as the item of measurement, the Spaniards were ensuring, if only inadvertently, that the two systems of counting would be as closely commensurate as practicable.[151]

But our evidence is precisely that they were not. The document in question plainly demonstrates that the Spaniards and the Indians put wildly variant numbers to what from all appearances were the same entities. Any Tarascan success in withholding information about small settlements is immaterial to this puzzling state of affairs, and explanations must be sought elsewhere. Several questions remain to be asked, even if they are unanswerable. Why did the Spaniards include the Indian numbers without comment if they regarded them as unacceptable? And if they regarded them as acceptable, then what do their own numbers mean?[152] This might seem an insoluble puzzle, at least on the basis of the known evidence; still, anyone intending to use either set of figures for extrapolation must at least address these questions.[153] Did both groups count the same way? Did both groups agree on the meaning of *casa*?

More telling, the Michoacán case, as limited as it might be, would seem to have a devastating effect on the practice of extrapolating population from such counts or even of using such counts in a generic way to support an impression of dense populations. Any belief in the Spanish house counts for these particular settlements carries with it the dubious burden of believing as well that the Indians expected to be able to gull the Spaniards into thinking that five of every seven houses were temporarily unoccupied.[154] Or of believing that they could continually offer counts that were less than one-half the actual number with relative impunity.

In their efforts to estimate the population of Michoacán, Cook and Borah first used the story in a single late source of an army of "200,000, evidently first-line" Tarascans and allies who set out to assist Moctezuma against the Spaniards but then withdrew. They regarded the implied figure of 1 million for the total Tarascan population as possibly an underestimate.[155] Later they were a little more precise, estimating a population for Michoacán in 1519 of 1,258,154, based on projections from "the Central Plateau less Tenochtitlán" in which they assumed exactly the same depopulation rate between 1519 and 1532, despite the considerably different ecological, epidemiological, and ergonomic environments.[156] In neither case did Cook and Borah refer to the count of 1523–24 and its implications, but treated Michoacán as lacking any such data.

In their study of the Tarascan state, Shirley Gorenstein and Helen Pollard noted that "[t]he native estimate [in the Caravajal *visita*] is always smaller than the Spanish" one and decided to use figures "between the two."[157] In some ways this is at least a sensible, and probably a necessary, temporary expedient, but it is an expedient nonetheless, and one that does not attempt to come to terms with the source of the discrepancies. It would have been a helpful procedure if it could be shown that one side in the matter fortuitously happened to underestimate to the very extent that the other side overestimated, and the process very definitely does not allow for valid extrapolation.[158]

Are the differences between the Spanish and native counts epistemological? What is a count, or, for that matter, a "house[hold]?"[159] Or are the differences political—a contest of wills, fought out over the question of local population? The last might have seemed worthwhile initially, but surely it would not have continued on this ground for the entire duration of the visit—almost a year. Among other things, accepting the Spanish counts in this instance implies that they had less reason to exaggerate than the Indians had to underestimate, or that they were more capable of counting accurately, or both. Either way, it seems an instance of the spoils (in this case posterity's willingness to believe) accruing to the victors.

Whatever conclusions we might eventually reach, this document on the Michoacán count allows us the rare chance to see how counting is a negotiation. Its precise numbers make it what the High Counters are wont to call a "census," the same kinds of data that constitute the *suma de visitas* of 1548, of which Borah and Cook made so much use.[160] Yet both sets of precise numbers can hardly be true—in the typical negotiation *neither* would be. Borah and Cook, however, see all such counts—at least as they are preserved—to be accurate in the event and then transmitted without any possibility of serious error.

Giving Disease a Bad Name

It is impossible to allow him to go through life supposing that all the zeroes of the zeta function were real.

—G. H. Hardy,
Collected Papers, referring to the
Indian mathematical wizard Srinivasa Ramanujan

It is otherwise with Khorasan and Iraq, which countries are afflicted with a hectic fever and a chronic ague: every town and every village has been several times subjected to pillage and massacre . . . so that even though there be generation and increase until the Resurrection the population will not attain to a tenth part of what it was before.

—ᶜAla a-Din ᶜAta-Malik Juvayni,
History of the World-Conqueror,
referring to the effects of the Mongol conquest

By the mid-1960s Sherburne Cook and Woodrow Borah had ceased revising themselves and were largely content to try—with considerable success—to convince interested parties that the population of central Mexico in 1519 was as high as 25 million and could well have been even higher. It remained for others to carry the battle forward and outward. Henry Dobyns grasped the passed baton with alacrity. Whereas Cook and Borah had confined themselves to Mesoamerica, Dobyns conceived his own charge as covering the entire hemisphere. He published a paper in *Current Anthropology* in 1966 in which he attempted to make a hemispheric case for depopulation of the magnitude of 95 percent or more over time.[1] There he argued that such rates were applicable virtually everywhere in the New World.[2] The stakes, then, were substantially higher than they were for central Mexico, yet the evidence was far more exiguous. In this chapter I look at how well Dobyns coped with this dilemma.

Dobyns's paper merits close attention for several reasons. It was clearly a manifesto, designed to push a particular argument and to encourage others to corroborate his conclusions with specific case studies. The paper was well received by the High Counters and, more importantly, probably helped to create other High Counters, since it has been widely influential and frequently cited for its methodological contributions to the debate. Thus it deserves—literally—Linda Newson's characterization of "seminal."[3] It displays as well certain techniques by which the High Counters, among whom Dobyns has remained prominent, move from text to calculation. Even thirty years later it stands as an unsurpassed microcosm of the High Counter movement, and looking at the paper and its reception can serve as a useful gauge of the epistemological and methodological ebb and flow that have characterized the High Counter movement.[4] I approach Dobyns's arguments and those of his critics seriatim; thus this chapter is organized in much the same way as his paper and the comments that accompanied it.

In undertaking his enterprise, Dobyns aped Cook and Borah, beginning by claiming that "[t]he idea that social scientists hold of the size of the aboriginal population of the Americas directly affects their interpretations of New World civilizations and cultures."[5] Dobyns had set himself a formidable task—nothing less than developing an argument that could demonstrate that contact populations were much greater *all over* the Americas than anyone had previously imagined. He began by discussing "conservative hemisphere-wide estimates." In particular, this meant criticizing the work of A. L. Kroeber, whose eminence and low estimates have made him the perpetual prey of the High Counters—not, it must be said, without some reason, although he has long since resembled the proverbial dead horse. Dobyns went on to couple Angel Rosenblat with Kroeber, thereby giving himself a larger target.

A leading aspect of Dobyns's strategy was to bring Bartolomé de las Casas' various estimates into play, again a standard operating method of the High Counters. Dobyns noted that in various of his writings Las Casas proffered a wide range of figures.[6] These were invariably high, and sometimes impossibly witnessed.[7] Dobyns found it difficult to present Las Casas' various estimates as part of a coherent argument, and he wisely made no effort to demonstrate their accuracy or even the possibility of their accuracy; instead, he was content merely to have Las Casas' highest numbers on the table.

As he left him temporarily, Dobyns wrote that "[i]n 1560, Las Casas raised his estimate of Indian mortality to that date to 40,000,000." This is quite true (except that Las Casas said "over 40 million"), but Dobyns neglected to add that Las Casas went on to say that "more than 4,000 leagues of land [were] depopulated," a figure that can have no relationship to reality whether we treat it as areal or lineal.[8] Las Casas thus compromised whatever credibility his depopulation figure might have had, and it is a pity that Dobyns tore this statement, the parts of which Las Casas clearly preferred to be corroborative, asunder.

Dobyns soon returned to Las Casas in a section entitled "area population estimates," that is, figures assigned in the chronicles to specific places in the New World. For Venezuela, Dobyns pointed out that Las Casas estimated Indian deaths there at between 4 million and 5 million from 1526 to 1541, but again failed to notice that Las Casas added parenthetically "(according to my belief)," a belief that is not supported by other estimates or by any independent evidence.[9] One of Las Casas' more ridiculous estimates, it was ignored in his time and has been ever since.

Dobyns went on to cite a 1685 estimate of Indian losses by the Marqués de Varinas.[10] Calling it "contemporary comment," Dobyns observed that "[t]he contrast between the views of modern social scientists and of a colonial authority whose active career spanned a score of years about the time that American Indian population probably began to recover is very marked."[11] At best, Dobyns missed a chance to explain why Varinas's figures were likely to be reliable or what their significance might have been, or what recovery after a population nadir had to do with contact population levels. This would have proved difficult, since Varinas himself offered no justification and no sources. Dobyns remarked that Varinas cited a loss of 8 million "in the valleys of Peru and nearby areas," but this is hardly a fair translation of Varinas's "los valles del Perú y *Tierra-Firme,*" which was a term generally applied by that time to all of North and South America (it had once been applied only to the isthmus of Panama).[12] In short, it is not easy to see why Varinas was called to the witness stand, except for the saving altitude of his numbers.

———

In dealing with "projection methods" Dobyns addressed several estimates of the pre-Columbian population of Yucatán.[13] In particular he was pleased with the estimate offered by Oliver and Edith Bayles Ricketson, who, on the basis of projections from the site of Uaxactun, suggested that the peak population of Yucatán was probably between 13.3 million and 53.3 million.[14] Dobyns presented this part of the Ricketsons' arguments fairly, but did not question them.[15] He failed to note, however, the several caveats raised by the Ricketsons, who all but destroyed their own arguments by showing the improbability of most of their premises.

Dobyns continued that Sylvanus Morley had accepted the Ricketsons' projections, and then noted a dissenting voice.[16] George Brainerd, who edited later editions of Morley's work, disagreed with Morley, and therefore with the Ricketsons. In contrast to their views, Brainerd "[a]ssum[ed] occupancy of one out of eight houses, with five persons per house, giv[ing] a density of 136 [persons] per square mile," thereby halving the Ricketsons' lowest estimate at a single stroke.[17] He went on to halve it again by pointing out that the typical Maya household "consists of two of more houses." All in all, Brainerd thought, an average density of about thirty persons per square mile was all that the area's carrying capacity could accommodate.[18] Thus he reduced the Ricketsons' minimum population level, accepted by Morley, by eight-ninths.[19]

Dobyns noted all this reasonably accurately but went on symptomatically: "This guess by Brainerd clearly conflicts with the carefully worked out estimates based on actual archaeological survey data."[20] This was disingenuous, as well as demeaning, because Brainerd, following Morley, had relied on the very data for Uaxactun that the Ricketsons had collected—or, rather, created, since the data represented the results of a test they had conducted based on a sample segment of the larger survey. In effect, both the Ricketsons and Brainerd were "guessing," but Brainerd supported his guess by observing that the site of Uaxactun had been occupied for more than a millennium, a fact that significantly affected the odds of simultaneous occupation. The Ricketsons, on the other hand, made their calculations only to all but disavow them.[21] While concerned with Brainerd's revisions of Morley's interpretations, Dobyns failed to note that others—for example, J. Eric S. Thompson—had offered much lower estimates of their own.[22]

Dobyns concluded his section on the "dead reckoning" method by assuring readers that Cook, Simpson, and Borah had "demonstrated fairly conclusively" that the population of central Mexico was more than 25 million, without further comment. He then moved on to the longest part of his analysis—"cross-checking source consistency."[23] He was impressed by Sherburne Cook's work on the aboriginal population of California and used the opportunity to make a claim that at the time was incorrect and which the passing of more time would prove preposterous: "The methodological assumptions made by 'skeptical' analysts excused them from engaging in such a laboriously scientific method as systematic cross-checking of sources."[24]

In fact Dobyns immediately illustrated the difficulties in carrying out such exercises by explaining away one of Carl Sauer's estimates that happened to be lower than Kroeber's for the same people. Sauer he absolved by making an argument that was quickly to become central to the High Counters' enterprise: those imputing high population levels could not "go back in time earlier than extant documentation . . . , which lagged behind the spread of Old World disease agents which almost certainly reduced the aboriginal population even before literate explorers arrived on the scene."[25] Since early figures, whether accurate or not, were unavailable for much of the Americas, Dobyns was forced to extrapolate even more than was usual for the High Counters.

In looking at Cook's work on Baja California, Dobyns referred to Cook's reliance on an estimate published in 1771 by the Jesuit Jakob Baegert.[26] Cook had correctly noted that Baegert had reckoned that the Baja Indians could never have numbered above 40,000 to 50,000, but Dobyns twisted this slightly to read, "a colonial estimate by Baegert of 40,000 to 50,000."[27] Cook regarded Baegert's estimate as "an intelligent guess," but it is clear from Baegert's conspective work, and even more from the series of letters he wrote to his brother while in lower California, that the figure is best treated as an allegory on the way Baegert regarded both the people of lower California and the sterile and arid environment—an expression of his contempt for both, and not at all a serious effort to speculate on earlier population levels.[28]

At the same time Dobyns made it clear that he conceived of "cross-checking" as including the procedure by which Cook had devised a population density, as if this were an independent operation— a common but dangerously erroneous practice of the High Counters, who often fail to understand the impact of their own objectives on their arithmetic.[29] In this case Cook had carried out a series of unabashedly "if/then" and "but" operations, the objective of which was to achieve consistent estimates among methods. Take this example:

> But this figure [15,000] is certainly low. . . . We are conservative if we raise the number to 20,000. If we then add 2500 each (1000 × 2.5) for Loreto, Francisco Xavier, Comondú, and Santa Rosalía de Mulegé, or

10,000, we get a total of *48,000*. Approximately this number seems indicated if we accept Meigs's value of 2.5 times the maximum known census figure.[30]

This, of course, is not "cross-checking" but outright tampering, which, however plausible in its parts, has as its purpose only to create a self-consistent picture. Dobyns did fault Cook for "obscur[ing] the actual scale" of depopulation by "assuming that it was a constant and uniform ratio . . . over the entire area."[31] Perhaps he had not written the last part of his own paper at the time.

Dobyns then moved on to central Mexico, where he quickly engaged in an orgy of multiplication and addition regarding the number of baptisms that a given number of Spanish clergy could have carried out. In this exercise he undoubtedly had allegations by the missionary chroniclers of prodigies attributed to themselves and their brethren. Interestingly, and ultimately symptomatically again, Dobyns was not content to rehearse these accounts but insisted that the missionaries had been even more productive than they had realized. As Dobyns put it in disagreeing with one of his principal sources: "It may be seen that Motolinía himself very possibly failed to appreciate the total magnitude of postconquest mass conversion in New Spain, even though he credited himself with baptizing 400,000 Indians."[32]

Dobyns cited a report by Alonso de Zorita who, as *oidor* of the audiencia of New Spain from 1556 to 1566, worked and wrote on behalf of the Indians there. As Dobyns interpreted Zorita: "The Spaniards forced the Indians living within a 30–40 league radius of Mexico City to erect a great wall to contain their cattle."[33] Here Dobyns mixed up Zorita's account, sometimes to his own disadvantage. In fact Zorita spoke of two construction projects—a causeway in Mexico City and a cattle pen in the Toluca valley, and it was in the context of the former that he spoke of the 2 million Indians.[34]

On the other hand, Dobyns tripled Zorita's 2 million Indians by a series of familiar maneuvers—treating the figure as representing men only, and then only some of the men—and this in turn eventually enabled him to deduce that there must have been about 190 persons per square mile in the area. In this Dobyns used a league that was too short (2.5 miles), which increased the imputed density, but more importantly, he ignored Zorita's explicit comment that "all the people of the land [*toda la tierra*] were summoned." If Zorita had meant to say part of the men and none of the women, one would imagine that he would have found a way to do it that did not contradict himself.[35]

The real issue, though, is hardly the length of a league, or even Dobyns's unauthorized multiplying, but the likelihood that Zorita's account is accurate. Who would have counted the Indians? How did they distinguish one levy from another in the first place? Why would they have bothered? Dobyns does suggest that "[p]resumably the Spaniards or the Indian foremen kept books on the work crews so the figure talked about should have been fairly accurate," but this is too casual and too optimistic to persuade skeptics that Indian hordes of such size worked on this project, particularly since neither this number nor any number like it is mentioned in any other source for the period, and it is—as usual—very much in the round.[36] The modern translator of Zorita's *Breve y sumaria relación* found himself in sympathy with Zorita's arguments but also saw "palpable exaggerations" in his work that resulted from Zorita's commitment to the welfare of the Indians.[37]

Turning to the Inca state, Dobyns expressed the opinion that P. A. Means's estimate of its population was "one of the most original estimations of the size of an aboriginal American population using an ethnohistoric method."[38] That meant that Means had calculated high. In doing so, Means had employed an idealized model of the Inca administrative system in which each administrative unit along the hierarchy was held to have approximately the same population over time. This view of things could well be thought "original," but hardly realistic.[39] Dobyns pointed out a couple of criticisms of Means's approach and thought them "undoubtedly valid" in certain respects, but argued that even so "they do not seriously impute the utility of Means's method for obtaining an approximation of the actual population."[40]

As Dobyns noted, Means's method derived a range of 16 million to 32 million, and Dobyns suggested that "the higher figure is consistent" with Cook and Borah's recently published central Mexican figure.[41] He did not elaborate. In recruiting Means, Dobyns was being unfair to the former's overall argument, for Means went on: "Assuming, for caution's sake, that it was much closer to the lower of these two figures than to the higher, we find that the population of the empire was approximately twice as great as that of the same territory to-day."[42] Thus Dobyns robbed Means of what little caution he had showed and imputed his own lack of it to him.

———

Having set the stage with a panoply of very large but impressionistic numbers drawn from an extremely limited number of unexamined historical sources, Dobyns turned to the real task of his paper. As he put it: "The civilized Indians subject to the native American empires were by far the most numerous of all New World groups, and estimations of their pre-Columbian magnitude must rest upon methods adapted to documentary analysis."[43] These methods involved devising a way to use later, and better understood, population figures and extrapolate them back to the contact or precontact period. In this way they would give substance and validity, even precision, to the estimates of Las Casas and others.

The title of the last section of Dobyns's paper, "Scale of Depopulation by Disease," provided a clue to his approach. Certainly other students of American Indian depopulation had included epidemic mortality as an important factor (although others, like Kroeber, had not, as Dobyns showed), but no one before Dobyns—and no one since—grants this factor such explanatory centrality and potency. As he put it: "Any interpretation of reported native populations during the early years of contact with Europeans which ignores the tremendous mortality caused by epidemics inevitably underestimates the size of the aboriginal populace."[44]

Dobyns began his task in this section by briefly discussing Cook's revision of his earlier estimates of the population of California owing to the ravages of an epidemic, possibly of malaria, that struck Oregon and California in the 1830s.[45] Cook had been able to amass an impressive litany of eyewitness accounts of the effects of this epidemic, particularly in the Sacramento valley.[46] There can be no doubt that mortality was great, but Cook sometimes pushed the evidence too far, as when he calculated a mortality rate of "40 to 60 percent" in one refugee village by guessing at both the total number of refugees and the duration of the mortality there; only one night's mortality was included in his sources.[47]

Throughout his study we find a dichotomy between Cook's exposition and his calculations. For instance, he recognized that some of the claims of very high, even total, mortality could probably be explained by flight, but he insisted that this did not affect the overall picture.[48] At any rate, Cook decided that "[f]orty percent seems too low" and referred to estimates for the earlier Oregon phase of the epidemic.[49]

Apparently Cook forgot that these very estimates were also his own calculation. Since he regarded the situation in California as "very similar" to that in Oregon, he naturally concluded that "we may set the mortality [there] at the same value as for Oregon, that is, 75 percent." This would mean, he concluded, that "fully 20,000 natives of the great Central Valley died in 1833; my own opinion is that this figure is too small," although why he should think that he never declared.[50] We readily discern a heady circularity in this reasoning, but Dobyns missed it. In his view, Cook had "found that Indian mortality" was about 75 percent in both areas; Dobyns failed to realize that although this figure was not impossible, it was nonetheless the result of a series of highly interconnected calculations, often lacking the requisite evidence.[51]

To bolster his case Dobyns pointed out that early observers had seen disease as a factor in depopulation, but he chose to concentrate on one who had not—Bartolomé de las Casas, whom Dobyns ambiguously described as "merely the earliest and best-known commentator upon the biological plight of the Indian."[52] He then berated Las Casas—and Kroeber—for failing to see that most Indians had really died of disease rather than ill treatment or warfare. But he could not explain why Las Casas so studiously turned a blind eye to this phenomenon, which, at least for Dobyns, far exceeded all other causes of Indian decline and must, by his argument, have been raging before Las Casas' eyes day in and day out.

———

Dobyns's paper reached a crescendo with his discussion of "depopulation ratios," the aspect for which it is best remembered and most often cited. Dobyns began by admitting that he felt it "incumbent . . . to indicate a workable method." In aid of this he suggested "another projection method employing a depopulation ratio established by comparison of relative numbers of a given group at two points in time. One such time should be that when the population analyzed fell to its lowest numerical strength [nadir]."[53]

He rightly preferred to establish local depopulation levels that would reflect particular conditions, "but that is impossible for lack of records." Establishing regional ratios, however, lay "beyond the scope of this paper." He was left, then, with "a 'standard' hemispheric depopulation ratio for demonstration purposes," which entailed establishing a ratio "between the known or confidently estimated preconquest population in 1 area and a known or closely estimated nadir population in that same area." Once this was done, "the ratio thus obtained will then be tested for consistency against comparable ratios for other areas in order to arrive at what appears to be a generally applicable ratio."[54]

With a few exceptions, Dobyns's test cases came from areas he had already addressed earlier in his paper. He noted that Cook and Simpson in 1948 had postulated an 86.4 percent decline (from 11 million people to 1.5 million) for central Mexico, only to give way to Cook and Borah's later estimate of a 94.1 percent decline (from 25.3 million to 1.5 million). But he was sure that Cook and Borah's figure was actually too low. In fact, "[s]ince those calculations ignored the tremendous depopulation" caused by the 1520 smallpox epidemic, a more realistic contact population would have been 30 million.[55] This produced "a depopulation ratio of at least 20 to 1" from acme to nadir, which, he pointed out hopefully, also happened to be the same ratio that Cook and Borah had calculated for one town (and one alone) in central Mexico.

Dobyns then retraced his steps to the Incas, where, following John Rowe this time, he reported that the population of the Rimac area, measured in families, had declined by a factor of sixteen to one, and that of another area, by twenty-five to one. Once again he argued that these figures were actually too low, because family *size* had also declined from pre-Spanish days. And once again he chose only the portion of Rowe's argument that suited his own.[56]

At this point Dobyns turned his attention to population estimates for Potosí. Following Jehan Vellard's data, Dobyns concluded that there had been a population decline there "on the order of 9 to 1" between 1575 and 1690, and that this was largely attributable to epidemic disease.[57] The Potosí case, as well as Dobyns's use of it, is especially indicative of the problems inherent in estimating population decline and assessing the reasons for it.[58] In order to provide the detail required without overwhelming the central argument, I defer discussion of it to an excursus at the end of this chapter.

Dobyns next quoted again from the tract of the Marqués de Varinas, who, Las Casas-like, spoke of mounds of skulls along the roads in southern Peru and asserted that from an original population of 2 million there remained but 20,000 Indians, a decline of 99 percent. Dobyns regarded the Peruvian case as similar to that of central Mexico and went on to improve the similarity by arguing that both estimates were too low for one reason or another.

Returning to Sherburne Cook's study of the California Indians, Dobyns casually doubled Kroeber's ratio of 8[.3] to 1 because of the 1833 (he called it the 1830–33) epidemic. He then remarked, almost *en passant* and decidedly without relevance, that "this [new calculation] is very close to Rowe's Rimac River Valley ratio."[59] Again, the implication is that one unwarranted manipulation serves to corroborate another, wherever they occur in the postcontact Americas. Dobyns then multiplied Kroeber's depopulation rate by three in order to get a twenty-five-to-one ratio, which he compared with "Rowe's Chincha ratio from Peru."[60] Another hit.

Dobyns moved to new territory by discussing the Tierra del Fuegians, Amazonians, and northern Pimans. Lucas Bridges had estimated that the aboriginal population of Tierra del Fuego in the early 1870s was between 7,000 and 9,000 but provided no source or details—and counting the scattered and nomadic Indians in the area must have been virtually impossible.[61] The Ona Indians of Tierra del Fuego were reported to have had only 40 members in 1950 and 2,000 at the end of the nineteenth century. This decline provided Dobyns with a useful depopulation ratio—fifty to one.[62] Dobyns's source, Vellard, thought that the data on Fuegian depopulation were "fairly secure," but this is clearly not the case.[63] None of the earlier data for purported apogee figures were contemporaneous; those for the Ona, for instance, were based on an unsupported assertion made more than half a century later.[64]

Dobyns also confined himself to recent times when dealing with the Amazon region, for which he cited numbers for some groups that suggest ratios of 20 to 1, 222 to 1, 15 to 1, 16.6 to 1, and 25 to 1. For these he relied on two sources (one of whom, Vellard, he followed closely, but who provided no sources of his own) rather than attempting a more comprehensive analysis of the numerous groups in the area.[65] One group of northern Pimans in Arizona purportedly suffered a loss of 51 to 1 in the course of the eighteenth century. Dobyns regarded this ratio as the highest one possible before the slippery slope to extinction would have set in. Even so, "aboriginal disease conditions ended among the Northern Piman Indians long before 1700, so survival of even greater population losses seems possible."[66]

To many this ensemble might seem an extraordinary grab-bag of examples, ranging in size from fewer than a hundred to some 30 million, in time from early in the sixteenth century to 1950, and in area from Tierra del Fuego to Arizona. Certainly it is not the "encyclopedically-based" exercise that one observer thought it.[67] Moreover, if we exclude the central Mexico case, where Dobyns raised the highest existing figure arbitrarily by more than 15 percent solely to create an exact depopulation ratio, we are left with a few hundred thousand people, much less than 0.5 percent of the total that Dobyns was to impute to the Americas at contact. Dobyns, however, was undaunted by all these anomalies and, indeed, tried to turn them to advantage: "From the wide range of depopulation ratios encountered for various native American populations in widely scattered portions of the hemisphere, it appears that a ratio of 50 to 1 over a century marks the approximate outer limits of human survival and population recovery."[68]

Dobyns left himself no option but to conclude with his own ratio: "The depopulation ratio of 20 to 1 appears to be a sound, if perhaps conservative, tool to employ as a hemispheric minimum."[69] All these assumptions he put into a table in which, beginning with a set of nadirs—none verified—and conversion factors of 20 and 25, he coaxed out a hemispheric contact population of either 90,043,000 or 112,553,750.[70] In passing he offered another covering principle—that a period of 130 years was "frequently the time" that must elapse between apogee and nadir, or at least, so he argued, this was the case among the California Indians (whose time of apogee he had not established) and in central Mexico.[71]

In essence then, Dobyns argued for a set of covering laws with respect to the degree and duration of population decline. By assuming such a "standard" depopulation ratio, he implied that it was possible to ascertain the timing and substance of the population nadir, multiply this figure by twenty or, preferably, twenty-five, tally the regional results, and determine hemispheric totals with a reasonable degree of accuracy.[72]

—————

With this coda, Dobyns gave way to his respondents, who addressed his paper in the same issue of *Current Anthropology*. Not surprisingly, the comments were mixed. Several respondents praised Dobyns for reprising earlier estimates of contact population, some regional and some hemispheric, and for exposing the biases of those who would count low. Typical of these was John W. Bennett, who remarked that these earlier attitudes "became a source of consistent bias which objective analysts like Dobyns and Borah have now overcome."[73] Others praised the method by which Dobyns set to work—Olemar Blasi called it "the most coherent one," for instance, if applied discriminatingly.[74] Given Dobyns's reliance on his work, Sherburne Cook predictably appreciated Dobyns's efforts in return. In particular he found Dobyns's belief in the high estimates of early observers encouraging, since, for Cook, to think otherwise would be to accept "an incredibly perfect conspiracy, one which has never been detected by some of the most powerful ecclesiastical and civil organizations the world has ever seen."[75]

Frederick L. Dunn expressed a common sentiment when he termed Dobyns's results "reasonable or at least plausible" in most respects, and he "applaud[ed] his emphasis on disease as a contributory factor."[76] Bruce Trigger thought the paper to be "a well-executed and highly enlightening study," although he had doubts as to the extrapolative value of some of Dobyns's examples.[77]

There was also criticism. Several respondents regarded Dobyns's standard depopulation ratio as an ambitious and simplistic expedient, and one not supported by the available data.[78] Richard Forbis was particularly trenchant, regarding the ratio as "totally unconvincing, merely resulting in estimates based upon other estimates," while Blasi thought that a ratio as low as two to one was likely in areas that had never been capable of supporting dense populations.[79] In all this there was an undercurrent implying that contact population levels must be, and could be, determined locally before valid hemispheric estimates could be made.[80] Also expressed was the view that Dobyns had an obligation to discuss the likely degree of error in his calculations and to express them as ranges.[81] As Driver put it, "[a]nyone bold enough to estimate aboriginal population ought to be bold enough to estimate his own error."

Thomas F. and Alice B. Kehoe and Peter Kunstadter emphasized the crucial role that Dobyns had given to the so-called nadir population figures and thought he had paid insufficient attention to the difficulties of specifying what these actually were, since he was, after all, proceeding to multiply them by twenty and twenty-five.[82] Along these lines, Helmuth Fuchs presented the case of the Panare of Venezuela, whose numbers had been estimated four times in the 1940s and 1950s, each time differently, and suggested that anthropologists give more attention to improving the accuracy of such contemporary counts before moving on to heroic extrapolation.[83]

Interestingly, only William Denevan and Bruce Trigger commented on Dobyns's use of sources—Denevan to point out that he had ignored Rowe's less palatable ratios, and Trigger to suggest that Dobyns had not "cross-check[ed]" the Iroquois case very well.[84] Only a single respondent wondered how Dobyns's use of cases separated so much in time could be fruitful, and only one other chose to disagree with Dobyns's optimistic assessment of the credibility of eyewitnesses.[85] Perhaps Nathan Keyfitz and A. Carmagnani best captured the ambivalent spirit of several of the responses when they wrote that "[o]ne cannot but admire the man who boldly struggles with inadequate data when no better are to be had; but if he expects our admiration for scientific restraint as well as for courage, he must present the outcome of his struggle in a form which accords with the modesty of his materials."[86]

As is so often the case in multilateral exchanges of views, Dobyns's reply to his critics and supporters was more revealing than his original presentation. In this instance, he became more intransigent. He began by agreeing with those who "tax[ed]" his hemispheric estimates and he called his ratio "a first approximation" and its results "tentative."[87] He might have thought so at the time, but he has since abandoned his estimate and his ratio only in order to increase them.[88] Dobyns enthusiastically agreed with one commentator's "indictment of past methods of estimation in terms of rules of statistical inference," whatever that meant.[89] Finally, he professed to accept the criticism that by concentrating on zenith and nadir population figures and eschewing more complex population dynamics, his results might not have been worth the labor.[90] Characteristically, Dobyns disagreed with Denevan's suggestion that his Andean population estimates were too high, while in turn finding Denevan's "Amazon [depopulation] ratio reasonable" because it projected population levels that surpassed Dobyns's own by several millions.[91]

Dobyns followed with twin arguments that were to become quintessentially his in the debates of the next twenty years or so. The first was that there was scarcely a disease incident that was not also an epidemic, and very few epidemics that did not evolve into pandemics. He turned reports of smallpox on the eastern seaboard of North America in 1764 into the suggestion that it had also struck the Indians of the Great Plains and mountain areas of the west. Even more dubiously, he continued that "[this] disease was also reported from distant points in the Spanish colonial empire, such as the Guaraní missions [of Paraguay]."[92] Tying one outbreak of a disease with another more than six thousand miles away merely on the basis of rough simultaneity enabled Dobyns to imply that other, but unreported, outbreaks in the great distances between served to reduce the populations of these areas further.[93]

In attempting to identify yet another smallpox pandemic, this time in 1780, Dobyns displayed a slackness in his use of sources that was to become habitual.[94] "I suspect," he wrote, "that this epidemic was the same one that killed over 40,000 individuals in Mexico City in 1779 and perhaps 50,000 in Puebla."[95] Checking his stated source shows the magnitude of his error. Angel Rosenblat wrote:

En 1779 las viruelas mataron más de 9,000 personas en la ciudad de Méjico. El matlazáhuatl [which he defined as "una especie de tifus, de origen indígena"], que se manifestaba de siglo en siglo, se desencadenó en 1736–1737, y a él se atribue—sin duda exageradamente—la muerte de las dos terceras partes de la población del verreinato.[96]

In a footnote Rosenblat added that Mexico City lost 40,157 persons to this earlier epidemic and its attendant famine, and Puebla another 50,000.[97] In short, the epidemic that Dobyns attributed to 1779–80 had actually occurred more than forty years before Dobyns wanted it to and before the date at which he portrayed it in his exposition in order to make a case for yet another pandemic.

There was a smallpox epidemic in Mexico City in 1779–80, and in a work published the year before Dobyns's article appeared, Donald B. Cooper cited mortality for the epidemic: the death toll was "somewhat higher" than the 8,821 officially reported near the end of the epidemic. In other words, Rosenblat had been correct.[98]

In placing one phase of this pandemic in the northern Great Plains, Dobyns referred to an account in the work of David Thompson and implied that this was eyewitness testimony.[99] In fact, as Thompson himself wrote, he arrived in the area only six years later at the tender age of sixteen and, more to the point, wrote his account another sixty or more years after that.[100] Thompson's published version was an "adaptation" of journals he had kept, and other recensions do not include the details Dobyns cited.[101] Perhaps an exceptional memory accounts for Thompson's much belated and numerous elaborations of his earlier notes, but we can hardly know this, nor should we suspect it.[102]

Similarly, Dobyns responded to his commentators with the argument that there were no significant precontact population checks in the Americas, a view that he has reiterated many times since, in the face of a rapidly growing body of evidence to the contrary. Of course this position is required by his premise of a contact population in the neighborhood of 100 million people, but it also benefited from Dobyns's own vision of life before the arrival of the Europeans.

To the suggestion that in colonial times it was difficult to count Indians because it was difficult to define and classify them, Dobyns was forced to replies such as that he had "considerable confidence in the accuracy of identification of an Indian by a 16th- or 17th-century Spanish gentleman concerned over the purity of his blood lines."[103] In any event, the question is hardly one of distinguishing Indians from

Europeans but of distinguishing one group of Indians from another, since the estimates on which Dobyns and other High Counters rely are often so particularistic. That counts invariably referred to precisely the same eponymy over a period as long as four centuries is a presumptive burden that the High Counters have manfully carried but scarcely addressed, and certainly have not, even in a single case, demonstrated to be true.[104]

Turning a sow's ear into a silk purse, Dobyns found that one of his critics "reinforces my argument for cross-checking data by questioning some of mine."[105] The case was that of the number of baptisms it was possible to conduct in a single day, and Dobyns claimed that answering this depended on knowing "minimum ceremonial requirements."[106] He did not claim to know these, or how they were practiced in colonial times, and thereby did not claim to validate his calculations by such knowledge. Instead, he referred to a modern Peruvian example of mass marriage—a case of wrong place, wrong time, wrong sacrament. In fact, the instance is quite anomalous—the result of an annual "roundup" of couples living in sin, who are forced by church authorities to marry. The marriage is "mass" because the roundup itself is conducted only once a year, and surprise and swiftness are a concern. The marriages themselves are merely the mopping-up phase of the campaign.[107]

Dobyns closed his reply by expressing gratification that his commentators agreed that the question of the contact population was "an open one to be discussed in terms of evidence and methods not heretofore employed." He added: "To the extent that I manage to stimulate fresh research on Indian population trends, and to inhibit facile utilization of misleading estimates, I shall feel amply rewarded for this effort."[108]

Experience was to show that this was a case of petard self-hoisting. It is possible to see a good deal of ironic ambiguity in both these statements. The fact remains, though, that Dobyns did stimulate—and validate—a fresh and persistent outburst of interest in establishing contact and nadir populations and, along with them, depopulation ratios.

Despite his repeated obeisance to "cross-checking," a serious flaw in Dobyns's research in 1966 and since has been his own tenuous relationship with the evidence. His practice of choosing his sources gingerly, and of relying on a single friendly piece of evidence, was abundantly clear in this paper, not least in the Potosí example that I

discuss in the excursus at the end of this chapter. Whether he truly regarded his method as "cross-checking" is impossible to know, and
more or less beside the point. It is more important to judge how other
students of contact population regarded it. In effect Dobyns treats his
sources—in the 1966 paper and elsewhere—as a species of silly putty,
to be shaped to conform to his predispositions.

Dobyns's essay was gratefully accepted by many who sympa-
thized with the Indians' plight. Calvin Martin considered the piece "a
compelling critique" of previous estimates and claimed that Dobyns
had used "a highly sophisticated calculus of his own devising," which
Martin termed "the bichronic method," that is, the depopulation
ratio.[109] Martin then betrayed his own unfamiliarity with just about
everything by going on to surmise that "the areas [Dobyns] analyzed
were naturally those from which we have the most complete and trustworthy population figures."[110] In fact, whatever Dobyns's criteria of
choice had been—the appearance of high depopulation ratios seems
the most influential one—he ignored many areas (Paraguay, Central
America, the eastern seaboard of the United States, Colombia, northwestern Mexico) about which a great deal more is known than is the
case for Amazonia, Tierra del Fuego, and other areas.[111] More recently, Alfred Crosby has spoken of the "admiration and malice
[Dobyns] has aroused," thus attributing base motives to his critics,
though not to his supporters.[112]

Nicolás Sánchez-Albornoz, while he did not claim necessarily
to agree with Dobyns's results, nonetheless approved of his method,
which he called "simple and clear," and added that Dobyns did "not
disguise its theoretical nature nor hide his basic assumptions." He
found that Dobyns's reasoning was "actually less haphazard" than it
might appear and credited him with "rais[ing] to the status of a generalization the results reached by the detailed historical studies of
Cook, Borah, and Simpson," who, he added (whether in praise or
condemnation is not clear), "were themselves too cautious to apply
their conclusions to the continent as a whole."[113]

As noted, Dobyns raised Cook and Borah's newly advanced figure of more than 25 million for central Mexico yet again, this time to
30 million, because "early chroniclers thought half the Indian population died" in the first smallpox epidemic there in 1520–21.[114] However, although calling on their testimony, Dobyns cited no "early
chroniclers" at all. Instead he referred to the work of Juan Nuix, published late in the eighteenth century. This is essentially what Nuix had
to say, although he was even vaguer than Dobyns: "The [unnamed]

historians say that this evil [smallpox] was introduced into New Spain in the year 1520, and that it wiped out half the inhabitants of the affected provinces."[115] The claim of 50 percent mortality is so crucial to measuring depopulation—that is, to testing Dobyns's use of the depopulation ratio—that it is extraordinary that he failed to consult any of the original sources.

Robert McCaa has recently done this, and his study shows that whereas all observers agreed that the impact of the smallpox was devastating, they seldom specified mortality rates.[116] In light of this, McCaa concludes that "[w]hether the fraction of smallpox deaths was one-tenth or one-half, we have no way of knowing, but from my reading of the texts discussed here, the true fraction must fall within these extremes, perhaps near the midpoint."[117] Accepting McCaa's 30 percent for the sake of argument, as against Dobyns's 50 percent, means that for every million survivors there had been 1,428,571 people alive before the epidemic rather than 2 million, a reduction of nearly 30 percent.

Despite all this, it can hardly be denied that Dobyns's article lived up to his own hopes by persuading those of like mind that arithmetic could indeed win the battle with the sources. Dobyns reinforced this piece with further studies and claims. Most notably, he steadily upped the ante, including his own previous estimates, for the area north of central Mexico until, in 1983, he announced that at contact this population was in the vicinity of 18 million, which, as he noted, implied a depopulation ratio of about seventy-two to one.[118]

The Maya case discussed earlier and the Potosí case still to come each point out the futility of regarding precontact population as ever-growing and postcontact population as ever-shrinking, each in its own way defying the normal laws of population dynamics. Even so, in his later work Dobyns continued to hold to each of these premises, particularly in his interpretation of the demographic history of sixteenth-century Florida.[119] Indeed, the argument that Dobyns's earliest critics found least tenable, and the one that has continued to attract the greatest criticism, is his notion that very similar depopulation ratios can be applied to any area of the Americas. Numerous regional studies have demonstrated the inapplicability of this concept, but Dobyns has shown no disposition to concede the near universality of his ratio.[120] Ironically, Dobyns's ratio gains exposure every time it is paraded in such discussions, which grant it renewed life even as it is being criticized.

To the extent that Dobyns has responded to these criticisms, his argument has been uniform and staunchly predictable: his critics do not take sufficient account of the damage wrought by unrecorded epidemics that occurred before any population estimates could be made. This is the perfect argument—irrefutable in the most profound sense of the word, in much the same way as belief in heaven and hell and the soul is irrefutable. Almost as good, it is infinitely malleable as well, since the number and effects of these postulated, inevitably imaginary epidemics can readily be manipulated to suit particular lines of reasoning; they are in no way subject to the normal constraints of evidence. For Dobyns such manipulation has always been upward.[121]

Excursus

Dobyns's treatment of alleged depopulation in Potosí was virtually throwaway, yet it serves well to suggest the limitations of his approach. As Dobyns put it:

> Another useful example [of depopulation] is the work force compelled to dig ore from the Potosí mines and extract metals from it. Viceroy Toledo designated 16 Andean highland provinces to provide this labor in 1575, a generation after conquest, assigning 95,000 Indians. By 1663 the number had fallen to 40,115, and by 1689 it was down to 10,633. While other factors, such as out-migration from these provinces to avoid compulsory mine labor, helped to lower their population, the toll of disease is certainly reflected in the indicated depopulation ratio on the order of 9 to 1 over 115 years.[122]

Even at first glance this seems a strange argument.[123] The rationale of the *mita* system was to provide a fluid work force responsive to changing needs, and it was in no way a biologically reproductive group; nor did it relate, after the initial calculation, directly to any reproductive groups. Rather, the numbers at Potosí, as at any site producing raw materials, depended on market conditions, technology, and resource abundance.[124] As well, they related to both production and productivity—the first difficult to measure at this distance, the second impossible.[125]

Whatever the provenance of the 95,000 figure—and Vellard provided no sources by which to test his accuracy, nor did Dobyns (it represents the total for the first septennial cycle)—only three years later the Spaniards established the annual *mita* level at 14,181, slightly up from the 13,500 that constituted the initial allotment.[126] This figure fluctuated until 1633, when it was set at 12,354, where it remained until it was drastically reduced in 1688; it was reduced further in 1692.[127] These figures were notional and were not always met, for reasons that had nothing to do with absolute population decline (which in turn often resulted from flight and not death and therefore was absolute only in terms of the recruitment areas around Potosí). When Vellard wrote that the figure of 1,633 *mitayos* in 1689 represented the traditional one-seventh, he was being anachronistic, which shows the inutility of using such data to calculate any demographic matters.[128]

In short, there is need to distinguish between the nominal level at which the *mita* levels were set, the actual need to fulfill these from year to year, and the total Indian population in and around Potosí. Looking at the last in contrast to the formal *mitayo* labor force, real or presumed, is of little help except to illustrate how pointless it is to attempt to measure population decline using Potosí as a microcosm. In 1577, just two years after Dobyns would have 95,000 *mitayos* in place, it was reckoned that there were only some 20,000 adult male Indians in the area and another 20,000 women and children.[129] At the turn of the century the number of adult male Indians was put at more than 50,000.[130] By 1611 this figure had increased to about 76,000.[131] Only seven years later the number had again grown, to 84,462 Indians just "in personal service."[132]

Of course, neither the stability of the *mitayo* levy nor the wildly oscillating non-*mitayo* Indian population of Potosí signifies in itself that depopulation was not occurring elsewhere in the viceroyalty. Originally, the *mita* was established to allow a seven-year cycle of corvée labor, but as time passed such depopulation compressed the cycle.[133] In fact, there is a great deal of circumstantial evidence regarding population decline, but its degree we cannot know from counts of Indians at Potosí, even accurate counts, because the numbers waxed and waned independently of population inhibitors like disease.[134] Thus Dobyns's confident assertion that "the toll of disease is certainly reflected in the indicated depopulation ratio on the order of 9 to 1 over 115 years" has no basis in fact. Potosí's Indian population can be diagnostic of nothing of the kind.

To put it another way, the number of *mitayos* could increase by aggressive recruitment even when the designated population pool actually shrank. Conversely, the number of *mitayos* could decrease even when the pool was increasing if members of that pool were particularly successful in avoiding service by flight or alternative employment, or if fewer *mitayos* were required at the mines.

The trouble in calculating the number of Indians in Alto Perú in the 1680s demonstrates the futility of relying on such counts for a century earlier. By then the number of *mitayos* had fallen drastically, not, *pace* Vellard and Dobyns, largely because of an absolute decline in population but because the Indians were taking advantage of new economic opportunities by residing in *mita*-exempt areas or by becoming peripatetic *forasteros* (migrant laborers) in order to evade the *mita,* and because the supply of silver was proving not be be inexhaustible after all.[135]

Previous efforts to count the Indian population and reassert the *mita* had failed both because of increasing Indian recalcitrance and because many Spanish and Indian authorities preferred that such figures not become known. A *numeración* was finally carried out in 1683, but so dubious were the civil authorities that it would be accurate that they ordered a parallel and secret census by the ecclesiastical authorities. Even then the Indians were remarkably successful in avoiding being officially observed and thereby made eligible for the *mita.*[136] The results of the enumeration showed a 50 percent decline from 1573, that is, a two-to-one population decline rather than a nine-to-one decline. The provinces susceptible to the *mita* showed the greatest decline, but the degree to which this decline was due to the death rate as opposed to the flight rate was not determined then and certainly cannot be determined today. One thing that the count certifies is that there was never an arithmetical connection between the overall population and the nominal or actual number of *mitayos* available for work in the mines.[137]

If we accept the raw numbers of the 1680s enumeration, we must conclude that population decline was in the area of 2:1 to 3:1 for the period concerned. In fact, even this ratio might be too high, for in 1692 it was determined that there were 33,423 *originarios* (descendants of the first *mitayo* cohort) and another 31,031 *forasteros* (incomers), which could mean that in the century or so that had passed since the Potosí *mita* was established, the adult male population had declined by only one-third.[138] It might well be that population decline in the area was greater before 1575, although this is as irrelevant as it is indeterminate, since it was not the issue that Dobyns addressed.

Some of these data have become more generally accessible only as a result of research carried out since Vellard and Dobyns published their work, but more than enough evidence was abroad even then to negate Vellard's conclusions about the degree and cause of population decline in the Potosí area. Dobyns's error was in using Vellard's erroneous conclusions for his own purposes without attempting to consider them thoughtfully. In treating the numbers of the late seventeenth century as applying to the same body of people as those of more than a century earlier, Vellard, and thereby Dobyns, ignored all population dynamics of the most demographically volatile area in Spanish colonial America. In concentrating on the counts of *tributarios*, they helped their own cases along immensely, because, owing to flight and death, this group declined more rapidly in the Potosí area than did the population as a whole.[139] Beyond this, by specifying what Vellard only implied—a nine-to-one population decline—Dobyns completely misconstrued the nature of Vellard's data, a lapse that could perhaps have been avoided had he looked at Vellard's sources rather than at his conclusions. All in all, his method was not much different from using the rolls of the United Mine Workers to estimate the population trends of the coal-producing areas of the United States, or even of the country as a whole.[140]

Rashomon the Chronicler

Herodotus gives the losses as 6400 Persian and 192 Athenian dead. The latter figure we can surely accept.

—J. F. Lazenby,
The Defence of Greece, referring to the battle of Marathon

The flagrant[ly] contradictory statements of eye-witnesses had reached my ears and amazed me, and my difficulties increased. . . . Where an event had equal weight of testimony on both sides, or anything reached me opposed to my own view of the question, I submitted it to His Majesty [the Mughal emperor Akbar] and freed myself from responsibility.

—Abu al-Fazl,
ᶜAin-i-Akbari

The day after Custer's last stand, other United States Army units took possession of the battlefield and its grisly remains. During the next several days measures to identify and bury the dead began. The first order of business was a body count. The results of this count were recorded by eight different participants and observers, who testified in the series of hearings that ensued. The conditions would seem to have been ideal for unanimous agreement about the number of bodies left behind by the victorious Indians. Not so. The eight witnesses offered five different numbers, ranging from 206 to 212.[1] The range of difference—about 3 percent—might seem small, but in the circumstances it can also be regarded as uncommonly large.[2]

If, since 1876, evidence and scholarly opinion have coalesced, in the popular mind the numbers increased at the same time. As a scholar of the Custer myth puts it: "For the number of the hero's band the age preferred 300, or occasionally its multiple."[3] This choice was hardly accidental—it had a specific etiology—Herodotus reported that 300 Spartans perished at Thermopylae, while some thought that 600 men had made the Charge of the Light Brigade.[4] In short, 300 became a symbolic number, the shorthand way of recreating the myth of Custer's last stand in its own image.[5]

———

The claim that it is impossible to take seriously the numerical evidence in the chronicles regarding the numbers of Indians to be found anywhere in the Americas is sweeping and cannot be shown to be true— or false. But we are not faced, therefore, with a matter simply of deciding whether believing is more satisfying and more appropriate than doubting. By looking at another body of evidence, we might at least come closer to judging the *likelihood* that the chroniclers and their sources were adept at other, less complex and more direct kinds of estimating and measuring.

For instance, in addition to estimating the sizes of Indian armies, towns, and populations, the Spaniards often provided figures relating to their own forces—the sizes of detachments, expeditions, and other smaller groups of men that were constantly being gathered together and marched off on some new adventure. Here, it would surely seem, the evidence would be much less equivocal. The authorities needed to know how many men were in various units for arming them, victualing them, paying them, and recording their services for future preferment. And when chroniclers were actually members of these bodies of men, it would seem that they would be able accurately to count their comrades at various points in time. Moreover, there ought not to be so many uncertainties about the categories being measured—no need to extrapolate from some often unknown unit of measurement to something much larger.

The expedition of Hernando de Soto provides a test of this seemingly unexceptionable notion. This expedition was separated in space from all other forms of Spanish authority, it maintained itself for about four years, and four chroniclers reported on its operations. Two of them were named participants, the third an unnamed participant, and the fourth a nonparticipant who claimed to have done little more than edit the reminiscences of someone who was a participant.[6] Two of the accounts were recorded almost immediately after the remnants of the expedition reached New Spain, in accordance with the Spanish practice of gathering data as soon as possible in order to assess blame and, occasionally—although hardly in this case—credit.

In these circumstances we would expect to find solid agreement among the four chronicles regarding the number of Spaniards involved in various activities along the route, beginning with the very number of men who sailed from Santiago in Cuba in May 1539. Ominously, precision and agreement are already absent at this stage. The account of Rodrigo Ranjel, who served as de Soto's secretary during the expedition and whose account is probably to be regarded as the most authoritative, recorded that 570 men disembarked in Florida.[7] Luis Hernández de Biedma, the expedition's factor, recorded that the number was 620.[8] An anonymous Portuguese participant known as the Fidalgo de Elvas, who published an account about fifteen years after the return of the survivors, remembered that there were 600 in the expedition at its outset.[9] Inca Garcilaso de la Vega, purportedly basing his account on that of yet another member, wrote that 1,000 men were present on the occasion.[10]

Ignoring Inca Garcilaso, we find a fairly tight range, at least by the standards of the genre: the range is only 8.8 percent of the smallest number. Still, the extremes of this range are the estimates of Biedma and Ranjel, whom we might have expected to have had privileged access to the same set of data. Elvas's figure of 600 may be seen as a rounding-off. All things considered, it is probably safe to assume that between 570 and 620 Spaniards landed in Florida, but it is hardly possible to be any more precise than the sources themselves are.

During their four years abroad in the American Southeast, the members of de Soto's expedition fought many skirmishes, a few minor battles, and one major conflict at Mauvila, where the army suffered severe losses. How severe? Twenty-two Spaniards died, according to Ranjel.[11] Biedma's statement that "more than twenty" died neither agrees nor disagrees with Ranjel's.[12] Elvas remembered that only eighteen were killed that day.[13] Inca Garcilaso, again in a world of his own, tried to persuade his readers that forty-seven soldiers perished during the battle itself and another thirty-five died later from wounds received on the field, thereby being both precise and anecdotal—a nice touch, even though it conspicuously disagrees with all other sources.[14]

The range here—again omitting Inca Garcilaso in order not to taint the results—is tolerably tight, although not quite so narrow as the range for the number of expeditionaries at embarkation. Of all the numbers generated by the de Soto chronicles, it is surely reasonable to expect that these would be the nearest to identical, given the implications. Possibly, however, the differences here lie once more in interpretation rather than in calculaton. Following Inca Garcilaso, it is probably the case that some Spanish soldiers died as a result of, rather that at, the battle of Mauvila. Thus, Elvas may have recorded only battlefield deaths, whereas Ranjel and Biedma were thinking in terms of battle-related deaths. But this can be only modern speculation and rationalizing. Once again, the best sources we have fail to answer our needs as fully and precisely as we would wish.[15]

The case of the de Soto chroniclers raises a larger question: are the discrepancies discussed here the result of a simple failure to record, or do they spring from a more profound lack of interest in knowing and transmitting the kind of information needed to fuel the modern appetite for precision? Did Ranjel, for instance, actually know at one time how many men disembarked in Florida and how many died at Mauvila but let the memory slip away in the stress of campaigning? Or did he regard these data as momentarily utilitarian but not as knowledge worth preserving accurately and indefinitely? These are not questions that can be answered, any more than we can know whether Ranjel was representative of other chroniclers in this regard. Nor can we even know whether Ranjel (or Biedma or Elvas) got the numbers right in the first place, or that he felt the need to. Still, we can look at other cases to get a better fix.

Before invading the Inca state, Francisco Pizarro sent out several reconnoitering parties. One of these landed on the Ecuadorian coast early in 1531. Two sources (one, Cieza de León, probably dependent on the other, Jérez) recorded that 180 men and 36 horses comprised the party.[16] Cristóbal de Mena was, like Jérez, a participant, but he thought there were 250 men.[17] Pedro Pizarro, a relative of Francisco Pizarro's who, like Cieza de León, came to Peru later, stated that there were 200 men in this advance party.[18]

Early in 1519 Hernán Cortés landed on the coast of Mexico with a contingent of 530 (or 400 or 500 or 508 or 560 or 600, etc.) men.[19] Months later the Spaniards had been reinforced, had fought their way to Tenochtitlan, and had captured the Aztec emperor Moctezuma, who died in custody. Eventually the Aztecs rose against the Spaniards and drove them out of Tenochtitlan on the famous *noche triste,* killing hundreds of the Spaniards and even more of their Tlaxcalan allies. How many hundreds? The observers of the time were uncertain and offered an unusually wide range of figures: 150, 200, 290, 300+, 400, 450, 450+, 500, 500+, 600, 600, 600, 680, 800, 860 (or 870), 1,000, and 1,170.[20]

Interestingly, both the lowest and the highest numbers were offered by participants in the affair. Cortés himself offered the lowest number—in fact, the two lowest numbers, thereby disagreeing with himself in testimonies provided later the same year.[21] It is hardly surprising that Cortés would minimize Spanish loss of life, since any losses would be debited to his account by the Spanish authorities, with whom his relations were at that moment troubled. On these grounds alone most students of the Spanish conquest of Mexico have rejected these lowest casualty figures, even while some of them seem willing to accept Cortés's extraordinarily high figures for Indian fighting units.[22]

There is at least inferential evidence that a list of Spanish deaths was compiled sometime after the occasion; it would have been an entirely appropriate thing to do.[23] If so, it would have been Cortés who commissioned it, yet his figures are implausibly low—not believed in our time and probably not widely believed in his. And he contradicted himself later in a way that suggested much higher figures than those he formally advanced. Whether such a list was itself accurate, and whether any of the other estimates was based on such a list, is impossible to know, but clearly no more than one of them could have been right. This reinforces the notion that even such a specific attempt to reach accuracy at the time had no visible effects on the loss figures that have come to us via the chronicles.

Be that as it may, the range of estimates is especially astonishing for the *noche triste* battle. In part this range is so broad because the Spaniards did not retain possesson of the battlefield and never had the chance to bury most of the dead. Just the same, presumably there were at least rudimentary muster rolls, obsequies in absentia, and other ways of pinpointing fairly closely the number of Spaniards who never appeared again—the likely definition of "killed" in this instance. Yet the range is about eightfold, and this must be attributed either to political purposes (the use of the occasion to salvage or discredit Cortés's actions), to the lack of memory (a convenient but necessarily ubiquitous explanation for disparity in numbers), to faulty transmission (always possible, but apparently very less often probable), or to indifference.[24] In reality, it hardly mattered how many Spaniards had perished, only how many had survived, and on that number the historical record is considerably more consistent, ranging from 340 to 440.[25]

It is easy enough to sum up the numerical data available for various Spanish activities during the two-year-long conquest of the Aztec empire: in no single instance is there perfect harmony among sources as to the numbers of Spanish men and horses involved in any one of the several activities for which such numbers are provided. In not one of the numerous opportunities do our sources, most of them deriving from participants in the events or from their testimony as recorded by others, manage to agree with one another. From our perspective this might seem extraordinary but, although perhaps such a unanimous lack of unanimity is unusual, it can hardly be considered entirely unexpected. Indeed, this body of examples can be seen to represent a microcosm of two different—and in this instance competing—fields of thought about the opportunity costs of reaching and maintaining numerical accuracy.[26]

In terms of Spaniards counting other Spaniards, the campaign ended just as it had begun—with confusion and contradiction. Details of the Spaniards' losses during their three-month final siege of Tenochtitlan present the usual array of numbers. Not surprisingly, Cortés's apologist, López de Gómara, offered the lowest casualty figure, "about fifty."[27] This figure was repeated with slight variations by Cervantes de Salazar and Herrera y Tordesillas, while Torquemada wrote of "fewer than one hundred."[28] Bernal Díaz del Castillo offered no overall figure for this occasion, but his account is a tantalizing embodiment of the problem. Speaking only of the number of captured Spanish soldiers sacrificed at the final siege of Tenochtitlan, he first wrote that there had been 66 of these, then later 72 or 78, and finally 62.[29] The discrepancies seem not to have bothered him, and perhaps they should not concern us particularly either, so long as we do not attempt to extrapolate grandly from these figures, the highest of which is more than 25 percent greater than the lowest.[30]

The conquest of Chile began in the same way from Peru as that of Peru had begun from Panama—as reconnaissance followed by invasion. A small group of mounted Spaniards under Pedro de Valdivia set out in 1540, acting on rumors of riches to the south. How many men did this group comprise? As usual, there are about as many answers as sources—ranging from as few as 138 men to as many as 170.[31] In this case the issue is more than usually complicated, because the final little army consisted of smaller contingents collected at different points along the route—which only emphasizes the challenges that are to be expected from sources dealing with these matters.[32]

Once in Chile, Valdivia and his men, and the reinforcements that followed over the years, found themselves facing far stiffer opposition from the Araucanians than the Incas had managed to mount against Pizarro's force. In the process the Spaniards lost a number of pitched battles and sieges. In one of these the Araucanians massacred every member of a Spanish detachment in the Copiapó valley in 1549. Annihilation has its appeal, and instances of the forlorn hope seem to find their way indelibly into the historical record (Mount Gilboa, Thermopylae, Cremera, Masada, Roncesvalles, the Alamo, Little Big Horn); at least seven shorter or longer accounts of the debacle at Copiapó have survived. The figures quoted for the dead in these sources range from twenty-seven to forty, and no two of them are the same.[33] Inevitably, modern renditions of the conquest of Chile have been at no little variance themselves.[34]

Valdivia's career had only a few more years to run before he himself was killed by the Araucanians at Tucapel, along with all his men. The records of this defining event in the early history of the colony are considerably more consensual than those for the battle of Copiapó. The widely proposed view was that forty Spaniards had perished at Tucapel. As we know, forty is a popular, even symbolic, number in history, forcing at least some suspicion from even the most equable historians.[35] Fortunately for the skeptical, other numbers from 35 to 151 were also current at the time.[36] Once again, modern views of the number of Spaniards lost at the battle of Tucapel vary, presumably according to the sources consulted.[37]

There are no Spanish eyewitness accounts of the casualties at these two battles, but the testimony that has survived comes from officials and settlers close at hand to the events and presumably in a position to offer definitive figures. The only reasonable conclusion is that the kind of precision modern scholars take for granted and insistently seek out seldom exists.[38] And even if we choose to assume that at least one of the proffered figures for each of the two battles was right, what then? It is easy enough to be democratic and vote with the majority for Tucapel, but for Copiapó we are allowed only to be intuitive.

Fired by exaggerated reports of the wealth and populousness of "seven cities" in Cíbola, north of New Spain, Francisco Vázquez de Coronado mustered an army in the town of Compostela early in 1540. The force then moved to Culiacán, nearer its objective. From there Coronado left with an advance party, and the main body followed shortly after. How large was this advance party? It depends entirely on which source we consult. Pedro de Castañeda, a participant who wrote an account of the expedition some twenty years later, remembered that Coronado started north "with about fifty cavalry and twenty-five foot soldiers and most of the Indian allies."[39] On the other hand, Juan Jaramillo, a captain in the expedition who probably wrote earlier than Castañeda and who was perhaps a member of the advance party, wrote of "sixty cavalrymen" accompanying Coronado, failing to mention either the foot soldiers or the Indians.[40] Another source, an anonymous *relación*, offered yet a different figure: "eighty horsemen and twenty-five foot soldiers."[41] Finally, an anonymous source, probably not a participant or observer, noted that Coronado left Culiacán with "only seventy-five companions on horseback and thirty foot soldiers."[42]

Four sources, four variant sets of figures. Apparently there was no real interest at the time in knowing and transmitting the exact details of the composition of Coronado's party. The writers of all four sources were interested in the cavalrymen even while they provided discordant numbers; three of them carried data about accompanying infantry; but only one thought it worth mentioning that there was a group of accompanying Indians, the largest of the three groups. In the circumstances it comes as no surprise that modern accounts of Coronado's expedition maintain and exacerbate this ambiguity, often picking some numbers from one source and some from another.[43] No wonder the modern editors of these very sources wisely decided to temporize by stating that Coronado set out "with approximately 75 horsemen and 25 foot soldiers, some Indian allies, and with cattle for food."[44]

All this might seem to be no more than just another coat of gold on the proverbial lily. But for Coronado there are a couple of twists that make the case especially intriguing. In the first place, a muster roll of the expedition, carried out at Compostela, exists. It is naturally very detailed, precise, and specific. It relates that Coronado's force then comprised exactly 225 horsemen and 62 infantry, along with 558 horses.[45] This would seem definitive; certainly greater faith must be placed in this document than in any of the others discussed in this chapter. And it clearly is to be preferred to other estimates of the size of Coronado's force, such as that of 250 "cavalry" at Culiacán made by Viceroy Antonio de Mendoza.[46] Isn't it?

Maybe not. It has long been known that more than 287 men accompanied Coronado. In fact, a recent study has identified at least 338 members of the expedition.[47] Presumably the additional fifty-odd men (and one woman) joined the expedition after the muster, which after all was held very early and far from the front in order to suit the viceroy's convenience. Thus the muster roll was at best accurate for one moment and one place, and neither of these was particularly relevant to succeeding events. Yet in its exactitude the muster roll beguiles and thus misleads.[48]

———

Before closing this discussion, it might be well to point out that the Spaniards had trouble counting each other from the very beginning of the colonial enterprise. A small detachment of men went missing when Columbus stopped at Guadeloupe in November 1493 on his return voyage to Hispaniola. Two eyewitnesses mentioned the occasion. According to Diego Alvarez Chanca, seven men were lost for four days; however, Michele de Cuneo reported that the incident involved eleven men who were missing for five or six days.[49] Later, Ferdinand Colón and Las Casas, secondary witnesses and one probably relying on the other, both recorded that nine men went off and became lost.[50] Modern accounts of Columbus's brief sojourn at Guadeloupe are satisfied to mention the incident, sometimes to cite a number, but never to discuss the discrepancies. For their purposes it is enough to note that a small group of Spaniards became lost—a vanguard of the repeated expeditions after treasure that were to characterize the exploration of the Americas. All well and good, but in terms of an interest in the numbers in the Spanish sources, this incident is not entirely insignificant, since it effectively established a pattern in accounts of the conquest of the Americas. Indeed, it can best be seen as a tiny first symptom of what was quickly to become a well-developed, chronic, and contagious syndrome.

As if for emphasis, the problem reasserted itself only a few days later when the fleet met some Caribs on a canoe. Nine accounts of the occasion survive, and the number of Caribs ranges from five to sixteen, with the only agreement appearing in sources dependent on one another. As a result, seven different estimates of the size of this single crew are available for those who would use it, for instance, to estimate the population of the Lesser Antilles in 1493.[51]

It would be downright unfair to suggest that only the Spaniards had trouble counting each other. The English settlers in Virginia seem also to have had unexpected difficulties in tabulating themselves—were there 1,200 or 1,500 of them in two settlements during the 1620s?[52] Later in Virginia, two sets of figures were derived for the census of 1682—one from the colony as a whole, the other covering nine of its counties. In only one instance of the nine do the two figures agree; in all other cases the county lists are consistently higher, so that their total is 5,905 male adults while that derived centrally is only 5,273.[53]

At the same time, the problem was manifesting itself farther north. In 1632 Thomas Morton estimated that there were 12,000 English in New England, while another source dating from the same year gave the total as "about 2,000."[54] Just two years later, the incident repeated itself. This time John Winthrop, the governor of the Bay

Colony, thought that the colony had about 4,000 residents.[55] A prospectus touting further settlement disagreed: there were at least 20,000 Europeans in Massachusetts and another 10,000 elsewhere in New England.[56] And so it went.

Given its provenance and odd fit with other figures from the time, it is easy enough to discount the figure of 30,000. At the same time it is necessary to keep in mind that the impetus for this figure was not, after all, much different from the motives that actuated Cortés to proffer such high figures for Aztec armies—figures that the High Counters have accepted and energetically defended. Nor was it very different from the motives that prompted Motolinía and other missionaries to gather far more souls for heaven than was practicable at the time, but these figures, too, have been defended and justified in the interests of counting high.[57]

Turning to New France, we find a similar interest in the seventeenth century in knowing how many whites were permanently settled in the seven populated clusters along the St. Lawrence river. Censuses of these were held in 1666 and 1667. The recorded figures differed by 5.3 percent and 9.6 percent, respectively, from the likely actual figures derived from consulting the manuscript records, probably because of the inclusion or exclusion of particular groups and the season at which the count was made. Despite the best efforts, probably one-quarter of the population there was left uncounted.[58] The French thus join the English and the Spanish in their inability to count small numbers of their own citizens accurately, as well as to define their terms of reference precisely and clearly.[59]

Having looked at the surprising degree of conflict in the sources' measurement of relatively small groups of Europeans, we can look at another category measured and reported by the chroniclers. In this case it is the sizes of things rather than of groups of people. Since these things were immovable and in most cases potentially subject to an unlimited amount of scrutiny, we should again have the right to expect nearly unanimous consistency.

We begin with the details in the chronicles of the conquest of Peru about the size of the chamber that Atahualpa agreed at Cajamarca to fill with various sorts of treasure. Several weeks passed between the time of the promise and its fulfillment. During those weeks, we might reasonably suppose, the room was the cynosure of all Spanish eyes, since each member of the expedition would be entitled to a share in the treasure. Francisco de Jérez, Francisco Pizarro's secretary, estimated that it was "22 ft. in length and 17 ft. in width."[60] Another expeditionary, Cristóbal de Mena, came close to agreeing, recording it as 25 feet by 15 feet.[61] Writing less than a year later, Hernando Pizarro, Francisco Pizarro's half-brother, remembered matters much more generously: according to his testimony the room was some 30 to 35 feet by 17 or 18 feet.[62] An anonymous account published in France in 1534 wrote of a house that was "twenty feet in height [*aulteur*] and eighteen feet in width."[63] In recording his recollections several years later, Juan Ruiz de Arce suffered the opposite effect—for him the treasure room was only 20 feet by 15 feet.[64] Finally, Fernando Montesinos, who wrote a century later, whose work is necessarily derivative, and whose reputation does not stand high, expressed it in different terms: the house or room was "7 $\frac{1}{3}$ varas in width, 5 $\frac{1}{4}$ varas in length, and 3 $\frac{3}{4}$ varas in height."[65] The pattern here is slightly unusual—normally such calculations tend to increase as time passes—but the scattershot effect is typical of multiple testimonies.[66]

In terms of how high the room was to be filled, Jérez had it as an "estado and a half," along a "white line" that ran along the perimeter halfway up. For Mena it was "que un hombre alto no allegava a ella con un palmo."[67] John Hemming is inclined to accept Jérez's estimate, and there are reasons for agreeing with him.[68] As Francisco Pizarro's secretary, Jérez was officially responsible for assuring the accuracy of details of this kind. On the other hand, Hernando Pizarro's account was, so far as we can tell, offered the nearest in time to the events at Cajamarca, albeit not more than several months before the accounts of Jérez and Mena.[69] Ruiz de Arce's account would probably be considered the least reliable, because it was offered later and by an illiterate informant. But it is Pizarro's apparently inflated account that most requires explanation.

Four testimonies, then, produced as many different results. Looking at these a little more closely, we see that even the apparently close agreement between Jérez and Mena is merely adventitious, the result of countervailing differences of opinion about length and width. While Hemming's argument that Jérez is likely to be most accurate is contextually reasonable, his further conclusion that the "other writers [Pizarro and Ruiz de Arce] agreed roughly with [Jérez's] measurements" is decidedly odd.[70] After all, in square area, Pizarro's estimate is about 1.9 times greater than Ruiz de Arce's, while these two differ from Jérez's by +52 percent and -19.8 percent, respectively.

If three record books showed Ted Williams's lifetime batting average as .276, .344, and .523 respectively, or if three atlases recorded the height of Mount Everest as 23,263 feet, 29,002 feet, and 44,083 feet, or if three historical dictionaries showed Louis XIV as ruling 58 years, 72 years, and 109 years, their users would have every right to be thoroughly bemused and would be justified in rejecting them all, even though research could show that in each case one of the figures was correct. Yet these differences are of exactly the same magnitude as those among the sources for the size of Atahualpa's treasure room that Hemming finds tolerable.

Each of them in fact represents substantial *dis*agreement. Hemming's lack of concern about this level of incommensurateness indicates that he is perhaps too eager to see silk purses where sometimes there are only sows' ears. Beyond that, his use of the word "measurement" calls for comment. Given the disparity of opinion, we are hardly able to argue strongly that any of these figures was the result of actual measurement, even while we can concede that some measuring was probable. But whose? If Jérez's, then none of the others'. If Pizarro's, then none of the others'. And so on. None of the figures given in the sources is congruent enough with any of the others to allow us to assume that more than a single measurement was taken and that all the other specifications were the result either of gazing at the room or of word of mouth. In the circumstances we are left with nothing more than to agree with Hemming, in this case on the basis of Jérez's status, but this can by no means be an argument of closure.

It is also worth remembering that eyewitness accounts that were prepared within a year or so of the observation are relatively rare things among the chronicles of the Indies. It was true for Cortés, Pizarro, and Valdivia, but the accounts of Cabeza de Vaca, Díaz del Castillo, and the other chroniclers of Peru, and all four de Soto chronicles, were recorded years after most of the events they purport to describe, sometimes in wondrous detail. The case of the treasure room at Cajamarca, then, is more minatory than encouraging. The object being measured—or at least given measurements—was probably observed by these four chroniclers hundreds of times within a very short period and observed with a particular, even enthralled, interest. Yet this alone was not enough to produce even one reported measurement that fully corroborated another.[71]

The cases cited here are only a handful of a much larger universe of accounts (including accounts of size, number, and color) that in some way describe or measure objects that came within the purview of the reporters. But are they representative? The short answer is that they are. Ordinarily, or so it might seem, the existence of independent testimony is a boon to the historian intent on fixing with a degree of certainty some aspect of the past. Paradoxically, searching for multiplicity in numbers entails finding variation, difference, contradiction, and disappointment.

Measuring is a universal impulse, but mismeasurement seems to be the usual result, especially in the days before the advent of measuring devices more accurate than the human eye.[72] Measuring the size of an object or natural wonder requires calculation rather than counting and so is inherently more difficult. On the other hand, if the object remains in place, it is possible to test the acuity of ocular estimates. Take the case of Niagara Falls; the two main cataracts are known to be 167 feet high and 158 feet high, respectively. However, this is a modern measurement. The many early descriptions of the falls misapprehended their actual height, sometimes by orders of magnitude and most often by magnifying it.[73]

Europeans' first impressions of the Grand Canyon were similar. In August 1540 Coronado, en route to Cíbola, dispatched a party to seek out the Colorado river. Led by Garcí López de Cárdenas, the party chanced on the Grand Canyon. Castañeda, who recorded the episode, said that the Spaniards estimated the width of the canyon to the north to be "three or four leagues" as the crow flies "across to the other bank of the stream which flowed between [the rims]."[74] This was not a bad guess, but the Spaniards, presumably unaware of how far above the Colorado they stood, went on to estimate the river to be only an arm's length across, although the Indians accompanying them insisted that it was no less than a league (more than three miles) wide. After some investigation, the Spaniards decided that the Indians were right after all.[75]

———

Twice in the chronicles of the conquest of Mexico we find mention of immense numbers of skulls arrayed in particular public places as mementos of past triumphs; presumably they were no more mobile than the treasure room at Cajamarca. Díaz del Castillo reported that in Xocotlán he saw "piles of human skulls so regularly arranged that one could count them, and I estimated them at more than a hundred thousand. I say once again that there were more than a hundred thousand of them."[76]

Another participant chronicler, Andrés de Tapia, reported a similar case at the *templo mayor* in Tenochtitlan and provided even more circumstantial detail. He described how he and a companion came upon five huge racks of skulls, which they proceeded to count—or, rather, they extrapolated from one of the racks to include all five. By this procedure they arrived at a total figure of 136,000 skulls, without, Tapia said, including those on two adjacent towers.[77]

These are astonishing numbers, to be sure, and they have been used both to justify large population counts and for other purposes, presumably not much different from their original purpose—to over-awe.[78] For instance, at a very early stage in the High Counter revolution—when the population of central Mexico was still estimated at about 2 million and had not yet become more than twelve times greater—Sherburne Cook took account of this evidence. He noted that not everyone took these estimates seriously but argued that "[a]s much discretion is necessary . . . in rejecting as in accepting them."[79] He went on to comment, in what not unfairly might be considered to be one of the core tenets of the High Counters' credo:

> Bernal Díaz and Andres de Tápia [sic] . . . were actual participants in the conquest, eyewitnesses of the events they described. Both can be accused of personal bias with reference to the politics of the day, . . . [b]ut they both state emphatically that they actually counted [sic] the skulls in question and as accurately as they were able. They had no motive for falsification and both were reliable, competent soldiers. I can therefore see no reason for not accepting their figures at face value.[80]

Later, Woodrow Borah expressed much the same opinion. He thought that "[t]he sobriety and seriousness of [Tapia's] testimony is impressive" and went on, in one of the great statements of the movement: "When a men seriously says he counts, his evidence is worth a hundred guesses by historians four hundred years thereafter."[81]

Given the logistical impossibilities (to be discussed shortly) that Tapia's "sober" testimony entails, this argument is eloquent testimony to an indomitable will to believe, as well as to a certain naiveté concerning the rhetorical devices of the time. Nigel Davies provides a series of logistical problems that human sacrifice on this or even a much lower level would have created. He concludes that the extremely high numbers in the chronicles for precontact sacrifice, as well as Tapia's number of skulls, are "invariably vastly inflated."[82]

Still others have picked up on the data regarding the skulls, most notably Michael Harner, who found them to be irresistible support for his arguments about protein-driven cannibalism in precontact Mexico. In turn, his argument fed on, and fed, the propositions of the High Counters regarding the population of central Mexico at the time of conquest. It needed to, since he speculated that human sacrifice accounted for as many as a quarter of a million victims annually toward the end of the preconquest period.[83]

Unlike other matters discussed in this chapter, the issue here is not one of discrepant figures offered by different witnesses to the same event but more simply a matter of straightforward credibility. It is true that the skulls in these purported depositories were fixed objects that could, in theory, be counted by observers. The question to be considered is the likelihood that Díaz and Tapia were actually relating the numbers of skulls they observed "as accurately as they were able." This is not a question that can be answered directly, but the testimony of the sources certainly begs for critical analysis in the context of the larger problem addressed here.

Pace Cook, Díaz del Castillo did not write that he "actually counted" the skulls, but only that he could have. Instead, or so he says, he estimated their number—on what grounds is quite unclear. Consider the implications of Díaz's description. There were no fewer than 100,000 skulls in "the plaza" of what was apparently a modest provincial town, arrayed, he says, in some fashion that permitted easy counting. What would this have been? If they were laid out flat, they would have consumed as much as 100,000 square feet of area, likely to be much greater than the size of a country town's plaza. If they were piled, how were they piled to be easily calculated? In particular, if they could be counted, why was Díaz satisfied only to estimate them?[84]

Tapia's account seems even more outlandish, despite the profusion of detail, if not because of it. Despite the detail, his description is elusive, but he seems to claim that he actually counted as many as 27,200 skulls before multiplying that figure by five to obtain his final total.[85] Early in the twentieth century Genaro García discussed Tapia's description and concluded that the construction described by Tapia could have supported no more than 2,760 skulls.[86] More recently, Ortiz de Montellano looked at the matter again and calculated that Tapia's testimony would require a rack that was about six hundred feet tall![87] It seems, then, that Tapia's flood of detail was specifically designed to persuade readers who would not have the opportunity to test his calculations.

Beyond the physical impossibility of the scenarios sketched by Díaz and Tapia there is the simple argument from silence, which in this case must at least be considered. It can only be reckoned peculiar that of the participant chroniclers, Díaz alone mentioned the impressive cache of skulls in Xocotlán, and Tapia alone the contents of the "famous" skull rack in Tenochtitlan. At the very least, one would expect each chronicler to have mentioned both cases—certainly one would expect Díaz, who professedly exhibited such an interest at Xocotlán, to have continued that interest in the Aztec capital, where an even larger aggregation of skulls must have been anticipated by all hands. And is it credible that Cortés himself, who strained every literary sinew to present his case to Charles V, would have failed to mention numbers of such magnitude?

In contrast, there is an impressive reticence on the matter in the chronicles. Díaz mentioned evidence of sacrifices "in every town they reached," and there are a few other scattered comments, but nothing at all to indicate skulls preserved in such enormous numbers.[88] This widespread silence, precisely where we would not expect to encounter it if Díaz and Tapia were "accurate," suggests that in fact they were not.

We can accept that Díaz encountered a large number of skulls at Xocotlán and that there was an even larger number at Tenochtitlan for Tapia to record—and no more. The numbers that each put to their observations can be regarded only as one of the more piquant examples of exaggeration encountered in the sources. In this case, the purpose of such hyperbole—to discredit the Aztec political and moral system—is patently evident. That so many modern commentators have taken these particular numbers so seriously (Harner actually regards them as probably on the low side) bespeaks the power of numbers to persuade and to be used in turn to persuade others.[89] We do not know how successful Díaz and Tapia were in convincing their readers that Spanish Christian morality required that the Aztecs be overthrown, but were they to know of their success more than four centuries later, if with slightly different effect, they might be amused.[90]

Do any number of mismeasurements, however well documented, matter? Is it not possible to assume, for instance, that the Spanish chroniclers and their informants were, if inexplicably, considerably more careful and accurate in their efforts to measure others than their counterparts discussed earlier were in counting themselves? Of course we can assume just that; as we have seen, many of those seeking contact population levels make this very assumption time and again.[91] Unfortunately, in granting the chronicles of the Indies unconditional amnesty, we would also be underwriting a kind of historiographical miracle, since the propensity to mismeasure—and not just aggregations of people—and to do so on the high side can be documented from the very beginnings of the historical record—in ancient China, Mesopotamia, Egypt, and elsewhere. In this sense, the inability of four or five eyewitnesses who proved unable to measure in situ or to recall later the dimensions of an easily accessible empty space is completely unsurprising. Indeed, had all these sources agreed exactly, it would be so suspicious as to lend almost irrefutable credibility to the notion of their interdependency.

———

I close this discussion by citing a few other examples—just a sampling—of problems in measurement. Islands are a useful test of measurement skills, since they vary in size and shape among themselves but present the same front over time. The tendency of the early explorers, beginning with Columbus, was to overstate their size and so their significance, but another aspect is the observers' inconsistency in comparing islands with each other. A case from the Philippines illustrates this well. A report from the 1590s, some thirty years after Spaniards began to settle there, attempted to estimate the sizes of many of the islands, as well as the number of Filipinos who had been brought into the encomienda system.[92] In Table 2, the islands are arranged by size as reckoned in this report.

By any standard, the variation here is noteworthy; its patterns suggest that the author of the report, Francisco de Ortega, tended to overestimate the sizes of small islands while underestimating the sizes of larger ones, but that he did neither with any predictability. Thus he reckoned that Luzon was only three-quarters the size of Mindanao, whereas it is over 10 percent larger. Similarly, Ortega estimated that Maripipe and Samal were roughly the same size; in fact Samal is almost ten times larger. And so on, all showing that at least some Spaniards were not particularly competent in measuring fixed bodies of land.[93] To most of us this is not a surprise.[94] And yet the sizes of bodies of land directly affect estimates of their population whenever such expedients as density per areal unit are employed.

More mobile than islands, yet larger and less mobile than men, ships would seem to offer little impediment to being counted accurately. Two instances from the English Channel, widely separated in time, however, suggest that this is not so.[95] William of Normandy's invasion of England was recorded by several observers and by others within a few years of the event. Yet in the chronicles describing the occasion, the number of ships he employed ranges from 696 to "quite eleven thousand"![96]

After looking at all possible aspects of the matter, C. M. Gill-

Table 2. Estimated and Actual Sizes of Philippine Islands

Island	Est. "League in Circuit"	Actual Size (km2)	Ratio of Est. to Actual Size (as %)
Ambil	5	28	5.6
Ilin	8	77	9.6
Romblon	8	82	10.3
Fuga	9	93	10.3
Camiguin	10	164	16.4
Capul	10	35	3.5
Banton	10	28	2.8
Cuyo	12	58	4.8
Maripipe	15	28	1.9
Samal	15	248	16.5
Tablas	18	686	38.1
Bohol	24	3,865	161.0
Masbate	25	3,269	130.8
Catanduanes	30	1,431	47.7
Marinduque	30	898	29.9
Leyte	60	7,214	120.2
Mindoro	80	9,735	121.7
Cebu	100	4,422	44.2
Negros	100	12,705	127.1
Panay	100	11,515	115.2
Luzon	300	104,689	348.0
Mindanao	400	94,730	236.9

Source for estimates: Francisco de Ortega, "Report concerning the Filipinas Islands," 1594.

mor concluded that "[t]he numerical strength of the fleet is impossible to estimate accurately through an analysis of ship capacity and naval logistics."[97] Just the same, he calculated that building even seven hundred ships would have imposed impossible demands on the forests of northern France, and that the procurement of raw materials and the maintenance of those employed in building the ships would have turned Normandy into "an economic wasteland."[98]

Nearly nine hundred years later, another large fleet was required to evacuate British and allied troops from the beleaguered port of Dunkerque. This successful operation was famously impromptu, but there was a hastily improvised purview, if not overall control, and ample documentation survives. Even so, there has been no finality concerning the number of ships and boats involved in the operation—one author has referred to the matter as "[p]robably the most vexed of all Dunkirk questions."[99] The official version is that 693 "British" ships participated, but other estimates run to more than 1,200 ships.[100] These estimates do not always address precisely the same issue (in this case, what was being counted), which only underscores the complexities of measuring, especially during war.[101]

Finally, there are the usual problems in measuring distances from point to point. Sometimes these were recorded as durations of travel and sometimes in measurements whose exact modern equivalents are uncertain—for example, leagues. Further problems arise because the figures for the same routes, however they might be expressed, are often discrepant or otherwise inconsistent. This condition has contributed significantly to the disputes over the course of Columbus's first voyage or of Hernando de Soto's travels through parts of the southeastern United States. In this insouciant plurality the early chroniclers and explorers were merely imitating what had come before.[102]

In terms of measuring distances, the Great Wall of China offers an interesting case. The only manmade object visible from the moon, its sheer size should make it easy to measure. Travelers to China in late medieval–early modern times estimated its length variously at between 40 leagues and 400 leagues, that is, from about 120 to about 1,200 miles. This range is wide but not exceptional, since these reports were based on brief encounters at best and imagination at worst. Moreover, the concept of the Great Wall is itself fluid because there are many local offshoots to the main wall. Arthur Waldron, who has studied the matter thoroughly, concluded that "in the absence of surveys and reliable cartography, it must be admitted that the figure cannot be known."[103] This makes it only a little surprising that estimates made since 1970 have ranged from as low as 1,684 miles to the official Chinese figure—31,250 miles![104]

The examples discussed here speak well to the problems of choosing from among a series of disparate numbers. In most cases we cannot be certain whether the differing numbers represent unsuccessful efforts to measure the same thing or whether the issue is more complex—that in some cases different things were being measured without our knowledge, or possibly even that the same units of measurement were used but were treated idiosyncratically.

The case of Díaz del Castillo's account of casualties suffered at the time of the *noche triste* underscores some of the taxonomic problems. Many modern accounts of the *noche triste* speak of Díaz as remembering that 870 (or 860) Spaniards died then; in fact he wrote something different. Three versions of Díaz's manuscript survive. In one of them he wrote: "I assert that within a matter of five days over 870 soldiers were killed and sacrificed."[105] In this casualty count he clearly includes *noche triste*, the battle of Otumba four days later, and any losses suffered between these two events. It is less clear whether he refers only to battlefield deaths or includes wounded who later died. In that regard, his mention that some of the Spaniards were sacrificed after being captured by the Aztecs points up another facet of the issue—prisoners of war who did not survive their captivity.

Díaz's account raises issues at two levels. First, he, more than others, attempted to clarify the limits of the occasion he was describing, and in doing so he inadvertently underscored the complexities of definition with which all modern attempts to grapple with numbers in these sources must come to terms. Second, and more ominously, his disagreements with himself (in numbers as much as in anything else), as betrayed in the surviving texts of his work, forcefully remind us that we have no such textual history for most of the other chronicles. We tend to work on the assumption that however problematical the figures themselves might be, the process that has brought them to our attention has been straightforward and discernible. The fortuitous survival of no fewer than three manuscript variants of Díaz's history demonstrates that this can be more presumption than assumption and more assumption than reality.

The range of choices that have been made regarding grounds for accepting certain numbers from a set of variants and rejecting the remainder is scarcely uninteresting. As we have seen merely from the few examples noted in this chapter, these choices have been several.

The most common expedient, and the most justifiable, is to accept certain testimony because of the authority of the observer. Thus the measurements of Atahualpa's treasure room recorded by Jérez are judged superior to those of others because he was presumably responsible for this kind of administrative detail. Likewise, although the range of variation for Spanish deaths at Mauvila is narrow, if exactitude really mattered then it is likely that Ranjel's figures would be accepted because he was Jérez's counterpart. In the absence of other criteria, this approach seems reasonable, always remembering that it is a clear case of *faute de mieux* and is based on modern concepts of what constitutes authoritativeness.

Another criterion, which at first glance seems hardly less reasonable, is to judge the reliability of a number by the proximity of the observer to the phenomenon being measured or counted. But in the case of Atahualpa's treasure room, all the accounts emanate from observers who had ample occasion to view and measure the room, yet no two agreed. The same applies to the casualty figures for Mauvila and to the disparate reckonings of the height of Niagara Falls.

A better definition of proximity would be the alacrity with which the account was written down. Inevitably, for instance, accepting what Díaz had to say must be tempered by the fact that he wrote his account(s) many years after the events he described. In the case of the de Soto chronicles, the expedition itself ended only three years after the battle of Mauvila, and although Ranjel's and Biedma's accounts were transcribed into the historical record shortly afterward, three years is a long time to remember one set of facts when there were so many subsequent activities also to remember. Perhaps, though, Ranjel, Biedma (and Elvas, for that matter) maintained written accounts which they were able to consult when preparing their synoptic versions. Perhaps indeed, but we do not know this; we can merely choose to believe it in order to justify firmer belief in their versions.

In some manuscripts from this period we can see that the authors frequently crossed off or erased matter owing to second thoughts.[106] For the vast majority, however, we have available only the results of the final transmission—the published version—and cannot be aware of authorial or editorial changes and transcriptional errors that might have occurred, to which integers are the most vulnerable. In short, "proximity" is a dangerously protean concept, and one whose implications are too often outside our ken. For Oviedo, eyewitnessing was a powerful notion that he often used to combat the views of Las Casas, who in turn used it himself to deflect criticism of his own numerical estimates. The samples here tend to suggest that for modern historians the "eyewitness" account is to be at once valued and feared.

A third standard by which to judge the authority of numerical data in the sources has been the concordance of more than one source. Certainly concordance is not to be despised—if it can be shown to result from independent testimony and is not the result of interdependence and borrowing. This can seldom be shown in the case of numbers, which tend to be rounded off in ways that resist the tracing of influences. Beyond this, there is a certain whiff of desperation in choosing to accept a particular number simply because it is the only one repeated from a menu of several choices. After all, that the figure six hundred appears three times in estimates for Spanish losses during the *noche triste* means only it does *not* appear fourteen other times.

This example leads to another common procedure—averaging. It might be said that in this case six hundred is not only the mode but virtually the median and the mean as well. For some these might be powerful statistical credentials, but they have no value in deciding which of the estimates of *noche triste* losses, if any, is to be deemed the most accurate. Even if every figure had been the same, it would not be an unimpeachable warranty for their validity but would provide only a different point of departure for efforts to determine this.

Yet another criterion for preferring a particular numerical testimony is our knowledge—again, if any—of details about the views of particular authors that, we think, might have influenced their choice of numbers. The case of Cortés's anomalous—and reciprocally discrepant—estimates for *noche triste* is the clearest example cited here. Intuitively we recognize that Cortés had good reason for minimizing Spanish losses, and this, combined with the fact that his numbers are substantially lower than all the remaining available estimates, virtually forces us to suspect that their value is ideological rather than arithmetical.

By the same token, though, even this realization does not require that we reject them as impossibly incorrect. However unlikely, it is not inconceivable—and the point must be stressed both for fairness and for methodological rigor—that one or another of them is correct. It is even conceivable that both are correct—that they represent different notions of the time span involved. It is doubtful that any historian would actually advance this argument—as I am not advancing it here—in preference to alternatives. That it cannot be ruled out simply illustrates the inveterate scantiness of our knowledge about the origins, context, and content of all these estimates.

Finally, there is another, little used but in some ways exceptional means of testing the accuracy of numerical estimates in our sources. This is the *accidental* concurrence—or in some cases lack of concurrence—of other information that might come unbidden into play. These apparently incidental data need not themselves be demonstrably correct to serve this purpose. At the very end of 1520 Cortés reassembled his remaining forces in Tlaxcala in preparation for returning to Tenochtitlan. According to him, this muster comprised 40 cavalry and 550 infantry.[107] As C. Harvey Gardiner noticed many years ago, "[t]he numbers given by Cortés on this occasion become an indirect but nonetheless real contradiction of previous figures stated by him."[108] Since *noche triste,* a contingent of 175 men had been added to a force that exceeded 1,000 men on the eve of *noche triste,* which should mean, in light of the information available to us (viz., that no other significant losses had occurred in the meantime), that the Spanish force at that moment was around 1,000 strong, if Cortés's earlier low estimates were correct. In effect, Cortés is here inadvertently telling on himself, and this circumstance makes the argument powerful. Had one set of figures been his and another someone else's, a case adding to the unreliability of Cortés's estimates would still be possible, but it would lack much of the *gravitas* that results from a common source.

Suggestively discrepant testimony of this kind may well be widespread, but it remains underused because it requires canvassing the available sources more broadly, specifically in search of evidence designed to cast doubt on other evidence. Like the argument from silence, exercises of this nature appear to be regarded as unprofitable—something in the nature of 1 + 1 (or even 2 + 2) = 0. Instead, the idea is clearly to accumulate evidence rather than to test it: 1 + 1 should equal 2, or even more if possible.

Still another factor comes into play in dealing with wildly inaccurate assessments of physical objects such as Niagara Falls and the Grand Canyon. All observation is conditioned: it is the outcome of a private negotiation between experience and expectation. Larger than any waterfall known to the English or French at the time, Niagara Falls would ineluctably have been seen in exaggerated terms until the conditioning of the observer was given time to conform. Conversely, if paradoxically, the Grand Canyon is so large and so deep that even to today's visitors it appears almost an optical illusion. Viewed from the rim, the Colorado river seems like a small stream indeed, and if the distance between viewer and object is not known, then it will be interpreted very much as it appears—precisely the astronomers' distinction between absolute and apparent magnitude.

———

In one of the passages heading this chapter, Lazenby accepted the fact that the Athenians knew exactly how many of their fellow citizens they had buried and then recorded this number accurately for posterity, beginning, at least for us, with Herodotus. On the face of it, his assumption and conclusion are reasonable, but the examples cited here suggest that in these matters reasonable is not always right. No doubt the Athenian body count was more accurate than that for the Persians—beyond that perhaps no more ought to be said, except that words like "surely" do not fit well into the lexicon of quantitative military history.[109]

Recently Hasok Chang has discussed "the circularity in observation itself," that is, the problem in mensuration of using the instrument to validate the measurement and the measurement to certify the instrument. He notes, among other things, what is obvious enough when stated: "[T]he validity of a measurement method cannot be established without relying on its own result." In short, "the burden of justification is merely pushed around among different measurement methods."[110]

Chang was addressing measurement by highly calibrated equipment. A fortiori, the dilemma is all the greater when the measuring devices are the human eye, human memory, and human fallibility. To complicate matters, Atahualpa's treasure room, Montezuma's armies, or the dead Spaniards on the field at Mauvila no longer remain available as a means to test this equipment. In short, there exist no certain means by which to draw even probable conclusions about the accuracy of particular evidence. The problem, while insoluble, is not one to be regarded lightly for its lessons.

The examples cited here merely remind us of the obvious—that wide ranges of estimates emanate from almost identical sets of circumstances.[111] Of these estimates, only one could have been right in any specific set of circumstances, and it is Panglossian to imagine that it is this correct estimate that has managed to survive, or even that enough contextual evidence has also survived to allow us to choose correctly from the available variants on evidentiary grounds alone.

The Spanish observers' troubles with numbers of Spaniards—and this is only a small sample of the evidence available—bodes ill for those who wish to rely on the same observers for numbers of Indians. In deploying these numbers, particularly as mere points of departure, such scholars make several assumptions, each of which is counterintuitive: that the Spaniards counted quickly better than they counted slowly; that they were much better at estimating in the tens of thousands than in the tens; and that they were more adept at counting others than at counting themselves. Short of demonstrating the validity of these strange notions, there is no realistic way to devise calculations based on the numbers in the chronicles. And turning a blind eye hardly qualifies as a substitute.[112]

Antipodean Antics

Consequently, here we have a case in which, despite the complete lack of useful, positive information, we are still able to state definite figures with great certainty. The relationships are so simple . . . that with today's perfected methods of scientific research we are able to fill the missing parts of the source accounts and to estimate the numbers of Germans better than the Romans could when they saw them before their very eyes and had daily dealings with them.

—Hans Delbrück, *Geschichte der Kriegskunst in Rahmen der politischen Geschichte*, vol. 2

People very frequently magnify or belittle, without regard to reality, things which they have heard, perhaps from those who were not familiar with them.

—Pedro Castañeda Nájera, in Hammond and Rey, *Narratives of the Coronado Expedition*

"Whatever the errors and exaggerations of the sources and local differences, it is possible to estimate without fear of contradiction that the native population of Chile had declined by at least 80% around 1598. . . . From 800,000 it had fallen to 160,000."[1] With this confident assertion, Sergio Villalobos R. ended his discussion of the contact population of Chile. At about the same time—the early 1980s—another Chilean historian, Jorge Hidalgo, was writing about the population of a smaller area in Chile, with hardly less panache:

Pedro de Valdivia [conquistador and first Spanish governor of Chile] wrote in a letter to Hernando Pizarro in 1545 that there were 15,000 Indians between Copiapó and the Río Maule valley; assuming then an average of five persons in each domestic unit, the total population would have been 75,000. Valdivia adds, however, that an equal number had died in the intervening years since the conquest of Chile began, which brings the total retrospectively to 150,000 in 1540. If we exclude from this figure an estimated 20,000 Chilean Diaguita and the estimated Aconcagua valley population of 7,500, we arrive at 122,500 Picunche. [Gerónimo de] Bibar [an early chronicler] writes that in 1558 in the jurisdiction of Santiago (i.e., from the valley of Aconcagua to that of the Río Maule) there were more than 25,000 Indians when the Spanish entered the land in 1540. If we make the same calculation as above, there would have been a total population of 125,000 in 1540, or, excluding once again the inhabitants of the Aconcagua valley, 117,500 Picunche. The earliest historical figures for the Picunche, therefore, can be amplified within a range of 117,500 to 122,500. According to both authors, however, population decline was devastatingly rapid: 50 per cent in five years, according to one, and 72 per cent in eighteen years according to the other.[2]

These passages are not from any of the main players in the contact population game. They appear only as passing features of a broader focus; they deal with an area of the Americas largely overlooked by the High Counters; and the numbers they produce are not particularly large in the scheme of things. Despite all this, Hidalgo's passage in particular repays study because it is very much a reflection of the High Counters' methodology.

Hidalgo revives a notion that has long proved serviceable to those who would count high. The argument that the word *indio* represents males of fighting or working age receives unambiguous textual support only occasionally but is clearly appealing withal. In Hidalgo's case the *indios* mentioned by Valdivia and Bibar become one-fifth of a "domestic unit."[3] The size of this unit is strictly the determination of the modern observer—there is no adequate ethnographic or census evidence from the time. The only constraint is that its size be plausible—anything from three to seven might do. In this case the other four members are never mentioned in the sources, even implicitly. They are, in effect, multiple doppelgängers brought into play, if not into existence, in aid of multiplying the unattractively low numbers in the historical record. Only if there were a discernible context—for example, a battle—or some grammatical hint that the term was being used in its narrowest sense would it be possible to indulge in this particular conceit.

The four-to-one ratio assumes that adult males declined more rapidly than the rest of the Indian population. In particular, it fails to take into account labor migration or, in the case of Chile, flight to avoid subjection to colonial authority. If one were to analyze the sex and age distribution among, say, various southern African ethnic groups in their traditional domiciles, one would find a low percentage of adult males, not because of death but because they travel to South Africa to find work in the mines and other industrial pursuits.

Villalobos demonstrates the potentially dizzying effects of this assumption when he refers to Pedro Mariño de Lobera's comment that the Indian population around Imperial was 4,400 *indios* and that the warrior part did "not reach" 14,000.[4] Villalobos sums these as "28,400" and multiplies by five, which "yields a number of 142,000 inhabitants." But, he goes on, "[t]his quantity must be about half of the population existing at the beginning of the conquest." And so the population in 1540 quickly spirals to "about 280,000," that is, nearly twenty times the raw figures in the source.[5]

In this case Mariño de Lobera did specify that the Indians about whom he spoke were adult males, but this is exceptional. Just the same, equating the term *indios* in the chronicles and other records with adult males between eighteen and fifty or so has been standard operating procedure in estimating the contact population. For Chile the practice appeared in the work of Tomás Thayer Ojeda, who was emphatic on the matter: "It would be a grave error to believe that [certain encomienda figures] represent the true number of the indigenous population; it corresponds only to that of the *tributarios*, that is, strictly speaking, to the adult males between 18 and 50 years of age."[6] At the same time, Thayer Ojeda was more discriminating in seeking a multiplier. Weighing several circumstances, he finally decided that sometimes the factor should be three and other times four, depending on the age range, which he thought varied from one time and one encomienda to another, although he usually multiplied by three.[7]

Even in cases where *indios* might mean *tributarios*, we can hardly be sure that this category was invariably confined to adult males. When Valdivia first arrived in central Chile, the local cacique offered him twelve hundred male *and five hundred female laborers* to work the newly discovered mines.[8] Valdivia refused the women at the time, but with the Spaniards' increasing voracity for gold and the equally increasing scarcity of Indians, especially male Indians, who were either dying or fleeing southward to join the armies of resistance, we can hardly be sure that women and even children were not then recruited to fill the need. As it happens, there is no need to rely entirely on inference. As early as 1559 the *oidor* Fernando de Santillán complained that children as young as "seven and eight years old" were being forced to work in the mines in Chile.[9] Under the circumstances, even in cases where *indios* refers to laborers, the ratio could only be around 2 or 2.5 to 1, which would reduce population figures projected from it by as much as half.

The central, and possibly fatal, problem with using multipliers, whether they spring from thought or from reflex, is simply that they are contextually undiscriminating. It seems most reasonable to assume that in *some* cases (encomienda counts probably, warrior counts almost certainly) the sources indeed typically referred to adult male Indians, but that at other times (e.g., when estimating gross populations of various areas, or converts) they intended to be more inclusive, without ever realizing the distinction they were making. Such variant usage is demanded by the nature of the language, by common sense, and, in cultures other than Spain, by the use of the masculine to incorporate the feminine.

Moreover, it would be hard to find a population anywhere in which adult males constitute as little as one-fifth of the population, except as the temporary consequence of war.[10] The proportion would only climb in societies where age fifty was seldom reached and infant mortality was high. Modern counters have studiously ignored this issue, yet simply increasing the multiplier from a plausible three to an unlikely five increases every projection based on them by two-thirds.

Getting back to Hidalgo's assertion, we note that since Bibar did not specify a minimum number for the unaffected population, it is impossible to calculate any rate of depopulation at all except on the lines of a "more than *x* percent" basis. He did write that about 9,000 Indians survived in 1558, which would be a reduction of 64 percent, not 72 percent, if we use 25,000 as the dividend.[11] Apparently Hidalgo decided that "more than 25,000" actually meant 32,142, since 9,000 is 28 percent of that number—surely a strange way of proceeding. Hidalgo went on to add that "the upheaval in Araucanian society [between 1550 and 1555] resulting from war combined with high mortality, drought, the destruction of crops, famine and a smallpox epidemic, slashed the population by over 60 per cent."[12] He concluded that 1 million "seems to be the closest approximation" to the population of Araucania on the eve of the Spanish invasion, and presumably it was even higher in the 1520s.[13]

It is unclear where the 60 percent decline originates, unless it is simply a raw average of 50 percent and 72 percent. Assuming this for the moment, if both Valdivia and Bibar were talking about roughly the same group(s) of Indians, it seems odd that their population would have declined by half in the first five years and then by only 15 percent more in the next thirteen, when the fighting, hunger, and maltreatment were more intense. Yet that is precisely what these figures imply if they are taken seriously. Moreover, the two chroniclers appear to contradict each other. Valdivia says that there were about 50,000 Indians in the area in 1540, while Bibar is content to speak of "more than 25,000." There is no contradiction only if "more than 25,000" was Bibar's way of saying "50,000," an alarming contingency for those intent on belaboring the numbers in the chronicles. Hidalgo subtracts an "estimated" 27,500 from the figures he derives from Valdivia but tells us nothing about how his estimates were formed. In the circumstances it would be fair to suggest that they were designed to bring the first of the calculations into close, but not suspiciously exact, harmony, with Hidalgo's second set of figures.

The palpable question behind all of this is, where did Valdivia and Bibar secure their estimates of the 1540 Indian population? Did the former rush to the area to find the Indians politely waiting to submit to a body count before they began to resist the Spaniards? Hardly. It was late 1540 before Valdivia and his party reached Copiapó in far northern Chile, and another several months before they arrived at the future site of Santiago. That city, hardly founded, was destroyed by the Indians the following September, and for two years the Spaniards were virtually beleaguered there, hardly in a position to indulge in demographic investigation, had they been so inclined.[14]

Perhaps, then, Valdivia was in a position to count the survivors in 1545 in time to write off about it to Pizarro? Perhaps after he did so, they obligingly told him that as many as he had counted had not survived? If so, how did they know this? Had they kept a running tab since the arrival of the first Spaniards—a tab that reached equilibrium with the survivors at the very time Valdivia happened to be counting? Couched facetiously perhaps, these are not facetious questions but the sort that must be asked as part of the process of testing the sources for this kind of information. Apparently no testing occurred in this case.[15]

Pace Hidalgo, it is far from clear that Bibar was referring to "the jurisdiction of Santiago." In order best to appreciate this allusive passage it is necessary to quote it *in extenso.* Although parts of it might seem irrelevant, this irrelevancy is germane. Bibar's comment occurs as the last part of the last paragraph of a short chapter dealing with the appointment of the first bishop of Santiago in 1558:

En la ciudad Imperial está fundado otro monasterio de la invocación de Nuestra Señora de la Merced, el cual fundó el padre Diego Rondón. En la ciudad de Valdivia está otro monasterio de la invocación de Nuestra Señora de la Merced, el cuya fundó fray Pedro Olmedo. Hacen mucho provecho su doctrina a la conversión de estos naturales. Cuando los españoles entraron en esta tierra había más de veinte y cinco mil indios, e no han quedado en los términos de esta cuidad [Santiago] ni a ellos sirven, sino es nueve mil indios, porque con las guerras pasadas y también el trabajo de las minas ha disminuido su parte.[16]

In the previous paragraph Bibar had just described several religious establishments in Santiago, and he went on to mention those in two other cities in the new colony. That is, his focus had changed from the city of Santiago to Chile as a whole, and it was in this context that he referred to "this land." This instance of one obiter dictum piggybacking on another should give pause, for it is not unusual to find this kind of textual imbroglio in the chronicles, which, after all, were seldom written to the high literary standards demanded by posterity.

It is peculiar that Bibar would descend from the general ("this land") to the specific (Santiago and its environs), rather than the reverse. It is hard to avoid concluding that these two phrases are in opposition rather than apposition, and that Bibar's population figure of twenty-five thousand refers to the entire colony as it was then organized, and not merely to the city of Santiago. By the same token it seems clear that his figure of nine thousand applies only to Santiago—"this city."

It is not hard, then, to discern a shift in emphasis here, or to find a plausible reason for it. A major preoccupation of the Spaniards was to establish encomiendas and to collect Indians in them. Most of these were in or near the few newly established towns. Between 1541 and 1558, Indians from scattered sites had been moved closer together for improved administrative control and security. As early as 1546 they had already been organized, and reorganized, into *repartimientos*.[17] In this sense, Bibar's two figures would refer to roughly the same aggregations, but under different circumstances.

Nor is there any strong suggestion that Valdivia and Bibar were both measuring depopulation from the same beginning point. Valdivia speaks specifically of the region "from Copayapo to Mauli" but gives no clear assurance that he is measuring depopulation there from any particular point in time.[18] Bibar, on the other hand, is more pointed, but without being definitive. He dates the decline from the time when "the Spaniards entered this land," by which he must mean either 1540 or 1541. When he was writing, in about 1558, the term *tierra* probably was meant to refer to the entire jurisdiction of Chile (which was coterminous with the Santiago see, the principal focus of his chapter), by then an area running from the viceroyalty of Peru down at least as far as the Bíobío, well south of the Río Maule. This was an area much larger than Valdivia specified, rather than one only half the size, as Hidalgo argues.

───────

Hidalgo's clear assumption—and the implicit argument of most others who have postulated a specific contact population for Chile—is that all losses were net losses, the result of death. Thus, for instance, when Bibar speaks of a decline of sixteen thousand (or eighty thousand) Indians, he is held to mean that these had died from one cause or another. While this is not impossible, there are certainly other, more likely possibilities. The most obvious of these is that in many cases Indians in Chile did not die but fled to areas beyond Spanish control. Indeed, this explanation is far likelier for Chile than for almost anywhere else in the Americas, since some areas there were brought under effective central control only well into the nineteenth century.

To some degree the language of the early chroniclers fosters such an assumption, for death is seldom mentioned. Thus, Bibar says that in the 1550s the area of the city of Imperial "lacked of the Indians three parts of the five" that were supposedly in residence when Valdivia first arrived there.[19] In other cases Bibar could be more explicit, if not definitive. Referring to the area around Santiago elsewhere in his work, he wrote: "There are not as many people in this province [n.b.: not "land"] as when the Spaniards arrived because of the wars and uprisings they had with the Spaniards. . . . [O]f three parts there is not [now] one." He added that work in the mines had combined with warfare to effect their "destruction."[20]

The opportunities for flight to still independent areas and Spanish redistributions on behalf of the encomienda system remind us that when they estimated present Indians, or noted absent ones, the Spaniards were operating within a dynamic demographic situation that would have made it virtually impossible to count accurately. In fact, the Spanish authorities in Chile in these earliest years were painfully aware of local migration patterns. Leonardo León has deployed an array of laments by Spanish officials in the sixteenth century, deploring the fact that Indians from the occupied territories were fleeing south or even across the Andes in order to escape the encomiendas.[21] As Bibar put it, describing the situation around Santiago after the Indians burned it in September 1541, "the Indians, seeing that they would not have even an hour of peace or quiet, worked to get away."[22] And they continued to "get away" for at least the next sixty years.

Failure to consider the demographic consequences of migration is apparent in a table Thayer Ojeda constructed after testimony in the chronicle of Mariño de Lobera. While Thayer Ojeda regarded these figures as exaggerated by as much as tenfold, he arrived at them largely by adding warrior counts from one region after another and at different times, implicitly accepting that the Indians never moved and therefore could never have been estimated twice, more often, or not at all.[23] Yet, as we will see in chapter 12, migration as an alternative to death in explaining population decline is missing in action in the work—and presumably the very thought—of the High Counters. Those who have studied the population dynamics in postcontact Chile generally think of decline in terms of outright "collapse" as a result of widespread mortality rather than in terms of migration as an unwilling expedient against compliant servitude or death. In this case, the very regions in Chile in which the greatest number of Indians were to live after the 1540s—and probably always had—were usually beyond the reach of the Spaniards.

Hidalgo also quotes Pedro de Valdivia to the effect that part of southern Chile was "all a town, a garden, and a gold mine." He neglects to mention that in the immediately preceding passage Valdivia claimed that those Spaniards who had seen Mexico "say that there is a much greater quantity of people [in southern Chile] than in [Mexico]."[24] In this way Hidalgo quarantines Valdivia's hyperbole in one sentence in such a way as not to infect what he claims in the next.

Although Hidalgo confined himself to citing the testimony of Valdivia and Bibar, other sources throw indirect light on population levels in the first years of Spanish rule in Chile. The declining population of Indians was frequently and pointedly noted at the time. The Spanish conquistadors quickly began to feel cheated and aggrieved at the shortage of Indians, since they were the chief means by which the Spaniards hoped to extract whatever natural wealth the new colony might bring. As early as 1545 Valdivia wrote to Charles V that he had secured information from the local caciques about "the quantity of Indians between the Mapocho valley and Mauli" in anticipation of establishing encomiendas. If he received specific numbers, he did not include them, but he did express surprise that there were not as many Indians as he had hoped.[25]

A year later the cabildo at Santiago urged Valdivia to redistribute the Indians because the district was more sparsely populated than had been supposed. Some *encomenderos* had as few as 20 to 30 Indians, and none more than 150, whereas, the petitioners argued, a single encomienda in Peru had more Indians than all those in Chile combined.[26] They advised Valdivia to consolidate and reassign the encomiendas and compensate the *encomenderos* with new distributions in the as-yet-unconquered south.[27] This picture clashes with Hidalgo's interpretation of Bibar's evidence as indicating a population of 117,500 in the Santiago area as late as 1540—that is, after the purported smallpox epidemic had struck the area. The corollary of his presumption that there was a population of around 45,000 (9,000 × 5) in and around Santiago in 1558 implies a population of at least 100,000 in 1546. In contrast, the palpable implication of the testimony of the petition is that it was considerably smaller than this.[28]

The two hundred or so words in Hidalgo's passage, albeit a minute fragment of the discursive torrent so far expended on the subject, raise several of the more important questions facing the work of the High Counters. This passage provides a surprisingly long menu of some of the problems that have always wracked the movement. Most obvious is the reflexive reliance on the numbers in the sources, with no attempt to assess their likely, or even possible, accuracy. Simple arithmetical procedures go awry as well. Unwarranted translations of words allow the introduction of interpretations that flout the evidence in order to multiply any numbers based on the chronicles. Disease is gratuitously, although in this case casually, introduced to provide the wherewithal for the population decline. Numerous relevant sources are ignored.

One of the first efforts—and still the most extensive—to calculate the contact population of Chile based on figures provided in the sixteenth-century sources was that of Tomás Thayer Ojeda.[29] However, Thayer Ojeda did not venture an opinion about the size of the contact population of Chile. He experimented with procedures that could have led him to that conclusion but instead chose to point out the inevitable dead ends. For instance, he demonstrated how easy it was to make various projections derived from discrepant data appear to agree merely by manipulating the extrapolative values.[30] He also showed that taking the highest values offered by Mariño de Lobera could result in a population estimate ten times that supported by the same chronicler's lowest figures.[31]

Even though Thayer Ojeda could demonstrate the exiguousness of the projection approach, as well as the inconsistency of the primary sources, he retained some faith in these sources. He could write, for instance, that "[d]espite the uncertainty of these notices, it does not appear excessive to accept the quantity of *100,000 tributarios* that Mariño de Lobera assigns to Concepción for the whole jurisdiction, comprising the province of Arauco and the part that was annexed to the town of Los Confines a little later." This permitted Thayer Ojeda to multiply this figure by a factor of 3.3 to arrive at a total Indian population of 330,000 for that area, a procedure that he repeated for other areas of southern Chile.[32]

In explaining his reorganization of the encomiendas, Pedro de Valdivia admitted to Charles V that he had made the first distribution "without having true information" about the state of affairs. He quickly had "a truer relation," however, and "saw the few people that [the land] had." Most of them, he reported, had scattered or died.[33] We are not in a position to be sure just what territory Valdivia was referring to, but since he used the term "the land" immediately previously, it appears that he had in mind all of Chile as he knew it. Nor can we know what he meant by "few people." Fewer than Peru? To be sure. Fewer than he had anticipated? To be sure. Fewer than there had been when he arrived in the area several years earlier? This time the answer can only be, probably.

In the absence of data needed to draw any conclusions, there is no way of knowing any of these things—most are more probable than the competing presumptions, no more. In the absence of the necessary information to weigh our conclusions, it might just be necessary to believe that Valdivia had the better chance of being correct, if only because he was appropriately imprecise. In contrast, Hidalgo has argued that "by 1540 our data are more abundant and precise" than they were earlier, which is to say nothing. He goes on to cite Mariño de Lobera as an example, saying that "he gives us various data, some exaggerated, and others, apparently closer to reality."[34] It is tempting to credit Mariño de Lobera, and all the other chroniclers as well, with being generally accurate, but to judge their accuracy we need criteria other than their apparent agreement with our own hypotheses.

Still, the tortuous course that the Spanish colonization of Chile took means that there should be a higher concentration of estimates of specific groups of Indians, made either in the course of wars or in the establishing of *repartimientos*, than there are overall estimates. There may well be as many as one hundred such references in the sixteenth-century chronicles and other sources from the period—for example, Valdivia's letters and the *probanzas de serviços* that have survived. Few of these estimates, if any, agree with each other or are particularly commensurate. Sometimes the discrepancies result from divergent estimates of what appear to be the same countable entity, but most often it is simply a matter of different things being counted or the same things being counted at different times, although the evidence is usually insufficient to reveal the particulars.

A recent attempt by Miguel Cervellino Giannoni to calculate population decline in the Copiapó area after contact points up well the difficulties that arise from failing to recognize the need for commensurable data before valid comparisons can be made. Citing a few references to population levels in the chronicles allows the author to compute various decline rates, such as "a percentage of decline on the order of 56.4 percent."[35] But why assume that one chronicler's "Copiapó" was nothing more and nothing less than the Copiapó of all the others? Cervellino does not—and cannot—demonstrate that the same categories of people were being counted, that the same political or physical entities were involved, or even that the estimates were made at the same time of the year. All these—and more—matter. And it matters too that the estimates cannot be made to approximate one another. In fact, the earliest—and highest—estimate made in this case is of Indians who fought in one of the first battles against the invading Spaniards. It seems entirely reasonable to assume that on the occasion Indians from a wider area came together to combat the invaders and then dispersed after the battle to defend their own habitats.

Given these imponderables, exercises that pretend to make such comparisons are attempting to interbreed estimates of dubious quality and differing ingredients and can only be misleading and futile. But perhaps it is quixotic to expect quantitatively usable data from chroniclers who often were "characterized by a perception of time distant from our own; its essential elements were a lack of precision [many did not even know their own age], comparison with events that occurred in the more or less remote past, an enormous gravitation toward the past, and the predominance of Christian cosmogony."[36]

Buffered behind the desert of Atacama, which the Spaniards referred to as the *despoblada*, the disease experience of Chile was likely to have been more self-contained than that of other areas of Spanish America. The first epidemic mentioned in the chronicles occurred in 1554–55, but Henry Dobyns will have none of that. Instead, on the basis of documented smallpox in central Mexico and the Caribbean, he believes that there was virtually a pole-to-pole pandemic in the 1520s.[37] There is no evidence in the chronicles to support this claim—no mention of pockmarked Indians, for instance—and no reference to any epidemic in any testimony by the Indians later on.[38]

Nonetheless, Dobyns's view has found supporters among Chilean historians. Hidalgo brings in smallpox as a factor in Indian decline, although without specifying what he means. In his turn Villalobos accepts that smallpox struck the Mapuche "before the conquistadors arrived."[39] Others, such as León, point out the absence of evidence and prefer to keep the matter open.[40] Those who would argue for a precontact smallpox epidemic would presumably at least double their extrapolations of Indian populations in the 1540s if they were estimating populations twenty years earlier, for they would regard the later people as remnants of the earlier.

Although none of the chroniclers mentions disease before 1540, all mention some kind of "pestilence" that struck the southern Araucanians shortly after Valdivia's death in 1553. If we discount phantom precontact pandemics, this epidemic was the first to strike the Indians of Chile, and it is worth exploring both contemporaneous and modern descriptions of it, particularly because they encapsulate certain interpretive strategies employed in the contact population debate.

Jerónimo de Bibar, who finished his work only four years after the epidemic, spoke of a "great pestilence" that combined with a drought to "diminish the Indians in such a manner that of three parts they lacked two."[41] His formula, "lacking two parts of three," was common to him and perhaps should be regarded as formalistic. Be that as it may, other chroniclers painted an even worse picture of destruction. Alonso de Góngora Marmolejo, writing in the 1570s, portrayed a particularly grim scene.[42] He spoke of a drought that occurred simultaneously with "an infirmity of pestilence" that the Indians called "chavalongo," which, he said, meant "a pain of the head." This caused the Indians to be "struck down," and being "without houses and without necessities, so many thousands died that the province remained depopulated, [and] where there had been a million Indians, there scarcely remained six thousand. So many were dead," he concluded, "that there did not seem to be anybody throughout the countryside, and in a repartimiento that had once had 12,000 Indians, there remained fewer than thirty."[43]

The work of Pedro Mariño de Lobera, the third of the earlier chroniclers, survives only in a copy made after his death.[44] Whether or not because of the added voice of the copyist, Mariño de Lobera's numbers are much higher than those of Bibar or Góngora Marmolejo, and his estimates of both the contact population and, inevitably, its rate of decline often differ by orders of magnitude from those of other witnesses. Indeed, he summarized his view of depopulation in Chile with the remark that "wherever there had been one thousand Indians, scarcely fifty now remain [in the 1590s]."[45] Later on, José Pérez García asserted that the epidemic was one of smallpox and even provided the detail that the Indians had a term for this, "piru cuthan," as well as another one, "charan," for measles.[46]

In addition to being mentioned in these formal attempts to recapture the past, this disease episode appears in testimony collected at the various hearings that so typified Spanish colonial administration. Perhaps the most interesting of these is the evidence of Juan Fernández de Almendras in 1558. He related that the scarcity of Indians in his time was due to the fact that many of them had died, "as much from hunger as from chabalongo, which is modorra," and that this had led to instances of cannibalism, so that in his particular encomienda not two hundred Indians were left from an original three thousand.[47] In a letter of 1577 Gonzalo Hernández de Bermejo volunteered the most apocalyptic vision of this epidemic, speaking of "a great famine" followed by "a great pestilence" that together "killed more than two million people."[48]

Accounts of this epidemic continued to reverberate through later generations of chronicles. Diego de Rosales, writing in the 1660s, offered yet another account. "There came those wild fevers which the Indians call Chabalongo, which was a species of plague [*peste*] which filed the tombs and cemeteries with an infinity of people."[49] In the 1740s, Pedro de Córdoba y Figueroa gave the matter the expected twist, treating it as divine retribution for the killing of Valdivia a few months earlier. "With this plague [*plaga*] God punished most of the [Indian] provinces . . . , wreaking terrible havoc on its inhabitants." The epidemic began late in 1554 and lasted until the end of the following year, and it was "the contagion of smallpox." Those who died were "numberless." Just the same, Córdoba y Figueroa passed along some numbers: in one encomienda 12,000 Indians (again!) had been reduced to a mere 100, while in another the Indian population had declined from 800 to 80. Besides those who died, many others fled into the forest far from settlements. Córdoba y Figueroa was certain that no epidemic in the history of the world could have been as "atrocious."[50] Finally, Miguel de Olivares, writing in the 1760s and 1770s, agreed—"to the evils of war was added an epidemic of smallpox [*viruelas*], and the first that there was in Chile, since before this they were ignorant of these contagions." Olivares then went on to cite by name the two *encomenderos* whose estimates were included in Córdoba's history, a sure sign of borrowing on the part of one or the other.[51]

From this brief sketch two things emerge. There was certainly an epidemic that resulted in a dramatic depopulation of the Arauco area from a combination of death and departure, and it is impossible to know just what that disease was or what its specific demographic effects might have been. The sources offer a variety of symptoms and diagnoses that should deter all but the most resolute from putting a name to it and thus perhaps better fixing its mortality rate, since the figures offered in the chronicles can hardly be exonerated from hyperbole.

Some modern students of early colonial Chile have attempted to do both. Crescente Errazuriz was content to quote Fernández de Almendras as to the nature of the disease and a few other witnesses as to specific cases of population decline.[52] But a committed interest in the size of the contact population and the mechanics of its decline brought further interpretation. One of the earliest of these was offered by Francisco Encina in his monumental history of Chile. Referring to the three-year-long drought that afflicted Araucanian territory in the 1550s, he continued: "To hunger was added an epidemic of typhus (chavalongo of the Indians) with features so great that almost all the sick died."[53] José Bengoa refers to "the first great plague of typhus, which the mapuches called chavalongo." He went on that "[i]t is said in the chronicles that it could have killed some 30 percent of the indigenous population." Bengoa repeats the diagnosis, if not the effects, concluding that "[w]e do not know what occurred in mapuche society before this demographic catastrophe. It is clear that a reaction must have existed. We can suppose it, but it would be to go too much farther in speculation."[54]

Tomás Bonilla Bradanovic agrees that *chavalongo* was merely the Mapuche word for typhus, and he is no more modest in supposing its effects, suggesting that "about one-third" of the Indian population succumbed to this disease and a variety of others between 1554 and 1561.[55] As well, Leonardo León asserts that the 1554–55 epidemic can be identifed as typhus, as does Carlos Valenzuela Solis.[56] H.R.S. Pocock, alone among modern observers but apparently following Diego Barros Araña, opts for typhoid fever.[57]

None of these authors cites sources for his identification of *chavalongo* with typhus, although it seems to stem from modern common usage in which the Mapuche word has been assimilated into Chilean Spanish as a synonym for typhus; the usage is then retrojected back anachronistically to the sixteenth century. Barros Araña was one of the first to comment on this. Although he equated *chavalongo* with typhoid fever rather than typhus, he dismissed the notion that the word had had such a meaning three centuries earlier.[58]

Writing on the history of smallpox in Chile, Enrique Laval decided that the epidemic had been, unsurprisingly, smallpox, solely on the basis of its apparently widespread incidence, since no relevant symptoms were recorded in the sources. Laval disagreed with those who argued that the Spaniards knew the symptoms of smallpox too well not to have referred to it by name if it had occurred. He argued that the clear distinction between smallpox and other eruptive fevers was a seventeenth-century phenomenon. Maybe so, but as he himself pointed out, an epidemic in Chile only a few years later was treated as smallpox in nearly all the chronicles.[59] Elsewhere, Laval suggests that "it appears . . . that the Araucanians term as chavalongo any infectious illness accompanied by headaches, general malaise, high fever, [or] a state of delirium." Noting that *chavalongo* is probably a nineteenth-century importation into Chilean Spanish usage, he wonders to what extent the Araucanians could "clearly distinguish" one infectious disease from another at a time when, he thought, the Spaniards were largely unable to.[60]

In this case Laval's question is well asked, for to identify *chavalongo* with typhus—or with anything else—is also to imply that the Araucanians of the 1550s had already developed a lexicon sufficiently nuanced to apply it to different congeries of symptoms even before they struck—and in some cases several centuries in advance of the formal distinction among certain diseases, one of them being typhus.

Despite this, could it be that modern scholarship has managed to determine that the epidemic of 1554–55 actually was typhus? It seems impossible. As a diagnostic symptom, "a pain in the head" is worthless, yet it is the only physical description we have. We can only conclude that there has been an unfortunately reflexive and anachronistic application of modern usage to texts and situations centuries older. Unless we come into possesson of more clinical details, we might presume that one disease, or a combination of heretofore unknown diseases, struck the Araucanians, but—it would seem—not the Spaniards. The precise nature of the disease hardly matters, and in this sense the relentless pursuit of chimerical precision is merely emblematic.[61]

———

The Spanish occupation of the island of Chiloé in 1567 provides a convenient opportunity to test the hypothesis that the Spaniards were not particularly interested in counting themselves and others with the degree of precision we might prefer.[62] The campaign lasted only a few days, and all the sources agree that the Indians there were parceled out by *repartimiento* soon afterward. All things considered, we might expect to find a high degree of conformity among the sources for this occasion. Let us look at three relevant kinds of measurements: the size of the Spanish force involved, the number of Indians counted, and the size of Chiloé itself.

Spaniards occupied Chiloé in late January and early February 1567. They did so with a force of—well, the sources vary widely. The earliest sources give figures ranging from 110 to 130. The lowest of these numbers was provided by Góngora Marmolejo, who, if he did not accompany the expedition, served as a *corrigedor* on the island only a few years later.[63] As part of the inquiry into the services of Martín Ruiz de Gamboa, who led the expedition, several of its members testified, and those who offered specific numbers gave figures ranging from 110 to more than 120.[64] Mariño de Lobera wrote that there were 130 Spaniards on this expedition, as did two *licenciados* in a letter written only nine months after the occasion, and as did the cosmographer Juan López de Velasco, hardly a primary source.[65] Sometime later there seems to have developed a radically different textual tradition. Several seventeenth- and eighteenth-century sources record that only sixty soldiers took part in this expedition.[66] Why such a strain developed is not at all clear, although the unusual repetition of the same anomalous number suggests the likelihood both of a common source—perhaps an oral one—and of the chroniclers' reliance on one another.

Moving on to the number of Indians on Chiloé at the moment of occupation, we find references to a *matrícula,* or census, that was soon carried out in preparation for establishing encomiendas. One count, one group of sedentary (for Chile at least) Indians—the circumstances seem propitious. It is not to be—the range is from "9 or 10,000 *indios de repartimiento*" to 160,000 "Indians." The highest figure by far was also among the first to be offered, by the *licenciados*

Venegas and Torres de Vera, who wrote that Martín Ruiz de Gamboa "distributed to the principals [who had accompanied him] a much greater number of natives, which were found after we arrived," since he "distributed almost 160,000 Indians, a little more," soon after occupying the island.[67] López de Velasco provided the lowest figure—roughly 6 percent of the highest—and this conceivably could refer to a slightly later period, his own time.[68]

About forty years later Antonio de Herrera y Tordesillas suggested a figure of twelve thousand, the same as that of Juan Diez de la Calle, whose estimate was later still.[69] Herrera had access to good sources, although he seldom tells us what they were. An estimate of twenty thousand comes from Mariño de Lobera, who may be on the high side when compared with Herrera, but not, in this case, when compared with most of the other early recorded estimates.[70] Later sources represent a quantum leap. According to Miguel de Olivares, writing around 1670, there were no fewer than fifty thousand "indios de lista."[71] Diego de Rosales apparently agreed: "fifty thousand Indians by matrícula."[72] The number continued to climb. Juan Ignacio Molina, writing in the 1770s, as he was lowering the number of Spaniards to sixty, increased the number of Indians to seventy thousand, "or so they say."[73] The number continued to creep still higher. A chorography of Chile published in 1776 reported that "seventy thousand Indians" submitted to the Spaniards.[74] Pedro de Córdoba y Figueroa, also writing in the eighteenth century, remarked that indeed Chiloé was "very populated, . . . whether in truth or fantasy, by seventy thousand Indians."[75] José Pérez García agreed with this highest figure.[76] Unfortunately for the historical record, Martín Ruiz de Gamboa forsook the opportunity to offer what should have been the most authoritative estimate, merely alluding in passing to his activities on Chiloé.[77]

It would be easy to suggest that all the earliest sources were referring to adult males whereas all the later sources meant to include the entire population. Such a solution would not only preserve the distinction between *indios* and human beings that the High Counters have imposed on the sources but would also allow the population of Chiloé in 1567 to be raised proportionately.[78] Unfortunately, there is no evidence to support this, other than the argument itself.

Modern assessments of these early estimates vary as well. Vázquez de Acuña surveys some of the early reports and decides that most of them are "absurdities and exaggerations," though he concedes that it is likely that Chiloé had "respectable population densities" at the arrival of the Spaniards. All in all, he thinks, the contact population was probably about fifty thousand, based on early estimates of twelve thousand *tributarios,* but he regards his figure as no more than "a compromise."[79]

Turning to the size that early observers imputed to Chiloé, we find more of the same. Chiloé was indisputably the largest island along the coast of southern Chile. Just how large was a matter of dispute in the sixteenth, seventeenth, and eighteenth centuries, long after the Spaniards had occupied it and had sailed past and around it many times. Góngora Marmolejo, who lived on the island for a time, estimated it at sixty leagues long and six or eight leagues wide.[80] Alonso González de Najera, Antonio de Herrera, and López de Velasco all agreed that Chiloé was fifty leagues long and from two to nine leagues wide.[81]

Diego de Rosales followed Góngora Marmolejo for its length but thought it only three leagues wide, four in places.[82] Miguel de Olivares, writing much later, thought it even larger, eighty leagues long ("so they say"), no width indicated.[83] The anonymous chorography attributed to Molina raised the stakes: Chiloé was "seventy leagues long and twenty [leagues] at its widest."[84] Other writers suggested that it might be either fifty leagues long by six leagues wide, or sixty leagues long.[85] Actually Chiloé is about ninety miles, or thirty leagues, long, and on average thirty miles, or ten leagues, wide.[86] Thus, while early observers as much as doubled the length of the island they were also halving its breadth.[87]

It is convenient to consider Mariño de Lobera's description of some islands apparently in the vicinity of Chiloé. Of these he wrote of a reconnaissance party of nine Spaniards and thirty Indians that departed from Chiloé in 1578 and almost immediately "found . . . more than 1500 islands, and some of them so populated that more than 200,000 Indians ordinarily live there."[88] He was probably referring to the numerous rather small islands south of Chiloé, now called the Chono islands. Despite the company it keeps, some have found Mariño de Lobera's population figure for these islands not wildly implausible, without considering that the Spaniards could hardly have "found" more than fifteen hundred islands in an archipelago that has only a few hundred at most, even by the most generous definition of "island."[89]

Moreover, how could Mariño de Lobera's sources have been able to calculate such a large population, especially if it was there only "ordinarily" and spread among so many venues? Clearly the estimates of both the number of islands—straight out of Marco Polo—and their population are wildly exaggerated responses to new discoveries and very reminiscent of the descriptions that Columbus was wont to give during his first and second voyages. But instead of being disregarded as instances of hyperbole, they have been accepted in their substance and ignored in their possible unreliability.

Another issue arises. Mariño de Lobera, in his "Crónica," as well as all the other chroniclers of the occupation of Chiloé, spoke of "indios," so that modern counters, if they are to be consistent in presuming *indios* to be adult males, must posit a total population for the islands in question in the neighborhood of 1 million. Since this is even more absurd than usual, consistency must give way. As it happens, Mariño de Lobera assists in its banishment by referring on other occasions to "tributarios," thereby making this distinction, alone among the chroniclers. This merely raises another issue, however: if Mariño de Lobera used the term *indios* to represent all ages and all genders, how can modern scholarship argue that the other chroniclers did not do so? Once again, the answer must be that these observers were undiscriminating in their application of the term, just as we would expect them to be. They were, after all, merely chroniclers of their time and place rather than demographers of our time and place.

As always, it is important to consider the purposes of the sources from which we would draw our information on the contact population of Chile. The letters of Valdivia, while hardly as interminable or as rhetorically vainglorious as those of Cortés, were intended to serve the same purpose. Valdivia and Cortés, and others who wrote to the Spanish court, did so from motives of self-advertisement and self-justification. These letters might justly be seen as forerunners of today's holiday letters which, ostensibly purveyors of news, are actually thinly disguised rodomontade.[90]

The conventional modus operandi among High Counters is to treat their sources not only as highly reliable and accurate but also as independent. For instance, when Bernal Díaz del Castillo happens to agree with Cortés, it is because they both were closely reflecting reality. As we will have more than one occasion to see, this sanguine attitude does not survive testing well. And, not unexpectedly, for Chile we see a great deal of interdependence among our sources. For instance, Jerónimo de Bibar relied heavily on Valdivia's letters, even to the extent of copying numerous passages verbatim.[91] By his own admission Góngora Marmolejo made use of Alonso de Ercilla y Zúñiga's *La Araucana,* which had been published about five years before Góngora

Marmolejo finished his own work.[92] In his turn, Diego de Rosales drew on Bibar, without acknowledging that he had done so.[93]

None of this—and further study is sure to uncover more of the same—can be considered surprising. It was common practice among writers of the time to borrow freely from one another, sometimes with acknowledgment and sometimes without. In the case of the chronicles of the conquest of Chile, textual evidence hardly seems necessary. Bibar, Góngora Marmolejo, Mariño de Lobera, and Ercilla all lived together in Chile for several years in the 1550s, and although we will probably never have evidence that they discussed their projects with each other over the dinner table (Bibar was already writing, as were perhaps the other three), it is hard to imagine that in this closed and isolated society, informal exchanges of opinion did not occur as a matter of course. If so, reciprocal influences underlay and blighted the texts that ultimately resulted. While the four chronicles frequently agreed with each other, this can hardly be said to be corroboration as well.

In the last analysis, the fatal flaw in all attempts to calculate the contact population of Chile based on later estimates of portions of it is simply that the Indians were far too mobile to permit us to make assumptions of commensurateness. Valenzuela (though hardly he alone) encapsulates the faulty logic well when he writes that "their [the Araucanians'] army, calculated at 40,000 men before [the battle of] Marigüeñu [in 1554], now [ca. 1558] no longer amounted to 14,000 warriors capable of bearing arms."[94] The argument might have force if this army had been functioning far from home—Alexander in Bactria or Hannibal in Italy or de Soto in the American Southeast—but this was a national levy operating at home, in a position continually to draw new conscripts, fluid enough to comprise different characteristics at different times and places, and sensible enough to divide and reunite to meet tactical and strategic exigencies. If the forty thousand warriors were apples, then the fourteen thousand warriors can only have been oranges.[95]

Long ago, John M. Cooper, writing in the *Handbook of South American Indians*, commented that "[e]stimates of *Araucanian* population at the time of first White contact vary from a half million to one and a half million." He went on to observe that "[t]hese estimates rest on very weak evidence, and it is impossible to say which of them is nearest to the truth."[96] Despite half a century in search of better evidence and more sophisticated means to interpret what evidence there is, this statement remains as true as when it first appeared in print.[97]

Evading History
through Language

Here was an archbishop with a warrior's eye to the main chance, shrewdly appreciative of the lie of the land, a historian for whom history was warfare, a master of camouflage, the perfect judge of the feint, connoisseur of the understatement, unblinking purveyor of the inconceivable.

—Peter Linehan, *Historians and the History of Medieval Spain*, on Archbishop Rodrigo of Toledo

It's really quite simple: every time you decide something without having a good reason, you jump to Conclusions whether you like it or not. It's such an easy trip to make that I've been there hundreds of times.

—Norton Juster,
The Phantom Toll Booth

Whatever their particular aims, all authors have an overriding purpose—to persuade readers to accept their general arguments or their representation of a true or fictional set of circumstances. Accomplishing this requires that they demonstrate that the available evidence suits their interpretation, that new evidence warrants their views, that their translation of sources betters all others, and so on. While the methods might be several and diverse, at heart any attempt at persuasion depends more on the ways in which authors are able to capture the goodwill of their readers than on any other quality. This expedient, the *captatio benevolentiae* of the ancient rhetoricians, encompasses a whole battery of discursive devices, each designed to complement and reinforce the others in making a case.[1] The yawning gap between the High Counters' pretensions and the evidence available to support these pretensions makes studying their rhetorical techniques particularly interesting, because they must rely on deploying them so insistently and because, it must be admitted, they have been extremely successful.[2]

Although examples of the High Counters' rhetorical handiwork appear throughout this work, it should be useful to coalesce the argument by focusing on a single example of the genre. Although any number of instances could be looked at, I have chosen a case that is by no means a central one, although it has not lacked influence. Nonetheless, because it is brief and yet so redolent of the discursive strategies of the High Counters in terms of its rhetorical appeal and conclusions, it encapsulates the larger enterprise remarkably well.

The work in question is a relatively short essay by Pierre Clastres entitled "Eléments de démographie amérindienne."[3] Clastres is best known for his work among modern hunting and gathering societies in Brazil and Paraguay, but he took time out to write on the historical demography, as he saw it, of the Tupi-Guaraní Indians of the area. Clastres is an anthropologist, sharing a disciplinary affiliation with several High Counters, few of whom have been specifically trained in the care and handling of historical sources. This deficiency manifests itself frequently in Clastres's argument, not least in his treatment of the early sources for Tupi-Guaraní population dynamics.

These data are unusually rich and diverse, although no less problematical than other such sources. Clastres ignores them completely—or rather he uses some of them but declines to tell his readers how, by actually citing them. Instead, he prefaces his brief bibliography of modern works with an extraordinary declamation: "For facts concerning the sixteenth, seventeenth, and eighteenth centuries, we refer throughout to the French, Portuguese, Spanish, German, etc., chroniclers, as well as to the writings and letters of the first Jesuits in South America. These sources are well enough known that it would be superfluous to detail them further."[4] Having put any pursuers off his trail, Clastres keeps his word as he offers his personal version of Tupi-Guaraní historical demography.

———

Although Clastres prefers to keep the chroniclers anonymous, he alleges a great respect for their work. "Almost all of them," he claims, "were learned and faithful observers." To this happy circumstance is to be added another: they observed societies which, although dispersed over many tens of thousands of square miles, possessed, nonetheless, "a relative uniformity."[5] Thus, to observe one group was to observe them all—a familiar and fundamental tenet of the High Counters' creed. Clastres proves an adept practitioner of several rhetorical expedients, especially the modesty trope. He professes to be suitably diffident about his own qualifications and, more to the point, about the plausibility of his conclusions.[6]

Just the same, he is astonished to find that not everyone believes in the chroniclers' fidelity and accuracy, although he misconstrues the nature of the doubt. He notes correctly that many scholars suspect the accuracy of the numbers in the chronicles, but he then seeks to destroy the reasonableness of this doubt by going on to conjure "a very strange situation—everything in the chronicles is acceptable but the numbers which they provide!"[7] By painting the critics as mindless numerophobes, he implants the notion that their doubts are not to be entertained. In truth, most critics of the chronicles have found a great deal more to question than their numbers.

Like so many other High Counters, Clastres's target of choice is Angel Rosenblat (whose name he invariably misspells), and he launches the usual attacks on Rosenblat's work, some of them well founded but also largely beside the point. In dismissing Rosenblat, Clastres again turns to the value of the unnamed chroniclers: "[S]ince no valid argument destroys the demographic data of the chroniclers—*who were eyewitnesses*—perhaps it is better, rejecting the usual prejudices, to take seriously for once what they tell us."[8] There are several ironies here. Despite assuming an aura of splendid isolation, in granting the chronicles implicit belief Clastres becomes a member in good standing of a practicing majority. Then, despite his emphasis, the very sources he relies on most—at least apparently—were not eyewitnesses, as we will see. Finally, the chroniclers scarcely ever provided data than could rightly be termed "demographic."

Clastres briefly abandons his "uniformity" thesis by conceding that "[t]he information of the chroniclers clearly indicates that the Tupi-Guaraní villages were of unequal size." Just as quickly, he regains the initiative: "But we can accept an average of 600 to 1000 persons per group [= village?], a hypothesis, we have to emphasize, that is deliberately *low*."[9] Here modesty trope number two comes again into effect: even though this estimate is "deliberately low," it will nonetheless "appear enormous to Americanists." In this way, what some might think high becomes "enormous," and then, by paradox, quite plausible.

Clastres immediately puts his presumption to work. He argues crucially that "the homogeneity" of the Tupinambá and the Guaraní "is such, and from every point of view, that the demographic dimensions of Guaraní and Tupi local groups were certainly very similar."[10] This piece of legerdemain ignores completely the very different habitats of the two groups but permits Clastres to move nimbly from the Tupinambá situation to that of the Guaraní.

Estimating, on no particular evidence, that the Guaraní occupied 350,000 square kilometers at an unspecified date, he continues: "Assuming this to be true, and knowing the *mean* density of the local groups [i.e., one equals all], can we determine the total population?"[11] His answer is an unequivocal yes, although he works by indirection. He speaks, for instance, of a "population census" for the island of Maranhão, a short-lived haven in northeastern Brazil, and actually cites a source for it, Claude d'Abbeville.[12] According to Clastres, d'Abbeville estimated that there were twelve thousand Indians on the island in 1612, or, by Clastres's calculation, a density of "exactly 10 inhabitants per square kilometer."[13] Actually, what d'Abbeville wrote is that there were twenty-seven "principal villages" on the island, there "being in number from two to three hundred in some villages, in others five or six hundred, in others sometimes more, sometimes less, so that on the whole island there *could be* some ten or twelve thousand souls."[14]

Clastres does not propose to carry this density over bodily to the entire Guaraní area—"(which would yield 3,500,000 Indians)"— but adds—the modesty trope again—"[n]ot that such a figure would worry us."[15] Fortunately, he is able to call to his aid "a priceless piece of information coming from [Hans] Staden," who led the life of an itinerant prisoner for about a year. According to Clastres, Staden wrote that the villages he saw were generally nine to twelve kilometers apart, which Clastres incorrectly converts to "about 150 square kilometers per local group."[16]

Clastres's minor arithmetical error, however, is nothing compared with his other misapprehensions in this passage. Although Staden did occasionally provide information about distances from one Tupinambá village to another, these data do not permit us to make conspective statements about the spatial relationships of Tupinambá villages (much less those of the Guaraní!). In contrast to the mindless symmetry that Clastres depicts, Staden in fact imputed to the Tupinambá more than a modicum of practicality: "They prefer to set up their dwellings in places where they have wood, water, fish, and game close at hand."[17] And they frequently relocated their villages as well.[18]

More to the point, Staden measured distances in German "Meilen," which were the equivalent of about 7.4 kilometers. In order to express himself as Clastres would have it, he would have had to use uncommon fractions; he did not even use common ones.[19] In short, Clastres's "priceless piece of information" is a phantom of his own making, based in part, it would seem, on his taking Staden's "mile" to represent 1.6 kilometers.

Proceeding nonetheless, Clastres made further calculations. He divided his guess that the Guaraní occupied 350,000 square kilometers by his guess that since each individual micropolity occupied an average of 150 square kilometers, there were 2,340 of these in toto. He then multiplied this figure by his guess that each of them contained an average of 600 persons.[20] Voilà, the Guaraní population in the early seventeenth century was 1,404,000.[21]

Seeking further to determine the density of Guaraní settlement, Clastres refers to various estimates of the sizes of Tupinambá (not Guaraní) villages. In the chronicles these estimates are expressed in terms of the numbers and capacities of large communal houses called *malocas*. The estimates vary in the sources, just as villages sizes must have on the ground. Clastres picks just two such descriptions for his sample. He claims that Fernão Cardim reported that the typical *maloca* housed one hundred people—an error, since Cardim actually wrote that they housed "two hundred and more persons."[22] In counterpoint, Clastres goes on to say that Jean de Léry spoke of five hundred to six hundred people per *maloca*.[23]

There are also differences of opinion in the sources as to the number of *malocas* per village, which ranges from four to eight.[24] This scarcely permits Clastres to make his next move, which is to express a range based on multiplying the two lowest estimates, on the one hand, and the two highest, on the other, since this grants arithmetical legitimacy to his random—and erroneous—sample. In fact, there are other estimates that tend, at least in the matter of the *malocas'* capacity, toward the lower end of the range, but Clastres overlooks these.[25]

Clastres's treatment of the number of inhabitants of the "typical" Tupinambá *maloca* actually points to a small but germane problem in using these data to estimate Tupinambá population density, since both ancient and modern practices in this respect have been notably erratic.[26] Both Florestan Fernandes and William Balée have listed the relevant information in several early sources.[27] The two list roughly the same sources but treat the data in them differently.[28] Where they overlap, Fernandes and Balée show the same numbers for each source (Cardim, 100–200; Nóbrega, 50; Pigafetta, 100; Staden, 40). For Balée these each represent "people," whereas Fernandes treats the smaller numbers as representing "polygynous families [*lares políginos*]," and the larger numbers (those of Cardim and Léry), "individuals."

At first it seemed as if this was just carelessness on the part of one or the other, but looking at the primary sources shows a more complex situation. One of the two earliest extant accounts is that of the so-called "anonymous pilot." This report was written by, or was based on, the recollections of a member of the expedition of Pedro Alvares Cabral in 1500.[29] Concerning the population of the large houses of the Tupinambá, the author struck a note of unintended ambiguity that was to be a hallmark. Dealing neither with individuals nor with families, he wrote that "in only one house there are 40 [to] 50 beds, set up like looms [i.e., hammocks]."[30] This is precisely the kind of datum that excites such interest because it can be held to represent anything from 40 to perhaps 250 or 300 people. For our purposes its value lies in the way it expands still further the variety of approaches in and to the sources.

Pero Vaz de Caminha, who also made his observations as a member of Cabral's expedition, wrote that two Portuguese crew members who had been sent off to fraternize with the Tupinambá "say that in each house there dwell thirty or forty persons [*pessoas*]," which seems at least unambiguous, if not necessarily correct.[31] After Caminha, things become less precise. Antonio Pigafetta, next in time, wrote that "each 'boii' held one hundred men with their respective wives and children," who created an "enormous din."[32]

Unlike Caminha, Pigafetta, and the anonymous pilot, the Jesuit missionary Manuel da Nóbrega was no passerby. Writing in 1549, he mentioned "very large palm houses, in which could be put fifty Indians with their women and children."[33] Thus he virtually quoted Pigafetta, but halved his number. Only a few years later, Hans Staden offered a different version. For him each house was like an entourage, since each chief "collects a group of forty men and women, as many as he can get," and with these he established a household based on fealty rather than kinship.[34] Staden's statement could hardly be more problematical. Were there forty men and forty women, or a combined total of forty? And what about children? If the size of a household depended on the popularity and might of a particular chief, as Staden implies, then why mention any particular number at all?[35] And did Staden mean to imply that the size and composition of Tupinambá households changed repeatedly, a by-product of local realpolitik?[36]

Writing much later, and not truly as an eyewitness, Fr. Vicente do Salvador included in his history of Brazil the obligatory comment on Tupinambá houses. These houses were "so long that seventy or eighty couples lived in each one." Later in the same passage he implied that in addition to these couples were "their families," but otherwise he was concerned with different matters such as the lack of privacy.[37] Fr. Vicente's comments are among the earliest to bear the stamp of being a generic intepretation of disparate data, and his number could have been the result of his own compromises with these data.

The latest author included in Fernandes's survey was Simão de Vasconcelos, whose history of the Jesuits in Brazil was published in 1663. Included in the ethnography of the proselytized was the comment that "from twenty to thirty couples" lived in a Tupi house.[38] Since Vasconcelos was essentially writing in the ethnographic present, we cannot know whether he was referring to his own time or to some time in the preceding 150 years, which renders his estimate interesting but unusable.

This ensemble of small-scale examples illustrates some troubling aspects of taking sources too seriously. The anonymous pilot and Pero Vaz de Caminha either saw exactly the same set of Tupi dwellings, saw different dwellings at the same time, or heard the same report from those who did. Yet the difference between Caminha's testimony, which must be taken as read, and that of the anonymous pilot, where the intepretive gamut is wide, could easily be as much as tenfold.

There is an even greater difference between the figures of Caminha and Léry (discussed shortly), which might or might not be accounted for by the fifty years or so that intervened between them. Whatever the reasons, granting both estimates equal reliability by averaging them is the irreversible triumph of mathematics over common sense. No less ominous is the fact that the description by Hans Staden, who, of all the chroniclers, could observe at the greatest leisure, not only offers a variation in numbers but also provides an explanation for the makeup of these houses which suggests that the size of their population could vary almost from one day to the next. It is possible, of course, that each of these observations was accurate but not typical of the Tupinambá area as a whole. Whatever else, it is monitory that Staden, who had the best opportunity to observe widely, not only presents one of the lowest figures for *maloca* occupancy but also provides an explanation that prohibits us from using *maloca* estimates for larger demographic purposes at all.[39]

This brief discussion of early descriptions of the occupancy of Tupinambá houses illustrates as well one of two other things, and most likely a bit of both.[40] The populations of these houses varied in size, even when the houses did not; that is, the same houses in the same locales contained different numbers of people at different times, and none of the European observers was in a position to detect this. The second point is that beyond the issue of the accuracy of these numbers, these observers had idiosyncratic ways of expressing themselves, leaving it to us to plumb their language for its meaning. It is surely the case that they were neither concerned with exactitude nor expected their readers to be. Once again, it also means that we cannot simply impose our meanings and our derived numbers on the sources and proceed apace from there.[41]

The example of Jean de Léry offers a special case. It is important to Clastres because, he says, "the number of inhabitants of each *maloca* . . . oscillated from 100 (according to Cardim, for example) to 500 or 600 (Léry)."[42] If this is true, Léry's figures would be considerably higher than those of any of the other chroniclers and, in the game of the golden mean, would permit much higher overall estimates. When we turn to Léry's text, however, we immediately confront one of those cruxes that make living among these sources so intriguingly unpredictable. The passage in question appears in Léry's work as follows: "[S]e trouvant tel *village* entre eux où il y a de cinq à six cents personnes, encores que plusieurs habitent en une même maison: tant y a que chaque famille . . ."[43] In other words, Léry stated that there were five hundred to six hundred people *per village* and that "several" (persons? families?) lived in each house.[44]

In line with his policy, Clastres does not cite a source, but it seems clear that this francophone author was not relying on Léry directly in the original French. Chances are that he was following the distinct lusophone tradition in the matter, as expressed in all the recent translations of Léry's *Histoire* published in Brazil, in which this passage reads: "Em algumas aldeias moram, *na mesma casa,* de quinhentas a seiscentas pessoas e ñao raro mais . . ."[45] The difference here is arithmetically significant, even momentous if pressed. More significant is the way in which Clastres has robbed Léry's text of its meaning simply by using a defective translation, even while several editions of the original text were available. Fernandes's standard ethnography of the Tupinambá credited Léry with writing that "500 to 600 individuals" occupied each *maloca,* and this misapprehension has ramified throughout the later literature that depends on his work.[46] Léry's houses containing five hundred to six hundred persons are phantoms—phantoms not of his making but created by his negligent translators and interpreters.[47] But the error has come to outshine the fact, and its undoubted utility all but ensures that this will continue to be so.[48]

Clastres is especially interested in demonstrating that the Guaraní population was reduced rapidly and dramatically under the impact of colonial rule, in particular by the establishment of the *reducciones,* towns in which the Indians were congregated. To do this he adopts what he calls "*the regression method,* brilliantly illustrated by the Berkeley School," which is to serve as "counterproof" to his own argument, which uses population density.[49] In other words, he proposes to work back from later counts to earlier ones in the hope that the latter will be larger. To do this he uses two recorded estimates, one from 1690 (about 240,000), the other from 1730 (about 130,000). As he uses them, they seem to prove his point—but only until we look at them a little more carefully.

For the earlier count he cites the Jesuit Anton Sepp, saying that Sepp "wrote that in 1690 [*sic*] there were thirty *reducciones* in all, of which none had fewer than 6,000 Indians and several of which surpassed 8,000 inhabitants."[50] Not quite so. Sepp did write on the matter, from Buenos Aires, ten days after arriving in the New World and while still en route to the mission field, but he did not write what Clastres credits him with. According to Sepp, "in each of these villages, our fathers have in their care from five to fifteen thousand souls."[51] And there were not thirty of these, but "twenty-four."[52]

In another letter, written perhaps two years later, Sepp, now more familiar with things, changed his mind—the Guaraní mission field comprised "twenty-six *reducciones*" and each *reduccion* "counts three, four, five, six thousand souls and even more."[53] Playing the average game, this would suggest a total population of somewhere around 120,000 to 130,000, rather than the 240,000 that Clastres asserts.[54]

Sepp's figures must not have been entirely congenial to Clastres, or he would not have overlooked what Sepp really said. But are any of them accurate as well? With a few exceptions, we possess annual population returns from the Guaraní missions for 1702, and for scattered years before that. One of these years is 1690, when a population of 77,646 was recorded for the twenty-four *reducciones,* or less than one-third of that reported in absentia by Sepp.[55] In 1702 the population of the *reducciones* was recorded as 89,501, for the then twenty-seven sites, which would work out to an average of slightly over 3,000 each.[56] All this suggests that Sepp was exaggerating, although not nearly so much as Clastres does.[57]

This does not appear to be a case of picking from data of equal value. The series of population returns from the Guaraní missions is entirely coherent and self-reinforcing.[58] It shows that the highest population these missions ever attained was just over 140,000 in 1732, just before a series of epidemics caused it to drop by more than 60,000 in the next decade.[59] These figures have long been available—that Clastres was unaware of them, or ignored them, suggests that he had an ideology of his own.[60]

In a threefold manner, then, Clastres falls short of practicing sound historical method with respect to these sources. First, he fails to avail himself of the full range of readily available, if not always congenial, evidence. Second, and worse yet, he sees no purpose in tying his assertions to the evidence he does use, thereby effectively interdicting ready scrutiny of the way he uses materials.[61] Thus, another untraceable assertion is Clastres's claim that "the archives of the Jesuits say that during a period of a few years [the *bandeirantes* from São Paulo] would have killed or captured 300,000 Indians."[62] The use of the conditional suggests that the figure is Clastres's rather than the unidentified sources', arrived at by cumulating references. Be that as it might, John M. Monteiro and others consider the figure of 300,000 Indians captured by Paulistas between 1628 and 1636 to be a canard, perhaps best divisible by ten.[63] And third, as if to mock his own lack of citation, Clastres's use of historical sources, so far as it can be checked, is remarkably ineffective, naive, and, to borrow his term, "ideological."[64]

————————

At various points in his essay Clastres supplements the arithmetical trope with the modesty trope. For instance, he assures readers that the density implied by his calculations is only 40 percent of that on the island of Maranhão, which, as he had already pointed out, was very much an anomalous case. He goes on to clinch the matter, in part by repeating himself for effect: "This figure will appear enormous, unreasonable, unacceptable to some, if not to many. Now, not only is there no reason (except ideological) to reject it, but we actually consider our estimate to be quite modest."[65]

Clastres's sentiment is strikingly typical of High Counter rhetoric—we are scholars, those who disagree with us are ideologues. Almost as reminiscent is the fact that the figure is based on a number of misconceptions, miscalculations, and textual encounters of the worst kind. To complete the parallel, Clastres allies his procedure even more securely with those of the High Counters when he closes by suggesting that "our figure of 1,500,000 Guaraní, hypothetical to be sure, is in no way unreasonable. On the contrary, it is the calculations of Rosenblatt [*sic*] that appear to us absurd, since he accepts 280,000 Indians in Paraguay in 1492."[66]

Clastres continues to pursue the modesty trope relentlessly. Citing Borah and Cook's estimate that the population of central Mexico dropped by 96 percent before beginning to recover, he proclaims that for the Guaraní, "on the contrary we must accept a relatively weak depopulation rate, compared to the Mexican case, of 9/10 in two centuries."[67] Not only does this rhetorical strategy allow him to present his results as unexceptional—and unexceptionable—but it also enables him to regard his earlier calculations as reinforced: "As a consequence, the 150,000 Indians of 1730 [he has added 20,000 gratuitously, but hardly aimlessly] were ten times more numerous two centuries earlier: they were 1 million 500 thousand." The onslaught continues as he goes on to observe that he considers the rate of decline "moderate, even if it is catastrophic."[68]

Of course, there was a specific purpose in all this. His guessing and his obeisance to moderation serve a logical purpose after all:

> The figure of 1,500,000 Guaraní in 1530, obtained in this way, is no longer hypothetical, as in the previous mode of calculation [i.e., population density]. We even think of it as a minimum. In any case, the convergence of results obtained by the regression method and by the method of average densities reinforces our conviction that we are not mistaken.[69]

After which he goes on yet again to castigate Rosenblat and others who had postulated lower populations.

This semantic and arithmetical frippery permits Clastres to close resoundingly: "One must thus, in order to reflect on the Guaraní, accept these basic facts: *before the conquest they were 1,500,000, spread over 350,000 square kilometers, with a density of a little more than 4 persons per square kilometer.* This fact is rich in consequences."[70] In the end, all Clastres's hypotheses, all his speculation, all his peculiar uses of sources are eclipsed by the arrival of facts. He is not, nor should his readers be, in any doubt whatever that he has made his case.

Attentive readers, however—doubters, hypercritics—are likely only to have their suspicions reinforced by both Clastres's methods and his exposition. Even so, Clastres's piece is unquestionably a tour de force of the particular style of rhetoric that has come to distinguish the writings of the High Counters. It is all there: the cavalier, slightly sneering dismissal of all those who insist on holding contrary opinions; the discursive spin that turns unsupported opinion into irrefutable facts; the appeal to readers' sympathies through a self-portrayal marked by diffidence; and, most of all, the emblematic failure to use sources responsibly.

If Clastres shows himself unequal to the complexity and variety of the sources, he wages another battle with panache and effect. As if realizing that the sources would not serve him well if he were challenged, he draws repeatedly and effectively on an impressive arsenal of rhetorical devices in which tentative handling of the sources is brilliantly overcome by practiced recourse to the arts of persuasion. Symptomatically, the appeal to readers anticipates the actual presentation of the argument by way of his choice of evidence. He prefaces his case study with the observation that "[t]he traditional image of South America . . . illustrates particularly well this mélange of half-truths, errors, and prejudices that lead to treating facts with a astonishing lightness."[71] Thus he not only primes readers to agree with him about the proponents of lower population estimates but also introduces the notion that he is about to produce a series of unexceptionable "facts" embedded in the sources.

Clastres closes his essay as he began it—with a potpourri of rhetorical moves. He begins by speaking of "our modest reflection on the Guaraní" but then goes on, rather more immodestly, to suggest that "it forces us to admit the higher demographic hypothesis *for all of America,* and not only for the High Cultures," that is, those studied by the Berkeley School.[72] In short, Clastres presents his work as both modest and pathbreaking, as both tentative and unexceptionable, as of both local and hemispheric consequence. But, it is clear, he wishes and expects his readers to ignore in each case the first term of these couplets while embracing the second.

Reactions to Clastres's calculations have been mixed. John Monteiro could not decide whether the exercise was "pure soothsaying or fantastic arithmetic," but he thought it probably didn't matter much.[73] Bartomeu Melià spoke of "simple, even ingenious, mathematics" but observed that "it has nothing of history about it."[74] Carlos Brandao, conversely, found Clastres's calculations easy to accept in all their parts.[75] William Denevan noticed Clastres's figures only in passing but seems to have considered them unexceptionable.[76] But if Clastres's numbers have not been widely adopted, the arithmetical and discursive methods he deployed in their pursuit have been granted the greatest compliment of all—repeated imitation.[77]

Rescuing History
from the Sources

*Again it is a case of picking and choosing among the literary references
to find one that "sounds about right," a method that is obviously too
subjective and arbitrary to be satisfactory in terms of historical demography.*

—Tim G. Parkin,
Demography and Roman Society

He's an academic; and if you're an academic you're trained to check—
check your sources, check your references, check your evidence.

—Colin Dexter,
Death Is Now My Neighbour

If looking at Vandals crossing the Strait of Gibraltar establishes a
perspective on credulity in the face of numbers, looking at another
circumscribed example can serve as a mise-en-scène to suggest the invincible tendentiousness—and worse—that seems invariably to accompany the High Counters in their combat with the written sources.
Rather in the way of William McNeill, Alfred W. Crosby has made a
successful habit of writing for the larger community interested in
intersocietal influences. Although not given to counting out loud,
Crosby clearly sees himself as a fellow traveler of those who do.
Nowhere is this more obvious than in his throwaway comment made
while discussing the debate over the size of the contact population of
the Americas:

> The burden of evidence rests more heavily on those who state (often on
> the basis of tradition rather than data) that there were only a few na-
> tive Amerindians in 1492 than on those who state (usually after much

research and analysis of original sources) that there were tens of millions of people in the New World when Columbus arrived.

Although avoiding numbers, Crosby then offered his own opinion about the size of this population, in which he clearly sided with those on whom, he had just argued, the burden of proof did not rest. "I doubt that there were any large areas in the New World suitable in soil fertility, climate, flora, and fauna for dense populations that were not already thoroughly populated in 1492."

Crosby had prepared the way for this opinion by considering the possibility that New World populations could plausibly have grown fast enough for the earth to have become an intergalactic "sphere of living flesh." In the finest rhetorical fashion, Crosby promptly rejected this notion, calling it "an old chestnut." But old or not, chestnut or not, it served to render his following argument plausible, if not downright modest.[1]

Crosby's paean to the High Counters' modus operandi is no more than a passing comment in a paper with a larger purpose. Its very offhandedness, though, enhances its credibility, as though the matter were not in any doubt and therefore required no further comment. In disagreeing with this assumption, I would like to discuss in particular the invidious contrast expressed in Crosby's parenthetical asides. In particular I want to treat his praise of the High Counters' source-critical method as if it might after all not be deserved. In doing so I will suggest that the notion that most High Counters have used "original sources" scrupulously is, well, an "old chestnut."

As it happens, the very point for which Crosby chose to praise the High Counters is the one where they have shown themselves most vulnerable. Ironically, the High Counters themselves would probably prefer to be remembered for their arithmetical prowess, not least because they implicitly assume by the way they work that clever mathematics can transcend unfriendly or nonexistent sources. But Crosby, however unwittingly, puts his finger on the quintessential problem of the High Counters: their apparent incapacity to deal rigorously with sources, whether by misinterpreting them, by ignoring them, or by using translations of doubtful value. The degree to which this is the case is quite extraordinary; here I can mention only a few paradigmatic examples while referring the reader to other examples cited throughout the present work.

An interesting example, perhaps less for its use of sources than for its methodological peculiarities, is N. D. Cook's widely accepted estimate that the area of present-day Peru had about 9 million people in it at around 1520. In his study, described recently, and correctly, as "the most sober study of the Peruvian case,"[2] Cook juxtaposes careful literary analysis and guarded discourse with highly dubious arithmetical assumptions and procedures. The problems lie in Cook's dating of continuous Spanish-Indian contact, since his back-projection method of accumulating population is overwhelmingly sensitive to the length of time it is devised to cover. In his definitive work on the subject Cook projected back to 1520 to reach his figure.[3] In doing so he offered no explanation for why he had decided to discard his own earlier date of 1530, which produces a figure of around 6 million.[4]

Cook is able to offer no documentary support for choosing 1520, with its 3-million-person difference. He accepts without demur the common but by no means universal tradition that the Inca ruler Wayna Qhapac died of smallpox, but his death has never been dated earlier than 1524 and is sometimes dated as late as 1530. To reach a population figure of around 9 million required that Cook take his projection back to 1520, at least five and possibly ten years too far; that he postulate uniform rates of decline within (though not among) ecological zones over time; that he ignore population recovery between epidemics; and that he overlook the effects of uncounted Indians, particularly migrant workers.[5]

In chapter 8 I discussed the case of Pierre Clastres, whose obstructiveness renders it difficult, and occasionally impossible, to test his assertions. How unusual is Clastres's dereliction? It is remarkable, certainly, in its crass insouciance, but his difficulties with sources are not unusual at all; they are merely made slightly more occulted by his operating method. A few other examples can serve to illustrate this. Most of them happen to emerge from recent studies of the American Southeast, but they are not otherwise atypical.

Ann Ramenofsky's study of the archaeology of decline in the lower Mississippi valley, central New York, and the middle Missouri is more soberly argued than most other High Counter literature, but she does conform to the inability to treat sources squarely. Take the following three examples, among several instances in which she cites early accounts that speak of depopulation in order to buttress her archaeologically based case. All relate to the lower Mississippi valley and occur with a few pages of each other. In the first, she quotes the missionary Henri Roulleaux de la Vente:

The Natchez . . . assure us that they came here to the number of more than 5,000. The other ones [*sic,* for nations] say that many centuries ago they were, some 3,000, others 2,000, others a thousand, and all that is reduced now to a very moderate number. What is certain is that our people in the six years in which they have been descending the river, know certainly that the number has diminished a third, so true is it that it seems God wishes to make them give place to others.[6]

Ramenofsky is here quoting by way of John Swanton, and except as noted, she does so accurately. But does she quote fairly as well? In fact, Swanton, who was quoting another source himself, actually had more to relay from that source. In Swanton the following passage immediately succeeds that just quoted:

The reason for this is very clear. It is that, for I do not know how many years, they have placed all their glory in carrying away scalps of their enemies on the slightest pretenses. Add to this that the English give [presents] to them and excite them to make war in order to obtain slaves by it.[7]

Since Ramenofsky was in the process of arguing for epidemic-based population decline, it was surely careless of her to overlook that her source was advocating quite a different cause.[8]

It appears that this may have been no accident after all. A few pages later Ramenofsky includes a quotation from another French missionary referring to roughly the same area and time:

We were deeply afflicted by [at] finding this nation of the Arkansas [Acansças], formerly so numerous, entirely destroyed by [war and by] disease. Not a month had elapsed since they had rid themselves of smallpox, which had carried off most of them. In the villages [village] are now nothing but graves, in which they were buried two together, and we estimated that not a hundred men were left. All the children had died, and a great many women.[9]

Notice Ramenofsky's trouble with this brief text. In particular notice her adroit omission of the phrase "by war," which correlates well with the instance previously cited. Note also the lack of ellipses. As well, by pluralizing the singular "village" she magnifies the effects of the disease.[10]

A third quotation on the same page is drawn from Simon Le

Page du Pratz's history of Louisiana, first published in 1758. The passage mentions "[t]wo distempers" ("smallpox and a cold") which afflicted the Natchez Indians and which, du Pratz observed, were "not very fatal in other parts of the world."[11] Wittingly or unwittingly, Ramenofsky follows an example set earlier by George Milner, precisely by beginning her abstract with the second sentence in the relevant paragraph from the English translation.[12] The first, omitted sentence reads: "I mentioned that nature had contributed no less than war to the destruction of these people." Indeed, du Pratz had spent two paragraphs detailing the effects of such wars—all of which Ramenofsky, like Milner, ignores in her haste to decontextualize.[13]

Ramenofsky's relentless sanitizing of her sources is as puzzling as it is gratuitous, and her pursuit of the single explanation both unnecessary and indefensible. Most scholars who have studied the demographics of contact have recognized the role that European diseases played in depopulation without treating it as a welcome excuse for arithmetical flights of fancy. By force-feeding their readers with distorted information, Ramenofsky and other champions of the disease model compromise their general argument by allowing those who would doubt it to demonstrate so easily at least one serious defect and so to imply others.[14]

Finally, for present purposes, there is the case of Thomas Hariot, who wrote of the activities and experiences of the expedition sent to find Roanoke colony. About an illness among the neighboring Indians he had this to say:

> There was no towne where wee had any subtile devise practised against us, we leaving it unpunished or unrevenged (because we sought be all meanes possible to win them by gentlenesse) but that within a few dayes after our departure from everie such towne, the people began to die very fast, and many in short space; in some townes about twentie, in some fourtie, in some sixtie & in one six score, which in trueth was very manie in respect of their numbers. This happened in no place that wee could learne but where we had bene where they used some practise against us, and after such time; The disease also was so strange, that they neither knew what it was, nor how to cure it; the like by report of the oldest men in the countrey never happened before, time out of minde. A thing specially observed by us, as also by the naturall inhabitants themselves.

Hariot went on that certain friendly Indians "were perswaded that it was the worke of our God through our meanes, and that wee by him might kil and slaie whom wee would without weapons and not come neare them." As a postscript Hariot added that "there was no man of ours knowne to die, or that was specially sicke."[15]

Hariot's description has drawn considerable attention from those propagating the disease model, and it is clear that he had some interesting things to say. His description certainly bears the likelihood that he was speaking of an illness that spread from the English to the Indians. Before looking at this, though, let us look at the way this passage has been treated *as a text* to see what kind of "analysis of original sources" has occurred.

Crosby himself noticed Hariot's comment and quoted from it. Indeed, he quoted the entire passage *except* the sentence "This happened in no place . . . after such time."[16] Marvin Smith, arguing that epidemics struck the Southeast from early in the sixteenth century, quoted Hariot by way of Crosby, but just as Crosby omitted part of Hariot's text, Smith omitted most of Crosby's transcription, recording only that "[w]ithin a few days after our departure from everie such towne, the people began to die very fast, and many in short space."[17]

In his turn, Henry Dobyns quoted only the line "which in trueth was very manie in respect of their numbers" (though not quite impeccably), cited Hariot's numbers correctly, and commented that "[t]he disease was strange to the natives, so that they knew neither how to cure it nor even what it was," which falls somewhat short of the Indians' testimony but at least was an effort. Finally, Dobyns referred to the sickness as a "contagious disease," which might well be correct but again is not quite what his source had to say.[18]

Francis Jennings, sympathetic to the High Counters' mission and to their argument that contact all but equaled contagion, also had occasion to quote Hariot's comment. In his case this citation comprised the portion "the people began to die very fast . . . which in trueth was very manie in respect of their numbers." Thus he, too, omitted much of Hariot that needs to be included to understand the flavor of the passage. In particular, he omitted the reference to the unprecedented nature of the disease.[19]

Peter Mires has looked at this occasion most recently and most extensively. He quotes the lines "within a few dayes . . . sixe score," and "the disease also . . . time out of minde."[20] Although citing Hariot's account as it appears in David Quinn's *Roanoke Voyages,* Mires apparently actually used Crosby's text as his source, since he commits the same telltale transcriptional errors. Seeking to identify this disease, Mires writes that "it seemed clear to Hariot and others [it is unclear whom he means] that the Europeans themselves were transmitting the disease," which, as we can see in looking at Hariot's testimony *en ensemble,* is hardly the case at all. Mires concludes that because the English "were unable to recognize" the disease, it must have been influenza, failing to note that an influenza epidemic had struck the British Isles less than thirty years before![21]

Mires notes what is indeed an intriguing point—that "outbreaks did not occur in villages where the English had not visited." From this he concludes that the vectors were people and not insects. Maybe so, or maybe the disease did spread further but Hariot was unaware of it. More to the point, taking Hariot seriously should lead to wondering *why* the disease did not spread. Surely the argument could not be that only Europeans could spread it by personal contact—that Indians could catch it but could not in turn disseminate it.

It is possible to go farther still and wonder why the disease was confined to those towns that had practiced "subtile devises" against the English, for that is precisely what Hariot asserts—"everie *such* towne."* Hariot's comment here, like that about the wrath of God, can only suggest that either his version is somehow garbled or it is infected by his own mistaken assumptions. Or it was intended as a parable. Or all three.

To return full circle, Ann Ramenofsky also quotes Hariot in an article intended for the general public. There she adheres to her customary policy by quoting most of the passage—not without error—but omits the part that follows "nor how to cure it."[22]

No reader of any of the foregoing authors could possibly become aware of the full extent of Hariot's comments by reading their quoted extracts alone. They will not learn that Hariot, who was a mathematician and astronomer, and so presumably a keen observer, spoke of a fairly circumscribed epidemiological occasion. The sickness followed behind the English but did not spread beyond those places they had visited. Moreover, if we are to believe Hariot, he regarded it as a kind of divine retribution for undisclosed but inimical behavior on the part of the Indians. In the circumstances this is so peculiar an outlook that it must throw some doubt on the passage as a whole.

Readers of Smith are especially badly off. They cannot know that the numbers involved not only were absolutely small but, thought Hariot, contextually large, suggesting a sparse population. Nor will they know that whatever the sickness was, it was thought to be entirely unprecedented in the area—unless there was an implausible lapse in the collective memory. Every author, if none so much as Smith, has adroitly excised embedded testimony damaging to his or her hypotheses while omitting some of Hariot's observation that would seem to help his or her cause.[23] Looking at the passage in toto leaves us with some perplexities. It was one thing for Hariot to note that the Indians blamed a Christian God and quite another for him to intimate that he agreed with them. Viewed conspectively, the story seems as much a morality tale, a fable, as a medically informed description of a disease episode. At any rate, it deserves considerably more scrutiny and understanding than Crosby, Smith, and the others have given it. And it must, too, make Crosby's readers wonder where his lavish praise originated. Certainly he could not actually have checked the High Counters' performance, and we can assume only that it is visceral praise from within the fellowship.

In the middle stages of the High Counters' movement, Woodrow Borah, from whom Crosby frankly drew inspiration, put their work in with some very fast company. Speaking of "the category . . . of historical evidence," he went on:

> [It] requires for proper study the application in full of very elaborate and exacting techniques of verification, painstaking reading, interpretation in the light of close knowledge of administrative systems and units of measurement used at that time, and of cross-comparison. They are the techniques that have been developed for the examination of historical materials over the centuries from Lorenzo Valla, the Bollandists, and the school of Saint-Maur to the present.[24]

In echoing this gratuitous claim, if with some loss of vigor, Crosby gives it renewed legitimacy. As such it must be accepted or challenged. Here I see no alternative but to choose the latter. I like to think that in doing so I have the support of all those whose names Borah so outrageously took in vain. Certainly users of their work are not likely so routinely to encounter examples of silent emendation, mistranscription, and excision—all in the name of pressing a particular argument that would lose credibility without these forms of textual molestation.

Fragments in Search of Preconceptions

We debated . . . what to make of the fact that our best hypotheses (especially those based on historical records) were inevitably subverted by an unforgiving and unobliging archaeological record.

—Alison Wylie,
"Facts and Fictions: Using Archaeology in a Different Voice."

I am convinced that the most productive clue to areas of critical ignorance derives from our skills in justifying a healthy skepticism. I do not mean a skepticism regarding what we can know—there, we must be totally optimistic—but a skepticism as to what we think *we know and understand. It is reasoned skepticism that leads us to the productive recognition of the nature of our ignorance.*

—Lewis R. Binford,
Faunal Remains from the Klasies River Mouth

If the amount of reliable firsthand evidence for contact population levels has relentlessly remained at nil during the past sixty years, the amount of archaeological evidence has inexorably increased, and with it the sophistication of the analytical techniques of the field. At the same time the rise, and sometimes the fall, of several schools of archaeological epistemology has stimulated waves of enthusiasm among practitioners. As a result, archaeologists are increasingly taking their places along with other scholars in assessing the post-1492 degree of Indian depopulation in the Americas.[1]

Inevitably, increasingly expansive claims concerning the sufficiency of archaeology to answer certain questions have been made along the way. Suspicions about the force of these claims spring from the intrinsic difficulty of the questions being asked, and they also go to the roots of the ways in which the work and the worldviews of historians and archaeologists differ. The extent of historical evidence, exiguous as it so often is, can never be matched by archaeological evidence, which is incredibly sparse, representative only by fiat, and depressingly expensive to unearth and analyze. Accordingly, archaeologists work by convention—by treating certain archaeological situations as having standardized causes and as representing other situations that have escaped archaeologists' ken. Some of these, such as the "meanings" of mass burials, will be discussed in this chapter.

While the High Counters' have expended most of their extrapolative arithmetic on the Americas from central Mexico south, archaeological inference flourishes more in the remainder of the hemisphere, owing to the lack of written evidence. At any rate, the examples I discuss here are drawn from the present United States and represent the main lines these arguments tend to follow.

Extensive early eyewitness accounts of Indian populations are confined in the Southwest to Coronado and in the Southeast to de Soto, both traveling in the 1540s. There is nothing more in the Southwest for another sixty years and in the Southeast for even longer, leaving archaeology to pick up the slack. Archaeologists and anthropologists have done this by using the chronicles of de Soto and Coronado to establish a baseline from which to posit precipitous decline.

Archaeologists of population decline have been prone to rely on the few sources that might complement their own evidence. Nowhere is this more obvious than in recent studies of de Soto's expedition, which has been left largely to anthropologists and archaeologists.[2] The approach has been to use the four chronicles of the expedition as if they complemented—rather than, as is more often the case, contradicted—one another, and to use them in translation. Improvements in critical analysis have been modest and cosmetic. For instance, where they once believed Inca Garcilaso de la Vega without hesitation, students of the expedition now believe him after offering token critical comments. David Anderson, an archaeologist, expresses this eccentric epistemology well: "Much has been made of Vega's inaccuracies, but this should not be used to discredit the source, since it stands as virtually the only sympathetic, detailed Spanish account of the southeastern Indians produced during the 16th century."[3]

———

In the past decade or so several works have been published that deal directly with the archaeology of postcontact population decline. In each case the author concentrates on the period between 1492 and some later time of direct contact, which is held to vary from one area to another. At their most extreme, proponents of the notion that disease everywhere foreshadowed European presence would argue that no European after Columbus saw intact American Indian societies. The break was so sudden and dramatic that it is useless to count on ethnohistorical sources to document it. Instead, only archaeological approaches can be used.[4] One of the tasks that contact archaeology in the Americas has set for itself, then, is to devise models to discover and explain any evidence of rapid depopulation between about 1500 and as late as about 1800.

So far at least, the boldest attempt to diagnose population decline and attribute it to the effects of the Indian encounter with Europeans is Sarah K. Campbell's study of the Columbia plateau, an area very far away from any known European-Indian contacts in the early sixteenth century.[5] One of Campbell's purposes is to lend much-needed support to Dobyns's argument that the smallpox epidemic that ravaged central Mexico in and after 1520 spread rapidly from one end of the hemisphere to the other.[6] Campbell is forthright in this: "My specific thesis, derived from Dobyns (1983) is that, in the Plateau, introduced epidemic diseases preceded other contact by a longer time than previously believed and were a decisive factor affecting protohistoric groups." Campbell goes on to state her conviction that "[d]isease-related mortality catastrophically reduced the size of the native population of the Plateau before the 1770s." This, she concludes, "render[s] ethnographic accounts unsuitable interpretive models for adaptations [and size] of earlier populations."[7] Archaeology is the only way out of this impasse.

Pursuing her objective, Campbell selects a "newer model [which] predicts that, because diseases spread well in advance of the frontier of direct contact, their impact was earlier and lengthier than suggested by historical records alone."[8] Campbell's self-imposed task is to find indications of such depopulation in the Columbia plateau before known European contact and to strengthen the model by attributing any posited depopulation to newly introduced European diseases. Campbell notes that epidemic disease was recorded along the Pacific coast as early as the 1770s, before which there are no contemporaneous records at all. Her sources had already concluded that there was no evidence for earlier diseases, and there is no substantive evidence about epidemics in Indian oral tradition. She rightly observes that the "lack of native oral traditions cannot be assumed to be reliable evidence regarding the occurrence of a catastrophic event [the first epidemic] nearly 300 years past."[9] Encouraged by this, in an extended exercise of if/might discourse Campbell evokes a scenario in which the spread of such diseases becomes probable, then virtually certain.[10]

Campbell focuses on the 1520 smallpox epidemic recorded for central Mexico, deliberately choosing a highest-mortality scenario as the model against which to test her evidence. In this her premise is—as indeed it must be—that "[s]uch dramatic changes in population should be detectable in the archaeological record even with data of relatively poor quality."[11] A further premise is that "in a sufficiently large region, immigration and emmigration [sic] can be assumed to be roughly equal and have little effect on long-term population trends."[12] Campbell concedes that "[n]o archaeological unit directly represents population," but she continues hopefully that "virtually any kind of archaeological remains could theoretically serve as a proxy variable."[13] This is a remarkably expedient line of reasoning, and one that might alarm even latent empiricists or anyone else who respects the complexity of historical evidence. At any rate, Campbell proceeds to discuss briefly several of these "proxy variables," including burial remains, food refuse, and utilized space, only to conclude, again rightly, that "these are conventions based on pragmatic considerations, not methodological absolutes."[14] These and other considerations precede and justify Campbell's main purpose, which is to analyze a number of sites in the area to determine prehistoric population patterns there. Campbell reassures her readers that from these sites emerges "[a] remarkably representative sample of different site types and time periods . . . as measured concretely by excavated volume and by artifact and feature assemblages, thus making the business of drawing regional generalizations not only possible, but likely meaningful."[15] Thus disarmed, she proceeds to her analysis.

It is crucial, of course, that she be able to date sites closely enough that certain of them can be confidently assigned to the first half of the sixteenth century. For this she uses the traditional tools of the archaeologist—radiocarbon dating, stratigraphy, ceramics—but also points out that "[o]ccupations of the early and middle 18th century are not readily distinguishable from late prehistoric sites dating between A.D. 1500 and 1700 except by radiocarbon dates."[16] Given the broad range in such dates that is needed for high probability, this seems as if it ought to be a major concern.[17] In the event, Campbell concedes that she "counted [a site] as protohistoric [i.e., pre-1700] only if there was archaeological evidence of protohistoric occupation," which seems a strikingly risky argument from silence, as well as circular tautology.[18]

Campbell preferred to "order habitation sites" by means of "pottery classes and other artifacts" but found these too scarce, forcing her to concentrate on "a single part of the study area, the Chief Joseph Reservoir, where a recently completed CRM [cultural resource management] project provides . . . sufficient chronological information on excavated components to date them independently."[19] Heroic extrapolation—and of a kind using methods that have been much criticized of late—is to serve in place of a greater abundance and variety of evidence.[20] To look at the longer range, Campbell establishes fifty-year intervals as a gross way to distinguish assemblages of variables. These include number and area of components, number of structured features, and the amount of shell and bone recovered. The operational premise which permits further investigation and analysis is that "[i]t is reasonable to assume that each of the above measures is positively correlated with the number of people who used an area."[21]

After listing variables and sites exhaustively, Campbell comes to the crux of her argument: "The discussion of chronological trends in the estimator variables addresses a restricted issue: are there any apparent demographic events between A.D. 1500 and A.D. 1775?" Going on, she concedes, perhaps fatally, that "[t]he trends in the estimator variables prior to A.D. 1500 is [*sic*] presented as a background context, but no attempt is made to evaluate the validity of magnitude of the post–A.D. 1500 events by comparison to earlier fluctuations."[22]

When Campbell aggregated and arrayed her pre-1525 data, she found that they "show[ed] a dramatic decrease between A.D. 1325–1375 and A.D. 1375–1425." She does not attempt to explain this, although she implies that perhaps the problem lies in the method or the data.[23] The evidence from food refuse accumulation alone, however, shows a slightly different pattern: there the decline occurs either after 1425 or after 1475, with "an extreme drop-off" in terms of maximums "from A.D. 1425–1475 to A.D. 1525–1575."[24] Campbell concludes, against her own hypothesis, that "[f]eature accumulation rates . . . are dramatically lower after A.D. 1425–1475 than before, but the decline begins earlier, after A.D. 1325–1375."[25] Site types, too, began to change after ca. 1375, with smaller sizes (Type 3) predominating in place of larger (Type 2) sites.[26]

This evidence leads Campbell to offer the following unexceptionable statement:

The decline in component numbers, component size, and food debris [after 1375] could possibly be due to factors other than population levels. Further, even if related to changes in population level, these changes might not be due to decimation by disease. Outmigration or population decline due to environmental change is possible, but no major environmental shifts have been noted in the regional pollen record for this period. A change in settlement pattern is also possible, although only shifts in house types have been remarked upon in the literature.[27]

Forced, *ex hypothesi,* into denying so early a decline, Campbell is left with little option but to ignore her own good advice. Having presented evidence suggesting that among the Indians of the Columbia plateau, serious if not steady depopulation began between 1375 and 1425, Campbell proceeds to her conclusions, which seem considerably at variance with her evidence. For instance, although she had written earlier that "[t]here is a very distinct reversal of the relative abundance of Site Type 2 and Site Type 3 sites *after A.D. 1375–1425,*" she now writes that "[s]ome kind of settlement pattern shift is apparent in this data *after A.D. 1475[–1525],* when the frequency of field camps (Type 2 sites) decreases and the frequency of locations/stations (Type 3) sites increases."[28] Thus she contrives to push the window of decline to a point just later than the earliest possible opportunity for the 1520 epidemic to reach the area if it hurried.

Such legerdemain encourages Campbell to draw further conclusions unjustified by the evidence she adduces or by her use of it. Thus, speaking of the "[d]emonstration of early population collapse in a portion of the North American intermontane west" requires going well beyond the evidentiary record, but she goes still further: "Given the nature of disease transmission, the finding [*sic*] of an early epidemic in one area of the Columbia Plateau virtually demands the conclusion that [the] pandemic occurred across a broader region," probably including the Great Basin and the Northwest Coast.[29]

To sum up: Campbell attributes a catastrophic depopulation on the Columbia plateau to an epidemic of smallpox that, by her own devised chronology, must have reached the area and done its damage no later than 1525. At the same time, the thrust of her own evidence is that depopulation began a century or so before this. Moreover, there were several periods of purported depopulation (i.e., a decline in her chosen indicators) extending as far back as the eleventh century, and this depopulation oscillated depending on whether number or weight

Table 3. Total Volume of Shell and Bone (in Cubic Meters) from Excavated Sites on the Columbia Plateau, 1275–1375 and 1425–1525

Duration of Settlement	1275–1325	1325–1375	Percentage of Decline	1425–1475	1475–1525	Percentage of Decline
Minimum	445	229	–48.6	309	190	–38.6
Mean	435	270	–37.9	348	190	–45.4
Maximum	596	375	–37.1	489	316	–35.4

Source: Tables 6–6 to 6–8 in Sarah K. Campbell, *PostColumbian Culture History*, 166–68.

of bone matter was considered, but there is no effort to account for these oscillations.[30]

When looked at overall, the data show few, if any, significant or consistent patterns, even if it were possible to correlate such patterns with levels of population. And the results vary, as Campbell notes, according to whether minimum, mean, or maximum durations are assumed for the accumulation of the volume of bone and shells collected.[31] As Campbell emphasizes, "[r]egardless of which estimate [minimum, mean, maximum] is used for duration [of settlements], all distributions show a marked drop in numbers between A.D. 1425–1475 and A.D. 1475–1525."[32] This is quite true, as is shown in Table 3, culled from Campbell's presented data, but, as it also shows, in terms of total volume the drop is even greater between the periods 1275–1325 and 1325–1375.

Looking at the data still differently, the total volume of bone and shells for the period ending 1475 was 18.0 percent less than total volume for the 1275–1325 period for the maximum duration, 20.0 percent less for the mean duration, and 30.6 percent less for the minimum duration. This evidence suggests that if we correlate these variables with population, then there had already been a steady decline before 1475.

Campbell does not explain why her fifty-year intervals begin with years ending in 25 and 75, or what effects using other intervals might have had on her hypothesis. What would the results have been had she used years ending in 15 and 65, so that one fifty-year period ended just before rather than just after the smallpox epidemic struck Mexico? If they were substantially the same, then her hypothesis would collapse on these grounds alone.[33]

Campbell's study is an example of failing to test serious variant data and conclusions in adversarial ways. Campbell's insistence on carrying her hypothesis through to a triumphant conclusion forces her to ignore her own results by failing to put the 1475–1575 period into the very context she provided. Her argument that the variables she was forced to choose reflect population trends is at best tenuous, and it places her squarely on the horns of a dilemma. Accepting it actually precludes accepting her primary hypothesis—that population dropped unprecedently between 1475 and 1525.

Despite this, Campbell's conclusions have gained a bit of a following. Most notably, Elizabeth Vibert credits Campbell with "mak[ing] a persuasive case for a hemispheric epidemic in the early sixteenth century having reached the [Columbia] Plateau."[34] Robert Boyd is slightly less enthusiastic, conceding that "the presence of a contemporary archaeological discontinuity in a sampled segment of the middle Columbia Basin suggests" that the smallpox epidemic of 1519–21 "might have" spread to the Pacific northwest.[35] The danger is that the attempt to enlist archaeological evidence to conjecture a spread of smallpox of some two thousand miles in less than five years could prove encouraging to further efforts.[36] For the High Counters, further efforts are no danger at all. If Campbell had argued her case better or been able to bring better evidence forward, they could have suggested that hundreds of thousands of square miles had been ravaged by smallpox long before the first outside observers were able to record population levels there.

Recently, William Green has examined the archaeological record for an area not otherwise intensively treated by archaeologists of the protohistoric period.[37] Like Campbell, Green confesses to having been influenced by Henry Dobyns's "remarkable" study of Timucuan "depopulation" during the sixteenth century, so it is no surprise that his conclusions parallel those of Dobyns, Ramenofsky, and Campbell.[38]

Green looks at the radiocarbon dates from eighty sites in Wisconsin, Iowa, and Minnesota and finds a "gap" in them covering most of the sixteenth and early seventeenth centuries. Ignoring warfare as a possible cause, he concentrates on climatic change and new diseases. About the data Green raises questions of representativeness and accident, but only to argue that there is no evidence that archaeologists have systematically ignored sites suspected of covering the period of the gap, which could account for it. He concedes that such sites might be "small or dispersed" or long since obliterated by subsequent building activity, but then brushes aside this possibility, which permits him to seek other explanations.[39]

Green concedes that "[o]ne of the many assumptions in [his] study is that the distribution of radiocarbon dates reflects population levels more than it might reflect the fluctuating production rates of atmospheric radiocarbon." In the circumstances he must conclude that the gap is to be construed as "reflecting lower population levels."[40] Too often Green finds himself in thrall to notions that lack direct support, however plausible that might seem to anyone plying an epidemic interpretation of depopulation. For instance, he refers to the de Soto expedition's "role in introducing smallpox to the Southeast," when in fact there is not the slightest evidence that this actually occurred.[41] In line with this, Green introduces much data indicating lines of communication along the Mississippi and other waterways, but this is irrelevant if there were no diseases to communicate.[42]

Finally, Green considers climatic change—in particular, the occurrence of the so-called Little Ice Age in the northern hemisphere during just this period. It is clear from his presentation that there is considerably more direct evidence for such an event than there is for any form of epidemic disease during this period. Nonetheless, Green is inclined to minimize its depopulative effects and concludes that various imputed population movements and losses "might be better explained by factors other than climatic change."[43] In the end, Green is not inclined to seek the singular explanation and suggests that environmental degradation and other factors be considered.[44] Withal, it is clear that he accepts the likelihood that various diseases struck the region in the sixteenth century and that they played a principal role in a significant population decline, which in turn is reflected in the archaeological record by the "gap."[45]

Of more concern is the central interpretive role he gives this gap. The implication is that there are few sites, perhaps none, that have been radiocarbon dated to the period from about 1520 to about 1650, but that beginning about the latter year the gap is closed by the appearance of more sites. If correct, the implication raises interesting questions. Why, after a century of depopulation, did sites reappear? Had population begun to increase and reached some point that produced sites? Or is immigration the explanation? If not, then the implied argument must be that the late-seventeenth-century population, by Green's argument much reduced from pre-1520 levels, still was able to generate sites that a larger, earlier population could not in the intervening 120 years. In turn this implies—yet at the same time discountenances—the idea that sites are the result of some threshold of population. Even worse, it casually confuses and equates sites and population—sites are being counted, but numbers of people are being inferred. This is an untenable position, but Green requires it for his argument because sites sometimes survive whereas evidence of individuals almost never does.[46]

The interpretation that the decline in the numbers or sizes of sites mirrors the rate of depopulation must sell itself by persuading others to accept the hypothesis that fewer sites discovered is the same as fewer sites occupied and, furthermore, that sites remained fixed enough in population that they can stand surrogate for real people. Clearly this notion is a tricky one, and it is refuted by common sense and by cases such as that of the Mohawk, where a combination of circumstances—which we have no reason to think unique—resulted in "a compacting of village populations."[47]

―――――

Mass burials have always interested archaeologists. In contact study archaeology, however, these have come to assume a more crucial diagnostic role. Nowadays, very much the default diagnosis is that such burials represent the victims of newly introduced diseases that were so devastating that traditional burial practices could not be carried out. Numerous examples of this line of reasoning have surfaced recently. Writing about the possible effects of early epidemics in the American Southeast, George Milner mentioned the evidence of mass burials. While he recognized that there might be several causes for such burials, he regarded most of these as exceptional and improbable and decided that the principal cause was the arrival of European diseases in the sixteenth or seventeenth century. Indeed, since disease was responsible for mass burials, these in turn served as support for his disease model—the most important archaeological evidence that such epidemics were frequent and widespread.[48] Ann Ramenofsky, also writing about the Southeast, followed suit.[49]

Then there is the case of the mass burial at Tatham Mound in Florida. Jerald Milanich argues that the deaths of the large number of people (70 bodies, plus parts of 240 others) found there are "good evidence" for "the contention that epidemics began almost as soon as the first Spaniard stepped ashore."[50] This robust statement is unfortunately weakened by the absence of an explanation for why the evidence in question, whatever it is besides the remains themselves, supports just this possibility and no other. Such an interpretation would also date the purported epidemic, even though there is no independent evidence to confirm such a dating, such as any mention in the chronicles of the de Soto expedition. On the other hand, further study of the burials at the King site in Georgia, once also attributed to the effects of an epidemic in de Soto's wake, have yielded a different possible interpetation.[51]

This remorselessly univocal approach inevitably carries with it certain consequences.[52] Essentially, it is an argument from silence and subject to all the defects of such arguments. Not the least of these is that the discovery of mass burials that cannot be accounted for in this way fatally undermines the argument by showing how other circumstances can cause the same effect. As it happens, there is much evidence of just this inconvenient circumstance, even though a single example would suffice as an effective counterfactual. In particular, there are numerous instances of mass burials in the American Southwest, all antedating 1492 and most attributed to massacres resulting from intertribal warfare.[53] For these reasons, and even more for environmental reasons, it is now believed that the population of the American Southwest reached its peak as early as A.D. 1250, after which it continued to decline until the arrival of the Europeans.[54]

The remains of at least thirty-five individuals were discovered at a site in the Northwest Territories of Canada that have been dated to A.D. 1370 ± 57 years. In these "the skeletal evidence of violence is . . . overwhelming," but not unique to the region.[55] There is also the case of Crow Creek in South Dakota, where nearly five hundred persons were massacred and buried sometime in the first half of the fourteenth century.[56] These cases bely not only the notion that mass burials were usually the result of epidemic deaths but also the Panglossian view that before contact American Indians were uncannily peacefully inclined and that their numbers tended to grow like Topsy.

Most interesting of all are the remains of several children aged four years and less excavated in northern Mexico. The burial dates to "sometime prior to A.D. 660," and Sheilagh and Richard Brooks have attributed the children's deaths to an unspecified epidemic.[57] The reasons offered are no better than those offered for similar postcontact situations, but the case serves to remind us that in any consideration of contact population and its antecedents, the incidence of epidemic disease before 1492 cannot be ruled out entirely.[58]

Routinely attributing mass burials to the effects of newly introduced epidemics, with all the implications thereof, is a salient example of the disease model advocates' penchant for saying that something happened merely because it *could have* happened. Of course diseases might have been responsible for such burials—and probably were in some cases.[59] But almost without exception it is impossible to determine such causation, especially for the many diseases that leave no osteological traces.[60] It must be said that the High Counters did not invent this explanation but in fact are following a tradition in archaeology. When Kathleen Kenyon encountered some mass burials at Jericho she decided that it was "probable that disease of some sort was responsible for the simultaneous deaths of entire families," merely because they appeared to be simultaneous and because the skeletons "show no signs of injuries," as though death and visible skeletal injuries were somehow not otherwise dissociable.[61]

All this suggests an unbridgeable epistemological gulf between the ways archaeologists and historians argue. Take the case of Livy's history of republican Rome. Only about a quarter of it is extant, yet historians do not see this as cause to regard events in Rome treated in the lost books as somehow similar enough to those about which information survives to allow them to extrapolate. Even less do they imagine that the lost books are evidence that nothing happened in Rome during these periods! Yet this is precisely how archaeologists of the protohistoric period in the United States operate. Theirs is an argument from silence par excellence.[62] When Ramenofsky, for instance, writes that "archaeologists are more likely to have identified a larger fraction of aboriginal settlements" from the protohistoric period than for earlier periods, and from that concludes that only depopulation can explain the fact that this number is low when by her argument it should be high, she is engaging in a classic argument from silence. And when she attributes the decline almost entirely to epidemics, most never mentioned in any source, there is serious risk of disingenuousness.[63]

Although of concern, these differences should not be surprising. Historians generally find evidence, whereas archaeologists generally create it. Historians seldom change the character of their sources, whereas archaeologists inevitably decontextualize, reorganize, and reclassify their data and impose meanings on them that cannot be shown to be inherent. Whereas historians are never satisfied that they have retrieved all relevant evidence, archaeologists can be certain that they have not even come close. From this conjuncture of factors comes the need for archaeologists to conventionalize their work, in particular by their own style of synecdoche (*pars pro omnia*). In this quest for theoretical sufficiency, what gets lost is variety, complexity, and diversity.

Indeed, the claims made by North American archaeologists

strike one as characteristically unseemly when compared, for instance, with the following comment made about Romano-British and Anglo-Saxon England, for which the data base for launching demographic arguments is nearly 45,000 excavated graves:

> Estimating population figures is probably one of the most hazardous exercises that archaeologists can undertake as there is rarely any absolute upon which such figures can be based. Generally, the figures that are given are guesses or result from deep, mystical "feelings" that some demographers of the past possess. The danger is that one person's estimate, perhaps based on logical reasoning, is adopted by some writers, giving it an air of respectability, whilst others merely add or subtract values because of equally abstract feelings.[64]

Recent and proceeding events continue to underscore the way in which at least one aspect of archaeological communication seeks to overcome these disadvantages. William Dever, a prominent warlord in the battle over the historicity of the biblical account of early Israel, is eager to chastise those who do not appreciate archaeological argumentation quite so much as he does. Of its sufficiency he is in no doubt whatever: "We [archaeologists] will write a history of ancient Israel, and we will also write the only competent histories of ancient Palestine. We shall not be deterred by the post-modern, relativist, deconstructionist malaise that affects so many social-science disciplines."[65]

This sublime confidence sits comfortably amid similar claims. Interpretations of Ebla, ᶜUbar, Alexander's tomb, and new cave paintings have presented just this face to the outside world, at least initially, as their excavators have pronounced each to have sensational characteristics. The trouble is that this enthusiasm has been followed by doubts expressed by other archaeologists, sometimes—as in the case of Ebla—from the same team, and by the occasional retraction. This dissent in turn has usually been met by silence, and eventually a new epistemological equilibrium develops that leaves the matter open. The cycle is a common, almost predictable, one, and damage is done each time it plays out. Even though this particular form of claim and counterclaim has not played a substantial role in the archaeological study of population decline, it does suggest the way in which archaeological evidence is granted power beyond its means—time and again.

Contact Does Not Equal Contagion

Whatever attacks can be made on his methodology, Griaule was the first to reveal to us the African cosmological vision.

—Luc de Heusch, in an interview by
Pierre de Maret, *Currrent Anthropology*, 1993

Most human demographic history happened before it could be recorded.

—Sheila Ryan Johansson, review of
Ole Jorgen Benedictow's *Medieval Demographic System*

An essential feature in the success of the High Counter enterprise is the ease with which it can dispose of the small numbers encountered in the sources. Two methods are practiced. The first is simply to regard them as small fractions of some larger, never counted whole. The second is to treat them as remnants of a larger population already ravaged by disease mortality. The estimates of the High Counters for population levels require, or at least benefit from, a single premise—that European diseases spread like wildfire over large parts of the Americas. If nothing else, the terms of the premise encapsulate well the epistemological wagers involved in their enterprise. For those less committed to the notion that closure is possible, the fact that this premise cannot be proved true in *any* case is a drawback; the High Counters, on the other hand, are content that it cannot be proved false.

Indeed, as a premise it can be hugely seductive in just this way. Those not enamored of the idea that a hypothesis cannot be taken as true unless and until it survives testing will be attracted to this form of escapism. Moreover, there is a substantial advantage in that critics of the High Counters' methods must attempt the impossible task of proving a negative. On the other hand, they could confine themselves to demonstrating the High Counters' failure to make even one ir-refutable case for contagion before contact, whether by a few years or a few centuries.

———————

Barring a few Scandinavian contacts, Europe first met the Americas early on the morning of 12 October 1492.[1] By the next day the irre-pressible impulse to estimate had already showed itself with an entry in the *diario* of the first voyage, a composite text—part Columbus, part Las Casas, and possibly part anonymous.[2] This entry also repre-sents the first effort to corrupt and deform the evidence regarding In-dian populations. The *diario* text, as transcribed by Las Casas, pur-portedly verbatim, reads: "As soon as [13 October] dawned, many of these people came to the beach."[3] This unadorned statement proved inadequate when Las Casas inserted the *diario* text into his portman-teau *Historia de las Indias*. Although he refrained from providing numbers, he managed to change the character of the original tableau; now, "the beach appeared to be full of people."[4] For the next several years the incipient Spanish colonial enterprise was centered on His-paniola, where Columbus returned late in 1493 and established a small settlement at Isabela to replace the burned-out settlement at Navidad. The Spanish-Indian experience on Hispaniola, which lasted until the virtual extinction of the Indians only thirty years later, offers a suit-ably small theater in which to look at the central explanatory role the High Counters grant disease.

At no point during this time did any of the extant eyewitness accounts estimate the population of the island—not surprising since they had seen so little of it. It was something of a surprise, then, when Sherburne Cook and Woodrow Borah took a look at the contact pop-ulation of Hispaniola and concluded that it was probably in the neigh-borhood of 8 million.[5] At eighty times the most commonly cited ear-lier estimate, this represents the single most dramatic leap upward by the High Counters.[6] Cook and Borah granted that this posited popu-lation decline was "startling and dramatic" and sought to explain it by referring to hunger, forced labor, and, above all, newly introduced European diseases.[7] Of the last they found no evidence in the relevant sources, but they managed to claim that "[f]rom the men of the first voyage of Columbus on, there was disease among the Spaniards. A large proportion of the men were ill at any given time, and there was a steady loss through death."[8]

Although in support of this claim they cited Ferdinand Colum-bus, Las Casas, and Peter Martyr, each of these sources referred to later voyages and none mentioned any illness that must be construed as a *disease*. Cook and Borah disregarded the only statement in the *diario* of the first voyage about the health of the Spaniards. Columbus wrote that at the end of November, at least, "of all my people there has been no one who has had a headache or been in bed with illness except one old man, from the pain of the stone which he suffered all his life."[9] At no point did Columbus comment adversely on the health of the Indians—quite the contrary, he frequently adverted to their good health, fine bearing, and so forth.[10] The weight of evidence, then, suggests strongly that whatever the later opportunities for infection, none occurred during the first voyage.

Columbus returned to Hispaniola about a year after he wrote about the good health of the crews. This time he was forced to write very differently, for indeed there was sickness among the Spaniards. Cook and Borah had alluded to this but were unable to specify just which "disease" this might have been. In a series of articles that appeared between 1985 and 1993, Francisco Guerra entered the lists on Cook and Borah's behalf, diagnosing the illness mentioned in the records as swine influenza.[11] The basis for his diagnosis was largely the fact that a large number of animals accompanied this expedition, and Guerra took the mention of some vague symptoms in the eyewitness accounts to resemble those of influenza. Thus he spoke firmly of "an acute infectious disease, extremely contagious, with a very short incubation period, affecting simultaneously a large population and characterized by high fever, ague, prostration, and excessive mortality."[12] Regrettably for his case, most of this information—and all the interpretation—is absent from his sources.[13]

Having found his epidemic, Guerra naturally felt obliged to make something of it, so that its detection might not be wasted. In doing so, he made Columbus and Las Casas complicit: although neither had a word to say on the subject, Guerra would have it that they "agreed . . . that many Spaniards died and that the Indians died in great numbers."[14] When questioned about his use of sources, Guerra became only more adamant: "[E]very quotation . . . was correct, the facts stand as they were first presented, and even the Spanish dead from the influenza epidemic . . . have been found and can be counted." But he could bring to his rebuttal no statement by Columbus regarding dead Indians.[15]

As far as mortality among the Indians is concerned, Guerra had already upped the ante. At first he had been satisfied to speak of "many" deaths, but later he wrote that "the epidemic starting the 9th of December 1493 at Isabela . . . killed over 500 Spaniards and afterwards *most* of the Indian inhabitants of the island."[16] Guerra's own estimates of the contact population of Hispaniola were considerably less than those of Cook and Borah, but the latter approved nonetheless, commending his work as "a fine piece of sleuthing."[17] And Hodges, Deagan, and Reitz accepted Guerra's approach by going it one voyage better, declaring stoutly that "it is nearly certain that during that time [January to perhaps November 1493]" the Spaniards left behind at Navidad "introduced alien European pathogens into the vulnerable Taino population."[18] They can offer no evidence on behalf of this rhetorical excursion, and do not try to.

———————

Despite his inability to cite sources correctly and his penchant for positing epidemic mortality indicated nowhere in the documentary record, Guerra's conclusions have proved influential—others besides Borah have found them convincing.[19] Of these, the person whose work is most important is N. D. Cook.[20] It is easy to agree with much of what Cook has to say. At first he is cautious about the likely size of the contact population, although not so cautious as to abstain from offering any estimate at all. He also takes care to express skepticism about claims of devastating epidemics that spread from the moment the Spaniards set foot on Hispaniola on their return voyage. Cook rightly points out the disparity between what the records say and what Guerra insists on making of them.[21]

There is also much to quibble about in Cook's own interpretation of the historical record. Despite his self-confessed belief that "[a]t the moment, caution is the best counsel," Cook sheds many of his expressed doubts as he proceeds.[22] In particular he emulates the notion of disease model advocates in offering peculiar interpretations of certain terms that recur in the historical sources. For instance, he claims that I am wrong when I state that Las Casas never made any connection between "disease" and mortality in Hispaniola. To demonstrate this, Cook quotes a passage from Las Casas' *Historia de las Indias* in which Las Casas deployed the terms *enfermedad* and *enfermedades*. These Cook translates as "illness" and "sicknesses," respectively. I have no quarrel with these choices; indeed, it was making the same choices that seemed to require denying to Las Casas any anticipatory support for the disease model.

Inevitably, arguments that anyone might advance along these lines become "wrong" whenever these expressions are translated in one way and interpreted in another. In line with the High Counters' modus operandi, Cook goes on intuitively—it can hardly be any other way—to equate "illness" with "disease," which is after all no more than one possible subset of "illness."

The immediate postcontact New World might also represent one of the rare occasions when the generic term could be held also to imply the specific. Certainly by about 1530 this was the case in many places, but to argue that this was true in Hispaniola as early as 1493, as Cook does (now following Guerra in face of his expressed reservations), is to argue in precariously circular fashion by allowing a preferred interpretation to impose itself on a body of evidence that is otherwise irremediably unforthcoming. Anyone who implies that Las Casas could not have meant "disease" when he wrote "enfermedad" is necessarily wrong, because it is impossible now to be certain of his intention. Still, it seems to me that when he used the plural (*enfermedades*), Las Casas must have been implying either that several epidemic diseases were already ravaging the New World or that the "illnesses" in question were environmental and/or idiosyncratic; that is, that they were not *diseases* in the normal sense of that term, which had a particular connotation even then.

Translating *enfermedad*, a broadly defined word in Spanish, into English, where finer semantic distinctions present themselves, well encapsulates the historical translator's intractable dilemma—the desire to be accurate even while operating in disconcerting ignorance of an author's intent, degree of knowledge, and discursive habits.[23] In the abstract, both "illness" and "disease" are possible and acceptable translations of *enfermedad*, but they are hardly equally likely ones. Despite the fact that the Spanish language encompasses both concepts in a single word, for the historical demographer the differences between their implications are profound.

This is clearly indicated in the disparate population estimates for Hispaniola already mentioned. Translating *enfermedad* as "disease" will always carry with it an *implication* that the death toll was much greater than if the term is translated as "illness." This is true whether we are discussing the fifteenth- and sixteenth-century Americas, nineteenth-century Hawaii, or twentieth-century Zaire. As terminology—and accordingly as interpretation—"disease" will inevitably imply greater numbers of affected persons and, since the High Counters' method is effectively programmed to provide a specific range of conclusions, a much larger total "contact" population to begin with.

Given this state of affairs, we might expect scholars studying the question to take pains to discuss the complexities of the issue of nomenclature and, when they attempt to bend evidence to their will, to justify their choices in necessary detail. Cook does not do this in his discussion of depopulation and its causes on Hispaniola. After equating "disease" with Las Casas' "enfermedad," and after arguing that Guerra's interpretations are to be taken cautiously, he goes on to state with enviable—if puzzling—confidence that "[d]isease raged among both Spaniards and the native peoples of Hispaniola, if not from 1492, then certainly beginning in November of 1493 with the arrival of the second expedition."[24] Here Cook effectively upstages Guerra by a month, if not a year.

The strategy of treating a generic word in the sources as having a specific or circumscribed or apocalyptic application is by no means new to Cook. As we have already seen, Woodrow Borah and Sherburne Cook decided that in the sources they used, *indio* invariably meant an adult male Indian, since to do so suited their hypothesis far better than the equally likely assumption that it often meant no more than an Indian of any age and either gender. And it is nothing novel to find *enfermedad* taking on a specific and *ex hypothesi* meaning throughout the High Counter literature. It is a thoroughly reasonable assumption that the chroniclers intended some of these references to speak of communicable disease and not just of illness. But it is not a reasonable *working* assumption, since it can seldom be demonstrated in specific instances with the certainty required to develop and mobilize plausible derivative hypotheses. And it is unacceptable merely to choose definitions intuitively, bereft of all context but the need to satisfy the demands of the argument on offer.

We can approach the penchant of Las Casas and other chroniclers for imprecise usage in yet another way. All the chroniclers had available to them alternative words they could use to express the notion of communicable disease as a *particular* form of illness. For example, words such as *contagión, epidemia,* and *peste* or *pestilencia* had already appeared in at least one dictionary available at the end of the fifteenth century.[25] In the circumstances it is surely reasonable to wonder why Las Casas and others were *invariably* careless enough to choose the general usage over the specific if they meant to refer to contagious diseases. While Cook points out that European medicine had not reached the stage of understanding the etiologies of most diseases, its practitioners recognized the characteristic ways in which they spread rapidly from person to person, as well as many of the more distinctive symptoms. Indeed, as early as 1348 Jacme d'Agrament, a Catalan doctor, had distinguished between smallpox and the plague.[26]

Among these practitioners, as Cook notes, was Diego Alvarez Chanca, who accompanied Columbus on his second voyage and on whose testimony Cook (as well as Guerra) relies heavily. Like Las Casas, Chanca forbore to apply a specific referrent to the illness he described among the Spaniards on Hispaniola at the end of 1493. He did not mention that it spread in a contagious fashion but only that most of the Spaniards were afflicted by it, a distinction that is indeed a difference. Nor, *pace* Cook, did Chanca or any other chronicler of this episode mention that this illness extended to the Indians. In the circumstances, these witnesses are perilously slender reeds to support Guerra's and Cook's claims that epidemic disease had struck *both* Europeans and Indians in Hispaniola by the end of 1493.

Finally, there is Juan Ginés de Sepúlveda, Las Casas' opponent on the nature of the Indians. Like Las Casas, Ginés de Sepúlveda was both theologian and historian; he was appointed official royal chronicler in 1536. Among his works was an account of Spanish activities in the New World through the conquest of Mexico, beginning with the four voyages of Columbus. He wrote that the Indians adopted a scorched earth policy on Columbus's return in 1493, resulting in many of them dying from "hunger." The scarcity eventually spread to the Spaniards, many of whom in turn also died of "hunger."[27] Ginés de Sepúlveda had nothing else to say about the health of either the Indians or the Spaniards in these early days.

Like all other chroniclers of the time, Ginés de Sepúlveda combined original materials—possibly including eyewitness accounts—with derivative information, some of it from Peter Martyr, Las Casas, and the royal chronicler Gonzalo Fernández de Oviedo y Valdés. His failure to mention any diseases among either the Indians or the Spaniards is not, of course, conclusive evidence that none struck. Nonetheless, Ginés de Sepúlveda added details about Indian and Spanish activities and attributed the mortality on the island to hunger, not to disease. Indeed, he was very precise in this: "a great part of the Indians died from hunger."[28] Ignoring the testimony in Ginés de Sepúlveda's brief account of Hispaniola in 1493–94 represents another lost opportunity to notice that some chroniclers did *not* mention disease and to take their testimony into account.

N. D. Cook concluded uncompromisingly that "Old World disease was brought to the Americas with the second expedition of Columbus in 1493."[29] He, like other High Counters, effectively denies to Las Casas and others—even to the medically trained Chanca—the capacity to be reasonably precise in description and nomenclature, including their declining to use specific words where, by Cook's argument, these should have applied. It is one thing to count accurately but quite a lesser matter merely to mention symptoms and attendant mortality, especially of the magnitude the High Counters propose. In the circumstances, this denial is genuinely odd considering how strikingly the High Counters have granted precision to these same chroniclers when they assigned very large numbers where such information could not have been known to them.

Such is the case with Nikolaus Federmann, whose estimate, offered forty years after the fact, Cook is strangely eager to accept at "face value."[30] Apparently Cook is beguiled by the fact that Federmann's figure of half a million is "remarkably close to some modern estimates," but a glance at Cook's table recapitulating these estimates shows that virtually any estimate under 1.1 million would fulfill this qualification.[31] Cook does not suggest why he believes that Federmann (or anyone else) could have had access to figures for the population of Hispaniola before the Spaniards had been able to gain effective occupation. Federmann cited no sources and was in Hispaniola only while in transit to and from Venezuela. Certainly his figure conflicts with the "official" estimates of the time. Moreover, his estimate of 500,000 is rounded in telltale fashion, probably to express something more like "a lot."

Most statisticians and historical demographers would be reluctant to grant Cook's sample of seven Indians—those who accompanied Columbus to Spain and back again—the reinforcing, almost corroborative, power that he grants it in assessing possible degrees of mortality on Hispaniola after 1493.[32] Beyond the matter of sample size, there is the usual source problem here as well. It is true, as Cook notes, that Chanca specifically stated that only two of seven Indians who began the voyage back from Spain survived, and that they were used as interpreters when the Spaniards reached the destroyed site at Navidad.[33] Cook might be granting Chanca an undeserved degree of authority here. Other sources for this leg of the second voyage, not used by Cook, tell a discrepant story. Ferdinand Columbus and Las Casas both wrote that Columbus put one Indian off the ship in Samaná in eastern Hispaniola with the aim of mediatizing the Indians of that area.[34] Columbus himself corroborated this version.[35] None of the three, however, speaks to the number of survivors or of Indians used as interpreters at Navidad, so that their versions merely raise suspicions that Chanca omitted part of the story or misremembered this detail.[36]

A significant means by which the High Counters could advance, or at least fortify, their case in this particular instance is simply to demonstrate that when the Spanish chroniclers and other sources used nonspecific terms to describe illness among the Spaniards, they actually intended to tell their readers that they were referring to epidemic disease among both Spaniards and Indians, as first Guerra and now Cook claim for Hispaniola. Until they make some progress along these lines, we can only continue to wonder about their irrepressible confidence. Failing this, they might resort to analogy, by illustrating, for instance, that other sources from this period did refer to known epidemics in the same kinds of generic terms. Given the nature of the evidence, this would be a difficult task under any circumstances, and it is not made easier by looking to Mexico as a test case. There we find that the chroniclers—even though they were generally missionaries and not trained medical personnel like Chanca, and even though they occasionally disagreed about the nature of a particular occurrence— seldom resorted to generic terms when describing the diseases they recorded but used the specific disease nomenclature available to them—the same nomenclature that had been available to the chroniclers of Columbus's second voyage.[37]

The notion that first contact and first contagion are always part of the same process was not born simultaneously with the High Counter movement but developed as a result of Henry Dobyns's arguments along these lines in his 1966 clarion call to arms.[38] At the time, Dobyns advanced it tentatively, if comprehensively, but it quickly became a central article of faith in his work and that of many others. Even those such as Ann Ramenofsky, with no apparent stake in the numbers game per se, could be found to argue, truly but trivially, that "[a]bsence of well-documented disease episodes from the sixteenth century does not disconfirm Dobyns's position."[39] The matter needs to be looked at more widely, because it is so important to the calculating exercise, because its application has become reflexive, and because it affords an example of the Art of the Possible as practiced in this field.

In her work on the archaeology of the transition from pre- to postcontact North America, Ramenofsky naturally addresses these issues. She admits that archaeological and osteological evidence by itself cannot provide strong support for postcontact epidemics but suggests that archaeological evidence of declining settlement activity should be allowed to convince readers that such decline was both real and the likely result of epidemics. Since archaeological dating is seldom fine enough to determine the timing of the diminution she perceives, she develops a table which she labels "known or probable epidemics in Florida and the Lower Mississippi Valley."[40]

Noting that using "known" is a bit disingenuous for the sixteenth century, for which there is documentary evidence (dubious at that) for only one of Dobyns's twelve postulated epidemics, Ramenofsky finds herself momentarily ambivalent: "One sixteenth-century reference to disease is slim evidence to argue for a century of decimation." She recovers quickly, continuing:

> The lack of direct historical evidence does not mean, however, that native populations did not experience the ravages of such infections as smallpox or malaria simultaneously or sequentially. Sixteenth-century Europeans were unaware of their microbial imports. Further, since parasites that erupt in disease have incubation periods prior to the expression of illness, it is possible that explorers simply did not observe the consequences of microbial introductions. Another possibility is that disease introductions, independent of European presence, diffused like spatial waves.[41]

This is an interesting and microcosmic sequence of argument. Ramenofsky begins by expressing caution but ends on an apocalyptic note. In the process she succinctly canvasses most of the arguments put forward by those espousing the contact-equals-contagion paradigm. Her five sentences are worth looking at a little more closely.

Ramenofsky is right to observe that one out of twelve is "slim evidence." She is equally correct, although by now on a different epistemological plane entirely, in arguing that absence of evidence is not neccessarily evidence of absence. There might well have been some epidemics—maybe even eleven—that failed to capture observers' attention, only to be retrieved by Dobyns. In fact Ramenofsky goes on to suggest just this, or even more—that Europeans were unaware of what they had wrought, failing to notice it time and again. By now she has reached slippery ground. It is by no means true that sixteenth-century Spaniards (and others) "were unaware of their microbial imports." However convenient this argument is as an undifferentiated explanation for the absence of documentary evidence, it cannot bear scrutiny. Intellectually and intuitively the Spanish explorers and settlers had ample experience at their disposal to recognize what was happening and, although to a lesser extent, to explain it, if not yet to prevent it.[42]

But by believing this, Ramenofsky is able to continue that the abject silence of the records is meaningless, to which she adds that incubation periods could have kept the Spaniards from realizing what was happening in their wake. The impression left is that de Soto's men—to cite the most prominent example—moved through the American Southeast so rapidly as to outstrip all incubation periods. Quite the contrary is true; not only did de Soto's men encamp for several months during each of four consecutive winters and spend many weeks at several other locations, but they also doubled back toward the end of their wanderings, visiting the same groups many months after earlier visits. All this was done without a single recorded observation of active disease.

Finally, Ramenofsky jettisons her initial caution entirely and adopts Dobyns's scheme of pandemic after pandemic radiating across the continent unfazed by distance, lack of population, or climate. In a single paragraph she has moved from token doubt to total embrace of a scheme that shatters any epistemological or epidemiological barriers to massive and repeated depopulation anywhere in the western hemisphere. Having done so, she is able to proceed with her three case studies, informed by a premise that brooks no halfway measures— disease is a ubiquitous and primary variable.

For better or worse, Ramenofsky is one of the saner partisans of precontact (but post-1492) pandemics. We have seen, for instance, how Sarah Campbell posits an epidemic of smallpox on the Columbia plateau in the 1520s, and other examples abound. Woodrow Borah is also an adherent of the notion, relying on rhetorical questions to make his argument. He suggests that "unrecorded as well as recorded vessels would make landings on the coast for supplies and other purposes, and, if they encountered Indians, engage in trade and other pursuits." This speculation is reasonable enough, but he follows: "Are we to believe that Europeans had no diseases among them in mild or more serious form and that they did not transmit them to the natives?"[43]

Borah then goes on to apply this principle to account for an extensive decline (unnoticed in the historical record) in the population of the Inca empire even before the death of Wayna Qhapac, possibly from smallpox, in the late 1520s.[44] Borah advances the likelihood that other Europeans had approached the Inca polity before Pizarro's force did so. In particular, he sees disease as emanating from the Río de la Plata and Amazon regions. Moreover, "[e]ven in so remote and unknown an area as California, Spanish exploration and the regular landing of the Manila fleet to replenish wood and water may well have left an epidemiological residue." And along with this another rhetorical question: "Did these movements have no epidemiological effects?"[45]

Borah concludes his discussion by bringing in the familiar notion of pandemics. He mentions nineteenth- and twentieth-century pandemics and adds his own epistemologically null comment that "the absence of records does not mean that pandemics did not occur" in the sixteenth-century Americas. He continues elliptically that "[o]n the contrary, their presence may reasonably be inferred from the outbreak of a virulent disease, especially one occurring under virgin soil conditions."[46] Concluding, Borah tracks the smallpox epidemic that struck Mexico in 1520 to the American Southwest; "even though we have no records to confirm this," he regards such hypotheses as "eminently reasonable."[47]

Jerald Milanich asks whether there were "pandemics that swept through the native populations in North and South America in the first decades after Columbus's initial voyage," and continues: "Did such pandemics precede Europeans into most regions of the Western Hemisphere, spreading from native group to native group?" His own view is cautious: "What is certain is that in the seventeenth century, numerous epidemics struck" Florida. Just the same, he concludes that "[t]he jury is still out," implying that eventually a verdict will be reached—he does not say how.[48]

Another example of the kind Campbell advances, though destitute even of the most basic defense, is Thomas Myers's statement that there were "at least four outbreaks of pestilence in the margins of the Amazon" between 1504 and 1531.[49] Claims like this (along with postulated mortality rates of 75 percent) make it easy for Myers then to calculate a contact population of more than 10 million just for the upper Amazon as late as 1524, with a decline to fewer than 700,000 just seven years later, and a steady decline thereafter.[50]

This belief in antecedent epidemics throughout the hemisphere encapsulates the extent to which the premises of the High Counters must constitute a belief system in which inferences become facts with little further ado. Dobyns, followed by Ramenofsky, Myers, and others, *believes* that prior epidemics occurred but is unable to support this belief with any independent evidence.[51] In turn, when others accept such beliefs as factually based, or even as probable rather than improbable, they establish second-generation belief systems in which decisions are made largely on the basis of predisposition and in which subchoices (e.g., rate of depopulation) are no longer independent of the primary choices (e.g., that one or more epidemics preceded the first recorded estimate).

———————

The idea that disease preceded its observation has also proved a favorite with writers of works that accompanied the Columbian quincentenary and are critical of European activities in the Americas. In one of the most popular of these, Kirkpatrick Sale argued that "European pathogens" had traveled with Columbus on his first voyage, and Sale embraced Cook and Borah's calculation of 8 million inhabitants for Hispaniola in 1492.[52] David Stannard, even more critical of European activities, likewise found the notion of early and frequent pandemic activity to be irresistible.[53] For these authors, the idea that disease raged uncontrolled helped justify the use of terms such as "genocide."[54]

That disease—and mortality—did precede the personal arrival of Europeans in various locales in the New World is almost certainly true, but by its very nature it must remain an abstract truth—probable as an inference but incapable of being demonstrated. The closest we can come is the accounts of Indians who spoke of epidemics occurring shortly before their evidence was recorded. This happened, for instance, in New England, in Peru, and in Yucatán.[55]

The accumulation of fragments of disparate evidence might also lead us to suspect that disease sometimes struck before there was opportunity to record it. Working on a limited temporal and spatial basis, Warren Dean tries to make a sympathetic case for this happening on the southern coast of Brazil before formal settlement took place. There, the fleet of Sebastião Caboto anchored for several months in 1526–27, and his account speaks of the "illness" of many crew members.[56] Dean turns this into a "fever" and concludes further that "[i]t seems quite possible that European infectious diseases were introduced" at the time.[57] This is unwarranted speculation, even in so circumscribed a case. It only emphasizes the extent to which even observers' testimony ignores the Indians, and it forces us to wonder whether they would have done so had they been dying in large numbers.

In estimating the Tupinambá population in 1555 as between 57,000 and 63,000, Dean wondered what it might have been in 1500, just before the arrival of the first Europeans. He suspects that it must have been much higher and turns to disease to account for the decline. He estimates that more than ten thousand Europeans, possibly many more, visited the Brazilian coast between 1501 and 1555. He speaks of the practice of abandoning sick crew members, as well as others as punishment. He points out, rightly, that "[a]bandoning sick crewmen on the beaches would undoubtedly increase the danger of contaminating the costal Indians" and concludes that "these contacts were enough to increase the mortality of the native population." Even while nothing Dean suggests is implausible, it remains hypothetical since, as he admits, he can cite no instances in the surviving record that such diseases did actually strike the Brazilian Indians.[58]

An episode recorded in the de Soto chronicles highlights the ambiguities so often overlooked in this matter. Describing the expedition's sojourn at Cofitachequi, two of the four chroniclers mention that a "plague" (*peste*) had depopulated a nearby town a few years earlier. One of the two, Elvas, spoke only of flight as a result of this *peste,* whereas Inca Garcilaso, notoriously undependable in all matters, asserted a high mortality.[59] Like most who adopt the disease model, Marvin Smith prefers to believe in Garcilaso and so in the incidence of fatal epidemics in the American Southeast no later than the 1530s.[60] Chester DePratter, on the other hand, offers reasons not to accept Garcilaso's testimony and concludes that there are "alternat[iv]e explanations" besides the purported epidemics—for example, simple abandonment owing to stress on resources.[61] DePratter's assessment of the logic of the case as refracted through the sources is cogent—certainly it can be preferred to Smith's argument, which consists solely of retailing the versions of Elvas and Garcilaso and choosing the latter.

Proponents of the widespread incidence of epidemics in the sixteenth century necessarily rely heavily on the few accounts of these in the sources.[62] Principally, these consist of the episode at Cofitachequi, that concerning the death of Wayna Qhapac mentioned elsewhere, and some postcontact testimony for the Maya areas of Mexico and Guatemala.[63] This meager data base is offset by other comments to the effect that certain later disease episodes were the first of their kind, such as Thomas Hariot's observation in 1587 noted in chapter 9.

Finally, many would agree with Stannard that "there is clear evidence that European diseases had a serious impact on California's native peoples throughout the sixteenth and seventeenth centuries."[64] In their study of the Chumash, for instance, Philip Walker and Travis Hudson repeatedly make the same claim but in the end can state little more than the obvious: "No doubt the opportunity existed for the introduction of European disease carried by members of [various] crew[s]" who visited, or might have visited, the area in the sixteenth century.[65] No doubt.

<hr>

Evidence suggests that the contact-equals-contagion equation is becoming increasingly a predisposing aspect of the algebra of the High Counters. That is, it is not only assumed but asserted, although with no stronger arguments than ever.[66] A recent example is Ramenofsky's attempt to impute a series of diseases to New Mexico between the time of Coronado's expedition and the Pueblo revolt of 1680.[67] Her argument consists largely of demonstrating that epidemiological principles could well have resulted in the spread of known incidents of diseases to this area, even while she is forced to concede that her hypothesis lacks credible historical evidence, forcing her into a remarkable number of "could have–might have" constructions. To her credit, Ramenofsky closes by admitting the obvious: "In the end, this analysis cannot proceed further than to specify what infectious parasites may have been present in New Mexico" before 1680.[68] Just the same, her rhetorical tactics to this point are a pretty good example of the principle that mentioning a long list of possible bad things makes none of them a bit more probable, although it probably does add a spurious plausibility to the argument.

Ramenofsky's example, only one of the latest, underscores that epidemic or, as some would have it, pandemic disease plays an absolutely fulcral role in the methods and conclusions of the High Counters. For them it provides a wide range of necessary services and takes on the character of a universal deus ex machina. Disease is used to explain both the fact and the degree of depopulation, but it serves other purposes as well. In particular it serves as explanation for discrepancies in population estimates. If, for instance, the population of place X in 1540 was estimated by the Spaniards as, say, 5,000, and the High Counters think it was 50,000 in 1520, then disease is hauled forward to account for the decline.

Clearly, depopulation of any magnitude whatever can be accommodated in this all-purpose fashion. When Cook and Borah needed to account for a 99.8 percent decline in the population of Hispaniola in just twenty years, they turned to disease as the major factor, despite the fact that there is not a single word in any of the relevant sources about such a disease or series of diseases among the Hispaniola Indians. For Florida, Henry Dobyns postulated almost as precipitous a decline between 1513 and the 1560s precisely as the result of a series of epidemics, none of which, once again, has found its way into the historical record for the area. Areas as remote from European settlement as the Pacific northwest are becoming depopulated, at least in the High Counters' writings, by diseases hurrying over thousands of miles in almost no time at all.

———————

Whereas it seems that interpreting strictly the evidence for early, frequent, and widespread epidemics can never succeed in arriving at plausible estimates, it is obvious that treating that evidence loosely can never *fail* to provide them. Treating historical evidence with a tempered imagination can spiral to an increased richness of perception. Too often, however, arguments never get beyond being self-sustaining in ways that systematically exclude other perspectives. In commenting on the relationship of evidence and theory in the study of history, Karl Popper wrote that

> although facts are collected with an eye upon the theory, and will confirm it as long as the theory stands up to these tests, they are more than merely a kind of empty repetition of a preconceived theory. They confirm the theory only if they are the results of unsuccessful attempts to overthrow its predictions, and therefore a telling testimony in its favor. So it is, I hold, the possibility of overthrowing it, or its falsifiability, that constitutes the possibility of testing it, and therefore the scientific character of a theory; and the fact that all tests of a theory are attempted falsifications of predictions derived with its help, furnishes the clue to scientific method.[69]

Historical method, of course, seldom aspires to mimicking scientific method in all its glory, although the High Counters have grown fond of dazzling with pseudo-scientific number-crunching. Even without claiming to replicate the method of the sciences, however, those practicing the methods of history need not be quite so zealous in avoiding the consequences of testing their hypotheses against all the data and against all the implications of those data.

Even those attempting merely to calculate the depopulation of the New World in generalized terms by pressing its beginning closer and closer to 1492 are confronted with refractory sources that do not provide them with the information they require. In this they are by no means unusually handicapped. Ever since the plagues of Egypt mentioned in Exodus or, more historically, the so-called Plague of Athens recorded in some detail by Thucydides, the available primary sources have frequently lacked the epidemiological detail required to infer high, even if still unmeasurable, mortality. Unfortunately, in transforming generalized references to illness among the Spaniards on Hispaniola into nothing less than an epidemic that had immediate and catastrophic effects on the island's Indian population, Guerra and Cook are treading a path already well worn by others attempting to do the same from the Andes to New England. Whatever virtues this unrestrained enthusiasm might have, as historical method it falls well short of defensibility.

This vulnerability to refutation is no light matter, for, as Popper implies, the process of justification inherently and invariably entails seeking out signs of falsehood and not signs of truth. To consider the operational tactics of the High Counters—or, for that matter, of any who seek to count—as avoidance behavior is scarcely to exaggerate. Although such an approach often gains adherents in the short run, in the long term this penchant to beg rather than ask questions, combined with a formidable lack of curiosity about the content and legitimacy of competing evidence and a concomitant failure systematically to engage the scholarship of others, can only render this the refuge of the credulous.

Surplus to Requirements

[T]he reason for the depopulation of these Provinces and towns lies . . . in the failure for so many years to repatriate migrant indians to their homes, so that today it would be impossible to find out the identity of each indian, since to disguise their origins they deny their home towns, and even those of newly born children, who are plausibly attributed to different unspecified regions.

—Petition from Indian caciques, 1656, quoted by Thierry Saignes in *Caciques, Tribute and Migration in the Southern Andes*

When we say that good historians accurately represent what they find in the archives, we mean that they look hard for relevant documents, do not discard documents tending to discredit the historical thesis they are propounding, do not misleadingly quote passages out of context, tell the same historical story among themselves that they tell us, and so on.

—Richard Rorty, "Does Academic Freedom Have Philosophical Presuppositions?"

The High Counters treat, or at least express, New World depopulation as a continuous process. The logic of the argument, and especially of the arithmetic behind it, requires two central assumptions: that the differences between the figures in the sources from one time to another represent Indian deaths, and that these figures are reasonably accurate—while a few Indians might have escaped being counted, their numbers were inconsequential. In short, it is assumed that the difference between two numbers represents true and general population decline, and nothing less.

Some have criticized this approach because, in its homogenization, it fails to account for either population recovery between epidemic episodes or the differential impact of disease from one environment to another.[1] Paradoxically, it actually fails, at least in graphic presentation, to treat disease episodes themselves as resulting in unusually rapid decline. In the process it ignores statements such as that made in 1592 by the *licenciado* Francisco Auncibay of the audiencia of Quito, shortly after a serious epidemic had struck the area. Auncibay was impressed by the fact that "[w]hen an epidemic strikes and kills part of the population, it returns to its previous size within a very brief time."[2]

On the other hand, Auncibay's impression might well have been unwittingly influenced by a phenomenon that he, like those interested in depopulation, failed adequately to consider. This is the marked degree of population mobility that characterized the American colonies from the imposition of Spanish rule and probably well before. This phenomenon was particularly marked in colonies where mining was a central feature of the economy. Here I treat largely the viceroyalty of Peru, for which labor migration has been most thoroughly studied. No one doubts that labor migration, whether forced or voluntary, was a salient phenomenon in colonial Peru, as it had been under the Inca regime. The debate concerns the timing, characteristics, and magnitude of migration, as well as—though this is less often considered—its effects on colonial counting. As N. D. Cook has pointed out, "[t]he Andean world the European entered was not a static, closed world, but a world in which there was much movement and change."[3]

In the viceroyalty of Peru the so-called *forasteros* ("outsiders") appear everywhere in the records, eventually to be carefully defined, though never to be as carefully counted. The ubiquity of *forasteros* in Peru introduces a wild card of uncertain significance for depopulation estimates. Generally, at least initially, the *forasteros* were not subject to the *mita* or other institutionalized forms of tribute, and they ranged widely looking for employment. For these and other reasons they either were not or could not be counted. It becomes necessary for those wanting to place faith in the "censuses" of the period to minimize their effect, and the effects of other uncounted groups.[4]

N. D. Cook's study of Peruvian Indian population trends to 1620 is quietly insistent on downplaying the numbers of all such groups before that date. Referring to *yanaconas* (servants of the Incas) and Cañaris (a group allied to the Spaniards, similar to the Tlaxcalans in New Spain), Cook argued that "[i]t is doubtful . . . that there were that many" *yanaconas* after the 1570s; the Cañaris could not have numbered "more than a few hundred"; and the number of descendants of the Incas "could not have been large."[5] He admitted that the *foras-*

tero population posed more of a "dilemma" for him, but he argued that "it is reasonable to believe that at the time of Viceroy Toledo [1569–81] the number of forasteros was insignificant and that almost all natives had been placed under the fiscal regime" as Toledo's reforms had intended.[6] Cook also conceded that by the late seventeenth century this group constituted "a large percentage" of the population in some jurisdictions, although he was confident that it was "highly unlikely the percentage [of *forasteros*] exceeded the percentage found in the returns of the 1750s."[7] At any rate, he preferred to think small in this respect and disregarded them in his calculations.[8] Most significantly for his estimation of overall population decline, Cook concluded that "[b]etween 1570 and 1620 Indian population counts during repartimiento reassessments were relatively accurate."[9]

Yet if the *forastero* proportion in many areas exceeded 50 percent by about 1650, it is difficult to accept that it was of so little significance demographically just thirty years earlier.[10] In discussing in greater detail the provenance of the numbers on which he based his contact population estimate, Cook reiterated his case. While at first conceding that "an undetermined number of males of tribute-paying age [and their dependents] were exempt" from tribute as early as the 1540s, he later retracted the *gravitas* of this by asserting only that "[s]ome Indians may have escaped the census-taker in sixteenth- and seventeenth-century Peru."[11]

By concentrating on Peru the modern state, Cook increased the validity of his statement, since it was to areas such as Potosí (now in Bolivia) that *forasteros* tended to gravitate.[12] But from where? Certainly from, among other places, those *corrigimientos* that remain within Cook's narrower purview. Indeed, by treating only present-day Peru and ignoring neighboring regions that were historically, linguistically, culturally, and economically similar, Cook creates an artificial situation in which many of the areas he studied show local, but illusory, population decline, regardless of other considerations. After all, some areas had to have contributed to the population explosion in mining centers like Potosí—in fact, many did by viceregal fiat. Moreover, other mining areas, such as Huancavelica, are in present-day Peru, and although the evidence is less abundant for them than for Potosí, it is unlikely that conditions there were much different in this particular regard. The most productive years at Huancavelica, as at Potosí, were precisely during the half century between 1570 and 1620.[13]

Others, less interested in determining contact population, have found the *forasteros*—if not always formally designated as such—to have been rather thick on this ground during the earlier period as well.[14] In particular, Karen Vieira Powers's study of the Quito area, far from the major mining centers, led her to conclude that "the total forastero population of the sierra must have been considerable at the turn of the seventeenth century."[15] In support of this conclusion, which directly contradicts Cook's working assumption, she brings to bear a large body of evidence.[16] In sum, she suggests that this evidence "brings into question both the vast depopulation rates in the sixteenth century . . . and the remarkable demographic recovery of the seventeenth century proposed by other historians."[17] William of Occam would likely approve. Even without this evidence the historian's intuition should suggest that regularizing and intensifying the *mita* tribute system in the 1570s would quickly have produced large numbers of Indians seeking to escape the *mita* proper while taking advantage of the economic opportunities the growth of mining in Alto Perú immediately and continuously produced.

Ignoring the *forastero* population, whatever it might have been, inevitably leads to underestimation of Indian population in Peru and contributes to a picture of depopulation that is illusory. Nicolás Sánchez-Albornoz, among others, has pointed this out.[18] Thierry Saignes, however, has been the most assiduous voice in this regard. He points out that "the spectacular impetus in the valleys and the urban-mining centers [of Alto Perú] can be explained only by the installation of a part of the 'natives' coming from the altiplano." Population "decline" in the altiplano, then, resulted in part from emigration rather than death. "In sum, we find in 1645 a number of tributaries that is close to that of 1575. These numbers must prompt us to look again seriously at estimates of depopulation in the southern Andean region."[19] Saignes's argument, and that of others, that we cannot treat depopulation *in vacuo* is palpably correct, yet it has not generally been heeded by those attempting just such estimation. Whether or not the *forastero* population was much less before 1620 than after, it can have resulted only in undercounts in most censuses. Cook reprimands several authors who failed to realize that some counts they imputed to 1591 properly belonged to the early to mid-1570s. He notes that as a result of this, "[a]ny population curve constructed for the 1570s to the 1590s would . . . be much flatter than it should be."[20] Yet ignoring the effects of *forasteros* on population counts has an even greater opposite effect in steepening the slope between 1570 and 1620.

The arithmetical consequences of this neglect are not insignificant. By virtue of a remorseless "arithmetic of the slope," positing a larger population around the turn of the seventeenth century for many regions of Peru is actually likely to have opposite effects on estimates of contact population. If one uses a depopulation curve, as N. D. Cook does for Peru (and Sherburne Cook and Woodrow Borah for central Mexico), then postulating high population levels after the conquest would tend to flatten the slope of that curve for the later period and, by extension, for the earlier period as well, reducing the contact population accordingly. Increasing the figures that Cook advances for Peru in 1620, then, results in a significantly lower estimate for 1520 in the kind of teeter-totter effect imposed by the methodology.

Cook is right in terming the *forastero* matter a dilemma. By its very nature the problem is intractable—after all, the *forasteros* themselves and those having an interest in unmonitored migrant labor made it impossible to count this group accurately. Thus their precise numbers, particularly in the earlier years before the *forasteros* became a recognized and denominated element of society, must remain little more than an academic curiosity. It would hardly be anachronistic to regard the *forasteros* as the undocumented aliens of their times. Inasmuch as U.S. authorities in the 1990s freely admit that they cannot know the number of undocumented aliens in the United States, it seems inappropriate to believe that we can somehow account for similar subterranean groups in Peru more than four centuries ago. This is hardly reason, though, to disregard the matter (or to speak reassuringly of "the constant vigilance" of the tax assessors), any more than attempts to calculate the dimensions of the Atlantic slave trade can omit consideration of the numbers of Africans transported by interlopers, smugglers, and other groups whose very purpose was to avoid detection.[21]

In her study of migrancy in the audiencia of Quito, Powers notes that rural-urban population movements "had the effect of creating an illusion of demographic growth in the central and north-central sierra."[22] Powers also speaks of numerous successful efforts to hide Indians, with the result that "much of the migrant population . . . did not appear in sixteenth-century demographics." More persistent Spanish efforts in the seventeenth century brought more of the *forasteros* into the tribute system, but Powers again does not infer the effects of this in projecting backward to seek a contact population; she views it only as "artificially inflating the highland statistics of the 1660s and 1670s."[23]

Finally, Powers speaks of refuges in the western and eastern lowlands of Quito right from the 1530s.[24] Then, of course, there was the rump Inca successor state at Vilcabamba, surely not counted by the Spanish—what was its population? And where did it go on the state's fall? Although the opportunities for flight in Peru were hardly as frequent and ready-to-hand as they were in, say, Chile, the occasions for other forms of evasive action were numerous and appealing. The implications of migration for population estimates is potentially especially severe whenever, as in the case of Cook's estimates of Indian population in Peru in the late sixteenth century, the totals are based on aggregating a large number of local counts taken over a period of many years.[25]

For New Spain, less has been done, but enough to suggest similar stimulus-response patterns. As early as 1962 José Miranda argued that Cook and Borah's proposed nadir of 1.2 million Indians about 1650 was both too low and too late. In large part he based his argument on his suspicion that they had not taken "the great mobility" of the Indians into account and that great numbers of "uncounted tributaries" would have increased their figure substantially.[26] More recent studies of the mining centers of New Spain, for the sixteenth century as well as the seventeenth, indicate that Miranda was right and that, as in Peru, these centers served as magnets for enforced and voluntary immigration.[27]

The High Counters tend to overlook evidence of population movement in precontact times as well. Thus Dobyns uses reports of abandoned pueblos in the chronicles of the Coronado expedition to argue for depopulation even while citing examples of population movement.[28] There is, however, a superfluity of evidence from the U.S. Southwest showing that population movement was an inevitable response to untoward climatic conditions—in particular, to aridity—for many centuries before contact.[29] Using abandoned sites as an argument for postcontact epidemics, then, is useless.

A measure of the High Counters' obstinacy regarding migration is Linda Newson's suggestion that migration might help to account for documented increases in population in the audiencia of Quito from the 1590s, without at the same time considering the fairly plain obverse.[30] Where, for instance, did these implied immigrants come from? Newson apparently does not care to address this question and its implications; indeed, her suggestion immediately follows a discussion of what she reckons—following Borah and Cook—as *absolute* population losses of between 13.18 to 1 and 26.02 to 1 in New Spain.

Elsewhere in the same article Newson mentions migration and flight as consequences of the Potosí *mita,* but still the penny does not drop.[31]

In another work Newson comments on a report from "several decades [fourteen years actually] after [the] Spanish conquest" that among the Cañaris of southern Ecuador the women outnumbered the men by fifteen to one. This disparity she—and her source—attribute solely to Inca massacres shortly before the Spaniards arrived, treating it as an absolute loss.[32] For others such a disparity would suggest that a thriving business in labor migration was at least partly responsible, mitigating the extent of real depopulation.[33] But again the notion seems not to occur.[34]

Likewise, Cook and Borah postulate depopulation rates of up to 70 percent for Yucatán during the sixteenth century, basing this on a few encomienda counts and early eyeball estimates of town sizes. In accounting for this decline they suggest that, based on their own calculations, "[t]he successful occupation of Yucatan by the Spaniards on their third entry and the great rebellion of 1545–1547 may have been much more destructive of Indian life than the prolonged fighting of the first two entries and must [*ex hypothesi*] have been much more devastating than is implied by the written records."[35]

Later Cook and Borah discuss the phenomenon of "fugitivism," which was particularly prevalent in Yucatán. They use it, however, only to account for otherwise inexplicable discrepancies in their estimates for the seventeenth century.[36] Although they duly note that some sources speak of large-scale flight before 1550, at no point does this fact enter their calculations derived from figures from the encomiendas, the very institutions that prompted such flight.[37]

Cook and Borah for Mexico, N. D. Cook for Peru, and Newson for Ecuador all make sharp distinctions between lowland and highland depopulation.[38] In each case they attribute this almost entirely to differential epidemiological patterns—certain diseases, especially malaria, did great damage in the hot and wet lowlands but had little effect in drier, cooler areas.[39] This makes sense, and this difference no doubt contributed to population decline. But it implies for the lowlands an absolute and catastrophic population loss of the kind that appeals to the High Counters.

Looked at in terms of migration, however, the loss is only relative—some part of the missing lowland Indians is counted in the highland areas, where most of the mines were, or was not counted at all, the Indians being in transit or in hiding. In this view of things the lowlands were a source of labor—quite like many rural areas in southern Africa whose men go off to the gold-producing Rand area, some temporarily, some permanently, because the population of the mining region is inadequate to supply all the mines' labor needs.[40] If anything, the pattern in early colonial America would have been more pronounced because of the labor-intensive nature of most extracting operations at the time.

─────────

When, as is most often the case for the High Counters, depopulation is measured by comparing population estimates at two periods of time, ignoring the possibility and effects of population movement merely turns the difference into an absolute loss. Ignoring the possibility that the loss in one place might have been compensated by gains elsewhere due to migration, the High Counters actually compound the damage by extrapolation, thereby imputing loss everywhere as people die with no effort to save themselves by flight.[41] Indeed, ignoring the possibility of internal and invisible migration in the sixteenth century has more than merely arithmetical consequences. It perpetuates and reinforces the notion that the Indians immediately fell into a kind of universal stupor that prevented them from acting in their own interests.[42] Instead, they simply allowed themselves to be acted upon in whatever ways the conquerors happened to choose. Thus, for instance, they allowed themselves to be herded to the mines for a tour of duty and either died during it or promptly returned home, to be counted, at its end.

This belief is not only unconsciously demeaning but is also contradicted by a host of evidence that has scarcely been tapped here. Statements such as that by a Spanish official in Peru in 1580 festoon the literature: "For every ten Indians that come to Potosí," he observed, "only six return home."[43] Chances are that the proportion of those preferring to stay rather than return home only increased—and not just in Potosí—along with new economic opportunities.

In looking at North America, where the opportunities were far fewer, Bruce Trigger made what ought to be a commonplace assertion: "In areas where contact became frequent, it does not appear to have been long before all native perceptions and behavior were significantly influenced by rational appraisals of Europeans and what they had to offer."[44] The procedures of the High Counters, which consist largely of undifferentiated arithmetic and which posit steady rates of decline among a helpless and hapless Indian population, turn this notion on its head.[45]

Colonial Cloning

*The least facet of bone, the slightest apophysis, have a determinate
character relative to the class, the order, the genus, and the species to
which they belong, to the point that, any time we possess merely a single extremity of a well-preserved bone, we are able, with diligence and
intelligent resort to analogy and effective comparison, to determine
[the missing parts] as surely as if we possessed the entire animal.*

—Georges Cuvier,
Discours sur les révolutions de la surface du globe

*In the space of one hundred and seventy-six years the Lower Missis-
sippi has shortened itself two hundred and forty-two miles. That is an
average of a trifle over one mile and a third per year. Therefore, any
calm person, who is not blind or idiotic, can see that in the Old
Oölitic Silurian Period, just a million years ago next November, the
Lower Mississippi River was upward of one million three hundred
thousand miles long, and stuck out over the Gulf of Mexico like a
fishing-rod. And by the same token any person can see that seven hundred and forty-two years from now the Lower Mississippi will be only
a mile and three-quarters long. . . . There is something fascinating
about science. One gets such wholesale returns of conjecture out of
such a trifling investment of fact.*

—Mark Twain, *Life on the Mississippi*

Mark Twain's satirical comment on the delights and dangers of extrapolation reads uncannily like another comment, this one by the historian Nicolás Sánchez-Albornoz, dealing only with the delights and
not, apparently, intended as satire:

> To obtain the total population figure for a locality or region from this
> fiscal information, the recorded numbers should be multiplied by a fac-

tor representing each individual's dependents. Then the omitted categories should be estimated and added. Finally, after using all the available sources, the gaps should be filled in by extrapolations.[1]

As Sánchez-Albornoz suggests, every estimate by a High Counter is quintessentially an exercise in extrapolation. No figure is this literature has been reached in any other way, since it is the High Counters' fundamental premise that the figures in the records never actually represent all the available Indians. Rather, they constitute a double residue. In the first place they are typically held to represent adult males—warriors and workers—rather than the population at large. Second, the populations in the sources are seen as remnants of much larger, but undetermined, precontact populations, diminished through disease and societal malaise.

If an estimate of Indian numbers is held to represent only 20 percent of the actual population, and if that population in turn is held to have been reduced by as much as one-half between 1492 and the time of the count (perhaps more if the count occurred after about 1550), then every number found in the sources must be multiplied by ten in order to approximate the population at the time of contact. Such numbers can be little more than an ideology that inheres in whatever multiplier is chosen. Ten or twenty might be common multipliers, but, as we have seen, they are sometimes higher, sometimes lower. The multiplier is unconditionally a creation of modern scholarship rather than the product of the sources, in which, by this definition, nine or more Indians always hide behind the tenth.

People-counting is an activity of great antiquity, but its scientific persona, the census, is much more recent, and the demonstrably accurate census continues to be an elusive phenomenon. Since extrapolation is inherently subjective, it might be useful to begin by looking at a few cases in which extrapolation has been used in ways that can be regarded only as nonsensical, at least from our present perspective.[2] Doing this will suggest how easily extrapolaters can fall victim to their devotion.

In 1837 the philosopher Thomas Dick published a work entitled *Celestial Scenery* as a contribution to an ongoing debate over the existence and nature of extraterrestrial life.[3] Dick was a dedicated believer in such life and in its demonstrability and scriptural justification. He began *Celestial Scenery* by advising readers that it was "intended for the instruction of general readers, to direct their attention to the study of the heavens, and to present to their view sublime objects of contemplation." Dick admitted that he had confined himself "chiefly to the exhibition of *facts*, the foundation on which they rest, and the reasonings by which they are supported."[4] Dick wished to establish populations for the other members of the solar system. Lacking figures, he was forced to project. He reckoned that the density of population of England was 280 persons per square mile, and he applied this figure to the remaining planets, to the largest of the asteroids, to the satellites of Jupiter, Saturn, and Uranus (Pluto was yet to be discovered), and even to the rings, and the edges of the rings, of Saturn. Armed with these premises, Dick calculated the population of each of fifteen units.[5]

Given his assumptions, it is no surprise that in every case but the asteroid Vesta his figures were immense. His method is demonstrated in the way he determined the population of Mercury:

> [T]he earth is above fifteen times larger than Mercury. Notwithstanding the comparatively diminutive size of this planet, it is capable of containing a population upon its surface much greater than has ever been supported on the surface of the earth during any time of its history. . . . At the rate of population now stated [280 per square mile], it is sufficiently ample to contain 8,960,000,000, . . . which is more than eleven times the present population of our globe.[6]

Dick continued with a minor caveat: "And although the one-half of the surface of this planet were to be considered as covered with water, it would still contain nearly six times the population of the earth." Having made this point, Dick ignored it in all his calculations aimed at estimating the population of the solar system. After repeating this exercise fourteen more times, Dick arrived at a total population— 21,891,974,404,480. He expected that this number would prove to be a minimum and would increase as further planets were discovered.[7]

From all appearances, Dick was deadly serious in all his presumptions and calculations. He anticipated and answered potential criticism about, for instance, the apparent lack of atmospheres in these heavenly bodies by postulating that they were invisible because, in contrast to earth's atmosphere, they were "perfectly pure and transparent."[8] True, not a single one of these twenty-two trillion people had ever been spotted, but Dick was convinced that it would be only a matter of time before that happened, and he found readers and reviewers who agreed with him, receiving public approbation and academic honors for his writings.[9] In fact, Dick was not yet finished. He continued to extrapolate and a few years later was able to conclude that "the living inhabitants" in the solar system numbered "60,573,000,000,000,000,000,000,000," a number which, he rightly noted, "transcends human conception."[10]

Before we succumb to the temptation to chuckle at these conclusions—the divine right of the present to judge the past—we need to apply context. Dick operated under certain hypotheses to which he added certain assumptions not wholly implausible for the time. To lend credibility to these he extrapolated on the basis of certain further assumptions about population density and surface area. In other words, he adopted a primitive carrying capacity argument to test his premises and, by virtue of thick helpings of *petitio principii,* he made it work to his satisfaction.

We have seen how the High Counters treat the numbers generated by historical sources as more likely to be true than the words that accompany them, as though it were actually more difficult to create a false number than a false narration. The notion that numbers, besides being exact, are less vulnerable to error or falsification carries over into the High Counters' arithmetical procedures, in which the appearance of exactitude, for instance, is fundamental. So, too, is their theory of the numbers behind the numbers. They treat phenomena such as Cortés's "more than 149,000" (discussed in chapter 15) as the result of some now-lost calculation rather than as a figure plucked from the thin air of Cortés's overall discursive strategy. This trust in numbers extends to a similar, but more widespread, belief in the objectivity of their own extrapolative measures. In a sense, they turn on its head the statistical rule that probabilities multiplied are probabilities lessened. In the process their own created numbers, each of which is usually the product of some number found in a source multiplied by some depopulation factor, assume a status that fails to account for their origins.

Stripped to its arithmetical bare bones, the High Counters' method can fairly by represented by the formula $X = e (a + b + c + d)$. In this formula X is the population at or just before the time of contact; a is the number in some recorded postcontact estimate; $b, c,$ and d, are all hypothesized uncounted elements of the population (women, children, the aged, other tribute-exempt individuals); and e is the factor by which depopulation has allegedly taken place—that is, the factor by which population was greater at the time of contact. The most palpable aspect of this is that the High Counters are seeking to solve for X on the basis of four unknowns (numbers not in the records) and one possibly known (the recorded estimate, about whose reliability they can only speculate). It is no less obvious that changing any of these has a profound ripple effect. These are hardly novel insights—no more than garden-variety arithmetical observations—yet their implications elude the High Counters and their adherents alike.[11]

Algebraically such a formulation "transcends human conception" no less that Thomas Dick's septillions. As a multiplicative chain, changing even the smallest value in it changes the total proportionately; changing "1" to "2" could result in changing 1 million to 2 million without any more manipulations at all. And of course, plugging in numbers subjectively reached (and there are virtually no numbers in the High Counters' canon that can escape this imputation) immediately renders the formula, and its results, dangerously unbounded, lacking discipline and an undistilled sense of moderation.[12]

———

A genus of extrapolation that the High Counters use heavily is back projection. An effect of the use of this method—adopted for Hispaniola, central Mexico, and Peru—is that the higher the estimates are after a certain point, the lower the projected contact population becomes, because the *rate* of depopulation becomes less precipitous. It is necessary only to establish a purported rate of decline for any segment of a population, or any span of time, and then extrapolate it to the remainder. We saw in chapter 12 how this has prompted the High Counters to ignore the effects of flight and labor migration in order to achieve the steepest possible line of population decline by preferring the smallest possible figures for the late sixteenth century and concomitantly higher figures before that.[13]

Conversely, imposing a one-size-fits-all depopulation ratio requires a different set of assumptions to serve its purpose. The first of these is to discern as high a "nadir" population as possible, since it is this number that is to be multiplied by the depopulation ratio. The second procedure is painfully obvious—increase that ratio. Again, multiplicative concatenation applies. Increase the nadir population—the simplest procedure—and the presumed contact population increases accordingly, with no need to tamper with the depopulation ratio. If circumstances preclude this, however, then the depopulation ratio is at hand, often assisted by adding an epidemic or two to the recipe. When needs demand, both the nadir population and the depopulation ratio can be increased: thus 1 × 10 becomes, say, 1.5 × 20, and the contact population is tripled forthwith.[14]

High numbers are deemed acceptable only if they occur early, say, in the first forty years or so after conquest. Should they occur later than that, they tend to be suspect because of their effect on the slope of the depopulation curve. Conversely, high numbers are always welcome in a depopulation ratio, because they can lead only to projections that are higher yet. Thus there has been no concern at all about the virtual certainty that the numbers the High Counters take to be "nadirs" must always represent a time either before or after the imperceptible moment of true nadir.

And what are the bounds on these procedures? There are none.[15] This open-endedness is illustrated in efforts to calculate population growth from one point in time to a later point in order to accommodate a later hypothesized population. David Stannard did this for Hawaii in suggesting a contact population of 800,000 there. In the process Stannard assumed a first-century discovery date by a party consisting of fifty men and fifty women, continuous settlement thereafter, and an average annual growth rate of 0.9 percent for the first three hundred years and 0.52 percent thereafter.[16] None of this seems wildly implausible, although none of it is demonstrably accurate either.

However, a more nuanced reading of the archaeological record suggests that it is "relatively certain" that "the establishment of Polynesian populations [that is, the attainment of viable population levels] . . . was accomplished sometime after A.D. 600."[17] Some colonizers might have arrived several centuries earlier but did not increase steadily, and the counting, whatever growth rate is postulated, should begin only after A.D. 600. O. A. Bushnell, on the other hand, argues that Stannard's one hundred people and his growth rates are both too high. Bushnell's estimate for Hawaii's contact population, like Stannard's, is neither implausible nor demonstrable, even though it is only one-eighth that of Stannard's.[18]

In their writings the High Counters complement extrapolative arithmetic with discursive strategies, numbers with words, in a way that has clearly proved highly effective. It would be impossible to address the totality of this work, although I have already cited some examples. Instead, I use Cook and Borah's study of the Mixteca Alta as a microcosm.[19] A brief study, it nonetheless manages to convey vividly the ways in which language is used to sell arguments and dispel doubts and dubious evidence.

Cook and Borah begin by asserting that "startling" and heavy preconquest soil erosion "must have been the work of a rather dense population over a very long span of time."[20] Maybe so, but there are certainly enough examples of erosion from other causes to make their use of "must have" unjustified. But "must have" and its rhetorical variations are commonplace constructions in the High Counters' discourse.[21] So is "agree(s)," as in the flat assertion that their population estimate of 600,000 to 800,000 in 1520 "agrees well with the evidence from the stratigraphic study of erosion that there was a dense population."[22]

Seeking to construct a depopulation curve ("depletion rate"), Cook and Borah alight on some "counts" of tributaries from the 1560s. Typically, they refer to these counts—and the much larger numbers that they squeeze from them—as "firm," "valid," and "solid"— in short, as usable.[23] As they note, though, these numbers derive from practically every year in the 1560s and thus are even farther from being censuslike than is usual in these cases. Taking them to be so merely implies that the male adults in the forty towns in question sat at home waiting for their turn to be counted. They did not, for instance, take advantage of labor opportunities, were not pressed into service elsewhere by the colonial authorities, did not choose to relocate their domiciles—they simply waited.[24] This would have been quite at variance with the alacrity with which the Indians were availing themselves of their legal remedies at the very same time.[25]

One sentence in the notes to one of the tables in *The Population of the Mixteca Alta* neatly crystallizes one of Cook and Borah's favorite rhetorical devices: "For pre-Conquest statements [of population] a factor of 4.5 [family members] per vecino or tributary has been used; for 1569 counts, a factor of 2.8 per tributary."[26] In this way any numbers found in sources from the colonial period are already arithmetically reduced by nearly 40 percent compared with estimates for earlier time periods, even before further calculations ensue. It is small wonder that the depopulation curves which Cook and Borah derive from such procedures are invariably about as steep as they can be without actually falling over. Looking at their language is useful here as well; when they speak of "pre-Conquest statements" they actually mean statements about preconquest populations emanating, in this case, from fifty years later—a very different, and much slighter, thing.[27]

Cook and Borah steepen the slope of their depopulation curve by taking 1569 "as the average date of the counts" in question. Conceding that the undated report that is their source is usually consigned to 1571, they demur: "Obviously the counts given in it are earlier."[28] Again, maybe so, but only "maybe," and not "obviously." We can assume that in making their decision the authors realized that pushing the date back even two years would have had significant ripple effects on the slope. Again, employing an unjustifiably strong term has presumably helped to deter criticism. At the least, Cook and Borah should have presented readers with an alternative curve based on the date 1571.

With respect to four of the largest towns in the area, Cook and Borah take heart in the fact that after a series of manipulations, none of them demonstrably valid, their calculations and earlier estimates differ "in no instance" by "more than 40 per cent."[29] Since the pairs of figures are, respectively, 12,000 and 18,900, 4,000 and 3,967, 25,000+ and 21,040, and 10,000 and 7,700, this is strictly the case only if measured the short way, if "more than 25,000" is taken to mean also less than 35,000, and if Cook and Borah's assumptions regarding Tlaxiaco, the town with the minimal difference, are correct. It also implies that a 40 percent discrepancy is insignificant.[30] When all is said and done, we most likely have another case in which both the early estimates—made from ten to fifty years after the fact—and modern calculations are indeterminably wrong.

Cook and Borah admonished Ronald Spores for believing, like George Kubler, in a population increase between 1550 and 1570. Such an increase, they insist, "flies in the face of all known population behavior."[31] By that they mean that it contradicts their own imposed population regime. Actually, Spores was making this argument for only a single town, Yanhuitlán, on the basis of a count there of 12,207 people "three years old and above," about 1546–48, a point which Cook and Borah ignore. Not exactly ignore, actually; this count emanates from the very *suma de visitas* that Cook and Borah had analyzed just eight years before.[32] In fact, they were then well aware of it—they had added 11.1 percent to it for "nursing infants" and derived a new figure, 13,563.[33] Now, however, this number suggested that population had not remorselessly declined after all, at least not in Yanhuitlán.[34] As a result they not only disregarded it themselves but also criticized Spores for doing exactly what they had earlier done themselves—using it.[35]

This odd performance hardly dampens Cook and Borah's opinion of their own work—and in the capacity of number-crunching to overcome every deficiency. Scattered throughout their discussion of the Mixteca Alta are statements reminiscent of others in the rest of their work. An example is the observation that "for the present purpose the exponential function is less complex to handle than the log-

log function, is adequate to cover the data at hand, and introduces no serious discrepancy."[36] More than an observation, this statement is a preemptive strike. Intended to justify their own procedures, these are also attempts to bludgeon possible resistance into submission. Presumably the hope is that such casual and iterated statements will deter others from challenging their work.

As we have seen several times, an important form of extrapolation in the High Counters' writings is their use of the term *indios*. The issue is exemplified well in their treatment of the Mixteca Alta, where they estimate the "population in persons" in eight towns as 216,900 at conquest. Of this figure they ascribe 90,000, or more than 40 percent, to the town of Yanhuitlán.[37] They do this on the grounds that in 1630 Bernabé Cobo wrote that the town "formerly had 20,000 Indians [*indios*]," adding that "now [1630] they have no more than 400."[38] Using their standard multiplier, they reach 90,000 for the total population. Thus, once again they treat the term *indios* as representing adult males, synonymous with *tributarios* or *vecinos*. They refer as well to a comment by Juan de Zumárraga in 1529 about the neighboring town of Tepozcolula in this way: "Zumárraga says vecinos = more than 25,000."[39] Wrong; Zumárraga wrote of "mas de veinte é cinco mill *indios*."[40] In an effort to maximize extrapolative possibilities, Cook and Borah simply insinuate the word *vecinos* into Zumárraga's mouth because it suits their purposes.

All this crystallizes the issue and raises a question: why would Zumárraga and Cobo, both clerics, think and write in terms of adult males when they surely regarded every Indian as a soul and not as a worker? More germanely, why do the High Counters treat Motolinía's millions of *indios* as an inclusive count while they regard smaller numbers advanced under roughly the same circumstances as exclusive? The simple answer is, because they have no choice. They can hardly treat the baptismal numbers discussed in chapter 18 as exclusionary—they are simply too large. Otherwise, though, they have more room for manuever. It is at least possible to think of 90,000 Indians in Yanhuitlán even though imagining 36 million Indians in New Spain is not.

This consistently inconsistent treatment of the most basic term in the sources reveals several rather unedifying aspects of the High Counters' method. The worst, but hardly the least common, is changing outright the testimony of their sources, as they do when they drag Zumárraga into their camp. The ways in which they multiply *indios* whenever they can, but are shrewd enough to avoid when they cannot—always without indicating their patterns of use—also points to a problematic discursive style. In most cases there is no way to know for sure whether *indios* was intended to be inclusive or exclusive. However, certain rough-and-ready distinctions seem reasonable. At one extreme, it should be assumed that missionaries talking about *indios* were talking about people of all ages and both genders. Conversely, when *indios* is used appositively with *tributarios* or the context is one of tribute or labor, it seems reasonable to treat the numbers as representing some portion of the population, though not necessarily only adult males.[41] Many, perhaps most, cases would fall between these extremes and require a delicate hand in interpreting them.[42] That light touch is largely absent from the High Counter literature.

———————

It would hardly be fair to suggest that the High Counters are alone in believing that extrapolation can overcome almost any deficiency in direct evidence. Quite the contrary; history and, especially, archaeology are replete with efforts to make too much from too little.[43] The theory that there is a necessary, if sometimes loose, correlation between roof and/or floor space and overall population has been debated for several decades, although no consensus has been reached.[44] As John Scarry shows for an Apalachee site, using various formulas can produce maximal estimates that are nearly four and a half times greater than minimal estimates for the same site.[45] In the same way, Keith Kintigh points out that he and others have demonstrated that for the Zuñi, "extant data can be used to support *drastically* different demographic reconstructions using alternative sets of plausible assumptions."[46] Thus, the degree of variance even at the lowest possible level of measurement precludes sensible population estimates.[47] It is a practice as well to treat pottery remains as somehow indicating the size of the population that left them.[48]

There are differences in both degree and kind, however, that tend to render the High Counters' efforts particularly suspect. First, they seldom are satisfied with a single extrapolation but string them together over both time and space.[49] While this can be arithmetically disastrous, the second characteristic premise is likely to be even more so. This is the idea that despite the argument for severe discontinuities, even ruptures, between pre- and postcontact periods, certain data from the latter—for example, tribute levels and household occupancy rates—remained consistent with those of the past.

The power of this fetish for extrapolation can readily be seen in the attempts made during the seventeenth and eighteenth centuries to deal with the dimensions of Noah's ark.[50] The ongoing discovery of more and more and larger and larger specimens of animal life imposed heroic measures on those intent on swallowing the biblical account whole. For instance, the notion of a single deck devoted to animals with smaller decks for supplies and people evolved into the notion of a ship with three decks for animals alone, and eventually even of five.[51] At the same time, the "cubit" used in the account also became larger and larger, so that eventually an ark emerged that looked, as one commentator put it, like "a shoebox or modern hotel."[52] Although efforts to accommodate the size of the ark to its purported residents eventually dropped out of mainline theological argumentation, they live on in certain literalist circles, growing ever more convoluted as they exceed the bounds of physical impossibility by greater and greater margins.[53]

Recently Rodney Stark has investigated certain aspects of early Christianity. Writing that even though the data are exiguous, "*[w]e must quantify,*" Stark goes on to do just that. "What we need is [sic] at least two plausible numbers to provide the basis for extrapolating the probable rate of early Christian growth." The first of these (1,000 Christians in A.D. 40) he constructs from a few biblical references, even though he duly recognizes that "[t]hese are not statistics." The second number he never really finds either, but uses a composite of modern estimates of from 5 million to 7.5 million Christians in about A.D. 300. Having already decided on a growth rate of 40 percent per decade, he produces a figure of 6,299,832 Christians in 300 and 33,882,008 in 350.[54]

Stark's beginning figure is important but emphatically problematic. He states that "several months after the Crucifixion there were 120 Christians" and notes a later reference to five thousand. The first number, however, offered by the author of the Acts of the Apostles and pertaining to several weeks after the crucifixion, is clearly not inclusive, apparently referring only to men and only to those locally available for a meeting called to elect a successor to Judas.[55] Moreover, in another book of the New Testament, Paul speaks of Christ's appearing to "more than five hundred" disciples at about the same time.[56] Whether this latter group included the 120 (a symbolic number in any case) mentioned in Acts no one knows. And if both groups included only men, then there were likely to have been well over one thousand Christians as early as A.D. 29. Thus Stark's estimate of one thousand more than a decade later must be too low by a large percentage.

In fact, Stark speaks of a "later" reference to "5,000 believers."

How much later is uncertain, but it is more likely to have been before
A.D. 40 than after.[57] The biblical account speaks of "the number of
men" as five thousand, allowing us once again to suspect that the actual number might have been twice this.[58] Stark thinks it "wise to be
conservative" in his initial estimate, but he is ridiculously so in light
of the evidence he chooses to rely on, which suggests a Christian population as much as ten times that which he posits.

Paradoxically, but symptomatically, this trouble with the
sources does not really matter, since Stark unabashedly manipulates
his growth rate in order to ensure that the figure it produces for
A.D. 300 falls within the range of other estimates based on different
criteria. Having done this, he is still able to find it "very encouraging
. . . that [his hypothesized growth rate] is exceedingly close to the average growth rate of 43 percent per decade that the Mormon church
has maintained over the past century." He goes on: "Thus we know
that the numerical goals Christianity needed to achieve are entirely in
keeping with modern experience, and we are not forced to seek exceptional explanations."[59] The element of mock surprise combined
with claims to actual source-based knowledge will surprise no one familiar with the procedures of the High Counters.

Borah and Cook are on record with the opinion that "[r]igid and uncritical extrapolation by whatever method . . . is likely to give misleading estimates of the pre-Conquest Indian population."[60] The observation comes late in their work on the problem and is in large part belied
by their methodology before and after the statement appeared in print.
Certainly it is belied by statements like Simpson's comment on depopulation late in the sixteenth century: "In the same 173 encomienda
towns the decline in population . . . [was] 44.3 per cent, which we
might accept as the standard rate of decline for all towns."[61]

Clearly, and despite the disclaimers, such mathematics lacks
subtlety and is carefully brewed to taste, and it betrays an unflagging
commitment to easy but vacuous extrapolative measures. Beyond this,
as we can see from examples cited throughout the present work, the
ways in which High Counters have applied these expedients could
scarcely be considered critical in any of the usual senses of the term.
They, and others like them, exemplify what M. M. Postan once called
"the lure of aggregates," a temptation that "inevitably incur[s] the risk
of errors on a truly heroic scale."[62]

It seems fitting to close this discussion by quoting part of the
debate over the Navigation Bill in the British Parliament in 1849:

[T]he lively impression was made on all minds . . . that there was hardly anything that might not be proved by such documents [trade statistics]; that they could be used equally by both sides; that, in short, you could prove anything and everything by their assistance. . . . It is easy to add a little here, and subtract a little there; gently to slip in a figure, it may be a cypher, among your data; slyly to make what seems a reasonable postulate in your premises, but which turns out in the result to be a begging of the question—and behold you gain your point, and triumph, unless it is found that your adversary, having access to the same stores of arithmetic, just proves his case and refutes yours with the same facility.[63]

The Jury Will Disregard

If there's anything I detest more than another, it is that spirit of historical inquiry which doubts everything, that modern spirit which destroys all the illusions and all the heroes which have been the inspiration of patriotism through all the centuries.

—Chauncey Depew, on the Columbian
quatercentenary, quoted by Howard Zinn
in "1492–1992: A Historian's Perspective"

Unto you it is given to know the mysteries of the kingdom of heaven, but to [the multitude] it is not given.

—Matthew 13:11

"Approximately 56 million people died as the result of European exploration in the New World."[1] With these words Francis Black launched a discussion of the reasons why New World populations were so devastated by new diseases. His paper appeared in *Science,* a journal with a wide readership interested in scientific or scientific-like matters but who need to be spoon-fed on occasion. Black not only wrote in a categorical fashion but also, in devising his number, placed 5 million deaths alone "in Australia and the Pacific" without further ado—or justification.[2] Black then proceeded to his argument; symptomatically, it was an argument that hardly required such large numbers, or any numbers at all, unless as an attention-getting mechanism.[3]

Black's discursive tactics, particularly his annihilation of alternatives, remind us that scholarly ideas, like diseases, need to find new carriers or they decline and disappear. Many arguments reach beyond their origins to seek out converts and a larger public domain. I look briefly at the effects of this in the contact population debate, for the High Counters have been both energetic and effective in reaching new audiences.

A recent series of showcase trials—those of the Menendez brothers, the police officers in the Rodney King beating case, and O. J. Simpson—has forced us to realize the quintessentially central role of the arts of persuasion and manipulation in playing to a jury. What we learned was probably disconcerting and disheartening to many. First, it became clear that the audience—the jury—was meticulously selected to make it amenable to particular arguments. We also learned that what the jury was permitted to hear and to ponder fell far short of the admitted circumstances of the cases. Indeed, it became clear that juries were forced to deliberate and conclude on the basis of carefully preselected packages of information. Finally, we learned that either by nature or by protocol, juries are a passive, even though decisive, part of the judicial process; however much they might feel deprived of basic information, however much they might resent it, there is little they can do about it, short of reaching a verdict that responds to these feelings.[4]

Selling a case to a jury marks even the best scholarship. Data are identified, gathered, assembled, treated, and finally presented to a prospective jury for judgment. This jury, the readership of books and articles, is usually content to rely on the case put before it rather than seeking to test the case itself. Like members of a courtroom jury, readers are relatively passive players in the game as it is actually played out. While this role is more a choice than a structural requirement, it is a choice very much tailored to, and shaped by, the difficulties involved in readers' testing the cases put before them. In turn, scholars putting a case often see it as a *particular* case and act like prosecutors or defense attorneys, but not both. They are satisfied to present one side of the case as if no others co-existed, and to summon up only the evidence required to support that side. It seems that this temptation becomes stronger when an audience is unfamiliar with a subject. The farther an argument reaches out from its rarefied and restricted ambiance to what we might call the public domain, the more unnuanced and unbalanced it becomes.

The public domain consists of many smaller domains, according to their distance from the home park of the argument. After trying to persuade those in their own field, scholars reach out to those in nearby disciplines, seeking to expand the effects of their case little by little. For the High Counters, who come from a variety of disciplinary backgrounds, these fields have been Latin American colonial history in particular, but also the history of European expansion and the historical demography of other areas of the world such as Oceania, the Far

East, and sub-Saharan Africa. Beyond this we have other academic disciplines not strongly interested in the problem as such but curious about how other scholars go about their business. Then we have the educated, interested public, in some ways the natural target of most arguments because success with this audience bodes well for enhanced status within a writer's own field. Finally, there is Everyman, whose latent interest is presumed capable of being aroused. I will discuss examples of each of these in turn, concentrating on the ways in which arguments adapt to their audiences.[5] Since the writings of the High Counters are extensive and their market share considerable, my own choices here can only be invidious, even tendentious.

A recent example of preaching to the convertible is Linda Newson's overview of the progress she sees being made toward establishing levels of contact population.[6] Included in one of the many collections of essays published to mark the Columbian quincentenary, it is directed, like its bookmates, toward a largely academic readership. Newson is an archaeologist whose principal interests have been in Central America and Ecuador, but in this essay she attempts to use historical arguments and speak to historians and others about New World depopulation at a level that seeks to avoid the intrusive detail while retaining necessary specificity.

Newson's conclusion is that depopulation was significant, was largely the result of new diseases, and is or will be—and this is the present point—measurable. Newson takes the obligatory potshots at Alfred Kroeber. Her devotion to high numbers is evident in her reference to the "so-called 'skeptical' group" of Kroeber, Angel Rosenblat, and Julian Steward, whose hemispheric estimates ranged from 8.4 million to 15.6 million.[7] Newson's claim that pre–High Counter estimators "dismissed early accounts as exaggerated, although generally without any critical evaluation of the evidence," exemplifies the High Counters' assiduous claims to higher ground as well as higher numbers.[8]

Newson embodies the High Counters' belief system and rhetorical strategy in several ways. Besides believing that demonstrably reliable estimates have already been made, she affirms her faith that unspecified evidence will come to light that will make an indefinite further number of such estimates possible. Nor is she averse to uttering certain truisms as though they were novel insights. She relies uncritically on the late-sixteenth-century engravings of Theodore de Bry and his sons for narrative and visual impact, despite a body of literature demonstrating the dangers in taking these graphic texts literally.[9]

Newson speaks of New World depopulation as "much more complex than is often recognized," even while she espouses a largely unilateral and sometimes simplifying, even monolithic, interpretation of it.[10] By believing in the value of closure, Newson studiously ignores critical comment both in her discussion and in her extensive bibliography of nearly 150 items.[11] Newson rightly praises Dobyns's 1966 article, discussed in chapter 5, as "seminal," and she demonstrates the accuracy of her choice of words by closely emulating his conclusions, his eclectic and Autolycan method of snatching an estimate here and a calculation there as if they were all true and equally significant, and his difficulties in understanding sources.[12]

Alfred W. Crosby has been one of the most influential exponents of the disease model, not only for the Americas but for the entire globe, or at least the European-colonized parts of it. Much of his work has been directed at audiences likely to be intellectually curious but not particularly well grounded in the subject at hand. A worst-case scenario benefits his most recent synthesis of these arguments, and he makes certain to bring into play the notion of early and widespread pandemics thoughout the Americas, asserting that "[s]mallpox may have ranged from the Great Lakes to the pampa in the 1520s and 1530s."[13] Not quite a categorical statement, and not one quite based on any evidence either, but it is enough to leave the notion lingering in the minds of his readers to the exclusion of all other possibilities.

In his immensely influential *Civilisation matérielle, économie et capitalisme* series, Fernand Braudel addressed the question of American Indian depopulation. Although he did not embrace the final Cook and Borah figures for central Mexico unreservedly (they are decribed as "inflated" in the English translation and as "fabuleux" in the French original), neither did he reject them out of hand. Certainly they were the only figures he cited, depriving his readers of the opportunity to judge other estimates or even to be aware of them. More significantly, perhaps, he went on to say, rather ambiguously, that "[n]o one is prepared to accept this [figure] blindly, despite the evidence of archaeologists and of so many of the chroniclers of the Conquest."[14] In short, the onus seems to be on those who dispute the figures of the High Counters: where was *their* evidence, Braudel seemed to ask.

Emmanuel Le Roy Ladurie, another prominent *Annaliste,* accepted one of Sherburne Cook's estimates for central Mexico, although, oddly, it was the lower figure of 11 million that Cook and Leslie Simpson proposed in 1948. He ignored Cook's later work with

Woodrow Borah entirely. As for Hispaniola, he thought Borah and Cook's work to be "a powerfully documented study" and he reproduced their table showing a "geometric rate" of decline. Ladurie also estimated that "perhaps one million" people lived in the New Hebrides alone "before colonization."[15] Immanuel Wallerstein repeated this semi-allegiance in his influential study of "the modern world-system," but thankfully, he had nothing to say about the New Hebrides.[16]

The High Counters' most influential convert at this level, however, was William McNeill, whose *The Rise of the West* and *Plagues and Peoples* have become widely assigned readings in history classes.[17] When McNeill published the first of these in 1963, he was still a catechumen. He cited only Cook and Simpson's lower figures for central Mexico enunciated in 1948 rather than Borah and Cook's much higher estimate that appeared in 1960. And he was cautious, wondering "if [they were] at all accurate" and referring to Rosenblat's lower estimates in counterpoint.[18]

Little more than a decade later McNeill pronounced himself an enthusiastic convert in *Plagues and Peoples,* the title of which explains why. Gone are the lower figures for central Mexico, and along with them the slightest hint of any doubt about the higher ones that supplanted them.[19] "Recent estimates," McNeill intoned, were based on "a sampling of tribute lists, missionary reports, and elaborate statistical arguments." These put the New World population at "about one hundred million," with "twenty-five to thirty million . . . assignable to the Mexican and an approximately equal number to the Andean civilizations." Even Hispaniola had a population of "somewhere between eight and fourteen million" in 1492.[20]

There is no telling where this farrago of misrepresentation originated; ominously, McNeill cited the "interesting summary of the evolution of opinion" in Dobyns's article in *Current Anthropology* but ignored all the "evolution" to concentrate on exaggerating what Dobyns had to say—something not at all easy to achieve. He argued that Cook and Borah's collection of essays in which the Hispaniola estimate appeared was no less than "a sort of climactic demonstration of statistical and critical evaluation."[21] The High Counters' claims—suitably elaborated, though hardly discussed—are by no means the only examples of McNeill's approach. Not surprisingly, given its line of argument, *Plagues and Peoples* is substantially a litany of recorded epidemics presented in their most apocalyptic resonance at every opportunity. And by 1990, the work had already sold more than 75,000 copies.[22]

The quincentenary produced a brief flurry of interest in contact population in the medical literature. Despite the expected incidence of factual errors, the results were not as extreme as might have been feared. Carlos Camargo, for instance, mentioned that estimates for the contact population were "understandably imprecise," adding that a "currently accepted figure is 54 million."[23] He noted estimates ranging from 5 million to 25 million for central Mexico and from 100,000 to 3 million for Hispaniola, without specifying his sources or his own preference.[24] He further suggested a maximum mortality rate of 30 percent for the smallpox epidemic in Mexico in 1520–21, roughly the same figure Robert McCaa has suggested as a reasonable average.[25]

On the other hand, Camargo spoke of "an outbreak . . . of highly infectious febrile illness with respiratory tract symptoms" on Hispaniola in late 1493, which "killed many thousands in Hispaniola and then spread to Cuba, Jamaica, and other Caribbean islands."[26] Here Camargo seems unwisely to depend—he cites no sources—on Guerra's phantom flu epidemic discussed earlier. Doctors and other medical practitioners who depend on such analyses for their views of the nature of disease transmission from Europe to the Americas can only be seriously misled about its timing.[27]

———

The success of the High Counters' work is well illustrated by the fact that their conclusions have reached the general public by way of the popular press. In anticipation of the quincentenary, *U.S. News and World Report* (circulation 2.4 million) addressed the question of the contact population: "Perhaps 40 million throughout the Western Hemisphere, including 10 million in central Mexico, 9 million in Peru and 2 million in the U.S. and Canada."[28] As matters stand, these are not unreasonable figures, which is perhaps why something happened to them on their way to an even larger audience. When *Reader's Digest* (circulation 28 million in 17 languages) adapted the *U.S. News and World Report* story a few months later, this is what it had to say: "By 1492, the Western Hemisphere may have contained 90 million people," of which "about 10 million inhabited what is now the United States and Canada [nothing on the rest of the hemisphere]."[29] This is an intriguing but disheartening state of affairs. What is intriguing is that in less than six months the same authors—or *Reader's Digest* for them—more than doubled one figure and quintupled another, without a word of explanation.[30] What is disheartening is how faithfully this minor episode mirrors so much of the High Counter enterprise in its multiplication without justification.[31] And *U.S. News* continues to present only the very highest figures to its readers.[32]

The quincentenary offered a special opportunity for writers to embrace high population levels in works that concentrated on the disastrous effects of 1492. For instance, Luis Rivera Pagán referred to Cook and Borah's figures for Mexico and N. D. Cook's for Peru as evidence of the magnitude of the catastrophe.[33] In his turn Robert Venables cited 72 million Indians in the Americas, 30 million for central Mexico, 7 million north of Mexico, and 5 million for the present-day United States as "minimum estimates" of the contact population, being careful to cite even higher alternatives as well.[34]

The impulse to increase numbers proportionally to a target audience is readily illustrated beyond the High Counters. Readers of the *Bookseller* in 1985 might have come across the following sensationalist advertisement, complete with a picture of a rat:

> Antioch, A.D. 1098, an army of 300,000 wiped out. Serbia, 1914, 150,000 dead within six months.[35]

The ad was touting the forthcoming re-publication of Hans Zinsser's enormously popular (36 printings between 1934 and 1963) *Rats, Lice, and History,* a history of typhus. Zinsser deferred to no one in bandying unqualified numbers, but in this instance the ad unfairly stated his position, which was that "[d]isease and famine killed so many [of a purported 300,000 at Antioch] and in such a short time that the dead could not be buried."[36]

Zinsser's work is entirely unprovenanced, but William of Tyre, an early chronicler, described the scene: "So frightful was the mortality that scarcely a day passed when at least thirty of forty corpses were not borne out for burial."[37] At this rate it would have taken nearly twenty-five years for 300,000 to die.[38] But then the Crusaders' army was nothing like 300,000 strong when it reached Antioch—desertion, death by starvation or in battle, and side excursions had reduced it so much from its original size of at most 100,000 people (including camp followers) that modern estimates run from 10,000 to 30,000, or 4 percent to 10 percent of Zinsser's publisher's figure.[39] In this way Zinsser's bad history was made worse in a retelling designed to seize the attention of a particular audience.[40]

The case of Will and Ariel Durant's multivolume *The Story of Civilization* offers a special case. Marketed under the imprimatur of the Book-of-the-Month Club for over thirty years, hundreds of thousands of volumes have been sold. Not professionally trained historians, the Durants devoted a shared lifetime to presenting history to those who might not otherwise become interested in it. The result is nearly nine thousand pages ranging from ancient Egypt to the French Revolution. Considering the magnitude of the undertaking, the Durants could ill afford to be both comprehensive and critical. We see this clearly in their use of numbers, in which they seldom challenged hoary tradition. The Helvetii facing Julius Caesar were "368,000 strong," while the relief army at Alesia consisted of "250,000 Gauls."[41] In like fashion the barbarians burst onto the scene in the traditional large numbers. It was, as they put it, a "barbarian flood." In addition to believing in the 80,000 Vandals discussed in chapter 2, the Durants had Attila fight the battle of the Catalaunian Plains with "half a million men," and "162,000 men are said to have died there."[42]

It is likely that more people know their history from the Durants' work than from any other single source, and if they believe all they read, they will be condemned to think that in the past very large numbers of people indeed died in battles with each other or with pathogens. So will those whose awareness of the matter is confined to any of the works discussed here, as well as a number of other, similar works. In particular, the *Reader's Digest* incident suggests that the tactic of feeding larger numbers to less-informed audiences is well understood by those who are purveying the high figures. One attraction of this is obvious: in these contexts no explanation or justification of the numbers is required.[43]

Two other corners of the public domain should be mentioned. It is probably fair to say that the impressions of most adults have been influenced by no source more than the textbooks consumed during their formal education. Much has been written lately about the defects of these; in terms of the present concern, I note only that one such work numbered the Persian army in 480 B.C. at precisely 2,641,610! Then there is the table-top book, designed to impress but also susceptible of imparting information. One such work, devoted to Hispanic civilization generally, has a section entitled "The Tragedy of the Native Peoples." Although it is generally well balanced and cautiously framed, users will still find in it statements such as "it is possible that Peru (within its present limits) held as many as 9 million people in the early 1520s; by 1620 the number had fallen to 600,000."[44]

All is not lost, however. In an unusual turn of events, readers of a recent encyclopedic treatment of Latin America will find a balanced, if brief, discussion of the issue. Robert McCaa, a demographic historian, resists the temptation to outrage his readers in the usual ways. Instead, he considers "demographic hell" probably a better description of pre-contact America than "paradise," and he speaks of "maximalists" and "minimalists" rather than just the former, suggesting at least that these are two extremes with similar probabilities of being correct.[45]

McCaa's approach is very much the exception, though. Almost by definition, the public domain is multifaceted, with many nooks and crannies. Largely it ranges from those who believe anything they read as a matter of course (the *Reader's Digest* crowd) to those who have more specific tastes and are not lacking critical instincts. The latter might well be attracted to Crosby's *Ecological Imperialism* because it is well written and broad-gauged in its approach and opportunistically combines in its title two words that have a contemporary cachet. In neither case are there any particular a priori reasons to doubt the arguments on offer, and it is likely that readers at both extremes will take with them the very impressions they are meant to receive. Sadly, few will have their interest piqued enough to persuade them to pursue matters to the point where their certainty will be abraded by the weight of evidence.

I Came, I Saw, I Counted

And we have not seen and we have not heard that any king had ever appointed anybody to count the numbers of those killed in any battle conducted between himself and his enemy, unless the number of the slain was one thousand or less. As for those killed in the battles of Hulaku, Ghazan, and Timur, the establishment of their numbers is sheer madness, and whoever believes in these numbers is nothing but a madman.

—Ibn Taghri Birdi, fifteenth-century Egyptian historian, quoted in David Ayalon, "Harb," *Encyclopaedia of Islam*

[W]hat a wreck he [the historian Barthold Georg Niebuhr] has made of the imposing structure of ancient history, as it comes to us from the hands of ancient art. Whether the simple fact, that what he gives us is more certainly true than what we had such perfect faith in before is, or should be, sufficient to compensate us for that of which he despoils us, cannot well be a question with those who have a better faith in art, as the greatest of all historians, and as better deserving of our confidence than that worker who limits his faith entirely to his own discoveries. We prefer one Livy to a cloud of such witnesses as M. Niebuhr.

—William Gilmore Simms, *Views and Reviews in American Literature, History, and Fiction*

While engaged in the arduous conquest of the Aztec state, Hernán Cortés found time to write several letters to the Spanish court trumpeting his triumphs and excusing his failures, of which there were about equal numbers until the end. These letters have been used to determine the population of central Mexico when Cortés landed on the coast in 1519, and their role as corroboration of the results of other techniques makes them worth some extra attention. So do certain claims that the figures in the letters are at least plausible and at most accurate. To determine the first—the second is beyond our capacity—we need to bring some much-needed context to the problem. It is hardly adequate, though possibly reassuring, merely to stipulate that Cortés had no particular reason to exaggerate. Baldly stated, this can only be a matter of uninformed opinion; we need to visit the crowded genre of war reports.

In purpose, content, and expression, Cortés's letters remind us of nothing so much as Julius Caesar's accounts of his two major wars—*The Gallic War* and *The Civil Wars*. The first is clearly more appropriate to the exercise.[1] Like Cortés, Caesar went off on his own, warring against enemies of unknown number, strength, and power. There was a greater variety of them, but basically they represented the same Other to Caesar that the Aztecs did to Cortés. Moreover, like Cortés, Caesar was immeasurably aided by allies drawn from this very Other. And, like Cortés, Caesar's numbers have been the springboard for several attempts to estimate the population of Gaul in the mid-first century B.C., at its supposed apogee.

The task is made easier and more rewarding by the fact that in *The Gallic War*, as in Cortés' letters, the antagonists invariably and exceedingly outnumber the protagonists. In *The Gallic War* Caesar provided figures for the opposition; these are always large, and sometimes very large. Indeed, if we are to believe Caesar, the armies of the various tribes he confronted and inexorably defeated often totaled hundreds of thousands and were accompanied by camp followers of even greater numbers.

Since his time, Caesar has been more often believed than doubted, and his work has been praised both as literature and as history. For some time *The Gallic War* has been a standard introductory text in Latin classes. Its *incipit*, "all Gaul is divided into three parts," has become so familiar that it is often plagiarized and modified without losing its identity—no mean feat in a world growing less and less acquainted with the works of classical antiquity.

The balance of critics and defenders of Caesar's writings is probably closer now than ever before.[2] Here I look at some of the numbers Caesar mobilized and the ways in which he tried to sell them to his audience, the Senate and citizens of Rome. This is not only because Caesar's figures have long been used to suggest population levels for ancient Gaul but also because the rhetorical strategies of Caesar and Cortés are so similar. The former's practice and its interpretation have given added credibility to the notion that warrior counts can be accurate indicators of overall population. If it could be demonstrated that

Caesar's numbers are likely to be at least roughly correct, it would validate some of the efforts to calculate the population of Gaul at the time and, by analogy, similar efforts in the Americas. On the other hand, if it is demonstrated that his figures are impossibly high, this would suggest the wisdom of doubting the reliability of other parts of his account, as well as the figures of Cortés. This inaccuracy cannot be proved, if only because, *ex hypothesi,* the evidence nearly all disappeared on the field of battle. Just the same, it is useful to look closely at a few examples of the way in which Caesar propelled numbers at his readers, and at the effects of this, before turning to the ways in which Cortés did the same.

Some sixty times in *The Gallic War* Caesar offered his readers estimates of the forces he was fighting, and occasionally of whole populations. Although Caesar's estimates of the fighting forces and the overall populations of several Germanic and Gallic tribes amount almost to a genre of their own within the larger context of *The Gallic War,* they have not been subjected to a great deal of close attention on their way to being accepted or rejected in aid of other pursuits. More to the point, while they have often been accepted in toto, they have been rejected only on a case-by-case basis.

As we will see, there is clearly a case for regarding all of them as indications of Caesar's penchant for the grandiose and not as the outcomes of accurate estimates on his part. I discuss only several of the more wildly implausible examples of Caesar's use of numbers, since these obviously best repay attention. I do not propose a plausible-implausible dichotomy by which to determine credibility, however.[3] While it might be true that plausible numbers resist critical attention more easily than implausible ones, it is no less true that all the numbers offered by a given source in a given set of circumstances need to be judged by the company they keep.

———

If we are to believe Caesar's own account, many of the groups he met and defeated he also annihilated, so that, he tells us, only their names were left behind. It could be unfair to criticize Caesar himself for the invincible credulity of some of his readers. After all, he made it easy enough for them to disbelieve him. His reiterated claims to having extirpated whole tribes has the ring of standard-issue rhetorical boasting rather than truth, and he never bothered to explain how he was able—or willing—to do this time and again.

Two of many possible examples suggest most compellingly the nature of the problem—and even suggest that Caesar was not above being a bit of a hoaxer. Certainly something like this seems to be operating in his account of his confrontation with the Helvetii and their allies in 58 B.C. To read him tell it, as a result of defeating these groups in battle and forcing the surrender of the survivors, certain information fell into his hands which indicated that there were 263,000 Helvetii and another 105,000 from allied groups.[4] Of this figure, 92,000, exactly one-quarter, were "fit to bear arms." Some of the Helvetii decided to remain in Gaul under Roman rule while others—110,000 by census, Caesar wrote—preferred to return home. The unenumerated remainder apparently died in combat

As unlikely as these numbers are, the way in which Caesar purportedly learned them is even more extraordinary. He wrote that "[i]n the camp of the Helvetii were found, and brought to Caesar, records [*tabulae*] written out in Greek letters, wherein was drawn up a register of names [*tabulis nominatim*] showing what number of them had gone out from their homeland, who were able to bear arms, and also separately children, old men, and women."[5] It is not completely clear from Caesar's way of expressing himself whether the listing of names was confined to those capable of bearing arms or included everyone. Either way, virtually nothing about this peculiar scenario makes much sense.[6]

Why record the names of all the members of the tribe, if indeed that was the case? For that matter, how would it have been possible to do this for so many?[7] And why Greek letters, and written by whom? Who among the Helvetii could read Greek letters, should they need to? When had this been done and how were names removed? Some modern editors of Caesar's text have suggested that this script reached the Helvetii by way of the Greek colony of Massilia, but this is believable only if we accept Caesar's story in the first place. Did itinerant Greek scribes travel about beyond the borders of the Roman empire hiring themselves out as registrars just in case someone like Caesar came along to record such information?

Furthermore, if these were actually "tablets," as Caesar's term suggests, where could they have been stored in transit? Presumably they would have been of wood or stone, and their sheer number and weight would have rendered them untransportable. And how, for that matter, would access to them have been gained? And how long would it have taken for them to be prepared before the migrants left home— no matter by whom?

Suppose, alternatively, that the "tabulae" contained only the names of those able to bear arms.[8] If this makes more sense logistically, it seems to make less sense practically. How were these individuals identified when the rolls were made, and how were names added? More to the point, what would the purpose of the lists, once compiled, have been? How would they have been consulted? Were they alphabetical? Was there an index? How could names have been retrieved from the list, and under what circumstances was this attempted? For that matter, how were names deleted from this running inventory? In short, why would such "tabulae," whose construction was presumably an arduous, time-consuming, and expensive process, have been created?

For that matter, how exactly did Caesar count the 110,000 who decided to return?[9] And why bother? And how did he determine who was capable of bearing arms and who was not? And is it not at least slightly suspicious that these turned out to be exactly one-quarter of the whole? Under the circumstances, this might seem too low a proportion; after all, according to Caesar the Helvetii were migrating en masse, fleeing enemies and seeking to establish themselves somewhere in western Gaul. Prudence would require that in such a state of affairs, the percentage of those bearing arms would be appreciably higher. Whatever the case, the proportion of exactly one to four cannot but appear suspect.[10]

Several later ancient historians provided figures that were lower than Caesar's. Plutarch, closest to Caesar in time, was also closest to him in his estimate (300,000). Orosius, writing in the fifth century, reduced the figure to 157,000. Even though we cannot know how each of these writers arrived at the figure he used (Orosius was probably abstracting from now-lost portions of Livy), each must ultimately have derived them from *The Gallic War,* and the differences between them would represent the particular degree of doubt that each author brought to his reading of Caesar.[11] Accepting this as natural in one sense, it remains odd that, contrary to many modern students, these writers chose to dispute the very figures for which Caesar claimed to have had documentary evidence.[12]

C. E. Stevens's discussion of the episode epitomizes the dualistic mien of much modern scholarship. He finds a lot to be skeptical about in all aspects of the Helvetii tale, including the overall figure of 368,000. But not the possibility that *some* accurate figure was found, recorded, saved, and transmitted. It is Livy's figure of 157,000, via Orosius, that Stevens finds "surely much more likely."[13] Lower, yes; more plausible because of that, yes again; but more likely to be accurate? The answer to this must be no.

Much earlier, Heinrich Kloevekorn had taken a similar position.[14] He scoffed at Caesar's numbers and argued that if the Helvetii were carrying with them a three-month supply of flour, they would have required more than eight thousand wagons to transport it over difficult terrain. He pointed out that Caesar's account of the reasons for the migration made little sense and added that Caesar had several good reasons for exaggerating the number of Helvetii: it would magnify his victory, justify his fighting in the first place, allow him to meddle in the internal affairs of other Gallic tribes, and justify his acting without waiting for the formal approval of the Roman Senate.[15] These points made, Kloevekorn still felt obliged to offer his own estimate of the Helvetians and their allies. He thought that 160,000 represented a reasonable compromise of the several numbers later writers had offered—without considering, for instance, that these themselves must have represented similar compromises made earlier.[16] Despite all the incongruities, unqualified belief in each of these numbers lives on in several recent discussions of the occasion.[17]

Three years after defeating the Helvetii, Caesar came into contact with two other Germanic groups, the Usipetes and the Tencteri. Manufacturing a casus belli, he attacked them unexpectedly, catching them unprepared in their encampment. Many were killed there, while others fled to the nearby confluence of the Rhine and Moselle rivers. There, or so says Caesar, "they gave up hope of escaping further [and] a large number were already slain, and the rest hurled themselves into the river, there to perish overcome by terror, by exhaustion, by the force of the stream."[17]

Extraordinary as these mass suicidal tendencies might appear, no less astonishing is Caesar's following comment—that in this action not a single Roman soldier died (not even from exhaustion!) and only a few were wounded, even though they had faced "an enemy whose numbers had been 430,000."[19] If we accept the details that Caesar provides, this carnage cum pursuit must have occurred in the few hours between midday and darkness on an early spring day. Well might J.F.C. Fuller, who knew his military history, label it "one of the most complete victories in history."[20] In terms of respective casualties it could hardly have known any peer.[21]

Here, then, is another large number—in fact, the largest number deployed in *The Gallic War*. This time, and more usually, Caesar offered no hint as to how he knew how many Usipetes and Tencteri there were. His narrative of the battle and of the events leading up to it do not suggest that the Romans had the leisure to count their adversaries (who would have been as many people as there are in Tucson or Long Beach), and doing so was clearly impossible in the chaos of the battle and its aftermath as described. In short, there is no reason whatever to suspect seriously that Caesar's number had any relationship at all to the actual numbers of Usipetes and Tencteri.

Here Caesar has met with at least some modern skepticism, if not always on entirely sensible grounds.[22] Ernest Desjardins sought the explanation in a remarkably unlikely transcriptional error, "CCCCXXX" for "XXXXIII," thus increasing the number tenfold.[23] Ferdinand Lot, on the other hand, noted that the same groups appeared later in the Roman records. On this occasion, Lot suggests, "it is absolutely certain that they were infinitely less numerous" than Caesar propounded.[24] For his part, Fuller seemed slightly less dubious of this figure than of that for the Helvetii, mentioning only that it was Caesar's.[25] Gustave Bloch and Jérôme Carcopino merely considered this an example of Caesar's "customary complaisance" with numbers, while Matthias Gelzer spoke of a force "supposedly 430,000" strong."[26] No wonder that in his study of the psychology of warfare, John Keegan wondered about modern military historians' credulity respecting Caesar's account of his battles.[27]

This body of skeptical opinion, though, remains a minority one. Despite the fact that in the same passages in which he adverted to 430,000 Usipetes and Tencteri, Caesar admitted to other forms of misrepresentation, and despite his having been called on it both at Rome in his day and in the scholarship of ours, his patently nonsensical statement regarding the numbers of the enemy that day have gone virtually unchallenged. In accounts of Caesar's campaigns and in editions of *The Gallic War,* his claim generally merits no particular attention at all, receiving the acquiescence of silence.[28]

Others, however, have been less silent than enthusiastic about both these numbers and the others that deface the text of *The Gallic War.* As we have already noticed, Robert Wallace incorporated several of Caesar's numbers—and challenged none of the others—in order to posit a population for Gaul at the time of not less than 48 million.[29]

And Wallace was only the first of many.[30] At the end of the nineteenth century Julius Beloch, whose estimates of the various provinces of the Roman empire still command attention, if not complete allegiance, turned to the question.[31] At first he estimated the Gallic population at 3,390,000, but a hail of criticism—Germans did not count

Frenchmen!—forced him to raise it, if only slightly, to 4.5 million.[32] Criticism has continued, and it is generally recognized that despite arraying Caesar's figures, Beloch's principal criterion was density per square kilometer, and that he tailored his other premises to ensure that Gaul had a lower density than other regions of the Mediterranean world.[33] This preordained methodology derived from Beloch's belief that "higher civilization" correlated well with high population densities because it allowed and encouraged the development of industry and commerce. Thus Gaul could not have been densely populated at the time of the Roman conquest, but only as a result of it.[34]

Shortly after this, Emile Levasseur, in introducing a general account of French population history, tried his own hand at determining the number of people living in Gaul at the Roman conquest. He began by conceding the obvious—that "[i]t is impossible to determine the number of inhabitants of Gaul before the conquest," but he thought that the country was not very densely populated. He also believed that the "numbers of combatants" cited by Caesar were "suspect" for the usual reasons. They emanated from "an ambitious general interested in boosting the prestige of his victories by exaggerating the numbers of the enemy."[35]

Despite these handicaps he felt a need to persist, "despite the small number and doubtful value of the documents that history disposes." He suspected that it might be useful, of all things, to rely on the unreferenced testimony of Diodorus Siculus that "Gaul is inhabited by many tribes of different size; for the largest number some two hundred thousand men [*andrôn*], and the smallest fifty thousand."[36] Levasseur transformed his source's clear use of "many" into "the sixty peoples of long-haired Gaul" of later times, allowing him to proceed by substituting one source's numbers for another source's words.

Adopting an average of 100,000 "inhabitants per tribe," which, he thought, seemed to accord not only with Diodorus Siculus but also with statements by Caesar and Strabo about the Belgae, and tacking on Gallia Narbonnensis, Levasseur concluded that there were "about eight million inhabitants for all of Gaul," or about twelve people per square kilometer.[37] He modestly concluded that "we do not present this [figure] as a certain fact, or even as a probable fact supported by ample proofs, but as a simple hypothesis expressed in numerical form."[38] Later references to Levasseur's work show that his number endured while his caveats found a quick death.[39]

Of the rest, one of the earliest, most indefatigable, and most influential was Camille Jullian.[40] In his massive history of Roman Gaul,

Jullian prefaced his discussion of Gallic population figures by addressing the credibility of the sources:

> Let us not tax the ancient writers who have preserved these numbers for us with error or exaggeration. They had them from the natives, and the peoples of the past, more so than the Christians, loved statistics and enumerations. Their religion demanded these one-by-one censuses [*sic*], all these scrupulous additions of men or of soldiers; the national gods wanted there to be made an exact accounting of the citizens who belonged to them.[41]

Despite the eccentric tenor of this argument, Jullian put his finger on one of the issues of the counts in *The Gallic War* and, by extension, in the chronicles of the Indies: whose numbers are they?[42]

T. Rice Holmes, too, was inclined to exonerate Caesar by blaming his informants and later copyists for those numbers he regarded as hyperbole. No doubt there were occasions when Caesar took such figures as given, while at other times he either improved on them or made his own estimates. Battlefield figures might especially have been products of the Romans, if not of Caesar himself. The case of the Helvetii can only suggest that Caesar was not above devising a tale to fit whatever figures he wished to purvey.

Two works on the ancient Gauls appeared in the immediate aftermath of the Nazi occupation of France, each meant to fortify the historical self-image of postwar France.[43] Both dealt with the vexed issue of population. The first of these, Albert Grenier's *Les Gaulois*, took umbrage at "a modern German" estimate that the population of Gaul was only 5 or 6 million.[44] Addressing the Helvetian count, he argued that "[i]f there is one number [in the sources] that appears to present exceptional guarantees of exactitude, it is that of the Helvetians."[45] Indeed, Grenier, like Jullian, was disposed to raise this number on the assumption that it excluded large numbers of slaves. Citing Plutarch and Diodorus Siculus at their most grandiloquent, he concluded, after some calculations of his own, that "about fifteen million inhabitants is a minimum that must certainly have been exceeded."[46]

Ferdinand Lot, a much more eminent historian, wrote the second work, published two years later. In contrast to Grenier, Lot not only rejected the tale of the Helvetian tablets but found it "astonishing that there are any historians who accept it."[47] He declined as well to believe that there could have been 430,000 Tencteri and Usipetes.[48]

Despite his doubts, however, Lot felt obliged to render an opinion about the probable population of Gaul at the time. Harking back to the method—if hardly the conclusions—of Beloch, he reckoned that on the basis of a "very weak" estimate of thirty people per hectare, it "would have been some twenty million."[49] Thus Lot's doubt produced a higher number than Grenier's credulity.

These two efforts, presumably achieved independently (at least in terms of overt method), might have lent credence to a population figure of about 15 million to 20 million if only each of them had not adopted a flawed methodology. For Lot it was the assumption that population was distributed in ancient Gaul uniformly enough to enable an "average" population density to be applied. Because he arrived at such a density already armed with knowledge of the number of hectares involved, Lot's task became merely a matter of applying a density that, when multiplied by this number, would result in a middle-range population figure.

Grenier's reasoning will be more familiar to students of the New World contact population debate. Like Levasseur, he was especially attracted to Diodorus Siculus's statement, noted earlier. "Many" does not work well as a multiplier, so Grenier turned it into two numbers: there were "some twenty great peoples and about forty small ones."[50] It was also necessary to change "men" into "people" by multiplying by four; indeed, "such a coefficient surely provides only a minimum." And voilà, 24 million inhabitants of Gaul step forward after the equal sign.[51] The problems here are painfully obvious; the assumption that every Gallic tribe minimally numbered either 200,000 or 800,000 is only the most palpable, since it seems likely that Diodorus Siculus intended only to suggest—we know not why—a continuum that ran from 50,000 to 200,000. Nonetheless, it allowed Grenier to present the figure of 24 million as a reasonable one, even though in the end he provisionally advanced a lower figure of 12 million to 15 million.[52]

Raymond Schmittlein has carried the high-counting banner forward.[53] Schmittlein regards the figures put forth by Strabo, which are among the highest of all, as "not exaggerated." He suggests, for instance, that the number of "warriors" who took part in the battle and siege of Alesia in 52 B.C., which effectively ended the conquest of Gaul, would be "on the order of two and a half million men." To this he adds another million men of fighting age and multiplies this number by about 5.7 to arrive at a total of "twenty-one million inhabitants" in ancient Gaul.[54] Despite taking the unusual position of correlating warrior counts and overall population directly, Schmittlein's overall approach resembles the High Counters' most closely.

More recently, John Drinkwater has criticized Beloch's assumption of an average of seven to eight people per square kilometer and substituted for it his own belief that Gaul was as densely populated as Italy, and so about fifteen people lived on the typical square kilometer. As a result, he estimates a population of about 8 million.[55] In short, Drinkwater's figure is as much tied to his estimates for other parts of the Roman empire as Beloch's were. Only the exact relationship differs.[56]

Looking at Caesar's account of the Gauls, Barry Cunliffe offers a particularly ingenuous reading. He speaks elusively of "documents" in the Helvetian case and concludes that "Caesar's figures may be exaggerated but there is no reason why he should have falsified them and the way in which he presents them has a ring of authenticity." After alluding to several other of Caesar's figures, none of which he disputes, Cunliffe concludes that "hundreds of thousands of Gauls were killed, hundreds of thousands were carried away to be sold into slavery, and incalculable numbers were maimed."[57]

Two French historians have recently treated Caesar's figures in typically friendly fashion. Jean-Noël Biraben thinks them to be of "acceptable orders of magnitude" and uses them explicitly to estimate the population of Gaul at 6,800,000 ± 500,000 at the time.[58] Robert Etienne is more circumspect, speaking of the "snare of numbers," but he goes on to quote Caesar on the Helvetii, speaking of "credible documents," namely the "tablets" mentioned earlier. Like Biraben, he uses Caesar's figures directly to extrapolate a general population, which he sets at between 4 million and 4.5 million.[59] While this is one of the lowest estimates offered in the matter, it shows how easily Caesar's numbers lend themselves to virtually any modern estimate.

Finally, there is the case of Christian Goudineau, who has written an extensive, archaeologically focused work on Caesar's campaigns.[60] Throughout the work Goudineau presents Caesar's numbers virtually without comment. At one point, though, he addresses the issue explicitly, observing rightly enough that "the problem is to know whether these numbers are credible or not." He concludes that "in my opinion, they are—approximately." Thus he believes that the Helvetian losses were 220,000, and he imputes losses of "several tens of thousands" to several other occasions, enabling him to conclude that Plutarch's claim that Caesar killed 1 million Gauls in battle is "acceptable." All this leads Goudineau to conclude that "various demographic estimates are not only reasonable but rather insufficient [i.e., understated]."[61]

In support of his argument Goudineau refers vaguely to "psychological and administrative limits that oppose any hyperbolic exaggerations," although just what these are he nowhere clarifies.[62] Oddly for an archaeologist, Goudineau engages none of the logistical cruxes implicit in his belief. He fails as well to undertake any serious textual criticism or rhetorical analysis, nor does he allude to any of the literature touching these issues.

It might be worthwhile to look at the ways in which Diodorus Siculus's testimony has been put to modern use. As we have seen, he failed to provide a multiplicand with actual numerical value. His testimony is seriously complicated by the fact it is partly qualitative ("many"), and even the quantitative matter is ambiguous (50,000 *to* 200,000? 50,000 *and* 200,000?). None of this, however, has diminished the ardor of those who have felt obliged to use these data as points of departure.

One of the first of these, as already noticed, was Robert Wallace, whose modus operandi, although over two centuries old, has decided modern overtones. To begin with, he replaced Diodorus's "many" with Appian's "400 nations or tribes." Combining these disparate data, he suddenly turned modest. Even though they seemed to suggest a very high figure, he did not feel "obliged to compute all the inhabitants of Gaul at much above 80 millions." Maybe there were many more small nations than larger ones. Instead, he decided on "a more moderate computation . . . only about 40 millions."[63]

In this particular exercise Wallace acted as a prototype both by combining incommensurate and dubious evidence and, especially, in a fit of seeming modesty, by backing off the ineluctable results of his procedure and producing a figure that he could call modest but which has ever since remained nearly twice as large as any later estimate. He could thereby convince both himself and his readers that he was operating at a minimal level and that further research or rumination might actually raise the figure considerably, for by his own premises the figure could be as high as $400 \times 125{,}000 \times 4$, or 200 million. Gaul would then have been inhabited by about as many people as the highest number estimated for the Americas.

No later student of the matter has been as cavalier as Wallace in blending sources, but those who have used Diodorus Siculus have routinely transformed his "many" into "60," the number of *civitates* awarded Gaul by Augustus, on the assumption that there was a straightforward correlation between these and the individual tribes in existence in the 50s B.C.[64] Clearly there must have been some such correlation, but the process entails a bouillabaisse of differing, if not discrepant, data.[65] Equal parts of Caesar, Augustus, and Diodorus Siculus are emulsified in order to create a composite estimate. In all these cases assumptions are necessarily made about Diodorus's meaning: did he intend to suggest that all polities had either about 50,000 or about 200,000 warriors, or was he merely indicating the minimum and maximum? No one seems sure.

Does it matter, though? How plausible—indeed, how possible—are Diodorus's figures?[66] The numbers of the contingents that, Caesar mentioned, were gathered together to relieve the siege of Alesia argue against accepting them.[67] Jacques Harmand argues that this number "is thus far from finding itself contradicting Gallic demographic possibilities."[68] There seems, though, to be a serious contradiction. These forces were the result of a national levy, or so Caesar says, but the total of about 280,000 represents only about 6 percent of the lowest estimate (Beloch's), and only about 1 or 2 percent of those estimates in the 15 million to 20 million range. That is, the figure ranges from only one-eighteenth to one-fourth of the available manpower based on various population estimates. Playing arithmetical games with Diodorus's information would only reduce that proportion still further. Considering that the occasion must have been viewed as a last-ditch effort to expel the Romans, this seems much too small to be even remotely likely. For that matter, if the potential strength of the Gallic armies was in the millions, as is implied in population estimates of about 20 million, then why did they not manage in seven years of fighting to combine forces to achieve a superiority that would have overwhelmed even Caesar?

––––––

We need to look at the figures for the siege of Alesia in *The Gallic War* for another reason.[69] There are varying manuscript traditions for this text, and, not surprisingly, these numbers have suffered in the process of multiple transmissions. Caesar first listed a number of tribes and the levies that were to be raised in order to relieve Alesia. Then he noted that one group, the Bellovaci, which had been allotted 10,000 men, agreed only to send 2,000. Several sentences later he stated what he thought was the actual number of troops that had been raised. Three numbers then present themselves: the aggregate of those levied; that aggregate minus 8,000; and the totals that, according to Caesar, actually came to do battle.

At the first and last of these stages, transmission problems enter the picture. It would be best to present the situation algebraically, with the first figure in each pair the number of tribes and the second the number of men. The "standard" manuscript tradition is this:

$$(2 \times 35{,}000) + (6 \times 12{,}000) + (2 \times 10{,}000) + (4 \times 8{,}000) + (8 \times 5{,}000) + (1 \times 4{,}000) + (3 \times 3{,}000) + (2 \times 2{,}000) + (1 \times 30{,}000) - 8{,}000 = 273{,}000$$

A lesser, but still used, tradition, however, shows the following state of affairs:

$$(2 \times 35{,}000) + (6 \times 12{,}000) + (2 \times 10{,}000) + (11 \times 8{,}000) + (3 \times 5{,}000) + (3 \times 4{,}000) + (1 \times 3{,}000) + (2 \times 2{,}000) + (1 \times 10{,}000) - 8{,}000 = 286{,}000$$

In addition, there are two separate manuscript traditions for Caesar's last set of figures: one shows 8,000 cavalry and 240,000 infantry, and the other, 8,000 cavalry and 250,000 infantry. Thus, in referring to the numbers of this relief force, modern scholars can offer at least six legitimate numbers (i.e., authorized by manuscripts): 248,000, 258,000, 273,000, 281,000, 286,000, and 294,000, or a range of 18.5 percent from bottom to top. A particular choice will be grounded on whether the author uses the levied figures, the levied figures minus the shortfall of the Bellovaci, or the "final" assimilated figures offered by Caesar.[70]

In part, students of the Gallic wars have chosen differently because they have used editions based on different manuscripts.[71] Differences in the two equations just shown issue almost entirely from scribal choices for that frequently overlooked variable, punctuation—in particular, different decisions regarding commas and semicolons. Lists are peculiarly vulnerable to this type of "error," and numbers themselves, even (or especially?) Roman numerals, to *lapsus calami*.[72] The earliest extant manuscripts of *The Gallic War* date from the ninth to the twelfth centuries.[73] Would it not be reckless to assume that all previous but lost versions maintained Caesar's figures, right or wrong, unscathed for century after century? The circumstances add luster to the notion that the figures cannot be treated literally even though it is impossible to replace them with anything that can be regarded as more pristine, let alone more accurate.

Despite these anomalies and contradictions, Caesar's recorded muster of the relieving army has been widely used to establish population limits, or at least to suggest the distribution of population among the Gallic peoples.[74] In one of the most formula-driven discussions of the issue, Eugène Cavaignac proposed that ancient Gaul probably had a population of about one-third the *rural* population of France of his own time, or from 9 million to 12 million. In doing so he accepted that most numbers in *The Gallic War* were transmitted accurately *as numbers,* but he occasionally saw fit to interpret them differently from the way Caesar had—rather an inverted approach.[75] In turn, though Cavaignac asserted otherwise, this argument was buttressed by another—that the figures for Alesia represented roughly one-third the available troops for the tribes represented.[76] In the nineteenth century Theodor Mommsen, often revisionist in his arguments, had no problem in accepting Caesar's figures, because for him Caesar was the embodiment and culmination of everything good in the Roman character.[77] Even Beloch, denounced as a hypercritic by those who preferred higher estimates than his, accepted these figures at face value, even though he drew a different set of conclusions from them.[78]

Again we can explain this reliance on the fact that the figures seem plausible even if rounded. Like the so-called census of the Helvetii, they seem to imply documentary authority rather than an eyeball estimate. They vary from tribe to tribe, presumably (to suggest more would indeed be to argue in a vicious circle) to represent at least roughly the relative population levels of these groups as the Romans came to know them later. Few students of the matter have discussed explicitly how Caesar came to know the details of this levy, but Jullian, who had explanations for most things, thought "such precision" left "no doubt that [Caesar] had before his eyes a public document, transmitted to him by some deserter from the assembly of [Gallic] chiefs."[79]

———

Viewing the literature conspectively, then, we find a range of opinion that the population of Gaul at the imposition of Roman rule was anywhere from about 4 million to 48 million. Each proposed figure along this spectrum is based on virtually the same evidence: Caesar's figures plus the odd piece of unprovenanced information in later sources such as Plutarch, Strabo, and Diodorus Siculus, each of whom "improved" on Caesar. The range itself is peculiarly the result of modern suppositions regarding the means by which to extrapolate. By accepting most figures at face value, by preferring larger or smaller numbers when there is a choice, by varying the proportion of fighting men to overall population, by varying the degree of density of Gauls per square measure, and by introducing whole "uncounted" segments of society such as slaves, modern scholarship has imposed itself on evidence that is helpless to resist.

To sum up, all modern estimates of the population of ancient Gaul derive ultimately, and most often directly, from the figures found in Caesar's *Gallic War*. Some of these estimates employ the concept of inhabitants per square kilometer by assuming some kind of relationship between ancient and modern density, but this approach is almost always checked against Caesar's figures. Deciding which of these to accept, how to extend them to the population at large, and how to relate the results both to the Roman empire and to modern France in whole or in part has created limitless opportunities to manipulate the raw data. In the circumstances it is no wonder that the range of total population in modern estimates is so great that the highest estimate is twelve times the smallest. That most opinion clusters in the more restricted range of 10 million to 20 million can hardly be taken as an assurance of greater probability, but only of a greater propensity toward the high end of verisimilitude.[80]

The observation that Caesar's numbers are more plausible when divided by ten is a serious indictment of his accuracy, as well as of the credulity of those who have taken him seriously. But neither he nor his interpreters stand alone. Like Caesar, Hernán Cortés employed and enjoyed the advantages of being the chronicler of his own exploits. The circumstances in which Cortés left a record of his impressions of the populations of various parts of Mexico bear uncanny resemblances to the circumstances surrounding the work of Caesar. Like Caesar, Cortés found himself attempting to conquer a world never before within his own imperial ambit. Like Caesar, Cortés also found himself in danger of being an outcast while he was doing it. In his time Caesar had chronic disputes with the Roman Senate over the limits of his authority, the legal bounds of which he certainly transcended.[81] In turn, although nominally under the authority of the governor of Cuba, Cortés lost no time in effectively renouncing that authority, even defeating a force the governor sent against him. To solidify his shaky legal authority, Caesar sent triumphant communiqués to the Roman Senate, although the Roman people were his intended audience. In like fashion Cortés decided to bypass Cuba by addressing his letters to the Spanish king.

It is no surprise, then, how alike the two sets of letters turn out to be. Here we are interested only in the effects the respective situations had on the senders' uses of numbers to plead their cases. Having looked at Caesar's way and the ways of his interpreters, we can turn to the evidence in Cortés's writings and the manner in which it has been used. As we will see, the similarities do not end with the texts themselves but extend to the modern response to Cortés's numbers.

We are not lucky enough to find Cortés recording that he spent night after night in his tent poring over Caesar's writings while on the campaign to conquer Mexico.[82] Even so, we find that he treated the Mexica armies about the same way that Caesar wrote about the Gallic hosts. They were enormous, but in the open field they were as easily vincible as the Gauls. In the five letters that Cortés wrote to the Spanish king between 1520 and 1525 there are numerous references to the sizes of enemy forces. Some are plausible, some are not, and some are simply ludicrous. Of the last, the most outlandish example is Cortés's comment that just before the Spaniards were expelled from Tenochtitlan, they "calculated" that they were outnumbered more than twenty-five thousand to one.[83] Since there were several hundred Spaniards present at the time, Cortés was implying—though he probably never realized it, or cared if he did—that they were being hounded by several million Indian warriors.

This example is so clearly hyperbole that it almost seems justified—Cortés was simply making a point—and the comment has apparently never been used by the High Counters to support belief either in an exceedingly dense population in the valley of Mexico or in the credibility of Hernán Cortés. Nonetheless, it bespeaks a state of mind that was willing to use numbers that are risible, whatever the point being made.

Indeed, we see much the same outlook in several of the cases in which Cortés refers to enemy armies or local populations. Four times he uses the same expression, "more than 150,000," and in a fifth the curious locution "more than 149,000."[84] Are we to assume that in every case Cortés had been able to make an accurate estimate of aggregations that just happened to be about the same size each time? Or, rather, that he had been able to count up to 150,000 (or 149,000) but was forced to stop even though more Indians remained to be counted? Some have assumed just this kind of thing, at least by implication, by accepting the basic credibility of Cortés's account. A more likely explanation would be simply that for Cortés, some number around 150,000 represented the uncountable.[85]

A second contemporaneous account of the conquest of Mexico is Francisco López de Gómara's *Historia de la conquista de Mexico,* first published in 1552. Contemporaneous, but hardly independent. In fact, Gómara's *Historia* can safely be regarded as the textual alter ego of Cortés's letters.[86] Gómara was Cortés's chaplain and amanuensis, and he dedicated the work to the conquistador's heir, Martín Cortés. In the dedication Gómara placed Cortés and the conquest of Mexico in the constellation of other great conquests of the past, real and imagined, and spoke of his determination to see its glories preserved for posterity.[87] In the circumstances, the similarities between the two accounts mean far less than any differences might, and I concentrate on the differences in respect to the numbers that López de Gómara chose to ignore or change in his clone account.

The third contemporaneous account that the High Counters have put to use is Bernal Díaz del Castillo's *Historia verdadera de la conquista de la Nueva España.* The work was the product of Díaz's old age, but it is generally agreed that it holds up well under scrutiny—far better, for instance, that the similar account of de Soto's campaigns by Inca Garcilaso de la Vega, allegedly based on similar reminiscences. If Caesar had later annalists who offered lower numbers even though they were not Caesar's, then Cortés had Díaz del Castillo. Díaz traveled with Cortés as a common soldier and saw the same things Cortés saw, but he disagreed frequently and vehemently with Cortés's estimates of the sizes of armies and towns. In his own work Díaz took pains to disagree with Cortés on this very matter, even though the issue was not central to Diaz's own narrative. It comes as a surprise, then, to learn how much the High Counters have taken to Díaz and have enlisted his testimony on their own behalf, as I discussed in chapter 4. Of course, they have been unable to do this by quoting Díaz, but only by vague, but hearty, intimation.

From all appearances, the High Counters think highly of Díaz's account, recognizing it as more independent of Cortés's than is López de Gómara's.[88] Cook, Simpson, and Borah were among the first to embrace Díaz, speaking of his narrative as being "full of firsthand observation which supplements the statements of Cortés to an extraordinary degree." They continue that "the testimony of two such experienced witnesses must be accepted . . . as probably coming fairly close to the truth." Finally, all restraint disappears as they further assert that "the size of Indian armies . . . as stated throughout the accounts of Cortés and Díaz corresponds with the values given for the preceding decades by native historians."[89] In short, instead of appreciating the great differences of opinion between Díaz and Cortés and undertaking to explain why they prefer the former, Cook and Borah merely co-opt Díaz by denying them.

The matter of "values" and "native historians" is discussed in chapter 4. Cook and Borah's comments about Díaz del Castillo, however, are best dealt with in the present context, since truly independent corroboration of contact and postcontact numbers is exceedingly rare, perhaps even nonexistent.[90] In fact, beyond their approving general comments, Cook and the others ignore Díaz in detail.[91] Their embrace is the kiss of Judas. To understand this duplicity we need only look closely at Díaz's account, where we find that in every applicable case Díaz disagrees with Cortés via López de Gómara. Although Díaz disputes Gómara on various points throughout the work and on various matters, he is scathingly outspoken with regard to the very issue of numbers.[92] Díaz had hardly begun his work when he commented that Gómara's version of things was "very much contrary" to what really happened, and that this was especially true when he wrote "of great cities and such large numbers of their inhabitants." He observed that it seemed to him that Gómara would just as soon write "eight" as "eight thousand."[93] Later in his work he was even more excoriating and dismissive:

> The chronicler [Gómara] says that so many thousands of Indians opposed us on the expedition, [but] there is neither rhyme nor reason in the high numbers he gives. And he also speaks of cities and towns and villages in which there were so many thousands of houses, when there was not a fifth part of them.

He presciently added that "if one were to add together all that he puts into his history, there are more millions of men than there are in the entire universe."[94] He closed by repeating his earlier charge: "[Gómara] would as soon write eight [or one] thousand as eighty thousand. By his boasting he believes that his history will be pleasing to those who hear it, by not saying what really happened." Let the reader decide, he concludes.[95] One set of readers, it seems, has decided—not so much that Díaz del Castillo was wrong and Cortés and López de Gómara right, but that the two do not even disagree. Apparently, Cook and his associates decided to regard the word "supplement" as a rough synonym for the word "contradict."

Bernal Díaz's differences of opinion with Cortés manifest themselves throughout his account of the campaign, except in his figures for the first pitched battle, when the Spaniards met Mayan forces at Centla in March 1519. After the battle, Cortés wrote, the Indians told him that 220 of their men had been killed, whereas Díaz reports, also on the basis of Indian informants, that 800 had died.[96] After that, the opposite pattern emerges. Cortés estimated that Cempoala fielded

50,000 warriors; Díaz recollected only 14,000.[97] When the Spaniards reached the territory of Tlaxcala, they were confronted by local forces on three occasions. For Cortés, the enemy numbered 100,000 on the first two occasions and "more than 149,000" on the last.[98] Not true at all, retorted Díaz—there were 3,000, 40,000, and 50,000, respectively, on these occasions.[99] As the Spaniards neared Tenochtitlan, Cortés reckoned that the town of Iztapalapa had 12,000 to 15,000 inhabitants.[100] Díaz was satisfied to regard it as "very large."[101] And so on, throughout the course of the two works (treating Cortés and López de Gómara as one).[102]

It is hardly possible to decide whether Cortés or Díaz was the more accurate, or whether either was accurate at all.[103] What matters is that Díaz provides an important counterpoint to the testimony of Cortés, but his evidence has been first compromised and expropriated and then ignored. Instead, we find López de Gómara being used to corroborate his own source.

Although proving the most popular, Cortés's numbers are not always the highest available. That honor probably goes to Francisco de Aguilar, who counted houses rather than people. Writing in the 1560s, when he was in his eighties, Aguilar remembered that he saw—and presumably counted—20,000 houses in Cempoala, 60,000 in Cholula, 80,000 in Texcoco, and 100,000 in both Tlaxcala and Tenochtitlan.[104] Multiplying these numbers by a suitable occupant multiplier (say, five to eight) would produce some truly impressive numbers.[105]

In the same way that accepting Caesar's estimates of the enemy is a prerequisite to estimating the population of ancient Gaul, so believing in Cortés, López de Gómara, or even Aguilar has become a necessary component in arguments that multiply the population of the New World—and central Mexico in particular—by as much as twentyfold. Certainly this increase is premised on other features as well, some of which are discussed elsewhere in this book, but the recourse to warrior counts is both obvious and long-standing. More than that, it encapsulates the demeanor behind the methodology by wrenching these figures forcibly from their intellectual context and treating them entirely as chronologically displaced reportage.[106]

The High Counters use Cortés's figures in the same ways that those seeking the elusive population of ancient Gaul use Caesar's evidence. They make no attempt to correlate these numbers directly with the purported total population, since this would produce figures that are far too small.[107] Instead, Cortés's figures, and those of other observers, are introduced and sometimes defended, though never rejected, as a foregrounding designed to persuade the reader that the larger calculations which follow have a built-in plausibility, or at least are not compromised by the recorded warrior counts.

The modern return to belief in the numbers in the chronicles can be dated to at least 1935, when Carl Sauer, writing about northwestern Mexico, had this to say: "Modern students commonly have been inclined to discount early opinions of native numbers, but rarely have specified their reasons for doing so. I have found no general reasons for suspecting that the first observers were given to exaggeration." Sauer conceded that some, like Las Casas and López de Gómara, "who had a case to defend," would be the "[l]east trustworthy." But, he concluded optimistically, "[e]motional bias and romantic narrative . . . are not long concealed from the attentive reader."[108] Thus disarmed rather than armed, Sauer proceeded to estimate the contact population of the area "between Gila and Río Grande de Santiago" as "in excess of half a million," on the basis of "the record, as interpreted."[109] In the process, he defended his choice to believe no more than he accused the skeptics of doing.[110]

Although it was concerned with a different time and place, and even more with a different order of magnitude, Sauer's posture on the credibility of the early sources inspired work elsewhere in Mexico. More than a decade later there appeared the first work of the High Counters devoted to central Mexico. It was here that Simpson and Cook brought Díaz del Castillo into their fold as part of a general discussion of "military estimates." They found that these estimates "correspond very closely in size . . . with those cited by the codices" and therefore that "[s]uch uniformity negates the assumption of serious error or deliberate falsification by any one observer." They then proceeded to cite the warrior counts of Cortés, López de Gómara, Herrera, and others. They seemed to be unaware of, or unconcerned by, the possibility (and in Gómara's case, the certainty) that these figures were not independent but derivative.[111] Nor did they do more that cite variant figures without addressing the implications of the variance.[112]

In 1957 Cook and Borah first suggested that the population of central Mexico might be much higher than even they had recently thought—maybe as much as 25.3 million. As we have seen, they arrived at this figure by retrojecting back from later estimates, and they were slightly reluctant to believe it themselves. They realized that "[t]here is no immediate evidence to justify" certain of their assumptions and added that the procedure which yielded this new figure should be regarded as a "calculation . . . of theoretical significance only, . . . presented simply as one possible way of approaching the problem."[113] Only a few years later, any doubts had vanished. In the lengthiest of their works devoted to the problem, they reduced their earlier figure by 100,000, or 0.4 percent, but more than compensated for this by a new assurance.[114]

Cook and Borah addressed the issue for the last time in 1971.[115] The arguments are largely the same as previously, except that Díaz is no longer named as agreeing with Cortés. Cook and Borah conceded that "[t]he large size of the contingents reported has aroused vigorous objections by some scholars," but they cited only Angel Rosenblat. They further admitted that modern estimates of crowd size vary, but they insisted that Cortés's estimates were "eminently reasonable. He was on the spot and a far better witness than a scholar [Rosenblat] four centuries later who has not even inspected the terrain."[116] What is remarkable about this claim is how uncannily it resembles John Calvin's much earlier defense of a similar figure in the Book of Isaiah:

> A hundred and eighty-five thousand. That the army was so vast need not make us wonder, as ignorant people do, who reckon it to be incredible and fabulous when they are told that so great a multitude went into the field of battle, because we are accustomed to carry on war with much smaller troops. . . . Nor ought we to be astonished at the vast forces which they led into battle, for they are much more capable of enduring heat, and toil, and hunger, and are satisfied with a much smaller portion of food.[117]

At any rate, Cook and Borah then turned to estimates of urban population sizes—usually house counts. Again they found little with which to disagree, even bringing Aguilar's estimate for Cempoala, admittedly his lowest, into the discussion.[118] Finally, Cook and Borah looked at "indirect" population indicators, in particular the figures that Cortés and Díaz cited for marketplace attendance and their comparisons with cities in Spain. They closed by citing Tapia's estimate of 136,000 skulls at the *templo mayor* in Tenochtitlan, adding as a Parthian shot that "[i]f one remembers that this temple, although the main one, was but one of many where human victims were sacrificed, it becomes clear that such numbers presuppose a dense aboriginal population."[119]

Notable in this extensive reliance on numbers in the chronicles is the absence of justification. There is no interest in how these numbers were derived or why they are so very round, no thought given to their context in either military and literary terms, no recourse to a long history of numerical exaggeration under precisely the same kinds of circumstances that characterized the Spanish conquest of Mexico. In short, Thomas Whitmore is twice mistaken when he claims that these studies, and others like them, "are characterized by methodological sophistication, including the explicit identification and careful assembly of sources and the cross-checking of their validity."[120]

One way to put Cortes's Indian numbers into perspective is to consider their tactical implications.[121] How, for instance, would "more than 150,000" men be disposed on the battlefield? If they formed themselves into a body 1,000 men long and 150 men deep, and if we assume an irreducible minimum of one yard between individuals, its front would be nearly two-thirds of a mile wide and 150 yards deep. A more practical arrangement—say, fighting men five or ten deep—would result in a front either eight or sixteen miles wide. Various other permutations would produce similar quadrilaterals of a size impossible to control centrally, and if the distance between individuals were increased, the problem would simply become greater.[122] Beyond this there would presumably be large numbers of camp followers and logistical support personnel (e.g., how many porters would be necessary to support such numbers in the field, and where would the food and water in sufficient quantities come from?).[123] And all this, for the Aztecs, would have been done without draft animals and the wheel.[124]

Finally in this respect, there is the question of weaponry and tactics—the usual reasons offered for Cortés's apparently phenomenal success in defeating armies three hundred times the size of his own. Admittedly, in weaponry at least the advantages were largely to the Spaniards. Even so, the astounding inefficiency of firepower then, and even now, should not be overlooked.[125] Horses could terrorize temporarily, but it required men and weapons to inflict serious casualties.

The Spanish estimates of the size of Tenochtitlan and other cities used so promiscuously by the High Counters remind us of other such examples. That of Babylon is discussed elsewhere, but there is the analogous case of Nineveh, the last Assyrian capital. If we were to believe Jonah, professedly an eyewitness, the city was so large that it "requir[ed] three days to cross."[126] Diodorus Siculus, though not an eyewitness, seemed to agree—for him Nineveh was the largest city ever built, a full 480 stades, or more than 50 miles, in circumference. Moreover, its walls were 100 feet high, and there were no fewer than

1,500 towers, each in its turn 200 feet tall.[127] This all sounds positively Cortesian, especially when we learn that excavations at the site
of Nineveh have shown that the city was about seven to eight miles in
circumference, encompassing some 1,850 acres—by no means tiny,
but still small enough that the average Assyrian of the time could have
strolled across it in little more than an hour.[128] In this case of archaeology versus history, it is hard to avoid according the laurels to archaeology. Once a site has been positively identified, determining its
superficies is not one of the more challenging tasks confronting
archaeologists.[129]

Caesar's commentaries and Cortés's dispatches exemplify and exploit
a topos that Rolena Adorno has addressed for the Americas and
Michael Murrin for the Renaissance more generally.[130] This is what
Murrin calls "the heroic few," in which warfare is envisaged as the triumph of godliness, represented by the few, over godlessness, represented by numberless and faceless masses. In this scenario the odds
are so great that victory can only be the verdict of fortune. And the
greater the odds, the surer the sign.[131]

A necessarily related theme is that even when the sizes of the
contending forces are roughly equal, the casualties are not. This occurs in several of Caesar's accounts of the defeat of various Gallic
groups, and he carried on the work in the accounts attributed to him
of the ensuing civil war with Pompey.[132] As it happens, Caesar had an
able mentor in all this, his predecessor as dictator, L. Cornelius Sulla.
By his own account at least, Sulla was one of the most efficient field
commanders in history. During these wars, for instance, he managed
to kill 70,000 opponents in a battle near Capua in 83 b.c. at a cost of
only 70 (some said 124) of his own troops.[133] The next year saw a like
success—at the battle of Sacriportis the enemy's losses were 20,000 or
25,000 dead and another 8,000 captured, while Sulla lost only 23 of
his own men.[134]

Notwithstanding these fortunate occasions, Sulla's crowning
military achievement was his defeat of the Pontic army at Chaeronea
in 86 b.c. The sources, based on his own memoirs, now lost, record
that the Pontic force was either 100,000 or 110,000 strong and that all
but 10,000 of these were killed, even though the Romans numbered
fewer than 20,000. The Romans' losses? According to Plutarch, Sulla
at first thought that he had lost fourteen men, but two of these turned
up before the day was out.[135] Small wonder that P. A. Brunt observed
recently that "Sulla evidently had a penchant for keeping his own

losses within two figures."[136] And even smaller wonder that Hans Delbrück referred to the ancient accounts of the battle as "fantasies."[137]

All things considered, it is no surprise to read so many comments in the European chronicles of expansion that betray a stupefying confidence in the fighting ability of Europeans as compared to the lesser races.[138] As early as 1128 Bernard of Clairvaux, no doubt inspired by the figures in the chronicles of the Crusades, wrote that two Christian knights could put to flight ten thousand unbelievers.[139]

Other, less perceptible reasons existed for downgrading casualties. Pushing for a conscript civilian army and charging that the *condottieri* of his time were seldom willing to risk their lives for their employers, Machiavelli claimed that at the battle of Anghiari in 1440, only one *condottiere* had been killed, and he by accident rather than bravery.[140] In fact, contemporaneous accounts bely Machiavelli's confident claim and show that there were several hundred casualties that day.[141]

Those chroniclers who could read neither Greek nor Latin and thus had no access to Plutarch, Caesar, and others could find heady alternatives in the Spanish chroniclers of the *reconquista,* in which, these sources avow, Spanish armies routinely killed hundreds of thousands of Muslims in battle. One of the greatest triumphs of the *reconquista* was the battle of Las Navas de Tolosa in 1212. Many accounts from both sides report on the battle, and in these we find all the expected things. Spanish accounts of Muslim numbers range from 60,000 men "in the first line" alone to 186,000 cavalry plus 925,000 infantry plus porters "without end." Muslim losses are recorded as concomitantly high. As for the Spaniards, the same chronicles assert losses ranging from "a few" to 200.[142]

Not to be outdone, the Spaniards in the Philippines, perhaps besotted by the easy successes in America, plied Philip II for permission to invade China. According to Hernando Riquel, writing in 1572, it would be an easy matter: "There are very many populous cities on the way, but if his Majesty would be pleased so to command, they could be subdued and conquered with less than sixty good men."[143] This hubris was no aberration; just a few years later another Spanish official repeated the boast. Yes, China held "millions of men," was more populous than Germany. But this was of little consequence: give the writer "two or three thousand men" and he could "take whatever province he pleases." Better yet, "[i]n conquering one province, the conquest of all is made."[144] Closer to home, Bartolomé de las Casas partook of this argument, claiming that 200 Spaniards could, and did, rout and destroy a Taino army of 100,000 in 1494.[145] In like fashion, the chronicler of the first Spanish expedition to New Mexico about the same time saw things much the same way. As he put it: "The Lord willed . . . that the whole land should tremble for ten lone Spaniards, for here were over 12,000 Indians."[146] In this way the fantasy worlds of the chivalric romances were reincarnated.

In these cases the Spaniards were not only re-creating the chivalric romances but were continuing a tradition begun by Columbus. Only some forty-eight hours in the New World, he was already boasting that fifty Spaniards could keep the island of Guanahaní in subjection. This was probably true, since it was small and sparsely populated, but six weeks or so later Columbus's boasts had grown apace. Now, after visiting a village on Cuba whose inhabitants had fled at his approach, "the Admiral assured the sovereigns that ten men make ten thousand flee, they are so cowardly and fearful" and lacking in serious weaponry.[147]

Examples of such grotesque disparities in battlefield numbers abounded in the models most familiar to the chroniclers of the Indies.[148] What is of concern is that what Murrin calls "epic" is removed in content and attitude only slightly from the testimonies of Caesar and Cortés. All the texts deal with historical and quasi-historical events in ways that dramatize them. In surveying the battle accounts in several epics or epic-like productions, some from the Americas, Murrin concludes that "[e]pic statistics correspond to what the chroniclers relate, and the battles the poets narrate are typical."[149] A difference is that whereas the epicists wrote only occasionally in hope of personal advancement, virtually every word in Caesar and Cortés was calculated to evoke first exculpation, then edification and admiration, and finally elevation and gratification.[150] In light of this state of affairs, the comments of the High Counters cited earlier are both extraordinary and anachronistic, redolent of nothing so much as the style of past panegyrists. Even they, however, were content to allow praise to be its own end and did not proceed from it to vast arithmetical exercises.

The estrangement of battle descriptions from any necessary reality is starkly illustrated by the so-called Battle Scroll, one of the Qumran documents, or Dead Sea Scrolls. In it a battle is described in the most minute detail: anticipatory strategies, sizes and deployments of contingents, battlefield tactics, and outcome. The numbers are normative, but no more so than in any number of other battle accounts. The battlefield maneuvers are inherently plausible, no doubt based on descriptions of real battles. But the battle itself happened only in the mind(s) of the author(s) of the scroll—it was Armageddon, anxiously awaited and thought imminent by some, but otherwise quite outside all historical experience.[151]

When the High Counters speak of the massacre at Cholula, they remind us of yet another category in which inflated numbers have flourished throughout history. An early example is the case of Mithridates of Pontus's massacre of Italian traders in Greece and Asia Minor in 88 B.C., a prelude to his attempt to oust the Romans from these areas. The numbers involved range from 80,000 to Plutarch's 150,000 "Romans [alone!] . . . massacred in a single day."[152] Some modern authorities are inclined to accept at least the lowest figure, but most agree with Brunt when he writes that "[d]oubtless a few thousand . . . perished."[153] More familiar is the St. Bartholomew's Day massacre in France in 1572. It is unlikely that many more than 4,000 Huguenots died in Paris proper at the time and perhaps a like number outside the capital, but already in the following decade Protestants were claiming that 300,000, even 765,000, people had been slain, while Catholics were denying that anything at all had happened.[154]

A number of other "massacres," great and small, that have been studied show two similar patterns emerging.[155] The first is that eyewitness numbers are often inflated. A good example is that of the infamous Black Hole of Calcutta. Contemporaneous accounts held that nearly 150 English were incarcerated there in 1756 and that 123 of them died overnight. Closer attention to the attendant arithmetic of the siege and fall of Calcutta, which occasioned the incident, show in fact that "*at the most* only sixty-four persons were confined in the Black Hole, of whom twenty-one survived."[156] The second pattern is that those with sensationalist purposes seldom take these findings into account.[157]

Putting Caesar's and Cortés's dispatches—not to mention those of Sulla and others discussed here—to quantitative uses underscores the general problem of deriving objective information from self-reportage. Six hundred years ago, Ibn Khaldun precociously commented on just this issue. Earlier historians had "strayed from the truth and found themselves lost in the desert of baseless assumptions and errors." He continued: "This is especially the case with figures, either of sums of money or of soldiers, whenever they occur in stories. They offer a good opportunity for false information and constitute a vehicle for nonsensical statements. They must be controlled and checked with the help of known fundamental facts."

Ibn Khaldun then went on to cite examples of the problem from earlier Islamic historiography. In refuting them he relied on logistical arguments. For instance, Moses' Israelites could not have numbered 600,000 because if they "were in battle formation, [they] would extend two, three, or more times beyond the field of vision." He continued in this vein at some length, all the while adducing arguments that are perhaps even more valid in the state of the present evidence than they were in his time.[158] It is instructive to compare these views with those of the High Counters, for whom logistical considerations, whether tactical or strategic, never weigh heavily, on the rare occasions when they weigh at all.

Caesar's accounts of his wars have recently been described by Michael Grant as "extremely potent, subjective and clever works of self-advertisement and personal propaganda, disguised beneath apparent self-restraint and modesty."[159] Change "Caesar" to "Cortés" and the sentiment could be transposed bodily to Mexico.[160] The key to their acceptance lies, I think, in the matter-of-fact, understated style to which Grant refers. Caesar and Cortés developed a discursive style that is "modern" enough to win acceptance.[161] Thus both Caesar and Cortés provided enough circumstantial detail to account for the incredible numbers they thrust at readers to convince them that the core of their narrative must be accurate. This is no different from the strategy of many of the authors of the utopian tales discussed in chapter 19. As A. J. Woodman rightly pointed out, "we must . . . remember that descriptive detail is the hall-mark of the fabricator of history."[162]

In yet another way Caesar's reports to the Roman Senate and Cortés's dispatches to Charles V seem extraordinarily up-to-date. Consider contemporary "coachspeak," for instance, which consists so largely of telling fans that the opposing team is really better than its record indicates. The coach is warning fans not to be surprised if the home team does poorly, as well as hinting that they should be suitably impressed if the team does well—one-downmanship in aid of one-upmanship.

With the exception of Central America, the High Counters have not directly used warrior counts recently in assessing population, if for no other reason than that these numbers, however high, are never high enough for that purpose. Just the same, observing the way they have swallowed these accounts almost whole—certainly without in the least exploring the history of the matter—offers a discouraging window on the ways in which they think, if not calculate. Most dejecting of all are the ways in which they evade the basic responsibility to seek out for comparison similar kinds of data and their intepretation.[163] Failure to do this has resulted in a style of discourse and an epistemological stance that seems numberless scholarly generations behind the times.[164]

In trying to discern reasons why belief is so often preferred to doubt when there is no independent evidence sustaining either, it seems certain only that the large numbers in the sources are seen as, as indeed they are, congenial to the general argument.[165] By itself, this raison d'être is hardly unusual, but it is also a line of operation that cannot resist criticism so much as it must simply ignore it.[166] To this must be added the care with which both Caesar and Cortés couched their reports. As one scholar of rhetoric has put it:

> Cicero recommends that the speaker ingratiate himself through a careful arrangement of appeals: the accentuation of personal merit (but without arrogance), the diminution of personal faults, the stress on one's misfortunes and difficulties, and finally the use of prayer, entreaties, and expressions of humility.[167]

Far more fascinating than Cortés's implausible numbers leading to implausible triumphs on the field is the way in which he managed to out-Caesar Caesar even though the latter was a colleague of Cicero's for half a lifetime.[168]

By Wonder Inflamed

Ancient historians were not like modern historians, especially in their handling of numbers.

—Catherine Rubincam,
"Casualty Figures in the Battle Descriptions of Thucydides"

He used, too, to play jokes on his slaves, even ordering them to bring him a thousand pounds of spiders-webs and offering them a prize; and he collected, it is said, ten thousand pounds, and then remarked that one could realize from that how great a city Rome was.

—*Scriptores Historiae Augustae*,
referring to the emperor Elagabalus

Canvassing the High Counter literature easily reveals how radically these writers have forsaken the opportunity to contextualize their work within the much larger historiography of numbers—whether they refer to the sizes of armies and cities or to epidemic mortality. Beyond the occasional reference to purported mortality in such places as Iceland, the High Counters seem unaware of the great tradition of quantitative history outside the Americas that has thrived since the time of the earliest surviving evidence.[1] It is hardly possible to overcome this studied ignorance here, but offering in brief compass some relevant comparative work will contribute to assessing the probability that the High Counters' modus operandi can achieve success beyond the self-declared.

What follows in this and the subsequent two chapters is a "numbers in history" *tour d'horizon* intended to sketch the nature and extent of the problem. I make no attempt to be thoroughgoing, since that would be impossible. Even so, I hardly know where to begin. Chronologically, for instance, the predisposition to overestimate the number of enemies defeated or killed in battle is manifested about as early as it possibly could be—in one of the first surviving battle reports, in which Rameses II proclaimed his own valor and the superiority of his gods over those of the Hittites at the battle of Kadesh. Rameses spoke of "millions" of Hittites but modestly claimed to have killed—by himself—only the occupants of twenty-five hundred chariots.[2]

The practice endured after Rameses' time, though without need for his precedent.[3] Slight variations in number, though hardly in substance and purpose, appeared in the Assyrian royal annals, in the writings of Herodotus, and, for that matter, in the works of all the Greek and Roman historians.[4] As we have seen, Julius Caesar was an able and relentless practitioner of the art of exaggeration, a practice that was indefatigably followed by his successors at the helm of the Roman empire. And the Chinese annals for the "warring states" period are replete with virtually identical descriptions.

The breakup of the Roman empire, the conquest of the west by Germanic tribes, and the conquest of much of the east by the forces of Islam had no effect on this topos. Whether it was Christian monastic chroniclers or Islamic historians, the numbers remained larger than reality allowed, greater than logistics permitted, rounder than logic could reasonably accept. In all this, the concept of army size clearly bore no relationship to commonplace practicalities. Numbers that would have fighting forces occupy square kilometers in combat or urban populations that required unlivable densities and impossible numbers of food providers were thrust at readers as if the numbers themselves were sufficient sanction. They proved to be precisely that, in epistemological systems that preferred the easy weight of received authority to the dubious pleasures of doubting. An inevitable result was that the weight of numbers became ever greater because the impediments to such magnification remained inconsequential for so long.

This state of affairs reached a crescendo just about the time that Spanish chroniclers began to write about the numbers of peoples they were encountering in a dazzling new world. Just as the *res gestae* of antiquity were being recovered and revered, the chance to repeat these—or to believe that they were being repeated—providentially appeared. Cortés could not only admire Caesar but could also emulate him in accounts of his own activities. Even if spoilsports like Bernal Díaz del Castillo came along later to disagree, it was really too late, except for posterity, and posterity, in the person of the High Counters, has chosen to believe Cortés.

We can look at some of the corpus of work that the High Counters have so largely managed to overlook. Its size alone renders this neglect puzzling unless we assume that the High Counters have become so enamored of the potential of their arithmetic that critical source evaluation simply appears to be of little value to their enterprise. The corporate feeling might have been that however much this work addressed similar problems, it did so in ways that they had rendered obsolete by a renewed belief in the evidence, ably fortified by mathematics.

———

For several good reasons we might begin with the matter of battlefield numbers. It is the most extensive genre of its kind, as well as the easiest to falsify. Not surprisingly, it is well represented in the writings of the chroniclers of the Indies. Finally, it is a category on which the High Counters rely repeatedly—even though they use it symbolically, because however high the numbers are, they are ordinarily too low to be used arithmetically to calculate huge populations.

The world of the Greeks and Romans was the cynosure of the Renaissance and therefore of many of the chroniclers. In the literature of classical antiquity are satisfyingly large figures for the sizes of armies. The natural point of departure is Herodotus' account of the Persian invasions of Greece.[5] These occasions were the earliest in which Greeks fought non-Greeks, and repelling the invasions marked, by the view of the time, the saving of western civilization. Thus it was a story to be told and retold. Telling it Herodotus' way—and Herodotus had virtually a monopoly then as now—requires that the Persian invasion armies in 480 B.C. numbered no fewer than 2,080,000 fighting men, plus another 541,610 seamen, as well as equivalent numbers of camp followers—a horde so vast, over 5 million in all, that defeating it could only have been miraculous.[6] A critical modern perspective shows another miraculous side to the story—the feat of moving so many people so far so quickly. It could not have been done, and was not.[7]

The Renaissance found the acme of Greek military genius in the person of Alexander the Great, whose armies defeated vastly superior numbers time and again. These victories were due to superior discipline, weaponry, and fearlessness, as well as consummate campaign strategy and battlefield tactics. Although Alexander's reputation could easily have stood on these mere facts, this was scarcely ever permitted, and along the way things like the numbers of his opponents grew to mythic proportions. Thus, if we were to believe Alexander's chroniclers, he and his army of about 35,000 faced and routed as many as 110,000 Persians at Granicus, 600,000 at Issus, and over a million at the climactic battle of Gaugamela.[8] Based on logistics, topography, and battle detail, more likely numbers are 25,000, 50,000, and 80,000 to 120,000, respectively, but these are modern observations.[9] No one could be a second Alexander without defeating vastly superior forces on the battlefield. None of the Spanish leaders claimed quite this rarefied status, but they were all aware of the attractions of the victory of the vastly outnumbered army.[10]

Hannibal's defeat of the Romans at Cannae in 216 B.C. is the classic execution of the encirclement and annihilation of a superior force—battlefield tactics at their purest. How superior were the Romans at Cannae, and how many died on the field? Carthaginian accounts have not survived intact, and with them have been lost probably the highest estimates.[11] But the Roman chroniclers are not without their interest in this regard. In his account of the Punic wars Livy spoke of 45,500 or 50,000 casualties.[12] Polybius, who wrote only a few generations after the battle and long before Livy, but who was a Greek and not a Roman, offered a higher figure—70,000—and other ancient historians chose numbers between these extremes.[13] Modern estimates are more modest still—perhaps as few as 25,000 Romans and allies were left dead on the field.[14] Living off the countryside in hostile territory, Hannibal would have found that the forage requirements of his pack animals alone taxed his ability to support a large army, especially because he would have been competing with the Roman armies in the field at the same time, which in turn would have affected their own maximum size.[15]

Between the second Punic War and Caesar's campaigns in Gaul, the Roman armies fought several wars against Germanic tribes, the Cimbri and Teutones in particular. Gaius Marius defeated these groups between 103 and 100 B.C.[16] To read the sources, these peoples put enormous armies into the field, far greater than the Romans could respond with. We read of armies hundreds of thousands strong, all of which, however, were eventually all but annihilated by consular armies, a foretaste of what Caesar had in store for the Gallic tribes he faced.[17]

Later Roman estimates of other "barbarian" armies from the fourth to the sixth century were similarly overstated.[18] These frequently ran into the hundreds of thousands, topping out at half a million or so.[19] Early chroniclers recorded that as many as 300,000 combatants died in the battle of the Catalaunian Fields in 451, in which the Romans and Visigoths defeated the Huns.[20] Most modern estimates credit Attila with from 15,000 to 30,000 combatants, although a few moderns who have written on the subject bandy figures as high as 750,000, with 300,000 casualties.[21]

Nor was the urge to exaggerate confined to the West. The annals of the "warring states" period in China (403–221 B.C.) are rife with accounts of armies as large as 600,000 and battles in which hundreds of thousands of people lost their lives and only very small numbers survived. The annals record that one of these states, Qin, inflicted battle casualties of about 1.5 million in 130 years, even though the record is admittedly incomplete.[22]

It is not hard to suggest reasons why such numbers are so high. From the literary point of view, battles offer unparalleled set-pieces for dramatizing and moralizing. High numbers were often accompanied by rousing speeches presented verbatim, by reports of often impossible individual acts of heroism, and by lengthy discussions of why outmanned armies carried the day.[23] Very high numbers of combatants and casualties were often no more than minor dramatis personae. It is not distinctly odd that the High Counters have been so indulgent with respect to the sizes of armies and towns as cited in their sources. Just the same, they might have been expected to recognize the logistical implications of their acts of faith.

———

Even Herodotus, while he was assessing the size of the Persian hordes at precisely 5,283,220, took time to muse on the problems that such numbers must have created:

> I marvel how there were provisions sufficient for so many tens of thousands; for calculation shows me, that if each man received one choenix of wheat a day and no more, there would be every day a full tale of eleven hundred thousand and three hundred and forty bushels; and in this I take no account of what was for the women and eunuchs and beasts of draught and dogs.[24]

Herodotus was content to live with his puzzlement because the unwelcome alternative was to reduce the size of the Persian force.[25] He did not address the *en marche* implications of a force of the size he calculated. Modern scholars, unable to demonstrate on textual grounds alone that such figures are impossibly high, have begun to fall back on showing instead that it would have been physically impossible to provide the wherewithal to keep such armies going forward.

The case of Xerxes' invasion mirrors this well. By one calculation—among an infinite variety of possible scenarios—if the infantry marched ten abreast and the cavalry five abreast, the column would have been 1,320 miles long.[26] And even a column this wide would have been impossible at many stages along the journey because of topographical limitations.[27] By making his numbers absurdly high, Herodotus guarantees the success of exercises of this kind. Just the same, using substantially lower figures for the sake of argument, Young has shown that it would have taken literally millions of pack horses to victual the marching Persian army, requiring reductions to figures no larger than about 2–3 percent of those Herodotus advanced.[28]

Herodotus' estimate of the enemy was only the forerunner of innumerable such estimates right up to the present. A single example must suffice to strengthen the point. In 1402 Timur, the ruler of Samarkand more famously known as Tamerlane, invaded the Ottoman domains and defeated and captured the Ottoman sultan. Contemporaries were much struck by this cataclysmic occasion, and this reaction appeared forcefully in the numbers they ascribed to the combatants. Timur's army likely did not exceed 140,000 troops, but this scarcely inhibited estimates at the time, which ranged from 400,000 to 1.4 million. The highest—somewhat ominously—was that of an eyewitness. Bayazid's force, perhaps about 85,000, was estimated to have been as much as five times greater by the same sources.[29] In no case did the estimate in any exogenous source approximate the likely fighting strength of either force.

For estimates of urban population, we can turn to the worlds of both classical antiquity and the medieval and early modern traveler's account. (The observations of Cortés, Díaz del Castillo, and others fall clearly within the latter genre.) Frequently, figures are adduced that require little skepticism to doubt. Such a case is Josephus's statement that the district of Galilee contained in the first century A.D. exactly 204 villages, the smallest of which had 15,000 inhabitants.[30] This multiplies out to a minimum population of 3,060,000 (over 3,000 persons per square mile). Small wonder, then, that even those who would treat Josephus seriously as a historical source have had some trouble with his calculation.[31] Some who reject Josephus's population figures as "fanciful exaggerations" still accept, if sometimes only by implication, his number of villages, which, strictly speaking, has no more credibility.[32] Relying on Josephus to one degree or another, early modern estimates of the population of New Testament Palestine ranged from 2.5 million to 7 million.[33] Some, with latent ideological purposes, relied on him more than others.[34] Further recognition of the absurdities of Josephus's testimony and of the logistics of the particular situation has led to a series of new estimates of between 250,000 and 1 million at the low end and 1.5 million at the high end.[35]

Interest in total urban populations is modern—few early records of cities provide even rough estimates, forcing interested parties to seek proxy data on which to build. For early and medieval Islamic cities, typical surrogates are statements about the number of mosques or public baths in a given city. Both the raw data and the results of using them are often amusing, but no less minatory for that.

One of the most extensive exercises is that of André Raymond, who looked at the available evidence for several cities in the Ottoman empire. Since direct population data were "almost non-existent before 1850," he thought it "not unuseful" to look at the land areas of various cities and the numbers and munificence of civic monuments and public baths. When faced with choices, Raymond preferred to accept those estimates of population density and numbers of baths that reinforced one another. Not surprisingly, in the end his ratio of baths to persons was in every case between 1:3,500 and 1:4,500, and it is virtually impossible to determine whether Raymond was extracting population from baths or baths from population. Although admitting that population probably oscillated more frequently and rapidly than the number of baths, in the end Raymond virtually imposed a public bath master plan on the Ottomans—"one bath per 4,000 inhabitants constitutes an average number."[36]

If public baths played such a role, then medieval Muslims were a sanitary lot indeed. Yazdagird b. Mahbandar somehow believed that there were no fewer than 60,000 baths in Baghdad. Aggravating the situation, he allocated each of them 200 households of 8 persons each. The result—Baghdad's population in the eighth century was 96 million![37] Another historian of the period agreed and went on to claim that "[f]or each bathhouse there were five mosques, making a total of 300,000."[38] Slightly less fantastic, though hardly yet sensible, is Ibn cAbd al-Hakam's (d. 870/871) claim that at the Arab conquest Alexandria had 4,000 baths, 40,000 Jews, 400 royal pavilions, and 600,000 taxpaying adult males. These numbers are suspiciously symbolic as well as impossibly large.[39]

The numbers and sizes of mosques could also be seen as measures of piety, so it is hardly a surprise that enormous numbers of these were attributed to other important Muslim cities besides Baghdad. Thus Ibn al-Saci attributed 36,000 mosques to Fustat, a precursor of Cairo, and another 20,000 to Alexandria.[40] When the number of mosques or public baths is not recorded, observers have used the square superficies of particular extant mosques as an index of the population of the urban area they served. Using this method, Ibn al-Faqih (ninth century) produced populations for Córdoba, Damascus, and Baghdad of 1 million, 400,000, and 2 million, respectively.[41]

The approach has found a modern following. Josiah Russell tested this out for Damascus:

> The great mosque of Damascus had an inside surface of about 11,000m². Such a Friday mosque was expected to accommodate the entire adult Islamic male congregation of the city, perhaps a trifle less than a third of the civic population. Allowing about two m² to each worshipper, since he had to prostrate himself on his knees, there should have been room for about 15,000, thus about the same as the city area suggests.[42]

How inviting this approach is to circular reasoning! Why not more or less than two meters per worshipper? Did they fill the entire mosque? What happened when population grew or declined? Why were adult males "a trifle less" than one-third of the total population? What of non-Muslims?[43]

In archaeological contexts another expedient has been to estimate the possible water supply and from it the number of people drinking it. John Wilkinson attempted this for first-century Jerusalem. Necessarily, he was forced to work from a series of assumptions such as that water was brought from certain points to the city (no physical evidence available), and that the average daily consumption was, as he put it, "at the low rate" of twenty liters per capita. Having made these and other assumptions, each of which effectively raised the imputed population, Wilkinson estimated the city's population at more than one hundred thousand.[44] Like all such arguments, this was ineluctably circular because effectively it was designed to suggest the possibility of corroboration by independent means.[45]

For both archaeologists and historians, however, the principal method for estimating urban populations has been to estimate the area of a city and then apply an average density to it. The data are, as always, delightfully exiguous. Take one of the earliest examples of this approach—Herodotus' claim that Babylon was a square 120 by 120 stades, or a total area of nearly 200 square miles.[46] In his turn, Ctesias, who actually lived in Babylon for a time, reduced Herodotus' figure by a quarter.[47] In fact, more than a century of archaeological work on the site has revealed that the outer walls of Babylon were less than eight miles in circuit. Thus the city contained only about one-fiftieth the area that Herodotus claimed.[48]

In addition to estimating the size of Babylon, Herodotus provided a fairly detailed description of the city's layout and buildings as these were reputed to have been in the middle of the fifth century B.C.[49] Here archaeology has vindicated him to a surprisingly large extent, so it seems that Herodotus was able accurately to describe all he saw—or heard about—except matters relating to the *size* of Babylon. Some have exculpated him on the grounds that, as O. E. Ravn put it, this information "was doubtless given to him by informers [*sic*] or derived from combinations of figures he had heard."[50] By this argument, Herodotus was such a good eyewitness that when the evidence goes against him, he must not have been operating by autopsy. Although possible, of course, this hardly seems likely; if Herodotus was able to see, as well as to describe, the public buildings and gardens, he was also in a position to estimate for himself the length of the circuit of the city. That he failed so miserably more likely bespeaks a tendency to see the exotic in larger-than-life terms.

———

Pompeii offers a particularly fascinating example of the genre of urban population estimates. It is the best preserved city from ancient times—a fossil buried in ash that allows conclusions to be based on almost optimal archaeological conditions. This fortunate circumstance has not helped much in estimating Pompeii's population, and modern guesses range from less than 7,000 to as high as 30,000.[51] Giuseppe Fiorelli, the first serious excavator, estimated the population of Pompeii at about 12,000, deduced from the number of houses that had been unearthed multiplied by an average number of people per household, and then extrapolated to account for the presumed number of houses yet to be excavated.[52]

A few years later Heinrich Nissen, arguing that Fiorelli had not taken sufficient account of the second stories of these houses, tried to do so himself by raising Fiorelli's estimates to a minimum of 20,000 and a maximum of 30,000, even 50,000 seasonally.[53] Nissen's estimate resulted in a very high average population per household, which he attributed to large numbers of slaves. Julius Beloch disagreed, suggesting instead a population of 15,000.[54] Outside this line of descent, estimates of Pompeii's population in A.D. 79 have tended to be on the high side, coalescing at between 20,000 and 25,000 in the general and guidebook literature.[55] But then further excavation seemed to imply that large portions of the city were not residential areas after all, leading to estimates as low as 8,000, or even 6,400, permanent residents.[56] Wieslaw Suder considered that the population oscillated between 10,000 and 20,000, while most recently Andrew Wallace-Hadrill has also argued for the likelihood of small numbers, since continuing excavation has reduced the number of dwellings likely to have been full-time residences.[57]

Some estimates for Pompeii have also been based on the seating capacity of the amphitheater there, which the principal early excavator of the site calculated to be 12,807 but which is now thought to have been some 20,000.[58] The assumption seems to be that the size of the amphitheater, like the sizes of mosques, is somehow directly related, even over time, to the population of the city.[59] Even the sizes, numbers, and placements of beds have been brought into action to determine the "average" number of persons per household.[60]

Inevitably, though, both in the beginning and still, the number of—and number of stories in—buildings calculated to be residences and the total area of the city have been the starting points for most discussions. Both are subject to wide ranges of interpretation.[61] As noted, further excavations have shown that early projections of the number of households were too high, while determining the limits of the city has proven to raise issues that, although they have demographic implications, can hardly be addressed simply as a demographic issues. In general, however, estimates of total population in Pompeii have declined in recent years and are now usually about one-half earlier guesses. All in all, despite their unique state of preservation, the ruins of Pompeii have managed to defy every effort to yield an unexceptionable population figure. On the whole, estimates of the populations of ancient cities have tended to decline recently. As with army sizes, this has been a direct effect of employing more realistic logistical schemata for the evidence at hand. There is also a palpable freeing from the thrall of the ancient sources.[62]

The seductiveness of high numbers in an ancient setting is illustrated in the dispute over the population of Roman Britain. In 1929 R. G. Collingwood set a cat among the pigeons by arguing that 500,000 was "something like a maximum estimate."[63] Collingwood's new low estimate, as one observer put it, "arouse[d] opposition and incredulity."[64] Attacks on it were promptly forthcoming; the *gravitas* of these was that Collingwood had let the side down.[65] Collingwood's estimate had the effect of lowering further estimates, though not to his own proposed level. Whereas only a few years earlier Edward A. Foord had suggested that the Romano-British population at its height was "more than from 3,000,000 to 3,500,000," Mortimer Wheeler, in replying to Collingwood, thought it must have been around a million and a half.[66] In 1936 Collingwood met Wheeler halfway by changing his own figure to "a round million." More recently, others have suggested figures as high as 2 million.[67]

The contrast between the understanding of figures like those just cited and those used by the High Counters is striking. Many decades have passed since the scholarly study of the ancient and medieval art of war took the numbers in the sources so uncritically. Some have withstood modern testing, but most have not. Estimates of 600,000 Crusaders, 700,000 Huns, or more than 1 million Persians in Greece are now seen as ideas to be investigated rather than numbers to be believed and set into a frenzy of extrapolative motion.[68]

In the area of reported expenditures, which should ordinarily be more restricted in its opportunities than warrior counts or estimates of urban population, Walter Scheidel found very similar patterns in an extensive survey of classical allusions. This literature, he found, "is permeated by conventional or symbolic monetary valuations to an extent that seriously restricts the range even of tentative calculations and quantifying comparisons." To what extent? "[B]etween ninety and one hundred percent of all existing financial numerical data are merely conventional figures which cannot automatically be accepted as rough approximations or rounded variants of actual figures." Scheidel surmised that this game of conventions was shared between authors and readers—that the latter took the numbers presented to them with tongue pressed firmly in cheek. And he wondered why modern scholars have been so reluctant to participate in the exercise by these rules.[69]

———

In sheltering themselves against doubt through a studied unawareness of scholarly progress in the broader genre of numbers in history, the High Counters permit themselves the luxury of treating numerical evidence in a largely bygone fashion. In this way they can offer up, apparently seriously, such statements as "[w]ith this revision, if we calculate the aboriginal population, we arrive at 7,975,000, or in round numbers eight millions" for the population of Hispaniola in 1492.[70] Or, in a fashion that even Herodotus and Moses of Khorene would have found risible: "Perhaps 58,178,666 Amerindians inhabited [central Mexico] just before the malarial parasite attacked in 1516 [*sic*]."[71]

Yet none of the problems with numbers that has been been suggested here should come as a surprise. Thomas Burns expressed the reason succinctly when he described the numbers imputed to the Germanic invaders during the later Roman empire, writing that only one chronicler of the period "avoided the temptation to inflate the size of the German armies in order to increase the magnitude of the Roman victories or explain Roman defeats."[72]

More than fifty years ago Michael Rostovtzeff concluded gloomily, but realistically, that "the evidence at our disposal . . . does not allow us to form even an approximate idea of the density of the population of the Hellenistic world, of its fluctuations, or of the relative size of the various elements in the population, such as the proportion of free citizens to metics [immigrants] and slaves in the cities, and of natives to immigrants in the eastern monarchies."[73] Given the great advantages in terms of evidence that the ancient world has on the world of the chroniclers of the Indies, the invulnerable optimism of the High Counters can only have a strong tinge of rose to it.[74]

Epidemic Hyperbole

Now I am going to be liberal about this thing, and consider that fifty million whites have died in America from the beginning up to today— make it sixty if you want to; make it a hundred million—it's no dif-ference about a few millions one way or t'other.

— Mark Twain, "Captain Stormfield"

Numbers are so much the measure of everything that is valuable, that it is not possible to demonstrate the success of any action, or the pru-dence of any undertaking, without them.

—The *Spectator*, 19 September 1711

Having looked at figures deriving from warfare, we turn to estimates of deaths by disease, the victims of which were often seen in early times as casualties in the struggle with the forces of evil. Numerous epidemics afflicted the Mediterranean world before 1492. Death from disease most urgently drives the High Counters' calculations, to the point that they occasionally reach out to dredge in figures from else-where on their behalf. But whereas most ancient and medieval esti-mates of death from disease are purportedly eyewitness, the High Counters are generally forced to calculate theirs as by-products of other mathematical manipulations, or simply to assume that they occurred.[1]

The impact of the Black Death in Egypt and its concomitant ef-fects on modern efforts to determine the population at the time on the basis of reports of epidemic mortality shows this line of argument at work. In 1938 A. N. Poliak, using a familiar modus operandi, sug-gested that a report of 900,000 deaths, along with the further asser-tion that the Black Death killed off about one-third of the population, made it easy to calculate that there were about 3 million inhabitants of Egypt at the time.

Unfortunately, Poliak got most of his data wrong. In the first place, al-Maqrizi, an early source for this episode but not the source Poliak used, stated unambiguously that 900,000 had died just in Cairo itself, and then during only a two-month stretch. He went on: "This did not include those who died" in several places "outside Cairo, whose number was several times bigger than that."[2] Considering that the epidemic lasted for an entire year, David Ayalon, adopting Poliak's arithmetical premises for effect, calculated that getting the evidence right required a projected population for all of Egypt of between 108 million and 216 million. Another manuscript tradition reads that the loss was *two*-thirds of the population, which would in turn halve these figures. They would still be enormously too high, but the point is that Poliak failed to consider all the relevant sources and to get correct those that he did consult.[3]

Had Poliak cast his net more widely, he might have noticed that about a century after the Black Death struck Egypt, a local historian, Ibn Taghri Birdi, commented on epidemic mortality. When faced with discrepant numbers Ibn Taghri Birdi tended to prefer the higher choice (though often adding "but only God knows"). Still, he saw a problem in his sources: "In connection with [a later epidemic] I pondered about each epidemic that took place in previous generations and up to our own time [and I concluded that the] figures given were nothing but guesswork and conjecture, and I am ashamed to say, mere speculation."[4]

———

A recent and relevant development in the history of medicine is the trend to attribute specific diseases to incidents mentioned in works that are not usually regarded as historical. The effect, if not the purpose, is to lend credence to the whole by identifying some part of it as having a real-world counterpart. Thus, when F. Wessely recently put a modern name (in this case, leptospirosis) to the "pestilence" mentioned in the *Iliad,* he embraced a much larger hypothesis—that there was a Trojan war which lasted ten years (since the pestilence took place in its ninth year) and which progressed much as Homer described it in his work.[5]

Epidemiologically, the Trojan war is small potatoes: the well-known prelude to the flight of the Israelites from Egypt described in Exodus has caught the attention of historians most dramatically in this respect.[6] There it is recorded that Jahweh visited no fewer than ten punishments in quick succession on the Egyptians. The last of these was a pestilence that killed firstborn male offspring, both human and animal. The story, and the miraculous passage of the Red Sea, is familiar as a story; as history it is both dubious and doubted. But only recently: this biblical account is unquestionably the paradigm that for three millennia shaped concepts of disease etiology in the Judeo-Christian tradition, including concepts behind the accounts of epidemics that festoon the chronicles of the Indies. Along the way the plagues, and in particular the pestilence, have beguiled those who would accept the literal truth of the biblical account, and even those not so inclined.

A puzzling development is the recent urge to diagnose this episode retroactively in the pages of medical journals. Thus, in a tour de force, H. M. Duncan Hoyte not only identified the tenth plague, the pestilence, as typhoid fever but also found himself able to ascribe a medical or natural reason to each of the other nine.[7] John S. Marr and Curtis D. Malloy have done the same, although with different results in almost every case. In their scheme of things, the tenth plague resulted from "mycotoxins specific to stored grains" that "preferentially killed [the] first to access [the] store."[8] This ingenious argument accounts to their satisfaction for the biblical claim that the plague struck only the "eldest," by claiming that "eldest" and "first" were just two ways of saying the same thing. In short, the story of the ten plagues was substantially a true relation, missing in its own discourse only the naturalistic explanations that modern science can now provide.[9]

Of course there have been skeptics as well. Some, like Donald Redford, an Egyptologist who was struck by the anachronistic topographical features of the Exodus account and by other anomalies, doubt that there was an exodus at all and, a fortiori, a series of plagues that preceded and provoked it.[10] For his part, John Van Seters regards the plague narrative as a "literary creation" from exilic times, built on other biblical passages relating to later events.[11] Others have pointed out that other biblical allusions to these purported plagues differ substantially from the classical case in Exodus.[12]

Biblical accounts mention several other plagues, each of them described as an instance of God's aiding the Israelites—the righteous Israelites anyway. Again, modern attempts have been made to identify these. Among them was the plague recorded as striking the Philistines in retaliation for their kidnapping the ark of the covenant. Notably, or so the biblical account tells us, when the ark was returned, the plague subsided. Some modern scholars have suggested that this was the first known instance of the bubonic plague, although other candidates have been put forward.[13]

As Lawrence Conrad, a Semiticist, has pointed out, there are both textual and contextual reasons against accepting the very existence of this particular case of divine punishment of the Philistines. On the basis of textual analysis, Conrad concluded that "[t]here is simply not a shred of evidence indicative of bubonic plague which does not collapse into nothingness when subjected to critical examination."[14] He continued that it would be pointless to argue over the identity of the incident, since the account "is composed of a variety of didactic details provided in order to illustrate an overarching religious theme [God's righteous punishment] and not to describe any particular historical event."[15] Clearly, though, the commitment to belief and to retrospective diagnosis ensures that modern efforts to cure biblical patients will continue.[16]

If Exodus and the *Iliad* have provided pretexts for discerning identifiable diseases, then other, undeniably historical epidemics have provided similar opportunities to magnify their effects, most often in aid of seeing the hand of providence in action. Nowhere has this been more the case than in the so-called plague of Justinian, which ravaged the Byzantine empire and other areas of the Mediterranean world in the 540s. The modern consensus is that this epidemic represented the maiden voyage of bubonic plague into the western world. The principal source for the effects of the epidemic in the Byzantine world is Procopius, an eyewitness and historian of his times. Like Thucydides a thousand years earlier, Procopius reported that the epidemic had originated in "Ethiopia."[17] Be that as it might, the disease soon reached Constantinople, where, if we are to believe Procopius, enormous numbers of people fell victim to it.

Procopius subscribed firmly to the notion that this epidemic was "sent from Heaven" and in fact took pains to refute those who would "fabricate outlandish theories of natural philosophy"—that is, those who looked for a terrestrial cause. Procopius was certain that "[i]t is quite impossible either to express in words or to conceive in thought any explanation, except indeed to refer it to God."[18] In giving God due credit, Procopius offered numbers that can only be wildly exaggerated. Speaking of Constantinople itself, he wrote that the disease lasted four months there, of which three saw particular virulence. Eventually, "the tale of the dead reached five thousand each day, and again it came to ten thousand and still more than that."[19]

Procopius was thus vague as well as apocalyptic. His numbers could be used to support almost any calculation—and have been. In a general history of the Byzantine empire, Harold Lamb wrote that "[w]itnesses . . . say that more than 300,000 perished . . . out of a population of some three quarters of a million."[20] T. H. Hollingsworth, a historical demographer, paid more attention to Procopius but still came up with a figure nearly as high—244,000. He did this by taking Procopius's "still more than that" to represent 10,500, a dubious proposition but at least a conservative one, and by using mortality in seventeenth-century England and a series of other speculative conditions, none of them demonstrably correct—or incorrect.[21] Using Procopius's description as well, and adopting a population for Constantinople that was little more than one-half that which Hollingsworth had used, Timothy Bratton arrived at a figure of only 57,660 deaths.[22] Finally, Glanville Downey followed Procopius almost to the letter when he wrote of "5,000 deaths a day in the capital, and when the visitation was at its worst it was estimated that 10,000 people died every day."[23]

The range here is fivefold, but it could have been much greater, for Procopius's text allows almost endless possibilities.[24] For instance, one could assume 3,000 deaths a day for one month, 7,500 a day for two more months, and, say, 16,000 (to "corroborate" John of Ephesus) for the month of greatest intensity. This series of calculations—the spirit of which will seem familiar—leads to a mortality figure of 1,020,000, and with it the implied argument that this figure could be pushed even higher with a few additional twists.[25]

There is more to consider than mathematics here—for instance, the context and the author. When he was writing this account, Procopius had conceived a violent hatred of Justinian and his wife, even writing a diatribe that came to be called "the secret history," alleging numerous enormities on their part.[26] At one point in this, Procopius plainly wrote that as a result of the Byzantine conquest of the Vandal kingdom in North Africa, "if one should venture to say that five million men perished in Libya alone, he would not, I imagine, be telling the half of it." If this seems outlandish, bear in mind that the chapter in which this very Lascasian accusation occurred was entitled "How Justinian Killed a Myriad Myriads of Myriads of People." Since a myriad was 10,000, Procopius was in effect alleging that one trillion $(10,000^3)$ people had died.[27] Should we assume optimistically, if paradoxically, that while Procopius could think in terms of trillions he could also be accurate in terms of thousands? Of course we can, but it would be a perilous and self-indulgent conceit.[28]

If the effects of Procopius's antipathy toward the Byzantine court create credibility problems, so do other aspects of his account. For instance, it was consciously based on Thucydides' narrative of the Plague of Athens.[29] While this is not implausible—though hardly the stuff for grand theorizing—it has the character of a topos, and in any case it would seem unwise to grant literal belief to *any* description that professes to be literary imitation.[30]

Similar exaggerations marked accounts of epidemics in the Islamic world. These accounts are anecdotal and conventionalized in their details, as well as marked by reports of enormous casualties. Thus, according to one account, Basra was struck by an epidemic in 689 during which "[e]very day for three days 70,000 perished."[31] In a later account of the same occasion, the numbers crept upward—now they were 70,000, 90,000, and 93,000, and "on the fourth day the population was snuffed out."[32] In describing another plague, this same author wrote that "on the first day of the plague 70,000 died, on the second day seventy-some thousand died, and on the third day the people were snuffed out," no luckier in their turn than Caesar's Usipetes or Ramesses' Hittites.[33] And according to the Icelandic chronicles, London fared little better during the Black Death, with only "fourteen men" surviving the ordeal.[34]

Later compilers of plague mortality estimates tended to add episodes as well as to inflate casualties; sometimes, for instance, authors writing under one dynasty sought to discredit its predecessor for provoking God's wrath. Invariably, in one way or another, Muslim historians treated epidemics as signs of divine displeasure and frequently associated them with other terrestrial and extraterrestrial portents.[35] As Lawrence Conrad puts it: "Plagues and pestilence were subjects surrounded by an aura of legend and superstition, and the Black Death [which occurred during Ibn Abi Hajala's lifetime] and later plagues ensured that tales of epidemics and prophecies of doom would remain topics of great interest."[36] This tendency was noticed as early as the fifteenth century, when Ibn Hajar al-ᶜAsqalani chastised earlier compilers of plague chronologies for incorporating floods, famines, and droughts into their definitions of plagues.[37]

Writing in A.D. 166, Lucian of Samosata spoke of a contemporary historian, Crepereius Calpurnianus, who was such "a keen emulator of Thucydides" that he had "brought down on the people of Nisibis" in Mesopotamia "a sort of plague" that he had "lifted . . . from Thucydides in its entirety," except for a minor detail.[38] Lucian's implication is that the plague was a fictional device that Calpurnianus had adopted in a frankly imitative spirit. Just the same, several students of the Antonine plague that ravaged the Roman empire and its environs about that time take Lucian to be describing an actual event, if at the same time criticizing its telling, and imply that the event was part of the larger epidemic.[39] Some have even gone so far as to attribute to Lucian himself the provenance and description of the plague, completely ignoring Lucian's scathing comments.[40]

These authors take heart in the fact that Lucian failed to call Calpurnianus a liar in so many words, but it is a slender reed, since Lucian was clearly accusing him of producing a pastiche of Thucydides even to the point of introducing absurd anachronisms.[41] Moreover, the passage on Calpurnianus is in the very midst of a section in which Lucian lampooned historians who, he felt, had sacrificed accuracy to artifice, and he certainly says as much when treating Calpurnianus. The alleged plague at Nisibis is a minor affair in the historiography of disease, but it suggests that epidemic as metaphor needs to be considered in attempting to give life to death.

––––––––––

Another important recent stimulus to creating phantom plagues has been the production of several histories of particular diseases in which the authors seem irresistibly drawn to epidemiological imperialism. Of these perhaps the most determined is Donald Hopkins's history of smallpox.[42] In this work Hopkins's disease of choice takes on a time-depth and universality heretofore unknown as he co-opts virtually every major recorded epidemic from the earliest times. Thus, for him the Plague of Athens was smallpox; so were the Justinianic plague and any number of other epidemics recorded in one place or another. Not satisfied with this, Hopkins turns historical incidents that were clearly not instances of epidemic disease into smallpox. Hopkins follows Eusebius in according an epidemic—smallpox, he is sure—to Palestine and Syria in A.D. 312, although other sources, equally likely to mention such an event, all fail to do so.[43] As an argument from silence this is only middling, but Hopkins was remiss in overlooking the silence.

Other of Hopkins's imputations merit less benefit of any doubt and might truly be disbelieved. For instance, he sees an episode of smallpox in Quintus Curtius Rufus's account of Alexander the Great's campaign in India. Again, no other source mentions this particular incident, but it hardly matters since Quintus Curtius's account can stand alone as an example of something that was *not* smallpox. He had little to say about the occasion, mentioning only that the attack followed immersion in "a salt lake" and that applying oil to the affected areas proved to be a "cure." This scarcely sounds like smallpox, or infectious disease of any sort, but Hopkins compounds the error by describing the incident as "a fatal illness," even though Quintus Curtius mentioned no deaths either.[44]

Hopkins again discerned smallpox in the Qur'anic account of the miraculous destruction of an invading Ethiopian army by the citizens of Mecca in A.D. 570. The Qur'an speaks not of disease but of hordes of birds who dropped "stones of baked clay" on the invaders. Early Islamic accounts treated the story literally, but later exegetes decided that it was more fitting to regard the occasion as a divine visitation of smallpox designed to mark Muhammad's birth and, as it happens, the heroics of his grandfather in the campaign.[45] In none of these cases—and others—is Hopkins alone in his belief that these were recollections of epidemics, although he was the first to weave them into an overarching argument of a specific disease transmission. Regrettably, in citing precedents and sources, he is too often content to rely on modern secondary materials, especially those from the nineteenth century, rather than seeking out the original texts.[46]

Subtler changes more often account for the continuing belief in epidemics that probably never were. A good example relates to the purported epidemic at Antioch in 1098, the casualties from which I discussed earlier. Matthew of Edessa, an Armenian historian who wrote within a generation of the events, described the losses proportionately. Most scholars are likely to gain an awareness of Matthew's testimony through a recent military history of the First Crusade. There, relying on a translation into French from the Armenian original, John France writes that "Matthew of Edessa actually says that during the siege of Antioch the Franks lost one in seven of their men to plague."[47] The French passage, however, is not nearly so explicit epidemiologically: "Following the famine, sickness [*maladie*] was introduced among the Crusaders; of seven men they lost one."[48] A recent translation of this source from the original Armenian into English is even vaguer, as well as clearly different: "[B]ecause of the scarcity of food, mortality and affliction fell upon the Frankish army to such an extent that one out of five perished."[49]

Neither of the translated texts, however they might otherwise differ, speaks of a plague or an epidemic but only of sickness and mortality under trying conditions. In using the term "plague" France exceeds his evidence, perhaps because he is aware that other sources mention an epidemic at about this time. He might well be correct in believing in a plague, but he is clearly incorrect in attributing such a belief to Matthew of Edessa.

As these examples suggest, plagues, epidemics, and pestilences were all indiscriminately adopted topoi—standard tools of literary license. As metaphors they were ideal, as apocalypses they were unparalleled, as examples of the gravity of the divine they were irresistible.[50] Small wonder, in the circumstances, that they are a great deal more ubiquitous in literature than in life.[51]

———

This magnification of the effects of disease was almost a matter of religion, since episodes of epidemic disease were so frequently seen as the punitive hand of God made manifest. Daniel Denton, a minister's son, synthesized the comments of centuries of observers when he wrote in apparent puzzlement about the Indians on Long Island late in the seventeenth century:

> [I]t is to be admired, how strangely they have decreast by the Hand of God, since the *English* first setling of those parts; for since my time, where there were six towns, they are reduced to two small Villages, and it hath generally been observed, that where the *English* came to settle, a Divine Hand makes way for them, by removing or cutting off the *Indians,* either by Wars one with the other, or by some raging mortal Disease.[52]

In seeing things this way, Denton—and all those for whom he stands surrogate—was only reprising the biblical account in which Moses had it directly from the mouth of God that the plagues visited on the Egyptians were signs of divine displeasure from which the Israelites were providentially exempted.[53] In couching the description as a struggle between believers and unbelievers, good and evil, life and death, what could be more natural than to accentuate the disparity of the two sides—the good side becoming commensurately better as the bad becomes worse?[54]

A failure to consider disease in the historical record as an epistemological as well as an epidemiological phenomenon leads irresistibly to a broad-gauged willingness to accept both its existence in every case and the apocalyptic results attributed to it. Having ascribed a supernatural origin to the "plague," Procopius could hardly do less than describe its effects in equally apocalyptic fashion. But nearly fifteen centuries have elapsed since Procopius thought and wrote—long enough that thinking along with him is indefensibly anachronistic.[55]

Careful Errors

We thus publish this statistic [that 340,960 Kongolese were baptized from 1672 to 1700] in a purely documentary way and without any pretension that it can serve as the basis for any scientific work whatever.

—E. de Jonghe and T. Simar,
Archives congolaises

[I]t was said that there were eighty thousand Moors gathered in this village of Manilla when this occurred. Indeed, one should subtract seventy-eight thousand from the eighty thousand mentioned in order to reach the two thousand that there might have been from the said village of Manilla and surrounding villages, including women and children, who were many.

—"Relación de la conquista
de la isla de Luzon"

While Spanish military men were estimating the sizes of Indian armies, and while Spanish administrators were trying to count *tributarios* and others, Spanish religious were advancing their own estimates of the numbers of Indians with whom they came into contact. It is only to be expected that the High Counters would be attracted to the baptismal figures that appear in several of the missionary chronicles. The appeal is obvious—these numbers are impressively and congenially large. As early as 1948 Cook and Simpson turned to this category. They admitted that "[n]o actual count of baptisms has come down to us," but they were not discouraged, since there were "certain summaries or estimates of totals made by the participating friars." They noted the existence of modern skepticism regarding these numbers; because they are "so large" they "have been considered grossly exaggerated." They thought it unlikely that there was a "willful desire to magnify the exploits of the missionaries"; as a result, the chroniclers, "particularly such men as Motolinía [their main source], must be absolved."[1]

Such arguments overlook any number of reasons why the missionaries would inflate baptismal figures. They needed to justify their activities and to seek continued financial support from the crown. Moreover, each of the missionary orders in Mexico saw its counterparts as much as competitors for official goodwill as co-workers in proselytization. Even more did they feel the need to escape the baneful authority of the bishops and diocesan clergy. Finally, they saw themselves as the instruments for the greatest accession of souls to the mystical body of Christ in many centuries.

Uninterested in this state of affairs, Cook and Simpson went on to suggest that the missionaries needed to know "who had been converted and who not; that is to say, the number of conversions at any particular time." In addition, they thought, the authorities were "too well acquainted with their territories to tolerate gross misrepresentation in the baptismal claims." Their reasoning led them to conclude, confidently if more than a little optimistically, that "no one at the time, or since, was or is in a better position than the early missionaries to estimate the number of conversions, and to ignore their testimony would be a strange departure from historical method."[2]

Failing to notice that blindly accepting this testimony was even stranger, Cook and Simpson immediately followed their own advice. They used whatever baptismal figures they could find to support their own estimate of central Mexican population during the sixteenth century—an estimate that was little more than half their final estimate reached fifteen years later.[3] In doing so they took several liberties with this evidence and failed to notice the numerous discrepancies in the testimony of Motolinía and the other missionary chroniclers that should have alerted them at once to the dangers of using this kind of evidence undiscriminatingly.[4]

Cook and Borah, and later Henry Dobyns, continued the theme. In an essay devoted specifically to the value of the sources for demographic reconstruction, Cook and Borah returned to the matter, albeit more briefly. Here they adopted a tactic common to their work—asserting that the various baptismal estimates were independently derived and thereby mutually corroborative. This is hardly the case, since Torquemada relied heavily on both Mendieta and Motolinía, Mendieta on Motolinía, and Motolinía on we know not whom.[5] In the process Cook and Borah expressed the only kind of doubt they knew:

they decided to regard Motolinía's estimates as "too conservative" and promptly more than doubled them.[6]

Cook, Simpson, and Borah dealt with baptismal figures at the local and regional levels and did not wonder about the logistics of baptism as the chroniclers occasionally presented them. These described prodigies of stamina and time management in rendering their accounts. It was left to Henry Dobyns to follow this line of thought. Dobyns began with a familiar claim: "[I]nternal evidence . . . suggests that [Motolinía], and probably other priests, *under*estimated the number of baptisms actually performed during the first 15 years of mass conversion" in Mexico.[7] The evidence in question consisted entirely of a few anecdotal accounts. For instance, Motolinía happened to relate one case in which two priests purportedly baptized 14,200 Indians in five days, or one Indian per priest per minute throughout the entire period.[8] Dobyns admitted that for him this "rings true."

Dobyns went on to cite a second instance in which, according to him, "another priest" was credited with baptizing 14,000 Indians in a single day—one baptism every six seconds nonstop.[9] Here we encounter yet another of those instances in which a High Counter comes to grief for failing to engage the sources effectively, although in this case Dobyns is hardly without companionship. Operating at fourth-hand, Dobyns misread his source, Rosenblat, who in turn had apparently mistaken his own source. According to this last source, the missionary in question, Pedro de Gante, "and another companion" baptized "more than 200,000 [Indians] and even more, that I [Gante] myself do not know the number . . . in one day 14,000 persons, other times 10[,000], other times 8,000."[10] Going back even farther, to the Latin original, we find it even more emphatically expressed: "I [Gante] and another friar, my companion" did the baptizing.[11]

There are still more complications to this apparently innocuous account. Just as Gante seemed to make his case more plausible by introducing a second missionary to divide the labor, he made it less credible in another way. This was not obvious to Rosenblat, and therefore to Dobyns, since they relied on an account that happened to omit two words, "con frecuencia." Ultimately, then, we learn that Gante claimed that he and a colleague not only baptized 14,000 Indians on one particularly efficient day, but that they did it "frequently."[12]

Perhaps it is too much to expect that Dobyns would trace back the content and meaning of this particular brief account, on which he depended so heavily. Oddly, if he had, he would have found it all the easier to continue, as he did, in a whirlwind of extrapolative energy that concluded with the calculation that "[s]ixty priests would have baptized 2,184,000 Indians annually."[13] The "internal evidence," then, turned out to be Dobyns's own calculations rather than data in the sources—categories he frequently treats as interchangeable.

———

In deciding what "rings true," Dobyns apparently failed to sense the logistical difficulties in his argument, but in response to a comment published with his article, he referred to "the pertinence of knowing 'minimum ceremonial requirements' for the sacrament" and cited a modern example of marriage practices in Peru on his behalf.[14] He failed to elaborate, presuming that readers would acknowledge that he knew these "requirements," whatever they were. His implication, though, was clearly that the Spanish clerics cut procedural corners in order to accommodate the tens of thousands of clamoring Indians.

Studies of baptismal practices in New Spain in the 1520s and 1530s, however, do little to support the notion that the missionaries treated baptism peremptorily, whatever they might have done about other sacraments.[15] True, they did not offer the same degree of pre-baptismal instruction that was later to be the case. In part, of course, the chance to baptize thousands of adult converts was a new departure.[16] Nonetheless, even though Robert Ricard could refer to "a more or less summary, more or less hasty, instruction" that "always preceded" baptism, it is clear that carrying this out would by itself have stretched the resources of the small number of priests in New Spain in the first decade after the conquest.[17]

In terms of daily output rates, it is the actual administration of the sacrament that needs to be considered. Dobyns's argument would require that the missionaries merely tossed holy water and chrism in the direction of the Indian masses, but this was hardly the case. As Motolinía himself related, an elaborate ritual accompanied the occasion, even if, as Ricard notes, it was limited to "the strictly essential."[18] But, as Ricard goes on, paraphrasing Motolinía, the occasion nonetheless entailed much:

Motolinía tells us that they assembled all candidates for baptism and placed the children in the front row, upon whom they performed [the rite of] exorcism. Thereupon they selected only a few upon whom to perform the ceremonies preliminary to the essential rite: the insufflation of the Holy Ghost (*flato*), the sign of the cross (*cruz*), the introduction of salt into the mouth (*sal*), and the rite of ephphatha (*saliva*). They [the candidates] were dressed in a white robe, the symbol of innocence, which normally was not done until after baptism by water. When these ceremonies were completed, the infants were baptized one by one with holy water and were sent away. Then the adults were given a second instruction in the significance of the sacrament they were about to receive and the obligations it implied, and in their turn were baptized one by one.[19]

After this there was a sermon, and some of the adults would be questioned about their understanding of the purpose and effects of baptism. Motolinía went on to add that "[t]his procedure has always been followed, so far as I know."[20] Fourteen thousand baptisms in one day under these circumstances? It seems not even remotely possible. Just the mention of white robes is enough to give serious pause. Were there at least fourteen thousand of these, so that all the Indians could don them beforehand? Or did they need to be passed from one person to another hundreds of times throughout the ceremony?[21] Motolinía, then, much the same as Bernal Díaz del Castillo, proves a slender reed when his testimony is consulted *en ensemble*. We can hardly know whether the disparity between his numbers and his descriptions ever occurred to Motolinía, who, after all, was neither a scholar in the modern sense nor dispassionate in any sense.[22]

Even these procedures became less widespread (although not immediately extinct) when a conclave of high-ranking ecclesiastics met in Mexico City in 1539 and reaffirmed papal directives against mass baptism without a full panoply of instruction.[23] Although Motolinía and others threatened to disregard the directives, and probably did on occasion, such mass baptisms could no longer have been considered the norm once the official weight of the church was against them.[24]

With respect to baptismal counts, even more than for warrior and *tributario* estimates, there is the unknown and unknowable variable of multiple counting. It might well have been that Indian fighting men tried not to encounter the Spaniards more than once, and even more likely that potential *tributarios* did the same. But if Indians tended to regard baptism as a defense against disease—as at least some evidence suggests—then what better tactic than to flock to baptism sites time and again in an effort to ensure immunity?[25] In the crowd conditions implied by the descriptions of Motolinía and others, it would have been impossible for the missionaries to be fully aware of this phenomenon, however much they might suspect it.

There is also evidence that as late as 1540 the proportion of Indians who had been baptized was still small in places. Studying several towns in Morelos, Sarah Cline concluded that "if [these towns] are taken as models of communities in the early stages of evangelization, then the Indians cannot be said to have embraced Christianity en masse."[26] Her sample is small, to be sure, and perhaps the missionaries somehow overlooked the Morelos area (only about fifty miles from Mexico City) in their frenetic activity, but it has yet to be contradicted by similar microstudies showing that large numbers of Indians were baptized in these early years—the very years about which Motolinía wrote.[27] James Lockhart agrees that before about 1540 the progress of conversion was "unhurried . . . tending ultimately toward universal baptism."[28]

Figures from other times and places in the Americas, perhaps most of all from Peru, contrast sharply with the Mexican figures. As late as 1565 one observer calculated that only about 300,000 adults had been baptized in Peru. This is a much lower percentage of postulated contact population than that attributed to Mexico, and over a period half again as long. Pedro Borges suggested that this "slow rhythm" was the result of the civil instability that marked the area until after 1550, but it seems equally likely that such instability would have motivated the Indians toward baptism.[29]

Although a Franciscan himself and sympathetic to the aims and claims of Motolinía and his confreres, Borges remained skeptical of their baptismal figures. "Naturally," he concluded his discussion of them, "many of these numbers cannot be taken literally." He went on:

> It is well known that in the sixteenth century, along with a lack of the numerical sense that we have today, there was a strong tendency to exaggerate, either by excess, as in this case, or by absence. The writers of the time, and not only the missionaries, spoke with the same facility of millions of Indians converted as of millions of Indians unbaptized, according to whether each approached the question from an optimistic point of view or from the opposite.

All was not entirely bleak in this regard, however. Some figures— Borges mentioned two thousand and four thousand as examples— accorded well with the pace of conversion that the sources suggested. He noticed that figures in sources not intended for immediate consumption tended to be more realistic and concluded that the missionaries could count fairly accurately when it suited them.[30]

In the High Counters' appraisal of missionary baptismal statistics and in their extrapolation from them, two characteristic methods emerge. The first is the errant use of sources; the other is the credulity with which the High Counters approach these data. We see how they are satisfied to dare their readers to doubt the goodwill, and therefore the essential accuracy, of the missionaries' claims. If they believed this themselves, it suggests an unawareness of work on such statistics done in other mission fields, which gives further reason to doubt whether the testimony of Motolinía and others can be taken as more than pious hyperbole.[31] If the daily figures cited by the chroniclers are impossible to credit, could their aggregate figures be more credible? They could, if there were reason to accept that inaccurate subtotals can lead to accurate totals. This seems distinctly counterintuitive, but discussing briefly the history of baptismal figures from other mission fields could strengthen the credibility of the Mexican figures.[32]

In the kingdom of Kongo, similar prodigies were reported. For instance, in 1704 a historian of the Capuchins wrote that a single Capuchin missionary, Félix de Villar, had baptized "more than 600,000" people in "only four years [1648–52]." The author went on: "[W]ho can say how many they baptized before and since, since it has been the case that for more than seventy years the sacrament has been administered continuously."[33] Another missionary claimed that he had baptized 100,000 persons in nineteen years, but even this contextually modest figure has been characterized as "an unintended exaggeration."[34]

Impressive numbers, but they can hardly compare with the accomplishments of another Capuchin, Cherubino da Savona. Savona was in Africa from 1759 to 1774 and was later to claim that he ("I myself") baptized some 700,000 people.[35] Indeed, it would seem that these were uncommonly productive years for all the Capuchins; just twelve years later, another missionary estimated that a further 388,000 Africans had been baptized in the previous eight years, including, it was added, more than 200,000 baptized in the month of April 1785 alone.[36] Similar, if not quite so astonishing, numbers continued to be recorded into the nineteenth century.

Baptismal numbers have been used to produce population trends for Kongo and its vicinity just as they have for central Mexico. Duarte Lopes was one of the first to offer an overall estimate. He had resided in the Kongo briefly from 1578 to 1583, and in 1588 wrote to Sixtus V regarding conditions there. In this letter he conjectured that there were "more than two million baptized Christians" in the kingdom—presumably the total population was considerably larger even than that.[37] Similar numbers crop up during the following two centuries.[38]

Several modern scholars see these figures as at least evocative.[39] Louis Jadin, for instance, though professing himself of two minds, conceded the benefit of his doubts and eventually accepted the basic accuracy even of Cherubino da Savona's claim that the population of the Kongo state "counted six million inhabitants" as late in the eighteenth century.[40] He exhibited some initial skepticism: as "a witness originating from the Mediterranean coast," Savona might have been prone to "some exaggeration."[41] Further, Jadin noted that Savona's estimate was more than twice that of any other recorded, and, as he observed, other contemporary estimates were much lower. On the other hand, Jadin was impressed by some of the details Savona presented—the names of chiefs and "even those of their wives," as well as data on churches and hospitals. In all, Savona seemed a responsible, even authoritative, witness on these matters, so why not on population levels? Jadin concluded that it would be "well-founded" to accept Cherubino da Savona's numbers provisionally.[42]

Still, he agonized further, the demographic circumstances of the nineteenth century gave him trouble: "[they] affirm the presence of several hundred thousand inhabitants [in an area] presently inhabited by several thousand."[43] He went to ask a familiar question: "Must we attribute to the homicidal epidemics of the nineteenth century, smallpox, *bexigas,* so often noted by the explorers, and later to sleeping sickness and other epidemics, the overwhelming disappearance of these populations?" He also considered that the slave trade contributed to depopulation, although his numbers, "17,000 to 29,000" per year, are much too high. He could only conclude that "the problem remains open."[44]

In accepting the missionaries' figures as well, W.G.L. Randles found it difficult in his turn to explain what they seemed to require—a precipitous population decline from the seventeenth to the nineteenth centuries.[45] He implicated all the usual culprits for this imputed depopulation. Foremost among these was the slave trade, which, according to Randles, had acted with "astonishing rapidity" as early as the first quarter of the sixteenth century. To the slave trade mortality was to be added casualties in the incessant civil wars that marked the area. Moreover, "an epidemic (doubtless smallpox)" ravaged the area in the 1650s, reducing the population, he thought, by "more than half."

Randles was not disconcerted by the lack of data for each of his hypotheses or by a 1675 estimate of "around 2,500,000" Kongolese: "If non-Christians were included in this number, it would represent a considerable decline compared to the estimate of Lopes in 1588."[46] As far as Randles was concerned, the total population in 1588 "must have greatly surpassed" those identified as Christian. Finally, Randles accepted that the population of Kongo had doubled during the intervening century, thanks to new food crops—food crops, oddly enough, that had been introduced quite some time before—since he, like Jadin, judged Savona's "five million" to be "perhaps a little exaggerated, but not impossible."[47] Then, again following Jadin, he posited that in the nineteenth century the slave trade and disease conspired once again to plummet the population to about one-tenth of Savona's figure within less than a century. All in all, his is a very familiar pattern underpinned by equally familiar arguments.[48]

Suspecting another possibility—that the missionary estimates were too high—John Thornton sought an alternative approach, using yearly figures for infant baptisms, as recorded in local registers, to project estimates of the population of Kongo around the turn of the eighteenth century.[49] As it happens, this method generated a figure of about half a million, or one-quarter of that which some observers advanced and one-twelfth that proclaimed by Cherubino da Savona.[50]

———

Not long after Motolinía and other Franciscans were proselytizing in the Americas, the newly founded Jesuit order began to send its first missonaries to other parts of the world. The most extensive venture was Francis Xavier's efforts in south and southeast Asia and Japan. The voluminous Jesuit archives and a sustained interest by modern Jesuit historians have led to extensive work on these mission fields. Along the way, specific attention has been paid to the issue of baptism statistics. The results are hardly encouraging for anyone yearning to believe in their essential accuracy.

Georg Schurhammer collected all the historical information on Jesuit baptisms under Francis Xavier—nearly twenty estimates in all. In the seventeenth century two competing "official" estimates developed. One had it that he had been responsible for 700,000 baptisms; the other put the number at 1.2 million. In the wake of these, "a riotous profusion" of further estimates ensued, running from 100,000 to 10 million, a range of a hundredfold.[51] After ransacking the local Jesuit materials, Schurhammer came to a strikingly different conclusion. In ten mission fields ranging from Sokotra to Japan, the Jesuits had, during the lifetime of Francis Xavier, baptized no more (Schurhammer regarded it as the highest possible figure) than 28,800 individuals.[52] This number is only about one-seventh of that which a single missionary claimed to have baptized "with [his] own hands."[53]

Further studies have reinforced Schurhammer's estimates.[54] On the island of Timor the Dominicans were claiming 100,000 baptisms at the same time the Dutch estimated them at only 12,250.[55] The low numbers are no surprise—most of these areas had well-developed religions of their own—but the important point is not how many or how few were baptized or why, but that the baptismal figures transmitted first by the missionaries and then by later apologists are completely without foundation yet continue to elicit credit.[56]

As Schurhammer pointed out, high numbers originally developed during the successful move to canonize Francis Xavier and were hagiographical emanations. Is there any reason to regard the numbers of Motolinía and others for New Spain as inherently likely to be more reliable? It is hard to imagine why. After all, they too were writing in one hagiographical tradition and trying to create a new one. Were not the first Franciscans to reach New Spain promptly christened "the twelve apostles?"

———

The converse of baptism is martyrdom—the ultimate vindication of baptism. Official opinion was that the growth of the early church was fueled by the blood of martyrs, and martyrdom automatically brought with it entry into heaven and thus sainthood. As John Phelan pointed out, "[t]he pre-Constantinian Church was the ultimate yardstick with which the friars of the sixteenth century measured the achievement of their own Indian Church."[57] From Nero to Constantine, written and epigraphic records of martyrdoms have survived. In the latter case, the numbers are usually relatively small, while in the former they are generally vague, using terms such as "countless" and "innumerable."[58] This has not inhibited some grandiose modern estimates. One of these—that 100,000 Christians had been martyred by the year 313— is reminiscent of the additive impulse.[59]

Although on a much smaller scale, martyrdom also featured in the expansion of Europe. The success of the Jesuits in Japan in the late sixteenth and early seventeenth centuries was remarkable but came to an abrupt end in 1614, when the missionaries were ordered to leave. There had been martyrs before this, but the persecution during the next forty years was particularly intensive.

Predictably, the number of martyrs during this period has been estimated to have been very high—as high as 300,000, a figure that Johannes Laures, the author of the most extensive study of the subject, regarded as "horrendously exaggerated."[60] In contrast, he calculated that, on the basis of the surviving documentation from the period, only a few more than 4,000 Japanese were actually executed as martyrs, even though several thousand others might have died as a result of the civil disorders that accompanied the suppression of Christianity.[61] Concomitantly, the size of the Christian population as a whole has also been variously estimated. The range at the time that persecution became overt is from 300,000 to 2 million, with even the first probably an exaggeration.[62]

Baptisms for China, Indochina, and various parts of India were at the same time inflated both in the contemporary records and in later efforts to calculate totals for these regions.[63] It is no wonder that Alexandre Brou, looking at the baptismal figures for several areas, concluded that such figures "only confirm the wholly negative conclusion that, alas, we cannot accept blindly the figures that routinely appear in the histories of the early missions." He added that "it is difficult to criticize" these figures constructively in the absence of any reliable evidence either way.[64]

The analysis of all baptismal statistics requires that other factors be brought into play.[65] Some missionary orders (e.g., the Capuchins) tended to baptize more readily and so more often than others (e.g., the Jesuits). Moreover, official policy—and even more, unofficial practice—regarding the instruction for, and administration of, the sacrament varied from time to time and place to place. Facile comments like that of Dobyns cited earlier are little more than means to evade coming to terms with this potentially debilitating complexity.

———

Missionary writing has received severe buffeting of late. Writing about the testimonies of twentieth-century missionaries, which are often used for ethnographic study, Charles Taber warns that "it turns out that there is often a considerable discrepancy between what missionaries intend to do, think they are doing, and report that they have done, and what actually takes place on [*sic*] the field as understood by the missionaries' audiences."[66] Taber identifies an important set of epistemological encounters: missionaries with the missionized; missionaries with their expression of this encounter; missionaries with their goals and their accomplishments; missionaries with their readers, whether these be potential contributors or scholars; and readers with their own vision of faith triumphant. Interacting, these several pairs of partial mismatches underscore the problems inherent in taking missionary writings as seriously as the High Counters have accustomed themselves to do. Whatever else might be the case, close, sustained, and critically informed scrutiny of these writings is likely to bear fruit, but it will not be the fruit of literal truth.[67]

Numbering the Imaginary/
Imagining Numbers

In the multitude of people is the king's honor; but in the want of people is the destruction of the prince.

—Proverbs 14:28

So that if we have a Series of numbers beginning at eight (for so many Souls surviv'd the Deluge) and doubling themselves in 60 years at a mean from the Flood till David, i.e., for about 1300 years, and thence forward to our own times in 400 years, i.e., for about 2700 years; we shall pretty nearly obtain the Sum total of Mankind in every corresponding year after the Flood.

—William Whiston,
A Short View of the Chronology of the Old Testament

The following passage by Simon Tyssot du Patot, published in 1710 in his *Voyages et aventures de Jaques Massé*, typifies a particular genre of writing associated with the expansion of Europe:

> [B]y a calculation made *en gros*[,] we have in this country 41,600 villages, in each village there are 22 families, at nine persons on average, each village would contain almost 200 inhabitants: thus in the entire kingdom 8323000. . . . It is a wonderful thing how many people are struck down by this pest [smallpox]. Not one of ten of them escape it. . . . [S]o few are exempt that hardly anyone dies of any other disease.[1]

The author went on to explain that these periodic epidemics of smallpox served as effective checks on further population growth in the land he was describing. To anyone familiar with the recent course of American Indian historical demography, this passage will seem uncannily reminiscent. In almost all its aspects there is a similarity to early, and even more to modern, descriptions of aboriginal American Indian populations—for instance, in the repeated and insistent use of first-person, "eyewitness" discourse in the attempt to persuade readers of the innate accuracy the observation.[2] It reminds us of an even stronger declaration in *Pilgrim's Progress:* "Yea, I think I may truly say, that to the best of my remembrance, all the things that here I discourse of, I mean as to matter of fact, have been acted upon the stage of this world, even many times before mine eyes."[3]

This passage, however, is not from one of the chronicles of the Indies, nor is it any modern attempt to calculate aboriginal population at contact. Instead, it comes from one of the many narratives of imaginary voyages that were so popular in the seventeenth and eighteenth centuries. These works are not historical sources in the usual sense, but bringing them into the discussion helps us understand better the premises of both the High Counters and the sources on which they are obliged to depend. It is no accident that the discursive strategies employed by the authors of these imaginary voyages strikingly resemble sources for, and interpretations of, population levels of the Americas at contact or thereabouts.

Most such works marshaled a formidable array of contemporaneous and conventional rhetorical weaponry in an effort—sometimes serious, sometimes only conventionalized—to convince readers that they were true accounts of true happenings. The most common device, virtually a topos, was the claim that an author of record was actually no more than the editor of a manuscript that had somehow come into his possession and which he was transmitting virtually untouched for readers' edification. Often complementing this was an appeal to authority by means of citing various travelers' accounts, as well as more conventional historical works, in order to reinforce the plausibility of the narrative in question.[4]

An unusual but effective tactic designed to bolster the purportedly testimonial aspect of a work was to explain carefully how the writer came by knowledge of certain events that, by the terms of the tale, could not have been witnessed personally. After the middle of the seventeenth century, more and more maps, usually with great political and physical detail and sometimes of impressively large scale, were featured in these works. Sometimes a picture of the traveler even served as frontispiece—a sort of guarantor of the whole. For instance, in some of the earliest editions of *Gulliver's Travels* a frontispiece portrait of none other than "Capt. Lemuel Gulliver" himself stared out at the reader, looking just as one might imagine had he been as real as Jonathan Swift. His address and the name of the artist were also included—powerful sureties indeed that Lilliput, Brobdingnag, Laputa, even the Houyhnhnms existed somewhere just beyond the ken of the accumulated exploration of the earth.[5]

Meant largely in parody, *Gulliver's Travels* fooled few readers of the time. Nonetheless, it remains the case that repeated assertions of truth, claims of authenticity, and modest editorial disguises evolved into a special form of "lying truth"—sophisticated, imaginative, and persuasive, a literary art form in itself.

In virtually always masquerading as first-person observations, if suspiciously often posthumously, and in trading heavily on that assertion, these works resembled—as we have seen—the discursive strategies of chroniclers such as Las Casas, Cortés, Díaz del Castillo, and Oviedo. Such ocular warrants were persuasive rhetorical tools then and, if anything, have been made to be even more persuasive after their times, in particular among those who lack a guarded awareness of the conventional views and suffusive role of these mechanisms in writings during and after the Renaissance.

Arithmetically, it can hardly be disputed that Tyssot du Patot's approach, which is standard operating procedure for its genre, bears almost a mirror image of the extrapolative techniques so necessarily adopted by the High Counters. Clearly the narrator had no opportunity to see and count every town in his imaginary kingdom of Bustrol, somewhere around Australia, but this hardly mattered, since reliable informants had assured him that each was identical with all the others—all that was required was to know the total number of towns, and the necessary computations could proceed without hindrance. This notion of symmetry pervades the High Counters' calculations because it must.[6]

The number at which Tyssot's narrator, Jaques Massé, arrived was large but not impossibly large, was exact but not suspiciously so, and was expressed as the unavoidable consequence of multiplying several smaller numbers which, readers would have felt sure, the narrator could easily have observed, verified, and calculated from his sources. Furthermore, as Massé took pains to explain to his readers, the crucial demographic information had been vouchsafed by the most reliable of sources.

Finally, there is the recurring mention of disease to explain why the population never grew to unmanageable proportions—although hardly to explain how the population of each town remained at par with that of every other town. This is what makes Tyssot's account so peculiarly redolent of recent investigations into the contact population of the Americas. Disease is the deus ex machina that makes their calculations seem at first reasonable, and in Bustrol the specter of smallpox threw the only pall over an otherwise well-regulated society.

Lest it be thought that Tyssot's description is wholly anomalous to the genre to which it belongs, it is necessary to cite some other examples that in aggregate underscore the similarities between the two arenas of discourse and at the same time suggest some reasons why this should be so.[7] Since so many High Counters and their noncounting allies have bestowed on precontact America a character that often is truly utopian, it seems analytically useful, as well as fair, to draw out this line of reasoning.

The first known, and still the most notable, utopia was Atlantis as Plato described it.[8] According to Plato, Atlantis was a very populous place indeed. He made no attempt to estimate its size other than to relate that "the number of men in the mountains and in the rest of the country was countless." He did provide, though, a piece of information that might allow us to do it for him. He wrote that "it was ordained that each allotment should furnish one man as leader of all the men in the plain who were fit to bear arms; . . . and the total of all the allotments was 60,000." From this single, but suggestive, datum we can extrapolate.[9] Let us say, for instance, that each allotment provided only twenty fighting men and the leader. These, multipled by 60,000, gives us 1,260,000 as the size of the Atlantean standing army. Let us say furthermore that one in five inhabitants in the country was fit to bear arms. This would bring the total population to 6.3 million. But is this really the total population? In Athens it was customary to include only free men when assessing population levels, so it might well be necessary to increase this figure appreciably, if we only knew whether there was a slave element on Atlantis—Plato leaves the question open.[10]

At any rate, Plato then goes on to speak of 10,000 chariots and 1,200 ships, and he closes by stating that "[s]uch . . . were the military dispositions of the royal City; and those of the other nine [metropoles] varied in various ways, which it would take a long time to tell."[11] Since he does not take the time to tell, anyone wishing to calculate the total free and unfree population of Atlantis's capital and other cities might feel obliged to multiply the tentative figure of 6.3

million by a factor of 10, 15, or even 20, in this way arriving at an estimate that might be as high as 126 million.[12]

The patronymic of much that was to follow is Thomas More's *Utopia,* first published in 1516. Like his imitators, More used the work to advance his personal moral and political agenda in a manner lightly, but adequately, disguised. In it he set the tone for the matters that are of concern here—his Utopia was made more relevant and more plausible in a number of ways, not least by including a profusion of details designed to convince willing readers that Utopia was a real place and therefore that its society could be replicated in the known world.

More made it clear that even though its economy was largely agricultural, Utopia was a populous place. Although Raphael Hythlodaeus, More's traveler mouthpiece, did not prove interested enough to calculate the total population, he too provided the rudiments for doing so. Utopia consisted of fifty-four cities, "all spacious and magnificent." No city could have more than "six thousand households (exclusive of the surrounding countryside)." In turn, these could consist of "between ten and sixteen adults." Besides these there are minor children in each family, whose number was unregulated.[13]

Given these data, determining the overall population of Utopia becomes mere calculation: $54 \times 6,000 \times 13 + x + y$.[14] Thus Utopia had a population of 4,212,000 adults plus an unknowable number of minor children and country folk. Assuming that there were eight minor children per household adds another 2,592,000 people ($54 \times 6,000 \times 8$). Assuming that the population of the countryside was one-half that of the cities adds a further 3,402,000, allowing us to arrive at a total population of 10,206,000. Since Utopia was an island (pseudo-Britain) with a circumference of 500 miles, this clearly represented a dense population.[15]

The exercise of projecting population figures for Utopia would scarcely be possible if More had not assured his readers that "[i]f you know one of their cities, you know them all, for they're exactly alike, except where geography itself makes a difference."[16] The notion that the whole is discernible from any of its parts is the keystone of an extrapolative methodology like that which characterizes modern attempts to discover the contact population of the Americas. Without this premise, usually implied though often made explicit, little could be accomplished in this enterprise in light of the exiguity of the data. Even truer to the form that he had re-created, More provided numerous measurements. It seems that hardly anything in Utopia did not have a size that Hythlodaeus was able to ascertain, remember, and eventually record.[17]

Many later utopian tales followed More's in positing large and/or dense populations for their particular corners of the imagination.[18] Even when figures for total population were missing, there were other indications that this was high. *The Free State of Noland,* published anonymously in 1701, merely told readers that in that particular republic there were no fewer than 32,600 local and national officials alone.[19] One might speculate on the likely ratio of elected officials (like that of *indios*) to the general population; instead I merely point out that Noland must have been heavily populated.

The Enlightenment and the period immediately preceding it were the heyday of imaginary voyage accounts, and Australia and its vicinity were frequently their locus. One of the earliest of these accounts was Gabriel Foigny's *La terre australe connue,* published in 1676. Foigny posed as editor of a discovered manuscript rather than as author of record.[20] The country was divided into 15,000 "seizains," each encompassing sixteen quarters, each with twenty-five houses, and each including four divisions of four persons each. Thus each "seizain" contained 6,400 persons; multiplying this by 15,000, as Foigny wrote, "gives a total of 96,000,000." But in the Southern Land, as in Utopia, large numbers of people remained uncounted—"the young people living with their masters." These totaled "a further 48,000,000" individuals, leading to a total population of 144,000,000.[21] All these figures had a biblical significance, Foigny being more relentless in his symbolisms than most other writers of utopian novels.[22]

Although Foigny differed somewhat from More by producing a population figure (which, until recently at least, would have seemed absurd on the face of it), he replicated More, Tyssot du Patot, and others in one crucial sense. Just before producing his overall population figures he pointed out that "[i]t is enough to know one quarter in order to be able to judge all the others." Because of the rigidly uniform characteristics of the inhabitants, knowing the composition of one seizain, and the numbers of these scattered throughout the country, made calculating total population merely a matter of extrapolation.

Foigny devoted an entire chapter to detailing recent wars between the "Australians" and their inveterate enemies, the Fundians. In these wars large armies—if small in proportion to the total population—were the rule; contingents of 200,000 to 300,000 were not uncommon. Battles were hard-fought and casualties high. At one war's end "a final count was made of the dead [and] it was found that a total of 398,956 [bodies] were piled up on the seashore for the flesh-eating birds to dispose of."[23]

Foigny also followed More in providing exact measurements for buildings and open spaces, as well as for various kinds of fauna.[24] Scarcely one of these is mentioned without at the same time being carefully sized up for readers' benefit. Finally, Foigny's conveniently deceased narrator, Jaques Sadeur, had the chance to observe "more than five hundred" foundered ships that were "preserved around the coasts from time immemorial," the remnants of unsuccessful invading fleets. All in all, the Southern Land was a revelation to Sadeur as well as to the readers of Foigny's book, who might have expected these remote lands to be sparsely inhabited.

In 1821 there appeared an account of Pluto—neither the planet nor the dog, both as yet unknown, but an underground world in the center of the earth. Albur was the largest and most populous polity in Pluto. Albur was not very large, only about 360 miles by 225 miles, or slightly smaller than the state of Utah.[25] Nonetheless, it supported a population of not less than 45 million.[26]

Since most utopias were pictured as relentlessly unwarlike, warrior counts, from which overall populations might be projected, were not often provided. An exception was the Oceana of Joseph Harington. Harington provided only a single datum from which to estimate the population of Oceana: "The Agrarian in Oceana without interruption of Traffique, provides us in the fifth part of the Youth an annuall source or fresh spring of 100000 [soldiers]."[27] Supposing that the male "Youth" of Oceana constituted at any given time about 10 percent of the general population allows us to speculate that this latter was in the neighborhood of 5 million. It could be more or less, depending on how we intuit the Oceanan definition of youth—the narrower it is, the greater the general population. Knowing nothing about that concept permits courses of action that attune well with whatever the intentions of the counters happen to be.

Occasionally, warfare entered other accounts of imaginary voyages, particularly voyages to Africa. Diderot wrote about the kingdom of Congo (no relation to the Kongo mentioned in chapter 18) in central Africa, where warfare was endemic and armies commensurately large. For instance, Diderot mentioned that the ruler of this state was able to put into the field an army of "1,600,000 [men] on foot."[28]

A largely uninhabited Australia continued to beguile writers of this genre. A work "edited" by Mary Fox, published in 1837, gave the world for the first time the story of a civilization that had descended from Englishmen fleeing the Reformation. Very English in culture and manner, "[t]heir numbers were reported at between three and four millions," all descended from a handful of fugitives and organized into "eleven distinct communities."[29] It would be another sixty years or so before the population of Australia as we know it reached this level.[30]

Although better known for other achievements, Giacomo Casanova published in 1788 an account of an imaginary voyage to the land of Protocosmo. Situated deep under the northern oceans, Protocosmo was just a bit smaller than the earth in which it was embedded, but oddly enough, it was considerably more populous. It consisted of eighty kingdoms and ten republics, as well as 216 "fiefs." Each of these last contained a minimum of 10 million inhabitants, so that simple multiplication gives us a total population of more than 2,160,000,000 people for the fiefs alone.[31] To this is to be added the information that each of the other ninety states had "about one hundred twenty million" inhabitants of their own, making for a population of nearly 11 trillion.[32] These figures resemble national debts more than population levels, but they have the advantage of being patently false.[33] Still, the argument can be made that the difference is more of degree than of kind.[34]

Although no terrestrial population figures, real or imaginary, rivaled those of Protocosmo, some utopian writers looked outward and found extraterrestrial worlds. By the eighteenth century, outer space might not have seemed much greater a surprise to Europeans than the New World had two centuries earlier.[35] In detailing the early history of the debate over extraterrestrial life, Michael Crowe draws attention to a large number of early efforts to impute populations to other units of our solar system—and beyond.[36] Of these the most egregious was Thomas Dick's bizarre effort mentioned in chapter 13. Dick threw cosmic numbers around precociously. At first, he estimated that there might well have been 21,894,974,404,480 inhabitants of the eight planets of his day plus some of their larger satellites, all calculated on the basis of population density in England, after forgetting to subtract for oceans and the like.[37] Raising his sights as he proceeded, Dick then turned to the universe as a whole. There, he thought, "there would be the following number of living inhabitants . . . , 60,573,000,000,000,000,000,000,000,000." This number, he granted, "transcends human conception."[38]

As already noted, a common means to convey verisimilitude in the imaginary voyage literature was the use of specious precision for numbers of people and animals or linear measurements. Early—and still egregious—examples of this approach appeared in Rabelais's *Gargantua* and *Pantagruel,* where it was clearly used to mock the very notion of precision.

On a much smaller canvas we see the technique employed in an account of the republic of Roncador, supposedly situated where Argentina, Brazil, and Paraguay intersect. Roncador was a small state, only some 30,000 square miles, with a population of between 50,000 and 60,000. With respect to the capital, also named Roncador, however, these vague estimates are replaced with a wonderful, almost cadastral-like precision. The observer was able to state that "[t]he census I immediately had made revealed a population of 754 families, 3,064 souls, possessing an aggregate of 4,632 tame cattle, 1,780 oxen, 1,510 horses, 3,791 mares, 501 mules, 198 asses, 4,648 sheep and a few goats."[39]

Although aimed at children, the Oz series by L. Frank Baum reflected numerous utopian demographic concepts. It also used well various forms of discursive validation, among them the persuading detail. One of these concerns the population of the city of Oz: "It has nine thousand, six hundred and fifty-four buildings, in which lived fifty-seven thousand three hundred and eighteen people, up to the time my story opens. . . . Altogether there were more than half a million people in the Land of Oz."[40] However the descriptions of the mores of Oz and the happiness and prosperity of its people cast utopian shadows, details such as these counter them with plausible statistics— an impression that Oz was only partly imagination. Baum's verifying detail, offered casually as an intrinsic part of the narrative thread, yet projecting a piquant lifelikeness, shows the legacy of the demographic aspects of earlier utopian work.

The use of authenticating quantitative detail reached a peak with the publication of *The Goddess of Atvatabar,* a work so laden with detail that it reads like a technical report—appearing at times to be more science than fiction.[41] As part of its general discursive fabric, there was the usual interest in numbers of people. The land of Atvatabar lay under the western hemisphere by way of the North Pole and was quite large in both extent and population. During the course of his visit, the narrator visited the capital city of 500,000 and observed armies 100,000, 217,000, 300,000, even 500,000 strong. Some naval forces consisted of as many as 10,000 of the local inhabitants.[42]

The island of Bensalem lay in the southern Pacific and was large for a Pacific island, but rather small just the same—"190 miles long, and 70 miles at its greatest width," and shaped like an ellipse.[43] Yet its population was "about two millions," or a density of something like 300 persons per square mile.[44] In tune with the symmetrical pattern of utopian demography, this population was confined largely to 39 coastal towns of about 40,000 people each, except for the capital, which had 60,000 people, and another town that had 50,000.[45] Even northern Siberia could not escape being densely populated in the imaginative voyage literature. In an imaginary voyage described by Osip Senkovsky in the middle of the nineteenth century, the protagonists came across an account of a local army of half a million men and learned that there were more than 3,000 cities in the area.[46]

Occasionally a counterfactual past was presented instead of alternative presents and hypothetical futures. One such work was Louis Geoffroy's *Napoléon et la conquête du monde*. Published in 1836, this work rewrote recent history to be more in tune with reviving French imperial aspirations. Here Napoleon, having united Europe, campaigns against the united Islamic world under the Ottoman sultan. In a great battle at Jerusalem in 1821, he defeats the Muslims, who lose over 300,000 men, at the expense of only 1,500 of his own soldiers.[47]

These numbers would not sound unfamiliar to a reader of Cortés's self-declaiming letters back home, in which he frequently estimated the sizes of Mexica armies he had defeated. Geoffroy was idealizing a past and Cortés a present, but there are further similarities. For example, both Cortés and Napoleon were able to triumph in part because of advanced technology. In Napoleon's case it was stream engines and dirigibles; in Cortes's it was armor, guns, and horses. Both Napoleon and Cortés represent triumphant Christianity, and their opponents, the faithless. A difference between the two accounts is that Geoffroy could not be believed, however much some Bonapartists might have wanted to, whereas Cortés still commands strong belief in some quarters.

———

One subcategory of imaginary voyages of interest here is that which bases itself on phenomenal, indeed impossible, fecundity and population growth. The locus classicus of this genus is Henry Neville's *The Isle of Pines,* published in 1668. As a result of a shipwreck in 1569, one Englishman and four women became marooned on an island "near to the Coast of Terra Australis." At once the man, George Pine, set about supplying his posterity, with remarkable success. In forty years he had 560 descendants; in fifty-nine years the total reached 1,789 descendants; and by the time the island came to the attention of the outside world, some ninety-eight years after Pine's landing, it was inhabited by between 10,000 and 12,000 of his progeny "by outside estimate."[48]

Compare this with the growth on two real islands—Pitcairn and Norfolk. The first was settled by mutinous crewmen of the *Bounty* in 1790, and the other more than sixty years later from Pitcairn Island. The *Bounty* party, which had stopped briefly at Tahiti, reached Pitcairn with not four women but twelve, yet by 1856 the original population of 27 had grown only to 194.[49] These people left Pitcairn to settle on Norfolk Island, recently abandoned as a penal colony and left uninhabited. Shortly afterward, several families returned to Pitcairn, the rest remaining. The latter's descendants, along with various immigrants, numbered only 1,880 persons by the 1980s.[50]

Just a few years after the publication of *The Isle of Pines*, there appeared Denis Veiras d'Allais's *The History of the Sevarites*.[51] In terms of population growth at least, the land of Sevarambia was the Island of Pines, but writ larger. Veiras's narrator reported that during the thirty-eight-year reign of Sevarias, "his People increas'd so prodigiously, that the Number of his subjects, which he caus'd to be taken exactly every seven Years, rose to above two Millions; tho' at the beginning of his Reign, the whole Amount was not but about eight hundred thousand."[52]

On Orphan Island there were "about 40" orphans in residence in 1867. Less than sixty years later this number had mushroomed to "one thousand and twenty-five, of whom five hundred and ninety-three were children under fifteen." The observer seemed to have an explanation for this explosive growth: "That's on the basis of an average of about five children to each [married] pair, taking four generations and given approximate equality of sexes, and a few deaths."[53]

Spectacular as the proliferation of the Pine family and the orphans was, it pales when compared with population growth in Galligenia, the creation of Charles François Tiphaigne de la Roche. There, more than 100,000 inhabitants claimed descent from a single Frenchman and his son and daughter, who practiced incest in a glorious way, if with absurd results.[54] This growth in Galligenia's population by a factor of 50,000 took place in less than two centuries, but unfortunately it did not seem unusual enough for Tiphaigne de la Roche to explain the mechanics.[55]

Notions of high population density reached zenith with John Holmesby's account of an imaginary voyage to the land of Nimpatan, a large island situated in the south Atlantic. In some parts of the Nimpatan's capital, Kelso, population density was reported as twenty to thirty persons per five square yards.[56] Neither the population of the city nor that of the country as a whole is mentioned, but extrapolative wonders have been carried out on the basis of little more than a single piece of information like this one.

———————

The novels in the Middle-Earth cycle of J.R.R. Tolkien have achieved virtually scriptural status among devotees. One result of their enormous popularity is an endogenous convention that treats Middle-Earth as "real" in order to support pseudoscholarly writings about various aspects of it, all complete with at least a surface seriousness of purpose.[57] Among these are demographic matters. To these Tolkien did not devote explicit attention, but aficionados of his work have stepped in to grasp the few nettles.

The Elves feature prominently in the Middle-Earth cycle—in particular, contingents of Elf warriors are mentioned in *The Silmarillion,* the last work of the cycle. Recently, Tom Loback made an effort to determine the Elf population on the basis of this scattered information. He writes that "it is plausible to assume the estimated size of the entire field army of Gondolin at the time of its fall must have been around 24,000 to 30,000." This assumption paves the way for a familiar multiplicative process. There were other armed Elves, perhaps another 2,000, and perhaps an additional 10 percent of the population that were unfit for duty. So much for the men; the female population was probably slightly larger, say another 40,000. Thus there were about 75,000 adults Elves at the time. and maybe "at the outside" 3,000 to 5,000 children, all aggregating to a population of as much as 80,000. "This figure with some adjustment," Loback goes on, "will give a theoretically possible average population" of an elf "House." But there was more than one Elf house in Gondolin, and when all the extrapolations are carried out, "it seems plausible" that the total Elf population at its height "can be estimated as 800,000 to 1,000,000," a figure thirty to forty times the size of the reported elf contingents.[58]

Other races were also denizens of Middle-Earth. One of these was the Orcs. There are several references to Orc fighting units in Tolkien's work, but invariably without numbers. Instead, there are vague references to "legions," "armies," and "hosts." The task of the intending Middle-Earth demographer is to put numbers to these labels. This, of course, requires a series of assumptions, the greatest of which is that Tolkien did not use these terms casually but implicitly related them to each other almost algebraically, and that every legion, every army, and every host was the same size as the others.[59]

Armed with this modus operandi, Loback determines, sometimes by referring to the size he himself had postulated for Elf armies, that "legions" are 10,000 to 15,000 strong; that "armies" ("SOAs" or "standard Orc armies") are, with "a bit of rounding off, up and down," from 20,000 to 30,000 Orcs in size; and that "hosts" represent two armies. In this way concepts—and the numbers springing from them—that are absent in the sources are imposed to further the exercise.[60] Since all Orcs seem to have been soldiers, there is no need to extrapolate to a larger population. But the sizes of Orc armies—and therefore of Orc populations—changed over time; at its peak the number of Orcs seems to have been as much as 650,000.

The author of this analysis of Orc population concludes by explaining his methodology: "[I]t can be seen that the use of a Standard Orc Army is a distinct possibility and that its form and size as suggested here, stands up well, in the face of such evidentiary numbers that are available."[61] What impetus lies behind this effort to impute certain unstated meanings of certain words to the original sources, then to turn these words into numbers, and finally to impose on these derived numbers certain algebraically defined and related patterns that facilitate larger-scale "demographic" exercises? The answer has a familiar ring: "By knowing how many folk lived here or there at this time or that, some more insight may be gained as to the dynamics of life and culture in Middle-Earth, for those of us that want to walk further along the road that 'goes ever on.'"[62]

––––––

The most important question raised by this discussion is just where to draw the line between "chronicler" and ("imaginary") traveler. After all, their discourses can be, and often are, dismayingly similar, and it would be unfruitful to think of them as being anything like mutually exclusive—one menacingly false, the other comfortingly true. In his study of the genre Neil Rennie expressed this concern many times, such as when he commented that "[t]he question worth pursuing . . . is . . . why the difference between a narrative and a novel is so hard to tell."[63] The impetus for verisimilitude became so dominant that some imaginary voyages were long accepted as real and the idealized societies they encountered as correctly depicted.

Yet, while modern readers of *Pilgrim's Progress* will probably greet Bunyan's assertion with a bemused smile—who did he think he was kidding anyway?—High Counters read astonishingly similar expressions in the work of Las Casas regarding the contact population of Hispaniola and swallow them whole—no bemused smile, no raised eyebrows, merely a nod of satisfaction.

Of course, similar expressions need not betoken similar intentions, but it would be unwise to presume intuitively that they cannot—that the chroniclers of the Indies were historians in our modern sense of that word, whereas More, Bunyan, Tyssot du Patot, and their innumerable counterparts were writers of fiction, again in the modern sense. To do so merely polarizes, for the sake of convenience, discursive and mental processes that, for the period of relevance here, were not at all poles apart.[64]

———

Closely related to the chronicles of the Indies, but not much different from the imaginary voyages, are the so-called romances of chivalry. Irving Leonard, among others, has shown what a profound effect these works had on the conquistadors' self-image.[65] They shared much with the imaginary voyages. For instance, their authors generally made more than token attempts at authenticity by claiming to be editors of newly found manuscripts. They also sought plausibility by devoting attention to the persuasive detail.

The archetypal, and most influential, example of the genre was *Amadís de Gaula,* written by Garcí Rodríguez de Montalvo and first published in 1508, and countless times since. Many of the adventures in *Amadís* take place in a locale called Insula Firme. To give the account a further touch of plausibility (it was, said Montalvo, a touched-up, recently discovered manuscript), Insula Firme is sized up for readers—twice in fact. Symptomatically, the figures vary: once (in chapter 44) it is described as "seven leagues long and five wide," but it nearly doubles as the story proceeds, so that by chapter 63 it is "nine leagues long and seven wide."[66] This growth, whether spontaneous or induced, hardly matters in tales of this kind, but the specification of worldly dimensions reminds us again that the urge to quantify is best treated distinctly from the notion that whatever results is necessarily, or even probably, real.[67]

Nothing could have been more efficacious in inducing at least some ambivalence in the minds of the readers of these romances of chivalry than to produce for them a few precise measurements every now and then. To give Insula Firme a specific size and a specific shape was to tease it from the realm of the completely fantastic by reducing the opportunities for readers to imagine for themselves what its size might have been. Given the chance, some might have regarded it as continental in size, while others might have thought it quite small. But with a few well-chosen words (and numbers are generally well-chosen words) Montalvo obliged his readers to agree with him in this.[68]

The utopian cum imaginary voyage literature discussed here is only a small fraction of an enormous corpus. It is possible that the cases addressed here happen to be entirely unrepresentative, although one example after another conforms to the pattern. In effect, each of these works includes several of the following as part of their fabric: they provide high total population figures for the worlds they have created; they provide the raw materials with which to calculate some kind of minimum or maximum total population;[69] they speak of densely populated worlds even when they provide no specific figures; they specify or imply extraordinarily rapid population growth; they use demographic data and other kinds of measurements (with plenty of examples) for rhetorical verisimilitude; and in support of all this they repeatedly claim to rely on actual records.[70]

In all these they resemble the worlds that the High Counters and others have created for themselves in the Americas. Consider the following passage in light of the utopian demographics discussed here:

> The *Puric* household has been variously estimated to contain from five to ten individuals. From this it follows that the *Chunca* contained from 50 to 100 people, the *pachaca* . . . from 500 to 1,000, the *huaranca* from 5,000 to 10,000, the *hunu* from 50,000 to 100,000, and the *guamán* or province ruled by a *tucuiricuc* consisting of four *hunu-cuna* from 200,000 to 400,000. In an attempt to arrive at some notion of the total population of the realm at the time of its greatest extension we are hampered by a lack of knowledge as to how many *guamán-cuna* were contained in each of the four *suyu-cuna* or quarters ruled by the four viceroys or *apu-cuna*. A careful study [of some modern maps] convinces me that each *suyu* must have contained at least twenty *guamán-cuna*. This figures gives to each *suyu* a population of between 4,000,000 and 8,000,000 and to the Empire of Ttahau-ntin-suyu a population of between 16,000,000 and 32,000,000.[71]

Another population estimate straight from the literature of imaginary voyages? Not at all; it is an apparently serious attempt to calculate the population of the Inca state. As a methodology it would not embarrass Plato, More, Tyssot, or even Loback, yet despite its odd premises, this estimate enjoyed thirty years of respectability, and as late as 1966 its method and its results were vigorously defended against all comers.[72]

Few real places have enjoyed utopian status as frequently and for quite so long as the pre-European Americas. It began with Columbus, whose rhapsodic descriptions of his own discoveries convinced himself, and others like Peter Martyr, that the Americas were little less than the Garden of Eden reborn for the edification of the deserving Christian Spaniards.[73] After a period of dormancy, a similar view took hold during the Enlightenment, the heyday of the "noble savage." Finally, the notion of a New World utopia (or at least an antidystopia) has enjoyed a robust rebirth during the past thirty years or so. This latest manifestation began, unwittingly, with claims that the precontact population of the Americas was much greater, and the level of civilization much higher, than the balance of opinion then was willing to concede. Introducing belief in a disease-free ("virgin soil") environment that was ravaged and destroyed by newly introduced European diseases made explicit what for a while had only been implied.

The quincentenary of Columbus's first voyage encouraged a wide variety of responses, from the reiteration of the *mission civilatrice* argument, made popular during the imperialism of the nineteenth century, to its radical denial and replacement with a *mission anéantise* alternative, in which Europeans destroyed, both wittingly and unwittingly, but certainly uncaringly, civilizations that were their equal or superior in all the things that really matter. Two works were especially prominent in this revisionism: Kirkpatrick Sale's *The Conquest of Paradise* and David Stannard's *American Holocaust*. Their titles tell all.

Another strand in this way of viewing the precontact Americas argues that the American Indians had developed an extraordinarily sharing and nurturing relationship with their environment, only to have the primeval forests, the bison, and the beaver exploited and annihilated by the heavy hand of the white man or by the newly debased Indian, who combined a newfound greed with an equally newfound technology to accomplish this.

A central work in this movement is Calvin Martin's *The Keepers of the Game,* in which he speaks, rather hopefully and certainly anachronistically, of an "environmental ethos" practiced by the Indians.[74] In pursuit of this, Martin argues that prior to the arrival of the Europeans, the Indians had developed a spiritual bond between man and environment, so that people, animals, and the physical environment existed in symbiotic harmony. Since there are early records testifying to Indians killing fauna for reasons other than mere survival, however, this bond must have been abrogated, because, *ex hypothesi*, such behavior was a departure from prevous norms. Martin suggests that the Indians came to blame the animals for the onset of new epidemic diseases, thereby breaking the compact. In short, although this utopian relationship had reached equilibrium, unanticipated stresses proved it to be a fragile thing.[75]

Martin's eccentric use of evidence, anachronistic interpretations, and ultimately condescending attitude toward presumed American Indian mores soon brought criticism of his work.[76] Undaunted, Martin developed his arguments, most of them undemonstrable given their nature, in two further works.[77] With its presentist implications, the question of American Indian beliefs and their effects before and after 1492 has spilled over into fields as seemingly diverse as religion and ecology.[78] The purportedly utopian nature of much of the Americas (the Aztecs grudgingly excluded) is central to the premises of much of the argumentation, for the society Martin and others portray is not very different from some of those that surface in the traditional utopian literature.[79] And for Oceania, archaeological evidence exists aplenty to indicate that the precontact Polynesians hunted to extinction more than fifty animal species.[80] Among the evidence is one site in New Zealand that might contain the remains of as many as 90,000 moas.[81]

———

The production of fantastic voyage literature during the past two millennia or so has been enormous, as is the range of approaches its authors have adopted and their critical success in securing an audience. One of the principal topoi of this body of writing is that the imaginary lands described were extraordinarily, even preposterously, populous.[82] As the relatively small body of examples educed here shows all too clearly, many of these stories are virtually indistinguishable from the chronicles of the Indies in this and other regards. To read Inca Garcilaso de la Vega or Alvar Núñez Cabeza de Vaca or Hernán Cortés is very much to proceed along a path blazed by an entire cohort of "fiction-is-truth" writers.[83] Wrenching these chroniclers from their natural habitat merely to invest them with indigent authority is simply retrograde.

How Many Wrongs
Make a Right?

Oh incredulitie the wit of fooles, that slovingly doe spit at all things faire, a sluggards Cradle, a Cowards Castle, how easie it is to be an Infidell.

—Quoted in Bradford Smith,
Captain John Smith: His Life and Legend

When an opinion has once become popular, very few are willing to oppose it. Idleness is more willing to credit than inquire; cowardice is afraid of controversy, and vanity of answer.

—Samuel Johnson,
"Mary Queen of Scots"

Many, if not most, hypotheses, arguments, and interpretations survive, sometimes even thrive, without scrutiny simply because their propagation outstrips the ability or the inclination of others to question them. The most effective way for an interpretation to prolong itself is to be ignored. Nonetheless, the acid test of scholarship is its capacity to withstand criticism of the most unfriendly sort. Scrutiny will often uncover errors of conception, faulty use of sources, arithmetical miscalculations, simple mistranscriptions, and the like. In one context or another, all these are important. Although typographical errors, for instance, seldom actually impede or misdirect understanding, they can suggest an alarming carelessness if too frequent. In reference works they can be more troublesome, especially if the format happens to be electronic—and especially if the errors are in numbers.

In short, even for simple problems consumers of information find it necessary to adopt differing levels of tolerance depending on circumstances. For other kinds of errors, intolerance must rise, since these more seriously affect the essence of an argument. Indeed, one obvious means to measure the value of an argument is the degree to which it is vulnerable to elementary falsification. To put it another way: how wrong can a hypothesis be in small ways before it becomes unacceptable in general—*as an argument?*[1] Or, for that matter, how are we to distinguish between "small" and "large" errors, and who is to decide? The issue has had several explicit airings of late—cases in which ambitious large-scale arguments have been subjected to such substantive and detailed criticism that they can be seen as seriously compromised at best and at worst mortally wounded.

———

The case of *Roots* is a apt place to begin. *Roots* was a phenomenon in the true sense of the word, sparking interest and enthusiasm across all segments of American society in the mid-1970s. Both the book and the television series were blockbusters to a degree then unprecedented and still without equal. Beyond the overall narrative thread of the story, which was unexceptional, lay the special appeal of *Roots.* Its author, Alex Haley, claimed that he had traced an ancestor named Toby back to a village in Africa, where he had been called Kunta Kinte and from which he had been kidnapped and brought to Virginia as a slave in the 1760s. By doing so, Haley produced a powerful symbol demonstrating that African Americans could engage in family genealogizing just as successfully as Americans who had come from western Europe.

To my mind, Haley's single most important achievement in *Roots* was his success in claiming that Kunta Kinte arrived in Virginia on a particular ship at a particular time. According to Haley, the ship was the *Lord Ligonier,* outbound from The Gambia, which arrived at Annapolis on 29 September 1767. That the *Lord Ligonier* arrived there and then is a matter of public record; that Kunta Kinte was on board was Haley's deduction based on a field trip to The Gambia, as well as, he reported, archival research in Virginia. During the latter, Haley's epiphany took place:

> I went to Richmond, Virginia. I pored through microfilmed legal deeds filed within Spotsylvania County, Virginia, after September 1767, when the *Lord Ligonier* had landed. In time, I found a lengthy deed dated September 5, 1768, in which John Waller and his wife Ann transferred to William Waller land and goods, including 240 acres of farmland . . . and then on the second page, "and also one Negro man slave named Toby."[2]

In the circumstances Haley's reported response ("My God!") was appropriately heartfelt and understandable. It was only the latest of a long line descended from Archimedes' "Eureka!"

Haley's exclamation proved to be less triumphant than tragic, however, for it soon eventuated that his research was fatally compromised. Apparently he had failed to consult records from before the arrival of the *Lord Ligonier* as well as after. If he had, he might have discovered what two critics ascertained with little difficulty—that Toby "appeared in six separate documents of record over a period of four years *preceding* the arrival of the Lord Ligonier"—forcing them to conclude that "Toby Waller was not Kunta Kinte."[3]

Given the particular nature of Haley's argument, these pre–*Lord Ligonier* appearances—even one of them—were entirely devastating, destroying his case without hope of restitution. It was a classic case of what can happen to the defective argument from silence. Two other criticisms followed, each of which pursued different lines, but to the same effect.[4] The sum of these was further to destroy Haley's claim that Toby was the same person as a certain Kunta Kinte—the core argument of his work. When they first appeared, Haley promised to refute these criticisms, but nothing came of this—nothing could. Just the same, until his death he was able to trade on the story in *Roots* that told how he had discovered how one particular ancestor had traveled from one known village in Africa on one known ship and arrived at one known place on a known date.[5] Since this entire scenario had been utterly refuted many years before, this was a remarkable testimony to the power of incumbency and popular appeal.

────────────

Most historical arguments, of course, are more complex structures than Haley's presentation. They can be wounded with a single shot, but not killed. Like a sophisticated computer system, they come with backup mechanisms, damage controls, and circumscribed access. While it is easy to see how harmful the criticism of Haley's tale was, most other cases require a great deal more criticism in order to be refuted, and even then might manage to stay afloat—they are less like the *Titanic* than the *Monitor*.

The ongoing case of Martin Bernal's work is an intriguing example of the latter case. Bernal, a Sinologist and political scientist, changed fields abruptly when he published in 1987 the first of several projected volumes with the umbrella title *Black Athena*.[6] In this volume, devoted to the modern historiography of Greek origins, Bernal proposed a radical change in prevailing wisdom, for he argued that virtually no aspect of ancient Greek civilization was homegrown. Instead, it emanated from either Egypt or Phoenicia. Bernal made no claims of originality or even of being radical; in fact, he termed his argument the "Revised Ancient Model" to indicate that he saw it as an overdue return to the views of the ancient Greek historians, primarily Herodotus, whose discussion of Egypt, allegedly derived from prominent Egyptians, has always fascinated his readers. Whereas others tended to see the growing skepticism of ancient Greek sources in the nineteenth century as an outgrowth of post-Enlightenment modes of thinking, Bernal saw those sources as crucially informed by implicit, reflexive, and mounting racism.

Criticism of Bernal's thesis, not least his faith in Herodotus, mushroomed almost spontaneously.[7] Much of it pointed out that he was more successful at discerning possible racist undertones in some modern Greek historiography than in demonstrating that Herodotus was right in his claims after all.[8] Whether deserved or not, Herodotus' reputation for accuracy, they argued, has declined no more than the reputations of many other sources based largely on oral tradition, hearsay, and encounters with cultures distinct from their own, recorded by observers supplied with ample curiosity but without the training or experience to satisfy it properly. In short, Herodotus was too etic and too gullible to be taken quite at his word regarding Egypt or anywhere else. It was pointed out that Herodotus himself made fewer claims of truth than many of his modern supporters have made for him.[9]

Bernal probably did his cause no good by writing such things as "I have found it helpful to take as working hypotheses those of Herodotus' statements that were unchallenged in antiquity."[10] This tenuous argument from silence fails to consider counterarguments that would render it meaningless. It could be that Herodotus was not criticized in antiquity because certain of his arguments were not taken seriously or simply were unknown to many authors. Or maybe he was criticized, but the works of the critics have not survived—after all, only a tiny fraction of ancient historical writing has come down to us.

Bernal raised his argument a notch or two in the second volume of *Black Athena*. There he attempted his own assessment of what he regarded as the primary sources. In this instance it proved embarrassingly easy to illustrate Bernal's unfamiliarity with the range and substance of these sources and with archaeological argumentation, as well as his linguistic and epigraphic incompetence. This irretrievably crippled his attempt to turn to his advantage the evidence he chose to consider.[11]

Whatever might be said about Bernal's line of argument, his willingness to engage his critics constantly in debate has been commendable.[12] Although he has claimed rather wistfully that his critics "have not come up with effective arguments," it would be rash to suggest that he has persuaded any of them.[13] It would be even more foolhardy to suggest that they have in turn convinced him. Nonetheless, even for those unfamiliar with the details of the arguments and counterarguments, the extended debate over *Black Athena* reveals the ebb and flow than can characterize scholarly debate at its most intense.[14]

—————

Such colloquy is not always possible, however, at least not at first-hand. Perhaps the most celebrated scholarly controversy of the past few years is that which followed the publication of Derek Freeman's extensive critique of the work of Margaret Mead on Samoa.[15] Freeman's book appeared several years after Mead's death, but her iconic stature in the profession and beyond ensured that others would pick up the cudgels on her behalf. Very early in the debate, for instance, George Marcus accused Freeman of creating "great mischief," not by being wrong but by being tendentious, as though he could be otherwise in the particular circumstances.[16] The Freeman-Mead case introduces yet another dimension into the issue at hand—the role of coteriship and personal animus in such debates.

Freeman faulted Mead on two particular grounds. The first was that she, an impressionable graduate student in her early twenties, had gone to Samoa predisposed to find evidence to support the theories of her teacher, Franz Boas, that culture was more important than nature in forming behavior—in short, that she had found exactly what she was looking for. Second, in his own fieldwork on Samoa, Freeman had interviewed several of Mead's informants, to be told that they had gulled her with stories of behavior that were tailored to meet her expectations but were not otherwise particularly true. It was immediately clear that Freeman's shafts had found chinks in anthropology's armor. This, combined with an abrasive and occasionally righteous style, ensured that a spirited, sometimes venomous, debate ensued.[17]

Freeman's argument left little room for maneuver; he was not prepared to take prisoners. If he was right, Mead's work was flawed by defects of theory and of practice and could no longer be accepted as valid—not that this was any longer entirely the case anyway. Beyond that, Freeman implied, its long-time centrality to the development of certain lines of anthropological thought indicated only that anthropologists and other social scientists were more gullible than they should be. Freeman intimated that Mead's work should long ago have been the object of a restudy rather than of continued uninformed credulity. Recently, however, Paul Shankman has accused Freeman of "neglect[ing] significant passages in source after source," in effect hoisting him with his own petard and reopening the debate.[18]

In 1989 Edwin Wilmsen published *A Land Filled with Flies: A Political Economy of the Kalahari.* There Wilmsen argued that the San (ex-Bushmen) were not the archetypal hunter-gatherers they were portrayed to be in numerous works of anthropology, and they had not really existed in pristine isolation, holdovers from an earlier evolutionary stage, but had become isolated by being marginalized by the effects of colonial expansion in the area. To support his hypothesis Wilmsen cited, among other things, a series of nineteenth- and early twentieth-century travelers' accounts and ethnographies which, he asserted, sustained his thesis.

Other anthropologists of the area took exception to Wilmsen's interpretation and sought to discredit it by, again among other things, looking at the same written sources he had adduced on his behalf. A brisk exchange of views ensued, which seemed to go against Wilmsen on this score, since his critics were able to illustrate several ways in which he had misunderstood German and vernacular terms, had misread maps, misconstrued handwriting, and the like.[19] Two of Wilmsen's most vociferous critics, Richard B. Lee and Mathias Guenther, directed their argument toward historians rather than anthropologists.[20] Recapitulating their previous charges and adding others, they were able to make an answerable case that Wilmsen had, unwittingly or not, committed a long series of errors in using his sources and thus had failed to show that San political economy was significantly different before the mid-nineteenth century than it was later. To this there has as yet been no response.[21]

In the debate over the San, ideologies lurk nearer the surface than they do in many other cases, although they are reminiscent of the Mead-Freeman controversy. Historians might intuitively warm to Wilmsen's portrayal of a dynamic and opportunistic San society, forced to change and eventually rendered marginal only as a result of outside forces.[22] On the other hand, they would probably agree with Lee and Guenther (and others) that Wilmsen has yet to make his case on one of the grounds he chose—in fact has injured it by his own care-lessness in using sources.[23]

Just the same, although his troubles with sources unquestion-ably weaken Wilmsen's arguments, they do not *by themselves* destroy the notion of economically thriving San groups that were, and remain, far from paradigmatic "primitive" societies, but only his attempt to demonstrate the case by using a particular set of documentary sources. Unlike the case of *Roots,* bereft of his interpretations of them Wilm-sen's written sources merely revert to being neutral, since he is not ar-guing from a silence that is not really there, as Haley did, but dis-cerning evidence that seems unable to survive his critics' onslaught. On the other hand, it would be no surprise if his credibility on other points were to suffer on the grounds that his enthusiasm for his argu-ments had outstripped his critical sense too often.[24]

It is unusual to see anthropologists debating issues on the basis of conventional historical evidence. At least this seems to be the point of a recent observation on another work dealing with the Kalahari San. There the reviewer expressed surprise, if not concern, that "even the content and veracity of specific historical documents, not to men-tion translations of them, has [*sic*] been hotly disputed."[25] The use of "even" in this passage might concern historians in its turn.

———————

The sins that Wilmsen's critics have charged him with are remarkably similar to those leveled against David Abraham several years earlier. Like the Derek Freeman–Margaret Mead controversy, the David Abra-ham case is most interesting because it shows once again that there is no necessary relationship between the degree of error and the toler-ance of it. In 1981 Abraham published *The Collapse of the Weimar Republic: Political Economy and Crisis,* a work on the reciprocating influence of big business and the National Socialist party in interwar Germany. It was at first greeted by mixed, but generally favorable, re-views, until other workers in the field discovered that Abraham had made a certain number of scholarly faux pas—misidentification of certain individuals, misdating of documents, incorrect archival cita-tions, appearing to quote when only paraphrasing, and so forth. With remarkable celerity the case became a cause célèbre within the pro-fession and without.[26] A second, revised, edition of the work ap-peared, but critics found it even less palatable than the original.[27]

Abraham's critics were not so much numerous as in a position to be influential and of a disposition to be indefatigable, and ulti-mately he was forced to seek employment outside his profession. Even so, many of them were willing to concede that his errors did not directly affect his argument but were ominous signs of a dangerously unscholarly and ideological turn of mind.[28] While Abraham defended himself against some charges, he made what in retrospect must be seen as the tactical error of admitting others and promising repentance, which proved not at all welcome.

During its course the debate transcended the specific instance to become polarized on conservative-radical lines.[29] Peter Novick, who had been Abraham's advisor in the writing of the dissertation that was to become *The Collapse of the Weimar Republic,* used the Abraham case in discussing the possibilities for practical objectivity on the part of historians. In the process he commented that "nothing could more infuriate empiricists than th[e] demonstration of the relative autonomy of the argument from the details of the evidence."[30] This in turn evoked a belated response from Henry Turner, one of Abraham's most trenchant critics, and there the matter seems to rest.[31]

———————

This small sampling illustrates the unpredictability of error tolerance and its effects.[32] Alex Haley's case was utterly destroyed, but few have noticed or cared, and it is likely that most people today still believe that he was able to trace his ancestry back to Africa—not because they willfully ignore the evidence to the contrary but because they are unaware that it exists.[33] At the other extreme, David Abraham's errors were admittedly unnecessary and careless, but they were not crucial to his general argument.[34] Even so, his academic career was irretrievably damaged because of them, although it might be that his interpretations continue to have influence. As an abstract argument, Edwin Wilmsen's view of San history remains possible, perhaps even the more credible alternative, but the damage done to his arrayal of it damages its credibility. Martin Bernal's case resembles that of Wilmsen, although writ larger. The number and seriousness of his errors has been demonstrated again and again, but this has not deflected him from pursuing his case to a variety of constituencies and has not destroyed the validity of his eclectic approach in the eyes of a large number of laypersons and some scholars.

Why this disparity? Certainly it is not to be explained merely by the reactive strategies of the four authors. Haley survived by saying nothing. Bernal survives by saying much. Abraham failed because he said the wrong things, while Wilmsen, like Bernal, has answered his critics—although he has been silent of late. Part of the answer must lie in the degree of receptivity that exists for particular arguments—a receptivity that is clearly detached from the inherent merits of the arguments themselves. *Roots* and Abraham are the clearest examples of this. Trading on public opinion, the first became a media phenomenon, and we tend not to destroy that which we invent in the first place. Scholarly interpretations of business in interwar Germany, however, must succeed or fail with a much smaller and much sterner audience, even though we might well suspect that the rigor of this audience is not without tactical, if not ideological, aspects.

The response to this kind of criticism is nearly always—if the imputation of errors cannot be rebutted—to argue that the criticism only nibbles around the edges of what remains a viable argument. Almost as popular is to adopt an Olympian hauteur, as was the case with Alex Haley, who could remain assured that the forums where his synthesis of his ancestry was demolished were largely beyond the interest and reach of most of his readers.

Most scholarly debates tend to run their course before they are resolved; both sides declare victory and quit the battlefield.[35] Even the case of *Roots,* where the evidence is undeniable and damning, scarcely reached a stage beyond the occasional brief artillery barrage, and these days it is a matter of sniping for the sake of making one's presence known.[36] At this point few will be convinced—or perhaps need to be. All the other cases remain in flux. Except for Abraham, a special case resolved less on its merits than on academic realpolitik, they drift on, battles of attrition unlikely to be won or lost before being abandoned in favor of another skirmish.[37]

———————

How does the work of the High Counters fit in here? It has been demonstrated often enough that their rate of accuracy in interpreting sources is no better than David Abraham's and usually a good deal worse.[38] Unlike Abraham, though, the High Counters seldom admit this, and unlike Bernal and Wilmsen, they have shown little appetite for engaging criticism in open debate. In fact they most closely resemble Alex Haley—in the seriousness of their errors, in the studied silence with which they respond to attacks, and, it must be conceded, in the general success of this tactic.

In this they have been ably assisted even by many of those who have shown their work to be faulty. To cite only a recent example: in detailing at great length that a popular High Counter correlative notion is wildly in error—the notion that disease and illness were virtually absent from the precontact Americas, allowing population to grow almost unchecked—Clark Larsen is content merely to allude politely to their arguments without attempting to consider their implications.[39] The cause of this immunity is baffling—at least it must be located outside strictly academic circles. One effect of it is certainly to encourage further work that fails to treat sources rigorously. Indeed, it might well lead other High Counters to claim privileged status for their work.[40]

Another category against whch we might measure tolerance is what we might call the tyranny of the conditional. The writings of the High Counters are festooned with phrases such as "if/then," "seems" or "appears," "might have been," "could have been," "must have been," and the like. Each of these is precisely an admission of doubt—in these cases very much appropriate, but unrecognized.[41] When the phrases are extensively concatentated, the uncertainty becomes insurmountable.

But somehow this almost never proves to be the case. Take Linda Newson's recent study of depopulation in the audiencia of Quito during the sixteenth and seventeenth centuries. In her overview of the sparse demographic data for this area she uses such locutions more than sixty times when referring to population estimates—hers or others'.[42] But in the three tables that synthesize her argument and array her calculations, the numbers suddenly lose all qualification, all doubt, and stand as unexceptionable addends in a mathematical rather than a historiographical world.[43] In this labyrinth a sentence such as "Assuming demographic decline during the sixteenth century, these figures suggest that the [Macas] region's aboriginal population may have been a conservative 10,000 but was probably higher" is transformed into an unadorned "10,000" in the ensuing table.[44] This dichotomy between words and figures, which inhabits so much of the High Counters' rhetorical world, is necessary if their arguments are to command belief.

Once upon a time Catholic doctrine treated venial and mortal sins as exclusive categories. The erring Catholic could commit any number of venial sins without fear of damnation, but a single slip over the line would ensure hellfire. In real time, this Draconian division was mitigated because mortal sins in one context were often treated as venial in another, and "intention" had a lot to do with things as well. Even so, veniality could never accumulate to the point of no return—its carrying capacity was infinite. The High Counters have been fortunate in finding that their readers have applied this doctrine, however unwittingly, to their work.

Numbers Do Lie

Il est plus d'hommes qui savent calculer que raisonner.

—Moheau,
Recherches et considérations sur la population de la France

I mean Negative Capability, *that is when man is capable of being in uncertainties, Mysteries, doubts, without any irritable reaching after fact & reason . . .*

—John Keats to George and Tom Keats, 27 December 1817

On Labor Day of 1995 a Chicago Cubs' player was awarded a home run on a ball that, the umpires ruled, had curved fair around the foul pole before landing in foul territory. Those watching on television were treated to a replay in which the ball was not visible—according to the announcers, it was behind the foul pole on the way from going from fair to foul. In the circumstances, observers were being urged to believe that the call was correct *because* the evidence was invisible. It provided an interesting occasion for partisan epistemology. Cubs' fans could believe that the ball was there, whereas fans of the opponent of the day could argue that the television shot had not even been taken during the flight of the ball. "Where's the beef?" they might well have asked. The invisible baseball is reminiscent of all the invisible Indians whose very invisibility is held to prove their existence, along with the equally invisible epidemics that killed them off.

The case of the invisible baseball reflects the fact that my quarrel with the methods—and necessarily with the results—of the High Counter movement is at root very much an epistemological one. Fundamentally, the issue between us is that we disagree about what can provisionally be believed and to what degree hypotheses can be formulated on the basis of such belief. A. G. Hopkins noted in passing one of the cruxes in this when he observed that "[i]mproved information has thus created a problem: bad data sustain simple theories of a complex world; good data inhibit easy generalization."[1]

This truism continues to elude the High Counters. Despite a signal increase in improved editions of (as well as additions to) the primary sources, and despite an increasing colloquy between literary and textual critics on the one hand and some historians on the other, they continue to move in a world in which sources are simple things, in which belief is a low-cost, readily available commodity, and in which notions such as "proof" are no less easy to find on well-stocked shelves.

Inevitably, the High Counters' case is riddled with unstable and untestable hypotheses. One of their fundamental claims, for instance, is that epidemic diseases spread so quickly and widely that they preceded opportunities to observe and record them. That they have been unable to demonstrate this even once is certainly not inconsequential, but, more seriously yet, they cannot disprove its polar opposite—that in *no* case did this occur. The claim, then, is epistemologically vacuous, existing merely of and for itself, with ideological status only. For the High Counters, this is enough.

———

Carl Haub has observed that "there are, of course, absolutely no demographic data available for 99 percent of the span of the human stay on earth."[2] On the evidence, it would be difficult to exempt the aboriginal Americas from this injunction.[3] It seems fair and necessary, albeit speculative as well, to ask why so many scholars who have chosen to distance themselves from standard historiographical operating principles then find a very large contact population in the Americas. The most obvious answer is that the quest represents a commonplace phenomenon—scholarship in tune with its times. Whereas an appreciation of the tragic effects of the "discovery" is by no means a new thing, its coalescence into something with so many characteristics of a movement marked by a sovereign complacency is a departure, one only reaffirmed by much of the recent work commemorating 1492.

Correlative to this is the High Counters' natural affiliation with the "world history" movement. In emphasizing the reciprocal effects of regions of the world on each other over time, exponents of world history have seized on New World depopulation with alacrity. The "discovery" of large numbers of American Indians and their post-contact decline is inevitably seen as exemplifying the benefits of the world history approach. Alfred Crosby is perhaps the prime proselytizer of this aspect of world history, and although he offers no numbers of his own, he invariably cites the High Counters and their results with approval, and those with whom they disagree or who disagree with them, with disdain, if at all.

If this is the case, then the High Counters have given away much to gain little. For in their explicitly reiterated premise about the effects of disease on American Indian populations is another premise, necessarily implied, even though never confronted. Perhaps the High Counters simply have never noticed that their arithmetical procedures and the presumptions that underlie them all but anesthetize the Indians. For success, their operations require several unlikely contingencies. By their arguments Indians simply watched themselves die off in droves, lamenting but not otherwise responding. Nor would the High Counters have the Indians respond to a host of new economic opportunities by choosing to move from place to place rather than being forced to do so as the result of some imposed obligation—the *mita* at Potosí, for instance. Then again, the High Counters insist that the Indians always paid tribute and taxes in the amount assessed, both before and after the conquest, since such a state of affairs is required just to begin to turn potential tribute into real people.

In arguing thusly, the High Counters re-create certain observations of the time, notably those of Las Casas, but others as well. This they do with scant concern for the intellectual ethos in which these observations were made, and in face of the logistical impossibilities they create. The comments on which they base their arguments (the occasional mention of mass suicide or a lethal resignation, for instance) sprang from mental worlds that clearly regarded the Indians as innocent and uncaring for their own souls because, if they had souls at all (a matter of considerable debate for some time), they were unaware of their significance or that suicide was a mortal sin. In short, speaking of docile, reactive, despairing, and irrational Indians, more often than not, was and is simply another way of distinguishing them pejoratively from Europeans by denying them full membership in the human race.

———

With a few exceptions only the lead singers have been discussed here, though as many as half a hundred others have lent their voices from the choir. My argument is that the paean to numbers they have produced is the last gasp of a tradition that, after a long life, has all but died out. Anachronistic though the movement might be, it raises questions about belief and doubt that need to be considered. As Iris Macfarlane put it in respect to another set of numbers: "The Black

Hole of Calcutta does not matter; it is believing in it that matters."[4] And, it seems, much the same is true with the High Counters, for whom believing is preferred to knowing. The degree of solidarity among them is impressive, but coterie scholarship seldom leads to new insights that can withstand scrutiny because it is nurtured on reciprocal aye-saying and mutual admiration rather than tempered by adverse commentary that can lead to more rigorous standards. It is no secret that constantly being assured of our worth is likely to convince us that there is no need for improvement. But the result could be a set of arguments that are little more than "highly imaginative piece[s] of intellectual fun."[5]

Of equal concern are such questions as, is there really anything to be gained by all these recent efforts to establish contact population levels?[6] The fact of fairly precipitous decline has almost always been accepted and can be built into arguments about reasons and effects regardless of whether the magnitude was 80, 95, or 96 percent.[7] And what about the risk of demonstrating to readers that when an author is so intent on finding certain information, standards are disregarded? Does this not influence readers' views of the rest of the author's work?

Indeed, an exceptional characteristic of the High Counter movement is its recidivist tendencies. It is no secret that numbers attract belief, no matter how implausible or implausibly secured. In general, though, the degree of critical acumen inculcated into scholars, and their disposition to apply it to numbers in the historical record, has tended to increase over time. But the methods and attitudes of the High Counters irresistibly remind us of another era, one, for instance, like that described by Jan Huizinga: "[M]en of the Middle Ages . . . could not for a moment dispense with false judgments of the grossest kind. . . . It is in this light that the general and constant habit of ridiculously exaggerating the number of enemies killed in battle should be considered."[8]

As we have seen, the great weight of evidence shows that Huizinga's comment is apropos. But there are few latter-day Froissarts who believe that the French army at Crécy numbered better than 100,000 men, and they generally do not have academic credentials.[9] In short, the numbers of fighting men reposing in the chronicles are no longer believed simply because they are there. But clearly, the conditions for belief have not vanished entirely. Reading Cook and Simpson's spirited, if ultimately fruitless, defense of Cortés's numbers captures well what is nothing less than a recrudescence of the medieval spirit of uncritical habits. In this scheme of things, to criticize at all is to doubt, and to doubt at all is to risk losing all, since the epistemic system in place is seamless, geodesic, and vulnerable.

Of course no number of examples of the inability of observers to count accurately or of being very interested in doing so (despite the interest posterity might take in their counts) can demonstrate beyond cavil that this is true for the sources on which the High Counters depend so heavily. Just the same, their repeated surprise—which we might treat as a rhetorical ploy—that some might doubt the reliability of the chroniclers' numbers demonstrates a decontextualized ignorance of the manifold ways in which numbers have been abused throughout history.

─────────

A clear premise of the present study is that access to actual or estimated population figures can be gained only through the available sources, which will range in quantity from none to few to many and in quality from worthless to apparently authoritative. No source can be considered incontrovertible, even though some might prove worthless, at least for demographic purposes. But every source must be tested as thoroughly as possible. As the pronouncements of Sauer, Cook, Dobyns, and others cited earlier suggest, however, the High Counters have shown a chronic inability to regard their sources as complicated and complicating. In the movement there is little zest for examining sources closely and no appetite at all for cross-examining them. Yet every source must be contextualized in its own time and place, not in ours. It must at least be inherently consistent and plausible, although this alone is no warrant of its reliability. It must be able to bear the brunt of close scrutiny, and the more it seems useful, the more demanding the scrutiny must become. Above all, the hunt for the congenial source cannot end as soon as such a source seems to be found and is warmly embraced.

While it is certainly permissible to stretch our sources, attempt to circumvent them, and even to believe in them provisionally during this process, in the end every source has a boundary—a carrying capacity if you will—and many will fail these tests. So be it. Historians must be able to feel some satisfaction in forcing their sources to fail, as well as in allowing them to pass.

A typical strategy relevant to this point is the propensity of the High Counters, as well as others who put historical numbers to use, to operate under a dichotomy in which those numbers that are not patently absurd are taken as reasonably accurate. Thus, if Procopius had not gilded the lily by claiming the loss of one trillion lives in North

Africa, but had offered a lower figure, perhaps several hundred thousand, he would have found any number of believers who operated on the premise that if a number is plausible and cannot be refuted on the basis of the available evidence, it is likely, ipso facto, also to be true. This is both uncommonly ingenuous and disingenuous. At the same time it is remarkably simple-minded, for it studiously ignores the complexities that characterize all historical evidence. In essence, it virtually exempts numerical evidence from the kinds of laborious critical study that all historical evidence warrants.

The importance of discourse in inducing belief is nowhere more apparent than in the case of the accounts of the Trojan war by Dares and Dictys, discussed in chapter 16. Strange as it might seem nowadays, these works, including their fantastic numbers, were the accounts of choice for well over a thousand years until Homer's *Iliad* replaced them. The reasons for this lie almost entirely in their discursive strategies. As Stefan Merkle recently put it:

> Both works have survived in sober Latin prose versions, each one prefaced with a dedicatory letter informing the reader that the respective text was discovered under lucky circumstances and translated from Greek into Latin. . . . The authors present "plausible," rationalistic accounts; the gods do not appear personally, and the archaic heroism of the protagonists is reduced to human scale. Laying claim to autopsy [eyewitnessing], Dictys and Dares . . . pick up the literary tradition of unpretentious records of individual combatants, or war diaries similar to the Latin genre of the *commentarius.*[10]

Dares and Dictys, then, quite like Caesar and Cortés, sold themselves to their readers by adopting a successful pretense that was reinforced by the style in which they couched it. What is of concern is that many twentieth-century students of the Caesar and Cortés have reacted alarmingly like the third-century readers of Dares and Dictys.

———

Patricia Nelson Limerick has recently written about the perdurability of incumbency as represented by Frederick Jackson Turner's famous frontier thesis. She points out how extraordinarily well Turner's interpretation has withstood criticism—first "a devastating set of critiques in the 1930s and 1940s," followed by a steady stream of similar commentary. She argues that "if the outcome had been governed by the usual set of historiographical rules, the Thesis would have been finished." She continues that in fact the most recent criticisms, including her own, had served only to "revitalize Turner's reputation." She concluded: "The more forcefully one said that Turner was wrong, the more one provided in the way of well-publicized opportunities for his admirers to praise him."[11]

There are certainly parallel currents in the ebb and flow of the debate over the size of the contact population of the Americas.[12] There are differences too—the triumph of the higher population estimates shows that incumbency is not inviolate but can be the victim of changing ways of thinking inside and outside scholarship. As well, the output of the High Counters is orders of magnitude greater than Turner's noted essay.

———

More than twenty-five years ago John Murra surveyed several recent editions of Andean chronicles and found himself encouraged. Murra was particularly gratified that a "characteristic of recent work by historians is the necessary job of systematically tracing who copied what and from whom." He went on that "'[c]orrespondences' and *concordancias* have long been noted between the chroniclers, but only in recent years has it become important to verify [for instance] how much Cobo had borrowed from Polo or Pedro Pizarro."[13] A few years earlier, the iconoclastic Åke Wedin had made similar observations and backed them up by citing several examples of clear but unenunciated reliance.[14] In addition, the editors of the better editions of the Andean chronicles have provided examples of intertextuality, although without trying to be comprehensive and without being particularly interested in the historical implications of their findings.[15]

Although Wedin and Murra addressed only work on the Andean chronicles, their remarks apply equally and forcefully to all the early writings on the Americas. Much historiographical work done since has advanced this trend, although much still remains to be accomplished.[16] As we have seen, almost to a person the High Counters prefer to ignore the conclusions of the editors of the texts they use in favor of treating these as unvarnished reportage. Nor do they distinguish between one edition and another in their work, again treating complicated texts as unproblematical—often in fact relying on translations.

Besides scarcely ever questioning the numbers in their sources, the High Counters are also wont to treat concurring opinions as mutually corroborative and validating. Thus they all believe that Wayna Qhapac died of smallpox because several sources say as much. But about an equal number of sources do not—some through silence, others by mentioning other causes of death. Until all the sources for

Wayna Qhapac's reign and death are closely compared and contrasted, and especially until it can be demonstrated that the accounts of his death by smallpox were actually generated independently, this interpretation can only remain a curiosity. But not an insignificant one withal, since declining to attribute Wayna Qhapac's death to smallpox has, by itself, enormous demographic consequences by the rules of the High Counters' game. N. D. Cook's estimate of the population apogee in Peru, for instance, would drop from some 9 million to about 6 million if one were to do no more than bring forward his date for the death of Wayna Qhapac by a few years, because doing so would shorten the depopulation curve.

In exercises of this kind, textual agreement means much less than textual disagreement. The case of the size of Atahualpa's treasure room shows this clearly. Had all the chroniclers who offered an estimate agreed, it would by itself have meant little, since they all had opportunities to observe the room in question and then to discuss and harmonize their opinions before they expressed them in print. Consequently, their inability to agree on a figure takes on more significance. Yet N. D. Cook, who has done much work on the contact population of the Inca state, has never taken the trouble to subject the sources even to routine scrutiny. In this he typifies well the work of the High Counters at large.

When this work is looked at conspectively, it emerges that one of the defining marks of the High Counters is a credulousness toward sources and arithmetical methods that can be sustained only by indifference. They evade the grueling work of thorough source criticism in favor of emphasizing the quantitative aspects—the regression analyses, the projections, the log logs—of their enterprise. So seldom have they rejected a numerical datum in a source—unless to make it higher—that I am unable to cite an instance, though I concede that at least some must exist. Yet a thorough canvass and scrutiny of their principal sources readily show how fragile their numerical information almost always is. Above all, this virtually medieval stance toward the sources marks the High Counters' work and renders it unacceptable in light of all the methods of source criticism now available.[17]

A natural corollary of the notion that estimates of contact population are crucial is that dependable contact population estimates are potentially, if not actually, practicable. Even some critics of the High Counters' work accept this premise. A reviewer of Daniel Reff's account of population decline in northwestern Mexico, for instance, while finding his conclusions dubious, held out hope still: "For a region as massive as northwestern New Spain, the creation of the relevant numbers is going to take a long time. Until then, there will be no easy answers."[18] Until when, one is stimulated to ask. Until new sources become available? What might these be? Or until more sophisticated methods of massaging existing sources are devised? Again, what might these be, and will they, too, result in distorting plain evidence so readily?

Such a premise seems especially to reflect the need to have the hope of answers even in the absence of reasonable grounds. In referring to an author's estimates of the populations of several Spanish cities in the twelfth century, Hugh Kennedy writes: "Here again he is definite where others might be cautious, [but] . . . it is probably better to have an estimate and treat it as a statistic rather than give up and admit that we do not know."[19] Similarly, in discussing the extremely vexed question of the population of the Roman empire at any time, Michael Jones frankly admits that "[w]e are forced either to argue our historical intepretations without the vital consideration of population or make the best estimate possible and risk the retribution of critics who justifiably denounce dubious methods and evidence. The second choice," he goes on, "seems better to me."[20] No less epistemologically peculiar is R. P. Duncan-Jones's comment on mortality during the so-called Antonine plague of the second century. Duncan-Jones inclines toward a higher mortality than do others who have considered the matter. He cites William McNeill as suggesting "a figure of 25–33% for mortality in places affected." Duncan-Jones considers that "the last figure is presumably closest to the truth [*sic*]," but he concedes that "there is no real basis for any numerical estimate."[21] Certainly it is tempting to see such an argument—that we can approach the truth in a matter like this, and know that we have—merely as befuddled hope. To some, at least, these are extraordinary positions: any port in a storm even if that port is teeming with pirates?

In the natural and physical sciences, to be sure, an onslaught of new evidence and new procedures has made once unanswerable—even unaskable—questions yield to its weight. And in history the same is true, if to a lesser degree. The discovery of new sources and of new elucidating techniques have thrown new light on many a dark corner. But is this reason to find hope of answers to the question of the contact population? The High Counters put that possibility straight out of the question by presuming huge population losses in areas far beyond the purview of any contemporary report that might have survived. By this they destroy one illusion only to sustain another.

For our purposes one of the most revealing and diagnostic comments in all the literature of population estimation comes from the discussion of the population of Roman Britain. Mortimer Wheeler, who was to become one of the most eminent archaeologists of his time, wrote that R. C. Collingwood's estimate of half a million was too small, but he was more concerned that one of Collingwood's critics, though he also thought that Collingwood had underestimated, had not finished the job. "After all," Wheeler went on, "one guess is as bad as another. Mr. Collingwood guesses half a million. Mr. Randall guesses . . . but on re-reading Mr. Randall I find that he doesn't guess at all. He passes lightly from persuasion to persuasion and ends with *x*." For Wheeler, *x* was not at all an adequate hypothesis, and he went on to provide a figure of his own: "[T]he population of Roman Britain was not half a million, but a million and a half."[22] Wheeler did not pretend that his figure was anything more than the product of a series of guesses or "axioms" for which there was not a shred of direct evidence. But, he seemed to imply, it was inadvisable to criticize a figure without replacing it, and so he replaced it. It is scarcely a surprise that Wheeler's guesstimate lived on longer than Randall's lack of one.

Addressing this line of reasoning, Marc Bloch, citing so recent an event as the battle of Austerlitz, cautions that it will not be easy to understand its course, noting that "[i]t will not do to exaggerate the advantages of the present" in this regard. He continues in an admonitory tone:

> Explorers of the past are never entirely free. The past is their tyrant. It forbids them to know anything that it has not itself, consciously or otherwise, yielded up to them. We shall never establish a statistical table of prices for the Merovingian epoch, for no documents have recorded these prices in sufficient number. We shall never be able to penetrate the minds of the men of eleventh-century Europe . . . because we have from them neither private letters nor confessions, for we have for some of them only some bad biographies, written in a conventional style.

Bloch went on: "It is always disagreeable to say: 'I do not know. I cannot know'." And he advised that we ought not to say it until we have "energetically, desperately searched" for evidence. Still, he concluded, "there will be some times when the sternest duty of the scholar, having tried everything, is to resign himself to ignorance and admit it honestly."[23]

"Disagreeable" is to put it mildly indeed! Bloch was decrying the simplifying notion that history is a science and so is cumulative. He was suggesting instead that it sometimes proves needful to remove ideas and conclusions from history's docket, even if this leaves a temporary, or even a permanent, blank space. Recognizing that the work of years leads nowhere because the connective tissue has decayed is an eventuality that the High Counters—in this case—simply exclude from consideration.[24] We can only wonder what Bloch would have thought of the notion that the contact population of the Americas could be known with any comfortable certainty. Doubtless he would immediately have recognized that the data he cited as inadequate surpass almost infinitely in quality and quantity those that the High Counters are eager to put into use.

In his study of the Plague of Athens, Robert Sallares expresses sentiments not unlike those of the High Counters. Decrying "counsel[s] of despair" that argue that it might be impossible for moderns to put a name to the disease that apparently struck on this occasion, Sallares writes: "Giving up when faced with a problem is never likely to add to the sum of knowledge."[25] In the abstract this is so true as to be a truism, but practically speaking we must see things differently. Is it possible to use the word "knowledge" to describe our understanding of this occasion, for instance? If it were, there would not be extant in the literature more than ten hypotheses about it, as there are, including some that regard Thucydides' accounts as more symbolic and metaphorical than real. The danger here is that the impulse to add to a putative "sum of knowledge" inevitably leads to redefining epistemological standards so that "knowledge" and "belief" come to be all but synonyms.

Speaking of early Germanic history, Walter Goffart observed the impulse to know, and thought it reckless:

> Like many other peoples, groups, and individuals, the early Germans are disadvantaged. Vast tracts of their past are unknowable for lack of evidence. Never mind. Only let what there is be as solidly founded as possible; let areas of ignorance be admitted and left vacant; and let the unavoidable conjectures be limited in number and strictly controlled.[26]

In one of Tom Stoppard's plays a character momentously announces a breakthrough: "I have found a truly wonderful method whereby all the forms of nature must give up their numerical secrets and draw themselves through number alone." Another character will have none of it: "Distortions, Interference. Real data is messy."[27] The High Counters seem to agree with both sentiments, for they are indefatigable in using "real" data as means to create many more of their own synthetic or proxy data. In contrast, these data are not at all messy but prove to be almost symmetrically neat and mutually corroborative. This feature of their work is probably most obvious in Cook and Borah's efforts to turn the sparse, incommensurate, and contradictory data in the *suma de visitas* into the proverbial silk purse. But the need to impose newly created data on the sources inevitably forms the cornerstone of all procedures that attempt to posit a contact population for any or all of the Americas.

Still, as a matter of fairness, a final question to ask is whether the work of the High Counters has improved during the past thirty years. In general, the answer must be that it has not (given their premises, it cannot). Take the work of Henry Dobyns. Suspect in 1966, it is no less suspect nowadays. If anything it is worse, because of his continued inability to absorb either the plain testimony of his sources or criticism of his work.[28] Simpson and Cook have died, but Woodrow Borah has occasionally written on the matter. He now tends to offer predictions and overviews instead of numbers, but he has not retreated at all despite the barrage of criticism leveled at him.

In the meantime a younger generation has emerged, imbued with a sense of mission and convinced both that the contact population was very, very large and that reasonably accurate estimates of it can be determined by the usual methods of extrapolation. To judge from their dedications and acknowledgments, many of these scholars see themselves as acolytes of the pioneer generation. A particular esprit de corps has arisen among those working in Central America, which would be worth a separate study looking at the epidemic effects of a cadre spirit.[29] In addition, Daniel Reff has studied northwestern Mexico, and Linda Newson, Ecuador. Both have proceeded very much in the Cook-Borah tradition of finding small numbers and making them large by synchronic and diachronic extrapolation. N. D. Cook has propounded a population estimate for Peru in 1520 using more demographically oriented techniques, but he has overenthusiastically projected these so far back in time that they have produced a number that cannot be justified on any count at all.

In archaeology, Ann Ramenofsky has tried to show that intensity of occupation—as determined from known sites—declined in three areas of North America in the sixteenth and seventeenth centuries. Her work is suggestive of postcontact population decline, although her conclusions only reinforce a generally accepted proposition and her heavy-handed use of written sources compromises her method.[30] More adventurously, Sarah Campbell has postulated that a smallpox epidemic struck the Columbia plateau before 1525, but her evidence is exiguous, her methods peculiar, and her conclusions spurious.

In sum, although numbers as high as those which Dobyns and the central Mexico triumvirate advanced are rarer these days, efforts to postulate earlier and more virulent epidemics on a regional basis—and thus higher initial numbers and greater rates of depopulation—continue unabated. Despite this change in emphasis, the methods adopted have necessarily remained very much the same. Find numbers, believe them, multiply them. In the process brush off skepticism like a troublesome gnat.

Among other things, the debate over the contact population of the Americas reminds us of a fundamental, if unfortunate, paradox. In an open scholarly community, no idea should be rejected until it has been thoroughly bruited. This is especially true of ideas that are out of step with their zeitgeist and, conversely, least true of those that are advanced largely as detritus of their times. Yet for few scholarly hypotheses is it possible to assemble the evidence required for them to survive the appropriately cutthroat scrutiny they might engender, whether it is immediately forthcoming or is centuries in the making. This dialectic is the ideal; the real is something quite different. Even the most absurd ideas are never fully jettisoned, even when the evidence mounted against them is incontrovertible. Instead they remain suspended, ready to be used should an occasion permit. Bad ideas, like bad money, never completely leave the marketplace: the High Counters' numbers—and worse, the notions underpinning them—are here to stay, not only because they fit so well into the High Counters' preferred surroundings but also because these numbers, like any numbers, fill so well an epistemological vacuum.

—————

I leave the penultimate word to Theodore Porter, a historian of science interested in quantification and its effects on scientific epistemology: "Numbers form a rhetoric within disciplines, and help to order them; and at the same time they give shape to the processes they purport to describe. Numbers have power; otherwise they're ineffective. Otherwise they can't be made true."[31]

The final word, however, must go to the journalist Stephen Powers. Having estimated that the maximum population of the California Indians (in 1769; therefore he was no High Counter) was 705,000, Powers found himself promptly challenged. His reply has elements of the classic about it. He was delightfully agreeable. "You may reduce my estimate by one half," he wrote, but "I do not see how I can concede any more."[32] His willingness to debate might inspire us all.

Notes

Chapter 1: Do Numbers Lie?

1. Plato, *Republic* VII.522.

2. White, review of Thornton, *American Indian Holocaust*, and Ramenofsky, *Vectors of Death*, 66. For other such views see chapter 11, and for the ancient world, Gomme, *Population of Athens*, 1.

3. Jacobs, "Tip of the Iceberg," 128, expressed this typically: "It is hard to imagine that our history can ever be the same again."

4. Larsen, "In the Wake of Columbus," 121.

5. Or, as Lovell, "'Heavy Shadows and Black Night,'" 437, puts it: "[C]ontroversy is generated not so much by the numbers themselves as by the divergent views of history that any particular choice of numbers represents."

6. Cook and Borah, "Hispaniola."

7. Robinson and Licate, review of Cook and Borah, "Hispaniola."

8. Essays I have published on the subject include "Contact Population"; "If Pigs Could Fly"; "Primary Source"; "When Did Smallpox Reach the New World"; "Their Numbers Become Thick"; "Current Devaluation"; "Native American Population at Contact"; "Counting the Encounter"; "Biological Effects"; and "Nescience, Belief, Quantification."

9. Some highlights of the career of the High Counters' arguments in the public domain, and the arguments of others like them, are discussed in chapter 14. For another case of coterie scholarship see Long, *Planting and Reaping*.

10. Recently Crosby, *Measure of Reality*, has argued that one of Europe's great advantages in its early expansion was a desire to measure everything material within time and space. The examples cited in this book, especially in chapter 6, underscore the usual gap between desire and its fulfillment.

11. Newson, "Pre-Columbian Settlement," 130.

12. Cook and Borah, "Credibility," 230.

13. At the same time similar works have had a more cometary experience: see, for example, Bacque, *Other Losses*.

14. E.g., Stannard, *American Holocaust*, 267, praised Cook and

Borah's work as "a pathbreaking revolution in historical demographic technique" that "examin[ed] enormous amounts of data from a great variety of sources." Sale, *Conquest of Paradise*, 315, speaks of "a rough academic consensus" that the contact population of the New World exceeded 60 million.

15. Loayza in Molina, *Crónicas*, 81–82n, emphases in original.

16. Loayza, however (in Molina, *Crónicas*), parts company with the High Counters in attributing all the population loss to "maltreatment." Loayza's wonderfully circular reasoning is unconsciously imitated by Sale, *Conquest of Paradise*, 316–17, when he writes on the nutritional requirements needed to satisfy his guess of "15 million north of Mexico." After laying out some numbers of what would be required, he immediately makes them real by proclaiming that "if this does not argue for Indian cultures a very special, an *intrinsic*, regardfulness for nature, it is hard to know what would" (emphasis in original).

17. Newson, "Demographic Collapse" 250.

18. Roman numerals, on the other hand, are easier to misread and miswrite, but the effects of doing so would typically be on a smaller scale (though hardly necessarily—e.g., "VI" turned into "MI" or "MVI"). For Hebrew numbers see, e.g., Wenham, "Large Numbers," 19–53.

19. Unless it happens to produce a nonsense number similar to the numbers that Rabelais used as a form of satire in his work. Perhaps the most work on the matter has been carried out in biblical research: see, e.g., Driver, "Abbreviations," 126–30, and Wenham, "Large Numbers." Work in this regard has often been apologetical, in aid of forgiving exaggeration on the part of the biblical authors in favor of later scribal errors, but it is useful in showing how easily such errors must have been made.

20. Those interested in examples should see chapters 16–18 and my other writings. In lieu of this let me simply point out that the High Counters have been busily at work in several areas mentioned here scarcely, if at all. These include the northern Andes, northwestern Mexico, the Amazonian basin, and—in particular perhaps—the former audiencia of Guatemala. For the last, see Lovell and Lutz, *Demography and Empire*, and for Amazonia, see Newson, "Amazon Basin."

21. At that, in many cases (e.g., the Plague of Athens), I have cited only a few more recent works that in themselves contain numerous references to earlier studies.

22. Martin, *Keepers of the Game*, 43, 47.

23. Postgate, "How Many Sumerians?" 47.

24. A recent and very summary, though reasonable, discussion of the present state of affairs is Thornton, "Aboriginal Native American Population."

25. Squier, "Monumental Evidence," 322, on claims that certain ar-

tifacts discovered in what is now West Virginia indicated a Viking presence there.

Chapter 2: The Historiographical Career of One Number

1. Victor of Vita, *History*, 3.
2. Procopius, *Procopius*, 2: 53.
3. The list is long and includes Hodgkin, *Italy and Her Invaders*, 2: 246; Piaget, *Histoire des etablissements*, 76–77; Lot, *Invasions germaniques*, 88 (while calling Victor a "contemporary"); Courtois, *Vandales*, 158; Brown, *Augustine of Hippo*, 424; Courcelle, *Histoire*, 117; Morazzani, "Essai," 539–60; Overbeck, *Untersuchungen*, 55–56 (slightly qualified); Schreiber, *Vandalen*, 121; Demougeot, *Formation*, 509; Mahjoubi and Salama, "Roman and Post-Roman Period," 500; Clover, "Carthage," 7: 3 ("swelled to perhaps eighty thousand"); García Moreno, *Historia*, 52–54; Bright, *Miniature Epic*, 10 (with a very slight reservation).
4. Delbrück, *Geschichte*, 2: 296.
5. Bury, *Later Roman Empire*, 1: 105.
6. Bloch, *Mélanges historiques*, 107.
7. Jones, *Later Roman Empire*, 1: 194–95.
8. Anderson, *Passages*, 113.
9. Russell, *Late Ancient and Medieval Population*, 75.
10. Riché, "Problèmes," 38. Riché went on to thank Victor for "this precious datum," while adding that modern historians have interpreted it "in different ways."
11. Claude, *Geschichte*, 37–38; Carson, "Kingdom," 336.
12. Orlandis, *Historia*, 32
13. Ferrill, *Fall of the Roman Empire*, 126. Ferrill was more inclined than most to accept the high numbers in the chronicles, since they provided the evidence for his principal argument.
14. Rouche, "Break-up and Metamorphosis," 53–77.
15. Thompson, *Romans and Barbarians*, 159. In contrast, Morales Belda, *Marina vándala*, 114–23 et passim, relies on Procopius's numbers for his own estimates, which are higher than 80,000, and for his calculations about Vandal vessel requirements.
16. Gautier, *Genséric*, 138.
17. Haury, "Stärke der Vandalen," 527–28; Schmidt, "Frage," 620–21. See also Schmidt, *Histoire des Vandales*, 42.
18. Seeck, *Geschichte*, 6: 416n21
19. Wolfram, *Goths*, 226
20. E.g., Hodgkin, *Italy and Her Invaders*, 2: 246; Schmidt, *Van-*

dales, 42; Courcelle, *Histoire,* 117; Courtois, *Vandales,* 216; Jones, *Later Roman Empire,* 1: 195; Bright, *Miniature Epic,* 253n16; Orlandis, *Historia,* 32–33; Wolfram, *Goths,* 226;

21. Randers-Pehrson, *Barbarians and Romans,* 153.

22. Others who have explicitly preferred Victor's testimony over that of Procopius include von Pflugk, "Belisar's Vandalenkrieg," 70–72.

23. If after, the case bears a close similarity to Byzantine accounts of failed efforts to count the effectives of the Second Crusade as they crossed the Bosporus in 1147. According to one chronicler of the period, "the hosts were so numerous that the officials appointed to the task gave up and returned unsuccessful" (Choniates, *Byzantium,* 38). A second chronicler turned "so numerous" into 900,000 men but agreed that "they could not count further" (Cinnamus, *Deeds,* 60). Yet recent estimates are that there were fewer than 10,000 (Choniates, *Byzantium,* 376n180).

24. Walter Goffart, *Barbarians and Romans,* 232n, finds the argument "unobjectionable, but . . . only that."

25. Marrou, "Valeur historique," 205.

26. Goffart, *Barbarians and Romans,* 231–34. Jones, *End of Roman Britain,* 268, cites Goffart and seems to attribute to him the sentiment that the figure 80,000 "is probably exaggerated but roughly credible," whereas Goffart suggests neither, certainly not the latter. An earlier discussion along these lines was that of Lepper, *De rebus gestis Bonifatii,* 88–90.

27. Courtois, *Vandales,* 215–17, was dubious but made no disabling argument against the figure. Musset, *Invasions,* 235, cited and exaggerated Courtois's reservations. Jones, *Later Roman Empire,* 1: 195, used the figure without comment but went on to cite an example in which a total population estimate of 80,000 was later transformed into 80,000 fighting men.

28. In a bit of a twist, modern estimates of the size of the Vandal army emanate from Victor's figures, rather than the reverse. Even so, there is little unanimity: Delbrück, *Geschichte,* 308–9 (8,000 to 10,000); Lot, *Art militaire,* 2: 250 ("not more than 10,000"); Lot, *Invasions,* 88 ("only 12 to 15,000 warriors"); Schmidt, "Sueves," 1: 305 ("about 15,000 armed men"); Bury, *Invasion,* 118 ("the fighting force might have been about 15,000"); Folz, *Antiquité,* 58 ("15 to 20,000"); Hodgkin, *Italy,* 2: 246 ("at the utmost 20,000 fighting men"); Demougeot, *Formation,* 509 (20,000); Anderson, *Passages,* 113 ("perhaps 20–25,000"); Courtois, *Vandales,* 216 (doubling the 80,000 would imply an army of "about 25,000"); Jones, *Later Roman Empire,* 1: 195 ("say 25,000").

29. *Pace* Gautier's airy claim of universal knowledge, there is a strong argument from silence working against this. Isidore of Seville, *History,* 33–35, writing sometime after 624, failed to mention the size of the Vandal host. Gregory of Tours, *History of the Franks,* 2: 39, writing late in the sixth cen-

tury, seems to have been unaware that there had been a count of the Vandals crossing to Africa, for he wrote only that they "crossed the strait." Earlier the chronicler Hydatius (d. 469), who wrote not long afterward—and before Victor—and who resided in Spain, merely recorded that Geiseric "abandoned Spain . . . with all the Vandals and their families" (Burgess, *Chronicle of Hydatius,* 91). A century later, Possidius was content to write only that "a great host of men, armed and trained for war," crossed over from Spain (Deferrari, *Early Christian Biographies,* 108).

30. It might be expected that a leader as "cunning" as Geiseric would see the advantages of spreading the dangers of shipwreck as thinly as possible, whatever the size of the group to be transported, once he had established a beachhead, which would not have required large numbers of fighting men.

31. Le Gall, "Itinéraire," 268–73. Courtois, *Vandales,* 159–60, estimated that about 2,500 ships would have been needed to transport the Vandals along the North African coast, but he estimated the numbers involved at 180,000, arguing that the crews of the ships would have outnumbered the passengers—and apparently were not drawn from among them.

32. Diesner, *Untergang,* 169–70; Morazzani, "Essai," 544–45. Dissenters include Schmidt, *Histoire,* 44–47, and Carson, "Kingdom," 337.

33. Wolfram, *Goths,* 226.

34. Goffart, *Barbarians and Romans,* 234.

35. A recent exchange about the number of Visigoths illustrates this. James, *Merovingian Archaeology,* 1: 194–95, argues that this was much less than the 100,000 or so often imputed to them. In contrast, Nixon, "Relations," 65–68, prefers a higher number: "[H]ow could it have been smaller, in light of the deeds of the Visigoths in Italy, and all that followed?" James and Nixon both used Victor's figure as a point of departure, Nixon because it provided a "safer order of magnitude" ("Relations," 65).

Chapter 3: Higher Numbers, Higher Ground

1. Dobyns, "Reassessing," 8–9.

2. Riccioli, *Geographiae Hydrographiae,* 679–80. For Riccioli in his times see Ducreux, "Premiers essais."

3. There were other early efforts to measure the earth's capacity to contain people. One of the most elaborate was that of Thomas Hariot, who, at the end of the sixteenth century, calculated that the earth could support 7,081,758,800 people. Most of his assumptions as to density, representativeness, and land area were incorrect, and he made some arithmetical errors. See Sokol, "Thomas Harriot." Cohen, *How Many People,* discusses a large number of past and present carrying-capacity estimates.

4. Montesquieu, *Lettres persanes*. For this aspect of Montesquieu's work see Young, "Libertarian Demography."

5. Montesquieu, *Lettres persanes*, 215.

6. Ibid., 214–15.

7. Ibid., 215.

8. The notion that the earth was anciently much more populous than it was later was much abroad. In Spain, for instance, two works published in the seventeenth century estimated declines from 78 million to 14 million and from 50 million to 19 million, respectively. The latter estimates themselves were more than twice too high. See Girard, "Chiffre."

9. Feijóo, "Senectud del mundo" and "Consectario a la materia del discurso antecedente, contra los filosofos modernos," in his *Obras escogidas*. Cf. Aldridge, "Feijoo."

10. Aldridge, "Feijoo," 134. For Petau, see Martin, *Petau*.

11. Even in the later nineteenth century there were attempts to justify the Bible literally by recourse to this kind of reasoning. See, for example, Ashpitel, *Increase of the Israelites*. Ashpitel (8) found no trouble in believing that after 215 years "sixty-eight males" had produced a population of "600,000 that were men, besides women and children." For other examples of the popular pastime of calculating drowned diluvians, see Egerton, "Longevity."

12. Wallace, *Dissertation*, 10.

13. Ibid., 6–9.

14. Ibid., 65.

15. Ibid., 58. For the Aeginetan case see Westermann, "Athenaeus."

16. Thus Wallace, *Dissertation*, 45–46, was able to transform Diodorus Siculus's already exaggerated estimate of Egypt's population of 7 million into 28 million.

17. For an argument that Caesar's numbers should never be taken at face value, see chapter 15.

18. Wallace, *Dissertation*, 72–74. And since Belgica was no larger "than the fourth part of Gaul," the ineluctable inference was that the population of the entire provinces in the 50s B.C. was 32 million (ibid., 74–75). Cf. chapter 15.

19. For Wallace's work and its influence see Bonar, *Theories of Population*, 175–78; Luehrs, "Population and Utopia"; Hartwick, "Robert Wallace"; and Winsor, "Robert Wallace."

20. Hume, "Populousness."

21. For the debate to which both Wallace and Hume contributed see Glass, *Numbering the People*, esp. 11–40. As Glass (24) pointed out, "the initiation, at least, of the argument of a higher population in the past derived far more from a desire to demonstrate the historical truth of the Bible, a nos-

talgia for a misconceived and over-glorified antiquity, and a distaste for the growing importance of manufacture and commerce."

22. Hume, "Populousness," 424.

23. Ibid., 459.

24. Ibid., 470–71, 468.

25. Ibid., 508.

26. Jennings, *Founders*, 85, traces "the beginning of sanity" to the work of H. J. Spinden, who estimated in 1929 that the hemispheric population in circa A.D. 1200 was "say 50,000,000 to 75,000,000 souls." Spinden, "Population," helped his own cause by making assumptions such as that the mounds in the Ohio valley area were built simultaneously, so that the area "must have supported several millions" just to accommodate this communal labor force.

27. For useful canvasses of twentieth-century activity in this area see Marino, "Aboriginal Population," and especially Daniels, "Indian Population."

28. Borah and Cook, "Conquest and Population," 177.

29. Clavigero, *Historia*, 369–90. Pauw, *Recherches philosophiques*. Clavigero saved a bit of ammunition for William Robertson, who, in his *History of America*, 4: 4–5, had mentioned both disease and internecine warfare as causes of depopulation.

30. Clavigero, *Historia*, 377.

31. Ibid., 388. For selections from Pauw, Robertson, and others see *Europa y Amerindia*.

32. Clavigero also criticized William Robertson on similar grounds. For the context of these fulminations see Commager and Giordanetti, *Was America a Mistake?*

Chapter 4: Damning the Torpedoes

1. Cook, *Demographic Collapse*, 53.

2. Newson, "Demographic Collapse," 249.

3. Larraín Barros, *Demografía*, 1: 51.

4. Ribeiro, *Americas and Civilization*, 98.

5. Mier, "Idea," 67.

6. For Mier's career see O'Gorman, *Seis estudios*, 59–148; Lombardi, *Political Ideology*; Brading, *Origins*, 24–65; and Jara, "Inscription."

7. Cook, "Interrelationship," 49. In this paper Cook used computed carrying capacity as the principal means by which he adjudged population levels. Just a few years earlier ("Population of Mexico," 514) he had accepted that "the pre-conquest population was somewhere near 2,00,000."

8. The *visitas* actually took place several years before and after 1548; Borah and Cook, *Population in 1548,* 19, considered this year to be "the average date," thereby closing off the question of the effects of population movements during the years in question.

9. E.g., Kubler, "Population Movements."

10. Borah stated this most unambiguously in his "Historical Demography," 29: "Let me hasten to add that for the period immediately after the appearance of the Europeans or their influence in any region, the entrance of Old World diseases meant a steady hammering downward for some decades."

11. Borah and Cook, *Population in 1548,* 57.

12. Ibid., 74. Since Borah and Cook used the word "population" to include both the "total" population and various portions of it, I cannot always be certain that I have interpreted them correctly.

13. Their argument, ibid., 60–65, implies that it so happened that the tributary population was at its lowest ebb just at the time when the *suma* was conducted, but they are unable to marshal much evidence on behalf of this argument beyond the "opinions" of a few contemporary observers. There are no other counts, for instance, that would justify this assumption. Their discussion of one possible dynamic of the *mayeques* (ibid., 71–73) likewise displays strained reasoning resulting from deficient evidence.

14. Cook and Simpson, *Population of Central Mexico,* 43.

15. The High Counters' use of warrior estimates is discussed in chapter 16.

16. Cook and Simpson, *Population of Central Mexico,* 3–4.

17. Borah and Cook, *Population in 1548,* 6.

18. Kubler, review of Cook and Simpson, *Population of Central Mexico,* 556–59.

19. Cook and Simpson, *Population of Central Mexico,* 22–38, the highest of several alternative calculations reached by projecting back from 1565.

20. Borah and Cook, *Aboriginal Population,* 88; idem, "Stratification." Although this range was given there, qualified by the statement that it was "an estimate with a wide range of error," in fact both the High Counters and their critics tend to express only the figure of about 25 million.

21. Borah and Cook, *Population in 1548,* 76.

22. Ibid., 76.

23. Ibid., 76n., citing *Epistolario de Nueva España,* 16: 83, "Relación de Xantetelco y sus sujetos," dd 2 February 1571.

24. Borah and Cook, *Population in 1548,* 76n; "Relación de Totolapan y sus sujetos," dd 11 February 1571, in *Epistolario de Nueva España,* 83–84. This takes the obviously incorrect locution "más cuento dos y dos" in the letter to mean "102," although "202" and even "104" cannot be ruled out.

25. The discrepancy between the numbers of widows and widowers could be explained by the fact that for one of the sites no number is given, but it is said only that "so many others" were there. Thus, in the space of a few lines this vague description became "60," hardly a likely contingency.

26. For a similar set of circumstances see the Michoacán example discussed at the end of this chapter.

27. Borah and Cook, *Population in 1548,* 76n.

28. Chaunu, "Population," 115.

29. Rosenblat, *Población de América.*

30. Ibid., 25–33.

31. Ibid., 33–49.

32. Borah and Cook, *Population in 1548,* 73. At least two of the four numbers and one of the two years in the table on that page are incorrect.

33. In fact, although Borah and Cook did not make the point, the *mayeques* are mentioned very infrequently in the early historical record—our knowledge comes almost entirely from Zorita's work, dating from the 1550s and 1560s. See, e.g., Hicks, "Dependent Labor," 251–55, and Carrasco, "Mayeques." From these it appears that not all *mayeques* were exempt from tribute, which would further lower their percentage of the population.

34. Rosenblat, *Población de América,* 49–68.

35. Ibid., 69–70. Rosenblat used 6,300,000 for Borah and Cook's final estimates.

36. Ibid., 71.

37. Rosenblat referred here to conclusions reached in Borah and Cook, *Aboriginal Population,* which is discussed later.

38. Rosenblat, *Población de América,* 71–81.

39. For the former see Borah, review of Rosenblat, *Población de América,* 475–77, where Borah largely confined himself to disagreeing with Rosenblat without providing much specificity.

40. Borah and Cook, "Conquest and Population," 177n.

41. Borah, "Historical Demography of Latin America," 200.

42. Borah, "Historical Demography."

43. Cook and Borah, *Essays,* 1: 1–72, 73–118, 119–200.

44. Sanders, "Central Mexican Symbiotic Region."

45. Ibid., 92.

46. Ibid., 94–101.

47. Ibid., 101–09.

48. Ibid., 112–14.

49. Denevan, "Epilogue," *NPA,* 291. Earlier, Sanders had suggested that the population of Mesoamerica "could not have been less than 12 million, with 15 million a more probable estimate" for an area of 1.25 million

square kilometers (Sanders and Price, *Mesoamerica*, 77). Even allowing for a slightly larger area—most of which had a lower population density—this figure seems markedly larger than his later estimate, as interpreted by Denevan, not least in terms of treating it as an irreducible minimum.

50. Coincidentally, Nutini, *Wages of Conquest*, 389, comes up with a figure of "between 12 and 13 million," but on the most exiguous evidence.

51. Slicher van Bath, "Calculation."

52. Ibid., 78–90.

53. Ibid., 80.

54. Cook and Borah, *Essays*, 1: 126.

55. Borah and Cook, *Population in 1548*, 90–102; Cook and Borah, *Essays*, 1: 237. Slicher van Bath, "Calculation," 90, offered evidence that such exclusions were the exception rather than the rule, which would reduce Cook and Borah's calculations by about 11 percent.

56. Slicher van Bath, "Calculation," 91–92; Cook and Borah, "Rate of Population Change," 463–70. The notion of an inexorable decline is less an assumption than an arithmetical imperative in calculating backward in time, and it has been widely used by the High Counters. In this methodology only the beginning and end points matter.

57. Rheenen, "Casados," took issue with Slicher van Bath, although not entirely at the expense of agreeing with Cook and Borah on all counts. For example, Van Rheenen argued that Slicher van Bath erred in using Cook and Borah's inaccurate transcription of the *suma*.

58. Zambardino, "Mexico's Population."

59. Ibid., 1–4.

60. Ibid., 8.

61. Ibid.

62. Borah and Cook, *Population in 1548*. The *suma* had been discussed earlier by Kubler, "Population Movements," 617–23. Kubler tended to be suspicious of the incipient move toward higher figures, arguing that depending on sources such as the *suma* "is not suitable for determining total populations." In support of this Kubler cited several circumstances that could have affected these counts one way or another. He also noted several instances in which the figures in these sources differed from those available elsewhere (607–11, 620–23).

63. Zambardino, "Mexico's Population," 12.

64. Ibid., 17.

65. Ibid., 18.

66. Ibid., 20.

67. Claims that results were achieved independently are frequent in the writings of Cook and Borah; see, e.g., their "Credibility," where they ap-

pear almost surprised to find that their estimate of 25.2 million for the contact population did not clash with the exaggerated estimates of early eyewitnesses.

68. Zambardino, "Mexico's Population," 24–25, emphasis in original.

69. As if to emphasize this, in a follow-up critique intended for a very different audience, Zambardino changed his own best estimate for the contact population by raising it to between 8 million and 10 million; see Zambardino, "Errors."

70. Zambardino repeated his criticisms more succinctly in a review of volume 3 of Cook and Borah's *Essays* (*AAAG* 70 [1980], 583–85). There he carried his case a step farther by arguing that Cook and Borah had used their 1623 population estimate as a means of "confirming" a pattern of very precipitous population decline, as they argued had happened between 1519 and 1548. He made another point worth bearing in mind: "[I]f [a] hypothesis is proved impossible then it must be abandoned, but being proved possible does not enhance its validity." Cf. Henige, "Native American Population," 11–12.

71. One response was that of Houdaille, "Population de l'Amérique." Houdaille pointed out that in light of the huge discrepancy between the lowest and highest figures, "it cannot be a question of taking the average and of holding forth on the result thus obtained," perhaps as an indirect comment on Cook and Borah's propensity for doing just that. The eight starters for the 1920 and 1921 New York Yankees hit a total of 223 home runs, for an average of about 28 each. Of these Babe Ruth hit 113—just one example of the fallaciousness of the averaging approach.

72. Borah, "Introduction," 7. Guerra posited an epidemic of swine flu in late 1493 to account for Indian depopulation. This is is taken up in chapter 11. Le Roy Ladurie, *Mind and Method*, 79, characterized Cook and Borah's work on Hispaniola as "a powerfully documented study," though he added enigmatically that "responsibility for [their figures'] accuracy I leave to them." He emulated the High Counters' discourse by referring to Verlinden's much lower estimate as "pure guesswork(?)."

73. Berdan, "Comparative Analysis," 132.

74. Ibid., 137–38.

75. Ibid., 138.

76. Ibid., 125n.

77. Borah and Cook, *Aboriginal Population*, 47.

78. The effects of their decisions are best seen in column 5 of their Table I in Borah and Cook, *Aboriginal Population*, 107–49. This result is despite their rhetorical claim that "[w]here no basis for decision exists, either in general pattern or the Spanish annotations and texts, we have chosen the lowest value in order to avoid possible exaggeration or inflation of values" (41).

79. E.g., the several essays in Berdan et al., *Aztec Imperial Strategies*.

80. Hicks, "Subject States." Hicks also cites a number of other recent studies that have compromised Cook and Borah's view of the tribute documents and that of their guide in the matter, Robert H. Barlow. Rojas, *A cada uno lo suyo,* illustrates, *pari passu,* the variety and complexity, and sometimes the inconsistency, of the tribute system inherited from the Aztecs. Many of the essays in Hodge and Smith, *Economies and Polities,* also treat complex tribute arrangements that are not amenable to straightforward arithmetical manipulation and extrapolation. Nielsen, "2.2.1 Tribute Distribution," 207–14, is another recent study showing the dangers of treating any tribute documents as necessarily either accurate or typical.

81. See further on this Hodge, *Aztec City-States,* 30–31, 51–53, 73–76, 110–13, 129–31, 145–47.

82. Hicks, "Subject States," 8, speculates that Spanish reorganization of the Triple Alliance in 1522 helped make it impossible to confirm the reliability of the *Codex Mendoza* and the *Matrícula,* which postdate that occasion.

83. Noguez, "Codex," 67–71.

84. The problem is treated briefly and inadequately in Henige, "Contact Population," 709–12.

85. Lunt, *Financial Relations,* 80–84, referring particularly to Peter's Pence, the Papal tithe. Russell, *British Medieval Population,* 8, was candid about this turn of events: it was "unfortunate, since the number of opportunities to secure large and accurate demographic information are few indeed."

86. A closely related case is hypothesized in Brumfiel, "Quality of Tribute Cloth," 453–62.

87. Terraciano and Sousa, "'Original Conquest' of Oaxaca," 67.

88. Ibid., quoting Wood, "Corporate Adjustments," 313.

89. Woodrow Borah was later to treat a group of just such fraudulent postconquest documents in his "Techialoyan Codices." For examples from Africa, where such fabricated sources were normative during colonial rule, see Henige, "Akan Stool Succession." And of course many medieval monastic charters are not authentic—or at least not true.

90. See, e.g., Paso y Troncoso, *Papeles de Nueva España.*

91. The many exiguities of tribute-levying and tribute-taking—and in a much better-documented situation—are treated in, among others, French, "Tribute of the Allies"; Unz, "Surplus"; and Lewis, "The Athenian Tribute-Quota Lists."

92. Denevan, "Native American Populations," xxi.

93. Whitmore, *Disease and Death,* 139. The arguments of this work are made more accessibly in Whitmore, "Simulation."

94. The High Counters have ignored Berdan's work even though her conclusions directly affect demographic issues.

95. E.g., Zantwijk, *Aztec Arrangement,* 285 ("at least 20 million people"); Miller, *Art of Mesoamerica,* 230; Berdan(!) and Anawalt, "The Codex Mendoza," 71 ("encompassing some 20 million people").

96. Hassig, *Trade,* 155–57.

97. Hassig, *Mexico,* 152.

98. Rabell Romero, "Estudios," 647–50. See also Rabell Romero, "Descenso."

99. Wilkie and Horn, "Interview," 415.

100. After the appearance of his article, Zambardino urged Woodrow Borah to respond but received instead a "'let us agree to disagree'" response (Rudolph A. Zambardino to David Henige, 12 March 1981). Cf. Calvin Martin's reaction to extended criticism of his thesis that the coming of European diseases broke a longstanding bond between Indians and the animals: "Each of the foregoing authors has challenged my interpretation in one way or another, and with one exception I intend to leave it to the reader of my book to decide on the merits of their case versus mine" (Martin, "Comment," 191).

101. Borah, "Historical Demography," 33.

102. Borah and Cook, "Hispaniola."

103. Jacobs is one of the few to comment favorably on Cook and Borah's Hispaniola work, professing to see in it "a painstakingly thorough analysis of data"; see Jacobs, "Indian and the Frontier," 55n3.

104. A good example of how this might be done is Whitmore, *Disease and Death.* Whether or not one agrees with his choices, the care with which he established and pursued alternative possibilities in making his own preferred choice is admirable.

105. E.g., Borah and Cook, "Conquest and Population," 177n., referring to Angel Rosenblat.

106. Chaunu, "Las Casas," 77–78.

107. Chaunu also confused Las Casas' accuracy with his goodwill. Because Chaunu was treating Hispaniola in particular, see Henige, "Contact Population," 222–25, where it is argued that Las Casas' own testimony—and a host of other considerations—require us to reject his figure globally, though not reflexively. After all, passing the sincerity test is hardly tantamount to passing the reliability test as well. For a discussion of Las Casas' unreliability at the basic transmissional stage, see Henige, "Las Casas as Transcriber."

108. Hassig, *Mexico,* 152n.

109. Baudot, "Percepción histórica," 3–6.

110. Wachtel, "Indian," 212.

111. Baudot, *Utopie,* 506, approximated this and at the same time reflected a common tactic when he gave detailed attention to Cook and Borah's

estimates and noted only in afterthought that others (he mentioned only Rosenblat) "strongly disagreed."

112. Melville, "Valle del Mezquital," 33–34. Cf. idem, *Plague of Sheep,* 4–5, where the debate is noticed but passed over in favor of the comment that "the estimated population decline in Mexico" between 1519 and 1620 "was "90–95 percent."

113. Berdan, *Aztecs,* 172, 172n. Oddly, in the text she mentioned that "the indigenous population plunged from an estimated 12–15 million to just over 1 million" and supported this with a footnote citing "[e]stimates [that] range as high as 25,200,000 (Cook and Borah 1963)."

114. Prem, Dyckerhoff, and Feldweg, "Reconstructing." The authors suggest that the population in 1519 was "nearly 15.1 million at its highest" (55).

115. Zantwijk, *Aztec Arrangement,* 285.

116. Zantwijk, however, was content to speak of a population of "at least 20 million people in central Mexico" (*ibid.,* 285).

117. Hassig, *Trade,* 155.

118. Prem, Dyckerhoff, and Feldweg, "Reconstructing," 50.

119. Or one can adopt an argument similar to that of Las Casas, who claimed, astoundingly, that one Spaniard consumed nine hundred times as much food as the average Indian on Hispaniola. See his *Brevísima relación,* 76.

120. The matter is also treated, with different premises and results, of course, in Super, *Food.*

121. In contrast to Cook and Borah's Panglossian portrayal of nutritional life in central Mexico, see the gloomy picture painted, on the basis of much better evidence, in Pearson, "Nutrition."

122. E.g., Cook and Borah, "Indian Food Production"; Williams, "Rural Overpopulation"; and Kobayashi, *Tres estudios,* 23–49. Evans, "*Plebs rustica,*" provides an interesting parallel discussion.

123. Ossorio y Redín, *Discurso universal.* Cf. Edge, "Population Records." Actually, the population of his own time was much less than he thought.

124. Borah, "Review of Rosenblat, *Población de América,*" 477.

125. Cook and Simpson, *Population of Central Mexico,* 1.

126. Ibid., 23.

127. Ibid., 47.

128. Borah and Cook, *Aboriginal Population,* 3–4, emphasis added.

129. Including their suggestion that a contextually impossible combination of "wholly different methods" produced estimates for central Mexico in excess of 27 million; see their "Essay on Method" in *Essays,* l: 114–15.

130. Borah and Cook's trouble with the concept of independence is

illustrated by comments such as "it is interesting that the values suggested by this interpretation fall close to the range of values shown in" an accompanying table, when these values are not in the sources but are calculated, adjusted, and imposed. It is also illustrated in an instance when a "trend line" produces a figure "remarkably close to that indicated by the statement of Bishop Fuenleal," which had dealt with one small aspect of tribute-taking. See Cook and Borah, *Indian Population,* 25, 27.

131. There is reason to suspect that Cook and Borah did not benefit from criticism at the front end of the process either. The volumes on Mexico were all published in *Ibero-Americana,* a series under their control, while the University of California Press—a house organ—published their other works.

132. Cook and Borah, "Credibility," 230.

133. Cook and Borah, *Indian Population,* 13.

134. Borah, review of Rosenblat, *Población de América,* 476.

135. Cook and Borah, *Indian Population,* 32.

136. Ibid., 42; cf. ibid., 45. "The best estimate for the number of casados in town *X* in 1568 is thus 55.7 per cent of 500, or 278 $\frac{1}{2}$. Obviously, the real number may have been 100 or 600, but our estimate must lie within the realm of reasonable probability. It does give an idea of the order of magnitude."

137. Cook and Borah, *Indian Population,* 39.

138. Borah and Cook, *Population in 1548,* 42–44.

139. For this argument see Henige, "Counting the Encounter," and sources cited there.

140. My own reading of the evidence leads me to think that Smith's assessment (*Aztecs,* 61) that "most scholars favor [lower] estimates" is, at least for the moment, too sanguine.

141. Crawford, *Antropología,* 61–63. In his hemispheric "minimum" estimate of 44 million, Crawford (65) allots 25 million, or 57 percent, to "Central America," 7 million to the Caribbean, 2 million to North America and 10 million to South America. The continued willingness to believe demonstrably incorrect information and the lingering effects resulting simply from the presence of that information in the literature are addressed in, among other places, LaFollette, *Stealing into Print.*

142. Bacon, *Novum Organum,* 57.

143. Cook and Borah, *Indian Population,* 14.

144. Levin, "Negative Evidence."

145. Warren, *Conquest of Michoacán,* 73–80, 248–59; idem, "Caravajal Visitation."

146. Warren, *Conquest of Michoacán,* 76. Warren also points out that several small settlements seem not to have been visited or counted at all.

147. Navarrete Pellicer, "Algunas implicaciones," 106.

148. Ibid.

149. Ibid., 107–8.

150. Ibid., 120.

151. It was customary in early modern Europe to count by houses or "hearths" as well. For an interesting contemporary discussion of the problems there, see Richard Forster to Birch, 2 December 1760, in Glass, *Numbering the People*, 78–89. Connell, *Population of Ireland*, 3–8, and Daultrey, Dickson, and O Gráda, "Eighteenth-Century Irish Population," discuss the difficulties in counting houses accurately in Ireland about the same time.

152. According to the report on Uruapán, visited about one-third of the way through the inspection tour, the Spaniards would ask the local headman for a count and then check it visually. If in fact the Spaniards had found that the actual numbers of houses/households were almost always much greater than the testimony of the headmen, it is odd that they would continue to solicit and record local opinion. See Warren, "Caravajal Visitation," 410–12.

153. Paredes Martínez, "Tributo indígena," 26–27, mentions Caravajal's inquest but ignores the matter of discrepant numbers.

154. Warren, *Conquest of Michoacán*, 76, wonders whether the difference resulted from the way in which the Tarascans counted their numbers before the arrival of the Spaniards. This was discussed in the *Relación de Michoacan* (early 1540s). Certain officials called *ocámbechas* were responsible for the counting: "And they did not count these houses by hearth or adult male, but by how many belong to a single family, for there are in some house[s] two or three adult males with their relatives. And there are in other houses no more than a husband and wife, and in others mother and son, and thus in this manner." While this is not terribly illuminating and is subject to more than one interpretation, it comes close to suggesting that a Tarascan-style count would result in a larger number of "houses" than the Spanish count, rather than the reverse, since one implication of the passage—though by no means the only possible one—is that such pre-Hispanic counts allowed for variations in family size. In contrast, there is no evidence that the Spaniards counted anything but structures, which should have produced the lowest raw numbers even while it could then generate higher numbers through creative extrapolation. Cf. *Relación de Michoacán*, 194.

155. Cook and Simpson, *Population of Central Mexico*, 29, citing Ixtlilxochitl, *Obras históricas*, 2: 418. Ixtlilxochitl's work was written more than a century after the conquest.

156. Borah and Cook, *Aboriginal Population*, 87. For environmental factors see Pollard and Gorenstein, "Tarascan State," and Pollard, *Taríacuri's*

Legacy, 79. In the latter, Pollard, on the basis of environmental considerations, estimates a maximum sustainable population of about one-third that postulated by Cook and Borah. Symptomatically, Cook and Borah added that this estimate "compares well with our 1532 estimate of 1,038,668" (in *Population in 1548,* 48) because of the smallpox epidemic and the "particularly ruthless [Spanish] conquest."

157. Gorenstein and Pollard, *Tarascan Civilization,* 36.

158. Later, Pollard apparently decided that the Spanish figures should be considered the more trustworthy: Pollard, *Taríacuri's Legacy,* 126, putting "'casas'" in quotation marks and assuming six persons per "household [= casa?]"

159. That is, it might be a household, a far more elusive concept, and one that raises issues like those already noted in terms of definition and therefore of size. Although the disparate ratios recorded in the *visita* do not support the notion, it is not entirely inconceivable that the Tarascans were counting extended families whereas the Spaniards were culling out nuclear families to be tabulated. Possibilities like this are dark clouds on the High Counters' horizon.

160. Cook and Borah, "Materials," 1: 10n, actually refer to the Caravajal *visita* as a "direct Spanish count," but, like Paredes Martínez, have nothing to say of its Indian counterpart.

Chapter 5: Giving Disease a Bad Name

1. I phrase this as a percentage deliberately, to show how doing so can mislead. In fact, for every 1,000 persons alive at a population nadir, there were 20,000 at apogee using a 95 percent depopulation ratio, whereas, by an apparently insignificant change to 96 percent, the number alive at apogee increases by 5,000, or fully 25 percent.

2. Dobyns, "Estimating," 395–416, with comments and reply, 425–44.

3. Newson, "Demographic Collapse," 249.

4. Even so, I am not convinced that it is entirely fair to treat Dobyns's paper as typical of later work by the High Counters. Just the same, Dobyns did set the methodological parameters and the general discursive tone; while others have shown themselves more cautious in their methods, these methods—and the hopes expressed by them—have clearly been influenced by Dobyns.

5. Dobyns, "Estimating," 395.

6. Ibid., 396–97.

7. Henige, "Contact Population."

8. Dobyns, "Estimating," 396; Casas/Pérez Fernández, *Historia de las Indias,* 3: 2439–2440.

9. Dobyns, "Estimating," 397. This follows the translation in the source that Dobyns used for Las Casas' *Brevísima relación:* McNutt, *Bartholomew de las Casas,* 384. Dobyns did not consult the original Spanish text.

10. Dobyns, "Estimating," 398. Dobyns called him "Varina."

11. Ibid.

12. Ibid., citing Varinas, *Vaticinios,* 36 (my emphasis). Like Las Casas' *Brevísima relación,* Varinas's work is a litany of unsubstantiated charges, some of which might well have been true but are not demonstrably so. For Varinas's views on depopulation and related matters see Falcón Ramírez, *Clases,* 65–74, and Varinas, *Estado eclesiastico,* 1–68 et passim.

13. Not "contact," since the period of peak population among the Maya antedated contact by centuries; see, e.g., Turner, "Population Reconstruction."

14. Ricketson and Ricketson, *Uaxactun,* 22–24.

15. In fact ("Estimating," 400), he referred to them as "applying a series of explicit assumptions to hard-won archaeological survey data," whatever that means.

16. Morley repeated the Ricketsons' argument and exemplification so closely that even though he acknowledged his source it all but amounted to unacknowledged borrowing. See Morley, *Ancient Maya,* 313–16.

17. Brainerd and Morley, *Ancient Maya,* 262–63. Morley's numbers continued to appear in the Spanish editions of the work until at least 1965. See Morley, *Civilización Maya,* 346–50.

18. Brainerd and Morley, *Ancient Maya,* 263.

19. The issue of contemporaneous occupation continues to exercise archeologists; for studies from an entirely different context see Helskog and Schweder, "Estimating," and Kardulias, "Estimating."

20. Dobyns, "Estimating," 401.

21. Morley's argument, following that of the Ricketsons, and Brainerd's disputing it both disappeared from the next edition of *Ancient Maya,* this time edited by Robert J. Sharer and published in 1983. In the most recent edition (1994), Sharer assumes sole authorship, and discussions of population levels become site-specific (467–73 et passim). If Dobyns had expressed concern that Brainerd had revised Morley dramatically without the slightest indication that he was doing so, he would have had a case, for the emendation in this respect was as silent as it could possibly have been. Just a brief "publisher's note" in the 1994 edition mentions that Brainerd "rewrote some material entirely," without further specification (ibid., v). Tikal, one of the most extensive Mayan urban sites, has been estimated to have had a maxi-

mum population of only about 60,000 (Culbert et al., "Population of Tikal"). In part Culbert and his colleagues reach this conclusion by adopting assumptions very different from those of the Ricketsons as to simultaneity, residential density, buildings per household, and so forth. The context for the Ricketsons' estimate is discussed in Black, "Carnegie Uaxactun Project." Among other things, Black notes the expressed concern of members of the project to validate the importance of the site—a set of circumstances that must be true of any archeological undertaking.

22. Cf. Thompson, *Rise and Fall*, 29, where he thought that his estimate of about 3 million might "be a bit low, but reliable data are so scarce that no figure is much better than a 'guesstimate.'"

23. Dobyns, Estimating," 403–8.

24. Ibid.

25. Ibid., 404.

26. Baegert, *Observations*, 53–58.

27. Cook, *Extent*, 7; Dobyns, "Estimating," 404. Cook, on the other hand, although he quoted Baegert correctly, treated him as if he had not by then taking "his mean estimate, 45,000," as his own working figure.

28. Cook, *Extent*, 7. Cf. Baegert, *Letters*, passim. In one of his early letters (115) he offered a much lower contact figure: "It is, however, certain that at the beginning of this mission, that is at the beginning of this [eighteenth] century, not more than 13,000 reasonable [*sic*, having reached the age of reason or about six years of age] souls lived in this huge territory" (dd 11 September 1752). Dobyns was later to estimate that the population of Baja California was a "minimum" of 87,760 (*Number*, 38).

29. Dobyns, "Estimating," 404.

30. Cook, *Extent*, 13–14, emphasis in original.

31. Dobyns, "Estimating," 405.

32. Ibid. For more on baptismal figures see chapter 18.

33. Ibid.

34. Zorita, "Breve y sumaria relación," 2: 114–15. For the history of this work see Vigil, *Alonso de Zorita*, 276–79, and Zorita, *Life and Labor*, 3–77. For context see Muñoz, "Obras hidráulicas."

35. For a more accurate translation see Zorita, *Life and Labor*, 211; cf. Zorita, *Señores*, 147.

36. Dobyns, "Estimating," 406. The need for such records is far from obvious, particularly since Zorita specifically stated that the Indians not only were not paid for their work but also were forced to provide the raw materials. Neither Zorita nor Dobyns offered any suggestions as to how such enormous masses would have been fed. In any case, just imagine the number and size of "books" required.

37. Zorita, *Life and Labor,* 69.
38. Dobyns, "Estimating," 408.
39. For approaches similar to Means's, see chapter 19.
40. Dobyns, "Estimating," 409.
41. Ibid., 408.
42. Means, *Ancient Civilizations,* 296.
43. Dobyns, "Estimating," 410.
44. Ibid., 411.
45. Not 1830 to 1833 as Dobyns implies; the first phase of this epidemic was in the Columbia and Willamette valleys, as Cook made clear enough.
46. Cook, "Epidemic of 1830–1833," 303–26.
47. Ibid., 320–21.
48. Ibid., 313–16.
49. Ibid., 321. For other estimates of the Oregon phase mortality see Boyd, "Another Look," and Spores, "Too Small a Place," 172, 190. For California see Philips, *Indians and Intruders,* 94–95.
50. Cook, "Epidemic of 1830–1833," 321–22.
51. Dobyns, "Estimating," 410. Over time Cook did the same for California as he and Borah and Simpson did for central Mexico. He began by estimating the maximum population at 135,000 and going so far as to say that "it is to be doubted seriously if Kroeber's conclusions can ever be subject to fundamental or drastic revision." His last estimate was 310,000, and along the way, of course, he thoroughly subverted Kroeber's work. See Cook, *Spanish Mission,* 161 et passim, and Hurtado, "California Indian Demography," and Cook's works cited there. For much lower estimates for Oregon see Robert T. Boyd, "Another Look."
52. Dobyns, "Estimating," 412.
53. Ibid.
54. Ibid.
55. There is no reason to suspect that Cook and Borah ignored this epidemic in formulating their conclusions, although they did not give it quite the same prominence that Dobyns did.
56. Rowe, "Inca Culture," 2: 184. Rowe, like Means, projected population on the basis of an idealized and decimalized Inca organization chart in lieu of any extant estimates. There were five estimates of population decline in the table to which Dobyns referred. The others, which Dobyns ignored, were 3:3, 3:1, and 4:3. He also ignored Rowe's conclusion that the overall population decline among the Quechuan-speaking peoples was about 4:1. For criticisms of both Rowe's numbers and his method see Smith, "Depopulation," and N. D. Cook, *Demographic Collapse,* 42–43.

57. Dobyns, "Estimating," 413; cf. Vellard, "Causas biológicas."

58. N. D. Cook, *Demographic Collapse,* 43–44, makes the same point in passing.

59. Dobyns, "Estimating," 413.

60. Ibid.

61. Bridges, *Uttermost Part,* 61, 521, 532. Bridges's own experience with the wraithlike Ona, the least peripatetic of the three groups in Tierra del Fuego, exemplifies the problem.

62. For other estimates of the region, almost every one different from any other one, see Lothrop, *Tierra del Fuego,* 25, 192–97; Pessagno Espora, *Fueguinos,* 143, 207, 209; and Gusinde, *Selk'nam,* 1: 131–35.

63. Vellard, "Causas biológicas," 82.

64. Dobyns, "Estimating," 413, following Vellard, who in turn cited Cooper, "Ona," 1: 108, who made the claim without further ado. Most recently, see Legoupil, "Indigènes."

65. Vellard, "Causas biológicas," 77–93.

66. Dobyns, "Estimating," 414.

67. May, "Prehistory," 19.

68. Dobyns, "Estimating," 414.

69. Ibid.

70. Ibid., 415.

71. Ibid., 414.

72. At this point Dobyns tended to use "'standard'" in single quotation marks, as if not quite believing in it, but in both this early paper and his later writings he invariably treated it as his principal methodological weapon.

73. Bennett in Dobyns, "Estimating," 426. Harold Driver, ibid., 430, felt that the High Counters' work in central Mexico was "based on unusually large samples of highly particularistic data and is a model of critical handling of materials."

74. Blasi in ibid., 426.

75. S. Cook in ibid., 427. Cf. Clavijero's similar comment noted in chapter 3.

76. Dunn in ibid., 430; cf. Peter Kunstadter and H. Paul Thompson in ibid., 436, 439.

77. Trigger in ibid., 440.

78. Driver, Thomas F. Kehoe and Alice B. Kehoe, and Kunstadter in ibid., 430, 434, 436.

79. Blasi and Forbis in ibid., 427, 431.

80. E.g., William A. Haviland in ibid., 433. On the other hand, Haviland thought that the highest estimates for Uaxactun, which Dobyns had regarded as implausible, might not be so.

81. Driver and Kunstadter in ibid., 430, 437. Cf. Zambardino's argument discussed in chapter 4.

82. Kehoe and Kehoe and Kunstadter in ibid., 434, 436.

83. Fuchs in ibid., 431–32.

84. Denevan and Trigger in ibid., 429, 440.

85. Eusebio Dávalos Hurtado and Thompson in ibid., 434, 439.

86. Keyfitz and Carmagnani in ibid., 435–36.

87. Dobyns's reply in ibid., 440.

88. E.g., 72 to 1 for North America; see his *Number,* 34–45.

89. Dobyns's reply in Dobyns, "Estimating," 440.

90. Ibid., 440–41.

91. Ibid., 441.

92. Ibid. For more on Guaraní demography see chapter 8.

93. To fill this yawning gap, Dobyns, "Estimating," 441, mentioned twenty-four deaths at one mission in Sonora, well short of the stuff of pandemics.

94. For a more extended discussion of Dobyns's relationship with his sources, see Henige, "Primary Source."

95. Dobyns, "Estimating," 441.

96. Rosenblat, *Población indígena,* l: 73. The degree to which *matlazahuatl* was endemic—and therefore possibly of precontact consequence—is disputed. For various arguments about whether the term represented an indigenous disease or was an existing term applied to a new disease, in particular to the case of the mortality in 1576 and following years, see, e.g., Cook, "Incidence," 321–22; Fernández del Castillo, "Tifus"; Hernández Rodríguez, "Epidemias"; Somolinos d'Ardois, "Epidemias"; Ocaranza, "Grandes epidemias"; and León, "Matlazáhuatl." If this disease did not antedate the Spanish arrival, the question arises as to why the Indians would have bestowed on it an existing Nahuatl term. The Indians also called this epidemic *cocoliztli* (Malvido and Viesca, "Epidemia"; Prem, "Disease Outbreaks," 38–42).

97. Citing in turn Orozco y Berra, *Historia,* 4: 64–67. Orozco y Berra referred to "parish registers, reputedly not very exact," for Mexico City, nothing for Puebla. For more on this episode see Alegre, *Historia,* 4: 380–85; González de Cossio, *Gacetas de Mexico,* 3: 78; Malvido, "Factores," 73–78. If it was intended to refer only to the *city* of Puebla, then the figure of 50,000 is greatly exaggerated: see Vollmer, "Evolución cuantitativa," 43–51; Malvido, "Despoblación"; Rabell Romera, *Población;* Caraviglia and Grosso, "Región," 560–62; Márquez Morfín, "Evolución cuantitativa, 38– 39; and Cuenya, "Peste."

98. Cooper, *Epidemic Disease,* 67–68.

99. Dobyns, "Estimating," 441. See Thompson, *Narrative*, 234–46.

100. Morton, *David Thompson;* Nickes, "David Thompson."

101. See, e.g., Thompson, *Travels*, 15–38, 82, 92–93, 96–97, 198–99, 302–3; Thompson, *Narrative*, xvi–xix, lxiv–lxxi (where the editor speaks of "the remarkable number of obvious inaccuracies" in the work), 49, 92–93, 236–37, 245–46, 367; Thompson, *Columbia Journals,* xii–xx.

102. Thompson's informants were Indians who also passed along the information that the Indians "had no idea of the disease and its dreadful nature," implying, it would seem, no previous contact with it. As well, Thompson was told that "the Bison, Moose, Red, and other Deer . . . also disappeared both in the Woods and in the Plains" (*Narrative*, 236–37). Among other things, Thompson appears to offer discrepant dates for this outbreak of smallpox: cf. Thompson, *Narrative*, 92, 92n, 236. Glover, "Witness," concludes that "the historian . . . must constantly walk delicately indeed when he relies on the unsupported word of David Thompson." For agreement with Dobyns that the epidemic of 1779–80 "diffused [from Mexico] as far as the Dakotas," see Ramenofsky, "Problem," 169.

103. Dobyns, "Estimating," 443. The remark seems particularly facile when contrasted with the difficulties in just this area invariably experienced by U.S. census-takers in the twentieth century. For this see, among others, Meister, "Misleading Nature"; Snipp, "Who Are American Indians?"; Anderson, *American Census;* and Thornton, "Aboriginal Native American Population."

104. Hacking, "Making Up People," discusses the difficulties in the value-laden process of categorizing people.

105. Dobyns, "Estimating," 444.

106. Ibid.

107. Price, "Trial Marriage."

108. Dobyns, "Estimating," 444.

109. Martin, *Keepers of the Game,* 44.

110. Ibid., 47.

111. On another occasion, Sempat Assadourian, "Crisis demográfica," 70, came straight to the point: Dobyns's estimates for Peru "must be rejected, since they are based on intolerable errors in the use of sources."

112. Crosby, "Summary," 278. Dobyns's numbers and arguments were borrowed whole by Vogel, *This Country Was Ours*, 251–53, and his conclusions influenced Jacobs, *Dispossessing*, 61–73.

113. Sánchez-Albornoz, *Population*, 34–35.

114. Dobyns, "Estimating," 407.

115. Nuix, *Reflexiones*, 81.

116. McCaa, "Spanish and Nahuatl Views."

117. Ibid., 429.

118. Dobyns, *Number*, 34–45. Since I have already commented on the methods of source criticism and general argument in this work, I will confine any discussion here only to any issues that help contextualize it. See Henige, "If Pigs Could Fly"; idem, "Primary Source." For Dobyns's comments on a couple of points raised in the latter, see Dobyns, "More Methodological Perspectives," and, in return, Henige, "Notion of Evidence." There the matter rests. In the meantime, Innes, "Disease Ecologies," 519–25, relies heavily on Dobyns.

119. Dobyns, *Number*.

120. Among the criticisms are those in Crawford, *Antropología*, 56–76; Newson, "Pre-Columbian Settlement," 132; and Smith, "Aboriginal Depopulation," 269–70.

121. Dobyns's views continue to get valuable air time; very recently Lord, "Ancient Puzzles," 9, referred to Dobyns's "detailed 1966 analysis" and cited his, and only his, estimates.

122. Dobyns, "Estimating," 413.

123. For the terms of the 1575 *mita* see, e.g., Cole, *Potosí Mita*, 7–22.

124. In fact, the establishment of the *mita* and the great expansion of the work force was stimulated by the introduction of new technology from Mexico: see Bakewell, "Technological Change." There were also communal strife, natural disasters, and unnatural disasters (e.g., the debasement of silver coinage) to consider. For incidents of these between 1622 and 1650 see Hanke, *Arzáns*, 36.

125. On the vagaries of the production of silver at Potosí and the problems in interpreting the available figures, see Arzáns de Orsúa y Vela, *Historia*, 3: 488–91.

126. Cañedo-Argüelles Fabrega, "Efectos," 240.

127. Cole, *Potosí Mita*, 111, 117, 120; Tandeter, *Coercion and Market*, 24–25.

128. Vellard, "Causas biológicas," 85. Thus Saignes, "Nota," 53, speaks of a reduction to 10,460 by 1617, a figure that was only a little more than one-half effected, a shortfall he thinks cannot be attributed to any specific reason in "so mobile and fluid" a set of circumstances. He suspects that "given the rapid decline in the extraction of silver," the actual supply of *mitayos* was negotiated up or down annually (55).

129. Juan de Matienzo to the king, 23 December 1577, in Levillier, *Correspondencia*, 1: 114–15; Cole, *Potosí Mita*, 15; Zavala, *Servicio personal*, 1: 103.

130. Bakewell, *Silver and Entrepreneurship*, 22; Arzáns de Orsúa y Vela, *Tales of Potosí*, xx.

131. Cole, *Potosí Mita*, 29. Cole (26n) discusses and dismisses certain early charges of very high population loss, perhaps in the very sources used by Vellard.

132. Rodríguez Molas, "Mitayos," 185. Rodríguez Molas presumably took this to imply a total Indian population of over 200,000. For an overview of various population estimates of Potosí during the colonial period, see Arzans, *Historia*, 1: lxix–lxx; Zavala, *Servicio personal*, 2: 96.

133. Tandeter, *Coercion and Market*, 24–26. Tandeter (27) points out another factor that helps to transcend any correlation between disease and population decline in this case: "massive human migrations and the abandonment of precisely those villages that were subject to the *mita* recruitment." Likewise, it seems that the majority of the conscripts from Pacajes were "absent" at various times; see Cañedo-Argüelles Fabrega, "Efectos," 244–47.

134. Sánchez-Albornoz, *Indios y tributos*, 26–34, calculated that the *originario* population around Potosí declined by about 42 percent between 1573 and 1683. Since the *originarios* represented the descendants of the *mitayos* of 1575, this figure is probably the closest it is possible to come to comparing like populations directly.

135. For the 1683–84 census see Evans, "Census Enumeration." This census, and particularly its effects during the next decade, are well discussed in Cole, *Potosí Mita*, 105–22, and Sánchez-Albornoz, *Indios y tributos*, 69–91. See as well Tandeter, "Forced and Free Labour," 101–3.

136. The viceroy's almost poignant defense of both the general accuracy and the equity of the census, and the measures he introduced on the basis of it, is found in his "Advertencias para la ejecución de los despachos de la nueva retasa y repartimiento de mitas de Potosí que han de tener presentes los corregidores y dar a entender a los Indios," dd 29 April 1689, in *Virreyes españoles*, 6: 231–38.

137. Other discussions that illustrate without emphasizing the unconnected fluctuations in both general and *mitayo* populations in colonial Potosí and its area include those of Bakewell, *Miners of the Red Mountain*, 104–30; N. D. Cook, *Demographic Collapse*, 236–45; Sánchez-Albornoz, *Indios y tributos*, 19–34; and Gisbert and Mesa, "Potosí," 160–64. For a more extended discussion see Abecia Baldivieso, *Mitayos de Potosí*, 57–90.

138. Cole, *Potosí Mita*, 117. This argument, of course, assumes that these figures are accurate, which they almost certainly were not, without knowing whether the inaccuracy was toward the low or the high side. It also takes into account immigration without knowing the degree of emigration, although to judge from the constant complaints of the mine operators, this was no small matter. In any case, as is argued in chapter 12, migration can

be as much a factor in measuring population growth and decline as disease, but is even harder to measure.

139. Sánchez-Albornoz, *Indios y tributos,* 22–34 passim.

140. Several documents illustrate the complexity and variety of the problem, including the fact that buyouts and other means of evading *mita* service were frequent; for these see Saignes, "Notes." Diffie, "Estimates," 275–82, discusses another kind of exaggeration.

Chapter 6: Rashomon the Chronicler

1. Gray, *Custer's Last Campaign,* 409–12; Hardorff, *Custer Battle Casualties;* Fox, "Custer's Last Battle."

2. Speaking of uncommonly large, the size of the Indian force at Little Big Horn has been estimated at anywhere from 400 to 9,000: Stewart, *Custer's Luck,* 309–12.

3. Rosenberg, *Custer,* 95.

4. Actually, 300 is merely the number conventionally adopted for Thermopylae; other estimates in antiquity ranged as high as 600; see Hammond, "Sparta at Thermopylae," 2–7.

5. For the alacrity with which "the last stand" became enmeshed in mythmaking, see, among others, Steckmesser, *Western Hero,* 163–237, 268–70, and, for more recent mythmaking, Linenthal, *Sacred Ground,* 127–71.

6. Numerous aspects of this corpus are addressed in the essays in Galloway, *Hernando de Soto Expedition.*

7. Oviedo, *Historia general* 1: 545.

8. Biedma, "Relación del sucesos," 213.

9. *Relaçam verdadeira,* ix^r. This edition is reproduced in Robertson, *True Relation.*

10. Garcilaso de la Vega, *La Florida del Ynca,* 27^r, 348^r.

11. Oviedo, *Historia general,* 1: 569.

12. Biedma, "Relación," 14: 233.

13. Elvas, *Relaçam,* 1: lxxx^v.

14. Garcilaso de la Vega, *Florida,* 204^r–v.

15. All four chronicles also recorded the number of arrow wounds treated after the battle: Ranjel, 648; Elvas, 700; Biedma, 760; Garcilaso, 1770. The range, sans Garcilaso, is 17.3 percent. A similar lack of agreement occurs in the accounts of the siege of Cuzco in 1536–37. Although the Spaniards in the city had a year to count themselves, they managed to offer estimates ranging from 150 to 240, and they counted their casualties with similar inconsistency. More accountably, they estimated that they had been attacked by from 50,000 to 300,000 besieging Indians: Flickema, "Siege of

Cuzco," 21–22nn, 32–33. Flickema's own research indicated that there were most probably 196 Spaniards in Cuzco at the beginning of the siege, a figure that does not appear in any of the surviving accounts. For similar troubles with a small-scale battle (were 39, 49, 59, or 400 colonists killed?), see Seybolt, "Note on Casualties."

16. Jérez, *Verdadera relación*, 322; Cieza de León, *Obras completas*, 1: 259 (ch. 30).

17. Mena, "Conquista del Perú," 79.

18. Pizarro, *Relación*, 13.

19. Thomas, *Conquest of Mexico*, 675n36, prefers the figure 530 because it was "given independently at the *residencia* against Cortés in 1539." Given the disparity of estimates in these cases, it is tempting to regard two instances of the same figure as corroborating one another, but we know too little of the opportunities for reciprocal feedback to do more than note such repetitions when they occur. In particular it is hard to judge just how "independent" any information offered at such *residencias* could have been—how were witnesses chosen? Were they sequestered? Were the questions unduly leading? In this case there is the additional imponderable of how the counting was carried out—that is, whether the sailors in the fleet, apparently about one hundred, were treated congruously in the various estimates. For the number of ships, itself at issue, see Gardiner, *Naval Power*, 17–21. As is usual, later attempts to transmit this information resulted only in further widening the degree of disagreement: e.g., Durán, *Historia*, 1: 3, thought that Cortés arrived with "only 300 men."

20. The range is arrayed in Wagner, *Rise*, 300, and Orozco y Berra, *Historia*, 4: 392n. See also Thomas, *Conquest of Mexico*, 410–13, 734–35, and Gardiner, *Naval Power*, 86–88. Thomas opts to accept the figure 600 as the most authoritative, whereas Wagner, *Rise*, 300, thinks that "600 or 650" is reasonable. Using a slightly different ensemble of estimates, Gardiner, *Naval Power*, 88, believes that the preponderance of testimony supports losses of about 800. Most secondary sources on the campaign seem to favor a figure of approximately 600, without noting the controversy and so their reasons for the preference—e.g., Innes, *Conquistadores*, 175. Symptomatically, the range of opinion regarding slain horses was much narrower; e.g., estimates that 150, 290, or 450 Spaniards were killed agreed that either 45 or 46 horses had also been killed (Martínez, *Hernán Cortés*, 273).

21. For the figure 150, see Cortés, *Cartas de relacion*, 187. On 20 August of the same year, during an adversarial proceeding in which he tried to cast blame on Pánfilo de Narváez for the debacle, Cortés testified under oath that "more than 200 Christians" were killed on the *noche triste*. See Conway, *Noche Triste*, 8. This occasion probably antedated his use of the figure 150

in his second letter, which, he wrote in his third letter, he completed on 30 October 1520. If so, then on reflection he recontextualized his already low figure. The number of horses lost was lowered as well, from 56 to 46, which seems to have become his own personal official figure, since it reappeared in López de Gómara's history-biography.

22. E.g., Wagner, *Rise,* 300. See chapter 15.

23. Gardiner, *Naval Power,* 86.

24. Even Cortés's biographer, Francisco López de Gómara, *Conquista,* 1: 312, seemed unable to swallow Cortés's patently low estimates, since he concluded that 450 Spanish deaths "is the most certain figure." He coyly added that "some say more, some less."

25. Wagner, *Rise,* 301–3. Cf. Davies, *Aztec Empire,* 186, 191, who mentions only 440; Berdan, *Aztecs,* 169 (600–700). Other discrepant estimates of the number of Spaniards under various circumstances during the conquest of New Spain are discussed in Konetzke, "Hernán Cortés," 355–67.

26. A related example, although involving names more than numbers, is that of the so-called "trece de Gallo," a group of men who remained behind on the island of Gallo in 1527, when the rest of Pizarro's expeditionary force returned to Panama, to serve as a warrant of Spanish commitment to explore the western coast of South America. The incident quickly became mythicized, and one result is that nineteen men compete in the chronicles for the thirteen vacancies: see Romero, "Isla del Gallo," 105–70; idem, *Héroes.* And in similar fashion, it was disputed how many missionaries (three to thirteen) comprised the Franciscans' advance party in Peru; for this see Tibesar, *Franciscan Beginnings,* 11–16.

27. López de Gómara, *Conquista,* 2: 66 (cxliv).

28. Cervantes de Salazar, *Crónica,* 3: 292 (5/197); Herrera y Tordesillas, *Historia,* 6: 176–77 (3/2/8); Torquemada, *Monarquía indiana,* 2: 312 (4/103).

29. Díaz del Castillo, *Historia verdadera,* 386, 402, 413. In a variant account preserved in another manuscript, Díaz was slightly more circumspect if no less inconsistent, writing of "sixty-odd" and "seventy-odd" (ibid.).

30. For an uncannily similar set of circumstances, see the discussion of the sources for Vasco da Gama's activities at Calicut and the numbers affected, in Disney, "Vasco da Gama." The eight contemporary or near-contemporary accounts show six different numbers—32, 34, 36, 38, "about 50" (three times), and 800. It is no surprise that this last has been repeated most often in modern accounts of the occasion.

31. Thayer Ojeda, *Conquistadores,* 1: 77. In the most thorough discussion of the issue, Thayer Ojeda, *Valdivia,* traced the fortunes of 150 of these men, and so this is probably to be regarded as the minimum number.

See also Errazuriz, *Pedro de Valdivia* 1: 131–32n. Modern historians have generally not concerned themselves with the discrepancy even while accepting a variety of numbers: Hancock, *Chile*, 41 (200); Elliot, *Chile*, 30 (150); Thayer Ojeda and Larraín, "Desastre de Tucapel," 25 (150); Thayer Ojeda, *Orígenes de Chile*, 197 (150); Faron, "Effects," 246 ("less than two hundred"); Korth, *Spanish Policy*, 238n6 ("some 150"); Pocock, *Conquest*, 64 ("up to 150 men in round numbers"); Armond, "Frontier Warfare," 52 ("fewer than 110"[!]); Villalobos R., *Historia*, 210 (152); León, *Lonkos*, 3 (156).

32. If the later chronicles are any indication, there grew up a tradition—probably some kind of Mayflower effect—that 200 Spaniards accompanied Valdivia from Peru. See Córdoba y Figueroa, *Historia de Chile*, 2: 44; "Informe de don Miguel de Olaverría," in *CDIHC* 2/4: 400; Olivares, *Historia militar*, 110.

33. Errazuriz, *Pedro de Valdivia*, 235–36n.

34. Encina, *Historia de Chile*, 1: 257 (30); Bonilla Radanovic, *Gran guerra*, 95 (40); Vernon, *Pedro de Valdivia*, 154 (30); Pocock, *Conquest*, 158 (29).

35. In the early Chilean chronicles the number forty is used far more often than any other to describe bodies of armed Spaniards.

36. Characteristically, Garcilaso de la Vega, *Royal commentaries*, 1: 451, provides the highest number by far; he wrote that "the first news" of the disaster reached Peru "on a scrap of paper" that said "'Pedro de Valdivia and 150 lances that were with him were swallowed by the earth.'" For Garcilaso's penchant for high numbers and counterfeit authentication see Henige, "*La Florida del Ynca.*"

37. Hancock, *History*, 53 (200!); Elliot, *Chile*, 43 (about 50); Thayer Ojeda and Larraín, "Desastre," 26 (40); Encina, *Historia*, 307 (37); Pocock, *Conquest*, 218 (40); Loveman, *Chile*, 53 ("about fifty"); Bonilla Bradanovic, *Gran guerra*, 128 (10 + 10 + 20); Vernon, *Pedro de Valdivia*, 177 (40); Galdames, *History of Chile*, 45 (40); Alvarez Vilela, "Expédition," 101n ("about sixty"). For more see Murrin, *History and Warfare*, 311n11.

38. Valdivia occasionally gave conflicting estimates of detachment numbers in his letters. See Valdivia, *Cartas*, 87–89n, 103n, 149–51n. A reasonable suspicion is that he was referring to slightly different circumstances in each case. One such instance is extensively discussed in Errazuriz, *Pedro de Valdivia*, 1: 188–93.

39. Castañeda Nájera, *Narrative*, 423.

40. "Relación hecha por el capitán Juan Jaramillo . . ." in *CDI*, 14: 304. Winship, *Journey*, 204, translated "sesenta" as "seventy," not an uncommon occurrence in the literature, as is the reverse.

41. "Relación del suceso de la jornada que Francisco Vázquez hizo en el descubrimiento de Cíbola," in *CDI*, 14: 318.

42. "Traslado de las nuevas y noticias que dieron sobre el descobrimiento de una cibdad, que llamaron de Cíbola, situada en la Tierra Nueva" in *CDI*, 19: 529.

43. Mimicking Castañeda, Bourne, *Spain in America*, 171, wrote of "about fifty horsemen, some foot-soldiers, and most of the Indian allies." Bolton, *Coronado*, 92, has "about eighty horsemen." In his introduction to the translated sources, Winship, *Journey*, 40, spoke of "seventy-five or eighty horsemen, . . . and twenty-five or thirty foot soldiers." Hammond, *Coronado's Seven Cities*, 23, wrote that "Coronado set out with about seventy-five horsemen, twenty-five foot soldiers, [and] some Indian allies." Day, "Mota Padilla," 93n, mentioned "a flying squadron of seventy horsemen." Day, *Coronado's Quest*, 97, spoke of "some seventy horsemen [and] twenty-five or thirty foot soldiers." None of these combinations of numbers is mentioned in any one of the sources. Likewise, Lecompte, "Coronado and Conquest," 288, uses the "Traslado's" numbers (75/30) but cites Castañeda. Bannon, *Spanish Borderlands*, 18, prudently mentions "about a third of the force." Lowery, *Spanish Settlements*, 296–99, is equally circumspect.

44. Hammond and Rey, *Narratives*, 15. In the latest discussion of the episode, Riley, *Rio del Norte*, 156, is content to refer to "perhaps two hundred to three hundred men in all"—including allied Indians.

45. Aiton, "Coronado's Muster Roll."

46. "Fragmento de la visita hecha á don Antonio de Mendoza," in *Colección de documentos para la historia de México*, 2: 118–19. Mendoza mentioned no infantry but did speak of 300 Indian allies. Aiton, "Coronado's Testimony," 314n, turned this into "1300" and changed Mendoza's estimate of horses and mules from 1,500 to 1,005. Bolton, *Coronado*, 69, seemed to regard Mendoza's report as canonical.

47. Inglis, "The Men of Cíbola."

48. Aiton, "Coronado's Muster Roll," 558, at least implies that individuals not listed on the roster did not accompany the expedition.

49. "Carta del doctor Diego Alvarez Chanca al cabildo de Sevilla" and "Relación de Miguel [Michele] de Cuneo" in Gil and Varela, *Cartas de particulares*, 159, 241.

50. Colón, *Life*, 114; Casas/Pérez Fernández, *Historia*, 2: 855. The accounts vary as well as to whether the men, whatever their number, wandered off accidentally or were sent in search of treasure, as well as both how the search was conducted and how the men turned up.

51. Eight of the estimates are collated in Gil and Varela, *Cartas de particulares*, 19–20. The ninth appears in a source since discovered.

52. Cohen, *Calculating People,* 57–64.

53. Morgan, *American Slavery,* 399–400. Morgan offers several suggestions to account for this pattern, but none seems wholly convincing, although in sum they underscore the numerous imponderables that underlie census-taking. See also idem, "Headrights and Head Counts." Other puzzling aspects of the numbers of settlers in Virginia during the first years are discussed and debated in Bernhard, "Men, Women, and Children"; Camfield, "Can or Two of Worms"; and Bernhard, "Forest and the Trees."

54. Morton, *New England Canaan,* 230; *Calendar of State Papers, Colonial Series, 1574–1660,* 1: 156.

55. Winthrop to Sir Nathaniel Rich, 22 May 1634, *Proceedings of the Massachusetts Historical Society* 20 (1882–83), 43. Winthrop declined to do more than estimate for fear of following the "sin of David."

56. "Relation Concerning the Estate of New-England," *New England Historical and Genealogical Register,* 40 (1886), 66–72. Various manuscripts of this account give different numbers.

57. On the baptismal counts see chapter 18.

58. Charbonneau and Légaré, "Population du Canada"; Pelletier, "Canadian Censuses"; Henripin, *Population canadienne;* Trudel, *Population du Canada.*

59. A minor, but suggestive, case of other small numbers gone awry is discussed in Houdaille, "Pertes dans la garde impériale."

60. Jérez, "Verdadera relación," 335.

61. Mena, "Conquista," 88. Cieza de León, *Obras completas,* 282 (c. xlviii), mentioned only "a large house."

62. Testimony of Hernando Pizarro, dd 23 November 1533, in Oviedo, *Historia general,* 4: 209. In translating this document, Clements R. Markham, *Reports,* 120, wrote "seventeen or eighteen feet wide, and thirty-five feet long." Porras Barrenechea, *Relaciones primitivas,* 73n, rendered it as "17 or 18 feet wide, 37 long."

63. Baldinger and Rivarola, "*Nouvelles certaines,*" 459.

64. Ruiz de Arce in Canilleros, *Tres testigos,* 95.

65. Montesinos, *Anales del Perú,* 1: 76. Since a *vara* is about 2.8 feet, Montesinos's measurements were (rounded off) 20 feet by 15 feet by 10.5 feet. These are virtually identical with those of Ruíz de Arce, suggesting a possible dependent relationship.

66. Cf. Hognesius, "Capacity of the Molten Sea."

67. Jérez, "Verdadera relación," 335; Mena, "Conquista," 88.

68. Hemming, *Conquest,* 551.

69. For brief biographies of these chroniclers, and details of their writings, see Lockhart, *Men of Cajamarca,* 133–35, 157–68, 268–70, 346–48.

70. Hemming, *Conquest*, 551.

71. For another example of problems in measuring captured treasure, see Ferrard, "Constantinopolitan Booty."

72. Cf. Crosby, *Measure of Reality.*

73. See Dow, *Niagara Falls.* In like fashion, if with considerably less justification, seven descriptions of Takakkaw Falls in British Columbia, all published in the 1990s, list their height from 254 to 384 meters.

74. Winship, *Journey,* 116.

75. Ibid.

76. Díaz del Castillo, *Historia verdadera,* 116 (ch. 61).

77. Tapia, "Relación," 2: 583.

78. And such descriptions of mass human sacrifice quickly became state policy to help justify the Spanish conquest of the Aztec state. This is illustrated in Motolinía's letter to Charles V designed to counter Las Casas' attack on Spanish practices. Motolinía wrote of an occasion during Ahuitzotl's rule (1486–1502) in which, he had heard, 80,400 victims were sacrificed "in one temple and in one sacrifice that lasted three or four days" (Motolinía to Charles V, 2 January 1555, in Motolinía, *Memoriales,* 404).

79. Cook, "Human Sacrifice," 88.

80. Ibid., 88–89. Having offered a rationale for belief, Cook, along with Woodrow Borah, accepted Tapia's statement in their "Materials," in their *Essays,* 1: 1–12, going so far as to suggest that this tower complex was only "one among many" in Tenochtitlan. They cite none of the studies noted later that show the impossibility of this calculation.

81. Cook and Borah, "Credibility," 232–33.

82. Davies, *Aztec Empire,* 227–41. Cf. idem, *Human Sacrifice,* 217–21, where he shows how impossible in practice the testimony of the records is. See also Vázquez, *Conquista de Tenochtitlán,* 109n101.

83. Harner, "Ecological Basis," 120–23. Harner's is a particularly undemanding reading of the sources and is couched in terms designed to confer far more authority on the claims of large skull deposits than they can possibly support.

84. Thomas, *Conquest of Mexico,* 694n36, calculates that a rack of 100,000 skulls that was 20 feet high, with the skulls 6 inches apart, would extend for 450 yards.

85. Tapia's English translator thought that "[t]here is no good reason to be skeptical of this figure," citing numbers in the Mexico chroniclers (e.g., Motolinía and Durán) purporting that tens of thousands of victims had been sacrificed on particular occasions in the past. See Fuentes, *Conquistadors,* 218n32.

86. García, *Antiguas relaciones,* xiii–xivn, found the possibilities "absurd."

87. Ortiz de Montellano, "Counting Skulls." Using information provided later by the missionary chronicler Diego Durán, Ortiz de Montellano estimated that, assuming a series of possible but least-likely assumptions, perhaps a maximum of 60,000 skulls could have been assembled at the *templo mayor* in Tenochtitlan. Berdan, *Aztecs,* 116–18, found Harner's arguments and figures "astonishing." Rosenblat, *Población indígena,* 90–91, offered some critical comments on skull-counting.

88. Harner, "Ecological Basis," 120–23, canvassed this meager literature, which he saw as sufficiently substantial evidence to support his thesis.

89. By this time, aggregations of skulls had become a bit of a topos. This was fueled by accounts of the results of the Mongol conquests in Iran in the 1220s and of Tamerlane two centuries later. As always, estimates varied, but sometimes they ran to over a million for each city. See, e.g., Juvayni, *World-Conqueror,* 1: 122–28, 151–78 passim; and Lambton, *Continuity and Change,* 16–21.

90. For the skull racks, or *tzompantlis,* as cynosures of much of the early historiography of Tenochtitlan and the *templo mayor,* see Boone, "*Templo mayor* Research," 6–13. Tapia's account has encouraged those seeking to find evidence of large-scale human sacrifice and even cannibalism among the Aztecs. In addition to Cook, "Human Sacrifice," and Harner, "Ecological Basis," see Duverger, *Fleur létale,* 191–95, 218–21.

91. For a recent study that resounds with enthusiasm for human sacrifice on the scale mentioned in the chronicles and which relies on Tapia and Díaz del Castillo for support, see Graulich, "Inauguration." For this particular case, Clendinnen, *Aztecs,* 322n7, considers that the number 80,400, as recorded in Diego Durán's history, "depends on a doubtful reading of a pictographic text." The dubious ability of pictures to tell as precise a story as words deserves more attention than those interested in the contact population of the Americas have given it.

92. Francisco de Ortega, "Report concerning the Filipinas Islands."

93. At almost exactly the same time, Juan López de Velasco, *Geografía,* 297–300, named most of the islands listed in Table 2 but did not try to give them dimensions (except for Mindoro, 75 leagues, and Mindanao, 300 leagues).

94. For a similar case, the island of Chiloé, see chapter 7.

95. Thereby excluding Julius Caesar's assertion in his *Gallic War* that he assembled no fewer than 800 vessels for his abortive invasion of Britain in 54 B.C.

96. For the latter figure, which implies that there were more ships than passengers, see Hardy and Martin, *Lestoire des Engles,* 2: 166.

97. Gillmor, "Naval Logistics," 106–7. Other modern guesses range

from 450 to 1,500: Fuller, *Military History,* 1: 371–74; Spatz, *Schlacht von Hastings,* 28; van Houts, "Ship List."

98. Gillmor, "Naval Logistics," 119. Eleven thousand ships would have required at least 650,000 trees, and so forth. Still, the range in ships is considerably less than that which the Norman chroniclers estimated for Harold's forces—from 4,000–7,000 to 1.2 million men (Freeman, *History,* 3: 498–500). Shortly before the Norman invasion, Harald Hardrada of Norway had invaded northern England, only to be defeated and killed by Harold. Contemporary estimates of his fleet ranged from 200 to 1,000 ships (Campbell, "Inquiry"). For the number of horses transported, also in dispute, see Bachrach, "Origins."

99. Collier, *Sands of Dunkirk,* 264.

100. Masefield, *Nine Days Wonder,* 50–51; Roskill, *War at Sea,* 1: 225–28, 603; Divine, *Nine Days of Dunkirk,* 251–53, 277; Collier, *Sands of Dunkirk,* 264; Turnbull, *Dunkirk,* 171–73; Gelb, *Dunkirk,* 310–11.

101. For instance, it is impossible to distinguish the number of ships from the number of trips, the latter being the only way to calculate capacity. As for the number of troops evacuated, the range is considerably smaller, but readers of accounts of the operation clearly have choices. They may, with Collier, *Sands of Dunkirk,* 264, believe that "[a]ll sources agree on the final count: 338,226." Or they might align themselves with Turnbull, *Dunkirk,* 172: "No two sources give the same figure for the exact number of men saved from Dunkirk, but if an *average* be taken then 338,226 would seem a safe approximation" (emphasis added). For other examples of differences of opinion about the size of cross-Channel fleets, see Runyan, "Naval Logistics."

102. E.g., Arnaud, "De la durée à la distance." For a fictional, but not thereby irrelevant, example of the difficulties in counting consistently, see Withrington, "'He Telleth the Number of Stars.'"

103. Waldron, *Great Wall of China,* 5–6.

104. Ibid., 4–5, 204–5. Already in the second century B.C., when it was far from complete, Sima Qian estimated it to be 2,600 miles in length, a wild exaggeration: see Bodde, "State and Empire," 61–63.

105. Díaz del Castillo, *Historia verdadera,* 1982, 1: 289. This is sometimes transcribed as "860," i.e., "sesenta," instead of "setenta." See ibid., 2: 26, for the textual variants.

106. A good example of this is Las Casas' transcription at about this very time of some form of Columbus's account of his first voyage. For details see Henige, *In Search of Columbus.*

107. Cortés, *Cartas de relación,* 1: 213–14.

108. Gardiner, *Naval Power,* 111.

109. One who would say a great deal more is Hammond; in his

"Marathon," 26, 28, he asserted that "it is certain that this record of the battle was correct in its facts" and that "the salient facts in Herodotus' narrative are completely unimpeachable." He could not understand why some scholars disagreed, unless it was "to fit the[ir] preconceived hypotheses."

110. Chang, "Circularity."

111. An interesting example of this phenomenon is amply chronicled in Good, *Lincoln.* As the editor points out (vii), these recollections show "some consensus in the earliest accounts," but this "gradually deteriorates as time progresses." See as well Wyatt, "Five Voices."

112. As I write this, the newspapers are full of headlines such as "Death toll remains mystery in Rwanda." Figures for a massacre at a refugee camp at Kibeho range from 338 from the perpetrators to between 2,000 and 8,000 by various outside authorities—both allegedly based on body counts, both advanced within a few days after the event.

Chapter 7: Antipodean Antics

1. Villalobos R., *Historia,* 2: 107.

2. Hidalgo, "Indians," 106n.

3. Although Hidalgo was silent on this point in his "Indians of Southern South America," he addressed the issue in his "Población protohistórica," 289: "[W]hen the chronicler speaks of 'indios' he generally refers to "adult males of working age, which later would be 'el indio de encomienda' or 'tributario.'"

4. For Mariño de Lobera see Casanueva, "Crónica." Casanueva (126) refers to "the enormous quantitative exaggerations (especially regarding the number of Araucanian warriors)" in Mariño de Lobera's chronicle, a point to which I will return.

5. Villalobos R., *Historia,* 1: 94–95n. Notice that Villalobos ignores Mariño de Lobera's more precise comment that the warrior population fell short of 14,000 by some unknown figure. Villalobos (ibid.) cites as well the suggestion of an *encomendero* that "the population of [Imperial] alone exceeded 150,000 Indians." See "Probanza de los méritos y servicios de Juan Beltrán de Magaña," in *CDIHC,* 16: 389. By Villalobos's arithmetic anyway, this means an overall population of 750,000.

6. Thayer Ojeda, "Ensayo crítico," 426–27.

7. Ibid., 428–38.

8. Pocock, *Conquest,* 85.

9. Santillán, "Relación," in *CDIHC,* 28: 287. Cf. Gil González, "De los agravios que los indios de las provinicas de Chile padecen," in *CHC,* 29: 461–66.

10. See, e.g., Reber, "Demographics of Paraguay," as well as post–World War I Europe. For the case of the Cañaris see chapter 12.

11. Bibar (or Vivar), *Crónica,* 351 (ch. cxli). Bibar's work, which, from early references, was known to have existed but was lost, was rediscovered in the 1960s and first published in 1969. As a result it has drawn more recent attention than the work of the other chroniclers, Ercilla of course excepted. See Zapater Equioiz, "Valor etnológico"; Michieli, *Comechingones;* Orellana Rodríguez, "Gerónimo de Bibar"; Berberián and Bixio, "Crónica"; Orellana Rodríguez, *Crónica;* Antei, *Invención;* Invernizzi Santa Cruz, "Trabajos."

12. Hidalgo, "Indians," 107. A case has been argued for smallpox "pandemics" in this area (see Dobyns, "Outline"). Hidalgo merely makes this statement, without arguments that might support it. I exclude it from consideration here as unproven and unlikely. Villalobos R., *Historia,* 2: 108, also accepts without demur that a smallpox epidemic struck Peru "before the conquistadors arrived." Its reality or not has no effect on the present discussion as offered, but underlines the matter of disease as a covering explanation, as discussed elsewhere in the present work. The evidence for such an epidemic in Peru itself is exiguous; that for any spread to Chile nonexistent.

13. Hidalgo, "Indians," 107. Cf. Villalobos R., *Historia,* 2: 107, citing the estimate of Steward, "Native Population," 658. Actually, Steward was doing no more than citing Angel Rosenblat with the less than enthusiastic comment that "[if] a native Araucanian population of 1,000,000 is not a gross error, Central Chile under Indian farming was far more productive than has been recognized." Perhaps he was right to doubt, since he had misquoted Rosenblat, who estimated the population of Chile at 600,000 in both 1492 and 1570: Rosenblat, *Población indígena,* 81, 92. For the identification of errors in calculating population density in Steward's work, see Miller, "Araucanian Population Density."

14. Details in Bibar, *Crónica,* 120–44. See also Pocock, *Conquest,* 92–104.

15. In a letter to Charles V dated 4 September 1545, the same date as his letter to Hernando Pizarro, Valdivia, *Cartas,* 43, wrote that "there are not three thousand Indians from Copayapo to the Canconcagua valley," just north of Santiago, implying either a much denser population from Santiago to the Río Maule or figures tailored to the recipients' needs as Valdivia anticipated them.

16. Bibar, *Crónica,* 351.

17. Errazuriz, *Pedro de Valdivia,* l: 341–55.

18. Pedro de Valdivia to Hernando Pizarro, 4 September 1545, in *Valdivia,* Cartas, 67.

19. Bibar, *Crónica*, 339.

20. Ibid., 236.

21. León, *Lonkos*, 7–20 et passim.

22. Bibar, *Crónica*, 132.

23. Thayer Ojeda, "Ensayo crítico," 143 (1919), 675.

24. Pedro de Valdivia to Charles V, 25 September 1551, in Valdivia, *Cartas*, 223.

25. Valdivia to Charles V, 4 September 1545, in Valdivia, *Cartas*, 44.

26. León, *Lonkos*, 18, uses the maximum as the average (though thinking it "optimistic") and assumes that the numbers refer to "male Indians." Certainly there is a stronger case for the latter equation whenever reference is directly to the encomienda system, but it can never be regarded as inevitable. At any rate, León thereby arrives at a total encomienda population of 25,000. Such a figure might seem reasonable, but it bears no discernible relationship to any earlier populations.

27. "Repartimiento hecho à Pedro de Valdivia," in *CDIHC*, 8: 120–32. For this reduction from 60 to 32 encomiendas see, e.g., Amunátegui Solar, *Encomiendas*, 1: 59–76; Korth, *Spanish Policy*, 22–28; Villalobos R., *Historia*, 1: 60–66; and León, *Lonkos*, 18–19.

28. For a brief survey of several early estimates for Chile, both in aggregate and of aggregations, see Medina, *Aborígenes*, 157–67. Medina concluded (160) that the contact population "must not have exceeded half a million."

29. Thayer Ojeda, "Ensayo crítico," 143 (1919), 673–724.

30. Ibid., 676–77.

31. Ibid., 679–80.

32. Ibid., 702–3, emphasis in original.

33. Valdivia to Charles V, 15 October 1550, in Valdivia, *Cartas*, 159.

34. Hidalgo, "Población protohistórica," 290. Hidalgo quickly proceeds to demonstrate in a series of extrapolations how easy it is to squeeze Mariño de Lobera's data (in this instance) onto Procrustean beds of modern design.

35. Cervellino Giannoni, "Población de Copiapó," 25–28.

36. Vergara Quiroz, "Edad y vida," 85. Coronado, testifying in 1547, stated his age as "over thirty years," when he was most probably 37: Aiton and Rey, "Coronado's Testimony," 292. Nor was he alone—Bartolomé de las Casas, for instance, and even Erasmus apparently did not know their own birthdates, or saw no reason to try to recall and record them accurately. For Las Casas (1484, not 1474) see Bishop and Weidman, "Correct Birthdate"; and for Erasmus (1466, not 1469 or 1470), Vredeveld, "Ages of Erasmus." The traditional birthdate of Vasco de Quiroga, first bishop of Michoacán, is

1470, but he was probably born closer to 1485; see Warren, *Vasco de Quiroga*, 8–9, and Hernández, *Don Vasco de Quiroga*, 30–31. See also Buckley, "John of Brienne," where it is shown that the canonical age of this Crusader is probably twenty-five years too high. Conversely, after his death the birthdate of St. Vincent de Paul was antedated by five years, against his own testimony, in order to make him appear not to have contravened the canonical age for ordination: Dodin, *Légende*, 141–44. For evidence that *most* people at this time did not know their true age, see Herlihy, "Population of Verona," 101–2, 119.

37. Dobyns, "Outline"; idem, *Number*, 11–16.

38. However, there is an interesting datum in Guaman Poma's chronicle (*Nueva corónica*, 1: 89–91) to the effect that an Inca army invaded Chile in the time of Pachacuti (traditionally died ca. 1471) and killed "100,000 Chilean Indians." In this, he went on, they were aided by "pestilence and hunger lasting ten years." Comments like these seem to need some explanation.

39. Villalobos R., *Historia*, 2: 108.

40. León, *Lonkos*, 17.

41. Bibar, *Crónica*, 317–18.

42. For Góngora Marmolejo's work see Antei, *Invención*, 106–14; Invernizzi Santa Cruz, "'¿Ilustres hazañas?'"; Aguilera G., "*Historia.*"

43. Góngora Marmolejo, *Historia*, 136–37. Thayer Ojeda thought that an extra zero had been added to both 100,000 and 1,200 to account for Góngora Marmolejo's high figures. While this is not an impossibility, it is counterintuitive to imagine two inaccuracies in transcribing, a relatively simple task, and at the same time a greater accuracy in counting large numbers of people, a much more difficult proposition.

44. Barros Araña, *Historia*, 2: 281–82.

45. Mariño de Lobera, "Crónica," 562.

46. Pérez García, *Historia*, 397–98.

47. Testimony of Juan Fernández de Almendras, 20 September 1558, in *CDIHC*, 22: 212–13. "Modorra" is a disease that appears several times in the colonial record but which has never been satisfactorily identified with a modern counterpart.

48. Gonzalo Hernández de Bermejo to the king, 2 January 1577, in *CDIHC*, 2/2: 316.

49. Rosales, *Historia*, 1: 455 (4/5). The bulk of this work was written between 1740 and 1745.

50. Córdoba y Figueroa, *Historia*, 2: 87.

51. Olivares, *Historia militar*, 161.

52. Errazuriz, *Chile sin gobernador*, 197–98.

53. Encina, *Historia*, 1: 347–49, 604. There is no support for his rough equation of morbidity and mortality.

54. Bengoa, *Conquista y barbarie*, 198.

55. Bonilla Bradanovic, *Gran guerra*, 169.

56. León, *Lonkos*, 17; Valenzuela S., *Paso*, 106, who writes that in "some localities" the epidemic "eliminated . . . up to 84 percent of the population."

57. Pocock, *Conquest*, 228.

58. Barros Araña, *Historia*, 2: 62–63n.

59. Laval Manrique, "Viruela," 209–12.

60. Laval Manrique, "Patología," 15–17.

61. Thayer Ojeda, *Ensayo crítico*, 190–202, briefly canvasses the early testimony about the nature and effects of this epidemic.

62. Further examples of this phenomenon are treated in chapter 6.

63. Gongora Marmolejo, *Historia*, 251. For Góngora Marmolejo's service as *corrigedor* see Vázquez de Acuña, "Descubrimiento," 160.

64. "Segunda información de servicios del General Martín Ruiz e Gomboa, 28 July 1569," in *CDIHC*, 19: 251, 266; "Tercera probanza de los méritos y servicios del Capitán Martín Ruiz de Gamboa," 18 January 1570," in *CDIHC*, 19: 309.

65. Egas Venegas and Juan Torres de Vera to the king, 20 November 1567, in *CDIHC*, 2/1: 104–5; López de Velasco, *Geografía*, 271. Mariño de Lobera, "Crónica," 468–70, described their inspection tour.

66. E.g., Córdoba y Figueroa, *Historia*, 130; Molina, *Compendio*, 255; Pérez García, *Historia*, 18. Rosales, *Historia*, 548, was content to speak of "men in sufficient numbers."

67. Venegas and Torres de Vera to the king, 20 November 1567, in *CDIHC*, 2/1: 106.

68. López de Velasco, *Geografía*, 271.

69. Herrera y Tordesillas, *Historia*, 1: 172; Diez de la Calle, "Noticias sacras," 372.

70. Mariño de Lobera, "Crónica," 448. Oddly, perhaps Góngora Marmolejo did not record the results of this count. See as well Vázquez de Acuña, "Descubrimiento," 150–58.

71. Olivares, *Historia*, 365. The editor of Olivares's work added the comment that "without doubt Olivares wished to say 50,000 Indians of all ages, which is the probable population of Chiloé at the moment of the conquest." Barros Araña, *Historia*, 2: 371n, argued that Rosales relied on Góngora Marmolejo for his own acount of the conquest of Chiloé, but on this matter Góngora Marmolejo was silent.

72. Rosales, *Historia*, 1: 244. Rosales added that a few years later the

population had dropped to 36,000 "tributarios," suggesting that his 50,000 should be interpreted as 200,000 or more. But then he continued further that in 1593 there were only "12,000 Indians," so that in 28 years the population had dropped by "38,000 Indians."

73. Molina, *Historia,* 256.

74. Hanisch, *Ataque.*

75. Córdoba y Figueroa, *Historia,* 131.

76. Pérez García, *Historia,* 19.

77. Gamboa to the king, 24 May 1569, in *CDIHC,* 2/1: 194–96.

78. Contreras A. et al., *Población,* 13–15.

79. Vázquez de Acuña, "Evolución," 404–6. As for Chile proper, our knowledge of encomienda distributions after the conquest does not support particularly high population estimates; see Góngora, *Encomenderos,* 22–25. Today the population of Chiloé is under 100,000.

80. Góngora Marmolejo, *Historia,* 252.

81. González de Najera, *Desengaño,* 13; Herrera, *Historia,* 1: 172; López de Velasco, *Geografía,* 271.

82. Rosales, *Historia,* 1: 548. And two leagues wide in still other places (498).

83. Olivares, *Historia,* 5; or maybe "70 or 80 leagues" (364).

84. Molina, "Compendio," 284.

85. Diez de la Calle, "Noticias sacras," 372; Pérez García, *Historia,* 115.

86. Schwarzenberg and Mutizábal, *Monografía,* 3. Cf. Urbina Burgos, "Rebelión."

87. For the later demographic history of Chiloé see Urbina Burgos, *Periferia,* 39–64, and Vázquez de Acuña, "Evolución," 408–52.

88. Mariño de Lobera, "Crónica," 500. What he meant by "ordinarily [de ordinario]" is also unclear.

89. Thayer Ojeda, "Ensayo crítico," 722, though, found it "fantastic" and eliminated it from his various calculations. Later population estimates have been in the hundreds rather than the hundreds of thousands: Cooper, "Chono," 1: 49.

90. For Valdivia's writings, by no means the worst of the lot in this respect, see, e.g., Soriano, "Perfil"; Goic, "Retórica"; idem, "Cartas." On the letter-report as an art form during this period see Guillén, "Notes."

91. Orellana Rodríguez, "Gerónimo de Bibar," 93–124.

92. Invernizzi Santa Cruz, "¿Ilustres hazañas?"

93. Orellana Rodríguez, "Influencia."

94. Valenzuela S., *Paso,* 106.

95. Later, the governor of Chile remarked that "all the enemy who can, move on horseback and therefore enter and leave our territory with in-

creasing ease and speed" (Alonso de Rivera to Philip III, 18 October 1613, quoted in Armond, "Frontier Warfare," 128–29). Earlier, of course, the Indians would have been somewhat less mobile, but hardly so much that this kind of movement would not have occurred routinely.

96. Cooper, "Araucanians," 2: 694. Emphasis in original.

97. The state-sanctioned figure is a round 1 million: Barros Araña, *Historia*, 3: ch. 12; *Historia Social y Económica*, 3: 391. A tertiary source recently spoke expansively of "at least 200,000 warriors" but cited no source: Clodfelter, *Warfare and Armed Conflicts*, 1: 57.

Chapter 8: Evading History through Language

1. E.g., Copenhagen, *"Exordium."*

2. For some general observations on this see Henige, "Native American Population." See chapter 14 as well.

3. The study first appeared as Clastres, "Eléments." It was republished the following year in a collection of Clastres's essays, *Société contre l'etat*, 69–87. This collection was in turn translated as *Society against the State*, and this essay, entitled "Elements of Amerindian Demography," is on pp. 64–82. For safety's sake, I use the original article.

4. Clastres, "Eléments," 24.

5. Ibid., 24–25.

6. For one replay of the modesty topos see Stannard, *Before the Horror*, 78–80 et passim.

7. Clastres, "Eléments," 25.

8. Ibid., 27, emphasis in original.

9. Ibid., 28, emphasis in original. Using a standardized local polity size of nine square kilometers, Dean, *Broadax*, 33, calculates an average density of nine persons per square kilometer.

10. Clastres, "Eléments," 27.

11. Ibid., 31; emphasis in original.

12. For the apostolic and ethnographic work of d'Abbeville, who spent only four months in Brazil, see Fishman, "Claude d'Abbeville and the Tupinambá." The most extended treatment of the episode is that of Pianzola, *Français*. For what it is worth, an eyewitness account from the same time estimated an Indian population of "more than twenty thousand": see "Carta . . . del Capitán Martín Suarez," in Suárez Moreno, "Informação," 168.

13. Clastres, "Eléments," 31. Using Clastres's imputed density against the actual size of this island, which is only 905 square kilometers, would result in an estimated 4,620,000 Guaranís. Observers' accounts from the time differed. According to one witness, the island was "more than fifty leagues

long and eight to ten wide," which would render it more than ten times its actual size ("Carta," in Suárez Moreno, "Informação," 168). The second-in-command of the French garrison thought differently: "[T]he extent of the island is twelve to fifteen leagues and [it is] more than forty leagues around," suggesting a total area of between about 2,000 and 3,000 square kilometers: see Pézieu, *Brief Recueil*, 7.

14. Claude d'Abbeville, *Histoire de la mission*, 185v, emphasis added. The Portuguese translation, *História da Missão*, 145, omits the "sometimes less" phrase. In his other account of Maranhão, *Arrivée*, d'Abbeville provided no estimates. Quite characteristically—indeed, classically—Clastres added that "according to Yves d'Evreux and Claude d'Abbeville, it did not at all appear as though the island's 12,000 inhabitants were endangered by a shortage [of food]." In fact, d'Evreux, *Voyage au Nord du Brésil*, provided no numbers at all. D'Abbeville also spoke of each village having four "lodges," and there is at least a hint that he multiplied the number of lodges by one hundred per lodge to arrive at his gross estimate. D'Abbeville and d'Evreux are treated extensively in Obermeier, *Brasilienreiseberichte*.

15. Clastres, "Eléments," 31.

16. Ibid. Using Clastres's own propensity for averaging, the distances between villages would average 10.5 kilometers, or about 110 square kilometers per polity.

17. Staden, *Zwei Reisen*, 117. For Staden see, among others, Wenzel, "Deutsche Conquistadoren," and Sousa, "Theatrics and Politics."

18. Relocation is mentioned frequently in the chronicles. E.g., Léry, *Journal de bord*, 273, wrote that the Tupinambá "ordinarily stay only five or six months in one place." For an overview see Ferguson, "Ecological Consequences."

19. For Staden's general problems in measuring distances see Campanário, *Hans Staden*, 103–12.

20. Such reasoning produces a calculable symmetry for the Guaraní area reminiscent of that which other authors produced for Atlantis and other imaginary places discussed in chapter 19.

21. Clastres, "Eléments," 31–32.

22. Ibid., 28; cf. Cardim, *Tratados da terra*, 90. Clastres is not alone in this; Balée, "Ecology," 255, shows "100–200 people/longhouse," citing Cardim. Both modern editions of Cardim's work, however, read the same: ". . . e casa ha qué tem duzentas e mais pessoas" (*Tratados*, 149). Métraux, *Civilisation matérielle*, 50n, recorded it as "100 to 200 persons."

23. A range repeated by Frank Lestringant in his edition of Thevet, *Singularités*, 99n. In contrast, Maestri, *Senhores do litoral*, 50, regards Léry's figures as logistically impossible. For Thevet see Assaf, "Specularity of Alterity."

24. The highest estimate, however, was nine or ten; see Balée, "Ecology," 255, citing Pero Vaz de Caminha.

25. In 1504, at least to judge from one eyewitness account, Indian villages on the southern coast of Brazil were configured differently from the way they were later and/or farther north. According to Paulmier de Gonneville, *Campagne*, 97, the people lived "in hamlets of thirty, forty, fifty, or eighty huts." I suspect that this would simply allow the High Counters to claim a dramatic decrease in population. It is more surprising that Clastres makes no mention of Anthony Knivet's account of his rather amazing adventures in Brazil in the 1590s. In it are reports of troglodytic pygmies and immense snakes, but also such information as figures for Indian armies "at least fortie thousand strong," Portuguese contingents of more than 500, battles in which 5,000 Indians were slain and others in which 16,000 prisoners were taken, longhouses over 600 feet long, and so forth. See Purchas, *Hakluytus Postumus*, 16: 233–65 passim. Dean, "Poblaciones indígenas," 31, rightly regards such numbers as "the products of fantasy."

26. Perhaps it is worth noting that a reasonable covering explanation of disparities in the sources would be that the number of inhabitants per *maloca* changed to fit changing exigencies. This happened, for example, with the longhouses of the Mohawk in the late sixteenth and early seventeenth centuries: see Snow, "Mohawk Demography."

27. Fernandes, *Organização*, 67–68; Balée, "Ecology," 255.

28. Fernandes lists Cardim, Léry, Nóbrega, Pigafetta, Salvador, Staden, and Vasconcelos, whereas Balée lists Caminha, Cardim, Nóbrega, Pigafetta, and Staden (as well as Montaigne, whom I do not consider).

29. See the argument in Greenlee, *Voyage*, 33–36.

30. Marcondes de Souza, *Descobrimento*, 306.

31. Arroyo, *Carta*, 57; other editions are identical.

32. Pigafetta in Visconde de Lagôa, *Fernão de Magalhais*, 2: 22. The same comment is in all versions and editions of Pigafetta's account. Clearly, though, Balée is wrong to credit Pigafetta with speaking of 100 "people"; perhaps he was following Métraux, *Civilisation*, 50n, who did the same. About the same time, Amerigo Vespucci was writing that he had encountered houses in which lived 600 persons (or, in another edition, that eight houses held 10,000 persons): Lester and Foster, *Americus Vespucius*, 122–23.

33. Nóbrega, *Cartas do Brasil*, 99. Métraux, *Civilisation*, 50n, rendered this as "50 persons."

34. Staden, *Zwei Reisen*, 117. In this case, then, it is unclear whether Fernandes or Balée is correct, if either. Métraux, *Civilisation*, 50n, has "40 persons."

35. Unless it was capacity, although it is well to bear in mind the powerful symbolic appeal of the number forty.

36. About this time Diogo Jácome spoke of Tupinambá "towns" ("povoções") of "400 souls or more": Diogo Jácome to the fathers and brothers at Coimbra, June 1551, in Leite, *Monumenta Brasiliae*, 1: 240.

37. Vicente do Salvador, *Historia do Brasil*, 86.

38. Vasconcelos, *Crônica* 1: 98. Métraux, *Civilisation*, 50n, translated "casais" as "families."

39. As, for example, in Dean, "Poblaciones indígenas," 28–31. Dean used an average of 40 "domestic units" per *maloca*, or 135 persons, and 4.5 *malocas* per village. On this basis he went on to estimate the Tupinambá population in 1555 as "between 57,000 and 63,000 persons." The numbers are modest but, like any other estimates, cannot be supported by the available evidence.

40. For a more general critical study of the chroniclers' accounts of the Tupinambá, see Fleischmann, Assunção, and Ziebell-Wendt, "Tupinambá," 125–45.

41. For similar estimates of Iroquois population by way of the size of their longhouses, see Bogaert, *Journey*, 3–9, 36–39.

42. Clastres, "Eléments," 28.

43. Léry, *Histoire d'un voyage*, 273, emphasis added. The same account in the first edition (La Rochelle, 1578) is worded slightly differently but is, if anything, even clearer: Léry, *Journal de bord*, 357; Lestringant, "Excursion brésilienne."

44. Elsewhere (*Journal de bord*, 241), Léry described an incident in which Indians assembling "from all parts," combined with those in the village where he was, aggregated only to the same number—"five or six hundred."

45. E.g., Léry, *Viagem*, 209, emphasis added.

46. Fernandes, *Organização*, 68. This may well have been Clastres's source. In Thevet, *Français en Amérique*, 116n, the editor incorrectly interprets Léry. However, the English translation of Léry is true to the original: Léry, *History of a Voyage*, 159.

47. Although Léry himself comes off badly in McGrath, "Polemic and History."

48. E.g., Hemming, *Red Gold*, 488.

49. Clastres, "Eléments," 33, emphasis in original.

50. Ibid.

51. Letter dd 15 April 1691, in Sepp, *Relación de viaje*, 122.

52. Not surprisingly, Sepp was correct here; the number of *reducciones* reached thirty only in 1716. From 1690 to 1702 there were 24 and then 26 and 27 *reducciones*. Sepp served among the Guaraní until his death in 1735.

53. Ibid., 189.

54. For aspects of Sepp's writings see Blankenburg, "German Missionary Writers," 40–45; Basalisco, "Culture a Confronto"; and Cardozo, *Historiografía paraguaya,* 263–69.

55. For the details see Furlong, *Misiones,* 630; Maeder and Bolsi, "Población de las misiones Guaraníes"; Vives Azancot, "Esplendor y la decadencia"; Maeder and Bolsi, "Población Guaraní"; Garavaglia, *Mercado interno,* 153–227; Velázquez, "Población del Paraguay"; Blumers, *Contabilidad,* 279–80 et passim; Maeder, "Población de las misiones de Guaraníes." For the Jesuit annual reports, from which these data come, see Cardozo, *Historiografía paraguaya,* 217–25.

56. In another letter from about the same time, Sepp, *Relación,* 197, offered yet another estimate—the number of Indians in a town "reaches from six to eight thousand and even more souls, without exaggerating, for the Indians are very prolific." Apparently, exactitude and consistency were not among Sepp's interests.

57. It is possible that Clastres misread one of the editorial notes to Sepp's *Relacion,* which states, correctly, that Sepp spoke of "6,000 and more inhabitants" in "the most populous reducciones" (231n9). If so, it is a symptomatic misreading.

58. This does not necessarily mean that they are also accurate; however, the attempt by Cardozo, *Paraguay colonial,* 125n, to double the reported figures to a maximum of 300,000, on the grounds that "women [and children?] were omitted from the censuses," seems decidedly odd.

59. Maeder and Bolsi, "Población de las misiones Guaranies," table opp. 138; Maeder, "Misiones de Guaraníes"; Carbonell, *Estrategias,* 91–101, 267–84, 377–78, 416–19, 451–63; Santos, "El Plata," 2: 673–90. Duviols, "Cultural Consequences," 76, 82, thinks that this highest number is "somewhat optimistic" and suggests that the population never exceeded about 110,000.

60. Whatever it was, Clastres's source for the 1730 population actually offered a number that is apparently too low. The year 1730 is one of the few years missing in the sequence, but the population in 1729 was reported as 132,685, and that in 1731 as 138,934.

61. I have been unable to trace the source for his statement that "as for Thevet, he speaks about certain villages that he visited that had 6,000, even 10,000 inhabitants" (Clastres, "Eléments," 28). There is, however, a statement about Tupinambá *armies* that seems remarkably reminiscent: "The number of combatants rises at times to 6,000, to 10,000, or even to 12,000 men" (Thevet, *Singularidades,* 123). Clastres considers the figure of 10,000 to be "exaggerated," but even the smaller number—if it is to be applied to villages rather than armies—is considerably higher than would be the product of multiplying the highest estimate of the number of *malocas* per village by

the highest estimate of their inhabitants. Clastres seems to be relying closely on Fernandes, *Organização*, 67–69, without acknowledging this.

62. Clastres, "Eléments," 30.

63. Monteiro, *Supply*, 5–6; idem, *Negros da Terra*, 73–76. Following Taunay, Simonsen, *História econômica*, 214, 245–46, suspects that the figure is a *lapsus calami* by some scribe, a view later adopted by Monteiro. Certainly such mistranscriptions would account for a certain number of errors in figures (both high and low) in the historical record, but a more likely reason in this case is simply that the Jesuits succumbed here to apocalyptic tendencies. Certainly the figure is completely incommensurate with the individual *reducción* populations (never more than a thousand families) reported in various correspondence of the period, for which see Vianna, *Jesuítas*.

64. Fleischmann, Assunção, and Ziebell-Wendt, "Tupinambá," discuss some of the problems facing those who would treat the sources on the Tupinambá as unproblematic reportage.

65. Clastres, "Eléments," 32.

66. Ibid., 33. Perhaps a target should also have been Villamarin and Villamarin, *Indian Labor*, 106, which estimated the Guaraní population at "about 200,000."

67. Clastres, "Eléments," 34.

68. Ibid.

69. Ibid.

70. Ibid., 35, emphasis in original.

71. Ibid., 23.

72. Ibid., 35–36, emphasis in original.

73. Monteiro, "Guarani," 478.

74. Melià, *Guaraní*, 48–51.

75. Brandão, "Guarani."

76. Denevan, "Native American Populations," xxvii. For brief critical comments on Clastres's argument see Hemming, *Red Gold*, 490.

77. Recently the numbers game for the Guaraní took a quantum leap when Jonathan D. Hill, in a foreword to Clastres, *The Land-Without-Evil*, 113, asserted that "[a]t the time of European peoples' arrival . . . the Tupí-Guaraní population was expanding and is estimated [by whom is not indicated] to have been around four million." The French original, published in 1975, made no such claim.

Chapter 9: Rescuing History from the Sources

1. Crosby, "Infectious Disease," 121.

2. Bakewell, "Conquest," 296.

3. Cook, *Demographic Collapse,* 75–114 et passim.

4. Cook, "Estimaciones," 37–60.

5. For a discussion of these and other points in Cook's analysis, see Henige, "Counting the Encounter."

6. Ramenofsky, *Vectors of Death,* 64–65.

7. Swanton, *Indian Tribes,* 39, citing a letter Roulleaux de la Vente dd 20 September 1704, as quoted in Gosselin, "Sauvages," 1: 37.

8. The frankly providential tenor of this passage should also give pause, since it suggests the possibility that de la Vente was exaggerating for effect.

9. Ramenofsky, *Vectors of Death,* 70, citing the letter of Jean François Buisson de Saint-Cosme, dd 2 January 1699, in Kellogg, *Early Narratives,* 359. Passages in brackets are as in Kellogg, but which Ramenofsky omitted. For the original text see Gosselin, "Sauvages," 35.

10. Which is represented by the unusual "picote" instead of the normal "petite vérole."

11. Ramenofsky, *Vectors of Death,* 70. Ramenofsky departs in about a dozen small ways from the text she does quote; in fact, few of the quotations (I found none) in *Vectors of Death* are transcribed *litteratim*—e.g., 65, 99 ("unwanted" for "unwonted"), 130, 133.

12. See Milner, "Epidemic disease," 45.

13. Le Page du Pratz, *History,* 305–6. Here, as well, Ramenofsky's transcriptions frequently (I counted eleven times) transgress the obligation to treat matter within quotation marks with strict rigor. Presumably the lethal colds antedated the arrival of the Europeans.

14. Since a diminution of settlements is an effect rather than a cause, it might be worth noting that other archaeologists, relying directly on bioarchaeological evidence, argue that any depopulation in the Mississippi valley in the sixteenth century was more likely to be the result of drought than of disease: see, for instance, Williams, "Vacant Quarter"; Burnett and Murray, "Death, Drought, and de Soto"; Hoffman, "Depopulation."

15. Quinn, *Roanoke Voyages,* 1: 378–79.

16. Crosby, *Columbian Exchange,* 40, where ellipses replace the omitted words.

17. Smith, "Aboriginal Depopulation," 259.

18. Dobyns, *Number,* 277.

19. Jennings, *Invasion,* 23.

20. Mires, "Contact and Contagion," 32.

21. For this epidemic see, among others, Creighton, *Epidemics,* 1: 399–411; Fisher, "Influenza"; Slack, "Mortality Crises"; and Moore, "Jack Fisher's 'Flu.'"

22. Ramenofsky, "Diseases of the Americas," 318.

23. Earlier, Sauer, *Sixteenth Century North America*, 303, quoted the passage fully from "There was no towne" to "time out of minde" and added Hariot's comment about the absence of effects on the Europeans. In his turn Milner, "Epidemic Disease," 46, quoted from "within a few dayes" to "respect of their numbers," from "The disease" to "time out of minde," and finally from "there was no man" to "sicke," all with modernized spelling.

24. Borah, "Historical Demography," 24–25.

Chapter 10: Fragments in Search of Preconceptions

1. Jennings, *Founders*, 89, suggests one reason for this quickened interest: "One must also consider a bias inherent in all archaeological work: i.e., it can go nowhere but up. Today's figures are minimum; tomorrow's new digs add new figures."

2. For some effects of this see Henige, "Millennarian Archaeology."

3. Anderson, *Savannah River Chiefdoms*, 62.

4. E.g., Dobyns, "Native New World"; Dunnell, "Methodological Impacts"; Ramenofsky, *Vectors of Death*.

5. Campbell, *PostColumbian Culture History*.

6. Dobyns, *Number*, 14–15, 24–26, 259–60.

7. Campbell, *PostColumbian Culture History*, 2–3; cf. 79.

8. Ibid., 5.

9. Ibid., 28. This is not to say that High Counters have not used such evidence to find just such epidemics. See, e.g., Dobyns, *Number*, 318–22, for the Naragansett.

10. Campbell, *PostColumbian Culture History*, 29–35 passim; cf. the discussion of similar discourse in Dobyns's *Number* in Henige, "If Pigs Could Fly."

11. Campbell, *PostColumbian Culture History*, 79, citing Ramensofsky, *Vectors of Death*.

12. Campbell, *PostColumbian Culture History*, 81; further undemonstrable assumptions follow (83–84).

13. Ibid., 86.

14. Ibid., 89.

15. Ibid., 107.

16. Ibid., 110.

17. Campbell, *PostColumbian Culture History*, 139–46, discusses the matter more extensively.

18. Ibid., 112.

19. Ibid., 115.

20. Campbell, *PostColumbian Culture History,* 117, cites several studies favoring pottery seriation as a means to establish chronology, but she mentions none of the studies that have questioned its universal applicability for determining relative chronology: see, for instance, Mason, "Historic Pottery."

21. Campbell, *PostColumbian Culture History,* 149.

22. Ibid., 169.

23. Ibid., 171.

24. Ibid., 172. Using bone weight instead of bone numbers produces a slightly different result, and also a question about which of the two matters more—that is, under what circumstances could an argument be made on behalf of either estimator at the expense of the other.

25. Ibid., 176.

26. Ibid., 181.

27. Ibid., 181. From what follows, it can be seen that the "after 1375" in brackets might be an unfair representation of Campbell's views, but not, it seems to me, of the evidence she offers.

28. Ibid., 181, 189, emphases added.

29. Ibid., 190. Or (190): "Dobyns' . . . hypothesis concerning a pan-hemispheric smallpox epidemic in the early 16th century is strongly corroborated."

30. E.g., figures 6–10 to 6–13, Campbell, *PostColumbian Culture History,* 173–75. Given the importance of bone matter in her analysis, Ringrose, "Bone Counts and Statistics," should be of interest.

31. Campbell, *PostColumbian Culture History,* 169.

32. Ibid.

33. It is interesting that all three measures increased for the 1525–1575 period, suggesting that the effects of the hypothesized epidemic were as swift to disappear as they were to appear.

34. Vibert, "Natives," 206, 222n1. Guilmet et al., "Legacy," 28n31, and Boyd, "Population Decline," 249, offer brief and not wholly unfavorable comments. Harris, "Voices of Disaster," 626n113, seems more dubious. More recently, Boyd, "Commentary," seems to renege, regards the epidemic of the 1770s as the first in the area, and disregards Campbell's work entirely.

35. Boyd, "Smallpox," 5.

36. Dobyns, "Disease Transfer," 277, asserts that "[r]egional specialists are convinced by [Campbell's] interpretation of the data," citing Boyd, who, as we have seen, was not quite so convinced.

37. Green "Examining."

38. Ibid., 292, referring to Dobyns, *Number;* for how remarkable see Henige, "If Pigs Could Fly;" idem, "Primary Source."

39. Green, "Examining," 296–97.

40. Ibid., 296.

41. Ibid., 300.

42. Ibid., 300–3.

43. Ibid., 304–7. For an instance of the effects of long-term (ca. 900–1100 and ca. 1200–1350) climatic change in other relevant areas, see Stine, "Drought." Both drought periods are considered to have been more extreme than any recorded during the historical period.

44. Green, "Examining," 308.

45. In contrast, in an accompanying paper, Sasso, "LaCrosse," 347, finds "little, if any, direct mortuary evidence suggesting large scale losses to disease within the region."

46. In the end it is impossible to disagree with Green's observation ("Examining," 297) that "[n]egative evidence provides exciting opportunities for unbridled speculation and inductive story-telling."

47. Snow, "Microchronology," 1602; and Pringle, "Plague."

48. Milner, "Epidemic Disease," 48–50. Cf. Mason, "Historic Pottery," 265–67.

49. Ramenofsky, *Vectors of Death*, 42–71. She does this only at the cost of inflicting some violence on the sources, for which see chapter 9. Ramenofsky, like Green, depends largely on settlement counts.

50. Milanich, *Florida Indians*, 103–4, where it becomes "probable evidence." Elsewhere (102) the author argues that "military engagements and epidemics clearly caused the deaths of many people." In this case, adding death in battle to death by disease is specifically designed to foster the author's attempt to equate Tatham Mound with the Ocale mentioned in the de Soto chronicles. See Mitchem, "Artifacts," 108, for virtually the same statement. See as well Mitchem, "Ruth Smith." The very dating of the site remains problematic.

51. Smith, "Aboriginal Depopulation," 261.

52. Borah, "Introduction, 15 (for California).

53. Examples (with archaeologically determined dates added in some cases) include Olson, "Burial," 822–26 (A.D. 1000–1200); Hartmann, "Preliminary Assessment," 305–6; Luebben and Nickens, "Mass Interment"; Nass and Bellatoni, "Burial"; Turner, "Taphonomic Reconstruction"; Turner and Turner, "Perimortem Damage"; Merbs, "Patterns"; and various essays in Owsley and Jantz, *Skeletal Biology*. As well, most areas of the Southwest are thought to have undergone significant oscillations in population from ca. 1100 to ca. 1500. For these see, e.g., Gumerman and Gell-Mann, *Understanding Complexity*, and Adler, *Prehistoric Pueblo World*.

54. E.g., Dean, Doelle, and Orcutt, "Adaptive Stress"; Dean, "Demography," 36–37.

55. Melbye and Fairgrieve, "Cannibalism."

56. Willey, *Prehistoric Warfare.*

57. Brooks and Brooks, "Palaeoepidemiology," 96–101. For the possibility of widespread pre-1492 disease see Kiple and Tarver, "Skeletal Biology."

58. Studies of skeletal populations representing mass burial in other parts of the United States antedating the arrival of the Europeans merely add grist to the mill. E.g., papers in Powell, Bridges, and Mires, *What Mean These Bones?;* and Larsen, "In the Wake of Columbus," 117–20. For a Mesoamerican case see Diehl, *Tula,* 94–95, there attributed to human sacrifice

59. Sasso, "LaCrosse," 347, expresses this well: "[A]s the ethnographic record for eastern North America contains ample indication of the cultural devastation wreaked by introduced disease, its potential role in bringing about population shifts . . . is worthy of further consideration, should more mortuary data become available as a result of further investigations." For a recent discussion of this and other paleopathological issues, see Boyd, "Skeletal Correlates." And there were other postcontact causes as well; for the nearly seven hundred skeletons found at Cholula and attributed to the Spanish massacre there in 1519, see Castro Morales and García Moll, "Entierro."

60. Galloway, *Choctaw Genesis,* 137, following Smith, *Archaeology,* 54–85, suggests that "multiple coeval burials of unusual demographic composition" might "indicate the depredation of disease." Presumably her statement refers to burials in which the old and the young predominate, but it is surely the case that massacres or natural disasters such as fire or flood would also involve just these more vulnerable segments of the population, rendering such a composition, should it be found, diagnostically unuseful.

61. Kenyon, *Excavations at Jericho,* 1: 267–68; Yasur-Landau, "Cemetery at Jericho," 238.

62. Given the argument, it is probably unfair for Snow, "Microchronology," 1603, to discredit the High Counters on the grounds that "[p]roponents of the higher estimates have not demonstrated that the sites exist to house that many [up to 18 million] people."

63. See chapter 9.

64. Arnold, *Roman Britain,* 122; cf. 121–41 for the discussion that encompasses this point.

65. Dever, "Identity," 19. For a reply see Whitelam, "Prophetic Conflict."

Chapter 11: Contact Does Not Equal Contagion

1. The presumption seems to be that any earlier encounters had no epidemiological effects that might have curtailed American Indian population growth before 1492.

2. For a discussion of this text see, among others, Henige, *In Search of Columbus.*

3. Columbus, *Diario,* 68–69.

4. Casas, *Historia,* 1: 145 (1/41). For this aspect of Las Casas' working methods see Henige, "To Read Is to Misread."

5. Cook and Borah, "Hispaniola."

6. For criticism of Cook and Borah's argument see Henige, "Contact Population."

7. Cook and Borah, "Hispaniola," 408.

8. Ibid., 409–10.

9. Columbus, *Diario,* 184–85, s.v. 17 November 1492.

10. Columbus, *Diario,* passim.

11. The articles by Guerra include "Epidemia americana"; "Intercambio epidemiológico"; "Cause of Death"; "Patobiografía de Colón"; "Origen de las epidemias"; "Earliest American Epidemic"; "Outline"; "Invasión de América"; and "European-American Exchange."

12. Guerra, "Earliest American Epidemic," 316, 323.

13. For a more detailed critique of Guerra's work see Henige, "Native American Population," 12–13.

14. Guerra, "Earliest American Epidemic," 316.

15. Guerra, "Early Epidemics," 19. Unfortunately, Guerra leaves undocumented his remarkable last assertion. For a reply see Henige, "Virtual Reality."

16. Guerra, "Early Epidemics," 21. Relying on Guerra, but citing Chanca (who said no such thing), Stannard, *American Holocaust,* 68, chimes in with the unsupportable claim that "natives everywhere were dead."

17. Borah, "Epidemics in the Americas," 3; idem, "Introduction," 7. In his "Outline," Guerra estimated that "most of the 3,500,000 Indians of the Antilles[!]" died in the wake of this "epidemic." This continues the constant rise in Guerra's own preferred figure, which began at 1 million and climbed to 3 million in the 1980s: cf. Guerra, "Earliest American Epidemic," 322, and idem, "Invasión," 221.

18. Hodges, Deagan, and Reitz, "Natural and Cultural Settings," 76.

19. E.g., López-Ríos Fernández, *Historia médica,* 105–14. Kiple and Ornelas, "After the Encounter," 51, offer Guerra's conclusions without comment.

20. Cook, "Depopulaton of Hispaniola."

21. Ibid., 222, referring in particular to Guerra, "Epidemia americana," and idem, "Earliest American Epidemic."

22. Cook, "Depopulation of Hispaniola," 219.

23. For a discussion of some implications of translating the Spanish

cielo, which can mean both "heaven" and "sky," in the chronicles, see Henige, *Maybe Heaven.*

24. Cook, "Depopulation of Hispaniola," 238.

25. Cf. Nebrija, *Vocabulario,* and Covarrubias Horozco, *Tesoro,* 352, 867–68.

26. Winslow and Duran-Reynals, "Jacme d'Agramont"; Agramont, "Regiment."

27. Ginés de Sepúlveda, *Historia del Nuevo Mundo,* 64–65.

28. Ibid., 64. Peter Martyr and Oviedo agreed.

29. Cook, "Depopulation of Hispaniola," 232.

30. Ibid., 219.

31. Ibid., 215. For five discrepant calculations of a 1514 "census" of the Indian population of Hispaniola, to which a sixth is then added, see Moya Pons, "Legitimación."

32. Cook, "Depopulation of Hispaniola," 223, 230.

33. Morales Padrón, *Primeras cartas,* 130–31

34. Colón, *Historie,* 1: 355.

35. Columbus, *Libro copiador,* 2: 454.

36. The problem of the number of Indians who traveled to Spain and then back to Hispaniola is briefly addressed in Morison, *Admiral of the Ocean Sea,* 2: 99n17. Morison concedes that the disparate evidence precludes firm conclusions. Columbus wrote that some Indians (number unspecified) died of smallpox in Cádiz as the fleet was set to embark, and he went on to explain that one Indian had survived of the four he had taken from the Samaná area just before returning to Spain the previous January. Columbus, *Libro copiador,* 2: 454; cf. Columbus, *Diario,* 342–43.

37. Prem, "Disease Outbreaks"; McCaa, "Spanish and Nahuatl Views."

38. Dobyns, Estimating," 395–414, 440–44. Dobyns has repeated the argument frequently, most recently in his "Native American Trade Centers." See chapter 5 for further discusssion of Dobyns's positions as staked out in this article.

39. Ramenofsky, *Vectors of Death,* 101, referring to central New York.

40. Ibid., 68. The table consolidates similar tables in Dobyns, *Number,* 15–16, 23, 270. The word "known" does not appear in the captions of any of Dobyns's tables, however.

41. Ramenofsky, *Vectors of Death,* 68. See now idem, "Problem."

42. For instance, the contemporary statement that smallpox struck Hispaniola for the first time in 1518 bespeaks knowledge of both the disease and its transmission. See Henige, "Smallpox."

43. Borah, "Introduction, 14. Alchon, *Native Society,* 12–18, 37, and Newson, *Life and Death,* 147–49, are only the latest to agree.

44. For more on this see Cook, *Demographic Collapse;* Henige, "Counting the Encounter."

45. Borah, "Introduction," 15. Cf. Borah, "Historical Demography," 176–77.

46. Borah, "Introduction," 15–16.

47. Ibid., 16.

48. Milanich, *Florida Indians,* 218.

49. Myers, "Efecto," 63.

50. Ibid., 77. Even so, Myers's work has struck responsive chords, e.g., Posey, "Environmental and Social Implications," 271–72. For a critique of Myers's methodology and conclusions (but not of the method behind the methodology), see Newson, "Amazon Basin," 15–18. Nonetheless, Newson (8) takes it for granted that disease "necessarily" preceded the earliest efforts to calculate the population of Amazonia.

51. The others include Jacobs, "Tip of the Iceberg"; Crosby, "Virgin Soil Epidemics, 289–93.

52. Sale, *Conquest of Paradise,* 160–61. Elsewhere Sale assumes that Europeans' diseases had preceded them virtually everywhere.

53. E.g., Stannard, *American Holocaust,* 24–25.

54. E.g., Sale, *Conquest of Paradise,* 161.

55. Perhaps the strongest case for pre-arrival disease can be made for the Inca area. Several High Counters address this and read much into it. Although it is mentioned by several early chroniclers, it was ignored by others, and before any serious judgments can be made it is necessary to apply standard textual criticism to these early sources to determine interrelationships and the like. Unfortunately, the chroniclers in question, even those who spoke of smallpox, displayed the usual indifference to confirming physical signs of disease among the Indians. For arguments based on accepting the case see, among others, Dobyns, "Outline," 495–97; Cook, *Demographic Collapse,* passim; Borah, "Introduction."

56. Medina, *Sebastián Caboto,* 1: 446–47.

57. Dean, "Indigenous Populations," 11. Dean cites no source for his use of the word "fever," although he may have borrowed it from Prado, *Primeiros povoadores,* 64–70, who used the term "fevers" in describing the episode.

58. Dean, "Poblaciones indígenas," 32–34.

59. For Garcilaso de la Vega, see Henige, "*La Florida del Ynca*"; idem, "Inca Garcilaso in Two Worlds."

60. Smith, "Aboriginal Depopulation," 258–59, 273n5.

61. DePratter, "Cofitachequi," 215–17, 225n95.

62. E.g., Jennings, *Invasion*, 15–31.

63. Early in the debate Crosby, "Conquistador y Pestilencia," set the tone in this regard by following Dobyns in accepting that Wayna Qhapac had died from smallpox and that the same pandemic had spread throughout the hemisphere. He offered some evidence for the former, none for the latter.

64. Stannard, *American Holocaust*, 24, citing a source (the record of Juan Rodríguez Cabrillo's voyage along the coast of California) that does *not* mention illness, let alone disease.

65. Walker and Hudson, *Chumash Healing*, 20–21. For the Midwest see Rafert, *Miami Indians*, 8.

66. And not only in the Americas; for the same argument for presettlement Australia see Butlin, *Economics and the Dreamtime*, 103–13.

67. Ramenofsky, "Problem." For a similar view see Upham, "Smallpox."

68. Ramenofsky, "Problem," 178.

69. Popper, *Open Society*, 2: 260.

Chapter 12: Surplus to Requirements

1. E.g., Thornton, *American Indian Holocaust*; Thornton, Miller, and Warren, "Aboriginal Population Recovery."

2. In Jiménez de la Espada, *Relaciones geográficas de Indias: Perú*, 3: 326. Whether Auncibay was referring to fecundity or to immigration is not clear.

3. Cook, "Migration," 43. The point is made more strongly by Powers, "Resilient Lords," 226, who speaks of "constant human movement," in the area both before and after the Spanish conquest. Powers (235–36, 249n74) also cites examples of "demographic fraud"—attempts to hide Indians by one stratagem or another—as do Saignes, "Politiques du recensement," idem, *Caciques*, and Andrien, "Corregidor de indios." The scale was relatively small (in the units and hundreds), but by how many instances are these occasions to be multiplied? Not by many, suggests Cook, *Demographic Collapse*, 88, who would argue that "at least for the 1570–1620 period, fraud was kept to a minimum during the tribute assessments," or that various kinds of fraud had countervailing effects. This is very hopeful thinking.

4. Mellafe, "Importance," was one of the first to deal with the matter, although he did so in a general way, intending only to draw attention to the lack of understanding of the issue.

5. Cook, *Demographic Collapse*, 81–83. The *yanaconas* were former royal servants of the Incas who had attached themselves to the Spaniards

(similar to the *mayeques* in New Spain), and the Cañaris had provided crucial support at the siege of Cuzco (thus the analog of the Tlaxcalans in New Spain), thereby earning exemption. By confining himself to the boundaries of modern Peru, Cook ignores the issue of how many Cañaris were there instead of in their traditional homeland in what is now Ecuador. Dealing with these, Newson, *Life and Death,* 53–55, credits them with a population of between 23,000 and 58,000 at the time. That the Cañaris and other ethnic groups were unaware of future national boundaries presents interpretative difficulties for Cook and Newson, though neither acknowledges them.

    6. Others disagree about the short- and long-term efficacy of the Toledan reforms in this respect.

    7. Cook, *Demographic Collapse,* 87–88. Cf. Cook, "Migration," 56, where he seems somewhat less categorical, perhaps taking into account the several studies on the matter published in the intervening decade.

    8. According to the book's index, the term *forastero* occurs nowhere else in *Demographic Collapse;* that is, Cook does not consider migration as a partial explanation for the precipitous decline he postulates for the coastal areas of Peru. Nor does he consider migration in other places (e.g., in discusssing the evolving Indian population of Cuzco, 216–19) where it would seem germane.

    9. Ibid., 89.

    10. E.g., Evans, "Migration Processses." Powers, *Andean Journeys,* is particularly germane in this regard.

    11. Cook, "Population Data," 75, 119.

    12. For Potosí see the excursus to chapter 5.

    13. Lohmann Villena, *Minas de Huancavelica,* 452–55 et passim; Whitaker, *Huancavelica,* 10; cf. Contreras, *Ciudad,* 78–113. As one observer put it for Oruro, a lesser mining center: "Many [Indians] go [there] because Indians always go where there is most to be gained" (Godoy, "Relación," 437, quoted in Zulawski, "Wages," 411). See as well Ramón, "Loja y Zaruma."

    14. Keith, *Conquest and Agrarian Change,* 42–49 et passim; Saignes, "Lupacas"; Sempat Assadourian, "Crisis demográfica"; Wachtel, "Men of the Water"; Saignes, "Ethnic Groups"; Ramírez, "*Dueño de Indios*"; Zulawski, "Wages," 405–30; Wightman, *Indigenous Migration,* 9–44; Andrien, "Spaniards"; Powers, "Resilient Lords," 225–49; idem, "Battle"; Saignes, "Politiques de recensement;" Hirschkind, "History," 329–30; Saignes, "Indian Migration"; Abercrombie, "Q'aqchas."

    15. Powers, *Andean Journeys,* 16.

    16. Ibid., 13–43 et passim.

    17. Ibid., 42–43.

18. E.g., Sánchez-Albornoz, *Indios y tributos,* 19–34, in a chapter entitled "Demographic contraction or diminution of the tributary mass?"

19. Saignes, "Parcours forains," 42; idem, "Politiques du recensement;" idem, *Caciques;* idem, "Etnias."

20. Cook, *Demographic Collapse,* 78.

21. Ibid., 90; for a discussion of the slave trade numbers see Henige, "Measuring the Immeasurable."

22. Powers, *Andean Journeys,* 23. Sensing the implications, Newson, *Life and Death,* 280, disagrees with Powers by claiming that "as yet insufficient evidence exists to suggest that migration to the sierra occurred on the massive scale Powers suggests." Since Newson says this in the process of calculating numerous populations levels for which there are no direct data, this appeal to evidence appears tendentious.

23. Powers, *Andean Journeys,* 23; cf. 95–105.

24. Ibid., 26.

25. Cook, *Demographic Collapse,* 75–107.

26. Miranda, "Población indígena," 182–89. See as well Haskett, "Taxco Tribute."

27. Cadenhead, "Mining Operations," 283–87; Berthe, "Minas de oro," 122–31; Bakewell, *Silver Mining,* 36–37, 124–29; Alberro, "Zacatecas"; Barrett, "King's Copper Mine"; Burnes Ortiz, *Minería.*

28. Dobyns, *Number,* 103.

29. E.g., Palkovich, "Historic Epidemics"; and Lipe, "Depopulation."

30. Newson, "Demographic Collapse," 253.

31. Ibid., 268–69.

32. Newson, *Life and Death,* 54, citing Pedro Cieza de León's *Crónica.* Cf. Hirschkind, "Indian Population," 314–16.

33. If 20 percent of the Cañari population at the time of Cieza de León's visit were children born after the massacres, then only 5 percent of the total would have been men and 75 percent women. This 5 percent would represent all adult male survivors of any Inca massacres plus any male children who had reached adulthood in the interim. In turn, this would imply a virtual annihilation of Cañari males by the Incas, a claim none of the sources makes. In short, only absenteeism would account for such an imbalance.

34. Interestingly, the Indian authorities advanced this ratio to Cieza de León to justify having conscripted women to serve the Spaniards as porters. Similarly, in a review of Alchon, *Native Society,* Caillavet comments that Alchon's failure to consult parish records and to consider the effects of migration "vitiates the credibility of the majority of [her] conclusions."

35. Cook and Borah, "Population of Yucatán," 64–65.

36. Ruz, *Rostro encubierto,* 56–68 et passim, and Farriss, *Maya So-*

ciety, 48–56, discuss the evidence for labor migration in sixteenth-century Yucatán.

37. Cook and Borah, "Population of Yucatán," 116–20.

38. Cook and Borah, *Indian Population,* 50–53; Cook, *Demographic Collapse,* 59–74 et passim; Newson, *Life and Death,* 3–22 et passim.

39. This argument is made particularly explicit in Newson, "Highland-Lowland Contrasts," 1187–95.

40. Several essays in Fetter, *Demography from Scanty Evidence,* address this issue in varying degrees, as does Fetter, "Missing Migrants."

41. It is unlikely to be coincidental that when deaths are recorded in situ, as in the case of the smallpox epidemic in Mexico City in 1779–80, the figures tend to be on the low side.

42. Until the publication of Genovese, *Roll, Jordan, Roll,* most historians held similar views of slaves in the antebellum South. Further work has reinforced Genovese's argument.

43. Comment from 1580 quoted in Saignes, *Caciques,* 22. High Counters are likely to assume that the others died rather than stayed on in private enterprise.

44. Trigger, "Responses," 1213. For similar views see, e.g., Axtell, *Invasion;* Bitterli, *Cultures in Conflict.*

45. For an attempt to factor migration into estimates of early modern population levels in the British Isles, see Wallwork, "Allowing for Migration."

Chapter 13: Colonial Cloning

1. Sánchez-Albornoz, *Population,* 40, describing the techniques of "the California school." The passage has a certain deadpan quality that might lead us to suspect it was not intended seriously. Either way, it captures the extrapolative method of the High Counters faithfully.

2. Robert Wallace, whose work is discussed earlier, anticipated these extrapolative frenzies with one of his own; see his *Dissertation,* 286–311.

3. For the context see Crowe, *Extraterrestrial Life Debate,* 167–215.

4. Dick, *Celestial Scenery,* 3, emphasis in original.

5. As a point of comparison, projecting the population of the United States using the density of New York City would produce a population of some 3.7 billion, whereas using Nevada would result in a projection of around 39 million.

6. Dick, *Celestial Scenery,* 63.

7. Ibid., 193.

8. Ibid., 344.

9. Crowe, *Extraterrestrial Life Debate,* 196–200.

10. Dick, *Sidereal Heavens,* 281–90. In this calculation human beings, like *indios,* stood surrogate for a larger group, in this case, "a number of beings . . . from the archangel and the seraph to the worm and the microscopic animalculum" (290).

11. Examples not otherwise mentioned here include Radell, "Indian Slave Trade," 93–94; Déléage, *Vie rurale,* 2: 1212–13; Butlin, *Economics and the Dreamtime,* 121–39, 215–20; and Manning, *Slavery and African Life.* Both Radell and Butlin use a single documented example as the basis for further guessing.

12. In effect this was the argument made by Zambardino, and couched in terms of probabilities, discussed in chapter 4.

13. At least one High Counter thinks that "the inverse-projection method . . . in the future is likely to figure more prominently in studies of Latin American populations" (Newson, review of Jackson, *Indian Population Decline,* 711).

14. For a minor instance that nicely encapsulates the problems, see Alchon, *Native Society,* 15–18.

15. The unboundedness of these methods can be illustrated by their obverse—predictions of future populations. In the eighteenth and early nineteenth centuries it was common to project the population of the United States to and beyond the millennium. In their enthusiasm for the unlimited prospects of the new republic, those who made such predictions usually overestimated wildly, in some cases for a factor of four or five. For instance, in 1775 Edward Wigglesworth, *Calculations,* predicted that the population of the then colonies would be 1.28 billion by the year 2000. See Spengler, "Population Prediction," and Schlesinger, "Casting the National Horoscope." On the larger stage, Cohen, *How Many People?* 402–18, surveys no fewer than sixty-six efforts between 1679 and 1994 to estimate the earth's carrying capacity. These range from 500 million to more than 1 trillion, the latter being over two thousand times greater than the former although the two calculations were made only four years apart (1967, 1971). To complicate matters, Cohen also includes twenty-six definitions of "carrying capacity." Cf. MacKellar, "On Human Carrying Capacity"; and Poursin, "Population mondiale en 2150."

16. Stannard, *Before the Horror,* 32–35.

17. Graves and Addison, "Polynesian Settlement."

18. Bushnell, *Gifts of Civilization,* 266–95. This kind of gamesmanship is parodied with amusing results in Belich, *Making Peoples,* 34–35. Cachola-Abad, "Orthodox Dual Settlement Model," postulates a considerably more complex population history for Hawaii—one not susceptible to simplistic projection.

19. Cook and Borah, *Mixteca Alta.*

20. Ibid., 17.

21. For examples see Henige, "If Pigs Could Fly"; idem, "Native American Population."

22. Cook and Borah, *Mixteca Alta,* 21.

23. Ibid., 23, 25, 28. Manifestly these were not counts at all, since all but one end in a zero, and most with two zeros. As our source says, these data were "as understood from the headman" of the town. See García Pimentel, *Relación de los obispos de Tlaxcala,* 64.

24. In one of the sources Cook and Borah cite, the largest town in the Mixteca Alta is Cuilapa, part of the encomienda of Martín Cortés, estimated to be as large as Yanhuitlán, the precontact Mixtec capital. As well, the compiler of the *Relación de los obispos de Tlaxcala* named thirteen ethnic groups and alluded to others, all constituting "a very great confusion" (64). This suggests the typically diverse composition of a migrant workforce.

25. Borah, *Justice by Insurance.*

26. Cook and Borah, *Mixteca Alta,* 70n.

27. Elsewhere (ibid., 31) they move to reinforce this impression by asserting that such belated population claims "were based on consultation of the archive [*sic*] or on a tradition from a pre-Conquest record and not too long separated from it." It seems more likely that in 1569, as in 1519, such "statements" were based simply on the desire to escape as much taxation as possible.

28. Ibid., 23n.

29. Ibid., 30; cf. 68.

30. The total population figures (taking "more than 25,000" to represent just 25,000 this time) are almost identical through the accidents of differences over and under, which might explain why Cook and Borah chose these towns and regard this as confirmation.

31. Cook and Borah, *Mixteca Alta,* 25n., citing Spores, *Mixtec Kings,* 73–75. For Kubler see chapter 4.

32. Paso y Troncoso, *Papeles,* 1: 131.

33. Borah and Cook, *Population in 1548,* 146, 159. In Cook and Simpson, *Population of Central Mexico,* 100, the number had been 13,733.

34. By the formula they devised, the population of Yanhuitlán in the late 1540s should have been two to three times the figure recorded in the *suma.* See Cook and Borah, *Mixteca Alta,* 29, 68.

35. This figure is absent from the list of recorded estimates for "Oaxaca-Mixteca" in Cook and Borah, *Indian Population,* 84.

36. Cook and Borah, *Mixteca Alta,* 29.

37. Ibid., 70n.

38. Cobo, *Obras,* 2: 467.

39. Cook and Borah, *Mixteca Alta,* 68n.

40. Carta á su magestad del electo obispo de Méjico D. Juan de Zumárraga, 27 August 1529, in *CDI* 13: 127, emphasis added.

41. See the discussion for Chile in chapter 7.

42. An example might be the numbers that figure in the "Relación de Guautla" from 1580, which Cook and Borah use. There, various figures for *indios* are given for "when the Spanish came," which does not seem like an economic context. The text is so inconsistent (e.g., sometimes *hombres* is used, and on another occasion *indios,* followed immediately by *indios tributarios*) that it seems unwise to assume that one and the same category was meant in every case.

43. E.g., for the notion that cooking pot size, of all things, can be used to infer population levels see Turner and Lofgren, "Household Size"; cf. Nelson, "Ethnoarchaeology."

44. E.g., Naroll, "Floor Area," 587–89 (the paradigmatic statement); Wiessner, "Functional Estimator"; De Roche, "Population Estimates"; Casselberry, "Further Refinement," 117–22; and Tourtellot, Sabloff, and Smyth, "Room Counts." Using both residential floor space and water supply, Becquelin and Michelet, "Demografía en la zona Puuc," estimate the population there at "30 to 50 percent" less than previously thought. Farther afield, see Postgate, "How Many Sumerians?" For a generalized critique of the problems involved in extrapolating from various kinds of areas see Hassan, *Demographic Archaeology,* 70–77.

45. Scarry, "Apalachee Homesteads," 212–14. Another example of falsely imputed simultaneity, and hence of lower population, is discussed in Park, "Thule Winter Site."

46. Kintigh, "Cíbola Region," 138, emphasis in original. Cf. Wetterstrom, *Food, Diet, and Population,* 44–46.

47. See Scheiber and Kintigh, "Test," who relate disparate densities to posited site functions.

48. See Tani, "Why Should More Pots Break?" For attempts at mound size correlations see Cook and Treganza, *Quantitative Investigation.* See as well the efforts to extract population from such things as water supply and amphitheater seating discussed in chapter 16, and note 44, this chapter.

49. Or sometimes, conversely, they treat a very few examples, sometimes only one, as representing a much larger reality: a relevant example of this is Radell, "Indian Slave Trade," 72, who uses one reference to a slave-trading voyage to extrapolate to hundreds of thousands of Indians lost. N. D. Cook, *Demographic Collapse,* 100–105, uses counts from two towns—fewer than three thousand people—and "appl[ies] what we have learned to all of Peru."

50. For examples of another species of eighteenth-century population extrapolation see Rusnock, "Quantification."

51. Cameron, *Legend of Noah,* 69–71, 143–47; Rex, "'Arche de Noé,'" 333–35; Rappoport, "Geology and Orthodoxy"; Browne, *Secular Ark,* 3–10.

52. Browne, *Secular Ark,* 5, referring to illustrations in Athanasius Kircher's *Arca Noë,* published in 1675.

53. E.g., Fasold, *Ark of Noah;* Windsor, "Noah's Vessel"; and, most astonishing, Woodmorappe, *Noah's Ark.*

54. Stark, *Rise of Christianity,* 4–5, emphasis in original.

55. See Acts 1:15. Cf. Wilcox, "Judas-Tradition," 439–41.

56. See 1 Cor 15:6. Cf. Gilmour, "Christophany."

57. E.g., Haenchen, *Acts of the Apostles,* 60–61.

58. Acts 4:4, emphasis added. For Acts as a source see Pervo, *Profit with Delight.* Pervo argues that it was written primarily for entertainment and edification rather than as a historical record.

59. Stark, *Rise of Christianity,* 6–7.

60. Borah and Cook, *Aboriginal Population,* 4.

61. Simpson, *Encomienda in New Spain,* 162.

62. Postan, "England," 161. Speaking of heroic, see Melville, *Plague,* esp. 78–84, for efforts to determine numbers of sheep in one area of central Mexico in the sixteenth century.

63. Henry, Baron Brougham and Vaux, 7 May 1849, in *Hansard's Parliamentary Debates,* 3d. ser.: 104 (London, 1849), 1332.

Chapter 14: The Jury Will Disregard

1. Black, "Why Did They Die?" p. 1739. Black relied on the average-based estimate of Denevan in *NPA,* xxviii–xxix.

2. Black, "Explanation," 293–94, was shortly to raise the stakes still further: "For present purposes, we can add to this [now 57 million] an estimate for Polynesia and Micronesia of six million and a similar number for Melanesia" and another million for Australia. He concluded that "the very round number of seventy million is currently the best available estimate of the population, outside Africa, that was newly exposed to Old World diseases since 1492." Cf. Le Roy Ladurie, *Mind and Method,* 72–80, on the New Hebrides.

3. Similar arguments in similar forums include, e.g., Jacquin, "Massacre," where the author speaks of "some sixty million Indians" in the Americas in 1492, 22 million of them in central Mexico and another 12 million or so in the Andean region. In an accompanying article in *L'Histoire,* a journal

of popular history, Anne Marie Moulin, "Choc microbien," propagates the notion that diseases struck many parts of the New World well before Europeans arrived in them.

4. A brief but useful discussion of this matter is that in Philips, "Evidentiary Standards."

5. A excellent study, drawn from an allied discipline, is that of Fahnestock, "Arguing in Different Forums."

6. Newson, "Demographic Collapse."

7. Ibid., 249.

8. Ibid., 249, citing Dobyns, "Estimating," 398. Cf. Crosby, "Infectious Disease," 121, for similar commentary.

9. For the work of the de Brys see the sources cited in Henige, "If Pigs Could Fly," as well as Duchet, *L'Amérique de Theodore de Bry;* Deak, *Discovering America's Southeast;* Conley, "De Bry's Las Casas;" and Iselin, "Reading Pictures."

10. Newson, "Demographic Collapse," 255. Speaking of temporal and spatial variations in this depopulation hardly compensates for her overarching conviction that it was continuous, pre–direct contact, and almost entirely disease generated. Newson, *Life and Death,* 353, expressed this conviction, perhaps unwittingly, in *petitio principii* statements such as this one: "The figure [for a part of Ecuador in 1549] is surprisingly low compared with later accounts, which suggests that the visita may have been less comprehensive than it appears." Like most High Counters, Newson fears evidence of population growth and so ignores most of the more complex population dynamics that likely operated—labor migration, fugitivism, and undercounts.

11. Newson, "Demographic Collapse," 247–88 passim. Thus she cites (252) Anna Roosevelt's work on Marajó Island without citing the work of Betty Meggers and others, which challenges Roosevelt's conclusions.

12. Newson has the alarming habit of yoking disparate modern sources as though they agreed with one another—and with her. Thus (ibid., 253, 263): "[G]iven a collapse to about 5.6 million in 1650 (Dobyns 1966: 415, Uberlaker [*sic*] 1988: 292)"; or, "The population of Hispaniola fell from about 1 million in 1492 to 250 in 1540 (Cook and Borah 1971: 401; Zambardino 1978: 707)." In fact, Dobyns's estimates (much challenged) of various nadirs range from the years 1570 to 1930, while Ubelaker discusses only North America and offers no estimate for 1650 at all, forcing Newson, in making her statement, to infer a number that Ubelaker did not supply and match it to a date that Dobyns did not provide. See Dobyns, "Estimating," 401; Ubelaker, "North American Indian Population Size." As for the population of Hispaniola in 1492, Borah and Cook, "Hispaniola," calculated it to be *eight* million, not one million, while Zambardino, "Critique," did no

more than suggest in passing that a figure of one million for Hispaniola should not be regarded as impossible. Newson's conclusions are entirely her own and do not find support in the sources she cites. An additional impediment to understanding is that Newson's syntax often combines with her referential practices in way that precludes knowing whether she is citing studies to criticize them or to lean on them for support. Newson has written a similar but shorter piece intended for a larger audience; see her "Pre-Columbian Settlement," 130–32. Cf. Newson, "Amazon Basin." Here Newson's leaps of faith are compounded by the fact that not one of her 169 citations includes page numbers.

13. Crosby, *Ecological Imperialism,* 201, citing Dobyns but no primary sources.

14. Braudel, *Structures of Everyday Life,* 35–36.

15. Le Roy Ladurie, *Mind and Method,* 72–80.

16. Wallerstein, *The Modern World-System,* 89–90. For another example from the same school see Biraben, "Essai."

17. For this success see McNeill, *Rise of the West.*

18. Ibid., 601.

19. As well as any explanation for his new line of reasoning.

20. McNeill, *Plagues and Peoples,* 180.

21. Ibid., 309n10.

22. McNeill, "Rise," 1. Recently the High Counters' numbers, as well as high numbers generally, have drawn yet another audience, for which see Katz, *Holocaust,* 65–100 et passim. Katz repeats his argument—and his figures—in his "Uniqueness of the Holocaust," 20.

23. Camargo, "1492," 547, referring to Denevan's compromise figures in *NPA,* xxvii–xxix.

24. Ibid.

25. Ibid.; cf. McCaa, "Spanish and Nahuatl Views." Coincidentally, the mortality rate for the first known smallpox epidemic in southern Africa has also recently been reduced from 75 percent to 30 percent: see Guelke and Shell, "Landscape of Conquest," 823–24.

26. Camargo, "1492," 547.

27. Günter Risse, a medical historian, in his "Columbus's Voyages," agrees with Camargo.

28. Lord and Burke, "America before Columbus," 31.

29. Lord, "Those First Americans," 100.

30. On querying, I was told by the editor in charge of the issue that "fact-checking" had turned up the higher, "more accurate" and "best estimates": Terry A. Kirkpatrick to David Henige, 6 February 1992.

31. E.g., relying on Parry, *Spanish Seaborne Empire,* 215, Issawi,

"Area and Population," 376, spoke of "the very large figures given . . . by the early Spanish writers" as being "rehabilitated."

32. Lord, "Ancient Puzzles."

33. Rivera Pagán, *Violent Evangelism,* 173–74.

34. Venables, "Cost of Columbus." For another, even more bizarre, example see Chicago Task Force on Central America, *Dangerous Memories,* 28–33.

35. *The Bookseller,* 29 June 1985, 630.

36. Zinsser, *Rats,* 155.

37. William of Tyre, *History,* 299. Albert of Aachen—but no other source—mentioned that a contingent of 1,500 Germans (0.5 percent of 300,000) fell victim to a plague. See Sybel, *History and Literature,* 206–54; Knoch, *Studien;* Morris, "Aims"; and Cahen, "Albert d'Aix," 31–33. Albert was not an eyewitness ("though not in body, yet in my whole heart and mind": Morris, "Aims," 100–101) but, like Peter Martyr, collected data from participants later on.

38. William and the other early chroniclers, several of them eyewitnesses, all stressed that lack of food and forage contributed more to mortality than disease did. Although there was certainly sickness, and possibly an epidemic, the most detailed modern account of the occasion does not even mention it: see France, "Crisis."

39. Delbrück, "Kreuzzuges," 423–28 (fewer than 10,000); Lot, *Art Militaire,* 1: 123–37 ("about 10,000"); Stevenson, "First Crusade," 297–99 (12,000–15,000); Oman, *Art of War,* 284–85 (25,000 to 30,000); Riley-Smith, *First Crusade,* 61–66 (20,000 to 30,000); Murray, "Godfrey of Bouillon"; cf. Raymond d'Aguilers, *Historia Francorum,* 125. Of course contemporary estimates were much higher—as high as 600,000. For recent discussions of the issues involved see France, *Victory,* 121–30; and Flori, "Problème de méthodologie." Flori focuses on the symbolic and metaphorical underpinnings of the various numbers, most of which had biblical associations, and seeks to exonerate the chroniclers from outright "fantasizing."

40. There was also the impetus of Christian jihad in western accounts of the Crusades. For this, and for the siege of Antioch in particular, see Siberry, *Criticism of Crusading,* 72–75. The chroniclers' credulity toward relics and portents is discussed in, e.g., Riley-Smith, *First Crusade,* 91–119. The contemporary chronicler Orderic Vitalis, *Ecclesiastical History,* 5: 109–13, credited the crusading army with 113,000 at Antioch. Verbruggen, *Art of Warfare,* 1: 7, 10, calculated that such a force would have required a column "of over twenty-eight miles." For high counting in other disease histories see chapter 17.

41. Durant and Durant, *Caesar and Christ,* 175, 177. For more on Caesar's estimates see chapter 15.

42. Durant and Durant, *The Age of Faith,* 40. Even worse is the comment in Creasy's *Battles,* 155, that "nor is there any reason to suspect the old chroniclers of wilful exaggeration in estimating Attila's army at seven hundred thousand strong." First published in 1851, this work has been reprinted nearly one hundred times since, most recently in 1992.

43. The myth-making mischief of such works is treated in Einbinder, *Myth of the Britannica.*

44. Bakewell, "Spanish America," 69. In the following sentence, Bakewell is slightly more circumspect, allowing that "[t]he population of central and southern Mexico was probably over 10 million in the early years of the sixteenth century." In his *Ride of the Second Horseman,* 198, O'Connell speaks of a population of "some ten millions souls' for the Inca empire, following Moseley, *Incas,* 9. Moseley, in turn, cited no source but likely relied on Cook, *Demographic Collapse.* Similarly, Kiple and Ornelas, "After the Encounter," 50–53, present a variety of numbers designed to suggest very high contact population levels for Cuba, Hispaniola, Florida, and the Lesser Antilles.

45. *Encyclopedia of Latin American History and Culture,* 4: 435–36.

Chapter 15: I Came, I Saw, I Counted

1. Comparing Caesar and Cortés is hardly new; it occurred both in Cortés's time and ours, the latter most explicitly in Alcalá, *César y Cortés.* The comparisons here differ in that they concentrate on the demographic implications of their writings and, even more, on the work of those who have made use of their writings. Both Caesar's and Cortés's writings might be compared as well to Napoléon's *Bulletin de la grande armée,* so notoriously hyperbolic that it gave rise to the saying "lying like a bulletin."

2. The most influential work of the critics is that of Rambaud, *Art de la déformation,* who includes a brief and generalized discussion of Caesar's numbers (179–82). Cizek, *Histoire,* 102–9, carries the argument forward. Dunham, "Caesar's Perception," 110–15, reminds us that Caesar was targeting an audience that wanted, and expected, to read very much what he ended up writing.

3. For an ambivalent view of just this distinction see Cameron, *Procopius,* 213: "There is just enough plausible detail, among the hearsay and the personal comment, to qualify as serious evidence, with sufficient distortion to make its interpretation highly problematic." In the passage in question Procopius referred to ghosts in Britain.

4. In addition to the sources cited here, the Helvetian episode is treated in Klotz, "Helvetierzug"; Pratt, *Hail Caesar!* 99–106; Stoessl, "Cae-

sars Politik"; Walser, *Caesar und die Germanen,* 1–7; Veith, *Feldzüge,* 75–85; Harmand, *Celtes,* 62–64.

5. "In castris Helvetorum tabulae repertae sunt litteris Graecis confectae et ad Caesarem relatae, quibus in tabulis nominatim ratio confecta erat, qui numerus domo exisset eorum, qui arma ferre possent, et item separatim pueri, senes [et] mulieresque": Caesar, *Gallic War,* 43–45. Some modern translations use "list," "lists," "records," or "documents" for "tabulae." These may broadly capture the spirit of the occasion but only at the expense of the letter.

6. T. Rice Holmes, generally an apologist for Caesar's accuracy, discusses some of the logistical monstrosities that would have attended the movement of this many people at once by wagon: Holmes, *Caesar's Conquest of Gaul,* 237–41; idem, *Roman Republic,* 2: 271–81. Even then, however, he is not fully willing to regard Caesar's numbers as wholly fictitious. See also MacKendrick, *Roman France,* 36–37 (over 12,000 tons of grain, 8500 wagons, and 24,000 draft animals required, for instance). Fuller, *Julius Caesar,* 101n, has the same reservations, but calculates that 36,800 wagons would have been required. He agrees that Caesar's figures, though widely accepted, are "extravagant." Bloch and Carcopino, *Histoire romaine,* 704, 704–5n, consider Caesar's numbers to be "rounded" and "palpably inflated," even though they speak of "the archives of the Helvetians." They regarded the numbers as "troublesome for the veracity of Caesar" and referred to the lower numbers of Appian, Orosius, and others, but this hardly seems to be a sensible approach, given the lateness and our lack of knowledge of the provenance of these sources, which in any case do not agree with one another. Cf. ibid., 714–15. The most bizarre grounds for accepting these figures are those offered by Hemmerdinger, "Dénombrement," 204–5: that the fact that the two sets of addends both total 368,000 means that the numbers are *"unshakable"* (emphasis in original).

7. Consider that modern telephone directories typically have no more than about 250 to 300 names per page, written much smaller than these tables could possibly have been. It would require about 350 directory pages to list 92,000 names, and 1,400 such pages to encompass 368,000 names, at four columns to the page.

8. E.g., Caesar, *Battle for Gaul,* 29.

9. While Julius Beloch, *Bevölkerung,* 450–52, was circumspect about the tablets, noting that they "supposedly" contained such information, he was willing to accept Caesar's "census" of the 110,000 survivors, since that number was "smaller" and seemingly was carefully secured.

10. Studies devoted directly to the count of Helvetii include Wachsmuth, "Zwei Kapitel"; Müller, "Zahl"; Quinche, *Helvètes,* 124–29;

Meyer, "Zahl," 65–70; Furger-Gunti, *Helvetier,* 101–4. The efficacy of Caesar's "documentary" approach is reflected in the comments of Hignett, "Conquest of Gaul," 550n. Although Hignett was critical of the figures in the histories of the Persian wars, and although he characterized other figures in *The Gallic War* as "wildly exaggerated" and "doubtful" (554, 558n), in the case of the Helvetii he mentioned instead that "[t]he figures are given by Caesar . . . on the authority of lists found in the Helvetian camp, and are now widely accepted as approximately correct."

11. Plutarch, *Plutarch's Lives,* 7: 487; Dio Cassius, *Dio's Roman History,* 3: 265–67; Orosius, *Seven Books of History,* 242. Plutarch actually has his defenders in this matter: see Pelling, "Plutarch's Method of Work," 93.

12. Jullian, *Histoire,* 2: 6n, believed that to this number should be *added* an unknown number of slaves, who were "very numerous" among the Helvetii. In a paper devoted to the spread of writing in western Europe during the last few centuries B.C., Greg Woolf, "Power," 90, has some comments on the episode.

13. Stevens, "'Bellum Gallicum,'" 168. Much earlier Hans Delbrück, *Geschichte,* 1: 487–89, had rejected Caesar's figure outright, among other things on the grounds that so many people moving would have required a wagon train not less than 180 miles long. Meier, *Caesar,* 241, is willing to divide Caesar's numbers by ten.

14. Kloevekorn, *Kämpfe Cäsars,* 3–24. And earlier than he, Napoléon III, *Jules César,* 62–64, expressed reluctant reservations on logistical grounds.

15. It hardly seems irrelevant to point out the stresses put on modesty by the system of triumphs that were awarded to successful generals during the last days of the Republic. According to Pliny, Caesar's archrival Pompey was even more successful in killing the enemy than Caesar was. Pliny, *Natural History,* 2: 565–71, wrote that Caesar had killed 1,192,000 "human beings," Gallic and otherwise. But this impressive figure was dwarfed by the totals accorded to Pompey—846 pirate ships destroyed in one battle alone, 876 towns vanquished in Spain, and 12,183,000 people killed or routed in battle or forced to surrender, along with another 1,538 towns! It would be a wonder indeed if Caesar did not feel obliged to exaggerate in this contest of impossibly high numbers. For Pompey's own unprecedented triumphs in the 70s and 60s see Seager, *Pompey,* 32–39; Greenhalgh, *Pompey,* 96–99, 168–71. For another example of high numbers as insistently groomed rhetoric at this time see Ramage, *Nature and Purpose,* 28–31.

16. Kloevekorn, "Kämpfe."

17. E.g., Hemmerdinger, "Dénombrement," and Kaenel and Paunier, "Bibracte," 153–58 (one concession—"about" 92,000 fighting men). For the myth-making use of the Helvetii for the later Swiss see Bergier, *Guillaume*

Tell, 121, who sees these numbers as "a certain exaggeration designed to enhance the military talent of Caesar and to justify the considerable expense" of the campaign.

18. Caesar, *Gallic War,* 196.

19. Ibid. Exhaustion is actually a serious consideration, one that might be likened to any of the inhibiting elements in a carrying capacity approach. Fuller, *Julius Caesar,* 90–91, thought that fifteen minutes was the maximum a legionnaire could fight in hand-to-hand combat before becoming exhausted, and more generally, Clausewitz, *On War,* 183–222, raised the time span only to twenty minutes. Keegan, *Face of Battle,* also treats the matter, as does Goldsworthy, "*Othismos,*" 20–21. For a related case, see Donlan and Thompson, "Charge at Marathon," 339–43, which shows through experimentation that Herodotus' account of the inception of this battle—a mile-long run in full armor—is well beyond physical endurance.

20. Fuller, *Julius Caesar,* 120. Among other things, Caesar's description implies that the Romans killed more than a thousand of the enemy every single minute of the engagement!

21. Caesar wasn't to know it, but his account of the annihilation of the Tencteri and Usipetes was given the lie by the reappearance of the latter in the historical record in A.D. 14, again fighting the Romans: Tacitus, *Annalen,* 1: 186; 3: 329–31. And finally they reappeared in A.D. 83, this time as renegade mercenaries in Roman Britain: see Tacitus, *Agricola,* in *Tacitus,* 1: 77–79.

22. Although in this case Napoléon III, *Jules César,* 138, seemed to have no doubts. Nor did Pratt, *Hail, Caesar!,* 146, who had the two groups "counted after" the battle!

23. Desjardins, *Géographie,* 2: 652. It would at least be easier to imagine achieving the same effect with Arabic numerals merely by misplacing a comma or a zero or two.

24. Lot, *Gaule,* 97.

25. Fuller, *Julius Caesar,* 118.

26. Bloch and Carcopino, *Histoire Romaine,* 2: 749; Gelzer, "Antrag," 47.

27. Keegan, *Face of Battle,* 62–69.

28. In addition to almost any modern edition of *The Gallic War* see Dion, "Migrations," 58–61. Lee, "Encounter," 100–103, deals only with the ways in which Caesar tried to sugarcoat his treachery and does not mention the imputed size of the enemy hosts. King, *Roman Gaul,* 42–52, accepts Caesar's figures, even those for the Usipetes and Tencteri, without demur. A more recent account of Caesar's Gallic campaigns that seems unable to decide whether or not to accept his figures is that of Jiménez, *Caesar,* 45, 56–57, 64–65, 72–75, 86–87, 182–85 et passim.

29. Wallace, *Dissertation,* 314–25.

30. Valentin-Smith, *Origine,* 34–38, listed fourteen such efforts ("to our knowledge") before adding a fifteenth—8,343,320. Several other earlier efforts are summarized in Holmes, *Caesar's Conquest of Gaul,* 340–43. Holmes himself, although not particularly skeptical of Caesar's number-mongering, concluded (341) that "to calculate the population of Gaul even approximately is impossible."

31. Most recently see Lo Cascio, "Roman Population." See as well, Gallo, "Beloch," and Goldsmith, "Estimate," 263–72. A fundamental difference between Beloch and those who advocate higher figures is that he regarded these census numbers as fairly comprehensive, whereas they (like most High Counters) hold that there was some serious degree of underrepresentation, with the degree they choose determining their total population estimates. On this issue in a smaller ambit see Jongman, *Pompeii,* 66–67.

32. Beloch, *Bevölkerung,* 448–60; idem, "Bevölkerung Galliens."

33. E.g., Drinkwater, *Roman Gaul,* 169–70.

34. Lo Cascio, "Roman Population"; Beloch, *Bevölkerung,* 454–57. In addition to the other responses, indirect or direct, to Beloch's conclusions discussed here, see Garofalo, "Popolazione."

35. Levasseur, *Population française,* 1: 99–101.

36. Diodorus Siculus, *Diodorus of Sicily,* 5: 163.

37. Levasseur, *Population française,* 100–101.

38. Ibid., 101.

39. E.g., Sée, "Population."

40. Jullian, *Histoire,* 2: 4–8; cf. 5: 25–27 for roughly the same argument.

41. Ibid., 2: 7.

42. For an appreciation of Jullian's *oeuvre* see Duval, *Travaux,* 1: 19–34. Duval (32) thought that Jullian expressed "too great a confidence in flattering numbers—for the population of Gaul, for towns and cities which it is impossible for us to calculate, for the number of victims in the war and in certain battles, and for the effectives in the armies; too much credit is given to the estimates offered by the sources, from which no serious deductions can perhaps by drawn with certainty, at least on a properly demographic scale."

43. For the context see Viallaneix and Ehrard, *Nos ancêtres les Gaulois;* Pomian, "Francs et Gaulois"; and Dietler, "'Our Ancestors the Gauls'," 584–605. Earlier, in the aftermath of the even more disastrous Franco-Prussian War, the Gauls were similarly idealized: see A. Simon, *Vercingétorix,* and Champion, "Power of the Picture."

44. Grenier, *Gaulois,* 225, probably referring to Beloch.

45. Ibid., 227.

46. Ibid., 229.

47. Lot, *Gaule,* 67–68. Lot tempered his skepticism by wondering whether Caesar's figure of 110,000 Helvetians who returned home might not have been "the real number of emigrants" before their defeat (106–7).

48. Ibid., 120.

49. Ibid., 68–69.

50. Grenier, *Gaulois,* 226.

51. Ibid.

52. In doing so, Grenier is reminiscent of Clastres, as discussed in chapter 8. A decade earlier Grenier, "Gaule romaine," 447–55, had undertaken much the same exercise. Relying on Strabo and Diodorus, he pegged the population at "15 to 20 million." Along the way he turned "many" into "sixty," rejected "the arbitrary calculations" of Beloch, whose method he regarded as "hypercritical," and quoted approvingly Jullian's speculation about the Gallic gods' expectations. He thought as well that "we must accept the enumeration of the Helvetians by themselves [*sic*]."

53. In the meantime, Thevenot, *Histoire,* 49–50, suggested a population somewhere between 10 million and 15 million. A little earlier Pareti, "Quanti erano," had suggested that the population of Belgica, one of the three provinces of Transalpine Gaul, was about 3 million in Caesar's time. Braudel, *Identité,* 64, speaks of "a dense population (*perhaps* 10,000,000 or more . . .)" (emphasis in original).

54. Schmittlein, *César,* 65–67.

55. Drinkwater, *Roman Gaul,* 170.

56. Drinkwater, ibid., does warn readers that his estimate "still involves a very considerable amount of guesswork" but adds that "at least it removes the impression of just a bare handful of millions of people which one is likely to get from the standard [=?] view."

57. Cunliffe, *Greeks, Romans, and Barbarians,* 115–24 passim.

58. Biraben, "Préhistoire," 44–46.

59. Etienne, "Gaule romaine," in ibid., 66–69. Here he relies on Bloch, *Histoire,* 34–35.

60. Goudineau, *César et la Gaule.*

61. Ibid., 259–60, 308–15.

62. Ibid., 308.

63. Wallace, *Dissertation,* 319–20. He eventually became slightly less "moderate," settling on a figure of 48 million.

64. For an overview of these see Béal, "*Bibracte*-Autun."

65. For details see Moreau, *Dictionnaire,* 373–85; Holmes, *Caesar's Conquest of Gaul,* 346–47.

66. Those who rely on Diodorus for all or part of their arguments

seem not to have noticed that elsewhere in his compilation (IV.19.1–2) he asserted that Herakles "founded a great city which was named Alesia after the 'wandering' (*alê*) on his campaign." This permitted him to go on that "at last Gaius Caesar, who has been pronounced a god because of the magnitude of his deeds, took it by storm and made it and the other Celts subjects of the Romans." Thus Diodorus not only has a claim but a story, buttressed by linguistic analysis. Presumably modern scholarship would reject the story on the grounds that Alesia was really an insignificant place before Vercengetorix holed up there, and because Herakles was not a historical figure. Without disagreeing, I would add that the evidence for Herakles is no weaker than the evidence that 60 to 400 Gallic polities each had a population somewhere between 50,000 and 200,000. On the contrary, evidence for Herakles is considerably more widespread that Diodorus's single voice on behalf of these population figures.

67. Caesar, *Gallic War,* 487–88.

68. Harmand, *Campagne,* 266. Harmand, "Composante," has written a more recent apologia for Caesar's writings.

69. For Caesar on sieges in general and on Alesia in particular, see Cipriani, *Cesare.*

70. The degree to which students of Caesar's activities at Alesia have availed themselves of the options is suggested by the following sampling: Napoléon III, *Jules César,* 292 (283,000); Jullian, *Histoire,* 3: 516n (276,000 or 288,000 on the basis of an unclear listing); Pratt, *Hail, Caesar!* 193 (250,000); Bloch and Carcopino, *Histoire romaine,* 2: 789 (300,000); Cunliffe, *Greeks,* 121 (281,000); Harmand, *Alésia,* 265–66 (248,000 or 258,000); Potier, *Génie militaire,* 271 (240,000); MacKendrick, *Roman France,* 51 (245,000); Holmes, *Caesar's Conquest of Gaul,* 341 (258,000); Hignett, "Conquest of Gaul," 569 (258,000); Fuller, *Julius Caesar,* 153 (266,000); Beloch, *Bevölkerung,* 455–56 (267,000); Markale, *Vercingétorix,* 230 (about 248,000); Grenier, *Gaulois,* 402 (about 248,000); Lot, *Gaule,* 122 (254,000); King, *Roman Gaul,* 52 (248,000); Markale, *Celtic Civilization,* 99 (240,000); Colomb, *Vercingétorix,* 272 ("more than 200,000"); Keppie, *Making,* 92 ("an alleged 250,000"). Jullian, *Vercingétorix,* 127, spoke of "nearly 300,000 men," only to deny it in a footnote.

71. For editions based on the two traditions, respectively, see Hering, *C. Iulii Caesaris Commentarii,* 140; Pontet, *C. Iulii Caesaris Commentariorum,* sub. VII, 75–76; and Seel, *C. Iulii Caesaris Commentarii,* 265–67.

72. Thus some manuscripts have "CCL," others "CCXL," and still others "CCXXX," accounting for the differences in Caesar's last figures.

73. For the text history of *The Gallic War* see, among others, Seel, *Caesar-Studien,* 27–37; Jullian, *Histoire,* 3: 149–52n.

74. A word about the number of Gauls within Alesia during the siege will not be inapropos. Caesar rendered this as 80,000, but the site most commonly thought to be Alesia is far too small (from 97 to 140 hectares depending on what is considered to have been defensible habitable space at the time) to have accommodated such a number, and many modern scholars reject his numbers on this basis. See, e,g., Delbrück, *Geschichte,* 531–32; Fuller, *Julius Caesar,* 150n; Markale, *Vercingétorix,* 226; Potier, *Génie militaire,* 265–68; Harmand, *Alésia,* 357–78. Yet Caesar's ability to know this figure is likely to have been greater than his ability to know the size of any army opposing him in the open field, or just campaigning elsewhere. Others (e.g., Jullian, *Histoire,* 507n) defend the notion on the basis that "exceptionally grave" circumstances required overcrowding. There is no mention of the victualing problems that must have attended the siege. Several other sites have been touted as being Alesia as well, sometimes on the grounds that they are commodious enough to have held 80,000 or more people. See, e.g., Carcopino, "Alésia;" Grapinet, "Alésia."

75. A good example of this modus operandi is Cavaignac's argument that Orosius' figure of 157,000 for the Helvetii proper is to be preferred to Caesar's estimate of 263,000 because 157,000 + 105,000 (the number of Helvetii auxiliaries claimed by Caesar) happens to total 262,000! Meyer, "Zahl," 68–70, also found it attractive to assume that somehow Orosius had happened on a source that more accurately recorded the Helvetian population. He saw it as a paleographic issue, with "CLVII" being turned into "CCLXIII" or even "CCCLXVIII" at some scribal stage. In this way the possibility that there was such a census is preserved, allowing further negotiation about the numbers it contained. Since Orosius lived in the fifth century, to prefer his unnamed source over Caesar is tantamount to taking a 1995 undocumented source for the population of central Mexico over the evidence of Cortés. However suspect the latter might be, there is at least the off-chance that it is reasonably accurate.

76. Cavaignac, *Population,* 137–54. After postulating this correlation several times, Cavaignac closed by claiming that "[t]hese results have been obtained by a method radically independent of the numbers given by Caesar for the levy of Alesia." He went on to say that he feared being reproached for arguing in "a vicious circle" (153). Actually he tried hard (e.g., 153) to maintain as close a ratio to one-third as he could by seeking to explain away apparent exceptions as the result of ancient or modern misunderstandings of the tribal units involved. Cavaignac went so far as to claim that we have a census in disguise in the figures of Plutarch and Appian, multiplied by four, suggesting, surely, that they had had the opportunity to know the entire population and from that had inferred the number of warriors, which they then addressed.

77. Mommsen, *History of Rome,* 5: 39, 60–61, 89.

78. Beloch, *Bevölkerung,* 450–60; idem, "Bevölkerung." A recent popular treatment also accepts every number in *The Gallic War* without comment: Le Bohec, *César,* 52–77.

79. Jullian, *Histoire,* 3: 516n. The notion of such an assembly is itself a modern retrojection of Gallic solidarity.

80. For a study of a set of circumstances not very dissimilar to the present one, see Burns, "Calculating," 187–90.

81. Sabben-Clarke, *Caesar,* treats Caesar's thorny relationship with the Roman Senate and the other triumvirs.

82. But for the general ambiance see Gil, "El libro greco-latino."

83. Cortés, *Cartas de relación,* 183. For a recent analysis of Cortés's rhetorical strategies in the letter which deals with the conquest of Tenochtitlan, see Checa, "Cortés."

84. Cortés, *Cartas de relación,* 183.

85. For Orderic Vitalis, the twelfth-century chronicler of Norman England, the surrogate figure was 60,000; see Murray, *Reason and Society,* 177, 179.

86. There is no lack of discussion of the close connections between the two works; among the most recent is that of Carman, "Voices of the Conqueror," which focuses on the speeches that Gomara put into Cortés's mouth.

87. López de Gómara, *Conquista,* 35–37.

88. But still, hardly as independent as one might wish; see, for instance, Brooks, "Motecuzoma Xocoyotl," who demonstrates the degree to which Díaz del Castillo was guided by earlier published sources of the campaign, to the point where his stated disagreements are sometimes actually out of character—a good sign of sincerity if not necessarily of accuracy. For more on Díaz see chapter 4.

89. Cook and Simpson, *Population of Central Mexico,* 23. Cook and Borah, "Materials," 11, accord Díaz the same heady accolade. In calling on Díaz, Cook and Borah emulate the strategy of Clavigero two centuries earlier in his history, discussed earlier.

90. Bearing in mind of course that Díaz del Castillo was not working *in vacuo* but wrote his work explicitly as comment on Lopez de Gómara's work, which struck him as glorifying Cortés at the expense of the rest of the Spaniards.

91. Much later Borah, "Historical Demography," 14, came to recognize that Díaz "objected scornfully to the reports of numbers by López de Gómara," but only to aid in recruiting him once again for another purpose.

92. For a sampling of various non-numerical examples see Díaz del Castillo, *Historia verdadera,* 220, 232, 303–4.

93. Ibid., 34.

94. Ibid., 296. In the other extant manuscript of the *Historia*, which differs in thousands of small and large ways, "the entire universe" is phrased as "in all of Castile." Díaz del Castillo worked on his history for the last twenty years or so of his life, and there are at least three surviving manuscripts, whose relationships to each other are far from resolved. Thus it is impossible to know whether "all of Castile" or "the entire universe" represents his final thoughts on the matter. For details see, most recently, Sáenz de Santa María, *Historia de una historia,* 15–43; Serés, "Textos."

95. Díaz del Castillo, *Historia verdadera,* 296.

96. Cortés, *Cartas de relación,* 84; Díaz del Castillo, *Historia verdadera,* 61–62.

97. Cortés, *Cartas de relación,* 106; Díaz del Castillo, *Historia verdadera,* 85–86.

98. Cortés, *Cartas de relación,* 115–17; as already noted, Cortés's locution is odd, almost bizarre. López de Gómara, *Conquista,* 1: 163–64, must have thought both that it was odd and that it was true, since he rephrased it to read "almost 150,000."

99. Díaz del Castillo, *Historia verdadera,* 116–21.

100. Cortés, *Cartas de relación,* 140–41.

101. Díaz del Castillo, *Historia verdadera,* 174–75.

102. For a study that goes beyond questioning the numbers to doubting the reality of several of these battles see Guzmán, *Visión crítica.*

103. It cannot entirely be ruled out that Díaz deliberately tried to minimize the numbers of Indians and so counter the *leyenda negra* of the time, although he was hardly reticent about commenting on Spanish atrocities and on the effects of the newly introduced diseases.

104. Aguilar, *Relación,* 68, 75, 76, 80, 95. For the argument, largely on logistical grounds, that the Tlaxcalan army "did not exceed 8,000" men see Muñoz Camargo, *Historia de Tlaxcala,* 199n. Cholula figures prominently in the early historiography of the conquest, because Cortés ordered the killing of numerous chiefs and townspeople there as an object lesson and later almost lost his estates in New Spain as a result. Needless to say, the figures vary as to the number slain: "many" (Díaz), 2,000 (Aguilar), 3000+ (Cortés), 4,000 (Sepúlveda and a member of Cortés's army), 5,000–6,000 (Las Casas, *Brevísima relación*), 6,000 (López de Gómara), 15,000+ (Las Casas in *De thesauri in Peru*), and 20,000 (Vázquez de Tapia). It is no surprise that Las Casas held different opinions at different times. The work in which his higher estimate appeared was completed about twenty years after the *Brevísima relación,* and the difference can be seen as one measure of Las Casas' increased commitment to the cause of the Indians, since it is unusual to find a number

in the rest of his corpus that is actually larger than its counterpart in the *Brevísima relación*. The substance of the sources for the event is discussed in detail in Marcus, "Conquête de Cholula," and Peterson and Green, "Massacre at Cholula."

105. Aguilar, *Relación*, 101–2, spoke of depopulation rates as high at 99.9 percent. For a recent view of the matter see Smith, "Size of Aztec Cities." Smith notes, among other things, that Cortés's estimate for Texcoco (30,000 household heads, or perhaps 150,000 total) is refuted by several archaeological studies that indicate a range of 18,500 to 30,000 persons. In line with my comments on archaeological interpretation in chapter 10, I should be circumspect. Still, it seems to me that archaeological interpretations resulting from several independent assessments can be treated as maximums, and, given the disparity, should also be regarded as refutations, to the degree that refutations are possible, of Cortés's (and Aguilar's and others') estimates in this case. For an earlier discussion see Rojas, "Cuantificaciones."

106. Early attempts to describe Tenochtitlan on maps underscores the medieval mores brought to so many matters of the Americas: see Palm, "Tenochtitlan"; Godbey, "New World"; and Leibsohn, "Mapping Metaphors."

107. This point is inadvertently made in Hassig, *Aztec Warfare*, 60, but by circular reasoning, taking the estimated total population for the basin of Mexico, derived partly from warrior counts, to demonstrate that it could support armed levies of over half a million.

108. Sauer, *Aboriginal Population*, 1.

109. Ibid., 32.

110. For a similar, though more extended, defense of the early sources for the same area, see Reff, *Disease*.

111. Cook and Simpson, *Population of Central Mexico*, 22–25.

112. In an aside, Cook and Simpson (ibid., 23n) refer to "an acute discussion of the credibility" of Cortés and Díaz in two works by Ramón Iglesia. In fact, in the work cited for Cortés, Iglesia had no trouble disbelieving Cortés on any number of matters (*Cronistas*, 17–69 passim). Any defense of Díaz's credibility with respect to numbers is ipso facto an attack on that of Cortés, a fact noted by Iglesia in the very work cited by Cook and Simpson: see Iglesia, *Hombre Colón*, 77–96. Thus Iglesia is joined to Díaz as a reluctant yokemate.

113. Cook and Borah, "Rate of Population Change," 466.

114. Cook and Borah, *Aboriginal Population*.

115. Cook and Borah, *Essays*, 1: 7–10.

116. Ibid., 8–9. This last observation is little more than a red herring. Like carrying capacity, terrain is a limiter more than an enabler. Cook and

Borah commented that Spanish estimates of allied troops and work parties are "better-grounded."

117. Calvin, *Commentary*, 3: 146, commenting on the biblical story that Jahweh had killed that many Assyrians during the night. This alleged event is not mentioned in Assyrian accounts of the campaign, which claim, in contrast, that 200,150 Israelites were taken captive: see, e.g., Sweeney, *Isaiah 1–39*, 477–79, and sources cited there.

118. Cook and Borah, *Essays*, 9–10.

119. Ibid., 10–12.

120. Whitmore, *Disease and Death*, 8–9. Conversely, it belies as well the comment that "[t]here is unanimity among scholars that the figures given for the time of the Conquest by contemporary writers cannot be trusted" (Prem, "Reconstructing," 50).

121. Similar exercises have been carried out for Xerxes' army, for those of the Persians at Cunaxa, Issus, and Gaugamela, and for the Helvetii discussed earlier in this chapter.

122. If, as Hassig, *Aztec Warfare*, 238, points out, the Aztecs used an "open formation" to counter the Spanish horses, these distances would increase accordingly.

123. Hassig, ibid., has little or nothing to say on these matters, even though the figures he offers for an army *en marche* (ibid., 66–70) suggest that 150,000 soldiers could constitute a column nearly 300 miles long! Yet he ignores the implications of his own case and accepts (e.g., ibid., 64) the existence of armies as large as 200,000 (plus 100,000 porters) in pre-Hispanic times—as filtered through Spanish sources.

124. For logistical problems involving much smaller armies with more efficient means of transport and supply, see the essays in Lynn, *Feeding Mars*. Earlier, Engels, *Alexander the Great*, 11–25 et passim, had shown how the number of pack animals and followers severely restricted the numbers of fighting men that could have accompanied Alexander in his campaigns. For the Roman armies see Peddie, *Roman War Machine*, 42–58. A very thorough study of the logistics of naval warfare is that of Gillmor, "War on the Rivers." Gillmor concludes that the topographical and victualling constraints involved means that the numbers in some of the chronicles must be tens of times too high.

125. See Raudzens, "Firepower Limitations." Even as recently as the Vietnam war it has been estimated (Lewis, *Assault Weapons*, 15) that 200,000 rounds were needed to kill one enemy soldier! During World War I, when the armies were immobile and entrenched, it required 1,400 artillery shells on average to inflict a single casualty (Holmes, *Acts of War*, 166–75).

126. Jonah 3:3. Cf. Wiseman, "Jonah's Nineveh," who translates the

phrase as "requiring a three-day visit," in hopes of rehabilitating Jonah's description.

127. Diodorus of Siculus, II.3.2 in *Diodorus Siculus*, 1: 357.

128. Madhloum, "Excavations at Nineveh," 76–79.

129. For a specific argument see Smith, "Hernán Cortés."

130. Adorno, "Warrior and the War Community"; Murrin, *History and Warfare*.

131. Among the paradigms for the chroniclers were the accounts of Josephus and the Books of Maccabees concerning the revolt of the Maccabees in the second century B.C. For the numbers involved, where "eye-witnesses habitually magnified the size of the enemy army and minimized that of their own," see Bar-Kochva, *Judas Maccabaeus*, 29–67.

132. E.g., at Thapsus in North Africa in 46 B.C., Caesar claimed that his forces killed 10,000 of the enemy at the cost of "fifty soldiers missing and a few wounded." For good measure Plutarch upped the 10,000 to 50,000, "without losing as many as fifty of his own men" (Plutarch, *Caesar* (liii.2), in *Plutarch's Lives*, 7: 567). A year later at the battle of Munda in Spain he had slightly more difficulty—33,000 Pompeian soldiers killed at the cost of "about a thousand men" (Caesar, *Alexandrian, African, and Spanish Wars*, 281, 369). Cf. Holmes, *Roman Republic*, 3: 267–70, 367–68, 531–34, 548–51; Kromayer, *Antike Schlachtfelder*, 2: 552–77, 3: 844–57.

133. Plutarch, *Sulla*, in *Plutarch's Lives*, 4: 413–15; Orosius, *Seven Books*, 216.

134. Plutarch, *Sulla*, in *Plutarch's Lives*, 4: 417; Orosius, *Seven Books*, 216.

135. Plutarch, *Sulla*, in *Plutarch's Lives*, 4: 389–91; Hirschfeld, "Typische Zahlen," 291–93; Hammond, "Chaeronea"; Sherwin-White, *Roman Foreign Policy*, 128–29; Baker, *Sulla*, 204 ("a remark which may be received in the sporting spirit in which it was made"); Bird, "Eutropius," 246–47. Through these later Roman authors, Sulla would thus have us believe that he had time to muster his entire force before dusk and determine the losses, and, pari passu, that he knew their numbers to a man.

136. Brunt, *Italian Manpower*, 697.

137. Delbrück, *Geschichte*, 1: 460. At about the same time Marcus Crassus reported killing 12,000 of Spartacus's slave army at the cost of three dead and seven wounded: see Ward, *Marcus Crassus*, 91n.

138. The roughly contemporaneous experience of the Portuguese in Africa, at least as adumbrated by their chroniclers, is uncannily similar. For instance, observers estimated that an army of fewer than 3,000 Portuguese and allies at the battle of Ambuila in Angola in 1665 managed to defeat an opposing force of not less than 100,000 men. Within a generation this num-

ber had reached 900,000, and the victory was attributed to the intervention of the Blessed Virgin. For the whole story see Saccardo, *Congo e Angola,* 2: 594–97; Toso, *Anarchia congolese,* 214–15; Thornton, *Kingdom of Kongo,* 75–76; Boxer, "Relação inédita."

139. Bernard of Clairvaux, "De Laude Novae Militiae," 927.

140. Machiavelli, *Le istorie fiorentine,* 227–29.

141. E.g., Simeoni, *Signorie,* 1: 400–404; Bayley, *War and Society,* 168–70; Prezzolini, *Machiavelli,* 41–42; Mallett, *Mercenaries and their Masters,* 196–97, 271. Block, *Condottieri,* addressed several such instances from the period.

142. For details on this and other battles of the period see Alvira Cabrer, "Muerte del enemigo." Alvira Cabrer discusses the mental world in which these numbers and proportions were all but ineluctable—a world not very different from that of the sixteenth-century chroniclers of the Indies. In the so-called Battle of Britain in the summer of 1940, the Germans tripled, and the British doubled, the number of casualties they claimed to have inflicted: see Hough, *Battle of Britain,* 310–11.

143. "News from the Western Islands," in Blair/Robertson, 3: 247.

144. Francisco de Sande, "Relación de las Filipinas [1576]" in Blair/Robertson, 4: 50, 58–59.

145. Casas, *Historia de las Indias,* 2: 928.

146. Pérez de Luján, *Expedition into New Mexico,* 97. Much earlier Balboa claimed that he had pacified much of the isthmus of Panama without losing so much as a single soldier: Pietro Martire de Anghiera, *Opera,* 115.

147. Columbus, *Diario,* 75, 193–95.

148. Murrin, *History and Warfare,* passim. An eyewitness account of the Ottoman siege and capture of Rhodes in 1522 claimed that in one engagement the Turks lost 20,000, the Christians 200, and that overall the Turks lost 114,000 men during the siege: Brockman, *Rhodes,* 133, 151.

149. Murrin, *History and Warfare,* 163.

150. Napoleon practiced the art remorselessly. Regarding the battle of Austerlitz, for example, he proclaimed in his *Bulletin de la grande armée* that 20,000 Russians perished in an icy pond; in fact the number was probably not much more than 200, or 1 percent of Napoleon's boast: see Manceron, *Austerlitz,* 297.

151. Yadin, *Scroll of the War,* 156–97 et passim; Davies, *War Scroll from Qumran;* Gmirkin, "War Scroll," 89–129.

152. Plutarch, *Sulla,* in *Plutarch's Lives,* 4: 405.

153. Brunt, *Italian Manpower,* 224–27. For other modern notices see Hatzfeld, *Trafiquants,* 45; Magie, *Roman Rule,* 1: 217, 2: 1103n37; Bowersock, *Augustus,* 1; Wilson, *Emigration from Italy,* 125–26; Sarikakis, "Vêpres

ephésiennes"; Amiotti, "Greci ed il massacro"; Keaveney, *Sulla,* 78–79; McGing, *Foreign Policy,* 113–14; Meier, *Caesar,* 84–85.

154. Weiss, "Seine"; Crouzet, *Nuit de la Saint-Barthélemy,* 32–34; Kelley, "Martyrs, Myths, and the Massacre," 199–200; Noguères, *Massacre of St. Bartholomew,* 158–60. For the wide range of estimates (20,000 to 150,000) of the number of Huguenot émigrés to England after the revocation of the Edict of Nantes in 1685 see Gwynn, "Huguenot Immigrants."

155. For a number of recent examples see Uekert, *Rivers of Blood.* Even for the Tiananmen Square massacre, widely covered live on television, the casualty figures range from 300 to over 1,000 (ibid., 31–32).

156. Gupta, "Black Hole Incident," emphasis in original. Cf. idem, *Sirajuddaullah,* 70–80, and Macfarlane, *Black Hole,* 228–31, 280–81, who is skeptical of more than just the numbers.

157. E.g., Barber's *Black Hole,* 206 et passim, is riddled with errors pointed out by Gupta, whose earlier work Barber had ignored. The later mythography is discussed in Hartmann, "'Black Hole' of Calcutta."

158. Ibn Khaldun, *Muqaddimah,* 1: 16–23.

159. Grant, *Greek and Roman Historians,* 64.

160. Grant, ibid., went on to point out how Caesar "quietly [took] credit for successes that his subordinates had won," which was the major thrust of Díaz's writing.

161. This approach makes it easier to think of Caesar and Cortés as war correspondents, for which see Knightley, *First Casualty.* More generally, see Woodman, "Hannibal to Hitler."

162. Ibid., 113–15. The work of Valerius Antias, now known only through Livy, is an early example of this strategy: see Howard, "Valerius Antias and Livy"; Laroche, "Valerius Antias"; and Ziolkowski, "Credibility of Numbers."

163. To provide a coda to this discussion, I return to Caesar's locale and Cortés's time to look at reports of the numbers at the battle of Grandson, in which the Swiss defeated Charles the Bold, Duke of Burgundy, in 1476. The Burgundian army did not exceed 20,000, and was probably smaller, but even the sober-sided Swiss chroniclers of the time fell victim and reported that it was as large as 120,000. Consonantly, the chroniclers reported Burgundian casualties of 7,000 when only a few hundred actually died in the battle. See Delbrück, *Perserkriege,* 156–59; Chabloz, *Bataille de Grandson;* Kurz, *Schweizerschlachten,* 96–107; Bächtold, "History, Ideology, and Propaganda."

164. For a general discusson of the discursive practices of Cortés's time and place see Abbott, *Rhetoric.*

165. That Cortés consciously worked to at least one model is demonstrated in Frankl, "Hernán Cortés." Moving forward into the very recent

past, the now notorious body counts during the Vietnam war were initially widely believed, even, it seems, by those who fabricated them. See, e.g., Lewy, *America in Vietnam,* 78–83; Gibson, *Perfect War,* 124–29, 156–59, 230–31; Spector, "Perception and Reality"; Hirschman, Preston, and Vu Manh Loi, "Vietnamese Casualties."

166. For this aspect of matters see chapter 4. For recent studies that treat Cortés's testimony as other than reportage see Clendinnen, "Cortés"; idem, "'Fierce and Unnatural Cruelty'"; Fernández-Armesto, "'Aztec' Auguries"; Pastor Bodmer, *Armature of Conquest,* 50–100; Prien, "Hernán Cortés' Rechtfertigung," 71–93; and Robles Mohs, "Adán, el Eden y Abel," 31–45. Each discusses the influences of classical and contemporary discourse, and of the extraordinary events of the conquest itself, on the style and content of Cortés's letters. Each author admires Cortés's rhetorical finesse a great deal more than he or she awards him points for accuracy.

167. Sargent-Baur, "Truth-Claims," 508.

168. Hulme, "Tales of Distinction," 170, refers to Cortés's "self-fashioning" and characterizes him as "the Benegeli to his own Quixote."

Chapter 16: By Wonder Inflamed

1. For the smallpox epidemic in Iceland early in the eighteenth century, which the High Counters frequently cite because of its presumed high mortality, see Henige, "If Pigs Could Fly," 701–20.

2. Gardiner, *Kadesh Inscription;* Ockinga, "Kadesh Record"; Goedicke, "Battle of Kadesh." Ramesses has been followed by some moderns in positing a very large Hittite army, though not large enough to accommodate Ramesses' own numbers: e.g., Burne, "Notes."

3. The genre in ancient Egypt is treated in Hall, *Pharaoh.* There are even earlier examples; for instance, an inscription relating to Naram-Sin of Akkad (ca. 2213–2176 B.C.) claimed that 270,700 of his soldiers were killed—to a man—over three years. See Foster, *Muses,* 1: 257–69; Longman, *Autobiography,* 103–29; Tinney, "New Look."

4. All aspects of the Assyrian numbers, some of which have been estimated to be over one hundred times too great, have recently been throughly investigated in De Odorico, *Use of Numbers.* Earlier studies include Olmstead, *Assyrian Historiography,* 7–9; Ungnad, "Zahl"; Gelb, "Prisoners of War"; Fouts, "Another Look"; and Laato, "Assyrian Propaganda." Millard, "Large Numbers," is more tolerant of at least some of these numbers, but in some cases only by regarding exactitude as a warrant of accuracy. For the numbers of animals in the annals see Wapnish, *"Seni ana la mani,"* who sees the numbers as meaning "a 'whole lot.'"

5. I could have begun instead with the so-called "Catalogue of Ships," exactly 1,186 of them, in the *Iliad*. This number has actually been used to calculate the number of Greeks transported to Troy. It seems that Homer mentioned the contingents on two ships, 50 and 120, respectively. Willcock, *Companion*, 26, saw promise in this: "[W]e might therefore take the mean of these two numbers (85) and multiply it by the total number of these ships (1,186) to find the strength of the whole force. The result is a little over 100,000 [100,810]." Cf. idem, *Commentary*, 66, where "c. 100,000 men" is treated as "a plausible calculation." Huxley, "Numbers," 316, also used this average and thought the result "not an absurdly large number, given the resources of Mycenaean Greece." Elsewhere ("Mycenaean Decline," 27) he argued that the two catalogs of ships in the *Iliad* "are a remarkable tribute to the accuracy of oral epic; . . . each springs from a single source at a single time, a source contemporary with a muster of Achaeans about 1240 B.C." Likewise, Willcock, *Companion*, 66–68, thought it "nearer the truth" to accept the catalog "as a miraculously preserved record of the historical army of Agamemnon" than as "a poor invention." In all cases these authors have merely improved the expedient first bruited by Thucydides, *Peloponnesian War*, I.x.5, that 50 and 120 were the smallest and largest crew sizes on the expedition. Thus these authors joined with Wallace, *Dissertation*, 38–39, for whose views on numbers see chapters 3 and 15.

All this seems hardly much better than the pseudohistorical account of the war by "Dares," which claimed that 866,000 Greeks and 676,000 Trojans had been killed during the ten years of conflict: Frazer, *Trojan War*, 168. More skeptical views include those of Gomme, *Historical Commentary*, 1: 114; and Kirk, *Iliad*, 237–40. Those who regard the *Iliad* as a reasonably accurate account of an essentially historical event take the ships' catalog at greater face value than those who do not. Simpson and Lazenby, *Catalogue*, 153–71, would trace the origins of the catalog to Mycenaean times while regarding its numbers as "far too high." Page, *History*, 151–52, accepted the accuracy of all the elements in the catalog except the numbers of ships and, by extension, the number of men transported in them.

6. Herodotus, *Persian Wars*, 3: 499–505 (vii, 184–87). As if to anticipate doubters, Herodotus recorded that the Persian troops were "counted" 10,000 by 10,000; cf. Burn, *Persia and the Greeks*, 326–31.

7. Modern estimates of Xerxes' army are about one-fifteenth to one-twentieth of Herodotus' figures: Maurice, "Size,"; Burn, *Persia and the Greeks*, 328; Georges, "Saving Herodotus' Phenomena," 49–50n; Hart, *Herodotus*, 76–77, 196; Lazenby, *Defence of Greece*, 173–75, 207, 227–28, 246–47. The most extensive discussion of the issue is that of Young, "480/479 B.C.," who

is followed by Balcer, *Persian Conquest,* 218–20. For the forces at the naval battle of Salamis see Labarbe, "Chiffres."

8. Fuller, *Alexander the Great,* 147–80; Bosworth, *Conquest and Empire,* 40–44, 58–62, 74–85; Green, *Alexander of Macedon.* 172–81, 226–35, 288–96; Lehmann, "Schlacht am Granikos"; Badian, "Granicus"; Hammond, "Battle of the Granicus River"; Janke, "Schlacht bei Issos"; Murison, Darius III"; Devine, "Grand Tactics"; Griffith, "Gaugamela"; Devine, "Battle of Gaugamela"; idem, "Macedonian Army."

9. E.g., Devine, "Demythologizing," and sources cited in note 8.

10. For other examples of number inflation in Greek historiography see Brown, *Timaeus of Tauromenium,* 71–73; Wiley, "Cunaxa and Xenophon"; and Dillery, *Xenophon,* 273n61.

11. On exaggerated estimates of the Carthaginian armies during the Second Punic War see Barreca, "Esserciti annibalici."

12. Livy, *War with Hannibal,* 149, 300. Livy's skillful use of numbers as palliation is treated in Rambaud, "Exemples de déformation."

13. Polybius, *Histories,* 2: 289–91 (III.117.1–6); Walbank, *Historical Commentary,* 1: 435–41.

14. E.g., Dorey, "Roman Casualty Figures"; Lazenby, *Hannibal's War,* 78–85; Caven, *Punic Wars,* 137–40; Schmitt, *Hannibals Siegeszug,* 238–47. Popular studies, e.g., Bradford, *Hannibal,* 114–16; Cottrell, *Enemy of Rome,* 128–29; and Lancel, *Carthage,* 390–91, tend to accept the highest reported numbers. Perhaps underlying the lower estimates is the fact that the ancients' numbers implied a killing rate of as high as 200 men per minute under impossible conditions; as the tactics are described, there would have greater and greater heaps of Roman bodies in a very small area, requiring a great deal of clambering to and fro by the Carthaginians. Indeed, the very notion of 70,000 or more bodies in such a confined area seems all but impossible. It is far more likely that the number of prisoners exceeded the dead, as at the battle of Tannenberg—the modern tactical equivalent of Cannae—in 1914: see Showalter, *Tannenberg.*

15. On this see Spean, "Hannibal's Mules."

16. Clerc, *Etudes critiques,* 34–37, 200–11; Völkl, "Taktischen"; Carney, "Marius' Choice of Battle-Field."

17. Donnadieu, "Campagne de Marius"; Demougeot, "L'invasion." Most of the details come from Plutarch's life of Marius: *Plutarch's Lives,* 9: 489–93, 503–5, 511–21, 531–39.

18. These are well discussed in Burns, "Calculating," 187–90. Hannestad, "Forces militaires," also addresses the case.

19. Bury, *Later Roman Empire,* 1: 104–5.

20. Gordon, *Age of Attila,* 107.

21. Groley, *Champs catalauniques!* 44–45, 50–51; Thompson, *Huns,* 154–55, 300. For references to the 750,000 and 300,000 figures see Thompson, "End of Roman Spain." The largest figures emanate from Hypatius, a contemporary chronicler: Burgess, *Chronicle of Hypatius,* 101. The battle has a long posthistory as well, in which high numbers feature: see Lukman, "Catalaunian Battle"; and Barnish, "Old Kaspars."

22. Parker, *Ancient China,* 31, 150–52; Bodde, *China's First Unifier,* 4–6; Loewe, "Campaigns," 90–97 (logistics); Bodde, "State and Empire," 98–100. For general questions see Yang, *Studies,* 75–84; Sima Qian, *Records,* 22–45; Sun Pin, *Military Methods,* 12–77, 246–61.

23. E.g., Walsh, *Livy.* 138–72, 197–200.

24. Herodotus, *Persian Wars,* 3: 505 (vii. 187). Here Herodotus engaged in the same kind of mathematical process that characterized Cook and Borah's attempt to estimate the contact population of central Mexico by way of the postcontact tributary codices discussed in chapter 4.

25. Young, "480/479 B.C.," 216–19, has a good discussion of why this alternative would have been unacceptable.

26. Maurice, "Size."

27. Not that any of this detracts from the fact that history is strewn with some fantastic numbers: perhaps the most outlandish, at least outside utopian writings, is the claim in an Armenian chronicle that Persian armies totaling 25,530,000 (Herodotus × 10) invaded Armenia during the A.D. 360s. See Hewsen, "Moses of Khoren," 59.

28. Young, "480/479 B.C.," 224–37.

29. Alexandrescu-Dersca, *Campagne de Timur,* 112–15; Matschke, *Schlacht bei Ankara,* 26–27. For the highest estimate see Langmantel, *Hans Schiltbergers Reisebuch,* 23–24.

30. Josephus, *Jewish War,* III.43.

31. E.g., Avi-Yonah, *The Holy Land,* 218–21 (who is otherwise quite credulous); Broshi, "Population de l'ancienne Jérusalem"; idem, "Estimating"; Hamel, *Poverty,* 137–40; Elsewhere (*Jewish War,* 6.420) Josephus added that the Romans killed 1.1 million Jews when they captured Jerusalem in A.D. 70. For a critique see Jeremias, *Jerusalem.*

32. Wilkinson, *Jerusalem,* 23; Reed, "Population Numbers," 206. Byatt, "Josephus," 53–55, strains especially hard to believe in these villages, finding it "by no means difficult to accept" the precise number. He then lists 14 of them by name and refers to "190 other villages and small towns, from a few hundreds to many thousands, but average of say, 1,500 each" to reach a population of 630,000 for Galilee, or about one-fifth of Josephus's implied minimum. Byatt's estimate of 2,665,000 for all of Palestine is "based on the figures of Josephus" (60).

33. Several estimates are arrayed conveniently in Byatt, "Josephus," 51–52; Avi-Yonah, *Holy Land,* 219–20; and Juster, *Juifs,* 1: 209–12.

34. A good example is Klausner, "How Many Jews?" Klausner was building a case for emigration to the newly established state of Israel, and he helped his cause by believing in Josephus's 204 villages and in every other number in the scriptural accounts, as well as by decreeing that if a certain number "is not a 'round' number, . . . it is not an exaggerated account." Along the way he displayed one of the more amusing characteristics of any movement. Those who had estimated low were mentioned without comment, but the three highest counters were characterized as "very careful," "important," and "great," respectively. His conclusion was virtually foreordained: Palestine "was populated and the land cultivated to an extent which to-day seems unbelievable." A similar case is that of Juster, *Juifs,* 209–12, who entitled his relevant section "The Numerical Importance of the Jews" and proceeded to make it come true.

35. E.g., Hamel, *Poverty,* 139; Broshi, "Role"; Applebaum, "Judaea," 376–77.

36. Raymond, "Signes urbains." Raymond constantly characterized his choices as "more reasonable" than others', on little other grounds than that they fit his Procrustean bed. See, as well, idem, "Population du Caire," where the basic argument is repeated.

37. Djandjgava, "Ways of Estimating," 65–66. Djandjgava (68) chose 1,500 to 1,600 as the number served by each bath in Cairo in the fifteenth century, largely to provide a corroborative total population by a different method. The true population of Baghdad at the time was probably between 200,000 and 600,000.

38. Lassner, *Topography,* 107. Other estimates of the number of baths in Baghdad ranged as high as 200,000 (ibid., 283).

39. Delia, "Population," 285. Once again, archaeology contradicts the chronicles: see Prominska, *Investigations.*

40. Djandjgava, "Ways of Estimating," 65.

41. Ibid., 66; Miquel, *Géographie humaine,* 153–87.

42. Russell, *Medieval Regions,* 203. Russell also adopted the expedient of estimating the whole from the unknown, but small, part, when he tried to calculate the size of the population of India in the seventh century on the basis of the monastic population there from figures provided by a Chinese pilgrim. Each step of the process involved providing actual numbers for vague accounts, forcing him to argue lamely at one point that "their numbers were in the same proportion as English clergy of 1377" (228–29). For several instances of Portuguese overestimates of Muslim cities see Aubin, "Chiffres." For underestimates see Doumani, "Political Economy."

43. Ancient Athens is treated in this way in Hansen, "Reflections."

44. Wilkinson, "Ancient Jerusalem."

45. Jeremias, "Einwohnerzahl Jerusalems," calculated the population of Jerusalem at 30,000 as an "upper limit," in part because of a "poor" water supply! For a sharp critique of using water supply calculations and amphitheater size to estimate ancient urban populations see Duncan-Jones, "City Population," 85–86. For the problematics of even a best-case scenario in this respect see Bruun, *Water Supply,* 97–114. For a related case see Amiran, *Early Arad,* 14–17.

46. Herodotus, *Persian Wars,* 1.178, assuming a stade of 600 feet. In 1990 fewer than twenty American cities were this large, and in about half these instances the area was a matter of administrative legerdemain unrelated to population size.

47. Bigwood, "Babylon." Pliny, *Natural History,* VI.xxx.121–22, more or less repeated Herodotus' figure and added that Babylon's successor city, Seleucia, numbered 600,000 people. For other ancient estimates of Babylon's size—all lower than Herodotus' but none by very much—see MacGinnis, "Babylon," 69–70.

48. Macqueen, *Babylon,* 155–60.

49. Historians are divided as to whether Herodotus' account, written in eyewitness style, was really that. Recent opinion tends to believe that it was, although the matter is not without contention. For the matter see, e.g., Macqueen, *Babylon,* 155; Ravn, *Babylon,* 84–87; MacGinnis, "Babylon," 67, 81–82; Rollinger, *Herodots babylonischer Logos,* 67–74; Arieti, *Discourses,* 172–77; Weitemeyer, *Herodots.*

50. Ravn, *Description,* 94.

51. Russell, "Pompeii."

52. Fiorelli, *Scavi,* 10–13.

53. Nissen, *Pompeianische Studien,* 374–79.

54. Beloch, "Città," 273–74.

55. Brion, *Pompeii and Herculaneum,* 111. A few studies estimated higher: Frank, *Economic History,* 245 (25,000); Cary, *History of Rome,* 625n6 (about 30,000, presumably following Nissen's lower maximum); and Tanzer, *Common People,* 2, who cited Nissen's higher, seasonal, estimate. The Michelin guide for Italy speaks of a population of "about 25,000."

56. Russell, *Control,* 1–8. Jongman, *Economy,* 108–12, thinks that based on an assumed proportion of city-dwellers to food-producers, even Eschenbach's estimate is too high for Pompeii proper. Less than two-thirds of the area of Pompeii consisted of buildings, whether residences or not: see Jashemski, "Gardens."

57. Suder, "Pompejów"; Wallace-Hadrill, *Houses and Society,* 92–103.

58. Fiorelli, *Scavi*, 14.

59. This is a concept that Wallace-Hadrill, *Houses and Society*, 95, rightly if optimistically characterized as "manifestly irrelevant." It was used by Frere, *Britannia*, 261, on the grounds that an amphitheater's seating capacity "might approximate to the adult population of [a] town," and more extensively in Forni, "Indagine." For early criticism of the notion see Latouche, "Aspect démographique," 684. Tacitus claimed that 50,000 people died when part of the amphitheater in the provincial town of Fidenae collapsed, a figure that a recent editor of Tacitus observed "will not bear a moment's examination." See Tacitus, *Annals*, IV.lxii–iii, in *Tacitus*, 4: 109–13; cf. Koestermann, *Cornelius Tacitus*, 2: 188–91. Ramsay, "Chroniclers' Estimates," 629, thought fifty a more likely number. The notion of size-population correlation can be dismissed simply by considering the sizes of cathedrals and parish churches in medieval western Europe vis-à-vis the communities they served.

60. Strocka, *Casa del labirinto*, 135–36. For arguments against this method see Wallace-Hadrill, *Houses and Society*, 96–97, 113–16.

61. This parlous state is emphasized for Ostia by Packer, "Housing and Population." Packer arrives at a population estimate about one-half that of previous ones.

62. E.g., Audin, "Population de Lugdunum," concluded that the city's population was "at most 40,000," in contrast to "the hundreds of thousands" advocated by earlier writers. Similar results are those of Jacoby, "Population de Constantinople" (from 1 million to 375,000). Thevenot, "Population des villes," 121–22, argued for higher numbers, but at the cost of redefining the concept of city.

63. Collingwood, "Town and Country."

64. Usher, "New Estimate," 674.

65. E.g., Randall, "Population and Agriculture."

66. Foord, *Last Age*, 66–67, immediately after noting that "[t]here are no solid grounds upon which to base any estimate of the population"; Wheeler, "Mr. Collingwood."

67. Collingwood and Myres, *Roman Britain*, 180, 181n; Frere, *Britannia*, 310–11; Jones, "Climate"; Salway, *Roman Britain*, 542–52. Archaeological evidence from newly discovered sites suggests that the figure might climb; for this see Higham, *Rome*, 18–21; Jones, *End of Roman Britain*, 13–17. At the same time, estimates of the number of Anglo-Saxon invaders has declined from about 100,000 or more to only 10,000: ibid., 17–32. For earlier periods, similar ranges of opinion seem to prevail: see Darvill, *Prehistoric Britain*, 160.

68. A number of such estimates are addressed in Gore, *Neglected Heroes*.

69. Scheidel, "Finances." Duncan-Jones, *Money and Government,* 16–19, propounds a similar argument.

70. Cook and Borah, "Hispaniola," 407.

71. Dobyns, "Reassessing," 9.

72. Burns, "Calculating," 187. Burns added an important point, which I discuss elsewhere, when he emphasized that high numbers are intrinsically no more unreliable that low ones—"the numbers are not less accurate simply because they have six digits rather than four" (188).

73. Rostovtzeff, *Social and Economic History,* 2: 1142–43.

74. A case that would be grist for any skeptic's mill was recently discussed by Conrad, "Arabs and the Colossus." Muslim historiography, followed by others, has it that the Arabs conquered Rhodes in the mid-seventh century and hauled away the remains of the fallen colossus. Estimates of the number of camels required ranged from 500 to 30,000, all impossibly high. Even worse, the dismantling and scrapping never took place!—fictional numbers applied to a fanciful situation. Cf. Maryon, "Colossus of Rhodes," 71–72, who considered that these numbers could "most probably, be accounted for by errors of transcription, assisted a little by wonder." For wildly variant estimates (150,000 to 900,000) of the population of Dahomey in the mid-nineteenth century see Herskovits, *Dahomey,* 2: 70–73.

Chapter 17: Epidemic Hyperbole

1. The trouble with epidemics, of the kind that leads to such estimates, is addressed in, e.g., Horden, "Disease, Dragons, and Saints," as well as in other papers in *E&I.*

2. Ayalon, "Population Estimates," 6, citing Poliak, "Demographic Evaluation," and al-Maqrizi, *Badhi al-Maᶜun.* In her *Cairo,* 37–38, Abu-Lughod tended toward high estimates for Cairo and Egypt generally, but found these particular figures to be "ludicrous exaggerations."

3. Ayalon, "Population Estimates," 1–19. Poliak's calculations evaded serious scrutiny for more than forty years.

4. Ibn Taghri Birdi, *History of Egypt,* 7: 92–95.

5. Wessely, "Peste d'Homère." Earlier, Krause, "Pest des Homer," identified it with pappataci fever.

6. Exodus 8:1–15:27.

7. Hoyte, "Plagues of Egypt."

8. Marr and Malloy, "Epidemiological Analysis," 21.

9. A similar view was held by, e.g., Hort, "Plagues of Egypt"; Ceccarelli, "Dieci piaghe d'Egitto."

10. Redford, "Perspective."

11. Van Seters, "Plagues of Egypt"; idem, *Life of Moses,* 77–112. See as well Cartun, "Who Knows Ten?"

12. E.g., Vater, "Plague"; Lee, "Genesis 1." See as well Fretheim, "Plagues." Each of these studies illustrates theological and rhetorical stimuli underlying the growth of the plague account to its final form.

13. These and other proposed identifications are discussed in Shrewsbury, *Plague of the Philistines,* 13–39.

14. Conrad, "Biblical Tradition," 281–82, 286.

15. Ibid., 287.

16. For inadvertently humorous examples see Levin, "Isaac's Blindness" (diabetic retinitis); Gordon, "Saul's Meningitis"; Schoental, "Mycotoxins"; Levin, "Speech Defect of Moses"; and Lieber, "Skin Diseases."

17. Since the Plague of Athens has drawn so much scholarly attention in the past thirty years, I mention a few recent studies—first those that attempt to diagnose the "plague" and then those that diagnose the text: Hopper, "Arenavirus"; Bellemore, Plant, and Cunningham, "Plague of Athens"; Morens and Littman, "Epidemiology"; idem, "Thucydides Syndrome"; Bellemore and Plant, "Thucydides"; Morgan, "Plague or Poetry?"; Swain, "Man and Medicine." On the early medieval view that "Aethiopia" (i.e., Africa) was the cradle of plague see, e.g., Allen, "'Justinianic' Plague," 6; Bratton, "Identity," 114–15.

18. Procopius, *History,* 1: 451–53 (II.xxii.1–5); cf. Cameron, *Procopius,* 40–43. Procopius's fixation with the miraculous is stressed in idem, "History as Text."

19. Procopius, *History,* 465 (II.xxiii.1). A contemporary, John of Ephesus, seemed to offer even higher numbers, topping off at 16,000 dead per day. See Bury, *Later Roman Empire,* 2: 64–65.

20. Lamb, *Constantinople,* 236.

21. Hollingsworth, *Historical Demography,* 366–67. Maas, *John Lydus,* 23, accepts Hollingsworth's calculations without comment.

22. Bratton, "Identity," 174–79. Although not citing a figure, Russell, "That Earlier Plague," implied a mortality in this range as well.

23. Downey, *Constantinople,* 20.

24. E.g., Stein, *Histoire,* 2: 759, accepted the figures in the sources and estimated that they represented a mortality rate of 40 percent to 50 percent. Mango, *Byzantium,* 68, reckoned that one-third of the population died but offered no specific numbers, while Diehl, *Justinien,* merely paraphrased Procopius and John of Ephesus. In contrast, although he ventures no numbers, Durliat, "Peste," deduces from epigraphic evidence that in the provinces the effects of the plague were "measured" and that the figures cited for Constantinople are "highly suspect."

25. Using a different sets of premises, Charanis, "Observations," 450, arrived as a figure of 675,000 casualties, which he then arbitrarily reduced by two-thirds—to reach a figure that "is not at all impossible." The population of Istanbul has been estimated numerous times since the Ottoman conquest. These are discussed—and reduced from as high as 1.2 million to as low as 212,000—in Stoianovich, "Cities," 61–68.

26. E.g., Fisher, "Theodora and Antonina"; Evans, "Justinian."

27. Procopius, *Secret History,* 89–90, 150.

28. Thus Procopius's trillion represents a number that is, by one account anyway, nearly ten times that of the total number of people who have ever lived on earth: see Haub, "How Many People?"

29. Allen, "The Justinianic Plague," 6; Evans, *Procopius,* 26–27; Cameron, *Procopius,* 40–43; Woodman, "Self-Imitation," 153.

30. For Thucydides' account as a stimulus for disease description well into modern times see Slack, "Introduction," in *E&I,* 9.

31. Conrad, "Arabic Plague Chronologies," 62, quoting al-Mada'ini (d. 840).

32. Ibid., 83, citing Ibn Abi Hajala (d. 1375). In his plague history Ibn Abi Hajala managed to discern exactly ten plagues, emulating the Exodus account.

33. Ibid., 86. Ibn Abi Hajala, at least, was suspicious, for he went on that a "similar description has already been given. . . . I do not know if it should be placed in this year [AH 131] . . . or whether it occurred as already mentioned.

34. *Islandske Annaler,* 223, 275, 404.

35. This is hardly peculiar to Muslim historians, of course; Gregory of Tours, to cite only one prominent example, had already done the same for the Franks.

36. Conrad, "Arabic Plague Chronologies," 92.

37. Conrad, "Taʿun and Waba," 272–73, 302.

38. Lucian, "How to Write History," in *Lucian.* 6: 23–25.

39. E.g., Gilliam, "Plague," 228–29n; Littman and Littman, "Galen," 243n.

40. E.g., Salmon, *Population et dépopulation,* 135. Debevoise, *Parthia,* 252, accepted this version, although without actually citing Lucian.

41. Woodman, "Self-Imitation," 153, regards the plague as "fictitious."

42. Hopkins, *Princes and Peasants.*

43. Ibid., 23, 166. For further details on this and the succeeding examples see Henige, "Early Epidemics."

44. Hopkins, *Princes and Peasants,* 17; Curtius Rufus, *History of Alexander,* 2: 450–51.

45. Hopkins, *Princes and Peasants*, 165–66; cf. Dols, "Plague," 375; Newby, "Abraha and Sennacherib"; Beeston, "Events in Arabia"; Kister, "Some Reports"; Simon, *Meccan Trade*, 52–55, 147–48n263. Even the reality of the campaign itself is in some doubt. Conrad, "Abraha and Muhammad," shows that the ascription of the campaign to 570 is merely a convention based on the number "40," Muhammad's age at the time of his first visions.

46. Karlen, *Plague's Progress*, 93–107 et passim, offers a more recent example of the apocalyptic penchant.

47. France, *Victory in the East*, 132.

48. Matthew of Edessa, "Chronique," 1: 33.

49. Matthew of Edessa, *Armenia*, 167–68, emphasis added.

50. For a particular example see Africa, "Worms and the Death of Kings," which treats the topos of phthiriasis to explain the deaths of particularly disliked rulers throughout history.

51. For other ancient examples see West, "Two Plagues"; Flintoff, "Noric Cattle Plague"; Todd, "*Famosa pestis.*" Even some eighteenth-century incidents were phantom, e.g., the alleged smallpox epidemic among the Miami Indians: see Peyser, "It Was Not Smallpox." The epidemic reappears in Rafert, *Miami Indians*, 29.

52. Denton, *Brief Description*, 6–7, emphases in original. John Smith had much the same to say about the epidemics that struck the Powhatans during the early years of the Jamestown colony: Smith, *Generall Historie*, 229.

53. For New Testament analogies see Amundsen and Ferngren, "Perception." Fernando Colón (*Life*, 150) attributed the decline of the Taino population on Hispaniola to "the favor of God, calculated to offset the disparity in numbers." For the general context see Entralgo, *Enfermedad*.

54. Studies of examples of this attitude abound; a sampling of modern studies, in roughly chronological order, would include Stark, "Epidemics"; Leven, "*Arthumia* and *Philanthrôpia*," 2: 393–407; Conrad, "Epidemic Disease"; idem, "Taᶜun and Waba"; Kroll and Bachrach, "Sin and Etiology"; Dols, "Comparative Communal Responses"; Ober and Alloush, "Plague at Granada"; Cipolla, *Faith, Reason, and the Plague*, 1–29; and Achinstein, "Plagues and Publication." Among the church fathers, whose works would have been familiar to the missionary chroniclers, see especially Cyprian, *Treatises*, 211–21, on an epidemic in Carthage in the 250s.

55. Jones, "Plague and Its Metaphors," demonstrates at some length how the "social imaginary" of that time, and ours, led "both contemporaries and historians to overestimate the impact of the disease, which provided an all too convenient catchall category and scapegoat for epidemiological and other catastrophes."

Chapter 18: Careful Errors

1. Cook and Simpson, *Population of Central Mexico,* 19. Crosby, "Conquistador y Pestilencia," 333, argues that the High Counters' estimates for central Mexico serve to "strengthen confidence in Motolinía's general veracity," effectively closing the circle.

2. Cook and Simpson, *Population of Central Mexico.* Evidently, for Cook and Simpson "ignore" and "accept" are the only two possible responses.

3. Ibid., 19–22.

4. For a discusssion see Henige, "Their Numbers Become Thick," 173–75.

5. Cook and Borah, "Materials," 12. For examples of such reliance see Henige, "Their Numbers Become Thick," 174–75.

6. Cook and Borah, "Materials," 12. Phelan, *Millennial Kingdom,* 143n11, found Cook and Borah's arguments at least suggestive. Noting that "[u]ntil recently, most scholars had dismissed Motolinía's figures as a pious exaggeration and a consequence of the friars' alleged faulty bookkeeping of baptismal records," he concluded that they might have exaggerated "somewhat" the number of conversions. For more jaundiced views see Baudot, "Amerindian Image," and Stephan, "Fray Toribio Motolinía," 97–100.

7. Dobyns, "Estimating," 405, emphasis added.

8. Motolinía, *Historia,* 126. Cf. more of the same in Motolinía's letter to Charles V of 3 January 1555, in Motolinía, *Memoriales,* 405, which made explicit comparison with biblical population figures. Cf. Ybot León, *Iglesia,* 1: 646–50.

9. Dobyns, "Estimating," citing Rosenblat, *Población indígena,* 1: 97n1. Rosenblat, who was actually dubious of all these numbers (ibid., 1: 96–100), in turn cited Chávez, *Pedro de Gante,* by way of yet another modern source.

10. Chávez, *Pedro de Gante,* 175. Rosenblat, *Poblacion indígena,* 97n1, has "other companions."

11. García Icazbalceta, *Bibliografía,* 101. The Latin expression is "[e]t baptizavimus ego cum socio fratre meo." This fuller, more explicit, sense is observed in Torre Villar, "Fray Pedro de Gante," 52. Cf. Verlinden, "Fray Pedro de Gante," 105–8.

12. Pedro de Gante to the Fathers, Brothers, and Sisters of the Province of Flanders, dd 27 June 1529, in García Icazbalceta, *Bibliografía,* 103. López de Gómara, *Conquista,* 2: 281, spoke of "two priests" who baptized "15,000" people at Xochimilco, either another case or one of those mentioned or implied earlier. López de Gómara went on to speak of "a Franciscan friar" who had, "himself alone," baptized 400,000 people, "although

over many years." Contrast this claim with the testimony of a Capuchin missionary in Kongo that "the number of baptisms in three years has been from fifteen to sixteen thousand"; he lamented that "it would have been considerably more had the missionaries been in greater numbers" (relation of Giuseppe da Busseto [1675], in Jonghe and Simar, *Archives congolaises,* 68). At the time there were about twenty missionaries in Kongo, yet, according to this report, they were unable to baptize in three years many more than two priests purportedly could baptize in one day in New Spain. Lopetegui and Zubillaga, *Historia,* 319, expressed an ambivalent—even paradoxical—view of these baptismal figures when they wrote: "Even reduc[ing] to a third the numbers indicated by these chroniclers of undeniable veracity, missionary efficiency seems extraordinary." Baptizing thousands in a single day is not unheard of in Christian tradition; e.g., Pope Gregory I, *Registrum Epistularum,* 551, credited St. Augustine with baptizing "more than 10,000" English on Easter of 598 and urged other bishops to heed his example.

13. Dobyns, "Estimating," 405. That is, he might have taken heart, and flight, in Gante's "frequently."

14. Dobyns, "Estimating," 444; see chapter 5.

15. See especially Ceccherelli, "Bautismo."

16. And one that caused much concern in official circles. For the Philippines, where Magellan's instant conversion attempts in 1521 aroused much theological handwringing in Spain, see Phelan, "Pre-Baptismal Instruction." More generally, see Fernández Rodríguez, *Dominicos,* 178–84.

17. Ricard, *Spiritual Conquest,* 85.

18. Ibid., 91.

19. Ibid., 91–92, with brackets as in original. Cf. Sylvest, *Franciscan Mission Theory,* 113.

20. Motolinía, *Historia,* 123–29. He repeated much the same account is his *Memoriales,* 123–24.

21. Or were the robes only for the select few? Motolinía's syntax leaves us in doubt.

22. See Baudot, *Utopia,* 276–79.

23. See, e.g., Gutiérrez Vega, *Primeras juntas,* 269–72.

24. Wagner and Parish, *Life and Writings,* 98–99; Greenleaf, *Zumárraga* 46–47; Gil, *Primeras doctrinas,* 221–30. The problem of hasty baptism without sufficient preparation continued to plague the mission field. In the early seventeenth century, for instance, Alonso de Sandoval criticized the Jesuits in west-central Africa for permitting inadequately instructed, but baptized, Africans to be sent to the Americas. See Sandoval, *De Instauranda,* 327–433 et passim.

25. E.g., Phelan, *Hispanization,* 54–55; Klor de Alva, "Spiritual Con-

flict," 360; Reff, *Disease,* 150, 157, 171–75, 210. As Ronda, "We Are Well as We Are," pointed out, this initial enthusiasm was often eventually replaced by doubt and resistance when the Indians realized that being baptized did not protect them from the new diseases.

26. Cline, "Spiritual Conquest," 477.

27. Cline's article is based on her contribution to *Book of Tributes.* There (43) Cline had stated that "a very small proportion" (4 percent and 9 percent, respectively) of the population of two locales was listed as baptized. She regarded this as evidence that the census was from the early 1530s (ibid., 8), but this flirts with circular argument, since it could just as easily be regarded as evidence that the missionary accounts of mass conversions outran the facts. Considerably more such local detail will be necessary before one or the other conclusion can approach competitive plausibility. McCaa, "Child Marriage," 3, agrees that the villages in question were "virtually untouched by the reformist zeal of Europeans."

28. Lockhart, *Nahuas,* 205.

29. Vaca de Castro to Philip II, 30 April 1565, *La Iglesia de España en el Perú* 2 (1944): 295; Borges, *Métodos misionales,* 461. Cf. Armas Medina, *Cristianización,* 243–67.

30. Borges, *Métodos,* 462–63.

31. For more on the millennarian perspective of the early missionaries in the New World see Phelan, *Millennial Kingdom;* Ricard, *Conquest;* and Sala Catala and Vilchis Reyes, "Apocalíptica española."

32. Using much smaller figures and estimates, which they take to be accurate, Guerra and Sánchez-Téllez, "Missionary Reports," conclude, rather unsurprisingly, that "the decline of the Indian population differed widely according to the lay of the land, population density, and agricultural resources."

33. Anguiano, *Misiones capuchinas,* 446. Kilger, "Taufpraxis"; Saccardo, *Congo e Angola,* 1: 491–92.

34. Guebels, *Jérôme de Montesarchio,* 203; Saccardo, *Congo e Angola,* 2: 43–44. For an even lower set of personal figures—about 2,500 per year from 1691 to 1701—see Rainero, *Congo,* 76–77. For other modest figures (20,000 all told), see Leitão, "Missão," 79.

35. Jadin, "Aperçu," 354, 389. Oddly, Savona claimed that he performed only 37,000 marriages during the same period. Jadin (354) regarded these numbers as "astonishing" but apparently not necessarily wildly inaccurate.

36. Ibid., 354.

37. Duarte Lopes to Sixtus V, 24 February 1588, in Brásio, *Monumenta missionaria africana,* 358–61; Cuvelier and Jadin, *Ancien Congo,*

166–70. Brásio thought the figure "clearly exaggerated," whereas Cuvelier and Jadin cited other figures in support of accepting it themselves.

38. Thornton, "Demography and History," 507n, mentions several of these, as does Toso, "Relazioni," 97–103. In addition see Jadin, "Aperçu," 354–57. For the nineteenth century see Filesi, "Epilogo."

39. Cuvelier, "Conversion."

40. Jadin, "Aperçu," 388. In the process Savona totaled the kingdom province by province, arriving at a slightly different, but hardly more likely, figure of 5,290,000, not counting the capital city of São Salvador (378–90). One must wonder where all these people lived. Thornton, *Kingdom of Kongo*, 38–39, notes that except for São Salvador, "the rural *mbanza* [towns] were scarcely more than overgrown villages"; even the seat of one of the most important provincial chiefs was "little more than a small collection of buildings." Cf. ibid., 54.

41. Jadin, "Aperçu," 355.

42. Cf. Toso, "Relazioni," 97–103, for further doubts about doubting.

43. Jadin, "Aperçu," 355.

44. Ibid., 357. See also Jadin, "Survivances." The title of this article derives from Jadin's belief in the higher figures of the eighteenth century as compared with the—therefore—much lower figures from the mid-nineteenth century and later.

45. Randles, *Ancien royaume,* 146–48.

46. Ibid., 147; cf. Giuseppe da Busseto in Jonghe and Simar, *Archives congolaises,* 67.

47. Randles, *Ancien royaume,* 147. Randles added in a footnote that he did not know how Jadin had "arrived at the number of six million," failing to note that it was Savona who contradicted himself.

48. Another familiar pattern was an inability of the missionaries to count themselves accurately. For an example of this see Giovanni Francesco da Roma's report, dated 1655, in Jonghe and Simar, *Archives congolaises,* 41–42. Frequent companions of large numbers of baptisms were claims about the advanced ages of many of the proselytized. This phenomenon occurs in the Capuchins' accounts of Kongo and neighboring Angola, where they were wont to speak of individuals allegedly as aged as 130 years. For examples see Giovanni Francesco da Roma, *Fondation,* 104, 104n. For the issue generally, and the mistaken belief placed in accounts of advanced centenarians in certain areas of the world, see Davies, *Centenarians;* Mazess and Forman, "Longevity"; Freeman, "Charlie Smith"; Garson, "Centenarian Question." These findings are ignored in works such as Milich, *Stranger's Supper.*

49. Thornton, "Demography and History," 507–30; idem, "Baptismal Register." Inevitably, Thornton was forced to declare certain assump-

tions as to the representativeness of his sample that he could not show to be true.

50. For a generally gloomy view of the value of the high encompassing numbers of the Capuchins, though not of the annually reported local figures, see Filesi and Villapadierna, *Mission antiqua*, 40–47.

51. Schurhammer, "Taufen," 37–38.

52. Ibid., 40–64.

53. Pedro Gonçalves, Cochin, to Ignacio de Loyola, 24 January 1555, in Wicki, *Documenta Indica*, 257. Gonçalves put his personal numbers at "more than 200,000." Cf. Quere, *Christianity in Sri Lanka*, 109–11, 166–67.

54. Schurhammer, "Bekehrung"; idem, *Francis Xavier*, 2: 300n31; 3: 187n255; Platenkam, "Tobelo, Moro, Ternate," 63; Schreurs, *Caraga Antigua*, 177–201; Jacobs, *Documenta malucensia*, 24n.

55. Boxer, *Fidalgos*, 175–76. Boxer drolly added that "[t]he lower estimate is the most likely to be the true one." Cf. Leitão, *Portugueses*, 75–87, 165–71, 183–91.

56. For the Philippines, where some early estimates exaggerated by as much as fivefold, see Gutiérrez, *Domingo de Salazar*, 57–63; and Sánchez Fuertes, "Franciscanos."

57. Phelan, *Millennial Kingdom*, 48.

58. A countertradition, however, spoke of smaller numbers: e.g., in the third century Origen, *Contra Celsum*, 133, wrote that "a few, whose number could easily be enumerated, have died occasionally for the sake of the Christian religion," since on the whole, "[God] always fought for them and from time to time stopped the opponents of the Christians and the people who wanted to kill them." Clearly the arguments about the number of martyrs could take opposite roads on behalf of roughly the same objective.

59. Hertling, "Zahl der Märtyrer." Hertling, "Zahl der Christen" and "Zahl der Katholiken," also estimated, by means of extrapolating from the fragmentary data in the literary sources (which remained unglossed), the number of Christians at various times in the first four centuries. For examples of fiction and exaggeration in the martyrologies see Barnes, *Diocletian and Constantine*, 175–91, and Davies, "Origin and Purpose."

60. Laures, "Zahl der Christen," 97. See Schütte, *Introductio*, 434–46, for an overview.

61. Laures, "Zahl der Christen," 97–101. For further details, and the numbers between 1614 and 1650 (2,128), see Boxer, *Christian Century*, 334–35, 448; and Brou, "Statistiques."

62. Boxer, *Christian Century*, 320–21, 492; Murdoch, *History of Japan*, 2/1: 70–73, 86–89, 237; Elison, *Deus Destroyed*, 54–55; Lach and Van Kley, *Asia*, 3/1: 171–72. Laures, "Zahl der Christen," 85–95, suggested divers

ways of calculating this figure, all of which presume an unlikely degree of representativeness in the surviving sources.

63. Brou, "Statistiques," 369–84. As Brou pointed out, totaling the available annual statistics for these areas almost invariably produces much smaller sums, suggesting that the exaggerated totals were no more than inspired guesses.

64. Ibid., 384.

65. For evidence that counting the baptized was difficult even in modern times see Benedict, "Catholics and Huguenots."

66. Taber, "Missionary Movement," 16. A similar agument has been made for the Kongo data discussed earlier: see Mudimbe-Boye Mbulamuanza, *Vocabulaire.*

67. A recent study that encapsulates and notes earlier literature is Peel, "Missionary Narratives."

Chapter 19: Numbering the Imaginary/Imagining Numbers

1. Tyssot du Patot, *Voyages,* 172–73, 269.

2. Extended studies of this phenomenon include Tieje, "Peculiar Phase"; idem, "Expressed Aims"; Adams, *Travel Literature,* 81–102 et passim; and sources cited in note 4.

3. Bunyan, *Pilgrim's Progress.* This virtually paraphrases the self-contradictory comments of Bartolomé de las Casas regarding the decline of the Taino population of Hispaniola; see Henige, "Contact Population."

4. The following works are, or contain, discussions of the various authenticating techniques. This is only a small sampling of the literature, designed merely to suggest the temporal and spatial magnitude of the phenomenon: Foley, *Telling the Truth;* Stadter, "Fictional Narrative"; Wiseman, "Lying Historians"; Laird, "Fiction"; Olsen, "Prologue"; Morse, *Truth and Convention;* Beltrán Llavador, et al., *Historias y ficciones;* Gómez-Montero, "¿Cuento, fábula, patraña o novela?"; Rothstein, "When Fiction Is Fact"; Marais, "Omnipotent Fantasies"; Racault, "Jeux de la vérité"; idem, *Utopie,* 310–24; Mylne, *Eighteenth-Century Novel,* 20–32 et passim; Beer, *Narrative Conventions;* Green, *Medieval Listening,* 237–58; Adams, *Travel Literature.*

5. Quintana, *Jonathan Swift,* 304; Downie, *Jonathan Swift,* 266–71.

6. An instance very much akin to Tyssot's is the effort of Dobyns, *Number,* 174–85, to extrapolate Timucuan population from a few estimates of small bodies of fighting men.

7. In particular compare this with chapter 4. For further on Tyssot, see Friederich, *Australia,* 23–25; Moors, "Imaginary Voyages," 12; Rosenberg, *Tyssot du Patot,* 101–34; Ronzeaud, "Formes et Enjeux."

8. A recent discussion, with useful bibliographical information, is that of Naddaf, "Atlantis Myth."

9. From time to time in this chapter I will engage in these arithmetical exercises. These are not intended to be serious attempts to calculate any of the populations in question but merely illustrate the use of this technique, so fundamental to the High Counters' methodology.

10. Plato, *Critias*, 119a.

11. Ibid., 119b.

12. Kukal, *Atlantis*, 33–36, performs a similar set of operations based on somewhat different premises and with consequently different results.

13. More, *Utopia*, 43, 55.

14. In this calculation, 13 is the average number of adults $(10 + 16 \div 2)$, including grown children and parents; x represents the total number of minor children, and y, the population of the surrounding countryside.

15. Britain's population at the time is generally estimated to have been less than 4 million: see Wrigley and Schofield, *Population History*. For the geographical similarities between Utopia and Britain see Parks, "More's Utopia."

16. More, *Utopia*, 45.

17. This is reminiscent of Inca Garcilaso de la Vega, who, in his *La Florida del Ynca*, included the most unlikely sets of measurements, allegedly by grace of his putative, but unnamed, informant. Henry Dobyns used these measurements to help calculate the Indian population of Florida at the time of the de Soto expedition. See Henige, "*La Florida del Ynca.*"

18. E.g., two islands described as about 2,000 square miles in extent each had more than 200 villages and, respectively, 9 and 11 larger cities: see Smeeks, *Krinke Kesmes*, 42, 44.

19. Davis, *Utopia*, 272–75. For more on Noland see Patrick, "Free State of Noland."

20. To bolster the claim, Foigny, *Terre australe*, resorted to the authenticating detail that characterizes the genre: the manuscript was "a kind of book made in folios, a half a foot long, six fingers wide, and two fingers thick." The work has recently been translated into English and annotated, as *Southern Land*.

21. Foigny, *Terre australe*, 71.

22. Ibid., lxx–lxxii, 71n. Ronzeaud, *Utopie*, 264–70, discusses at length Foigny's "mathematical game" and its underlying symbolism. See also Knen, "Utopie"; Demoris, "Utopie"; Ronzeaud, *Utopie hermaphrodite*, 264–65; Benrekassa, *Concentrique*; Fausett, *Writing the New World*, 130–44; Fonzeaud, "Formes et enjeux."

23. Foigny, *Terre australe*, 203.

24. Ibid., 71–72, 177 et passim; Ronzeaud, *Utopie*, 265–71. He even

provided details on the size of the flying Urgs who transported him to the austral land: Foigny, *Terre australe,* 184–85.

25. Using three miles per league, the unit of measure in the source.

26. Collin de Plancy, *Voyage.*

27. Harington, *Oceana,* 95.

28. Diderot, *Bijoux,* 159.

29. Fox, *Account,* 10.

30. For a real-time study that approaches Fox's argument, however unwittingly, see Butlin, *Our Original Aggression;* idem, *Economics and the Dreamtime.*

31. Casanova, *Icosameron,* 33.

32. Ibid., 62.

33. As might be expected, population tended to increase rapidly on Protocosmo. The titular couple of the tale alone produced 4 million descendants before they died: Ibid., 233.

34. See Diament, "Voies souterraines."

35. For the use of the Americas in utopian writings see, among others, Adams, "Outer Space."

36. Crowe, *Extraterrestrial Life Debate.*

37. Dick, *Celestial Scenery,* 276–80.

38. Dick, *Sidereal Heavens,* 290–91.

39. Read, *Green Child,* 118–19.

40. Baum, *Emerald City,* 29–30.

41. Bradshaw, *Goddess of Atvatabar.* This technique is oddly reminiscent of certain information in Marco Polo's account, particularly his description of Quinsay (the modern Hangchow). Polo's potpourri of apparently irrelevant, but precise, details persuaded Hollingsworth, *Historical Demography,* 245–47, to propose an estimate of "several million" as the population of the city in the 1270s. Marco Polo is perhaps a dangerous guide, though. The credibility of parts of his account has been repeatedly challenged lately, most comprehensively by Wood, *Marco Polo.* Wood argues that Polo did not even reach Mongolia. For another famous case, Jules Verne's use of the persuasive detail, see Hammerton, "Verne's Amazing Journeys."

42. Bradshaw. *Goddess of Atvatabar,* 73, 94, 250, 265. Some might recognize a certain similarity here with some early descriptions of central Mexico.

43. Samuel, *Unknown Land,* 69, with map opposite.

44. Assuming that its greatest width was twice its average width.

45. Samuel, *Unknown Land,* 69.

46. Senkovsky, *Baron Brambeus,* 102, 105.

47. Alkon, *Origins,* 131–37; idem, *Science Fiction before 1900,* 64–65.

48. Neville, *Isle of Pines,* t.p.; Aldridge, "Polygamy," 464–72; Rennie, *Far-Fetched Facts,* 66–68; Boesky, *Founding Fictions,* 141–61.

49. Nicolson, *Pitcairners.*

50. Terrell, *Prehistory,* 188–95.

51. It was first published in London in 1675. Veiras (or Vairasse) was a Frenchman resident in England, and two years later his work was republished in French at Paris.

52. Veiras d'Allais, *Sevarambians,* 1: 177. For this work see Fausett, *Writing the New World,* 113–29; Ronzeaud, "Formes et enjeux"; Mühll, *Denis Veiras,* 159–63.

53. Macaulay, *Orphan Island,* 24, 69. This striking increase did not prevent the local authority from expressing disappointment: "They haven't increased as much as one would have expected."

54. Tiphaigne de la Roche, *Histoire des Galligènes,* 72–78.

55. Such impossibly high population growth rates are reminiscent of similar arguments advanced more seriously by those intent on accepting a biblically based creation date. For instance, William Whiston projected back to Noah by starting off with a doubling of population every four hundred years and ending by having it double in less than every ten years in immediate postdiluvian times: Whiston, *Short View,* 65–67.

56. Holmesby, *Voyages.*

57. This unspoken agreement to treat Middle-Earth as "real" recalls the treatment accorded the Sherlock Holmes canon; for the extent of this see DeWaal, *World Bibliography,* and Baring-Gould, *Annotated Sherlock Holmes.*

58. Loback, "Kindreds," 34–38, 56.

59. See note 6, this chapter.

60. Loback, "Orc Hosts," 10–16, 26.

61. Ibid., 16; punctuation as in original.

62. Ibid.

63. Rennie, *Far-Fetched Facts,* 58 et passim.

64. A relevant debate that between Ahern, "Certification," and Reff, "Anthropological Analysis." Reff thinks that the relación of Fray Marcos de Niza, a highly fantasized text, has demographic utility.

65. Leonard, *Books of the Brave;* Weckmann, *Medieval Heritage.*

66. Rodríguez de Montalvo, *Amadís de Gaula,* 2: 364, 563. And, although no populations figures were given for Insula Firme, it was noted that it was "populated by so many . . . people."

67. See González, "Realismo y simbolismo"; Pierce, *Amadís de Gaula,* 151–55.

68. Just as visiting a place that we have only imagined thenceforth forces the imagination to operate within the bounds of any memory of that place.

69. Thus, e.g., an account of Antangil, published anonymously in 1616, described the kingdom as having 120 provinces, each with 100 cities, each of them divided in turn into groups ranging from 10 to 10,000: Lachèvre, *Antangil,* 39–40. Note the usual symmetry, not unlike that which Means, *Ancient Civilizations,* applied to the Inca state. Then there was Anatole France's anti-utopian Penguin Island, where all the excesses of rampant capitalism flourished—so much so that "fifteen million men labored in one giant town" (France, *Ile des Pingouins,* 416).

70. For this expedient see especially Mylne, *Eighteenth Century Novel,* and Adams, *Travel Literature.*

71. Means, *Ancient Civilizations,* 296; italics in original.

72. By Dobyns, "Estimating," 406.

73. See, e.g., Olmedillas de Pereiras, *Pedro Martir.*

74. Martin, *Keepers of the Game,* 47–65 et passim.

75. Ibid. In search of a larger audience Martin also wrote "War."

76. Especially Krech, *Indians.* For a critique of Krech's approach as "negative" see Dunnell, "Americanist Archaeological Literature," 518–20. Such covering arguments are spectacularly vulnerable to the countercase. The magnitude of the carnage in bison at the Head-Smashed-In site in southen Alberta, antedating the arrival of Europeans by more than a millennium, suggests that slaughter for its own sake was hardly unknown. Estimates are that the remains of at least 123,000 bison are at the site, implying that they were hunted on "a nearly industrial scale for many centuries." See Fagan, *Time Detectives,* 58–74; Frison, *Prehistoric Hunters.*

77. Martin, *American Indian;* idem, *Spirit of the Earth.* Cf. Sayre, "Beaver."

78. Exemplified, e.g., by Booth and Jacobs, "Ties That Bind," and more recently by Grinde and Johansen, *Ecocide of Native America.* In the latter (28) the great bison kills are attributed only to postcontact times, when the Indians had horses at their disposal.

79. For the argument that the Indians never possessed a "uniformly . . . genuine attitude of respect towards animals," and for nature generally, see Désveaux, "Indiens." See also Denevan, "Pristine Myth," and Butzer, "Ecology."

80. Belich, *Making Peoples,* 33–34; Gill, *Extinct Birds,* 15.

81. Anderson, *Prodigious Birds,* 131–34, 178–87. Then there is the case of the cloak of Kamehameha I, which is estimated to contain the feathers of 80,000 *mamos*—small wonder that the bird is "now extinct" (Te Rangi Hiroa, *Arts and Crafts,* 230–31). See also Athens and Ward, "Environmental Change"; Kirch, "Microcosmic Histories"; and Steadman, "Prehistoric Extinctions."

82. One particularly insistent strain, well known to the chroniclers of

the Indies, consisted of various medieval accounts of China. For instance, Marco Polo and Odoric de Pordenone described the city of Quinsay/Cansay as being 100 miles in circumference, with 12,000 bridges, each guarded by numerous soldiers, and 1,600,000 hearths (Polo) or 890,000 hearths, each with ten to twelve households (Odoric): Yule, *Cathay,* 2: 192–99. See note 41, this chapter.

83. For the influence of More's *Utopia* on Inca Garcilaso see Durán Luzio, "Tomás Moro," and Zamora, *Language,* 129–65.

Chapter 20: How Many Wrongs Make a Right?

1. In emphasizing this, I mean to suggest that an interpretation might eventually be proved correct by virtue of a different set of arguments.

2. Haley, *Roots,* 685, ellipsis in original.

3. Mills and Mills, "Roots," 9, emphasis in original.

4. Wright, "Uprooting Kinta Kinte"; Nobile, "Uncovering *Roots.*" Wright interviewed many of those whom Haley had named as informants, only to discover that they freely admitted to having misled Haley on virtually every point.

5. The nature and implications of this are treated in Taylor, "Griot from Tennessee."

6. Bernal, *Black Athena, I.*

7. Much of this occurred in the form of a flurry of published panel or symposia presentations: see, for instance, "The Challenge of *Black Athena,*" a special issue of *Arethusa* (Fall 1989) (seven papers plus responses); "Forum," *Arethusa* 25 (1992), 181–214 (one paper plus response); Keita, "*Black Athena,* 'Race,' Bernal and Snowden"; *Journal of Mediterranean Archaeology* 3 (1990), 53–137, 247–82 (seven papers plus responses); *American Historical Review* 97 (1992), 440–64 (two papers); and *Journal of Women's History* 5 (1993), 83–135 (five papers plus responses). See also Lefkowitz and Rogers, *Black Athena Revisited.*

8. However, the view that Bernal correctly identified early "racism" is hardly unanimous; see, for instance, Palter, "Historiography," Blok, "Proof and Persuasion," and Lefkowits, *Not Out of Africa,* who show that Bernal treated the work of a central figure in his argument very tendentiously

9. Herodotus' work has been the cynosure of a great deal of scholarly interest of late. Opposite extremes are represented by Fehling, *Herodotus,* and Pritchett, *Liar School.* Fehling claims that Herodotus was in no small measure a hoaxer, while Pritchett attempts to refute Fehling point by point. These two works are an interesting example of how the same sources can glint very differently depending on the light cast on them.

10. Bernal to *New York Review of Books*, 28 September 1989, 75. Symptomatically, Bernal turns this argument on its head in trying to antedate the development of the Greek alphabet by several centuries.

11. I venture to say that many Chinese historians would be astounded at the way in which Bernal attempts to date the end of the Xia dynasty, usually regarded as at least semimythical, on the basis of one of the dates postulated for the eruption of Thera; see *Black Athena, II,* 281–84, 307–9, 310–11. No less astounding is his view that "I see no reason why educated Egyptians should not have known of America at the time of Plato in the early 4th century [B.C.] or that of Solon in the late sixth [B.C.]" (298). (In fact, if Solon lived at all, he died before 560 B.C.)

12. Although this willingness is somewhat mitigated by his occasional tactic of deflecting criticism solely on the grounds that his critics are culturally prevented from appreciating his reasoning.

13. Allen, "*Black Athena*," 21.

14. This and other points are made in Palter, "*Black Athena*." The range of journals in which reviews and other comments have appeared is extraordinary, from popular news and opinion weeklies to African literature to women's studies to the *Quarterly Journal of Speech*. In April 1996 an Internet listserve emerged devoted entirely to discussion of *Black Athena* and its critics (athena-discussion@info.harpercollins.com).

15. Freeman, *Margaret Mead*.

16. Marcus, "One Man's Mead," 3.

17. Although largely exhausted, the debate lingers on. At its peak in the mid-1980s it consumed large sections of *Pacific Studies* 7 (1984), 91–196; 7 (1983–84), 118–56; and two full numbers of *Canberra Anthropology* 6 (1983) 1–192, as well as numerous other articles and reviews, including in such unlikely venues as *American Scholar, Academic Questions,* and *Skeptical Inquirer,* as well as most of the news weeklies. It has even generated three books: Holmes, *Quest;* Côté, *Adolescent Storm;* and Orans, *Not Even Wrong*.

18. Shankman, "Samoan Sexual Conduct."

19. See especially Wilmsen and Denbow, "Paradigmatic History," followed by several comments and Wilmsen and Denbow's reply; Lee and Guenther, "Oxen or Onions?"; Wilmsen, "Search"; Lee and Guenther, "Errors."

20. Lee and Guenther, "Problems."

21. In his "Search," Wilmsen is responding to Lee and Guenther's "Oxen." See Dickens, "The Case of the !Kung"; and Wilmsen, "Mutual Dependence."

22. For a debate concerning the size of population in the area at the turn of the twentieth century see Lau, "Uncertain Certainties"; Dedering, "German-Herero War."

23. Wilmsen and colleagues have also advanced an archaeological case. This debate is only the latest of many skirmishes regarding the role of the San in evolutionary and nonevolutionary schemata. For this see Barnard, *Kalahari Debate.*

24. Ironically, for instance, by his difficulties with printed sources Wilmsen might have weakened a stronger case from archaeology, although Sadr, "Kalahari Archaeology," argues that archaeological evidence is presently "insufficient" to support Wilmsen's case.

25. Simon, "Review," 167.

26. See "Communications," *American Historical Review* 88 (1983), 1143–49; Bowen, "Stormy Weather"; Winkler, "Brouhaha."

27. Hayes, "History in an Off Key."

28. As part of his defense Abraham arrayed his translations and paraphrases alongside the originals, which proved to support his arguments in any case.

29. E.g., "David Abraham Case"; various authors, "David Abraham's *The Collapse of the Weimar Republic,*" *Central European History* 17 (1984), 159–293; Abraham, "Business Wars"; idem, "Big Business."

30. Novick, *That Noble Dream,* 616–17.

31. Turner, "Peter Novick."

32. On the SABR listserve in 1996 and 1997 there was an intensive colloquy regarding the extent to which the errors (one estimate was of 500, 100 of them major) in Ken Burns's television documentary "Baseball" could be excused in the cause of art. A consensus was quickly reached that careless art had no place in something that called itself a documentary.

33. It is surely no exaggeration to say that many fewer than one percent of those who saw and/or read *Roots* have seen or read any of its refutations. While this is probably a greater disparity than usual in such cases, it remains that it is very rare for refutations to achieve the same degree of exposure as the claims they overturn.

34. An exchange on the use of evidence that is reminiscent of Abraham's case in its early stages is Shank, "Galileo's Day in Court"; Biagioli, "Playing with the Evidence"; and Shank, "How Shall We Practice History?"

35. Such a debate, now going strong, is that between Marshall Sahlins and Gananath Obeyesekere concerning the reasons why the Hawaiians killed Captain Cook. The principals have argued in books, and acolytes in book reviews, with utterly no likelihood of resolution, making it clear again that the modern perceptions of this occasion are far more weighty than the originals. For a useful review by a confessed outsider see Hacking, "Aloha, Aloha"; Brofsky, "Cook, Lono." Yet another debate, conducted on a smaller stage, rages over Ramón Gutiérrez's acclaimed *When Jesus Came.* In particular, see

the dozen commentaries in *American Indian Culture and Research Journal* 17 (1993), 141–77, esp. 143–50, 154–72, where Gutiérrez's use and interpretation of sources is vehemently criticized.

36. And those who do discuss it seem undisturbed by its unmasking; see, e.g., Courlander, "Kunta Kinte's Struggle," and Moore, "Routes."

37. A recent case, and one that relates directly to statistical procedures, is discussed in Peterson, "Re-Evaluation"; Weitzman, "Economic Consequences"; and Peterson, "Statistical Errors."

38. On this see chapter 14.

39. Larsen, "In the Wake of Columbus."

40. Thus following the lead of Woodrow Borah, who claimed that his and his colleagues' work deserves favorable comparison with the Bollandists and Maurists: Borah, "Historical Demography," 24–25.

41. For a discussion of this in Dobyns's work on the Timucua see Henige, "If Pigs Could Fly."

42. Newson, *Life and Death,* 32–112 passim.

43. Ibid., 59, 78, 114.

44. Ibid., 91; cf. 114.

Chapter 21: Numbers Do Lie

1. Hopkins, "Big Business," 130.

2. Haub, "How Many People?" p. 4. Oddly enough, Haub went on (perhaps in playful parody?) to suggest that 105,472,380,189 is the "number [of people] who have ever been born" (5).

3. As well as the ancient world, despite such breezy assertions as that the population of cities of more than 30,000 inhabitants "fell from 5,181,000 to 3,892,000" between A.D. 100 and 500: Sanderson, "Expanding," 268. Nearly all the essays in this work operate under similar assumptions that the past is quantifiable for the asking.

4. Macfarlane, *Black Hole,* 280–81.

5. Coleman, *History,* 133, referring to North and Thomas, *Rise.*

6. Crosby, "Summary," 278, seems to think so: "If further work ensues in the vein of which these papers are such fine examples, we may . . . look forward to the day when, after generations of scholarship, our hemispheric estimate will be accurate to a tolerance of plus or minus 30–50 percent." Perhaps his tongue was firmly in cheek as he wrote this; perhaps not.

7. Or, as Grumet, *Historic Contact,* 62, succinctly put it: "Whatever their actual number, North Atlantic Indian populations declined disastrously as Europeans migrated to the region." This is really all that can be, or needs to be, said.

8. Huizinga, *Waning*, 215.

9. For Froissart's inclinations in this regard—and he was only one of many—see Contamine, "Froissart."

10. Merkle, "Truth," 563; cf. idem, "Telling the True Story."

11. Limerick, "Turnerians All," 698.

12. For this in a nutshell one could do no better than consult Daniels, "Indian Population." Despite the geographical limits implied in the title, this article covers a wide variety of attempts to estimate this population. An example of according Cook and Borah's estimates "air time" even while accepting other estimates is Adams, *Prehistoric Mesoamerica*, 367. In the original edition of this work (Adams, *Prehistoric Mesoamerica* [Boston, 1977], 29, 311–12) Adams had refrained from citing the High Counters' figures at all.

13. Murra, "Current Research," 5.

14. Wedin, *Concepto de lo Incaico*, 32–94 passim.

15. For the peculiar citing habits of Inca Garcilaso de la Vega, and their implications, see Rodríguez Garrido, "Citas." Nonetheless, Inca Garcilaso remains well favored because of his plausible and assimilating detail: see Henige, "*La Florida del Ynca*," and Mazzotti, "Lightning Bolt."

16. Ironically but encouragingly, some of this involves the discovery and publication of additional texts. Murra had been too pessimistic when he wrote ("Current Research," 6) that "in recent decades we have made few discoveries of important new or unknown historical sources." Since his article appeared, further writings by Cieza de León and Betanzos, both of whom he praised, have been discovered, edited, and published.

17. Above all, criticisms of sources in this way must do battle with apparent feelings that are both widespread and deep-seated—your sources may indeed be in error, but I am positive that mine are not. It is a feeling on which lotteries depend—and thrive.

18. Williams, "Review," 97.

19. Kennedy, "Review," 466. Cf. the similar comment in a review of Reynolds, *Fiefs and Vassals* (*Historian* 58 [1995–96], 695): "[Reynolds] deliberately avoids suggesting any new paradigm to replace the one she has effectively destroyed. Consequently, teachers of medieval history will probably stick to the old model until something better comes along."

20. Jones, *End of Roman Britain*, 263.

21. Duncan-Jones, "Impact," 116n.

22. Wheeler, "Mr. Collingwood," 91, 95.

23. Bloch, *Apologie*, 105–6.

24. This helps to explain their studied avoidance of the logistical impossibilities created by their scenarios, several of which have been discussed here. But sheer impossibility is sometimes no hindrance. When W. J. Colenso,

the Bishop of Natal, wrote in the 1860s demonstrating how the numbers in several biblical books were quite impossibly large, he was reviled and almost excommunicated, on the grounds that he had no right to trivialize divinely inspired texts by making arithmetical exercises of them. For this interesting episode see, e.g., Hinchcliff, *John William Colenso,* 85–114; Guy, *Heretic,* 121–39; Rogerson, *Old Testament Criticism,* 220–38.

25. Sallares, *Ecology,* 245. Sallares follows his own advice by arguing that the disease was smallpox.

26. Goffart, "Two Notes," 29–30.

27. Stoppard, *Arcadia,* 43, 46.

28. For evidence of this see Dobyns, "Sixteenth-Century Tusayan"; Schroeder, "Comments"; Dobyns, "Superhuman Hearing." Dobyns's weaknesses as a counterpuncher show themselves particularly well in his "Building Stones and Paper."

29. For the moment see Lovell and Lutz, *Demography and Empire;* this very useful work is dedicated: "For Woodrow Borah and Murdo MacLeod, whose leads we try to follow."

30. For these see chapter 9.

31. Porter, "Statistics," 88.

32. Powers to John Wesley Powell, 3 November 1876, quoted in Hurtado, "California Indian Demography," 334.

Abbreviations

AA   *American Anthropologist*
AAAG   *Annals of the Association of American Geographers*
AAy   *American Antiquity*
AHSI   *Archivum Historicum Societatis Iesu*
AILC   *Amerindian Images and the Legacy of Columbus.* Eds. Nicholas
        Spadaccini and René Jara. Minneapolis: University of Min-
        nesota Press, 1992.
AJP   *American Journal of Philology*
ANRW   *Aufstieg und Niedergang der Römische Welt.* Eds. Hildegard Tem-
        porini et al. 86 vols. to date. Berlin: W. de Gruyter, 1972 to date.
ASR   *American Sociological Review*
BACH   *Boletín de la Academia Chilena de Historia*
Blair/Robertson   *The Philippine Islands, 1493–1803.* Eds. Emma Blair and
        George Robertson. 55 vols. Cleveland, Ohio: A. H. Clark,
        1903–9.
BSOAS   *Bulletin of the School of Oriental and African Studies*
CA   *Current Anthropology*
CC   *Columbian Consequences.* Ed. David Hurst Thomas. 3 vols. Wash-
        ington, D.C.: Smithsonian Institution Press, 1989–91.
CDI   *Colección de documentos ineditos relativos al descubrimiento, con-
        quista y organización de las antiguas posesiones españolas de
        América y Oceania.* 42 vols. Madrid, 1864–84.
CDIHC   *Colección de documentos ineditos para la historia de Chile.* 34 vols.
        Santiago: Imprenta Cervantes, etc., 1888–1960.
CHC   *Colección de historiadores de Chile y documentos relativos a la his-
        toria nacional.* 51 vols. Santiago: Dirección General de Pri-
        siones, etc., 1861–1953.
DDA   *Disease and Demography in the Americas.* Eds. John W. Verano and
        Douglas H. Ubelaker. Washington: Smithsonian Institution,
        1992.
E&I   *Epidemics and Ideas.* Eds. Terence Ranger and Paul Slack. Cam-
        bridge: Cambridge University Press, 1992.

EHEM   *Ensayos sobre la historia de las epidemias en México.* Eds. Enrique Florescano and Elsa Malvido. 2 vols. Mexico City: Instituto Mexicano del Seguro Social, 1982.

FC   *Forgotten Centuries: Indians and Europeans in the American South, 1521–1704.* Eds. Charles Hudson and Carmen Chaves Tesser. Athens: University of Georgia Press, 1994.

HA   *History in Africa*

HAHR   *Hispanic American Historical Review*

HM   *Historia Mexicana*

HSAI   *Handbook of South American Indians*

JAH   *Journal of African History*

JAOS   *Journal of the American Oriental Society*

JAR   *Journal of Anthropological Research*

JESHO   *Journal of the Economic and Social History of the Orient*

JHS   *Journal of Hellenic Studies*

JRS   *Journal of Roman Studies*

JSAS   *Journal of Southern African Studies*

JSH   *Journal of Southern History*

LAPHB   *Latin American Population History Bulletin*

NPA   *The Native Population of the Americas in 1492.* Ed. William M. Denevan. 2d ed. Madison: University of Wisconsin Press, 1992.

PPHML   *Precolumbian Population History in the Maya Lowlands.* Eds. T. Patrick Culbert and Don S. Rice. Albuquerque: University of New Mexico Press, 1990.

RHA   *Revista de Historia de América*

RI   *Revista de Indias*

TAPA   *Transactions of the American Philological Association*

VT   *Vetus Testamentum*

West/Woodman   *Creative Imitation and Latin Literature.* Eds. D. A. West and A. J. Woodman. Cambridge: Cambridge University Press, 1979.

WMQ   *William and Mary Quarterly*

ZAW   *Zeitschrift für die Alttestamentliche Wissenschaft*

Bibliography

Abbott, Don Paul. *Rhetoric in the New World*. Columbia: University of South Carolina Press, 1996.

Abecia Baldivieso, Valentín. *Mitayos de Potosí en una economía sumergida*. Barcelona: Técnicos Editorial Asociados, 1988.

Abercrombie, Thomas. "Q'aqchas and *la plebe* in 'Rebellion': Carnival vs. Lent in Eighteenth-Century Peru." *Journal of Latin American Anthropology* 2 (1996): 62–111.

Abraham, David. "Big Business, Nazis, and German Politics at the End of Weimar." *European History Quarterly* 17 (1987): 235–45.

———. "Business Wars." *Vierteljahrsschrift für Sozial- und Wirtschaftsgeschichte* 72 (1983): 329–52.

———. *The Collapse of the Weimar Republic: Political Economy and Crisis*. Princeton: Princeton University Press, 1981.

Abu al-Fazl b. Mubarak. *ᶜAin-i-Akbari*. Trans. H. S. Jarrett. 3 vols. in 4. Calcutta: Asiatic Society of Bengal, 1927–49.

Abu-Lughod, Janet L. *Cairo: 1001 Years of the City Victorious*. Princeton: Princeton University Press, 1971.

Achinstein, Sharon. "Plagues and Publication." *Criticism* 34 (1992): 27–49.

Acuña, Rene, ed. *Relaciones geográficas del siglo XVI: México*. 10 vols. Mexico City: UNAM, 1982–87.

Adams, John. "Outer Space and the New World in the Imagination of Eighteenth-Century Europeans." *Eighteenth-Century Life* 19 (1995): 70–83.

Adams, Percy G. *Travel Literature and the Evolution of the Novel*. Lexington: University of Kentucky Press, 1983.

Adams, Richard E. W. *Prehistoric Mesoamerica*. Boston: Little, Brown, 1977.

———. *Prehistoric Mesoamerica*. Rev. ed. Norman: University of Oklahoma Press, 1991.

Adler, Michael A., ed. *Prehistoric Pueblo World, A.D. 1150–1350*. Tucson: University of Arizona Press, 1996.

Adorno, Rolena. "The Warrior and the War Community." *Dispositio* 36/38 (1989): 225–46.

Africa, Thomas. "Worms and the Death of Kings." *Classical Antiquity* 1 (1982): 1–17.

Agramont, Jacme d'. "Regiment de preservacio a epidemia o pestilencia e mortaldats." Eds. and trans. M. L. Duran-Reynals and C.E.A. Winslow. *Bulletin of the History of Medicine* 23 (1949): 57–89.

Aguilar, Francisco de. *Relación breve de la conquista de la Nueva España.* Ed. Jorge Gurría Lacroix. 7th ed. Mexico City: UNAM, 1977.

Aguilera G., Francisco. *"Historia de todas las cosas que han acaecido en el reino de Chile y de los que lo han gobernado (1536–1575)* de Alonso de Góngora Marmolejo." *Revista Chilena de Literatura* 36 (1990): 105–12.

Aguilers, Raymond d'. *Historia Francorum qui Ceperunt Iherusalem.* Trans. John H. Hill and Laurita L. Hill. Philadelphia: American Philosophical Society, 1968.

Ahern, Maureen. "The Certification of Cíbola: Discursive Strategies in *La relación del descubrimiento de las siete ciudades* by Fray Marcos de Niza." *Dispositio* 38/39 (1989): 303–13.

Aiton, Arthur S. "Coronado's Muster Roll." *American Historical Review* 44 (1938–39): 556–70.

———. "Coronado's Testimony in the Viceroy Mendoza Residencia." *New Mexico Historical Review* 12 (1937): 288–329.

Alberro, Solange B. de. "Zacatecas, 'zone frontière,' d'après les documents d'Inquisition." *Cahiers des Amériques Latines* 24 (1981): 185–219.

Alcalá, Manuel. *César y Cortés.* Mexico City: Editorial Jus, 1950.

Alchon, Suzanne Austin. *Native Society and Disease in Colonial Ecuador.* Cambridge: Cambridge University Press, 1991.

Aldridge, A. O. "Feijóo, Voltaire, and the Mathematics of Procreation." *Studies in Eighteenth-Century Culture* 4 (1975): 131–38.

———. "Polygamy in Early Fiction: Henry Neville and Denis Veiras." *Publications of the Modern Language Association* 65 (1950): 464–72.

Alegre, Francisco Javier. *Historia de la provincia de la Compañia de Jesus de Nueva España.* 4 vols. Rome: Institutum Historicum, 1956–60.

Alexandrescu-Dersca, M. M. *La campagne de Timur en Anatolie (1402).* London: Variorum, 1977.

Alkon, Paul K. *Origins of Futuristic Fiction.* Athens: University of Georgia Press, 1987.

———. *Science Fiction before 1900: Imagination Discovers Technology.* Boston: Tusas, 1994.

Allen, Norm. "*Black Athena:* An Interview with Martin G. Bernal." *Free Inquiry* 10/2 (Spring 1990): 18–22.

Allen, P. "The 'Justinianic' Plague." *Byzantion* 49 (1979): 5–20.

Alvarez Vilela, Angel. "L'expédition à Ancud de don García Hurtado de Mendoza dans *La Araucana.*" *Etudes de Lettres* (Lausanne) (1992–93): 101–20.

Alvira Cabrer, Martín. "La muerte del enemigo en la Pleno Medioevo: Cifras y ideología." *Hispania* 55 (1995): 203–23.

Amiotti, Gabriella. "I Greci ed il massacro degli Italici nell'88 a.c." *Aevum* 54 (1980): 132–39.

Amiran, Ruth. *Early Arad.* Jerusalem: Israel Exploration Society, 1978.

Amunátegui Solar, Domingo. *Las encomiendas de indíjenas en Chile.* 2 vols. Santiago: Imp. Cervantes, 1909.

Amundsen, G. B., and D. W. Ferngren. "Perception of Disease and Disease Causality in the New Testament." In *ANRW,* 2/37: 2934–56.

Anderson, Atholl. *Prodigious Birds: Moas and Moa-Hunting in Prehistoric New Zealand.* Cambridge: Cambridge University Press, 1989.

Anderson, David. *The Savannah River Chiefdoms: Political Change in the Late Prehistoric Southeast.* Tuscaloosa: University of Alabama Press, 1994.

Anderson, Margo J. *The American Census: A Social History.* New Haven: Yale University Press, 1988.

Anderson, Perry. *Passages from Antiquity to Feudalism.* London: Verso, 1974.

Andrien, Kenneth J. "The Battle for Bodies and Souls in the Colonial North Andes: Interecclesiastical Struggles and the Politics of Migration." *HAHR* 75 (1995): 31–56.

———. "*El Corrigedor de Indios,* la corrupción y el estado virreinal en Perú (1580–1630)." *Revista de Historia Económica* 4 (1986): 493–520.

———. "Spaniards, Andeans, and the Early Colonial State in Peru." In *Transatlantic Encounters: Europeans and Andeans in the Sixteenth Century,* eds. Kenneth J. Andrien and Rolena Adorno, 121–48. Berkeley: University of California Press, 1991.

Anguiano, Mateo de. *Misiones capuchinas en Africa.* Ed. Buenaventura de Carrocera. Madrid: CSIC, 1950.

Antei, Giorgio. *La invención del reino de Chile: Gerónimo de Vivar y los primeros cronistas chilenos.* Bogotá: Instituto Caro y Cuervo, 1989.

Applebaum, Shimon. "Judaea as a Roman Province." In *ANRW,* 1/8: 355–96.

Arieti, James A. *Discourses on the First Book of Herodotus.* Lanham, Md.: University Press of America, 1995.

Armas Medina, Fernando de. *Cristianización del Perú, 1532–1600.* Seville: GEHA, 1953.

Armond, Louis de. "Frontier Warfare in Colonial Chile." *Pacific Historical Review* 23 (1954): 125–32.

Arnaud, Pascal. "De la durée à la distance: L'évaluation des distances maritimes dans le monde gréco-romain." *Histoire et Mesure* 8 (1993): 225–47.

Arnold, C. J. *Roman Britain to Saxon England.* London: Croom Helm, 1984.

Arroyo, Leonardo. *A carta de Pêro Vaz de Caminha.* São Paulo: Melhoramentos, 1971.

Arzáns de Orsúa y Vela, Bartolomé. *Historia de la villa imperial de Potosí.* Eds. Lewis Hanke and Gunnar Mendoza. 3 vols. Providence, R.I.: Brown University Press, 1965.

———. *Tales of Potosí.* Trans. Francis M. López-Morillas; ed. R. C. Padden. Providence, R.I.: Brown University Press, 1975.

Ashpitel, Francis. *The Increase of the Israelites in Egypt Shewn to be Probable from the Statistics of Modern Populations, with an Examination of Bishop Colenso's Calculations on This Subject.* Oxford: John Henry and James Parker, 1863.

Assaf, Francis. "The Specularity of Alterity: The Native Brazilian in André Thevet's *Les Singularités de la France Antarctique.*" *Romanische Forschungen* 103 (1991): 244–52.

Athens, J. Stephen, and Jerome V. Ward. "Environmental Change and Prehistoric Polynesian Settlement in Hawai'i." *Asian Perspectives* 32 (1993): 209–23.

Aubin, Jean. "Chiffres de population urbaine en Iran occidental autour de 1500." *Moyen-Orient et Océan Indien* 3 (1986): 37–54.

Audin, A. "La population de Lugdunum au IIe siècle." *Cahiers d'Histoire* (Lyon) 15 (1970): 7–14.

Avi-Yonah, Michael. *The Holy Land from the Persian to the Arab Conquests.* Grand Rapids, Mich.: Baker Book House, 1966.

Axtell, James. *The Invasion Within: The Contest of Cultures in Colonial North America.* New York: Oxford University Press, 1985.

Ayalon, David. "Harb." In *Encyclopaedia of Islam,* eds. Bernard Lewis et al., 2d ed., 3: 184–90. Leiden: Brill, 1971.

———. "Regarding Population Estimates in the Countries of Medieval Islam." *JESHO* 28 (1985): 1–19.

Bachrach, Bernard S. "On the Origins of William the Conqueror's Horse Transports." *Technology and Culture* 26 (1985): 505–31.

Bächtold, Ulrich. "History, Ideology, and Propaganda in the Reformation." In *Protestant History and Identity in Sixteenth-Century Europe,* ed. Bruce Gordon, 1: 46–59. Brookfield, Vt.: Scolar Press, 1996.

Bacon, Francis. *The Novum Organum, with the Great Instauration.* Eds. and trans. Peter Urbach and John Gibson. Chicago: Open Court, 1994.

Bacque, James. *Other Losses: An Inquiry into the Mass Deaths of Ger-*

man *Prisoners at the Hands of the French and Americans after World War II.* Toronto: Stoddart, 1989.

Badian, Ernst. "The Battle of the Granicus: A New Look." *Ancient Macedonia* 2 (1977): 271–93.

Baegert, Johan Jakob. *The Letters of Jacob Baegert, 1749–1761.* Eds. Elsbeth Schulz-Bischof and Doyce B. Nunis, Jr. Los Angeles: Dawson's Book Shop, 1982.

———. *Observations in Lower California.* Trans. and eds. M. M. Brandenburg and Carol L. Baumann. Berkeley: University of California Press, 1952.

Baker, G. P. *Sulla the Fortunate.* New York: Barnes and Noble, 1967.

Bakewell, Peter J. "Conquest after the Conquest: The Rise of Spanish Domination in America." In *Spain, Europe, and the Atlantic World: Essays in Honour of John H. Elliott,* eds. Richard L. Kagan and Geoffrey Parker, 296–315. Cambridge: Cambridge University Press, 1995.

———. *Miners of the Red Mountain.* Albuquerque: University of New Mexico Press, 1984.

———. *Silver and Entrepreneurship in Seventeenth-Century Potosí: The Life and Times of Antonio López de Quiroga.* Albuquerque: University of New Mexico Press, 1988.

———. *Silver Mining and Society in Colonial Mexico, 1546–1790.* Cambridge: Cambridge University Press, 1971.

———. "Spanish America: Empire and Its Outcome." In *The Hispanic World,* ed. J. H. Elliott, 65–84. London: Thames and Hudson, 1991.

———. "Technological Change in Potosí: The Silver Boom of the 1570s." *Jahrbuch für Geschichte von Staat, Wirtschaft und Gesellschaft Lateinamerikas* 14 (1977): 57–77.

Balcer, Jack M. *The Persian Conquest of the Greeks, 545–450 B.C.* Konstanz: Universitätsverlag, 1995.

Baldinger, Kurt, and José Luis Rivarola, eds. "*Nouvelles certaines des isles du Peru* (Lyon 1534): Edition et commentaire." *Revue de Linguistique Romane* 56 (1992): 439–73.

Balée, William. "The Ecology of Ancient Tupi Warfare." In *Warfare, Culture, and Environment,* ed. R. Brian Ferguson, 241–65. Orlando: Academic Press, 1984.

Bannon, J. F. *The Spanish Borderlands Frontier, 1513–1821.* New York: Holt, Rinehart, and Winston, 1970.

Bar-Kochva, Bezalel. *Judas Maccabaeus: The Jewish Struggle against the Seleucids.* Cambridge: Cambridge University Press, 1989.

Barber, Noel. *The Black Hole of Calcutta: A Reconstruction.* Boston: Houghton Mifflin, 1966.

Baring-Gould, W. S. *The Annotated Sherlock Holmes.* New York: C. N. Potter, 1977.

Barnard, Alan. *The Kalahari Debate: A Bibliographical Essay.* Edinburgh: Centre of African Studies, 1992.

Barnes, Timothy D. *The New Empire of Diocletian and Constantine.* Cambridge, Mass.: Harvard University Press, 1982.

Barnish, S. "Old Kaspars: Attila's Invasion of Gaul in the Literary Sources." In *Fifth-Century Gaul: A Crisis of Identity?* eds. John Drinkwater and Hugh Elton, 38–47. Cambridge: Cambridge University Press, 1992.

Barreca, Ferruccio. "Gli eserciti annibalici." *Civiltà Classica e Cristiana* 7 (1986): 43–68.

Barrett, Elinore M. "The King's Copper Mine: Inguarán in New Spain." *The Americas* 38 (1981–82): 1–29.

Barros Araña, Diego. *Historia jeneral de Chile.* 16 vols. Santiago: R. Jover, 1884–1902.

Basalisco, Lucio. "Culture a confronto: Guaraníes y Yaros visti da un gesuita alla fine del seicento." *Quaderni Ibero-Americani* 72 (1992): 709–20.

Baudot, Georges. "Amerindian Image and Utopian Project: Motolinía and Millenarian Discourse." In *AILC,* 375–400.

———. "La percepción histórica del drama demográfica de México en siglo XVI." *Quinto Centenario* 1 (1981): 3–24.

———. *Utopia and History in Mexico.* Niwot: University Press of Colorado, 1996.

———. *Utopie et histoire au Mexique; Les premiers chroniqueurs de la civilisation mexicaine, 1520–1569.* Toulouse: Privat, 1977.

Baum, L. Frank. *The Emerald City of Oz.* Chicago: Reilly and Lee, 1910.

Bayley, C. C. *War and Society in Renaissance Florence.* Toronto: University of Toronto Press, 1961.

Beckjord, Sarah H. "'Con sal y ají y tomates': Las redes textuales de Bernal Díaz en el caso de Cholula." *Revista Iberoamericana* 55 (1995): 147–60.

Becquelin, Pierre, and Dominique Michelet. "Demografía en la zona Puuc." *Latin American Antiquity* 5 (1994): 289–311.

Beer, Jeanette M. A. *Narrative Conventions of Truth in the Middle Ages.* Geneva: Droz, 1981.

Beeston, A.F.L. "Events in Arabia in the Sixth Century A.D." *BSOAS* 16 (1954): 431–41.

Belich, James. *Making People.* Auckland: Allen Lane, 1994.

Bellemore, Jane, and Ian M. Plant. "Thucydides, Rhetoric, and Plague in Athens." *Athenaeum* 86 (1994): 384–401.

Bellemore, Jane, Ian M. Plant, and Lynne M. Cunningham. "Plague of Athens: Fungal Poison?" *Journal of the History of Medicine* 49 (1994): 521–45.

Beloch, Julius. *Die Bevölkerung der griechisch-römische Welt.* Leipzig: Duncker and Humblot, 1886.

———. "Die Bevölkerung Galliens zur Zeit Caesars." *Rheinisches Museum für Philologie* 54 (1899): 414–45.

———. "Le città dell'Italia antica." *Atene e Roma* 1 (1898): 257–78.

Beltrán Llavador, Rafael, et al., eds. *Historias y ficciones.* Valencia: Universitat de Valencia, 1992.

Benedict, Philip. "Catholics and Huguenots in Sixteenth-Century Rouen." *French Historical Studies* 9 (1976–77): 209–34.

Bengoa, José. *Conquista y barbarie: Ensayo crítico acerca de la conquista de Chile.* Santiago: Ediciones Sur, 1992.

Benrekassa, Georges. *Le concentrique et l'excentrique.* Paris: Payot, 1980.

Berberián, Eduardo E., and Beatrix Bixio. "La crónica de Gerónimo de Bibar y los aborígenes de la provincia de Cuyo (República Argentina)." *Revista Española de Antropología Americana* 17 (1987): 197–234.

Berdan, Frances F. *The Aztecs of Central Mexico.* New York: Holt, Rinehart and Winston, 1982.

———. "A Comparative Analysis of Aztec Tribute Documents." *Proceedings of the Forty-first International Congress of Americanists,* 2: 131–42. Mexico City: INAH, 1975.

———. "The 'Tributary Provinces' in Aztec Imperial Strategies." In *Aztec Imperial Strategies,* eds. Frances F. Berdan et al. Washington, D.C.: Dumbarton Oaks, 1996.

Berdan, Frances F., and Patricia R. Anawalt. "The Codex Mendoza." *Scientific American* 266 (June 1992): 70–79.

Berdan, Frances F., et al., eds. *Aztec Imperial Strategies.* Washington, D.C.: Dumbarton Oaks, 1996.

Bergier, Jean-François. *Guillaume Tell.* Paris: Fayard, 1988.

Bernal, Martin. *Black Athena, I: The Fabrication of Ancient Greece.* New Brunswick, N.J.: Rutgers University Press, 1987.

———. *Black Athena, II: The Archaeological and Documentary Evidence.* New Brunswick, N.J.: Rutgers University Press, 1991.

———. *Cadmean Letters.* Winona Lake, Ind.: Eisenbrauns, 1990.

Bernard of Clairvaux. "De Laude Novae Militiae ad Milites Templi Liber." In *Patrologiae Latinae,* 2d ser. 182 (Paris, 1854), 921–40.

Bernhard, Virginia. "The Forest and the Trees: Thomas Camfield and the History of Early Virginia." *JSH* 60 (1994): 663–70.

———. "Men, Women, and Children at Jamestown: Population and Gender in Early Virginia, 1607–1610." *JSH* 58 (1992): 599–618.

Berthe, Jean-Pierre. "Las minas de oro del Marqués del Valle en Tehuantepec, 1540–1547." *HM* 8 (1959–60): 122–31.

Biagioli, Mario. "Playing with the Evidence." *Early Science and Medicine* 1 (1996): 70–105.

Bibar, Jerónimo de. *Crónica de los reinos de Chile.* Ed. Angel Barral Gómez. Madrid: Historia 16, 1988.

Biedma, Luis Hernández de. "Relación del sucesos de la jornada del capitán Soto a Florida." In Museo Naval Madrid, *Colección de documentos y manuscritos compilados por Fernández de Navarrete,* 14: 211–61. Nendeln: Kraus, 1971.

Bigwood, J. M. "Ctesias' Description of Babylon." *American Journal of Ancient History* 3 (1978): 32–52.

Binford, Lewis R. *Faunal Remains from the Klasies River Mouth.* New York: Academic Press, 1984.

Biraben, Jean-Noël. "Essai sur l'evolution du nombre des hommes." *Population* 34 (1979): 13–25.

———. "Préhistoire." *In Histoire de la population française, I: Des origines à la Renaissance,* 19–63. Paris: Presses Universitaires de France, 1988.

Bird, H. W. "Eutropius on Numa Pompilius and the Senate." *Classical Journal* 81 (1985–86): 243–48.

Bishop, Helen R., and Harold E. Weidman. "The Correct Birthdate of Bartolomé de las Casas." *HAHR* 56 (1976): 385–403.

Bitterli, Urs. *Cultures in Conflict: Encounters between European and Non-European Cultures, 1492–1800.* Trans. Ritchie Robertson. Stanford: Stanford University Press, 1989.

Black, Francis L. "An Explanation of High Death Rates among New World Peoples When in Contact with Old World Diseases." *Perspectives in Biology and Medicine* 37 (1994): 292–307.

———. "Why Did They Die?" *Science* 258 (11 December 1992): 1739–40.

Black, Stephen L. "The Carnegie Uaxactun Project and the Development of Maya Archaeology." *Ancient Mesoamerica* 1 (1990): 257–76.

Blankenburg, Sr. Mary Angela. "German Missionary Writers in Paraguay." *Mid-America* 29 (1947): 34–68.

Bloch, Gustave, and Jérôme Carcopino. *Histoire romaine, II: La république romaine de 133 à 44 avant J.-C.* Paris: Presses Universitaires de France, 1935.

Bloch, Marc. *Apologie pour l'histoire.* Paris: A. Colin, 1993.

———. *Mélanges historiques.* Paris: SEVPEN, 1963.

Block, Willibald. *Die Condottieri.* Berlin: E. Ebering, 1913.

Blok, Josine H. "Proof and Persuasion in *Black Athena*: The Case of K. O. Müller." *Journal of the History of Ideas* 59 (1996): 705–24.

Blumers, Teresa. *La contabilidad en las reducciones Guaraníes.* Asunción: Centro de Estudios Antropológicos, 1992.

Bodde, Derk. *China's First Unifier.* Leiden: Brill, 1938.

———. "The State and Empire of Ch'in." In *Cambridge History of China,* 1: 21–102. Cambridge: Cambridge University Press, 1986.

Boesky, Amy. *Founding Fictions: Utopias in Early Modern England.* Athens: University of Georgia Press, 1996.

Bogaert, Harmen Meyndertsz van den. *A Journey into Mohawk and Oneida Country, 1634–1635.* Trans. and eds. Charles T. Gehring and William A. Starna. Syracuse: Syracuse University Press, 1988.

Bolton, Herbert E. *Coronado on the Turquoise Trail: Knight of Pueblos and Plains.* Albuquerque: University of New Mexico Press, 1949.

Bonar, James. *Theories of Population from Raleigh to Arthur Young.* London: Allen and Unwin, 1931.

Bonilla Bradanovic, Tomás. *La 'gran guerra' Mapuche, 1541–1883.* Santiago: Instituto Geográfico Militar, 1988.

The Book of Tributes: Early Sixteenth-Century Nahuatl Censuses from Morelos. Los Angeles: UCLA Latin American Center, 1993.

Boone, Elizabeth Hill. "*Templo Mayor* Research, 1521–1978." In *The Aztec Templo Mayor,* ed. Elizabeth Hill Boone, 5–69. Washington, D.C.: Dumbarton Oaks, 1987.

Booth, Annie L., and Harvey M. Jacobs. "Ties That Bind: Native American Beliefs as a Foundation for Environmental Consciousness." *Environmental Ethics* 12 (1990): 27–43.

Borah, Woodrow W. "Epidemics in the Americas: Major Issues and Future Research." *LAPHB* 19 (Spring 1991): 2–13.

———. "The Historical Demography of Aboriginal and Colonial America: An Attempt at Perspective." In *NPA,* 13–34.

———. "The Historical Demography of Latin America: Sources, Techniques, Controversies, Yields." In *Population and Economics,* ed. Paul Deprez, 173–205. Winnipeg: University of Manitoba Press, 1970.

———. "Introduction." In *"Secret Judgments of God": Old World Disease in Colonial Spanish America,* eds. N. D. Cook and W. George Lovell, 3–19. Norman: University of Oklahoma Press, 1991.

———. *Justice by Insurance.* Berkeley: University of California Press, 1983.

———. "Review of Rosenblat, *Población de América.*" *HAHR* 48 (1968): 475–77.

———. "Sherburne Friend Cook." *HAHR* 55 (1975): 749–59.

————. "Some Problems of Sources." In *Explorations in Ethnohistory: Indians of Central Mexico in the Sixteenth Century*, eds. H. R. Harvey and Hanns J. Prem, 23–39. Albuquerque: University of New Mexico Press, 1984.

————. "Yet Another Look at the Techialoyan Codices." In *Land and Politics in the Valley of Mexico*, ed. H. R. Harvey, 209–21. Albuquerque: University of New Mexico Press, 1991.

Borah, Woodrow W., and Sherburne F. Cook. *The Aboriginal Population of Central Mexico on the Eve of the Spanish Conquest*. Berkeley: University of California Press, 1963.

————. "Conquest and Population: A Demographic Approach to Mexican History." *Proceedings of the American Philosophical Society* 133 (1969): 177–83.

————. *The Population of Central Mexico in 1548: An Analysis of the suma de visitas de pueblos*. Berkeley: University of California Press, 1960.

————. "Quelle fut la stratification sociale au centre de Mexique durant la première moitié du XVIe siècle?" *Annales: Economies, Sociétés, Civilisations* 18 (1963): 226–58.

Borges, Pedro. *Métodos misionales en la cristianización de América, siglo XVI*. Madrid: CSIC, 1960.

Bosworth, A. B. *Conquest and Empire: The Reign of Alexander the Great*. Cambridge: Cambridge University Press, 1993.

Bourne, Edward C. *Spain in America, 1450–1580*. New York: Harper and Row, 1904.

Bowen, Ezra. "Stormy Weather in Academe." *Time* (14 January 1985): 59.

Bowersock, G. W. *Augustus and the Greek World*. Oxford: Clarendon Press, 1965.

Boxer, C. R. *The Christian Century in Japan, 1549–1650*. Berkeley: University of California Press, 1951.

————. *Fidalgos in the Far East, 1550–1770*. 2d ed. Hong Kong: Oxford University Press, 1968.

————. Uma relação inedita e contemporânea da Batalha de Ambuila em 1665." *Boletim Cultural do Museu de Angola* 2 (1960): 65–73.

Boyd, Donna C. "Skeletal Correlates of Human Behavior in the Americas." *Journal of Archaeological Method and Theory* 3 (1996): 189–251.

Boyd, Robert T. "Another Look at the 'Fever and Ague' in Western Oregon." *Ethnohistory* 22 (1975): 135–54.

————. "Commentary on Early Contact-Era Smallpox in the Pacific Northwest." *Ethnohistory* 43 (1996): 307–28.

————. "Population Decline from Two Epidemics on the Northwest Coast." In *DDA*, 249–55.

————. "Smallpox in the Pacific Northwest: The First Epidemics." *BC Studies* 101 (Spring 1994): 5–40.

Bradford, Ernle. *Hannibal.* New York: McGraw-Hill, 1981.

Brading, D. A. *The Origins of Mexican Nationalism.* Cambridge: Cambridge University Press, 1985.

Bradshaw, William R. *The Goddess of Atvatabar.* New York: J. F. Douthitt, 1892.

Brainerd, George W., and Sylvanus G. Morley. *The Ancient Maya.* 3d ed. Stanford: Stanford University Press, 1956.

Brandão, Carlos Rodrigues. "Os Guarani, indios do sul: Religião, resistência e adaptação." *Estudos Avançados* (São Paulo) 10 (1990): 53–61.

Brásio, António, ed. *Monumenta missionaria Africa: Africa ocidental, 1570–1599.* Lisbon: Agencia Geral do Ultramar, 1963.

Bratton, Timothy L. "The Identity of the Plague of Justinian." *Transactions and Studies of the College of Physicians of Philadelphia* 5/3 (1981): 113–24, 174–79.

Braudel, Fernand. *L'identité de la France, 2: Les hommes et les choses.* Paris: Arthaud-Flammarion, 1986.

————. *The Structures of Everyday Life: The Limits of the Possible.* Trans. Siân Reynolds. New York: Harper and Row, 1981.

Bridges, E. Lucas. *Uttermost Part of the Earth.* London: Hodder and Stoughton, 1948.

Bright, David F. *The Miniature Epic in Vandal Africa.* Norman: University of Oklahoma Press, 1987.

Brion, Marcel. *Pompeii and Herculaneum.* New York: Crown, 1960.

Brockman, Eric. *The Two Sieges of Rhodes, 1480–1522.* London: J. Murray, 1969.

Brofsky, Robert, et al. "Cook, Lono, Obeyesekere, and Sahlins." *Current Anthropology* 39 (1997): 255–82.

Brooks, Francis J. "Motecuzoma Xocoyotl, Hernán Cortés, and Bernal Díaz del Castillo: The Construction of an Arrest." *HAHR* 75 (1995): 168–76.

Brooks, Sheilagh T., and Richard H. Brooks. "Palaeoepidemiology as a Possible Interpretation of Multiple Child Burials near Zape Chico, Durango, Mexico." In *Across the Chichimec Sea,* eds. Carroll L. Riley and Basil C. Hedrick, 96–101. Carbondale: Southern Illinois University Press, 1978.

Broshi, Magen. "Estimating the Population of Ancient Jerusalem. *Biblical Archaeology Review* 4 (June 1978): 10–15.

————. "La population de l'ancienne Jérusalem." *Revue Biblique* 82 (1975): 5–14.

————. "The Role of the Temple in the Herodian Economy." *Jewish Social Studies* 38 (1987): 33–37.

Brou, A. "Les statistiques dans les anciens missions." *Revue d'Histoire des Missic·ns* 6 (1929): 363–69.

Brown, Peter. *Augustine of Hippo*. Berkeley: University of California Press, 1963.

Brown, Truesdell S. *Timaeus of Tauromenium*. Berkeley: University of California Press, 1958.

Browne, Janet. *The Secular Ark*. New Haven: Yale University Press, 1983.

Brumfiel, Elizabeth M. "The Quality of Tribute Cloth: The Place of Evidence in Archaeological Argument." *AAy* 61 (1996): 453–62.

Brunt, P. A. *Italian Manpower, 225 B.C.–A.D. 14*. Oxford: Clarendon Press, 1971.

Bruun, Christer. *The Water Supply of Ancient Rome*. Helsinki: Societas Scientarum Fennica, 1991.

Buckley, James M. "The Problematical Octogenarianism of John of Brienne." *Speculum* 32 (1957): 315–22.

Bunyan, John. *A Pilgrim's Progress*. London: Nathaniel Ponder, 1678.

Burgess, R. W., trans. *The Chronicle of Hydatius and the Consularia Constantinopolitana*. Oxford: Oxford University Press, 1993.

Burn, A. R. *Persia and the Greeks: The Defense of the West, 546–478 B.C.* New York: Minerva Press, 1968.

Burne, A. H. "Some Notes on the Battle of Kadesh." *Journal of Egyptian Archaeology* 7 (1921): 191–95.

Burnes Ortiz, Arturo. *La mineria en la historia económica de Zacatecas, 1546–1876*. Zacatecas: UAZ, 1987.

Burnett, Barbara A., and Katherine A. Murray. "Death, Drought, and de Soto: The Bioarcheology of Depopulation." In *The Expedition of Hernando de Soto West of the Mississippi, 1541–1543*, eds. Gloria A. Young and Michael P. Hoffman, 227–36. Fayetteville: University of Arkansas Press, 1993.

Burns, Thomas S. "Calculating Ostrogothic Army and Population." *Ancient World* 1 (1978): 187–90.

Bury, J. B. *History of the Later Roman Empire*. 2 vols. New York: Dover, 1958.

———. *The Invasion of Europe by the Barbarians*. New York: Norton, 1967.

Bushnell, O. A. *The Gifts of Civilization: Germs and Genocide in Hawai'i*. Honolulu: University of Hawaii Press, 1994.

Butlin, N. G. *Economics and the Dreamtime: A Hypothetical History*. Melbourne: Cambridge University Press, 1993.

———. *Our Original Aggression*. Sydney: G. Allen and Unwin, 1983.

Butzer, Karl W. "Ecology in the Long View: Settlement Histories,

Agrosystemic Strategies, and Ecological Performance." *Journal of Field Archaeology* 23 (1996): 141–50.

Byatt, Anthony. "Josephus and Population Numbers in First-Century Palestine." *Palestine Exploration Quarterly* 105 (1973): 51–60.

Cabrero, Leoncio, ed. *Relación de Michoacán*. Madrid: Historia 16, 1989.

Cachola-Abad, C. Kenhaunani. "Evaluating the Orthodox Dual-Settlement Model for the Hawaiian Islands: An Analyis of Artefact Distribution and Hawaiian Oral Traditions." In *The Evolution and Organisation of Prehistoric Society in Polynesia*, eds. Michael W. Graves and Roger C. Green, 13–32. Auckland: New Zealand Archaeological Association, 1993.

Cadenhead, Ivie E. "Some Mining Operations of Cortés in Tehuantepec, 1538–1547." *The Americas* 16 (1959–60): 283–87.

Caesar, Julius. *Alexandrine, African, and Spanish Wars*. Trans. A. G. Way. Cambridge, Mass.: Harvard University Press, 1978.

———. *The Battle for Gaul*. Trans. Anne and Peter Wiseman. Boston: D. R. Godine, 1980.

———. *The Gallic War*. Trans. H. J. Edwards. Cambridge, Mass. Harvard University Press, 1958.

Cahen, Claude. "A propos d'Albert d'Aix et de Richard le Pèlerin." *Moyen-Age* 96 (1990): 31–33.

Caillavet, Chantal. "Review of Alchon, *Native Society*." *Annales: Economies, Sociétés, Civilisations* 50 (1995): 1362–65.

Calvin, John. *Commentary on the Book of the Prophet Isaiah*. Trans. William Pringle. 4 vols. Grand Rapids, Mich.: W. B. Eerdmans, 1948.

Camargo, Carlos A. "1492—the Medical Consequences." *Western Journal of Medicine* 160 (1994): 545–53.

Cameron, Averil. "History as Text: Coping with Procopius." In *The Inheritance of Historiography, 350–900*, eds. Christopher Holdsworth and T. P. Wiseman, 53–66. Exeter: University of Exeter Press, 1986.

———. *Procopius and the Sixth Century*. Berkeley: University of California Press, 1985.

Cameron, Don Allen. *The Legend of Noah*. Urbana: University of Illinois Press, 1949.

Camfield, Thomas M. "A Can or Two of Worms: Virginia Bernhard and the Historiography of Early Virginia, 1607–1610." *JSH* 60 (1994): 649–62.

Campanário, Manuel de Abreu. *Hans Staden: O homem e a obra*. São Paulo: Parma, 1980.

Campbell, Miles W. "An Inquiry into the Troop Strength of King Harald Hardrada's Invasion Fleet of 1066." *American Neptune* 44 (1984): 96–102.

Campbell, Sarah K. *PostColumbian Culture History in the Northern Columbia Plateau, A.D. 1500–1900.* New York: Garland, 1990.

Cañedo-Argüelles Fábrega, Teresa. "Efectos de Potosí sobre la población indígena del Alto Perú: Pacajes a mediados del siglo XVII." *RI* 48 (1988): 237–55.

Caraviglia, Juan Carlos, and Juan Carlos Grosso. "La región de Puebla/Tlaxcala y la economía novohispana (1670–1821)." *HM* 35 (1985–86): 549–600.

Carbonell, Rafael. *Estrategias de desarrollo rural en los pueblos Guaraníes, 1609–1767.* Barcelona: A. Bosch, 1992.

Carcopino, Jérôme. "Le site d'Alésia." *Revue des Deux Mondes* (July–Aug. 1958): 201–16, 424–39, 626–44.

Cardim, Fernão. *Tratados da terra e gente do Brasil.* Ed. Rodolfo Garcia. Belo Horizonte: Editora da Universidade de São Paulo, 1980.

———. *Tratados da terra e gente do Brasil.* Eds. Baptista Caetano, Capistrano de Abreu, and Rodolfo Garcia. 2d. ed. São Paulo: Companhia Editora Nacional, 1939.

Cardozo, Efraim. *Historiografía paraguaya.* Mexico City: Instituto Panamericano, 1959.

———. *El Paraguay colonial: Las raices de la nacionalidad.* Buenos Aires: Ediciones Nizza, 1959.

Carman, Glen. "The Voices of the Conqueror in López de Gómara's *Historia de la conquista de México.*" *Journal of Hispanic Philology* 16 (1992): 223–36.

Carney, Thomas F. "Marius' Choice of Battle-Field in the Campaign of 101 B.C." *Athenaeum* 36 (1958): 233–37.

Carrasco, Pedro. "Los Mayeques." *HM* 39 (1989–90): 123–66.

Carson, R.A.G. "The Kingdom of the Vandals." *History Today* 5 (1955): 334–40.

Cartun, Ari Mark. "Who Knows Ten? The Structural and Symbolic Use of Numbers in the Ten Plagues: Exodus 7:14–13:16." *Union Seminary Quarterly Review* 45 (1991): 65–119.

Cary, M. *A History of Rome down to the Reign of Constantine.* London: Macmillan, 1938.

Casanova, Giacomo. *Icosameron.* Ed. Rachel Zurer. New York: Jenna Press, 1986.

Casanueva, Fernando. "Crónica de una guerra sin fin: La 'Crónica del reino de Chile' del capitán Pedro Mariño de Lobera (1594)." *Bulletin Hispanique* 95 (1993): 119–47.

Casas, Bartolomé de las. *Brevísima relación de la destruición de las Indias.* Ed. André Saint-Lu. Madrid: Catedra, 1982.

———. *Historia de las Indias.* Ed. Agustín Millares Carlo. 3 vols. Mexico City: Fondo de Cultura Económica, 1951.

———. *Historia de las Indias.* Eds. Isacio Pérez Fernández et al. 3 vols. Madrid: Alianza, 1994.

Casselberry, Samuel E. "Further Refinement of Formulae for Determining Population from Floor Area." *World Archaeology* 6 (1974–75): 117–22.

Castañeda Nájera, Pedro. *The Narrative of Castañeda.* Ed. George P. Winship. Washington, D.C., 1896.

Castro Morales, Efraín, and Roberto García Moll. "Un entierro colectivo en la ciudad de Cholula, Puebla." In *Religión en Mesoamérica,* 381–86. Mexico City: Sociedad Mexicana de Antropología, 1972.

Catlin, George. *Letters and Notes.* Minneapolis: Ross and Haines, 1841.

Cavaignac, Eugène. *Population et capital dans le monde méditerranéen antique.* Strasbourg: Librairie Istra, 1923.

Caven, Brian. *The Punic Wars.* London: Weidenfeld and Nicolson, 1980.

Ceccarelli, G. "Le dieci piaghe d'Egitto e la loro interpretazione medica." *Minerva Medica* 85 (1994): 271–77.

Ceccherelli, Claudio. "El bautismo y los Franciscanos en México, 1524–1539." *Missionalia Hispánica* 12 (1955): 209–89.

Cervantes de Salazar, Francisco. *Crónica de Nueva España.* Ed. Francisco del Paso y Troncoso. 3 vols. Madrid/Mexico City: Tallares Gráficos, 1914–36.

Cervellino Giannoni, Miguel. "La población de Copiapó desde el siglo XVI al siglo XVIII (años 1535 a 1835)." *Mapocho* 28 (1990): 25–28.

Chabloz, Fritz. *La bataille de Grandson.* Lausanne: F. Payot, 1897.

Champion, Timothy. "The Power of the Picture: The Image of the Ancient Gaul." In *The Culture of Images,* ed. Brian Molyneaux, 213–29. London: Routledge, 1997.

Chang, Hasok. "Circularity and Reliability in Measurement." *Perspectives on Science* 3 (1995): 153–72.

Charanis, Peter. "Observations on the Demography of the Byzantine Empire." In *Proceedings of the Thirteenth International Congress of Byzantine Studies,* eds. J. M. Hussey et al., 445–63. London: Oxford University Press, 1967.

Charbonneau, Hubert, and Jacques Légaré. "La population du Canada aux recensements de 1666 et 1667." *Population* 22 (1967): 1031–47.

Chaunu, Pierre. "Las Casas et la première crise structurelle de la colonisation espagnole (1515–1523)." *Revue Historique* 229 (1963): 59–102.

———. "La population de l'amérique indienne (nouvelles recherches)." *Revue Historique* 232 (1964): 111–18.

Chávez, Ezequiel A. *Fray Pedro de Gante.* Mexico City: Editorial Jus, 1952.

Checa, Jorge. "Cortés y el espacio de la conquista: La *Segunda carta de relación.*" *MLN* 111 (1996): 187–217.

Chicago Religious Task Force on Central America. *Dangerous Memories: Invasion and Resistance since 1492.* Chicago: Task Force, 1991.

Choniates, Nicetas. *O City of Byzantium: Annals of Nicetas Choniates.* Trans. Harry J. Margoulias. Detroit: Wayne State University Press, 1984.

Cieza de León, Pedro. *Obras completas.* Ed. Carmelo Sáenz de Santa María. 2 vols. Madrid: Instituto Gonzalo Fernández de Oviedo, 1984.

Cinnamus, Joannes. *Deeds of John and Manuel Comnenus.* New York: Columbia University Press, 1976.

Cipolla, Carlo. *Faith, Reason, and the Plague in Seventeenth-Century Tuscany.* Ithaca: Cornell University Press, 1977.

Cipriani, Giovanni. *Cesare e la retorica dell'assedio.* Amsterdam: J. C. Gieben, 1986.

Cizek, Eugen. *Histoire et historiens à Rome dans l'antiquité.* Lyon: Presses Universitaires de Lyon, 1995.

Clastres, Hélène. *The Land-without-Evil: Tupí-Guaraní Prophetism.* Urbana: University of Illinois Press, 1995.

Clastres, Pierre. "Eléments de démographie amérindienne." *Homme* 13 (1973): 23–36.

———. "Elements of Amerindian Demography." In *Society against the State,* 64–82. New York: Urizen Books, 1977.

———. *La société contre l'état.* Paris: Editions de Minuit, 1974.

Claude, Dietrich. *Geschichte der Westgoten.* Stuttgart: Kohlhammer, 1970.

Claude d'Abbeville. *L'arrivée des pères capucins et la conversion des sauvages à nostre Saincte Foy.* Paris: L. Perrin, 1623.

———. *Histoire de la mission des pères capucins en l'isle de Maragnan et terres circonvoisins.* Paris: François Huby, 1614.

———. *História da missão dos padres capuchinhos na Ilha do Maranhão e terras circunvizinhas.* São Paulo: Livraria Martins Editora, 1945.

Clausewitz, Carl von. *On War.* Eds. and trans. Michael Howard and Peter Paret. Princeton: Princeton University Press, 1976.

Clavigero, Francisco Saverio. *The History of Mexico.* 2 vols. London: G.G.J. and J. Robinson, 1787.

Clendinnen, Inga. *The Aztecs: An Interpretation.* Cambridge: Cambridge University Press, 1991.

———. "Cortés, Signs, and the Conquest of Mexico." In *The Transmission of Culture in Early Modern Europe,* eds. Anthony Grafton and Ann Blair, 87–130. Philadelphia: University of Pennsylvania Press, 1990.

————. "'Fierce and Unnatural Cruelty': Cortés and the Conquest of Mexico." *Representations* 33 (1991): 65–100.

Clerc, Michael. *Le bataille d'Aix: Etudes critiques sur la campagne de Caius Marius en Provence.* Paris: Fontemoing, 1906.

Cline, Sarah. "The Spiritual Conquest Reexamined." *HAHR* 73 (1993): 453–80.

Clodfelter, Michael. *Warfare and Armed Conflicts: A Statistical Reference to Casualties and Other Figures, 1618–1991.* 2 vols. Jefferson, N.C.: McFarland, 1994.

Clover, F. M. "Carthage and the Vandals." In *Excavations at Carthage 1976–1978 Conducted by the University of Michigan,* ed. J. H. Humphrey, 7: 1–22. Tunis: Ceres, 1982.

Cobo, Bernabé. *Obras,* Ed. Francisco Mateos. 2 vols. Madrid: Sucesores de Rivadeneyra, 1956.

Cohen, Joel E. *How Many People Can the Earth Support?* New York: W. W. Norton, 1995.

Cohen, Patricia C. *A Calculating People: The Spread of Numeracy in Early America.* Chicago: University of Chicago Press, 1982.

Cole, Jeffrey A. *The Potosí Mita, 1573–1700: Compulsory Indian Labor in the Andes.* Stanford: Stanford University Press, 1985.

Coleman, D. C. *History and the Economic Past.* Oxford: Clarendon Press, 1987.

Collier, Richard. *The Sands of Dunkirk.* London: Collins, 1961.

Collin de Plancy, J.A.S. *Voyage au centre de la terre, . . . au pôle nord et dans des pays inconnus, traduit de l'anglais de Sir Hormidas Peath.* 3 vols. Paris: n.p., 1821.

Collingwood, R. G. "Town and Country in Roman Britain." *Antiquity* 3 (1929): 261–76.

Collingwood, R. G., and J.N.L. Myres. *Roman Britain and the English Settlements.* 2d ed. Oxford: Clarendon Press, 1936.

Colomb, Georges. *Vercingétorix: Histoire du pays gaulois depuis ses origines jusqu'à la conquête romaine.* Paris: Fayard, 1947.

Colón, Fernando. *Le historie della vita e dei fatti di Cristoforo Colombo.* Ed. Rinaldo Caddeo. 2 vols. Milan: Edizioni Alpes, 1930.

————. *The Life of the Admiral Christopher Columbus by His Son Ferdinand.* Ed. and trans. Benjamin Keen. 2d. ed. New Brunswick, N.J.: Rutgers University Press, 1992.

Columbus, Christopher. *The Diario of Christopher Columbus's First Voyage to America, 1492–1493.* Trans. and eds. Oliver Dunn and James E. Kelley, Jr. Norman: University of Oklahoma Press, 1989.

————. *Libro copiador de Cristóbal Colón*. Ed. Antonio Rumeu de Armas. 2 vols. Madrid: Testimonio, 1989.

Commager, Henry Steele, and Elmo Giordanetti, eds. *Was America a Mistake? An Eighteenth-Century Controversy*. New York: Harper and Row, 1967.

Conley, Tom. "De Bry's Las Casas." In *AILC*, 103–31.

Connell, K. H. *The Population of Ireland, 1750–1845*. Oxford: Clarendon Press, 1950.

Conrad, Lawrence I. "Abraha and Muhammad." *BSOAS* 50 (1987): 225–40.

————. "Arabic Plague Chronologies and Treatises." *Studia Islamica* 54 (1981): 51–93.

————. "The Arabs and the Colossus." *Journal of the Royal Asiatic Society* 3/6 (1996): 165–87.

————. "The Biblical Tradition for the Plague of the Philistines." *JAOS* 104 (1984): 281–87.

————. "Epidemic Disease in Formal and Popular Thought in Early Islamic Society." In *E&I*, 77–99.

————. "Taᶜun and Waba': Conceptions of Plague and Pestilence in Early Islam." *JESHO* 25 (1982): 268–307.

Contamine, Philippe. "Froissart: Art militaire, pratique et conception de la guerre." In *Froissart, Historian*, ed. J.J.N. Palmer, 132–44. Woodbridge, U.K.: Boydell, 1981.

Contreras, Carlos. *La Ciudad del mercurio*. Lima: Instituto de Estudios Peruanos, 1982.

Contreras A., Juan, et al. *La población y la economía de Chiloé durante la colonia, 1567–1826*. Concepción: Universidad de Concepción, 1971.

Conway, G.R.G. *Noche triste*. Mexico City: Gante Press, 1943.

Cook, N. D. *Demographic Collapse: Indian Peru, 1520–1620*. Cambridge: Cambridge University Press, 1981.

————. "Disease and the Depopulation of Hispaniola, 1492–1518." *Colonial Latin American Review* 2 (1993): 213–45.

————. "Estimaciones sobre la población del Perú en el momento de la conquista." *Histórica* 1 (1977): 37–60.

————. "Migration in Colonial Peru: An Overview." In *Migration in Colonial Spanish America*, ed. David J. Robinson, 41–61. Cambridge: Cambridge University Press, 1990.

————. "Population Data for Indian Peru: Sixteenth and Seventeenth Centuries." *HAHR* 52 (1982): 73–120.

Cook, Sherburne F. "The Epidemic of 1830–1833 in California and Oregon." *University of California Publications in American Archaeology and Ethnology* 43 (1956): 303–26.

————. *The Extent and Significance of Disease among the Indians of Baja California, 1697–1773.* Berkeley: University of California Press, 1937.

————. "Human Sacrifice and Warfare as Factors in the Demography of Pre-Colonial Mexico." *Human Biology* 18 (1946): 81–102.

————. "The Incidence and Significance of Disease among the Aztecs and Related Tribes." *HAHR* 26 (1946): 320–35.

————. *The Indian versus the Spanish Mission.* Berkeley: University of California Press, 1943.

————. "The Interrelationship of Population, Food Supply, and Building in Pre-Conquest Central Mexico." *AAy* 13 (1947–48): 45–52.

————. "The Population of Mexico in 1793." *Human Biology* 14 (1942): 498–515.

Cook, Sherburne F., and Woodrow W. Borah. "The Aboriginal Population of Hispaniola." In their *Essays,* 1: 376–410.

————. "An Essay on Method." In their *Essays,* 1: 73–118.

————. *Essays in Population History: Mexico and the Caribbean.* 3 vols. Berkeley: University of California Press, 1971–79.

————. "Indian Food Production and Consumption in Central Mexico Before and After the Conquest, 1500–1650." In their *Essays,* 3: 129–76.

————. *The Indian Population of Central Mexico, 1531–1610.* Berkeley: University of California Press, 1960.

————. "Materials for the Demographic History of Mexico." In their *Essays,* 1: 1–12.

————. "On the Credibility of Contemporary Testimony on the Population of Mexico in the Sixteenth Century." In *Summa Anthropologica en homenaje a Robert J. Weitlaner,* 229–39. Mexico City: INEH, 1966.

————. *The Population of the Mixteca Alta, 1520–1960.* Berkeley: University of California Press, 1960.

————. "The Population of Yucatán, 1517–1960." In their *Essays* 2: 1–179.

————. "The Rate of Population Change in Central Mexico, 1550–1570." *HAHR* 37 (1957): 463–70.

Cook, Sherburne F., and Lesley B. Simpson. *The Population of Central Mexico in the Sixteenth Century.* Berkeley: University of California Press, 1948.

Cook, Sherburne F., and A. E. Treganza. *The Quantitative Investigation of Mounds.* Berkeley: University of California Press, 1950.

Cooper, Donald B. *Epidemic Disease in Mexico City, 1761–1813.* Austin: University of Texas Press, 1965.

Cooper, John M. "The Araucanians." In *HSAI,* 2: 687–760.

————. "The Chono." In *HSAI,* 1: 47–54.

————. "The Ona." In *HSAI,* 1: 107–25.

Copenhagen, Carol A. "The *Exordium* or *Captatio Benevolentiae* in Fifteenth-Century Spanish Letters." *La Corónica* 13 (1984–85): 196–205.

Córdoba y Figueroa, Pedro de. *Historia de Chile* (*CHC*, 2). Santiago, 1862.

Cortés, Hernán. *Cartas de Relación*. Ed. Maria Vittoria Calvi. Milan: Cisalpino-Goliardica, 1988.

Côté, James E. *Adolescent Storm and Stress: An Evaluation of the Mead-Freeman Controversy*. Hilldale, N.J.: L. Erlbaum, 1994.

Cottrell, Leonard. *Enemy of Rome*. London: Evans Bros., 1960.

Courcelle, Pierre. *Histoire littéraire des grandes invasions germaniques*. Paris: Etudes Augustiniennes, 1964.

Courlander, Harold. "Kunta Kinte's Struggle to be African." *Phylon* 47 (1986): 294–302.

Courtois, Christian. *Les Vandales et l'Afrique*. Paris: Arts et Métiers Graphiques, 1955.

Covarrubias Horozco, Sebastián. *Tesoro de la lengua castellana*. Madrid: L. Sánchez, 1611.

Crawford, Michael H. *Antropología biológica de los indios americanos*. Madrid: MAPFRE, 1992.

Creasy, Edward S. *The Fifteen Decisive Battles of the World*. New York: Dutton, 1960.

Creighton, Charles. *A History of Epidemics in Britain*. 2 vols. London: Cambridge University Press, 1891–94.

Crosby, Alfred W. *The Columbian Exchange: Biological and Cultural Consequences of 1492*. Westport, Conn.: Greenwood, 1972.

———. "Conquistador y Pestilencia: The First New World Pandemic and the Fall of the Great Indian Empires." *HAHR* 47 (1967): 321–37.

———. *Ecological Imperialism: The Biological Expansion of Europe, 900–1900*. New York: Cambridge University Press, 1986.

———. "Infectious Disease and the Demography of the Atlantic Peoples." *Journal of World History* 2 (1991): 119–33.

———. *The Measure of Reality: Quantification and Western Society, 1250–1600*. New York: Cambridge University Press, 1997.

———. "Summary of Population Size Before and After Contact." In *DDA*, 277–78.

———. "Virgin Soil Epidemics as a Factor in Aboriginal Depopulation in America." *WMQ* 33 (1976): 289–97.

Crouzet, Denis. *La nuit de Saint-Barthélemy*. Paris: Fayard, 1993.

Crowe, Michael J. *The Extraterrestrial Life Debate, 1750–1900*. Cambridge: Cambridge University Press, 1986.

Cuenya, Miguel Angel. "Peste en un ciudad novohispana: El matlazahuatl de 1737 en la Puebla de los Angeles." *Anuario de Estudios Americanos* 53/2 (1996): 51–70.

Culbert, T. Patrick, et al. "The Population of Tikal, Guatemala." In *PPHML,* 103–21.

Cunliffe, Barry. *Greeks, Romans, and Barbarians: Spheres of Interaction.* New York: Methuen, 1988.

Curley, Michael J. *Geoffrey of Monmouth.* New York: Twayne, 1994.

Curtius Rufus, Quintus. *The History of Alexander.* Trans. John C. Rolfe. 2 vols. London: Heinemann, 1946.

Cuvelier, Jean. "Conversion en masse dans l'ancien royaume du Congo." *Bulletin de l'Union Missionnaire du Clergé Belge* 12 (1932): 63–69.

Cuvelier, Jean, and Louis Jadin. *L'ancien Congo d'après les archives romaines, 1518–1640.* Brussels: Académie Royale des Sciences Coloniales, 1954.

Cuvier, Georges. *Discours sur les révolutions de la surface du globe et sur les changements qu'elles ont produits dans le règne animal.* 6th ed. Paris: Heideloff, 1830.

Cyprian. *Treatises.* Ed. Roy D. Defarrari. New York: Fathers of the Church, 1958.

Daniels, John D. "The Indian Population of North America in 1492." *WMQ* 49 (1992): 298–320.

Darvill, Timothy. *Prehistoric Britain.* New Haven: Yale University Press, 1987.

Darwin, Charles. *The Life and Letters of Charles Darwin, Including an Autobiographical Chapter.* Ed. Francis Darwin. 2 vols. Edinburgh: A. and C. Black, 1888.

Daultrey, Stuart, David Dixon, and Cormac O Gráda. "Eighteenth-Century Irish Population: New Perspectives from Old Sources." *Journal of Economic History* 41 (1981): 601–28.

"The David Abraham Case: Ten Comments from Historians." *Radical History Review* 32 (1988): 75–96.

Davies, David M. *The Centenarians of the Andes.* Garden City, N.Y.: Doubleday, 1975.

Davies, Nigel. *The Aztec Empire: The Toltec Resurgence.* Norman: University of Oklahoma Press, 1987.

———. *Human Sacrifice in History and Today.* New York: Morrow, 1981.

Davies, P. S. "The Origin and Purpose of the Persecution of A.D. 303." *Journal of Theological Studies* 40 (1989): 67–94.

Davies, Philip R. *1QM, the War Scroll From Qumran.* Rome: Biblical Institute Press, 1977.

Davis, J. C. *Utopia and the Ideal Society*. Cambridge: Cambridge University Press, 1980.

Day, A. Grove. *Coronado's Quest*. Berkeley: University of California Press, 1964.

———, ed. "Mota Padilla on the Coronado Expedition." *HAHR* 20 (1940): 88–110.

Deak, Gloria-Gilda. *Discovering America's Southeast: A Sixteenth-Century View Based on the Mannerist Engravings of Theodore de Bry*. Birmingham, Ala.: Birmingham Public Library Press, 1992.

Dean, Jeffrey S., William H. Doelle, and Janet D. Orcutt. "Adaptive Stress, Environment, and Demography." In *Themes in Southwest Prehistory*, ed. George J. Gumerman, 53–86. Santa Fe, N.M.: School of American Research Press, 1994.

Dean, Warren. "Las poblaciones indígenas del litoral brasileño de São Paulo a Río de Janeiro: Comercio, esclavitud, reducción y estinción." In *Población y mano de obra en América latina*, ed. Nicolás Sánchez-Albornoz, 25–51. Madrid: Alianza, 1985.

———. *With Broadax and Fireband: The Destruction of the Brazilian Atlantic Forest*. Berkeley: University of California Press, 1995.

Debevoise, Nielson. *A Political History of Parthia*. Chicago: University of Chicago Press, 1938.

Dedering, Tilman. "The German-Herero War of 1904: Revision of Genocide or Imaginary Historiography?" *JSAS* 19 (1993): 80–88.

Deferrari, Roy J. *Early Christian Biographies*. New York: Fathers of the Church, 1952.

Delbrück, Hans. *Geschichte der Kriegskunst in Rahmen der politischen Geschichte*. 5 vols. Berlin: G. Stilke, 1920–28.

———. *Die Perserkriege und die Burgunderkriege*. Berlin: Walther and Apolant, 1887.

———. "Zur Geschichte des ersten Kreuzzuges." *Historische Zeitschrift* 47 (1882): 423–28.

Déléage, André. *La vie rurale en Bourgogne jusqu'au début de onzième siècle*. 2 vols. Macon: Protat Frères, 1941.

Delia, Diana. "The Population of Roman Alexandria." *TAPA* 118 (1988): 275–92.

Demoris, René. "L'utopie, autour du roman: *La terre australe connue* de Gabriel de Foigny (1676)." *Revue des Sciences Humaines* 155 (1974): 397–409.

Demougeot, Emilienne. *La formation de l'Europe et les invasions barbares, de l'avènement de Dioclétien (284) à l'occupation germanique de l'empire romain d'occident*. Paris: Aubier, 1979.

———. "L'invasion des Cimbres-Teutones-Ambrons et les Romains." *Latomus* 37 (1978): 910–38.

Denevan, William M. "Native American Populations in 1492: Recent Research and a Revised Hemispheric Estimate." In *NPA,* xvii–xxxviii.

———. "The Pristine Myth: The Landscape of the Americas in 1492." *AAAG* 82 (1992): 369–95.

Denoon, Donald. *Public Health in Papua New Guinea.* Cambridge: Cambridge University Press, 1989.

Denton, Daniel. *A Brief Description of New-York.* London: John Hancock and William Bradley, 1670.

De Odorico, Marco. *The Use of Numbers and Quantifications in the Assyrian Royal Inscriptions.* Helsinki: University of Helsinki, 1995.

DePratter, Chester. "The Chiefdom of Cofitachequi." In *FC,* 197–226.

De Roche, C. D. "Population Estimates from Settlement Area and Number of Residences." *Journal of Field Archaeology* 10 (1983): 187–92.

Desjardins, Ernest. *Géographie historique et administrative de la Gaule romaine.* 4 vols. Paris: Hachette, 1876–93.

Désveaux, Emmanuel. "Les Indiens sont-il par nature respectueux de la nature?" *Anthropos* 90 (1995): 435–44.

Dever, William G. "Identity of Early Israel: A Rejoinder to Keith W. Whitelam." *Journal for the Study of the Old Testament* 72 (1996): 3–24.

Devine, A. M. "The Battle of Gaugamela: A Tactical and Source-Critical Study." *Ancient World* 13 (1985): 87–116.

———. "Demythologizing the Battle of the Granicus." *Phoenix* 40 (1986): 265–78.

———. "Grand Tactics at Gaugamela." *Phoenix* 29 (1975): 374–85.

———. "Grand Tactics at the Battle of Issus." *Ancient World* 12 (1985): 39–59.

———. "The Macedonian Army at Gaugamela: Its Strength and the Length of Its Battle-Line." *Ancient World* 19 (1989): 77–80.

De Waal, Ronald B. *A World Bibliography of Sherlock Holmes and Dr. Watson.* Boston: New York Graphic Society, 1974.

Dexter, Colin. *Death Is Now My Neighbour.* London: Macmillan, 1996.

Diament, Henri. "Voies souterraines de l'imagination onomastique au Siécle des Lumières: L'*Icosameron* de Casanova." *Nouvelle Revue de l'Onomastique* 19/20 (1992): 173–80.

Díaz del Castillo, Bernal. *Historia verdadera de la conquista de la Nueva España.* Ed. Carmelo Sáenz de Santa María. Madrid: Instituto Gonzalo Fernández de Oviedo, 1982.

Dick, Thomas. *Celestial Scenery.* Philadelphia: E. C. and J. Biddle, 1847.

———. *The Philosophy of a Future State*. Philadelphia: E. C. and J. Biddle, 1847.

———. *The Sidereal Heavens*. Philadelphia: E. C. and J. Biddle, 1847.

Dickens, Patrick. "Why Anthropologists Need Linguistics: The Case of the !Kung." *African Studies* 54 (1995): 17–35.

Diderot, Denis. *Les bijoux indiscrets*. Paris: Au Monomatapa, 1771.

Diehl, Charles. *Justinien et la civilisation Byzantine au VI siècle*. Paris: E. Leroux, 1901.

Diehl, Richard A. *Tula*. London: Thames and Hudson, 1983.

Diesner, Hans-Joachim. *Der Untergang der römischen Herrschaft in Nordafrika*. Weimar: H. Böhlaus, 1964.

Dietler, Michael. "'Our Ancestors the Gauls': Archaeology, Ethnic Nationalism, and the Manipulation of Celtic Identity in Modern Europe." *AA* 96 (1994): 584–605.

Diez de la Calle, Juan. "Noticias sacras y reales de las Indias Occidentales." In *CHC*, 29: 351–95.

Diffie, Bailey W. "Estimates of Potosí Mineral Production, 1545–1555." *HAHR* 20 (1940): 275–82.

Dillery, John. *Xenophon and the History of His Times*. London: Routledge, 1995.

Dio Cassius Cocceianus. *Dio's Roman History*. Trans. Earnest Cary. 9 vols. London: 1914–27.

Diodorus Siculus. *Diodorus of Sicily*. Trans. C. H. Oldfather. 12 vols. Cambridge, Mass.: Harvard University Press, 1933–67.

Dion, Roger. "Migrations de peuples en Gaule au temps de César." In *Hommage à la mémoire de Jérôme Carcopino*, 55–63. Paris: Les Belles Lettres, 1977.

Disney, Anthony. "Vasco da Gama's Reputation for Violence: The Alleged Atrocities at Calicut in 1502." *Indica* 32 (1995): 11–28.

Divine, David. *The Nine Days of Dunkirk*. London: Faber and Faber, 1959.

Djandjgava, Gia. "Ways of Estimating Population Numbers in Medieval Islamic Cities as Exemplified in the Case of Fustat Cairo." *Al-Masaq* 5 (1992): 65–69.

Dobyns, Henry F. "Building Stone and Paper: Evidence of Native American Historical Numbers." *LAPHB* 24 (Fall 1993): 13–19.

———. "Disease Transfer at Contact." *Annual Review of Anthropology* 22 (1993): 273–91.

———. "Estimating Aboriginal American Population: An Appraisal of Techniques with a New Hemispheric Estimate." *Current Anthropology* 7 (1966): 395–416, 425–49.

————. "More Methodological Perspectives on Historical Demography." *Ethnohistory* 36 (1989): 285–99.

————. "Native American Trade Centers as Contagious Disease Foci." In *DDA*, 215–22.

————. "Native New World: Links between Demographic and Cultural Changes." In *CC*, 3: 541–60.

————. "An Outline of Andean Epidemic History." *Bulletin of the History of Medicine* 37 (1963): 493–515.

————. "Reassessing New World Populations at the Time of Contact." *Encuentro* 4/4 (Winter 1988): 8–9.

————. "Sixteenth-Century Tusayan." *American Indian Quarterly* 15 (1991): 187–200.

————. "Superhuman Hearing, Superhorses, and Miraculous Maize." *American Indian Quarterly* 17 (1993): 385–91.

————. *Their Number Become Thinned: Native American Population Dynamics in Eastern North America.* Knoxville: University of Tennessee Press, 1983.

Dodin, André. *Le légende et l'histoire de Monsieur Depaul à Saint Vincent de Paul.* Paris: OEIL, 1985.

Dols, Michael W. "The Comparative Communal Responses to the Black Death in Muslim and Christian Societies." *Viator* 5 (1974): 269–87.

————. "Plague in Early Islamic History." *JAOS* 94 (1974): 371–83.

Donlan, Walter, and James Thompson. "The Charge at Marathon: Herodotus 6:112." *Classical Journal* 71 (1976): 339–43.

Donnadieu, A. "La campagne de Marius dans la Gaule Narbonnaise (104–102 av. J.-C.)" *Revue des Études Anciennes* 56 (1954): 281–96.

Dorey, T. A. "Roman Casualty Figures at Trasimene and Cannae." *University of Birmingham Historical Journal* 7/2 (1959): 1–5.

Doumani, Beshara B. "The Political Economy of Population Counts in Ottoman Palestine: Nablus, circa 1850." *International Journal of Middle East Studies* 26 (1994): 1–17.

Dow, Charles M. *Anthology and Bibliography of Niagara Falls.* 2 vols. Albany: State of New York, 1921.

Downey, Glanville. *Constantinople in the Age of Justinian.* Norman: University of Oklahoma Press, 1960.

Downie, J. A. *Jonathan Swift: Political Writer.* London: Routledge and Kegan Paul, 1984.

Drinkwater, J. F. *Roman Gaul: The Three Provinces, 58 B.C.–A.D. 260.* London: Croom Helm, 1983.

Driver, G. R. "Abbreviations in the Massoretic Text." *Textus* 1 (1960): 126–30.

Duchet, Michèle, ed. *L'Amérique de Theodore de Bry*. Paris: CNRS, 1987.

Ducreux, Marie-Elizabeth. "Les premiers essais d'evaluation de la population mondiale et l'idée de dépopulation au XVIIe siècle." *Annales de Démographie Historique* (1977): 421–38.

Duncan-Jones, R. P. "City Population in Roman Africa." *JRS* 53 (1963): 85–90.

———. "The Impact of the Antonine Plague." *Journal of Roman Archaeology* 9 (1996): 108–36.

———. *Money and Government in the Roman Empire*. Cambridge: Cambridge University Press, 1994.

Dunham, Sean B. "Caesar's Perception of Gallic Social Structures." In *Celtic Chiefdom, Celtic State,* eds. Bettina Arnold and D. Blair Gibson, 110–15. Cambridge: Cambridge University Press, 1995.

Dunnell, Robert C. "Americanist Anthropological Literature, 1981." *American Journal of Archaeology* 86 (1982): 509–29.

———. "Methodological Impacts of Catastrophic Depopulation on American Ethnology and Archaeology" In *CC,* 3: 561–80.

Du Pontet, Renatus, ed. *C. Iulii Caesaris Commentariorum Pars Prior Qua Continentur Libri VII de Bello Gallico Cum A. Hirti Supplemento*. Oxford: Clarendon Press, 1900.

Durán, Diego. *Historia de las Indias de Nueva España y islas de tierra firme*. 2 vols. Mexico City: Editora Nacional, 1951.

Durán Luzio, Juan. "Sobre Tomás Moro en el Inca Garcilaso." *Revista Iberoamericana* 42 (1976): 349–61.

Durant, Will, and Ariel Durant. *Caesar and Christ*. New York: Simon and Schuster, 1944.

———. *The Age of Faith*. New York: Simon and Schuster, 1950.

Durliat, Jean. "La peste du VIe siècle." In *Hommes et richesses dans l'empire Byzantine,* 107–19. 2 vols. Paris: P. Letheilleux, 1988.

Duval, Paul-Marie. *Travaux sur Gaule, 1946–1986*. 2 vols. Rome: Ecole Française de Rome, 1989.

Duverger, Christian. *La fleur létale: Economie du sacrifice aztèque*. Paris: Editions du Seuil, 1979.

Duviols, Pierre. "The Cultural Consequences of the Expulsion of the Jesuits from the Río de la Plata." *Cultures* 7 (1980): 73–84.

Edge, P. Granville. "Precensus Population Records in Spain." *Journal of the American Statistical Association* 26 (1931): 416–23.

Egerton, Frank N. III. "The Longevity of the Patriarchs: A Topic in the History of Demography." *Journal of the History of Ideas* 27 (1966): 575–84.

Einbinder, Harvey. *The Myth of the Britannica*. London: McGibbon and Kee, 1964.

Elison, George. *Deus Destroyed*. Cambridge: Cambridge University Press, 1988.

Elliot, G.F.S. *Chile*. New York: Charles Scribner's Sons, 1907.

Encina, Francisco A. *Historia de Chile*. 20 vols. Santiago: Editorial Nascimiento, 1947–52.

Encyclopedia of Latin American History and Culture. Ed. Barbara A. Tenenbaum. 5 vols. New York: Scribners, 1996.

Engels, Donald W. *Alexander the Great and the Logistics of the Macedonian Army*. Berkeley: University of California Press, 1979.

Entralgo, P. Laín. *Enfermedad y pecado*. Barcelona: Ediciones Toray, 1961.

Errazuriz, Crescente. *Historia de Chile: Pedro de Valdivia*. 2 vols. Santiago: Imprenta Cervantes, 1911.

———. *Historia de Chile sin gobernador, 1554–1557*. Santiago: Imprenta Universitaria 1912.

Etienne, Robert. "Gaule romaine." In *Histoire de la population française, I: Des origines à la Renaissance*, 65–117. Paris: Presses Universitaires de France, 1988.

Europa y Amerindia: El indio americano en textos de siglo XVIII. Quito: Abya-Yala, 1991.

Evans, Brian M. "Census Enumeration in Late Seventeenth-Century Alto Perú: The *Numeración General* of 1683–1684." In *Studies in Spanish American Population History*, ed. David J. Robinson, 25–44. Boulder, Colo.: Westview, 1981.

———. "Migration Processes in Upper Peru in the Seventeenth Century." In *Migration in Colonial Spanish America*, ed. David J. Robinson, 62–85. Cambridge: Cambridge University Press, 1990.

Evans, J.A.S. "Justinian and the Historian Procopius." *Greece and Rome* 17 (1970): 218–23.

———. *Procopius*. New York, 1972.

Evans, John K. "*Plebs rustica*: The Peasantry of Classical Italy." *American Journal of Ancient History* 5 (1980): 19–47, 134–73.

Ewer, Charles R. "Continuity and Change: De Soto and the Apalachees." *Historical Archaeology* 30/2 (1996): 41–53.

Fagan, Brian M. *Time Detectives*. New York: Simon and Schuster, 1994.

Fahnestock, Jeanne. "Arguing in Different Forums: The Bering Crossover Controversy." *Science, Technology, and Human Values* 14 (1989): 26–42.

Falcón Ramírez, Javier. *Clases, estamentos y razas: España e Indias a través del pensamiento arbitrista del Marqués de Varinas*. Madrid: CSIC, 1988.

Faron, Louis C. "Effects of Conquest on the Araucanian Picunche during the Spanish Colonization of Chile, 1536–1635." *Ethnohistory* 7 (1960): 239–307.

Farriss, Nancy. *Maya Society under Colonial Rule.* Princeton: Princeton University Press, 1984.

Fasold, David. *The Ark of Noah.* New York: Wynwood Press, 1988.

Fausett, David. *Writing the New World: Imaginary Voyages and Utopias of the Great Southern Land.* Syracuse: Syracuse University Press, 1993.

Fehling, Detlev. *Herodotus and His "Sources": Citation, Invention, and Narrative Art.* Leeds: Francis Cairns, 1990.

Feijóo y Montenegro, Benito Jerónimo. "Senectud del mundo." In Feijóo, *Obras escogidas,* eds. Vicente de la Fuente and Agustín Millares Carlo, 1: 30–37. Madrid: Atlas, 1952.

———. "Consectario a la materia del discurso antecedente, contra los filosofos modernos." In Feijóo, *Obras escogidas,* eds. Vicente de la Fuente and Agustín Millares Carlo, 2: 89–101. Madrid: Atlas, 1961.

Ferguson, R. Brian. "Ecological Consequences of Amazonian Warfare." *Ethnology* 28 (1989): 249–64.

Fernandes, Florestan. *Organização social dos Tupinambá.* 2d. ed. São Paulo: Difusão Europeia do Livro, 1963.

Fernández-Armesto, Felipe. "'Aztec' Auguries and Memories of the Conquest of Mexico." *Renaissance Studies* 6 (1992): 287–305.

Fernández del Castillo, Francisco. "El tifus en México antes de Zinsser." In *EHEM,* 1: 127–35.

Fernández Rodríguez, Pedro. *Los Dominicos en el contexto de la primera evangelización de México.* Salamanca: Editorial San Esteban, 1994.

Ferrard, Christopher G. "The Amount of Constantinopolitan Booty in 1204." *Studi Veniziani* 13 (1971): 95–104.

Ferrill, Arthur. *The Fall of the Roman Empire: The Military Explanation.* London: Thames and Hudson, 1986.

Fetter, Bruce S., ed. *Demography from Scanty Evidence: Central Africa in the Colonial Era.* Boulder, Colo.: Westview, 1990.

———. "The Missing Migrants: African Seeds in the Demographers' Field." *HA* 11 (1984): 99–111.

Filesi, Teobaldo. "L'epilogo della 'Missio Antiqua' dei cappuccini nel regno del Congo (1800–1835)." *Euntes Docete* 23 (1970): 377–439.

———. *La "Missio Antiqua" degli cappaccini nel Congo, 1645–1835.* Rome: Istituto Storico Cappuccini, 1978.

Fiorelli, Giuseppe. *Gli scavi di Pompei dal 1861 ad 1872.* Naples: Tipografia Italiana, 1873.

Fisher, Elizabeth A. "Theodora and Antonina in the *Historia Arcana:* History and/or Fiction?" *Arethusa* 11 (1978): 253–79.

Fisher, F. J. "Influenza and Inflation in Tudor England." *Economic History Review* 18 (1965): 120–29.

Fishman, Laura. "Claude d'Abbeville and the Tupinambá: Problems and Goals of French Missionary Work in Early Seventeenth-Century Brazil." *Church History* 58 (1989): 20–35.

Fleischmann, Ulrich, Matthias Rohrig Assunção, and Zinka Ziebell-Wendt. "Os Tupinambá: Realidade e ficção nos relatos quinhentistas." *Revista Brasileira de Historia* 21 (1990–91): 125–45.

Flickema, Thomas. "The Siege of Cuzco." *RHA* 92 (1981): 17–47.

Flintoff, Everard. "The Noric Cattle Plague." *Quaderni Urbinati di Cultura Classica* (1983/1): 85–111.

Flori, Jean. "Un problème de méthodologie. La valeur des nombres chez les chroniqueurs du Moyen Age. A propos des effectifs de la première croisade." *Moyen-Age* 99 (1993): 399–422.

Foigny, Gabriel de. *The Southern Land, Known.* Ed. and trans. David Fausett. Syracuse: Syracuse University Press, 1994.

———. *La terre australe connue (1676).* Ed. Pierre Ronzeaud. Paris: Aux Amateurs des Livres, 1990.

Foley, Barbara. *Telling the Truth.* Ithaca: Cornell University Press, 1986.

Folz, Robert. *De l'antiquité au monde médiéval.* Paris: Presses Universitaires de France, 1972.

Foord, Edward A. *The Last Age of Roman Britain.* London: G. G. Harrap, 1925.

Forni, Giuseppe. "L'indagine demografica e gli anfiteatri in Dacia." *Apulum* 13 (1975): 141–54.

Foster, Benjamin R. *Before the Muses: An Anthology of Akkadian Literature.* 2 vols. Bethesda, Md.: CDL Press, 1993.

Fouts, David M. "Another Look at Large Numbers in Assyrian Royal Inscriptions." *Journal of Near Eastern Studies* 53 (1994): 205–11.

Fox, Lady Mary. *Account of an Expedition to the Interior of New Holland.* London: R. Bentley, 1837.

Fox, Richard A., Jr. "The Art and Archaeology of Custer's Last Battle." in *The Cultural Life of Images,* ed. Brian L. Molyneaux, 159–83. London: Routledge, 1997.

France, Anatole. *L'île des Pingouins.* Paris: Calmann-Lévy (1908).

France, John. "The Crisis of the First Crusade: From the Defeat of Kerbogah to the Departure from Arqa." *Byzantion* 40 (1970): 276–310.

———. *Victory in the East: A Military History of the First Crusade.* New York: Cambridge University Press, 1994.

Frank, Tenney. *An Economic History of Rome.* 2d ed. New York: Cooper Square, 1962.

Frankl, Victor. "Hernán Cortés y la tradición de las Siete Partidas." *RHA* 53 (1962): 9–74.

Frazer, R. M., Jr., trans. and ed. *The Trojan War: The Chronicles of Dictys of Crete and Dares of Phrygia.* Bloomington: Indiana University Press, 1966.

Freeman, Derek. *Margaret Mead and Samoa.* Cambridge, Mass.: Harvard University Press, 1983.

Freeman, Edward A. *History of the Norman Conquest of England.* 6 vols. New York: Macmillan, 1873–79.

Freeman, Joseph T. "The Old, Old, Very Old Charlie Smith." *Gerontologist* 22 (1982): 532–36.

French, A. "The Tribute of the Allies." *Historia* 21 (1972): 1–20.

Frere, Shepard. *Britannia: A History of Roman Britain.* London: Routledge and Kegan Paul, 1967.

Fretheim, Terence E. "The Plagues as Ecological Signs of Historical Disaster." *Journal of Biblical Literature* 110 (1991): 385–96.

Friederich, Werner P. *Australia in Western Imaginative Prose Works, 1600–1900.* Chapel Hill: University of North Carolina Press, 1967.

Frison, George. *Prehistoric Hunters of the High Plains.* Orlando, Fla.: Academic Press, 1991.

Fuentes, Patricia de, ed. and trans. *The Conquistadors: First Person Accounts of the Conquest of Mexico.* New York: Orion Press, 1963.

Fuller, J.F.C. *The Generalship of Alexander the Great.* New Brunswick, N.J.: Rutgers University Press, 1960.

———. *Julius Caesar: Man, Soldier, and Tyrant.* London: Eyre and Spottiswoode, 1965.

———. *A Military History of the Western World.* 3 vols. New York: Funk and Wagnall, 1954.

Furger-Gunti, Andres. *Die Helvetier. Kulturgeschichte eines Keltenvolkes.* Zurich: Neue Zürcher Zeitung, 1986.

Furlong, Guillermo. *Misiones y sus pueblos de Guaraníes.* Buenos Aires: n.p., 1962.

Galdames, Luis. *A History of Chile.* Chapel Hill: University of North Carolina Press, 1941.

Gallo, L. "Beloch e la demografia antica." In *Aspetti della storiografia di Giulio Beloch,* 115–58. Naples: Edizione Scientifiche Italiane, 1990.

Galloway, Patricia K. *Choctaw Genesis, 1500–1700.* Lincoln: University of Nebraska Press, 1995.

———, ed. *The Hernando de Soto Expedition: History, Historiogra-*

phy, and "Discovery" in the Southeast. Lincoln: University of Nebraska Press, 1997.

Garavaglia, Juan Carlos. *Mercado interno y economía colonial.* Mexico City: Grijalbo, 1983.

García, Genaro, ed. *Dos antiguas relaciones de la Florida.* Mexico City: J. Aguilar Vera y Comp., 1902.

García Icazbalceta, Joaquín. *Bibliografía mexicana del siglo XVI.* 2d. ed. Mexico City: Fondo de Cultura Económica, 1954 [1886].

García Moreno, Luis A. *Historia de España visigoda.* Madrid: Catedra, 1989.

García Pimentel, Luis, ed. *Relación de los obispos de Tlaxcala, Michoacán, Oaxaca y otros lugares en el siglo XVI.* Mexico City: Casa del Editor, 1904.

Garcilaso de la Vega, Inca. *La Florida del Ynca.* Lisbon: Pedro Crasbeeck, 1605.

———. *Royal Commentaries of the Incas.* Ed. and trans. Harold V. Livermore. 2 vols. Austin: University of Texas Press, 1966.

Gardiner, Alan H. *The Kadesh Inscription of Ramesses II.* Oxford: Griffith Institute, 1960.

Gardiner, C. Harvey. *Naval Power in the Conquest of Mexico.* Austin: University of Texas Press, 1956.

Garofalo, Francesco P. "Sulla popolazione della Galliae." *Revue Celtique* 22 (1901): 227–36.

Garson, Lea Keil. "The Centenarian Question: Old-Age Mortality in the Soviet Union, 1897 to 1970." *Population Studies* 45 (1991): 265–78.

Gautier, E. F. *Genséric roi des Vandales.* Paris: Payot, 1935.

Gelb, I. J. "Prisoners of War in Early Mesopotamia." *Journal of Near Eastern Studies* 32 (1973): 70–98.

Gelb, Norman. *Dunkirk.* New York: Morrow, 1989.

Gelzer, Matthias. "Der Antrag des Cato Uticensis, Caesar den germanen Auszuliefern." In *Festgabe für Paul Kirn,* ed. Ekkehard Kaufmann, 46–53. [Berlin]: E. Schmidt, 1961.

Genovese, Eugene D. *Roll, Jordan, Roll.* New York: Pantheon, 1974.

Georges, Pericles B. "Saving Herodotus' Phenomena: The Oracles and the Events of 480 B.C." *Classical Antiquity* 5 (1986): 14–59.

Gibson, James W. *The Perfect War: Technowar in Vietnam.* Boston: Atlantic Monthly Press, 1983.

Gil, Juan. "El libro Greco-Latino y su influjo en Indias." In *Homenaje a Enrique Segura Covarsi, Bernardo Muñoz Sánchez y Ricardo Puente Broncano,* 61–111. Badajoz: Departamento de Publicaciones, 1986.

Gil, Juan, and Consuelo Varela, eds. *Cartas de particulares a Colón y relaciones coatáneas*. Madrid: Alianza, 1984.

Gil, Fernando. *Primeras "doctrinas" del Nuevo Mundo: Estudio histórico-teológico de las obras de fray Juan de Zumárraga (1548)*. Buenos Aires: Universidad Católica Argentina, 1993.

Gill, Brian. *New Zealand's Extinct Birds*. Auckland: Random Century, 1991.

Gilliam, J. F. "The Plague under Marcus Aurelius." *AJP* 82 (1961): 225–51.

Gillmor, C. M. "Naval Logistics of the Cross-Channel Operation, 1066." *Anglo-Norman Studies* 7 (1984): 105–31.

———. "War on the Rivers: Viking Numbers and Mobility on the Seine and Loire, 841–886." *Viator* 19 (1988): 79–109.

Gilmour, S. MacLean. "The Christophany to More than Five Hundred Brethren." *Journal of Biblical Literature* 79 (1960): 248–52.

Ginés de Sepúlveda, Juan. *Historia del nuevo mundo*. Ed. Antonio Ramírez de Verger. Madrid: Alianza, 1987.

Giovanni Francesco da Roma. *La fondation de la mission des capuchins au royaume de Congo, 1648*, Ed. François Bontinck. Louvain: Editions Nauwaelaerts, 1964.

Girard, Albert. "Le chiffre de la population de l'Espagne dans les temps modernes." *Revue d'Histoire Moderne* 3 (1928): 420–36.

Gisbert, Teresa, and José de Mesa. "Potosí y su sistema hidraúlico minero." In *Obras hidraúlicas en América colonial*, 160–64. Madrid: Ministerio de Obras Públicas, 1993.

Glass, D. V. *Numbering the People: The Eighteenth-Century Population Controversy and the Development of Census and Vital Statistics in Britain*. Farnborough: D. C. Heath, 1973.

Glover, Richard. "The Witness of David Thompson." *Canadian Historical Review* 31 (1950): 25–38.

Gmirkin, Russell. "The War Scroll and Roman Weaponry Reconsidered." *Dead Sea Discoveries* 3 (1996): 89–129.

Godbey, Emily. "The New World Seen as the Old: The 1524 Map of Tenochtitlán." *Itinerario* 19 (1995): 53–81.

Godoy, Felipe de. "Relación e asiento, minas y población de San Felipe de Austria, llamados de Oruro. dd 1607." *Boletín de Oficina Nacional de Estadísticas* (La Paz): 7 (1912): 437.

Goedicke, Hans. "The 'Battle of Kadesh': A Reassessment." In *Perspectives on the Battle of Kadesh*, ed. Hans Goedicke, 77–121. Baltimore: Johns Hopkins University Press, 1985.

Goffart, Walter. *Barbarians and Romans, A.D. 418–584*. Princeton: Princeton University Press, 1980.

———. "Two Notes on German Antiquity Today." *Traditio* 50 (1995): 9–30.

Goic, Cedomil. "Retórica en las cartas de Pedro de Valdivia." In *Discursos sobre la "invención" de América,* ed. Iris M. Zavala, 101–21. Amsterdam: Rodopi, 1992.

———. "Retórica y representación: La carta VIII de Pedro de Valdivia." *Nuevo Texto Crítico* 5 (1990): 21–32.

Goldsmith, Raymond W. "An Estimate of the Size and Structure of the National Product of the Early Roman Empire." *Review of Income and Wealth* 30 (1984): 263–88.

Goldsworthy, A. K. "The *Othismos,* Myths and Heresies: The Nature of the Hoplite Battle." *War in History* 4 (1997): 1–26.

Gómez-Montero, Javier. "¿Cuento, fábula, patraña o novela?" *Iberoromania* 33 (1991): 75–100.

Gomme, A. W. *A Historical Commentary on Thucydides.* 5 vols. Oxford: Clarendon Press, 1945–81.

———. *The Population of Athens in the Fifth and Fourth Centuries* B.C. Oxford: Oxford University Press, 1933.

Góngora, Mario. *Encomenderos y estancieros: Estudios acerca de la constitución social aristocrática de Chile después de la conquista, 1580–1660.* Santiago: Editorial Universitaria, 1970.

Góngora Marmolejo, Alonso de. *Historia de todas las cosas que han acaecido en el reino de Chile y de los que lo han gobernado, 1536–1575.* Santiago: Ediciones de la Universidad de Chile, 1990.

González, Gil. "De los agravios que los indios de las provincias de Chile padecen." In *CHC,* 29: 461–66.

González, Javier R. "Realismo y simbolismo en la geografía del *Amadís de Gaula.*" *Letras* (Buenos Aires) 27–28 (1992–93): 15–30.

González de Cossio, Francisco, ed. *Gacetas de Mexico.* 3 vols. Mexico City: Secretaria de Educación Pública, 1949–50.

González de Najera, Alonso. *Desengaño y reparo de la guerra del reino de Chile.* Santiago: Imprenta Ercilla, 1889.

Good, Timothy S., ed. *We Saw Lincoln Shot: One Hundred Eyewitness Accounts.* Jackson: University Press of Mississippi, 1995.

Goodey, Brian R. "Mapping 'Utopia': A Comment on the Geography of Sir Thomas More." *Geographical Review* 60 (1970): 15–30.

Gordon, C. D. *The Age of Attila.* Ann Arbor: University of Michigan Press, 1966.

Gordon, Robert P. "Saul's Meningitis According to Targum 1 Samuel xix 24." *VT* 37 (1987): 39–49.

Gore, Terry L. *Neglected Heroes: Leadership and War in the Early Medieval Period.* Westport, Conn.: Greenwood, 1995.

Gorenstein, Shirley, and Helen P. Pollard. *The Tarascan Civilization: A Late Prehistoric Cultural System.* Nashville: Vanderbilt University Press, 1983.

Gosselin, Amédée. "Les sauvages du Mississipi [*sic*], 1698–1708." *Proceedings of the Fifteenth International Congress of Americanists* (Québec 1906) 1: 31–51. Quebec: Dussault and Proulx, 1907.

Goudineau, Christian. *César et la Gaule.* Paris: Errance, 1990.

Grant, Michael. *Greek and Roman Historians: Information and Misinformation.* London: Routledge, 1995.

Grapinet, Roger. "Mais où donc se situait Alésia." *Archeologica* 24 (September–October 1968): 24–31.

Graulich, Michel. "L'inauguration du temple principal de Mexico en 1487." *Revista Española de Antropología Americana* 21 (1991): 121–43.

Graves, Michael W., and David J. Addison. "The Polynesian Settlement of the Hawaiian Archipelago." *World Archaeology* 26 (1994–95): 380–99.

Gray, John S. *Custer's Last Campaign: Mitch Boyer and the Little Bighorn Reconstructed.* Lincoln: University of Nebraska Press, 1991.

Great Men and Famous Deeds. New York: Library for Young People, 1903.

Green, D. H. *Medieval Listening and Reading.* Cambridge: Cambridge University Press, 1994.

Green, Peter. *Alexander of Macedon, 356–323 B.C.* Berkeley: University of California Press, 1991.

Green, William. "Examining Protohistoric Depopulation in the Upper Midwest." *Wisconsin Archeologist* 74 (1993): 290–323.

Greenhalgh, Peter. *Pompey, the Roman Alexander.* Columbia: University of Missouri Press, 1981.

Greenleaf, Richard E. *Zumárraga and the Mexican Inquisition, 1536–1543.* Washington, D.C.: Academy of American Franciscan History, 1961.

Greenlee, William B., trans. and ed. *The Voyage of Pedro Alvares Cabral to India and Brazil.* London: Hakluyt Society, 1938.

Gregory of Tours. *The History of the Franks.* Trans and ed. O. M. Dalton. Oxford: Clarendon Press, 1927.

Gregory the Great. *Registrum Epistularum Libri VIII–XIV, Appendix.* Ed. Dag Norberg. Turnhout: Brepols, 1982.

Grenier, Albert. "La Gaule romaine." In *An Economic Survey of Ancient Rome,* ed. Tenney Frank, 3: 379–644. Baltimore: Johns Hopkins Press, 1937.

———. *Les Gaulois.* Paris: Payot, 1945.

Griffith, G. T. "Alexander's Generalship at Gaugamela." *JHS* 67 (1947): 77–89.

Grinde, Donald A., and Bruce E. Johansen. *Ecocide of Native America.* Santa Fe, N.M.: Clear Light, 1995.

Groley, Gabriel. *Ces fameux champs Catalauniques!* Troyes: La Rénaissance, 1964.

Grumet, Robert S. *Historic Contact.* Norman: University of Oklahoma Press, 1996.

Guaman Poma de Ayala, Felipe. *El primer Nueva Corónica y buen gobierno.* Eds. John V. Murra, Rolena Adorno, and Jorge Urioste. 3 vols. Madrid: Historia 16, 1987.

Guebels, Leon. *Jérôme de Montesarchio.* Namur: Grands Lacs, 1951.

Guelke, Leonard, and Robert Shell. "Landscape of Conquest: Frontier Water Alienation and Khoikhoi Strategies of Survival, 1652–1780." *JSAS* 18 (1992): 803–24.

Guerra, Francisco. "Cause of Death of the American Indians." *Nature* 326 (2 April 1987): 449–50.

———. "The Earliest American Epidemic: The Influenza of 1493." *Social Science History* 12 (1988): 305–25.

———. "Early Epidemics at La Hispaniola and Demographic Collapse." *LAPHB* 23 (Spring 1993): 23.

———. "La epidemia americana de influenza en 1493." *RI* 45 (1985): 325–47.

———. "The European-American Exchange." *History and Philosophy of the Life Sciences* 15 (1933): 313–27.

———. "El intercambio epidemiológico tras el descubrimiento de América." *RI* 46 (1986): 41–58.

———. "La invasión de América por virus." In *Maladie et maladies,* ed. Danielle Gourevitch, 219–25. Geneva: Droz, 1992.

———. "Origen de las epidemias en la conquista de América." *Quinto Centenario* 14 (1988): 43–51.

———. "An Outline of the Infectious Exchange of 1492." *Acta Belgica Historiae Medicinae* 5 (1992): 192–98.

———. "Patobiografía de Colón." In *Anales de las II jornadas de historia de la medicina hispanoamericana.* Cadiz, 1986, 259–60.

Guerra, Francisco, and M. C. Sánchez-Téllez. "Missionary Reports from Mexico (1550–1563): Estimates of Native Population Decline." *LAPHB* 25 (Spring 1994): 23–25.

Guillén, Claudio. "Notes toward the Study of the Renaissance Letter." In *Renaissance Genres,* ed. Barbara K. Lewalski, 70–101. Cambridge, Mass.: Harvard University Press, 1986.

Guilmet, George M., Robert T. Boyd, David L. Whited, and Nile

Thompson. "The Legacy of Introduced Disease: The Southern Coast Salish." *American Indian Culture and Research Journal* 15 (1991): 1–32.

Gumerman, George J., and Murray Gell-Mann, eds. *Understanding Complexity in the Prehistoric Southwest*. Reading, Mass.: Addison-Wesley, 1994.

Gupta, Brijen K. "The Black Hole Incident." *Journal of Asian Studies* 19 (1959–60): 53–63.

———. *Sirajuddaullah and the East India Company, 1756–1757*. Leiden: Brill, 1962.

Gusinde, Martin. *Los indios del Tierra del Fuego: Los Selk'nam*. 2 vols. Buenos Aires: Centro Argentino de Etnología Americana, 1982.

Gutiérrez, Lucio. *Domingo de Salazar, O.P.* Manila: University of San Tomas Press, 1979.

Gutiérrez, Ramón. *When Jesus Came, the Corn Mothers Went Away*. Stanford: Stanford University Press, 1991.

Gutiérrez Vega, Cristóforo. *Las primeras juntas eclesiásticas de México, 1524–1555*. Rome: Centro de Estudios Superiores, 1991.

Guy, Jeff. *The Heretic: A Study of the Life of John William Colenso, 1814–1883*. Pietermaritzburg: University of Natal Press, 1983.

Guzmán, Eulalia. *Una visión crítica de la historia de la conquista de México-Tenochtitlán*. Mexico City: UNAM, 1989.

Gwynn, Robin. "The Number of Huguenot Immigrants in England in the Late Seventeenth Century." *Journal of Historical Geography* 9 (1983): 384–95.

Hacking, Ian. "Aloha, Aloha." *London Review of Books* (7 September 1995): 6–9.

———. "Making Up People." In *Reconstructing Individuals*, eds. Thomas C. Heller et al., 222–36. Stanford: Stanford University Press, 1986.

Haley, Alex. *Roots*. Garden City, N.Y.: Doubleday, 1976.

Hall, Emma Swan. *The Pharaoh Smites His Enemies: A Comparative Study*. Munich: Deutscher Kunstverlag, 1986.

Hamel, Gildas. *Poverty and Charity in Roman Palestine*. Berkeley: University of California Press, 1990.

Hammerton, M. "Verne's Amazing Journeys." In *Anticipations: Essays on Early Science Fiction and Its Precursors*, ed. David Seed, 98–110. Syracuse: Syracuse University Press, 1995.

Hammond, George P. *Coronado's Seven Cities*. Albuquerque: University of New Mexico Press, 1940.

Hammond, George P., and Agapito Rey, eds. *Narratives of the Coronado Expedition, 1540–1542*. Albuquerque: University of New Mexico Press, 1940.

Hammond, N.G.L. "The Battle of the Granicus River." *JHS* 100 (1980): 73–88.

———. "The Campaign and Battle of Marathon." *JHS* 88 (1968): 13–57.

———. "Sparta at Thermopylae." *Historia* 45 (1996): 1–20.

———. "The Two Battles of Chaeronea." *Klio* 31 (1938): 186–201.

Hancock, Anson. *A History of Chile.* Chicago: C. H. Sergel, 1893.

Hanisch, Walter. *Un ataque dieciochesco a Juan Ignacio Molina.* Santiago: Ediciones Nihil Mihi, 1973.

Hanke, Lewis. *Bartolomé Arzáns de Orsúa y Vela's History of Potosí.* Providence, R.I.: Brown University Press, 1965.

Hanke, Lewis, and Celso Rodríguez, eds. *Los virreyes españoles en América durante el gobierno de la Casa de Austria: Perú.* 6 vols. Madrid: Atlas, 1978–80.

Hannestad, Knut. "Les forces militaires d'après la *Guerre Gothique* des Procope." *Classica et Medievalia* 21 (1960): 136–83.

Hansen, M. H. "Demographic Reflections on the Number of Athenian Citizens, 451–309 B.C." *American Journal of Ancient History* 7 (1982): 172–89.

Hardorff, Richard G. *The Custer Battle Casualties: Burials, Exhumations, and Reinterments.* El Segundo, Calif.: Upton and Sons, 1989.

Hardy, G. H. *Collected Papers of G. H. Hardy.* 7 vols. Oxford: Clarendon Press, 1966–79.

Hardy, Thomas D., and Charles T. Martin, eds. *Lestoire des Engles Solum la Translacion Maistre Geffrei Gaimar.* 2 vols. London: HMSO, 1889.

Harington, Joseph. *The Commonwealth of Oceana.* London: D. Pakeman, 1656.

Harmand, Jacques. *Alésia: Une campagne césarienne.* Paris: A. and J. Picard, 1967.

———. *Les Celtes au second age du fer.* Paris: Fernand Nathan, 1970.

———. "Un composante scientifique du corpus caesarianum: La portrait de la Gaule dans le *De Bello Gallico* I–VII." In *ANRW,* 1/3: 522–95.

Harner, Michael. "The Ecological Basis for Aztec Sacrifice." *American Ethnologist* 4 (1977): 117–35.

Harris, Cole. "Voices of Disaster: Smallpox around the Strait of Georgia in 1782." *Ethnohistory* 41 (1994): 591–626.

Hart, John. *Herodotus and Greek History.* New York: St. Martins, 1982.

Hartmann, Dean. "Preliminary Assessment of Mass Burials in the Southwest." *American Journal of Physical Anthroplogy* 42 (1975): 305–6.

Hartmann, George W. "The 'Black Hole' of Calcutta: Fact or Fiction?" *Journal of Social Psychology* 27 (1948): 17–35.

Hartwick, John M. "Robert Wallace and Malthus and the Ratios." *History of Political Economy* 20 (1988): 357–79.

Haskett, Robert S. "'Our Suffering with the Taxco Tribute'." *HAHR* 71 (1991): 447–61.

Hassan, Fekri A. *Demographic Archaeology*. London: Academic Press, 1981.

Hassig, Ross. *Aztec Warfare: Imperial Expansion and Political Control*. Norman: University of Oklahoma Press, 1988.

———. *Mexico and the Spanish Conquest*. London: Longman, 1994.

———.*Trade, Tribute, and Transportation: The Sixteenth-Century Political Economy of the Valley of Mexico*. Norman: University of Oklahoma Press, 1985.

Hatzfeld, Jean. *Les trafiquants Italiens dans l'Orient hellénique*. Paris: E. de Boccard, 1919.

Haub, Carl. "How Many People Have Ever Lived on Earth?" *Population Today* 23/2 (February 1995): 4–5.

Haury, J. "Uber die Stärke der Vandalen in Afrika." *Byzantinische Zeitschrift* 4 (1905): 527–28.

Hayes, Peter. "History in an Off Key: David Abraham's Second Collapse." *Business History Review* 61 (1987): 452–72.

Helskog, Knut, and Tore Schweder. "Estimating the Number of Contemporaneous Houses from ^{14}C Dates." *Antiquity* 63 (1989): 166–72.

Hemmerdinger, Bertrand. "Le dénombrement des tribus helvètes chez César (B.G., 1, 29)." *Bollettino dei Classici* 11 (1990): 204–5.

Hemming John. *The Conquest of the Incas*. New York: Harcourt Brace Jovanovich, 1970.

———. *Red Gold: The Conquest of the Brazilian Indians*. Cambridge, Mass.: Harvard University Press, 1978.

Henige, David. "Akan Stool Succession under Colonial Rule: Continuity or Change?" *JAH* 16 (1975): 285–301.

———. "The Biological Effects: Issues and Controversies." In *En ny verden Omkring Columbus*, eds. Jens Braarvig and Finn Fuglestad, 73–79. Oslo: Universitetet i Oslo, 1993.

———. "The Context, Content, and Credibility of *La Florida del Ynca*." *The Americas* 43 (1986–87): 1–23.

———. "Counting the Encounter: The Pernicious Appeal of Verisimilitude." *Colonial Latin American History Review* 2 (1993): 325–61.

———. "Early Epidemics and Modern Interpretations." Forthcoming.

———. "On the Contact Population of Hispaniola: History as Higher Mathematics." *HAHR* 58 (1978): 217–37, 709–12.

————. "If Pigs Could Fly: Timucuan Population and Native American Historical Demography." *Journal of Interdisciplinary History* 16 (1986–87): 701–20.

————. *In Search of Columbus: The Sources for the First Voyage.* Tucson: University of Arizona Press, 1991.

————. "Is Virtual Reality Enough or Should We Settle for Less?" *LAPHB* 23 (Spring 1993): 22–23.

————. *Maybe Heaven, Maybe the Sky, But Definitely Up.* Boston: African Studies Center, 1991.

————. "Measuring the Immeasurable: The Slave Trade, West African Population, and the Pyrrhonist Critic." *JAH* 27 (1986): 295–313.

————. "Millennarian Archaeology, Double Discourse, and the Unending Quest for de Soto." *Midcontinental Journal of Archaeology* 21 (1996): 191–215.

————. "Native American Population at Contact: Standards of Proof and Styles of Discourse in the Debate." *LAPHB* 22 (Fall 1992): 2–23.

————. "Nescience, Belief, and Quantification: A *ménage à trois* of Convenience?" *LAPHB* 23 (Fall 1993): 19.

————. "On the Current Devaluation of the Notion of Evidence." *Ethnohistory* 36 (1989): 304–7.

————. "Primary Source by Primary Source? On the Role of Epidemics in New World Depopulation." *Ethnohistory* 33 (1986): 293–312.

————. "'So Unbelievable It Has to Be True': Inca Garcilaso in Two Worlds." In *The Hernando de Soto Expedition: History, Historiography, and "Discovery" in the Southeast,* ed. Patricia K. Galloway, 155–77. Lincoln: University of Nebraska Press, 1997.

————. "Their Numbers Become Thick: Native American Historical Demography as Expiation." In *The Invented Indian: Cultural Fictions and Government Policies,* ed. James A. Clifton, 169–91. New Brunswick, N.J.: TransAction, 1990.

————. "To Read Is to Misread, to Write Is to Miswrite: Las Casas as Transcriber." In *AILC,* 198–229.

————. "When Did Smallpox Reach the New World (and Why does It Matter?)" In *Africans in Bondage: Studies in Slavery and the Slave Trade,* ed. Paul E. Lovejoy, 11–26. Madison, Wis.: African Studies Program, 1986.

Henripin, Jacques. *La population canadienne au début du XVIIIe siècle.* Paris: Institut Nationale d'Etudes Demographiques, 1954.

Hering, Wolfgang, ed. *C. Iulii Caesaris Commentarii Rerum Gestarum.* Leipzig: Teubner, 1987.

Herlihy, David. "The Population of Verona in the First Century of Venetian Rule." In *Renaissance Venice*, ed. John R. Hale, 91–120. Totowa, N.J.: Rowman and Littlefield, 1973.

Hernández Rodríguez, Rosaura. "Epidemias novohispanas durante el siglo XVI." In *EHEM*, 1: 215–31.

———. "Epidemias y calamidades en el México prehispánico." In *EHEM* 1: 139–56.

Herodotus. *Herodotus*. Trans. A. D. Godley. 4 vols. London: Heinemann, 1921–24.

Herrera y Tordesillas, Antonio de. *Historia general de los hechos de los Castellanos en las islas y tierrefirme de océano*. Ed. Antonio Ballesteros Beretta. 17 vols. Madrid: Tipografía de Archivos, 1934–57.

Herskovits, Melville J. *Dahomey: An Ancient West African Kingdom*. 2 vols.: New York: J. J. Augustin, 1938.

Hertling, Ludwig. "Die Zahl der Christen zu Beginn der vierten Jahrhunderts." *Zeitschrift für katholische Theologie* 58 (1934): 243–53.

———. "Die Zahl der Katholiken in der Völkerwanderungszeit." *Zeitschrift für katholische Theologie* 62 (1938): 92–108.

———. "Die Zahl der Märtyrer bis 313." *Gregorianum* 25 (1944): 103–29.

Hewsen, Robert H. "Moses of Khoren as a Historical Source." *Armenian Review* 39/2 (Summer 1986): 49–70.

Hicks, Frederic. "Dependent Labor in Prehispanic Mexico." *Estudios de Cultura Nahuatl* 11 (1974): 243–66.

———. "Subject States and Tribute Provinces: The Aztec Empire in the Northern Valley of Mexico." *Ancient Mesoamerica* 3 (1992): 1–10.

Hidalgo, Jorge. "The Indians of Southern South America in the Middle of the Sixteenth Century." In *The Cambridge History of Latin America, I: Colonial Latin America*, 91–117. Cambridge: Cambridge University Press, 1984.

———. "Población protohistórica del Norte Chico." *Actas del VI Congreso de Arqueología Chilena, 1971*, 289–94. Santiago: Editorial Universitaria (1973?).

Higham, Nicholas. *Rome, Britain, and the Anglo-Saxons*. London: Seaby, 1992.

Hignett, C. "The Conquest of Gaul." *Cambridge Ancient History* 9 (1932): 537–53.

Hinchliff, Peter. *John William Colenso, Bishop of Natal*. London: Nelson, 1964.

Hiroa, Te Rangi. *Arts and Crafts of Hawaii*. Honolulu: Bishop Museum, 1957.

Hirschfeld, O. "Typische Zahlen in der Uberlieferung der sullanistischen Zeit." In his *Kleine Schriften,* 291–93. Berlin: Weidmannsche Buchhandlung, 1913.

Hirschkind, Lynn. "History of the Indian Population of Cañar." *Colonial Latin American History Review* 4 (1995): 311–42.

Hirschman, Charles, Samuel Preston, and Vu Manh Loi. "Vietnamese Casualties during the American War: A New Estimate." *Population and Development Review* 21 (1995): 783–812.

Historia social y económica de España y América. Ed. Jaime Vicens Vives. 5 vols. Barcelona: Editorial Teide, 1957–61.

Hodge, Mary G. *Aztec City-States.* Ann Arbor, Mich.: Museum of Anthropology, 1984.

Hodge, Mary G., and Michael E. Smith, eds. *Economies and Polities in the Aztec Realm.* Albany, N.Y.: Institute for Mesoamerican Studies, 1994.

Hodges, William H., Kathleeen Deagan, and Elizabeth J. Reitz. "The Natural and Cultural Settings of Puerto Real." In *Puerto Real,* ed. Kathleen Deagan, 51–82. Gainesville: University Press of Florida, 1995.

Hodgkin, Thomas. *Italy and Her Invaders.* 8 vols. Oxford: Clarendon Press, 1880–99.

Hoffman, Michael P. "The Depopulation and Abandonment of Northeastern Arkansas in the Protohistoric Period." In *The Archaeology of Eastern North America: Essays in Honor of Stephen Williams,* ed. James B. Stoltman, 261–75. Jackson, Miss.: Department of Archives and History, 1993.

Hognesius, Kjell. "The Capacity of the Molten Sea in 2 Chronicles IV 5: A Suggestion." *VT* 44 (1994): 349–58.

Hollingsworth, T. H. *Historical Demography.* London: Hodder and Stoughton, 1969.

Holmes, Lowell D. *Quest for the Real Samoa: The Mead-Freeman Controversy and Beyond.* South Hadley, Mass.: Bergin and Garvey, 1987.

Holmes, Richard. *Acts of War: The Behavior of Men in Battle.* New York: Free Press, 1985.

Holmes, T. Rice. *Caesar's Conquest of Gaul.* 2d. ed. London: Oxford University Press, 1931.

————. *The Roman Republic and the Founder of the Empire.* 3 vols. Oxford: Clarendon Press, 1923.

Holmesby, John. *The Voyages, Travels, and Wonderful Discoveries of Capt. John Holmesby.* London: n.p., 1757.

Hopkins, A. G. "Big Business in African Studies." *JAH* 28 (1987): 119–40.

Hopkins, Donald R. *Princes and Peasants: Smallpox in History.* Chicago: University of Chicago Press, 1983.

Hopper, J.M.H. "An Arenavirus and the Plague of Athens." *Journal of the Royal Society of Medicine* 85 (1992): 350–51.

Horden, Peregrine. "Disease, Dragons, and Saints: The Management of Epidemics in the Dark Ages." In *E&I*, 45–76.

Hort, Greta. "The Plagues of Egypt." *ZAW* 70 (1958): 54–58.

Houdaille, Jacques. "Les pertes dans la garde impériale lors des cent jours." In *Historiens et populations. Liber Amicorum Etienne Hélin*, 705–8. Louvain: Academia, 1991.

————. "La population de l'Amérique avant Christophe Colomb." *Population* 41 (1986): 586–90.

Hough, Richard A. *The Battle for Britain*. London: Hodder and Stoughton, 1989.

Howard, Albert A. "Valerius Antias and Livy." *Harvard Studies in Classical Philology* 17 (1906): 161–82.

Hoyte, H. M. Duncan. "The Plagues of Egypt: What Killed the Animals and the Firstborn?" *Medical Journal of Australia* 158 (17 May 1993): 706–7.

Huizinga, Jan. *The Waning of the Middle Ages*. London: E. Arnold, 1924.

Hulme, Peter. "Tales of Distinction: European Ethnography and the Caribbean." In *Implicit Understandings*, ed. Stuart B. Schwartz, 157–97. Cambridge: Cambridge University Press, 1994.

Hume, David. "On the Populousness of Ancient Nations." In *The Philosophical Works*, 3: 421–508. Edinburgh: Black and Tait, 1826.

Hurtado, Albert L. "California Indian Demography, Sherburne F. Cook, and the Revision of American History." *Pacific Historical Review* 58 (1989): 323–43.

Huxley, George. "Mycenaean Decline and the Homeric Catalogue of Ships." *Bulletin of the Institute of Classical Studies* (University of London) 3 (1956): 19–31.

————. "Numbers in the Homeric Catalogue of Ships." *Greek, Roman, and Byzantine Studies* 7 (1966): 313–18.

Ibn Khaldun. *The Muqaddimah*. Trans. Franz Rosenthal. 3 vols. Princeton: Princeton University Press, 1967.

Ibn Taghri Birdi, Ibn al-Mahasin. *History of Egypt, 1382–1469 A.D.* Trans and ed. William Popper. 8 vols. Berkeley: University of California Press, 1954–63.

Iglesia, Ramón. *Cronistas y historiadores de la conquista de México*. Mexico City: Colegio de México, 1942.

————. *El hombre Colón y otros ensayos*. Mexico City: Colegio de México, 1944.

Inglis, G. Douglas. "The Men of Cíbola: New Investigations on the Francisco Vázquez de Coronado Expedition." *Panhandle Plains Historical Review* 55 (1982): 1–24.

Innes, Frank C. "Disease Ecologies of North America." In *The Cambridge World History of Human Disease,* ed. Kenneth F. Kiple, 519–25. Cambridge: Cambridge University Press, 1993.

Innes, Hammond. *The Conquistadors.* London: Collins 1969.

Invernizzi Santa Cruz, Lucia. "¿Illustres hazañas? ¿Trabajos e infortunios? La *Historia de Chile* de Góngora Marmolejo." *Revista Chilena de Literatura* 33 (1989): 7–22.

———. "'Los trabajos de la guerra' y 'Los trabajos de hambre': Dos ejes del discurso narrativo de la conquista de Chile (Valdivia, Vivar, Góngora Marmolejo)." *Revista Chilena de Literatura* 36 (1990): 7–15.

Iselin, Regula. "Reading Pictures: On the Value of the Copperplates in the *Beschryvinghe* of Pieter de Marees (1602) as Source Material for Ethnohistorical Research." *HA* 21 (1994): 147–70.

Isidore of Seville. *History of the Goths, Vandals, and Suevi.* Trans. and eds. Guido Donini and Gordon B. Ford, Jr. Leiden: E. J. Brill, 1970.

Issawi, Charles. "The Area and Population of the Arab Empire: An Essay in Speculation." In *The Islamic Middle East, 700–1900: Studies in Economic and Social History,* ed. A. L. Udovitch, 375–96. Princeton: Princeton University Press, 1981.

Ixtlilxochitl, Fernando de Alva. *Obras históricas.* 2 vols. Mexico City: Secretaria de Fomento, 1871.

Jacobs, Hubert, ed. *Documenta malucensia, 1, 1542–1577.* Rome: IHSI, 1974.

Jacobs, Wilbur R. *Dispossessing the American Indian.* New York: Scribner, 1972.

———. "The Indian and the Frontier in American History: A Need for Revision." *Western Historical Quarterly* 4 (1973): 43–56.

———. "Sherburne Friend Cook: Rebel-Revisionist (1896–1974)." *Pacific Historical Review* 54 (1985): 191–99.

———. "The Tip of the Iceberg: Pre-Columbian Indian Demography and Some Implications for Revisionism." *WMQ* 31 (1974): 123–32.

Jacoby, David. "La population de Constantinople à l'époque byzantine." *Byzantion* 31 (1961): 81–109.

Jacquin, Philippe. "Le massacre des indiens." *L'Histoire* 146 (July–August 1991): 119–24.

Jadin, Louis. "Aperçu de la situation du Congo et rite d'élection des rois en 1775." *Bulletin de l'Institut Historique Belge de Rome* 35 (1963): 347–419.

———. "Les survivances chrétiennes au Congo au XIX siècle." *Etudes d'Histoire Africaine* 1 (1970): 137–85.

James, Edward. *The Merovingian Archaeology of South-West Gaul.* Oxford: BAR, 1977.

Janke, A. "Die Schlacht bei Issos." *Klio* 10 (1910): 137–77.

Jara, René. "The Inscription of Creole Consciousness: Fray Servando de Mier." In *1492–1992: Re/Discovering Colonial Writing,* eds. René Jara and Nicholas Spadaccini, 349–79. Minneapolis: University of Minnesota Press, 1991.

Jashemski, Wilhelmina F. "The Gardens of Pompeii, Herculaneum, and the Villas Destroyed by Vesuvius." *Journal of Garden History* 12 (1992): 102–25.

Jennings, Francis. *The Founders of America.* New York: Norton, 1993.

———. *The Invasion of America: Indians, Colonialism, and the Cant of Conquest.* Chapel Hill: University of North Carolina Press, 1975.

Jeremias, Joachim. "Die Einwohnerzahl Jerusalems zur Zeit Jesu." *Zeitschrift des Deutschen Palästina-Vereins* 66 (1943): 24–31.

———. *Jerusalem in the Time of Jesus.* Philadelphia: Fortress Press, 1969.

Jérez, Francisco de. *Verdadera relación de la conquista del Perú y provincia del Cuzco.* Madrid: Atlas, 1947.

Jiménez, Ramón L. *Caesar against the Celts.* New York: Sarpedon, 1996.

Jiménez de la Espada, Marcos, ed. *Relaciones geográficas de Indias: Perú.* 3 vols. Madrid: Atlas, 1965.

Johansson, Sheila Ryan. "Review of Ole Jorgen Benedictow, *Medieval Demographic System.*" *Population Studies* 48 (1994): 527–34.

Johnson, Samuel. "Mary Queen of Scots." In *The Works of Samuel Johnson,* 13: 260–71. Troy, N.Y.: Literary Club, 1906.

Jones, A.H.M. *The Later Roman Empire.* 2 vols. Oxford: Blackwell, 1964.

Jones, Colin. "Plague and Its Metaphors in Early Modern France." *Representations* 53 (1996): 97–127.

Jones, Michael E. "Climate, Nutrition, and Disease." In *The End of Roman Britain,* ed. P. J. Casey, 231–51. Oxford: BAR, 1979.

———. *The End of Roman Britain.* Ithaca: Cornell University Press, 1996.

Jonghe, E. de., and T. Simar, eds. *Archives congolaises.* Brussels: Vromant, 1919.

Jongman, Willem. *The Economy and Society of Pompeii.* Amsterdam: J. C. Gieben, 1991.

Josephus, Flavius. *The Jewish War.* Trans. G. A. Williamson. New York: Penguin, 1981.

Jullian, Camille. *Histoire de la Gaule.* 8 vols. Paris: Hachette, 1908–26.

———. *Vercingétorix.* Paris: Cercle Historia, 1965.

Juster, Jean. *Les juifs dans l'empire romain.* 2 vols. Paris: Geuthner, 1914.

Juster, Norton. *The Phantom Toll Booth.* New York: Random House, 1961.

Juvayni, ᶜAla a-Din ᶜAta-Malik. *The History of the World-Conqueror.* Trans. John A. Boyle. 2 vols. Cambridge, Mass.: Harvard University Press, 1958.

Kaenel, Gilbert, and Daniel Paunier. "Qu'est-il arrivé après Bibracte." *Archäologie der Schweiz* 14 (1991): 153–58.

Kardulias, P. Nick. "Estimating Population at Ancient Military Sites: The Use of Historical and Contemporary Analysis." *AAy* 57 (1992): 276–87.

Karlen, Arno. *Plague's Progress: A Social History of Man and Disease.* London: Gollancz, 1995.

Katz, Steven T. *The Holocaust in Historical Context.* New York: Oxford University Press, 1994.

———. "The Uniqueness of the Holocaust: The Historical Dimension." In *Is the Holocaust Unique?* Ed. Alan S. Rosenbaum, 19–34. Boulder, Colo.: Westview, 1996.

Katzenstein, H. Jacob. *The History of Tyre.* Jerusalem: Schocken Institute, 1973.

Keats, John. *The Letters of John Keats.* Ed. Hyder Edward Rollins. 2 vols. New Haven: Yale University Press, 1958.

Keaveney, Arthur. *Sulla: The Last Republican.* London, 1982.

Keegan, John. *The Face of Battle.* London: 1976.

Keita, S.O.Y. "*Black Athena,* 'Race,' Bernal and Snowden." *Arethusa* 26 (1993): 295–334.

Keith, Robert G. *Conquest and Agrarian Change: The Emergence of the Hacienda System on the Peruvian Coast.* Cambridge, Mass.: Harvard University Press, 1976.

Kelley, Donald R. "Martyrs, Myths, and the Massacre: The Background of St. Bartholomew." In *The Massacre of St. Bartholomew,* ed. Alfred Soman, 181–202. The Hague: Nijhoff, 1974.

Kellogg, Louise P., ed. *Early Narratives of the Northwest, 1634–1699.* New York: Charles Scribner's Sons, 1917.

Kennedy, Hugh. "Review of Reilly, *Medieval Spains.*" *History* 80 (1995): 466.

Kenyon, Kathleen M. *Excavations at Jericho.* 2 vols. Jerusalem: British School of Archaeology, 1960–83.

Keppie, Lawrence. *The Making of the Roman Army from Republic to Empire.* London: B. T. Batsford, 1984.

Kilger, Laurenz. "Die Taufpraxis in der alten Kapuzinermission am Kongo und in Angola." *Neue Zeitschrift für Missionswissenschaft* 5 (1949): 208–14.

King, Anthony. *Roman Gaul and Germany.* Berkeley: University of California Press, 1990.

Kintigh, Keith W. "The Cíbola Region in the Post-Chacoan Era." In *The Prehistoric Pueblo world, A.D. 1150–1350,* ed. Michael A. Adler, 131–44. Tucson: University of Arizona Press, 1996.

Kiple, Kenneth F., and Kriemhild C. Ornelas. "After the Encounter." In *The Lesser Antilles in the Age of European Expansion,* eds. Robert L. Paquette and Stanley L. Engerman, 50–67. Gainesville: University Press of Florida, 1996.

Kiple, Kenneth F., and Michael Tarver. "Skeletal Biology and the History of Native Americans and African Americans." *LAPHB* 21 (Spring 1992): 3–10.

Kirch, P. V. "Microcosmic Histories: Island Perspectives on 'Global Change.'" *AA* 99 (1997): 30–42.

Kirk, G. S. *The Iliad: A Commentary, I, Books 1–4.* Cambridge: Cambridge University Press, 1985.

Kister, M. J. "Some Reports concerning Mecca from *Jahiliyya* to Islam." *JESHO* 15 (1972): 63–75.

Klausner, Joseph. "How Many Jews Will be Able to Live in Palestine?" *Jewish Social Studies* 11 (1949): 119–28.

Kloevekorn, Heinrich. *Die Kämpfe Cäsars gegen Die Helvetier im Jahre 58 v. Chr.* Leipzig: Gustav Schmidt, 1889.

Klor de Alva, Jorge. "Spiritual Conflict and Accommodation in New Spain." In *The Inca and Aztec States, 1400–1800,* eds. George A. Collier et al., 345–66. New York: Academic Press, 1982.

Klotz, Alfred. "Der Helvetierzug. Zur Glabwürdigkeit von Cäsars *Commentarii de bello Gallico.*" *Neue Jahrbucher für das classische Altertum* 35 (1915): 609–32.

Knen, Peter. "L'utopie entre 'mythe' et 'lumiéres'." *Papers on French Seventeenth-Century Literature* 14 (1987): 253–72.

Knightley, Phillip. *The First Casualty, from the Crimea to Vietnam: The War Correspondent as Hero, Propagandist and Myth Maker.* New York: Harcourt Brace Jovanovich, 1975.

Knoch, Peter. *Studien zu Albert von Aachen.* Stuttgart: Klett, 1966.

Kobayashi, Munehiro. *Tres estudios sobre el sistema tributario de los Mexicas.* Mexico City: Centro de Investigaciones, 1993.

Konetzke, Richard. "Hernán Cortés como poblador de la Nueva España." *RI* 9 (1948): 355–67.

Korth, Eugene H. *Spanish Policy in Colonial Chile: The Struggle for Social Justice, 1535–1700.* Stanford: Stanford University Press, 1968.

Kortmann, M. "Troy: Topography and Navigation." In *Troy and the Trojan War,* ed. M. J. Mellink, 1–16. Bryn Mawr: Bryn Mawr College (1986).

Krause, Paul. "Versuch einer neuen Deutung der 'Pest des Homer.'" *Medizinische Welt* 7 (1933): 1157–58.

Krech, Shepard III. *Indians, Animals, and the Fur Trade: A Critique of* Keepers of the Game. Athens: University of Georgia Press, 1978.

Kroll, Jerome, and Bernard Bachrach. "Sin and the Etiology of Disease in Pre-Crusade Europe." *Journal of the History of Medicine* 41 (1986): 395–414.

Kromayer, Johannes. *Antike Schlachtfelder.* 4 vols. in 5. Berlin: Weidmann, 1903–31.

Kubler, George. "Population Movements in Mexico, 1520–1600." *HAHR* 22 (1942): 606–43.

―――. "Review of Cook and Simpson, *The Population of Central Mexico in the Sixteenth Century.*" *HAHR* 28 (1948): 556–59.

Kukal, Zdenek. *Atlantis in the Light of Modern Research.* Amsterdam: Elsevier, 1984.

Kurz, Hans Rudolf. *Schweizerschlachten.* 2d ed. Bern: Francke, 1977.

Laato, Antti. "Assyrian Propaganda and the Falsification of History in the Royal Inscriptions of Sennacherib." *VT* 45 (1995): 198–226.

Labarbe, Jules. "Chiffres et modes de répartition de la flotte grecque à l'Artémision et à Salamine." *Bulletin de Correspondence Hellénique* 76 (1952): 383–441.

Lach, Donald F., and Edwin J. Van Kley. *Asia in the Making of Europe.* 3 vols. Chicago, University of Chicago Press, 1965–93.

Lachèvre, Frédéric, ed. *Le royaume d'Antangil (inconnu jusqu'à présent).* Paris: La Connaissance, 1933.

LaFollette, Marcel C. *Stealing into Print: Fraud, Plagiarism, and Misconduct in Scientific Publishing.* Berkeley: University of California Press, 1992.

Lagôa, João António Mascarenhas Judice, Visconde de. *Fernão de Magalhãis.* 2 vols. Lisbon: Seara Nova, 1938.

Laird, Andrew. "Fiction, Bewitchment and Story Worlds." In *Lies and Fiction in the Ancient World,* eds. Christopher Gill and T. P. Wiseman, 147–74. Exeter: University of Exeter Press, 1993.

Lamb, Harold. *Constantinople: Birth of an Empire.* New York: Knopf, 1957.

Lambton, Ann K. S. *Continuity and Change in Medieval Persia.* Albany: State University of New York Press, 1988.

Lancel, Serge. *Carthage: A History.* Oxford: Blackwell, 1995.

Langmantel, Valentin. *Hans Schiltbergers Reisebuch.* Tübingen: H. Laupp, 1885.

Laroche, R. A. "Valerius Antias: Livy's Source for the Number of Military Standards Captured in Battle in Books XX–XLV." *Latomus* 47 (1988): 758–71.

Larraín Barros, Horacio. *Demografía y asentamientos indígenas en la Sierra Norte del Ecuador en el siglo XVI.* 2 vols. Otavalo, Ecuador: Instituto Otavaleno de Antropología, 1980.

Larsen, Clark S. "In the Wake of Columbus: Native Population Biology in the Postcontact Americas." *Yearbook of Physical Anthropology* 37 (1994): 109–54.

Lassner, Jacob. *The Topography of Baghdad in the Early Middle Ages.* Detroit: Wayne State University Press, 1970.

Latouche, Robert. "Aspect démographique de la crise de grandes invasions." *Population* 2 (1947): 681–90.

Lau, Brigitta. "Uncertain Certainties: The Herero-German War of 1904." *Mibagus* 2 (1989): 4–9.

Laures, Johannes. "Die Zahl der Christen und Märtyrer in alten Japan." *Monumenta Nipponica* 7 (1951): 84–101.

Laval Manrique, Enrique. "Patología de los Araucanos durante la colonia." *BACH* 70 (1964): 5–42.

—————————. "La viruela en Chile desde la conquista hasta el regreso de Grajales a España en 1825." *Anales Chilenos de Historia de la Medicina* 9–10 (1967–68): 209–12.

Lazenby, J. F. *The Defence of Greece, 490–479 B.C.* Warminster: Aris and Phillips, 1993.

—————. *Hannibal's War.* Warminster: Aris and Phillips, 1978.

Le Bohec, Yann. *César.* Paris: Presses Universitaires de France, 1994.

Lecompte, Janet. "Coronado and Conquest." *New Mexico Historical Review* 64 (1989): 279–304.

Lee, Archie C. C. "Genesis 1 and the Plagues Tradition in Psalms CV." *VT* 40 (1990): 257–63.

Lee, K. H. "Caesar's Encounter with the Usipetes and Tencteri." *Greece and Rome* 16 (1969): 100–103.

Lee, Richard B., and Mathias Guenther. "Errors Corrected or Compounded? A Reply to Wilmsen." *CA* 36 (1995): 298–305.

—————. "Oxen or Onions? The Search for Trade (and Truth) in the Kalahari." *CA* 32 (1991): 592–601.

———. "Problems in Kalahari Historical Ethnography and the Tolerance of Error." *HA* 20 (1993): 185–235.

Lefkowitz, Mary R. *Not Out of Africa*. New York: Basic Books, 1996.

Lefkowitz, Mary R., and Guy M. Rogers, eds. *Black Athena Revisited*. Chapel Hill: University of North Carolina Press, 1996.

Le Gall, J. "L'itinéraire de Genséric." *Revue de Philologie* 62 (1946): 268–73.

Legoupil, Dominique. "Des indigènes au Cap Horn: Conquête d'un territoire et modèle de peuplement aux confins du continent Sud-Américain." *Journal de la Société des Américanistes* 81 (1995): 9–45.

Lehmann, K. "Die Schlacht am Granikos." *Klio* 11 (1911): 230–44.

Leibsohn, Dana. "Mapping Metaphors: Figuring the Ground of Sixteenth-Century New Spain." *Journal of Medieval and Early Modern Studies* 26 (1996): 497–523.

Leitão, Humberto. *Os Portugueses em Solor e Timor de 1515 a 1702*. Lisbon: Liga dos Combatentes da Grande Guerra, 1948.

Leitão, José Augusto Duarte. "A missão do P. Baltasar Barreira no reino de Angola." *Lusitania Sacra* 5 (1993): 43–91.

Leite, Serafim, ed. *Monumenta Brasiliae*. 3 vols. Rome: Monumenta Historica Societatis Iesu, 1956–68.

León, Leonardo. *Lonkos, Curakas, and Zupais: The Collapse and Remaking of Tribal Society in Central Chile, 1536–1560*. London: Institute of Latin American Studies, 1992.

León, Nicolás. "Qué era matlazáhuatl y qué el cocoliztli en los tiempos precolombinos y en le epoca hispana?" In *EHEM*, 1: 383–97.

Leonard, Irving A. *Books of the Brave*. 2d ed. New York: Gordian Press, 1964.

Le Page du Pratz, Simon. *The History of Louisiana*. Ed. Joseph G. Tregle, Jr. Baton Rouge: Louisiana State University Press, 1975.

Lepper, J.L.M. de. *De rebus gestis Bonifatii, comitis Africae et magistri militum*. Breda: W. Bergmans, 1941.

Le Roy Ladurie, Emmanuel. *The Mind and Method of the Historian*. Brighton: Harvester Press, 1981.

Léry, Jean de. *Histoire d'un voyage faict en la terre du Brésil, autrement dite Amérique*. Geneva: La Livre de Poche, 1580.

———. *History of a Voyage to the Land of Brazil, Otherwise Called America*. Trans. Janet Whatley. Berkeley: University of California Press, 1990.

———. *Journal de bord de Jean de Léry en la terre de Brésil, 1557*. Ed. M. R. Mayeux. Paris: Editions de Paris, 1957.

———. *Viagem à terra do Brasil*. Trans. Sérgio Milliet. 2d. ed. São Paulo: Livraria Martins (1941).

Lester, C. Edwards, and Andrew Foster. *The Life and Voyages of Americus Vespr cius.* New York: Baker and Scribner, 1846.

Lestringant, Frank. "L'excursion brésilienne: Note sur les trois premières editions de l'*Histoire d'un voyage* de Jean de Léry (1578–1585)." In *Mélanges sur la littérature de la Renaissance à la mémoire de V.-L. Saulnier,* 53–72. Geneva: Droz, 1984.

Levasseur, Emile. *La population française.* 3 vols. Paris: A. Rousseau, 1889.

Leven, Karl-Heiz. "*Arthumia* and *Philanthrôpia.*" In *Ancient Medicine and Its Socio-Cultural Context,* eds. P. J. van der Eijk et al., 2, 393–407. Amsterdam: Rodopi, 1995.

Levillier, Roberto, ed. *Audiencia de Charcas: Correspondencia de presidentes y oidores.* 3 vols. Madrid: Impr. de J. Pueyo, 1918–22.

Levin, Richard. "Negative Evidence." *Studies in Philology* 92 (1995): 283–310.

Levin, S. "Isaac's Blindness." *Judaism* 37 (1988): 81–83.

———. "The Speech Defect of Moses." *Journal of the Royal Society of Medicine* 85 (1992): 632–33.

Lewis, D. M. "The Athenian Tribute-Quota Lists, 453–450 B.C." *Annual of the British School at Athens* 89 (1994): 285–301.

Lewis, Jack. *The* Gun Digest *Book of Assault Weapons.* Northbrook, Ill.: DBI Books, 1986.

Lewy, Guenter. *America in Vietnam.* New York: Oxford University Press, 1978.

Lieber, Eleanor. "Skin Diseases: Contagion and Sin in the Old Testament." *International Journal of Dermatology* 33 (1994): 593–95.

Limerick, Patricia N. "Turnerians All: The Dream of a Helpful Discipline in an Intelligible World." *American Historical Review* 100 (1995): 697–716.

Linehan, Peter. *Historians and the History of Medieval Spain.* Oxford: Clarendon Press, 1992.

Linenthal, Edward T. *Sacred Ground: Americans and Their Battlefields.* Urbana: University of Illinois Press, 1991.

Lipe, William D. "The Depopulation of the Northern San Juan: Conditions in the Turbulent 1200s." *Journal of Anthropological Archaeology* 14 (1995): 143–69.

Littman, R. J., and M. L. Littman. "Galen and the Antonine Plague." *AJP* 94 (1973): 243–55.

Livy, *The War with Hannibal.* Trans. Aubrey de Sélincourt. Baltimore: Penguin, 1965.

Lo Cascio, Elio. "The Size of the Roman Population: Beloch and the Meaning of the Augustan Census Figures." *JRS* 84 (1994): 23–40.

Loback, Tom. "The Kindreds, Houses, and Population of the Elves during the First Age." *Mythlore* 51 (Autumn 1987): 34–38, 56.

———. "Orc Hosts, Armies, and Legions: A Demographic Study." *Mythlore* 62 (Summer 1990): 10–16, 26.

Lockhart, James. *The Men of Cajamarca*. Austin: University of Texas Press, 1972.

———. *The Nahuas after the Conquest*. Stanford: Stanford University Press, 1992.

Loewe, Michael. "The Campaigns of Han Wu-Ti." In *Chinese Ways in Warfare*, eds. Frank A. Kierman, Jr., and John K. Fairbank, 67–122. Cambridge, Mass.: Harvard University Press, 1974.

Lohmann Villena, Guillermo. *Las minas de Huancavelica en los siglos XVI y XVII*. Seville: Escuela de Estudios Hispano-Americanos, 1949.

Lombardi, John V. *The Political Ideology of Fray Servando de Mier, Propagandist for Independence*. Cuernavaca: Centro Intercultural de Documentación, 1968.

Long, Burke O. *Planting and Reaping Albright: Politics, Ideology, and Interpreting the Bible*. University Park: Pennsylvania State University Press, 1997.

Longman, Tremper. *Fictional Akkadian Autobiography*. Winona Lake, Ind.: Eisenbrauns, 1991.

Lopetegui, León, and Félix Zubillaga. *Historia de la iglesia en la América española*. Madrid: Editorial Católica, 1965.

López de Gómara, Francisco. *Historia de la conquista de México*. Ed. Joaquín Ramírez Cabañas. Mexico City: Robredo, 1943.

López de Velasco, Juan. *Geografía y descripción universal de las Indias*. Eds. Marcos Jiménez de la Espada and María del Carmen González Muñoz. Madrid: Atlas, 1971.

López-Ríos Fernández, Fernando. *Historia médica de las navegaciones colombinos, 1492–1504*. Valladolid: Universidad de Valladolid, 1993.

Lord, Lewis. "Ancient Puzzles and New Ones." *U.S. News and World Report* (24 February 1997): 9.

———. "Those First Americans." *Reader's Digest* 140/837 (January 1992): 98–102.

Lord, Lewis, and Sarah Burke. "America before Columbus." *U.S. News and World Report* 111/2 (8 July 1991): 31–37.

Lot, Ferdinand. *L'art militaire et les armées au Moyen Age en Europe et dans le Proche Orient*. 2 vols. Paris: Payot, 1946.

———. *La Gaule: Les fondements ethniques, sociaux et politiques de la nation française.* Paris: Fayard, 1947.

———. *Les invasions germaniques.* Paris: Payot, 1939.

Lothrop, Samuel K. *The Indians of Tierra del Fuego.* New York: Heye Foundation, 1928.

Lovell, W. George. "'Heavy Shadows and Black Night': Disease and Depopulation in Colonial Spanish America." *AAAG* 82 (1992): 426–43.

Lovell, W. George, and Christopher H. Lutz. *Demography and Empire: A Guide to the Population History of Spanish Central America, 1500–1821.* Boulder, Colo.: Westview, 1995.

Loveman, Brian. *Chile: The Legacy of Hispanic Capitalism.* New York: Oxford University Press, 1979.

Lowery, Woodbury. *The Spanish Settlements within the Present Limits of the United States, 1513–1561.* New York: G. P. Putnam, 1911.

Lucian of Samosata. *Lucian.* Trans. K. Kilburn. 8 vols. London: Heinemann, 1913–67.

Luebben, Ralph A., and Paul R. Nickens. "A Mass Interment in an Early Pueblo III Kiva in Southwestern Colorado." *Journal of Intermountain Archeology* 1 (1982): 66–79.

Luehrs, Robert B. "Population and Utopia in the Thought of Robert Wallace." *Eighteenth-Century Studies* 20 (1986–87): 313–35.

Lukman, Nils. "The Catalaunian Battle (A.D. 451) in Medieval Epics." *Classica et Medievalia* 10 (1948–49): 60–130.

Lunt, William E. *Financial Relations of the Papacy with England to 1327.* Cambridge, Mass.: Medieval Academy, 1939.

Lynn, John A., ed. *Feeding Mars: Logistics in Western Warfare from the Middle Ages to the Present.* Boulder, Colo.: Westview, 1993.

Maas, Michael. *John Lydus and the Roman Past: Antiquarianism and Politics in the Age of Justinian.* London: Routledge, 1992.

McCaa, Robert. "Child Marriage and Complex Families among the Nahuas of Ancient Mexico." *LAPHB* 26 (1994): 2–11.

———. "Spanish and Nahuatl Views on Smallpox and Demographic Catastrophe in Mexico." *Journal of Interdisciplinary History* 25 (1994–95): 397–431.

Macaulay, Rose. *Orphan Island.* London: W. Collins Sons, 1924.

Macfarlane, Iris. *The Black Hole, or the Making of a Legend.* London: Allen and Unwin, 1975.

McGing, B. G. *The Foreign Policy of Mithridates VI Eupator.* Leiden: Brill, 1986.

MacGinnis, John. "Herodotus' Description of Babylon." *Bulletin of the Institute of Classical Studies* 33 (1986): 67–86.

McGrath, John. "Polemic and History in French Brazil, 1555–1560." *Sixteenth Century Journal* 27 (1996): 385–97.

Machiavelli, Niccolò. *Le istorie florentine.* Ed. Pietro Ravasio. Firenze: G. Barbera, 1921.

MacKellar, F. Landis. "On Human Carrying Capacity." *Population and Development Review* 22 (1996): 145–56.

MacKendrick, Paul. *Roman France.* New York: St. Martins, 1972.

McNeill, William H. *Plagues and Peoples.* Garden City, N.Y.: Doubleday, 1976.

———. "*The Rise of the West* after Twenty-Five Years." *Journal of World History* 1 (1990): 1–21.

———. *The Rise of the West: A History of the Human Community.* Chicago: University of Chicago Press, 1963.

McNutt, Francis A. *Bartholomew de las Casas: His Life, His Apostolate, and His Writings.* New York: G. P. Putnam's Sons, 1909.

Macqueen, James G. *Babylon.* London: R. Hale, 1964.

Madhloum, Tariq. "Excavations at Nineveh: a Preliminary Report (1965–1967)." *Sumer* 23 (1967): 76–79.

Maeder, Ernesto J. A. "Las misiones de Guaraníes: Historia demográfica y conflictos con la sociedad colonial, 1641–1807." In *História e população,* eds. Sergio Odilon Nadalin, Maria Luiza Marcilio, and Altiva Pilati Balhana, 41–50. São Paulo: Fundação Sistema Estadual de Análise de Dados, 1980.

———. "La población de las misiones Guaraníes (1641–1682): Reubicación de los pueblos y consecuencias demográficas." *Estudios Ibero-Americanos* 15 (1989): 49–68.

Maeder, Ernesto J. A., and Alfredo S. C. Bolsi. "La población de las misiones Guaraníes entre 1702–1767." *Estudios Paraguayos* 2 (1974): 111–39.

———. "La población Guaraní de la provincia de Misiones en la época post-Jesúitica (1768–1810)." *Folia Historica del Nordeste* 5 (1982): 61–89.

Maestri, Mário. *Os senhores do litoral: Conquista portuguesa e agonia Tupinambá no litoral brasileiro.* Porto Alegre: Editora da Universidade, 1994.

Magie, David. *Roman Rule in Asia Minor.* 2 vols. Princeton: Princeton University Press, 1950.

Mahjoubi, A., and P. Salama. "The Roman and Post-Roman Period in North Africa." In *UNESCO General History of Africa II.* Berkeley: 1981, 465–512.

Málaga Medina, Alejandro. "Las reducciones en el virreinato del Perú." *RHA* 80 (1975): 9–42.

Mallery, Garrick. "The Former and Present Number of Our Indians." *Proceedings of the American Antiquarian Society* 68 (1877): 340–66.

Mallett, Michael. *Mercenaries and Their Masters: Warfare in Renaissance Italy*. London: Bodley Head, 1974.

Malvido, Elsa. "Factores de despoblación y de reposición de la población de Cholula, 1641–1810." *HM* 23 (1973–74): 52–110.

Malvido, Elsa, and Carlos Viesca. "La epidemia de cocoliztli de 1576." *Historias* 11 (Oct.–Dec. 1985): 27–33.

Manceron, Claude. *Austerlitz: The Story of a Battle*. New York: W. W. Norton, 1966.

Mango, Cyril. *Byzantium: The Empire of New Rome*. London: Weidenfeld and Nicolson, 1980.

Manning, Patrick. *Slavery and African Life*. Cambridge: Cambridge University Press, 1990.

al-Maqrizi. *Badhl al-Ma^{c}un fi fadl al-Ta^{c}un*. Cairo: Dar al-Kutub, n.d.

Marais, Mike. "'Omnipotent Fantasies' of a Solitary Self: J. N. Coetzee's *Narrative of Jacobus Coetzee*." *Journal of Commonwealth Literature* 21 (1993): 48–65.

Marcondes de Souza, T. O. *O descobrimento do Brasil*. 2d. ed. São Paulo: Grafica Editora Michalany, 1956.

Marcus, George. "One Man's Mead." *New York Times Book Review* (27 March 1983): 3–4.

Marcus, Raymond. "La conquête de Cholula: Conflit d'interprétations." *Ibero-Amerikanisches Archiv* 3 (1977): 193–213.

Maret, Pierre de. "Interview with Luc de Heusch." *CA* 34 (1993): 289–98.

Marino, C. "The Aboriginal Population of North America, ca. 1492: A Summary of Estimates." *International Journal of Anthropology* 5 (1990): 347–58.

Mariño de Lobera, Pedro. "Crónica del reino de Chile." In *Crónicas del reino de Chile*, ed. Francisco Esteve Barba, 225–596. Madrid: Atlas, 1960.

Markale, Jacques. *Celtic Civilization*. London: Gordon and Cremonesi, 1978.

———. *Vercingétorix*. Paris: Hachette, 1982.

Markham, Clements R. *Reports on the Discovery of Peru*. London: Hakluyt Society, 1872.

Márquez Morfin, Lourdes. "La evolución cuantitativa de la población novohispana: Siglos XVI, XVII y XVIII." In *El poblamiento de México: Una visión histórico-demográfica*, 2: 28–39. Mexico City: Consejo Nacional de Publicación, 1993.

Marr, John S., and Curtis D. Malloy. "An Epidemiological Analysis of the Ten Plagues of Egypt." *Caduceus* 12 (1996): 7–24.

Marrou, Henri Irenée. "La valeur historique de Victor de Vita." *Cahiers de Tunisie 57/60* (1967): 205–8.

Martin, Calvin. "Comment." In *Indians, Animals, and the Fur Trade: A Critique of* Keepers of the Game, ed. Shepard Krech III, 191–97. Athens, Ga.: University of Georgia Press, 1978.

———. *In the Spirit of the Earth: Rethinking History and Time.* Baltimore: Johns Hopkins University Press, 1992.

———. *Keepers of the Game: Indian-Animal Relationships and the Fur Trade.* Berkeley: University of California Press, 1978.

———. "The War Between Indians and Animals." *Natural History* 87 (June 1978): 92–96.

———, ed. *The American Indian and the Problem of History.* New York: Oxford University Press, 1986.

Martin, Jules. *Pétau (1583–1652).* Paris: Bloud, 1910.

Martín Hernández, Francisco. *Don Vasco de Quiroga, protector de los Indios.* Salamanca: Universidad Pontificia Salamanca, 1993.

Martínez, José Luis. *Hernán Cortés.* Mexico City: UNAM, 1990.

Martire de Anghiera, Pedro. *Opera.* Ed. Erich Woldan. Graz: Akademische Druck- und Verlagsanstalt, 1966.

Marx, Jacques. *Tiphaigne de la Roche.* Brussels: Université de Bruxelles, 1981.

Maryon, Herbert. "The Colossus of Rhodes." *JHS* 76 (1956): 68–86.

Masefield, John. *The Nine Days Wonder.* London: Heinemann, 1941.

Mason, Carol I. "Historic Pottery and Tribal Identification in Wisconsin: A Review of the Evidence and the Problems." *Wisconsin Archeologist* 74 (1993): 258–65.

Matschke, Klaus-Peter. *Die Schlacht bei Ankara und das Schicksal von Byzanz.* Weimar: Böhlau, 1981.

Matthew of Edessa. *Armenia and the Crusades.* Trans. and ed. Ara E. Doustourian. Lanham, Md.: University Press of America, 1993.

———. "Chronique." In *Recueil des historiens des Croisades: Documents arméniens,* 1: 33. Paris, 1869.

Maurice, F. "The Size of the Army of Xerxes in the Invasion of Greece, 480 B.C." *JHS* 50 (1930): 210–35.

May, Robert. "Prehistory of Amazonian Indians." *Nature* 312 (1 November 1984): 19–20.

Mazess, Richard B., and Sylvia H. Forman. "Longevity and Age Exaggeration in Vilcabamba, Ecuador." *Journal of Gerontology* 34 (1979): 94–98.

Mazzotti, Antonio. "The Lightning Bolt Yields to the Rainbow." *Modern Language Quarterly* 57 (1996): 197–211.

Means, Philip A. *Ancient Civilizations of the Andes.* New York: Gordian Press, 1931.

Medina, José Toribio. *Los aborígenes de Chile.* Santiago: Fondo Histórico y Bibliográfico José Toribio Medina, 1952.

———. *El veneziano Sebastián Caboto.* Santiago: Imprenta Universitaria, 1908.

Meier, Christian. *Caesar.* New York: Basic Books, 1995.

Meister, Cary W. "The Misleading Nature of Data in the Bureau of the Census Report on 1970 American Indian Population." *Indian Historian* 11 (December 1978): 12–19.

Melbye, Jerry, and Scott I. Fairgrieve. "A Massacre and Possible Cannibalism in the Canadian Arctic: New Evidence from the Saunaktuk Site (NgTn-1)." *Arctic Anthropology* 31/2 (1994): 57–77.

Melià, Bartomeu. *El Guaraní conquistado y reducido.* Asunción: Universidad Católica, 1986.

Mellafe, Rolando. "The Importance of Migration in the Viceroyalty of Peru." In *Population and Economics,* ed. Paul Deprez, 303–13. Winnipeg: University of Manitoba Press (1970).

Melville, Elinor G. K. "Environmental and Social Change in the Valle del Mezquital, 1521–1600." *Comparative Studies in Society and History* 32 (1990): 24–53.

———. *A Plague of Sheep.* Cambridge: Cambridge University Press, 1994.

Mena, Cristóbal de. "La conquista del Perú." In *Relaciones primitivas de la conquista del Perú,* ed. Raúl Porras Barrenechea, 79–101. Lima: Instituto Raúl Porras Barrenechea, 1967.

Mendoza, Antonio de. "Fragmento de la visita hecha à don Antonio de Mendoza." In *Colección de documentos para la historia de México,* ed. Joaquín García Icazbalceta. 2 vols. Mexico City: J. M. Andrade, 1858–66.

Merbs, Charles F. "Patterns of Sickness and Health in the Precontact Southwest." In *CC,* 1: 41–55.

Merkle, Stefan. "Telling the True Story of the Trojan War: The Eyewitness Account of Dictys of Crete." In *The Search for the Ancient Novel,* ed. James Tatum, 183–96. Baltimore: Johns Hopkins University Press, 1994.

———. "The Truth and Nothing but the Truth: Dictys and Dares." In *The Novel in the Ancient World,* ed. Gareth Schmeling, 563–80. Leiden: Brill, 1996.

Métraux, Alfred. *La civilisation matérielle des tribus Tupi-Guarani.* Paris: P. Geuthner, 1928.

Meyer, Ernst. "Die Zahl der Helvetier bei Caesar." *Zeitschrift für schweizerische Geschichte* 29 (1949): 65–70.

Michieli, Catalina Teresa. *Los Comechingones según la crónica de*

Gerónimo de Bibar y su confrontación con otras fuentes. San Juan: Universidad Nacional de San Juan, 1985.

Mier, Servando Teresa de. "La idea de la independencía." In his *Obras completas, 4: La formación de un republicano*, ed. Jaime E. Rodríguez O. Mexico City: UNAM, 1988.

Milanich, Jerald T. *The Florida Indians and the Invasion from Europe*. Gainesville: University Press of Florida, 1995.

Milanich, Jerald T., and Charles Hudson. *Hernando de Soto and the Indians of Florida*. Gainesville: University Press of Florida, 1993.

Milich, Zorka. *A Stranger's Supper: An Oral History of Centenarian Women of Montenegro*. New York: Twayne, 1996.

Millard, Alan R. "Large Numbers in the Assyrian Royal Inscriptions." In *Ah, Assyria . . . : Studies in Assyrian History and Ancient Near Eastern Historiography Presented to Hayim Tadmor*, 213–22. Jerusalem: Hebrew University, 1991.

Miller, Mary Ellen. *The Art of Mesoamerica*. New York: Thames and Hudson, 1986.

Miller, Sterling. "Araucanian Population Density: An Error in the *Handbook of South American Indians*." *AA* 80 (1978): 940–42.

Mills, Gary B., and Elizabeth S. Mills. "*Roots* and the New Faction: A Legitimate Tool for Clio?" *Virginia Magazine of History and Biography* 89 (1981): 3–26.

Milner, George R. "Epidemic Disease in the Postcontact Southeast: A Reappraisal." *Mid-Continental Journal of Archaeology* 5 (1980): 39–56.

Miquel, André. *La géographie humaine du monde musulman jusqu'au milieu du 11e siècle*. Paris: Mouton, 1967.

Miranda, José. "La población indígena de México en el siglo XVII." *HM* 12 (1962–63): 182–89.

Mires, Peter B. "Contact and Contagion: The Roanoke Colony and Influenza." *Historical Archaeology* 28 (1994): 30–38.

Mitchem, Jeffrey. "Artifacts of Exploration: Archaeological Evidence from Florida." In *First Encounters: Spanish Explorations in the Caribbean and the United States, 1492–1570*, eds. Jerald T. Milanich and Susan Milbrath, 99–109. Gainesville: University Press of Florida, 1989.

———. "The Ruth Smith, Weeki Wachee, and Tatham Mounds: Archaeological Evidence of Early Spanish Contact." *Florida Anthropologist* 42 (1989): 317–39.

Moheau, [unknown]. *Recherches et considérations sur la population de la France*. Paris: Moutard, 1778.

Molina, Cristóbal de. *Las crónicas de los Molinos*. Ed. Francisco A. Loayza. Lima: Imp. D. Miranda, 1943.

Molina, Juan Ignacio. *Compendio de historia de Chile.* In *CHC,* 11: 305–522; *CHC,* 26: 103–371.

Mommsen, Theodor. *The History of Rome.* Trans. William P. Dickson. 6 vols. New York: Scribners, 1895.

Monteiro, John M. "Os Guarani e a história do Brasil meridional, séculos XVI–XVII." In *História dos Indios no Brasil,* 475–98. São Paulo: Companhia de Letras, 1992.

———. *Negros da terra: Indios e bandeirantes nas origens de São Paulo.* São Paulo: Companhia de Letras, 1994.

———. *The Supply of Indian Slaves to Sao Paulo in the Seventeenth Century: Some Demographic Implications.* São Paulo: Associação Brasileira de Estudos Populacionais, 1989.

Montesinos, Fernando. *Anales del Perú.* Ed. Victor M. Maurtua. 2 vols. Madrid: Imp. de Gabriel L. y del Horno, 1906.

Montesquieu, Charles de Sécondat, Baron de. *Lettres persanes.* Ed. Henri Barckhausen. Paris: Hachette, 1913.

Moore, David C. "Routes: Alex Haley's *Roots* and the Rhetoric of Genealogy." *Transition* 64 (1994): 5–21.

Moore, John S. "Jack Fisher's 'Flu': A Visitation Revisited." *Economic History Review* 23 (1993): 280–307.

Moors, Derrick. "Imaginary Voyages." In *The Great South Land,* 8–14. Melbourne: Friends of the State Library of Victoria, 1988.

Morales Belda, Francisco. *La marina vándala: Los Asdingos en España.* Barcelona: Ariel, 1969.

Morales Padrón, Francisco, ed. *Primeras cartas sobre América, 1493–1503.* Seville: Universidad de Sevilla, 1990.

Morazzani, André. "Essai sur la puissance maritime des Vandales." *Bulletin de l'Association Guillaume Budé* 4/1 (1966): 539–60.

More, Thomas. *Utopia.* Eds. George M. Logan and Robert M. Adams. Cambridge: Cambridge University Press, 1989.

Moreau, J. *Dictionnaire de géographie historique de la Gaule et de la France.* Paris: A. and J. Picard, 1972.

Morens, David M., and R. J. Littman. "Epidemiology of the Plague of Athens." *TAPA* 122 (1992): 271–304.

———. "'Thucydides' Syndrome' Reconsidered: New Thoughts on the Plague of Athens." *American Journal of Epidemiology* 140 (1994): 621–29.

Morgan, Edmund S. *American Slavery, American Freedom: The Ordeal of Colonial Virginia.* New York: Norton, 1975.

———. "Headrights and Head Counts." *Virginia Magazine of History and Biography* 80 (1972): 361–71.

Morgan, Thomas E. "Plague or Poetry? Thucydides on the Epidemic in Athens." *TAPA* 124 (1994): 197–209.

Morison, Samuel Eliot. *Admiral of the Ocean Sea.* 2 vols. Boston: Little, Brown, 1942.

Morley, Sylvanus G. *The Ancient Maya.* Stanford: Stanford University Press, 1946.

———. *La civilización Maya.* Ed. Adrián Recinos. 5th ed. Mexico City: Fondo de Cultura Económica, 1965.

Morris, Colin. "The Aims and Spirituality of the First Crusade as Seen through the Eyes of Albert of Aachen." *Reading Medieval Studies* 16 (1990): 99–117.

Morse, Jarvis M. "John Smith and His Critics." *Journal of Southern History* 1 (1935): 123–37.

Morse, Ruth. *Truth and Convention in the Middle Ages.* Cambridge: Cambridge University Press, 1991.

Morton, Arthur S. *David Thompson.* Toronto: Ryerson Press, 1930.

Morton, Thomas. *New England Canaan of Thomas Morton.* Ed. Charles Francis Adams. New York: Burt Franklin, 1967 [1632].

Moseley, M. E. *The Incas and Their Ancestors.* London: Thames and Hudson, 1992.

Motolinía, Toribio de Benavente. *Historia de los Indios de la Nueva España.* Mexico City: Chávez Hayhoe, 1941.

———. *Memoriales.* Ed. Edmundo O'Gorman. Mexico City: Instituto de Investigaciones Históricas, 1971.

Moulin, Ann Marie. "Le choc microbien." *L'Histoire* 146 (July–August 1991): 128–32.

Moya Pons, Frank. "Legitimación ideológica de la conquista: El caso de la Española." in *De palabra y obra en el Nuevo Mundo,* eds. Manuel Gutiérrez Estévez et al., 63–78. Mexico City: Siglo Veintiuno, 1992.

Mudimbe-Boye Mbulamuanza. *Vocabulaire et idéologie dans les ecrits des missionnaires capucins aux 17e et 18e siècles.* Lubumbashi: n.p., 1975.

Mühll, Emanuel van der. *Denis Veiras et son histoire des Sévarambes, 1677–1679.* Paris: Droz, 1938.

Müller, B. A. "Die Zahl der Teilnehmer am Helvetierfeldzug im Jahre 58 v. Chr. Geb." *Klio* 9 (1909): 69–75.

Muñoz, Alvaro V. "Las obras hidráulicas en la valle de México: Siglos XVI y XVII." In *América: Encuentro y asimilación,* 237–56. Granada: Diputación Provincial de Granada, 1989.

Muñoz Camargo, Diego. *Historia de Tlaxcala.* 6th ed. Mexico City: Ateneo Nacional, 1947.

Murdoch, James. *A History of Japan.* 3 vols. New York: Ungar, 1964.

Murison, J. A. "Darius III and the Battle of Issus." *Historia* 21 (1972): 399–423.

Murra, John V. "Current Research and Prospects in Andean Ethnohistory." *Latin American Research Review* 5/1 (1970): 3–36.

Murray, Alan V. "The Army of Godfrey of Bouillon, 1096–1099: Structure and Dynamics of a Contingent on the First Crusade." *Revue Belge de Philologie et d'Histoire* 70 (1992): 301–29.

Murray, Alexander, *Reason and Society in the Middle Ages.* Oxford: Clarendon Press, 1978.

Murrin, Michael. *History and Warfare in Renaissance Epic.* Chicago: University of Chicago Press, 1994.

Musset, Lucien. *Les invasions: Les vagues germaniques.* Paris: Presses Universitaires de France, 1969.

Myers, Thomas P. "El efecto de las pestes sobre las poblaciones de la Amazonia Alta." *Amazonia Peruana* 15 (1988): 61–81.

Mylne, Vivienne. *The Eighteenth-Century Novel: Techniques of Illusion.* New York: Barnes and Noble, 1965.

Naddaf, Gerard. "The Atlantis Myth." *Phoenix* 48 (1994): 189–209.

Nagel, Joane. *American Indian Ethnic Renewal.* New York: Oxford University Press, 1996.

Napoléon III. *Histoire de Jules César.* New York: D. Appleton, 1866.

Naroll, Raoul. "Floor Area and Settlement Populations." *AAy* 27 (1962): 587–89.

Nass, G. Gisela, and Nicholas F. Bellatoni. "A Prehistoric Multiple Burial from Monument Valley Evidencing Trauma and Possible Cannibalism." *Kiva* 47 (1982): 257–71.

Navarrete Pellicer, Sergio. "Algunas implicaciones de los cambios en los patrones de asentamiento indígena durante el siglo XVI: Especulación aritmética e historia conjetural." In *Movimientos de población en el occidente de México,* eds. Thomas Calvo and Gustavo López, 103–21. Morelia: Colegio de Michoacán, 1988.

Nebrija, Elio Antonio de. *Vocabulario español-latino.* Madrid, n.p., 1951 [1495].

Nelson, Ben A. "Ethnoarchaeology and Palaeodemography: A Test of Turner and Lofgren's Hypothesis." *JAR* 37 (1981): 107–29.

Neville, Henry. *The Isle of Pines.* London: n.p., 1668.

Newby, Gordon D. "Abraha and Sennacherib." *JAOS* 94 (1974): 431–47.

"News from the Western Islands." In Blair/Robertson, 3: 231–49.

Newson, Linda A. "The Demographic Collapse of Native Peoples of the Americas, 1492–1650." In *The Meeting of Two Worlds: Europe and the*

Americas, 1492–1650, ed. Warwick Bray, 247–88. London: Oxford University Press, 1993.

———. "Highland-Lowland Contrasts in the Impact of Old World Diseases in Early Colonial Ecuador." *Social Science and Medicine* 36 (1993): 1187–95.

———. *Life and Death in Early Colonial Ecuador.* Norman: University of Oklahoma Press, 1995.

———. "The Population of the Amazon Basin in 1492: A View From the Ecuadorian Headwaters." *Transactions of the British Institute of Geographers* 21 (1996): 5–26.

———. "Pre-Columbian Settlement and Population." In *The Cambridge Encyclopedia of Latin America and the Caribbean.* 2d ed. New York: Cambridge University Press, 1992, 128–32.

———. "Review of Jackson, *Indian Population Decline.*" *Journal of Latin American Studies* 27 (1995): 710–11.

Nickes, John. "David Thompson." In *Canadian Dictionary of Biography* 8 (1985): 878–84.

Nicolson, Robert B. *The Pitcairners.* Sydney: Angus and Robertson, 1965.

Nielsen, Hjordis. "The 2.2.1 Tribute Distribution in the Triple Alliance." *Ancient Mesoamerica* 7 (1996): 207–14.

Nissen, Heinrich. *Pompeianische Studien.* Leipzig: Breitkopf and Hartel, 1877.

Nixon, C.E.V. "Relations between Visigoths and Romans in Fifth-Century Gaul." In *Fifth-Century Gaul: A Crisis of Identity?* eds. John Drinkwater and Hugh Elton, 64–74. Cambridge: Cambridge University Press, 1992.

Nobile, Philip. "Uncovering *Roots.*" *Village Voice* (23 February 1993): 31–38.

Nóbrega, Manuel da. *Cartas do Brasil, 1549–1560.* Rio de Janeiro: Officina Industrial Graphica, 1931.

Noguères, Henri. *The Massacre of St. Bartholomew.* London: Allen and Unwin, 1962.

Noguez, Xavier. "The 1531 Codex of Huexotzinco." In *Chipping Away on Earth: Studies in Prehispanic and Colonial Mexico in Honor of Arthur J. O. Anderson and Charles E. Dibble,* ed. Eloise Quiñones Keber, 67–71. Lancaster, Calif.: Labyrinthos, 1994.

North, Douglass C., and Robert P. Thomas. *The Rise of the Western World.* Cambridge: Cambridge University Press, 1973.

Novick, Peter. *That Noble Dream.* Cambridge: Cambridge University Press, 1988.

Nuix, Juan. *Reflexiones imparciales sobre la humanidad de los españoles en las Indias.* Madrid: J. Ibarra, 1782.

Nutini, Hugo G. *The Wages of Conquest.* Ann Arbor: University of Michigan Press, 1995.

Ober, William B., and Nabil Alloush. "The Plague at Granada, 1348–1349." *Bulletin of the New York Academy of Medicine* 58 (1982): 418–24.

Obermeier, Franz. *Französische Brasilienreiseberichte im. 17 Jahrhundert.* Bonn: Romanistischer Verlag, 1995.

Ocaranza, Fernando. "Las grandes epidemias del siglo XVI en la Nueva España." In *EHEM*, 1: 201–4.

Ockinga, Boyo G. "On the Interpretation of the Kadesh Record." *Chronique d'Egypte* 62 (1987): 38–48.

O'Connell, Robert L. *Ride of the Second Horseman: The Birth and Death of War.* New York: Oxford University Press, 1995.

O'Gorman, Edmundo. *Seis estudios históricos de tema mexicano.* Xalapa: Universidad Veracruzana, 1960.

Ohlin, Goran. "No Safety in Numbers: Some Pitfalls of Historical Statistics." In *Industrialization in Two Systems*, ed. Henry Rosovsky, 68–90. New York: Wiley, 1966.

Olivares, Miguel de. *Historia de la Compañia de Jésus en Chile (1593–1736) (CHC, 7).* Santiago: Imprenta Andrés Bello, 1874.

———. *Historia militar, civil y sagrada de lo acaecido en la conquista y pacificación del reino de Chile.* In CHC, 4: 13–402; CHC, 26: 1–101.

Olmedillas de Pereiras, María de las Nieves. *Pedro Martir de Angleria y la mentalidad exoticista.* Madrid: Editorial Gredos, 1974.

Olmstead, Albert T. *Assyrian Historiography.* Columbia: University of Missouri Press, 1916.

Olsen, Marilyn A. "The Prologue of the *Cauallero Çifar*." *Bulletin of Hispanic Studies* 62 (1985): 15–23.

Olson, Alan P. "A Mass Secondary Burial from Northern Arizona." *AAy* 31 (1966): 822–26.

Oman, Charles. *A History of the Art of War in the Middle Ages.* New York: B. Franklin (1959).

Orans, Martin. *Not Even Wrong: Margaret Mead, Derek Freeman, and the Samoans.* Novato, Calif.: Chandler and Sharp, 1996.

Orderic Vitalis. *The Ecclesiastical History of Orderic Vitalis.* Trans. and ed. Marjorie Chibnall. 6 vols. Oxford: Clarendon Press, 1969–80.

Orellana Rodríguez, Mario. *La crónica de Gerónimo de Bibar y la conquista.* Santiago: Editorial Universitaria, 1988.

———. "Gerónimo de Bibar y el origen de la historiografía Chilena." *Estudios Sociales* 54 (1987): 93–124.

———. "La influencia de Jerónomo de Vivar en la crónica del P. Diego Rosales." *Historia* (Santiago) 23 (1988): 253–66.

Origen. *Contra Celsum.* Ed. and trans. Henry Chadwick. Cambridge: Cambridge University Press, 1953.

Orlandis, José. *Historia del reino visigodo español.* Madrid: Rialp, 1988.

Orosius, Paulus. *The Seven Books of History against the Pagans.* Trans. Roy J. Deferrari. Washington, D.C.: Catholic University of America Press, 1964.

Orozco y Berra, Manuel. *Historia antigua y de la conquista de México.* 4 vols. Mexico City: Editorial Porrua, 1960.

———. *Historia de la dominación española en Mexico.* 4 vols. Mexico City: J. Porrua e Hijos, 1983.

Ortega, Francisco de. "Report concerning the Filipinas Islands, and Other Papers [1594]." In Blair/Robertson, 9: 95–119.

Ortiz de Montellano, Bernard R. "Counting Skulls: Comment on the Aztec Cannibalism Theory of Harner-Harris." *AA* 85 (1983): 403–6.

Ossorio y Redín, Miguel Alvarez. *Discurso universal de las causas que ofenden esta monarquía y remedios eficaces para todas.* (n.p., 1986), as reproduced from *Apéndice a la educación popular,* Pedro Rodríguez Campomanes, 4 vols.: Madrid: A. de Sancha, 1775, 1: 19–22.

Overbeck, Mechtild. *Untersuchungen zum afrikanischen Senatsadel in der Spätantike.* Frankfurt: Lassleben, 1973.

Oviedo y Valdés, Gonzalo Fernández de. *Historia general y natural de las Indias, islas y tierra-firme de mar océano.* Ed. José Amador de los Ríos. 4 vols. Madrid: Real Academia de la Historia, 1851–55.

Owsley, Douglas W., and Richard L. Jantz, eds. *Skeletal Biology in the Great Plains: Migration, Warfare, Health, and Subsistence.* Washington, D.C.: Smithsonian Institution Press, 1989.

Packer, James E. "Housing and Population in Imperial Ostia and Rome." *JRS* 57 (1967): 80–89.

Page, Denys L. *History and the Homeric Iliad.* Berkeley: University of California Press, 1959.

Palkovich, Ann M. "Historic Epidemics of the American Pueblos." In *In the Wake of Contact,* eds. Clark S. Larsen and George R. Milner, 67–95. New York: Wiley-Liss, 1994.

Palm, Edwin W. "Tenochtitlán y la ciudad ideal de Dürer." *Journal de la Société des Américanistes* 40 (1951): 59–66.

Palmer, Richard. "The Church, Leprosy, and Plague in Medieval and Early Modern Europe." In *The Church and Healing.* ed. W. J. Sheils, 79–99. Oxford: Blackwell, 1982.

Palter, Robert. "*Black Athena,* Afro-Centrism, and the History of Science." *History of Science* 31 (1993): 227–87.

————. "Eighteenth-Century Historiography in *Black Athena.*" In *Black Athena Revisited,* eds. Mary R. Lefkowitz and Guy M. Rogers, 349–402. Chapel Hill: University of North Carolina Press, 1996.

Paredes Martínez, Carlos S. "El tributo indígena." In *Michoacán en el siglo XVI,* 21–104. Morelia: Fimax Publicistas, 1984.

Pareti, Luigi. "Quanti erano i Belgi ai tempi di Cesare?" *Athenaeum* 22 (1944): 63–71.

Park, Robert W. "Thule Winter Site Demography in the High Arctic." *AAy* 62 (1997): 273–84.

Parker, Edward H. *Ancient China Simplified.* London: Chapman and Hall, 1908.

Parkin, Tim G. *Demography and Roman Society.* Baltimore: Johns Hopkins University Press, 1992.

Parks, George B. "More's *Utopia* and Geography." *Journal of English and Germanic Philology* 37 (1938): 224–36.

Parry, J. H. *The Spanish Seaborne Empire.* New York: Knopf, 1966.

Paso y Troncoso, Francisco del, comp. *Epistolario de Nueva España, 1505–1818.* 16 vols. Mexico City: Antigua Libreria Robledo de Porrua y sus hijos, 1939–42.

————, ed. *Papeles de Nueva España, Second Series.* 7 vols. Madrid, 1905–6.

Pastor Bodmer, Beatriz. *The Armature of Conquest: Spanish Accounts of the Discovery of America, 1492–1589.* Stanford: Stanford University Press, 1992.

Patrick, Max. "The Free State of Noland: A Neglected Utopia from the Age of Queen Anne." *Philological Quarterly* 25 (1946): 79–88.

Paulmier de Gonneville, Binot. *Campagne du navire l'Espoir' de Honfleur, 1503–1505.* Ed. M.A.P. d'Avezac. Paris: Challamel, 1869.

Pauw, Cornelius de. *Recherches philosophiques sur les Américains.* 2 vols. Berlin: n.p., 1770.

Pearson, Kathy L. "Nutrition and the Early-Medieval Diet." *Speculum* 72 (1997): 1–32.

Peddie, John. *The Roman War Machine.* Stroud: Sutton, 1994.

Peel, J.D.Y. "'For Who Hath Despised the Day of Small Things': Missionary Narratives and Historical Anthropology." *Comparative Studies in Society and History* 37 (1995): 581–607.

Pelletier, A. J. "Canadian Censuses of the Seventeenth Century." *Papers of the Canadian Political Science Association* 2 (1930): 20–34.

Pelling, C.B.R. "Plutarch's Method of Work in the Roman Lives." *JHS* 99 (1979): 74–96.

Pérez de Luján, Diego. *Expedition into New Mexico Made by Anto-*

nio de Espejo, 1582–1583. Eds. and trans. George P. Hammond and Agapito Rey. Los Angeles: Quivira Society, 1929.

Pérez García, José. *Historia de Chile (CHC, 22/23)*. Santiago: Imprenta Elzevieriana, 1900.

Pervo, Richard I. *Profit with Delight: The Literary Genre of the Acts of the Apostles*. Philadelphia: Fortress Press, 1987.

Pessagno Espora, Mario A. *Los Fueguinos*. Buenos Aires: Comando en Jefe de la Armada, 1971.

Peterson, David A., and Z. D. Green. "The Spanish Arrival and the Massacre at Cholula." *Notas Mesoamericanas* 10 (1987): 203–22.

Peterson, Richard R. "A Re-Evalutation of the Economic Consequences of Divorce." *ASR* 61 (1996): 528–36.

———. "Statistical Errors, Faulty Conclusions, Misguided Policy: Reply to Weitzman." *ASR* 61 (1996): 539–40.

Petty, William. "Political Arithmetic [1690]." In *The Economic Writings of Sir William Petty*, ed. C. H. Hull, 233–313. Cambridge: Cambridge University Press, 1899.

Peyser, Joseph L. "It Was Not Smallpox." *Indiana Magazine of History* 81 (1985): 159–69.

Pézieu, M. de. *Brief recueil des particularitez . . . de l'île de Marignan au Brezil*. Lyon: Jean Poyet, 1613.

Pflugk, Julius von. "Belisar's Vandalenkrieg." *Historische Zeitschrift* 61 (1889): 69–96.

Phelan, John L. *The Hispanization of the Philippines*. Madison: University of Wisconsin Press, 1967.

———. *The Millennial Kingdom of the Franciscans in the New World*. 2d ed. Berkeley: University of California Press, 1970.

———. "Pre-Baptismal Instruction and the Administration of Baptism in the Philippines during the Sixteenth Century." *The Americas* 12 (1955–56): 3–23.

Philips, George H. *Indians and Intruders in Central California, 1769–1849*. Norman: University of Oklahoma Press, 1993.

Philips, Susan U. "Evidentiary Standards for American Trials: Just the Facts." In *Responsibility and Evidence in Oral Discourse*, eds. Jane H. Hill and Judith T. Irvine, 258–69. Cambridge: Cambridge University Press, 1992.

Piaget, Edouard. *Histoire des établissements des Germains dans l'empire d'Occident*. Arnhem: Steendrukkerij, 1911.

Pianzola, Maurice. *Des français à la conquête du Brésil (XVIIe siècle): Les perroquets jaunes*. Paris: L'Harmattan, 1991.

Pierce, Frank. *Amadís de Gaula*. Boston: Twayne, 1976.

Pizarro, Pedro. *Relación del descubrimiento y conquista del Perú*. Ed. Guillermo Lohmann Villena. Lima: Pontificia Universidad Católica, 1978.

Platenkam, J.D.M. "Tobelo, Moro, Ternate." *Cakalele* 4 (1993): 61–89.

Plato. *The Republic*. Trans. Paul Shorey. 2 vols. London: Heinemann, 1937–42.

Pliny. *Natural History*. Trans. H. Rackham. 10 vols. London: Heinemann, 1938–62.

Plutarch. *Plutarch's Lives*. Trans. Bernadotte Perrin. 11 vols. London: Heinemann, 1914–26.

Pocock, H.R.S. *The Conquest of Chile*. New York: Stein and Day, 1967.

Poliak, A. N. "Demographic Evaluation of Middle East Population Trends since 1348." *Palestine and the Near East* 10 (1938).

Pollard, Helen P. *Taríacuri's Legacy: The Prehispanic Tarascan State*. Norman: University of Oklahoma Press, 1993.

Pollard, Helen P., and Shirley Gorenstein. "Agrarian Potential, Population, and the Tarascan State." *Science* 209 (1980): 274–77.

Polybius. *Histories*. Trans. W. R. Paton. 6 vols. London: Heinemann, 1922–27.

Pomian, Krzysztof. "Francs et Gaulois." In *Les lieux de mémoire*, ed. Pierre Nora, 3/1: 40–105. Paris: Gallimard, 1992.

Pontet, Renatus du. *C. Iuli Caesaris Commentarium*. Oxford: Clarendon Press, 1937.

Popper, Karl. *The Open Society and Its Enemies*. 2 vols. Princeton: Princeton University Press, 1963.

Porter, Theodore M. "Statistics and the Politics of Objectivity." *Revue de Synthèse* 114 (1993): 87–101.

Porras Barrenechea, Raúl. *Los relaciones primitivas de la conquista del Perú*. Paris: Presses Modernes, 1937.

Posey, Darrell A. "Environmental and Social Implications of Pre- and Postcontact Situations on Brazilian Indians." In *Amazonian Indians from Prehistory to the Present*, ed. Anna Roosevelt, 271–86. Tucson: University of Arizona Press, 1994.

Postan, M. M. "Medieval Agrarian Society in Its Prime: England." In *Cambridge Economic History of Europe*, 2d. ed., 1: 549–632. Cambridge University Press, 1966.

Postgate, Nicholas. "How Many Sumerians per Hectare? Probing the Anatomy of an Early City." *Cambridge Archaeological Journal* 4 (1994): 47–65.

Potier, René. *Le génie militaire de Vercingétorix et la mythe Alise/Alésia*. Clermont-Ferrand: Editions Volcans, 1973.

Poursin, Jean-Marie. "La population mondiale en 2150, ou les limites de l'incertitude démographique." *Le Débat* 75 (May–August 1993): 36–61.

Powell, Mary Lucas, Patricia S. Bridges, and Ann Marie Wagner Miles., eds. *What Mean These Bones? Studies in Southeastern Bioarchaeology.* Tuscaloosa: University of Alabama Press, 1991.

Powers, Karen Vieira. *Andean Journeys: Migration, Ethnogenesis, and the State in Colonial Quito.* Albuquerque: University of New Mexico Press, 1995.

————. "The Battle for Bodies and Souls in the Colonial North Andes: Interecclesiastical Struggles and the Politics of Migration." *HAHR* 75 (1995): 31–56.

————. "Resilient Lords and Indian Vagabonds: Wealth, Migration, and the Reproductive Transformation of Quito's Chiefdoms, 1500–1700." *Ethnohistory* 38 (1991): 225–49.

Pratt, Fletcher. *Hail Caesar!* New York: Smith and Haas, 1936.

Prem, Hanns J. "Disease Outbreaks in Central Mexico during the Sixteenth Century." In Cook/Lovell, 20–48.

Prem, Hanns, Ursula Dyckerhoff, and Helmut Feldweg. "Reconstructing Central Mexico's Population." *Mexicon* 15 (1993): 50–57, 70–71.

Prezzolini, Giuseppe. *Machiavelli.* New York: Noonday Press, 1967.

Price, Richard. "Trial Marriage in the Andes." *Ethnology* 4 (1965): 310–22.

Prien, Hans-Jürgen. "Hernán Cortés' Rechtfertigung seiner Eroberung Mexikos und der spanischen Conquista Amerikas." *Zeitschrift für Historische Forschung* 22 (1995): 71–93.

Pringle, Heather. "The Plague That Never Was." *New Scientist* 2039 (20 July 1996): 32–35.

Pritchett, W. Kendrick. *The Liar School of Herodotus.* Amsterdam: J. C. Gieben, 1993.

Procopius. *History of the Wars.* Trans. H. B. Dewing. 6 vols. London: Heinemann, 1953–62.

————. *Secret History.* Trans. Richard Atwater. Ann Arbor: University of Michigan Press, 1963.

Prominska, Elzbieta. *Investigations on the Population of Muslim Alexandria.* Warsaw: PWN, 1972.

Purchas, Samuel. *Hakluytus Postumus, or Purchas His Pilgrimes.* 20 vols. Glasgow: J. MacLehose and Sons, 1905–7.

Quere, Martin. *Christianity in Sri Lanka under the Portuguese Padroado.* Colombo: Colombo Catholic Press, 1995.

Quinche, Eugène. *Les Helvètes: Divico contre César (109 à 52 av. J.-C.).* Paris: Payot, 1948.

Quinn, David B., ed. *The Roanoke Voyages, 1584–1590.* 2 vols. London: Hakluyt Society, 1955.

Quintana, Ricardo. *The Mind and Art of Jonathan Swift.* New York: Oxford University Press, 1936.

Rabell Romero, Cecilia. "El descenso de la población indígena durante el siglo XVI y las cuentas del Gran Capitán." In *El poblamiento de México: Una visión histórico-demográfico,* 2: 19–35. Mexico City: Consejo Nacional de Población, 1993.

———. "Los estudios de demografía histórica novohispana: Una revisión crítica." In *Memorias del simposio de historiografía mexicanista,* 647–65. Mexico City: Comite Mexicano de Ciencias Históricas, 1990.

———. *La población novohispana a la luz de los registros parroquiales.* Mexico City: Instituto de Investigaciones Sociales, 1990.

Racault, Jean-Michel. "Les jeux de la vérité et du mensonge dans les préfaces des récits de voyages imaginaires." In *Métamorphoses du recit de voyage,* ed. François Moureau, 82–109. Paris: Champion, 1986.

———. *L'utopie narrative en France et en Angleterre, 1675–1761.* Oxford: Voltaire Foundation, 1991.

Radell, David R. "The Indian Slave Trade and Population of Nicaragua during the Sixteenth Century." In *NPA,* 67–76.

Rafert, Stewart. *The Miami Indians of Indiana.* Indianapolis: Indiana Historical Society, 1996.

Rainero, Romain. *Il Congo agli inizi del settecento.* Florence: La Nuova Italia, 1972.

Ramage, Edwin S. *The Nature and Purpose of Augustus' "Res Gestae."* Wiesbaden: F. Steiner, 1987.

Rambaud, Michel. *L'art de la déformation historique dans les Commentaires de César.* 2d. ed. Paris: Les Belles Lettres, 1966.

———. "Exemples de déformation historique chez Tite-Live." *In Colloque histoire et historiographie Clio,* ed. R. Chevallier, 109–26. Paris: Les Belles Lettres, 1980.

Ramenofsky, Ann F. "Diseases of the Americas, 1492–1700." In *Cambridge World History of Human Disease,* ed. Kenneth Kiple, 317–28. Cambridge: Cambridge University Press, 1993.

———. "The Problem of Introduced Infectious Diseases in New Mexico, A.D. 1540–1680." *JAR* 25 (1996): 161–84.

———. *Vectors of Death: The Archaeology of European Contact.* Albuquerque: University of New Mexico Press, 1987.

Ramírez, Susan E. "The *Dueño de Indios:* Thoughts on the Consequences of the Shifting Bases of Power of the 'Curaca de los Viejos Antiguos' under the Spanish in Sixteenth-Century Peru." *HAHR* 67 (1987): 575–610.

Ramón, Galo. "Loja y Zaruma: Entre las minas y las mulas, 1557–1700." *Revista Ecuatoriana de Historia Económica* 7 (1990): 111–45.

Ramsay, J. H. "Chroniclers' Estimates of Numbers and Official Records." *English Historical Review* 18 (1903): 625–29.

Randall, H. J. "Population and Agriculture in Roman Britain." *Antiquity* 4 (1930): 80–90.

Randers-Pehrson, Justine D. *Barbarians and Romans: The Birth Struggle of Europe, A.D. 400–700.* Norman: University of Oklahoma Press, 1983.

Randles, W.G.L. *L'ancien royaume du Congo.* Paris: Mouton, 1968.

Rappoport, Rhoda. "Geology and Orthodoxy: The Case of Noah's Flood in Eighteenth-Century Thought." *British Journal for the History of Science* 11 (1978): 1–18.

Raudzens, George. "Firepower Limitations in Modern Military History." *Journal of the Society for Army Historical Research* 67 (1989): 130–53.

Ravn, O. E. *Herodotus' Description of Babylon.* Copenhagen: A. Busck, 1932.

Raymond, André. "La population du Caire, de Maqrizi à la *Description de l'Egypte*." *Bulletin d'Etudes Orientales* 28 (1975): 201–15.

———. "Signes urbains et étude de la population des grandes villes arabes à l'époque ottomane." *Bulletin d'Etudes Orientales* 27 (1974): 183–93.

Read, Herbert. *The Green Child.* London: Heinemann, 1935.

Reber, Vera Blinn. "The Demographics of Paraguay: A Reinterpretation of the Great War, 1864–1870." *HAHR* 68 (1988): 289–319.

Redford, Donald B. "An Egyptological Perspective on the Exodus Narrative." In *Egypt, Israel, Sinai,* ed. Anson F. Rainey, 137–61. Tel Aviv: University of Tel Aviv Press, 1987.

Reed, Jonathan L. "Population Numbers, Urbanization, and Economics: Galilean Archaeology and the Historical Jesus." *Society of Biblical Literature 1994 Seminar Papers,* 203–19. Atlanta, 1995.

Reff, Daniel T. "Anthropological Analysis of Exploration Texts." *AA* 93 (1991): 636–55.

———. *Disease, Depopulation, and Culture Change in Northwestern Mexico, 1518–1764.* Salt Lake City: University of Utah Press, 1991.

"Relación de Guautla." *Tlalocan* 4 (1962): 3–16.

"Relación de la conquista de la isla de Luzon." In *Archivo del bibliófilo filipino,* ed. W. E. Retana y Gamboa, 4: 1–37. Madrid: Minuesa de los Ríos, 1898.

Relaciones geográficas: Perú. 4 vols. Madrid: M. G. Hernández, 1881–97.

"Relation Concerning the Estate of New-England." *New England Historical and Genealogical Register* 40 (1886): 66–72.

Rennie, Neil. *Far-Fetched Facts: The Literature of Travel and the Idea of the South Seas.* Oxford: Oxford University Press, 1995.

Rex, Walter E. "'Arche de Noé' and Other Religious Articles by Abbé Mallet in the *Encyclopédie.*" *Eighteenth-Century Studies* 9 (1975–76): 33–52.

Reynolds, Susan. *Fiefs and Vassals: The Medieval Evidence Reinterpreted.* New York: Oxford University Press, 1994.

Rheenen, Gerlof B. van. "The Term 'Casados' in Sixteenth-Century Sources and the Discussion around the Historical Demography of New Spain." *Boletín de Estudios Latinoamericanos y del Caribe* 30 (1981): 125–34.

Ribeiro, Darcy. *The Americas and Civilization.* Trans. L. L. Barrett and M. M. Barrett. New York: Dutton, 1971.

Ricard, Robert. *The Spiritual Conquest of Mexico.* Berkeley: University of California Press, 1966.

Riccioli, Giovanni Battista. *Geographiae Hydrographiae Reformatae Nuper Recognitae et Auctae Libri Duodecimi.* Venice: Typus I. LaNou, 1672.

Riché, P. "Problèmes de démographie historique du haut Moyen-Age (Ve–VIIe siècles)." *Annales de Démographie Historique* (1966): 37–55.

Ricketson, Oliver G., Jr., and Edith Bayles Ricketson. *Uaxactun, Guatemala: Group E, 1926–1931.* Washington, D.C.: Carnegie Institution, 1937.

Riley, Carroll L. *Río del Norte: People of the Upper Río Grande from the Earliest Times to the Pueblo Revolt.* Salt Lake City: University of Utah Press, 1995.

Riley-Smith, Jonathan. *The First Crusade and the Idea of Crusading.* Philadelphia: University of Pennsylvania Press, 1986.

Ringrose, T. J. "Bone Counts and Statistics: A Critique." *Journal of Archaeological Science* 20 (1993): 121–57.

Risse, Günter. "What Columbus's Voyages Wrought." *Western Journal of Medicine* 160 (1994): 577–79.

Rivera Pagán, Luis N. *A Violent Evangelism: The Political and Religious Conquest of the Americas.* Louisville: Westminster/John Knox Press, 1992.

Robertson, James A., trans. and ed. *True Relation of the Hardships Suffered by Governor Hernando de Soto and Certain Portuguese Gentlemen during the Discovery of the Province of Florida, Now Newly Set Forth by a Gentleman of Elvas.* 2 vols. DeLand, Fla.: Florida State Historical Society, 1932–33.

Robertson, William. *History of America.* 4 vols. Edinburgh: Peter Hill, 1818 (1777).

Robinson, David J., and Jack A. Licate. Review of Cook and Borah, *Essays in Population History,* vol. 1. *AAAG* 66 (1976): 464–69.

Robles Mohs, Ivonne. "Adán, el éden y Abel, o la estructura narrativa simbólica de las *Cartas de Relación* de Hernán Cortés." *Revista de Filología y Lingüística* 20 (1994): 31–45.

Rodríguez de Montalvo, Garcí. *Amadís de Gaula*. Ed. Edwin B. Place. 4 vols. Madrid: Instituto Miguel de Cervantes, 1959–69.

Rodríguez Garrido, José A. "Las citas de los cronistas españoles como recurso argumentativo en la segunda parte de los *Comentarios reales*." *Lexis* 17 (1993): 93–114.

Rodríguez Molas, Ricardo. "Mitayos, ingenios y proprietarios en Potosí, 1633." *Runa* 16 (1986): 179–262.

Rogerson, J. W. *Old Testament Criticism in the Nineteenth Century*. London: SPCK, 1985.

Rojas, José Luis de. *A cada uno lo suyo: El tributo indígena en la Nueva España en el siglo XVI*. Zamora: Colegio de Michoacán, 1993.

———. "Cuantificaciones referentes a la ciudad de Tenochtitlán en 1519." *HM* 36 (1986–87): 213–50.

Rollinger, Robert. *Herodots babylonischer Logos*. Innsbruck: Universität Innsbruck, 1993.

Romero, Carlos A. *Los héroes de la isla del Gallo*. Lima: Libreria Escolar, 1944.

———. "Los de la isla del Gallo." *Revista Histórica* (Lima) 6 (1918): 105–70.

Ronda, James P. "'We Are Well as We Are': An Indian Critique of Seventeenth-Century Missions." *WMQ* 34 (1977): 66–82.

Ronzeaud, Pierre. "Formes et enjeux de la réécriture dans les utopies du XVIIe siècle." *Dix-Septième Siècle* 47 (1995): 67–77.

———. *Utopie hermaphrodite*. Marseille: CMR 17, 1982.

Rorty, Richard. "Does Academic Freedom Have Philosophical Presuppositions?" *Academe* 80/6 (Nov.–Dec. 1994): 52–63.

Rosales, Diego de. *Historia general del reino de Chile, flandes indiano*. Ed. Mario Góngora. 2d. ed. Santiago: Editorial Andrés Bello, 1989.

Rosenberg, Aubrey. *Tyssot du Patot and His Work, 1655–1738*. The Hague: M. Nijhoff, 1972.

Rosenberg, Bruce A. *Custer and the Epic of Defeat*. University Park: Penn State University Press, 1974.

Rosenblat, Angel. *La población de América en 1492: Viejos y nuevos cálculos*. Mexico City: Colegio de México, 1967.

———. *La población indígena de América desde 1492 hasta la actualidad*. Buenos Aires: Institución Cultural Española, 1945.

———. *La población indígena y el mestizaje en América, 1492–1950*. 2 vols. Buenos Aires: Editorial Nova, 1954.

Roskill, W. S. *The War at Sea, 1939–1945.* 2 vols. London: HMSO, 1954.

Rostovtzeff, Michael. *The Social and Economic History of the Hellenistic World.* 2 vols. Oxford: Clarendon Press, 1941.

Rothstein, Marian. "When Fiction Is Fact: Perceptions in Sixteenth-Century France." *Studies in Philology* 83 (1986): 359–75.

Rouche, Michel. "Break-up and Metamorphosis of the West: Fifth to Seventh Centuries." In *The Cambridge Illustrated History of the Middle Ages I, 350–950,* 52–103. Cambridge: Cambridge University Press, 1989.

Rowe, John H. "Inca Culture at the Time of the Spanish Conquest." In *HSAI* 2: 183–330.

Rubincam, Catherine. "Casualty Figures in the Battle Descriptions of Thucydides." *TAPA* 121 (1991): 181–98.

Ruiz de Arce, Juan. "Advertencias." In *Tres testigos de la conquista del Perú,* ed. Conde de Canilleros, 67–115. 3d ed. Lima: 1964.

Runyan, Timothy J. "Naval Logistics in the Late Middle Ages: The Example of the Hundred Years' War." In *Feeding Mars; Logistics in Western Warfare from the Middle Ages to the Present,* ed. John A. Lynn, 79–102. Boulder, Colo.: Westview, 1993.

Rusnock, Andrea. "Quantification, Precision, and Accuracy: Determinations of Population in the *Ancien Régime.*" In *The Value of Precision,* ed. M. Norton Wise, 17–38. Princeton: Princeton University Press, 1995.

Russell, Josiah C. *British Medieval Population.* Albuquerque: University of New Mexico Press, 1948.

———. *The Control of Late Ancient and Medieval Population.* Philadelphia: American Philosophical Society, 1985.

———. *Late Ancient and Medieval Population.* Philadelphia: American Philosophical Society, 1968.

———. *Medieval Regions and Their Cities.* Newton Abbot: David and Charles, 1972.

———. "The Population and Mortality at Pompeii." *Bulletin of the International Committee on Urgent Anthropological and Ethnological Research* 19 (1977): 107–14.

———. "That Earlier Plague." *Demography* 5 (1968): 174–84.

Ruz, Mario Humberto. *Un rostro encubierto.* Mexico City: Ciesas, 1994.

Sabben-Clarke, James. *Caesar and Roman Politics, 60–50 B.C.* Oxford: Clarendon Press, 1971.

Saccardo, Graziano. *Congo e Angola con la storia dell'antica missio del Cappuccini.* 3 vols. Venice: Curia Provinciale dei Cappuccini, 1982–83.

Sadr, Karim. "Kalahari Archaeology and the Bushmen Debate." *CA* 38 (1997): 104–12.

Sáenz de Santa María, Carmelo. *Historia de una historia: La crónica de Bernal Díaz del Castillo.* Madrid: Instituto Gonzalo Fernández de Oviedo, 1984.

Saignes, Thierry. *Caciques, Tribute and Migration in the Southern Andes.* London: University of London, Institute of Latin American Studies, 1985.

————. "The Ethnic Groups in the Valleys of Larecaja: From Descent to Residence." In *Anthropological History of Andean Polities,* eds. John V. Murra, Nathan Wachtel, and Jacques Revel, 311–41. Cambridge: Cambridge University Press, 1986.

————. "Las etnias de Charcas frente al sistema colonial." *Jahrbuch für Geschichte von Staat, Wirtschaft und Gesellschaft Lateinamerikas* 21 (1984): 27–75.

————. "Indian Migration and Social Change in Seventeenth-Century Charcas." In *Ethnicity, Markets, and Migration in the Andes,* eds. Brooke Larson et al., 167–95. Durham: Duke University Press, 1995.

————. "Les Lupacas dans les vallées orientales des Andes: Trajets spatiaux et repères démographiques (XVI–XVII siècles)." *Mélanges de la Casa de Velázquez* 17 (1981): 147–82.

————. "Nota sobre la contribución regional a la mita de Potosí a comienzos del siglo XVII." *Historiografía y Bibliografía Americanistas* 28 (1984): 47–63.

————. "Notes on the Regional Contribution to the Mita in Potosí in the Early Seventeenth Century." *Bulletin of Latin American Research* 4 (1985): 65–76.

————. "Parcours forains: L'enjeu des migrations internes dans les Andes coloniales." *Cahiers des Amériques Latines* 6 (1987): 33–57.

————. "Politiques du recensement dans les Andes coloniales: Décroissance tributaire ou mobilité indigène?" *Histoire, Economie et Société* 6 (1987): 435–64.

Sala Catala, José, and Jaime Vilchis Reyes. "Apocalíptica española y empresa misional en los primeros franciscanos de México." *RI* 45 (1985): 421–47.

Sale, Kirkpatrick. *The Conquest of Paradise: Christopher Columbus and the Columbian Legacy.* New York: Knopf, 1990.

Sallares, Robert. *Ecology of the Ancient Greek World.* London: Duckworth, 1991.

Salmon, Pierre. *Population et dépopulation dans l'empire romain.* Brussels: Latomus, 1974.

Salway, Peter. *Roman Britain.* New York: Oxford University Press, 1981.

Samuel, Viscount Herbert. *An Unknown Land*. London: Allen and Unwin, 1942.

Sánchez-Albornoz, Nicolás. *Indios y tributos en el Alto Perú*. Lima: Instituto de Estudios Peruanos, 1978.

———. "La mita de Lima: Magnitud y procedencía." *Historia* 12 (1988): 193–205.

———. "Mita, migraciones y pueblos." *Historia Boliviana* 3/1 (1983): 31–59.

———. *La población de América latina desde los tiempos precolombinos al año 2025*. Madrid: Alianza, 1994.

———. *The Population of Latin America: A History*. Berkeley: University of California Press, 1974.

Sánchez Fuertes, Cayetano. "Los franciscanos y la evangelización de Filipinas, 1578–1600." *Archivo Ibero-Americano* 43 (1983): 311–51.

Sande, Francisco de. "Relación de las Filipinas [1576]." In Blair/Robertson, 4: 21–97.

Sanders, William T. "The Population of the Central Mexican Symbiotic Region, the Basin of Mexico, and the Teotihuacán Valley in the Sixteenth Century." In *NPA*, 85–151.

Sanders, William T., and Barbara J. Price. *Mesoamerica: The Evolution of a Civilization*. New York: Random House, 1968.

Sanderson, Stephen K. "Expanding World Commercialization." In *Civilizations and World-Systems: Studying World-Historical Change*, ed. Stephen K. Sanderson, 261–72. Walnut Creek, Calif.: Altamira Press, 1995.

Sandoval, Alonso de. *De Instauranda Aethiopum Salute*. Bogotá: Empresa Nacional de Publicaciones, 1956. Originally published as *Naturaleza*. Seville: Francisco de Lira, 1627.

Santillán, Fernando de. "Relación." In *CDIHC*, 28: 24–302.

Santos, Angel. "El Plata: La evangelización del antiguo Paraguay." In *Historia de la iglesia en hispanoamérica y Filipinas (siglos XV–XIX)*, ed. Pedro Borges, 2: 673–90. Madrid: Biblioteca de Autores Cristianos, 1992.

Sargent-Baur, Barbara N. "Truth-Claims as *Captatio Benevolentiae* in Villon's Testament." In *Conjunctures: Medieval Studies in Honor of Douglas Kelly*, 505–14. Rotterdam: Rodopi, 1994.

Sarikakis, Theodore C. "Les vêpres ephésiennes de l'an 88 av. J.C." *Epistemonike Epeteris Tees Philosophikees Scholas* 15 (1976): 255–64.

Sasso, Robert F. "La Crosse Region Oneota Adaptations: Changing Late Prehistoric Subsistence and Settlement Patterns in the Upper Mississippi Valley." *Wisconsin Archeologist* 74 (1993): 324–48.

Sauer, Carl O. *Aboriginal Population of Northwestern Mexico*. Berkeley: University of California Press, 1935.

―――. *Sixteenth-Century North America: The Land and the People as Seen by the Europeans.* Berkeley: University of California Press, 1971.

Sayre, Gordon. "The Beaver as Native and as Colonist." *Canadian Review of Comparative Literature* 22 (1995): 659–82.

Scarry, John F. "Apalachee Homesteads: The Basal Social and Economic Units of a Mississippian Chiefdom." In *Mississippian Communities and Households,* eds. J. Daniel Rogers and Bruce D. Smith, 201–23. Tuscaloosa: University of Alabama Press, 1995.

Scheidel, Walter. "Finances, Figures, and Fiction." *Classical Quarterly* 46 (1996): 222–38.

Schmidt, Ludwig. *Histoire des Vandales.* Paris: Payot, 1953.

―――. "The Sueves, Alans and Vandals in Spain, 409–429. The Vandal Dominion in Africa, 429–533." In *Cambridge Medieval History,* 1: 304–22. Cambridge: Cambridge University Press, 1957.

―――. "Zur Frage nach der Volkszahl der Wandalen." *Byzantinische Zeitschrift* 15 (1906): 620–21.

Schmitt, Tassilo. *Hannibals Siegeszug.* Munich: Tuduv, 1991.

Schmittlein, Raymond. *Avec César en Gaule.* Paris: Editions d'Artrey, 1970.

Schoental, R. "Mycotoxins and the Bible." *Perspectives in Biology and Medicine* 28 (1984): 117–20.

Scholes, France V., and Ralph L. Roys. *The Maya Chontal Indians of Acalan-Tixchel.* Washington, D.C.: Carnegie Institution, 1948.

Schreiber, Hermann. *Die Vandalen.* Bern: Scherz, 1979.

Schreiber, Katharina J., and Keith W. Kintigh. "A Test of the Relationship between Site Size and Population." *AAy* 61 (1996): 573–79.

Schroeder, Albert H. "Comments on Henry Dobyns' 'Sixteenth-Century Tusayan.'" *American Indian Quarterly* 17 (1993): 379–84.

Schreurs, Peter. *Caraga antigua, 1521–1910.* Cebu City: University of San Carlos, 1989.

Schurhammer, Georg. "Die Bekehrung der Paraver." *AHSI* 4 (1935): 201–33.

―――. *Francis Xavier: His Life and Times.* 3 vols. Rome: IHSI, 1973–82.

―――. "Die Taufen des hl. Franz Xaver." *Studia Missionalia* 7 (1952): 33–75.

Schütte, J. F. *Introductio ad Historiam Societatis Jesu in Japonia, 1549–1650.* Rome: IHSI, 1968.

Schwarzenberg, Jorge, and Arturo Mutizábal. *Monografía geográfica e histórica del archipiélago de Chiloé.* Concepción: Archivo Científico de Chile, 1926.

The Scriptores Historiae Augustae. Trans. David Magie. 3 vols. London: Heinemann, 1930–54.

Seager, Robin. *Pompey: A Political Biography.* Berkeley: University of California Press, 1979.

Sée, Henri. "Peut-on evaluer la population de l'ancienne France?" *Revue d'Économie Politique* 38 (1924): 647–55.

Seeck, Otto. *Geschichte des Untergangs der antike Welt.* 6 vols.: Berlin: Siemenroth and Worms, 1895–1920.

Seel, Otto, ed. *C. Iulii Caesaris Commentarii Rerum Gestarum.* Leipzig: Teubner, 1961.

———. *Caesar-Studien.* Stuttgart: Klett, 1967.

Sempat Assadourian, Carlos. "La crisis demográfica del siglo XVI y la transición del Tawantinsuyu al sistema mercantil colonial." In *Población y mano de obra en América latina,* ed. Nicolás Sánchez-Albornoz, 69–93. Madrid: Alianza, 1985.

Senkovsky, Osip. *The Fantastic Journeys of Baron Brambeus.* Trans. Louis Pedrotti. New York: P. Lang, 1993.

Sepp, Anton. *Relación de viaje a las misiones jesuíticas.* Ed. Werner Hoffmann. Buenos Aires: Editorial Universitaria, 1971.

Serés, Guillermo. "Los textos de la 'Historia verdadera' de Bernal Díaz." *Boletín de la Real Academia Española* 71 (1991): 523–47.

Seybolt, Robert. "Notes on the Casualties of April 19, and June 17, 1775." *New England Quarterly* 4 (1931): 525–28.

Shank, Michael H. "Galileo's Day in Court." *Journal of the History of Astronomy* 25 (1994): 236–43.

———. "How Shall We Practice History?" *Early Science and Medicine* 1 (1996): 106–50.

Shankman, Paul. "History of Samoan Sexual Contact and the Mead-Freeman Controversy." *AA* 98 (1996): 555–67.

Sharer, Robert J. *The Ancient Maya.* 5th ed. Stanford: Stanford University Press, 1994.

Sherwin-White, A. N. *Roman Foreign Policy in the East, 168 B.C. to A.D. 1.* London: Duckworth, 1984.

Showalter, Dennis E. *Tannenberg, Clash of Empires.* Hamden, Conn.: Archon, 1991.

Shrewsbury, J.D.F. *The Plague of the Philistines and Other Medical-Historical Essays.* London: Gollancz, 1964.

Siberry, Elizabeth. *Criticism of Crusading, 1095–1274.* Oxford: Clarendon Press, 1985.

Sima Qian. *Records of the Grand Historian: Qin Dynasty.* Trans. Burton Watson. New York: Renditions–Columbia University Press, 1993.

Simeoni, Luigi. *Le Signorie.* 2 vols. Milan: F. Vallardi, 1950.

Simms, William Gilmore. *Views and Reviews in American Literature, History, and Fiction.* New York: Wiley and Putnam, 1845.

Simon, André. *Vercingétorix et l'idéologie française.* Paris: Imago, 1989.

Simon, David. "Review of Gordon, *Bushman Myth.*" *JSAS* 19 (1993): 166–68.

Simon, Róbert. *Meccan Trade and Islam.* Budapest: Akadémiai Kiadó, 1989.

Simonsen, Roberto C. *História econômica do Brasil, 1500–1800.* 5th ed. São Paulo: Companhia Editorial Nacional, 1962.

Simpson, Hope, and J. F. Lazenby. *The Catalogue of the Ships in Homer's Iliad.* Oxford: Clarendon Press, 1970.

Simpson, Lesley B. *The Encomienda in New Spain.* Berkeley: University of California Press, 1966.

Slack, Paul. "Mortality Crises and Epidemic Disease in England, 1485–1610." In *Health, Medicine, and Mortality in the Sixteenth Century,* ed. Charles Webster, 9–59. Cambridge: Cambridge University Press, 1979.

Slicher van Bath, B. H. "The Calculation of the Population of New Spain, Especially for the Period before 1570." *Boletín de Estudios Latinoamericanos y del Caribe* 24 (1978): 67–95.

Smeeks, Hendrik. *The Mighty Kingdom of Krinke Kesmes (1708).* Ed. David Fausett, trans. Robert H. Leek. Atlanta: Rodopi, 1995.

Smith, Bradford. *Captain John Smith: His Life and Legend.* Philadelphia: Lippincott, 1953.

Smith, Colin T. "Depopulation of the Central Andes in the Sixteenth Century." *CA* 11 (1970): 453–64.

Smith, John. *The Generall Historie of Virginia, New-England, and the Summer Isles.* Cleveland: World Publishing Co., 1966.

Smith, Marvin T. "The Aboriginal Depopulation of the Postcontact Southeast." In *FC,* 257–75.

———. *Archaeology of Aboriginal Culture Change in the Interior Southeast: Depopulation during the Early Historic Period.* Gainesville: University Press of Florida, 1987.

Smith, Michael E. *The Aztecs.* Cambridge, Mass.: Blackwell, 1996.

———. "Hernán Cortés and the Size of Aztec Cities: Comment on Dobyns." *LAPHB* 25 (Spring 1994): 25–28.

Snipp, C. Matthew C. "Who Are American Indians? Some Observations about the Perils and Pitfalls of Data for Race and Identity." *Population Research and Policy Review* 5 (1986): 237–52.

Snow, Dean R. "Microchronology and Demographic Evidence Relating to the Size of Pre-Columbian North American Indian Populations." *Science* 268 (16 June 1995): 1601–4.

————. "Mohawk Demography and the Effects of Exogenous Epidemics on American Indian Populations." *Journal of Anthropological Archaeology* 15 (1996): 160–82.

Sokol, Barnett J. "Thomas Harriot, Sir Walter Raleigh's Tutor, on Population." *Annals of Science* 31 (1974): 205–12.

Somolinos d'Ardois, Germán. "Las epidemias en México durante el siglo XVI." In *EHEM*, 1: 205–14.

Soriano, Ramón L. "Perfil político de Pedro de Valdivia." *Anuario de Estudios Americanos* 34 (1977): 415–64.

Sousa, G. U. de. "Theatrics and Politics in Sixteenth-Century Brazil." *Journal of Dramatic Theory and Criticism* 8 (1993–94): 89–102.

Spatz, W. *Die Schlacht von Hastings*. Berlin: E. Ebering, 1896.

Spean, John F. "Hannibal's Mules: The Logistical Limitations of Hannibal's Army and the Battle of Cannae, 216 B.C." *Historia* 45 (1996): 159–87.

Spector, Ronald H. "'How Do You Know If You're Winning?' Perception and Reality in America's Military Performance in Vietnam, 1965–1970." In *The Vietnam War: Vietnamese and American Perspectives*, eds. Jayne S. Werner and Luu Doan Huynh, 152–64. Armonk, N.Y.: M. E. Sharpe, 1993.

Spengler, Joseph J. "Population Prediction in Nineteenth-Century America." *ASR* 1 (1936): 905–21.

Spinden, H. J. "The Population of Ancient America." *Annual Report of the Smithsonian Institution for 1929*, 451–70. Washington, D.C.

Spores, Ronald. *The Mixtec Kings and Their People*. Norman: University of Oklahoma Press, 1967.

————. "'Too Small a Place': The Removal of the Willamette Valley Indians, 1850–1856." *American Indian Quarterly* 17 (1993): 171–91.

Squier, E. G. "The Monumental Evidence of the Discovery of America by Northmen Critically Examined." *Ethnological Journal* 1 (1848): 313–25.

Staden, Hans. *Zwei Reisen nach Brasilien, 1548–1555*. Ed. Karl Fouquet. 2d ed. Marburg: Trautvetter, 1963.

Stadter, Philip A. "Fictional Narrative in the *Cyropaideia*." *AJP* 112 (1991): 461–91.

Stannard, David E. *American Holocaust: Columbus and the Conquest of the New World*. New York: Oxford University Press, 1992.

————. *Before the Horror: The Population of Hawai'i on the Eve of Western Contact*. Honolulu: University of Hawaii Press, 1989.

Stark, Rodney. "Epidemics, Networks, and the Rise of Christianity." *Semeia* 56 (1991): 159–75.

————. *The Rise of Christianity*. Princeton: Princeton University Press, 1996.

Steckmesser, Kent L. *The Western Hero in History and Legend*. Norman: University of Oklahoma Press, 1965.

Stein, Ernest. *Histoire du bas-empire*. 2 vols. Paris: Desclée de Brouwer, 1949.

Stephan, Jörg. "Fray Toribio Motolinía und die 'Geistliche Eroberung' Mexikos." *Wissenschaft und Weisheit* 58 (1995): 53–115.

Stevens, C. E. "The 'Bellum Gallicum' as a Work of Propaganda." *Latomus* 11 (1952): 165–79.

Stevenson, William B. "The First Crusade." In *Cambridge Medieval History*, 5: 265–99. Cambridge: Cambridge University Press, 1948.

Steward, Julian H. "The Native Population of South America." In *HSAI*, 5: 655–68.

Stewart, Edgar I. *Custer's Luck*. Norman: University of Oklahoma Press, 1955.

Stine, Scott. "Extreme and Persistent Drought in California and Patagonia during Medieval Times." *Nature* 369 (16 June 1994): 546–49.

Stoessl, Franz. "Caesars Politik und Diplomatie im Helvetierkrieg." *Schweizer Beiträge zur allgemeinen Geschichte* 8 (1950): 5–36.

Stoianovich, Troian. "Cities, Capital Accumulation, and the Ottoman Balkan Command Economy, 1500–1800." In *Cities and the Rise of States in Europe, A.D. 1000–1800,* eds. Charles Tilly and Wim P. Blockmans, 61–68. Boulder, Colo.: Westview, 1994.

Stoppard, Tom. *Arcadia*. London: Faber and Faber, 1993.

Storm, Gustav, ed. *Islandske Annaler indtil 1578*. Christiania [Oslo]: Grondahl and Sons, 1888.

Strocka, V. M. *Casa del labirinto*. Munich: Hirmer, 1991.

Suárez Moreno, Martín. "Informação sobre a Maranhão." *Anais da Biblioteca Nacional* (Rio de Janeiro) 26 (1904): 149–92.

Suder, Wiesław. "Pare uwag na temat demografii Pompejów." *Antiquitas* (Wroclaw) 11 (1984): 95–97.

Sun Pin. *Military Methods*. Eds. and trans. Ralph Sawyer and Meichun Sawyer. Boulder, Colo.: Westview, 1995.

Super, John C. *Food, Conquest, and Colonization in Sixteenth-Century America*. Albuquerque: University of New Mexico Press, 1988.

Swain, Simon. "Man and Medicine in Thucydides." *Arethusa* 27 (1994): 303–27.

Swanton, John R. *Indian Tribes of the Lower Mississippi Valley and Adjacent Coast of the Gulf of Mexico*. Washington, D.C.: Government Printing Office, 1911.

Sweeney, Marvin A. *Isaiah 1–39.* Grand Rapids: W. B. Eerdmans, 1996.

Sybel, Heinrich von. *The History and Literature of the Crusades.* Trans. Lucie Austin, Lady Duff Gordon. London: Chapman and Hall, 1861.

Sylvest, Edwin E. *Motifs of Franciscan Missionary Theory in Six-teenth-Century New Spain, Province of the Holy Gospel.* Washington, D.C.: Academy of American Franciscan History, 1975.

Taber, Charles R. "The Missionary Movement and the Anthropologists." *Bulletin of the Scottish Institute of Missionary Studies* 6/7 (1990–91): 19–32.

Tacitus, Cornelius. *Annalen.* Ed. Erich Koestermann. 4 vols. Heidelberg: C. Winter, 1963–68.

———. *Tacitus.* Trans. Clifford H. Moore and John Jackson. 5 vols. Cambridge, Mass.: Harvard University Press, 1925–37.

Tandeter, Enrique. *Coercion and Market: Silver Mining in Colonial Potosí, 1692–1826.* Albuquerque: University of New Mexico Press, 1993.

———. "Forced and Free Labour in Late Colonial Potosí." *Past and Present* 93 (1981): 98–136.

Tani, Masakazu. "Why Should More Pots Break in Larger Households?" In *Kalinga Ethnoarchaeology,* eds. William A. Longacre and James M. Skibo, 51–70. Washington, D.C.: Smithsonian Institution Press, 1994.

Tanzer, Helen H. *The Common People of Pompeii.* Baltimore: Johns Hopkins University Press, 1939.

Tapia, Andrés de. "Relación hecha por el Señor Andrés de Tapia." In *Colección de documentos para la historia de México,* ed. Joaquín García Icazbalceta, 2: 554–94. Mexico City: 1867.

Taylor, Helen. "'The Griot from Tennessee.'" *Critical Quarterly* 37/2 (1995): 46–62.

Terraciano, Kevin, and Lisa M. Sousa. "The 'Original Conquest' of Oaxaca: Mixtec and Nahua History and Myth." *UCLA Historical Journal* 13 (1992): 29–90.

Terrell, John. *Prehistory of the Pacific Islands.* Cambridge: Cambridge University Press, 1986.

Thayer Ojeda, Luis. *Orígenes de Chile: Elementos etnicos, apellidos, familias.* Santiago: Editorial Andrés Bello, 1989.

Thayer Ojeda, Tomás. *Los conquistadores de Chile.* 2 vols. Santiago: Imprenta Barcelona, 1913.

———. "Ensayo crítico sobre algunas obras históricas utilizables para el estudio de la conquista de Chile." *Anales de la Universidad de Chile* 139 (1916): 341–87, 655–69; 140 (1917): 173–208, 419–46; 141 (1917): 1509–36; 143 (1919): 445–76, 673–724; 144–45 (1919): 3–60, 545–77, 789–838.

———. *Ensayo crítico sobre algunas obras históricas utilizables para el estudio de la conquista de Chile.* Santiago: Imprenta Barcelona, 1917.

———. *Valdivia y sus compañeros.* Santiago: n.p., 1950.

Thayer Ojeda, Tomás, and Carlos J. Larraín. "El desastre de Tucapel." *BACH* 49 (1953): 27–30.

Thevenot, Emile. *Histoire des Gaulois.* Paris: Presses Universitaires de France, 1949.

Thevet, André. *Les Français en Amérique pendant la deuxième moitié du XVIe siècle,* Ed. Suzanne Lussagnet. Paris: Presses Universitaires de France, 1953.

———. *As singularidades da França antártica.* Trans. Eugênio Amado. Belo Horizonte: Livraria Itatiaia, 1978.

———. *Les singularités de la France antarctique,* Ed. Frank Lestringant. Paris: La Découverte/Maspéro, 1983.

Thomas, Hugh. *The Conquest of Mexico.* London: Hutchinson, 1993.

Thompson, David. *Columbia Journals.* Ed. Barbara Belyea. Montreal: McGill-Queens University Press, 1994.

———. *Narrative,* Ed. Richard Glover. Toronto: Champlain Society, 1962.

———. *Travels in Western North America, 1784–1812.* Ed. Victor G. Hopwood. Montreal: Macmillan, 1971.

Thompson, E. A. "The End of Roman Spain." *Nottingham Medieval Studies* 20 (1976) 5–28; 21 (1977): 3–31.

———. *The Huns.* Oxford: Blackwell, 1996.

———. *Romans and Barbarians: The Decline of the Western Empire.* Madison: University of Wisconsin Press, 1982.

Thompson, J. Eric S. *The Rise and Fall of Maya Civilization.* Norman: University of Oklahoma Press, 1966.

Thornton, John K. "Demography and History in the Kingdom of Kongo, 1550–1750." *JAH* 18 (1977): 507–30.

———. "An Eighteenth-Century Baptismal Register and the Demographic History of Manguenzo." In *African Historical Demography,* 1: 405–15. Edinburgh: Centre of African Studies, 1977.

———. *The Kingdom of Kongo: Civil War and Transition, 1641–1718.* Madison: University of Wisconsin Press, 1983.

Thornton, Russell. "Aboriginal Native American Population and Rates of Decline, ca. A.D. 1500–1900." *CA* 39 (1997): 310–15.

———. *American Indian Holocaust and Survival: A Population History since 1492.* Norman: University of Oklahoma Press. 1987.

———. "Tribal Membership Requirements and the Demography of 'Old' and 'New' Native Americans." In *Changing Numbers, Changing Needs:*

American Indian Demography and Public Health, eds. Gary D. Sandefur et al., 103–12. Washington, D.C.: National Academy Press, 1996.

Thornton, Russell, Tim Miller, and Jonathan Warren. "Aboriginal Population Recovery Following Smallpox Epidemics." *AA* 93 (1991): 28–45.

Tibesar, Antonine. *Franciscan Beginnings in Colonial Peru.* Washington, D.C.: Academy of American Franciscan History, 1953.

Tieje, Arthur J. "The Expressed Aims of the Long Prose Fiction." *Journal of English and Germanic Philology* 11 (1912): 402–32.

―――. "A Peculiar Phase of the Theory of Realism in Pre-Richardsonian Fiction." *Publications of the Modern Language Association* 28 (1913): 213–52.

Tinney, Steve. "A New Look at Naram-Sin and the 'Great Rebellion.'" *Journal of Cuneiform Studies* 47 (1995): 1–14.

Tiphaigne de la Roche, Charles François. *Histoire des Galligènes, ou mémoires de Duncan.* Amsterdam: Arkstee and Merkus, 1765.

Todd, Malcolm. "*Famosa Pestis* and Britain in the Fifth Century." *Britannia* 8 (1977): 319–25.

Torquemada, Juan de. *Monarquía indiana.* Ed. Miguel León-Portilla. 6 vols. Mexico City: UNAM, 1975–to date.

Torre Villar, Ernesto de la. "Fray Pedro de Gante." *Estudios de Historia Novohispana* 5 (1974): 9–77.

Toso, Carlo. *L'anarchia congolese nel secolo XVII: La relazioni inedita di Marcellino d'Atri.* Genoa: Bozzi, 1984.

―――. "Relazioni inedite di P. Cherubino Cassinis da Savona sul 'Regno del Congo e sue missioni.'" *Italia Francescana* 50 (1975): 97–103.

Tourtellot, Gair, Jeremy A. Sabloff, and Michael P. Smyth. "Room Counts and Population Estimation for Terminal Classic Sayil in the Puuc Region, Yucatán, Mexico." In *PPHML,* 245–61.

Toussaert, Jacques. *Le sentiment réligieuse en Flandre à la fin du Moyen-Age.* Paris: Plon, 1963.

Trigger, Bruce G. "Early Native North American Responses to European Contact: Romantic versus Rationalist Interpretations." *Journal of American History* 77 (1990–91): 1195–1215.

―――. *Natives and Newcomers.* Montreal: McGill-Queens University Press, 1985.

Trudel, Marcel. *La population du Canada en 1666: Recensement reconstitué.* Sillery: Septentrion, 1995.

Turnbull, Patrick. *Dunkirk, Anatomy of a Disaster.* London: Batsford, 1978.

Turner, B. L. "Population Reconstruction of the Central Maya Lowlands, 1000 B.C. to A.D. 1500." In *PPHML,* 301–24.

Turner, Christy G., II. "Taphonomic Reconstruction of Human Violence and Cannibalism Based on Mass Burials in the American Southwest." In *Carnivores, Human Scavengers, and Predators,* eds. Genevieve M. LeMoine and A. Scott MacEachern, 219–40. Calgary: University of Calgary Archaeological Association, 1983.

Turner, Christy G., II, and Lauren Lofgren. "Household Size of Prehistoric Western Pueblo." *Southwestern Journal of Anthropoplogy* 22 (1966): 117–32.

Turner, Christy G., II, and Jacqueline A. Turner. "Perimortem Damage to Human Skeletal Remains from Wupatki National Monument." *Kiva* 55 (1990): 187–212.

Turner, Henry A. "Peter Novick and the 'Objectivity Question' in History." *Academic Questions* 8/3 (Summer 1995): 23–25.

Twain, Mark. *Life on the Mississippi.* Ed. John Seelye. New York: Oxford University Press, 1990.

———. *Mark Twain's Quarrel with Heaven.* Ed. Ray B. Browne. New Haven: College and University Press, 1970.

Tyssot du Patot, Simon. *Voyages et aventures de Jaques Massé.* Bordeaux: J. L'Aveugle, 1710.

Ubelaker, D. H. "North American Indian Population Size, A.D. 1500 to 1985." *American Journal of Physical Anthropology* 77 (1988): 289–94.

Uekert, Brenda K. *Rivers of Blood: A Comparative Study of Government Massacres.* Westport, Conn.: Greenwood, 1995.

Ungnad, A. "Die Zahl der von Sanherib Deportierten Judäer." *ZAW* 59 (1942–43): 199–202.

Unz, Ron K. "The Surplus of the Athenian Phoros." *Greek, Roman, and Byzantine Studies* 26 (1985): 21–42.

Upham, Steadman. "Smallpox and Climate in the American Southwest." *AA* 88 (1986): 115–28.

Urbina Burgos, Rodolfo. *La periferia meridional indiana: Chiloé en el siglo XVIII.* Valparaiso: Ediciones Universitarias, 1983.

———. "La rebelión indígena de 1712: Los tributarios de Chiloé contra la encomienda." *Revista Tiempo y Espacio* (1990): 73–86.

Usher, Abbott P. "A New Estimate of the Population of Britain in Roman Times." *Geographical Review* 20 (1930): 674–76.

Valdivia, Pedro de. *Cartas de Pedro Valdivia que tratan del descubrimiento y conquista de Chile.* Ed. José Toribio Medina. Santiago: Fondo Histórico, 1954.

Valentin-Smith, James. *De l'origine des peuples de la Gaule transalpine et de leurs institutions politiques avant la domination romaine.* Paris: Imprimérie Impériale, 1866.

Valenzuela Solis, Carlos. *El paso de los guerreros.* Santiago: Zig-Zag, 1974.

van Houts, Elisabeth M. C. "The Ship List of William the Conqueror." *Anglo-Norman Studies* 10 (1987): 159–74.

Van Seters, John. *The Life of Moses.* Louisville, Ky.: Westminster/John Knox Press, 1994.

———. "The Plagues of Egypt: Ancient Tradition or Literary Invention?" *ZAW* 98 (1986): 31–37.

Varinas, Gabriel Fernández de Villalobos, Marqués de. *Estado eclesiástico, político y militar de la América.* Ed. Javier Falcón Ramírez. Madrid: Instituto de Cooperación Iberoamericana, 1990.

———. *Vaticinios de la pérdida de las Indias y mano de relox.* Ed. Joaquín Gabaldón Márques. Caracas: n.p., 1949.

Vasconcelos, Simão de. *Crônica da Companhia de Jésus.* Ed. Serafim Leite. 3d ed. 2 vols. Petrópolis: Editora Vozes, 1977.

Vater, Ann M. "A Plague on Both Our Houses." In *Art and Meaning: Rhetoric in Bible Literature,* eds. David J. A. Clines et al., 62–71. Sheffield: Sheffield Academic Press, 1982.

Vázquez, Germán, ed. *La conquista de Tenochtitlán.* Madrid: Historia 16, 1988.

Vázquez de Acuña García del Postigo, Isidoro. "El descubrimiento y conquista de Chiloé." *BACH* 44–45 (1977–78): 129–61.

———. "Evolución de la población de Chiloé (siglos XVI–XX)." *BACH* 102 (1990–91): 403–57.

Veiras d'Allais, Denis. *Histoire des Sévarambes.* Paris: C. Barbin, 1677.

———. *The History of the Sevarambians.* 2 vols. London: John Noon, 1738.

Veith, Georg. *Geschichte der Feldzüge C. Julius Caesars.* Vienna: Seidel, 1906.

Velázquez, Rafael Eladio. "La población del Paraguay en 1682." *Revista Paraguaya de Sociología* 24 (1972): 128–48.

Vellard, Jehan. "Causas biológicas de la desaparición de los indios americanos." *Boletín del Instituto Riva-Agüero* 2 (1953–55): 77–93.

Venables, Robert W. "The Cost of Columbus: Was There a Holocaust?" *Northeast Indian Quarterly* 5 (Fall 1990): 29–36.

Verbruggen, J. F. *The Art of Warfare in Western Europe during the Middle Ages.* 2 vols. Amsterdam: Elsevier, 1977.

Vergara Quiroz, Sergio. "Edad y vida en el grupo conquistador: Un estudio de la existencia humana en el siglo XVI." *Cuadernos de Historia* 1 (1981): 65–86.

Verlinden, Charles. "Fray Pedro de Gante y su época." *RHA* 101 (1986): 105–31.

Vernon, Ida. *Pedro de Valdivia, Conquistador of Chile.* Austin: University of Texas Press, 1946.

Viallaneix, Paul, and Jean Ehrard, eds. *Nos ancêtres les Gaulois.* Clermont-Gerrand: Faculté des Sciences et Lettres Humaines, 1982.

Vianna, Helio, ed. *Jesuítas e bandeirantes no Uruguai (1611–1758).* Rio de Janeiro: Biblioteca Nacional, 1970.

Vibert, Elizabeth. "'The Natives Were Strong to Live': Reinterpreting Early-Nineteenth-Century Prophetic Movements in the Columbia Plateau." *Ethnohistory* 42 (1995): 197–229.

Vicente do Salvador. *Historia do Brasil, 1500–1627.* Eds. Capistrano de Abreu, Rodolfo Garcia, and Venâncio Willeke. São Paulo: Editora Itatiaia, 1982.

Victor of Vita. *History of the Vandal Persecution.* Trans. and ed. John Moorhead. Liverpool: Liverpool University Press, 1992.

Vigil, Ralph H. *Alonso de Zorita: Royal Judge and Christian Humanist, 1512–85.* Norman: University of Oklahoma Press, 1987.

Villalobos R., Sergio. *Historia del pueblo chileno,* I. Santiago: Instituto Chileno de Estudios Humanísticos, 1980.

Villamarin, Juan A., and Judith E. Villamarin. *Indian Labor in Mainland Colonial South America.* Newark: University of Delaware Latin American Studies Program, 1975.

Vives Azancot, J. Pedro A. "Entre el esplendor y la decadencia: La población de Misiones (1750–1759)." *RI* 42 (1982): 469–541.

Vogel, Virgil J. *This Country Was Ours.* New York: Harper and Row, 1972.

Völkl, K. "Zum taktischen Verlauf der Schlacht bei Vercellae (101 v. Chr.)." *Rheinische Museum für Philologie* 97 (1954): 82–89.

Vollmer, Günter. "La evolución cuantitativa de la población indígena en la región de Puebla (1570–1810)." *HM* 23 (1973–74): 43–51.

Vredeveld, Harry. "The Ages of Erasmus and the Year of His Birth." *Renaissance Quarterly* 46 (1993): 754–809.

Wachsmuth, Curt. "Zwei Kapitel aus der Bevölkerungsstatistik der alten Welt." *Klio* 3 (1903): 281–85.

Wachtel, Nathan. "Men of the Water: The Uru Problem (Sixteenth and Seventeenth Centuries)." In *Anthropological History of Andean Polities,* eds. John V. Murra, Nathan Wachtel, and Jacques Revel, 299–310. Cambridge: Cambridge University Press, 1986.

———. "The Indian and the Spanish Conquest." In *The Cambridge*

History of Latin America, I: Colonial Latin America, 207–48. Cambridge: Cambridge University Press, 1984.

Wagner, Henry R. *The Rise of Hernando Cortés.* New York: Cortés Society, 1944.

Wagner, Henry R., and Helen R. Parish. *The Life and Writings of Bartolomé de las Casas.* Albuquerque: University of New Mexico Press, 1967.

Walbank, F. W. *A Historical Commentary on Polybius.* 3 vols. Oxford: Clarendon Press, 1957.

Waldron, Arthur. *The Great Wall of China from History to Myth.* Cambridge: Cambridge University Press, 1990.

Walker, Philip L., and Travis Hudson. *Chumash Healing.* Banning, Calif.: Malki Museum Press, 1993.

Wallace, Robert. *A Dissertation on the Numbers of Mankind, in Antient and Modern Times.* 2d. rev. ed. Edinburgh: Constable, 1809 (1753).

Wallace-Hadrill, Andrew. *Houses and Society in Pompeii and Herculaneum.* Princeton: Princeton University Press, 1994.

Wallerstein, Immanuel. *The Modern World-System: Capitalist Agriculture and the Origins of the European World-Economy in the Sixteenth Century.* New York: Academic Press, 1976.

Wallwork, Stephen C. "Allowing for Migration in Estimating Early Population Levels." *Local Population Studies* 56 (Spring 1996): 30–42.

Walser, Gerold. *Caesar und die Germanen: Studien zur politischen Tendenz römischer Feldzugberichte.* Wiesbaden: Steiner, 1956.

Walsh, P. C. *Livy: His Historical Aims and Methods.* Cambridge: Cambridge University Press, 1963.

Wapnish, Paula. "Is *Seni Ana la Mani* an Accurate Description or a Royal Boast?" In *Retrieving the Past: Essays on Archaeological Research and Methodology in Honor of Gus W. Van Beek,* ed. Joe D. Seger, 285–96. Winona Lake, Ind.: Eisenbrauns, 1996.

Ward, Allen M. *Marcus Crassus and the Late Roman Republic.* Columbia: University of Missouri Press, 1977.

Warren, Benedict. "The Caravajal Visitation: First Spanish Survey of Michoacán." *The Americas* 19 (1962–63): 404–12.

———. *The Conquest of Michoacán: The Spanish Domination of the Tarascan Kingdom in Western Mexico, 1521–1530.* Norman: University of Oklahoma Press, 1984.

Warren, Fintan B. *Vasco de Quiroga and His Pueblo-Hospitals of Santa Fe.* Washington, D.C.: Academy of American Franciscan History, 1963.

Weckmann, Luis. *The Medieval Heritage of Mexico.* New York: Fordham University Press, 1992.

Wedin, Åke. *Concepto de lo Incaico y las fuentes.* Göteborg: Akademiforlaget, 1966.

Weiss, N. "Le Seine et le nombre des victims parisiennes." *Bulletin de la Société de l'Histoire du Protestantisme Français* 46 (1897): 474–81.

Weitemeyer, Mogens. *Herodots og Berossos' Beskrivelse af Babylonien.* Copenhagen: Museum Tusculanum, 1996.

Weitzman, Lenore J. "The Economic Consequences of Divorce Are Still Unequal: Comment on Peterson." *ASR* 61 (1996): 537–38.

Wenham, J. W. "Large Numbers in the Old Testament." *Tyndale Bulletin* 18 (1967): 19–53.

Wenzel, Horst. "Deutsche Conquistadoren: Hans Staden in der Neuen Welt." In *Reisen und Welterfahrung in der deutschen Literatur des Mittelalters. Vorträge des XI. Anglo-Deutschen Colloquiums, 1989,* eds. Dietrich Huschenbett and John Margetts, 290–305. Würzburg: Königshausen and Neumann, 1991.

Wessely, F. "La peste d'Homère." *La Presse Médicale* 19 (10 November 1990): 1697–98.

West, David. "Two Plagues: Virgil, *Georgics* 3: 478–566 and Lucretius 6: 1090–1286." In West/Woodman, 71–88.

Westermann, William L. "Athenaeus and the Slaves of Athens." In *Athenian Studies Presented to William Scott Ferguson,* 451–70. Cambridge, Mass.: Harvard University Press, 1940.

Wetterstrom, Wilma. *Food, Diet, and Population at Prehistoric Arroyo Hondo Pueblo, New Mexico.* Santa Fe: School of American Research, 1986.

Wheeler, R.E.M. "Mr. Collingwood and Mr. Randall: A Note." *Antiquity* 4 (1930): 91–95.

Whiston, William. *A Short View of the Chronology of the Old Testament.* Cambridge: University Press, 1702.

Whitaker, Arthur P. *The Huancavelica Mercury Mine.* Cambridge, Mass.: Harvard University Press, 1941.

White, Richard. "Review of Thornton, *American Indian Holocaust,* and Ramenofsky, *Vectors of Death.*" *Ethnohistory* 37 (1990): 66–70.

Whitelam, Keith W. "Prophetic Conflict in Israelite History: Taking Sides with William G. Dever." *Journal for the Study of the Old Testament* 72 (1996): 25–44.

Whitmore, Thomas M. *Disease and Death in Early Colonial Mexico: Simulating Amerindian Depopulation.* Boulder, Colo.: Westview, 1992.

———. "A Simulation of the Sixteenth-Century Population Collapse in the Basin of Mexico." *AAAG* 81 (1991): 464–87.

Wicki, Jospeh, ed. *Documenta Indica, 1553–1557.* Rome: IHSI, 1957.

Wiessner, Polly. "A Functional Estimator of Population from Floor Area." *AAy* 39 (1974): 343–50.

Wightman, Ann M. *Indigenous Migration and Social Change: The Forasteros of Cuzco.* Durham: Duke University Press, 1990.

Wilcox, Max. "The Judas-Tradition in Acts 1: 15–26." *New Testament Studies* 19 (1972–73): 438–52.

Wiley, Graham. "Cunaxa and Xenophon." *Antiquité Classique* 61 (1992): 119–34.

Wilk, Richard R. "The Ancient Maya and the Political Present." *JAR* 41 (1985): 307–26.

Wilkie, James W., and Rebecca Horn. "An Interview with Woodrow Borah." *HAHR* 65 (1985): 401–41.

Wilkinson, John. "Ancient Jerusalem: Its Water Supply and Population." *Palestine Exploration Quarterly* 106 (1974): 33–51.

———. *The Jerusalem Jesus Knew: An Archaeological Guide to the Gospels.* Nashville: Thomas Nelson, 1978.

Willcock, Malcolm M. *A Commentary on Homer's Iliad, Books I–VI.* New York: St. Martins, 1970.

———. *A Companion to the Iliad.* Chicago: University of Chicago Press, 1976.

Willey, Patrick S. *Prehistoric Warfare on the Great Plains: Skeletal Analysis of the Crow Creek Massacre Victims.* New York: Garland, 1990.

William of Tyre. *A History of Deeds Done Beyond the Sea.* Trans. and eds. Emily A. Babcock and A. C. Krey. New York: Columbia University Press, 1943.

Williams, Barbara. "Contact Period Rural Overpopulation in the Basin of Mexico: Carrying-Capacity Models Tested with Documentary Data." *AAy* 54 (1989): 715–32.

Williams, Jack S. "Review of Reff, *Disease, Depopulation, and Culture Change in Northwestern Mexico.*" *Historical Archaeology* 29 (1995): 96–97.

Williams, Stephen. "The Vacant Quarter and Other Late Events in the Lower Valley." In *Towns and Temples along the Mississippi,* eds. David H. Dye and Cheryl A. Cox, 170–80. Tuscaloosa: University of Alabama Press, 1990.

Wilmsen, Edwin N. *A Land Filled with Flies: A Political Economy of the Kalahari.* Chicago: University of Chicago Press, 1989.

———. "On the Mutual Dependence of Anthropology and Linguistics." *African Studies* 54 (1995): 36–44.

———. "On the Search for (Truth) and Authority: A Reply to Lee and Guenther." *CA* 34 (1993): 715–21.

Wilmsen, Edwin N., and James R. Denbow. "Paradigmatic History of

San-Speaking Peoples and Current Attempts at Revision." *CA* 31 (1990): 489–507.

Wilson, A.J.N. *Emigration from Italy in the Republican Age of Rome.* Manchester: Manchester University Press, 1966.

Windsor, Samuel R. "Noah's Vessel: 24,000 Dreadnought Tons." *Catastrophism and Ancient History* 14/1 (January 1992): 5–31.

Winkler, Karen J. "Brouhaha over Historian's Use of Sources Renews Scholars' Interest in Ethics Codes." *Chronicle of Higher Education* 29 (6 February 1985): 1, 8–9.

Winship, George P. *The Journey of Coronado, 1540–1542.* Golden, Colo.: Fulcrum, 1990 [1904].

Winslow, C.E.A., and M. L. Duran-Reynals. "Jacme d'Agramont and the First of the Plague Tractates." *Bulletin of the History of Medicine* 22 (1948): 747–65.

Winsor, Mary Pickard. "Robert Wallace, Predecessor of Malthus and Pioneering Actuary." In *From Ancient Omens to Statistical Mechanics,* eds. J. L. Berggren and B. R. Goldstein, 215–24. Copenhagen: University Library, 1987.

Wiseman, D. J. "Jonah's Nineveh." *Tyndale Bulletin* 30 (1979): 29–51.

Wiseman, T. P. "Lying Historians: Seven Types of Mendacity." In *Lies and Fiction in the Ancient World,* eds. Christopher Gill and T. P. Wiseman, 122–46. Exeter: University of Exeter Press, 1993.

Withrington, John. "'He Telleth the Number of Stars; He Called Them by Their Names': The Lesser Knights of Sir Thomas Malory's *Morte d'Arthur.*" *Quondam et Futurus* 3/4 (1993): 17–27.

Wolfram, Herwig. *History of the Goths.* Berkeley: University of California Press, 1988.

———. *Das Reich und die Germanen zwischen Antike und Mittelalter.* Berlin: Siedler, 1994.

Wood, Frances. *Did Marco Polo Go to China?* London: Secker and Warburg, 1995.

Wood, Stephanie. "Corporate Adjustments in Colonial Mexican Indian Towns: Toluca Region, 1550–1810." Ph.D. diss., University of California at Los Angeles, 1984.

Woodman, A. J. "From Hannibal to Hitler: The Literature of War." *University of Leeds Review* 26 (1983): 107–24.

———. "Self-Imitation and the Substance of History." In West/ Woodman, 153.

Woodmorappe, John. *Noah's Ark: A Feasibility Study.* Santee, Calif.: Institute for Creation Research, 1996.

Woolf, Greg. "Power and the Spread of Writing in the West." In *Literacy and Power in the Ancient World,* eds. Alan K. Bowman and Greg Woolf, 84–98. Cambridge: Cambridge University Press, 1994.

Wright, Donald R. "Uprooting Kunta Kinte: On the Perils of Relying on Encyclopedic Informants." *HA* 8 (1981): 205–17.

Wrigley, E. A., and R. S. Schofield. *The Population History of England, 1541–1871.* London: E. Arnold, 1981.

Wyatt, David K. "Five Voices from Southeast Asia's Past." *Journal of Asian Studies* 43 (1994): 1076–91.

Wylie, Alison. "Facts and Fictions: Using Archaeology in a Different Voice." In *Archaeological Theory: Progress or Posture?* Ed. Iain M. Mackenzie, 3–18. Aldershot: Avebury, 1994.

Wynn, Phillip. "Rufinus of Aquileia's *Ecclesiastical History* and Victor of Vita's *History of the Vandal Persecution.*" *Classica et Medievalia* 41 (1990): 187–98.

Yadin, Yigael, ed. *The Scroll of the War of the Sons of Light against the Sons of Darkness.* London: Oxford University Press, 1962.

Yang, Lien-Sheng. *Studies in Chinese Institutional History.* Cambridge, Mass.: Harvard University Press, 1963.

Yasur-Landau, Assaf. "Socio-Political and Demographic Aspects of the Middle Bronze Age Cemetery at Jericho." *Tel Aviv* 19 (1992): 235–46.

Ybot León, Antonio. *La iglesia y los eclesiásticos españoles en la empresa de Indias.* 2 vols. Barcelona: Salvat, 1943.

Young, David B. "Montesquieu's Essay on Depopulation in the *Lettres persanes.*" *Journal of the History of Ideas* 36 (1975): 669–82.

Young, T. Cuyler, Jr. "480/79 B.C.—A Persian Perspective." *Iranica Antiqua* 15 (1980): 213–39.

Yule, Henry, ed. and trans. *Cathay and the Way Thither.* 4 vols.: Taipei: Ch'eng Wen Publishing Co., 1966.

Yves d'Evreux. *Voyage au nord du Brésil fait en 1613 et 1614.* Ed. Hélène Clastres. Paris: Payot, 1985.

Zambardino, A. "Critique of David Henige's 'On the Contact Population of Hispaniola: History as Higher Mathematics.'" *HAHR* 58 (1978): 700–708.

———. "Errors in Historical Demography." *Bulletin of the Institute of Mathematics and Its Applications* 17 (1981): 238–40.

———. "Mexico's Population in the Sixteenth Century: Demographic Anomaly or Mathematical Illusion?" *Journal of Interdisciplinary History* 11 (1980): 1–27.

———. Review of Cook and Borah, *Essays in Population History.* *AAAG* 70 (1980): 583–85.

Zamora, Margarita. *Language, Authority, and Indigenous History in the* Comentarios reales de los Incas. Cambridge: Cambridge University Press, 1988.

Zantwijk, Rudolf van. *The Aztec Arrangement: The Social History of Pre-Spanish Mexico.* Norman: University of Oklahoma Press, 1985.

Zapater Equioiz, Horacio. "Valor etnológico de la crónica de Gerónimo de Bibar." *Revista Chilena de Historia y Geografía* 139–40 (1971–72): 15–49.

Zavala, Silvio. *El servicio personal de los indios en el Perú.* 3 vols. Mexico City: Colegio de México, 1978–80.

Zinn, Howard. "1492–1992: A Historian's Perspective." In *Confronting Columbus: An Anthology,* eds. John Yewell, Chris Dodge, and Jan De Sirey, 1–14. Jefferson, N.C.: McFarland, 1992.

Zinsser, Hans. *Race, Lice, and History.* Boston: Little, Brown, 1963.

Ziolkowski, Adam. "Credibility of the Number of Battle Casualties in Livy, Books XXI–XLV." *Parola del Passato* 250 (1990): 15–36.

Zorita, Alonso de. *Breve y sumaria relación de la señores de la Nueva España.* Ed. Joaquín Ramírez Cabañas. Mexico City: UNAM, 1942.

———. "Breve y sumaria relación de los señores, y maneras, y diferencias que habia de ellos en la Nueva España, y de la forma que han tenido y tienen en los tributos." In *CDI,* 2: 114–15.

———. *Life and Labor in Ancient Mexico: The Brief and Summary Relation of the Lords of New Spain, by Alonzo de Zorita.* Trans. Benjamin Keen. Norman: University of Oklahoma Press, 1994.

———. *Los señores de la Nueva España.* 3d ed. Mexico City: UNAM, 1993.

Zulawski, Ann. "Wages, Ore Sharing, and Peasant Agriculture: Labor in Oruro's Silver Mines, 1607–1720." *HAHR* 67 (1987): 405–30.

Index